Transylvania

the Bradt Travel Guide

Lucy Mallows

Updated by
Rudolf Abraham

edition
2

www.bradtguides.com

Bradt Travel Guides Ltd, UK
The Globe Pequot Press Inc, USA

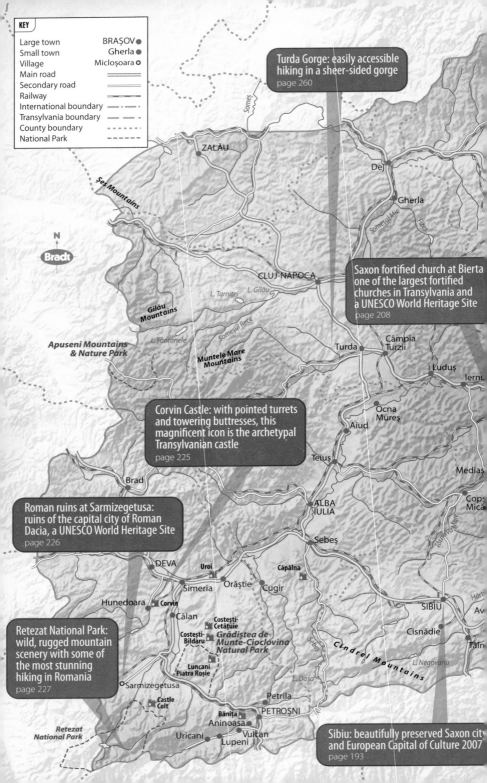

KEY

Large town	BRAŞOV ●
Small town	Gherla ●
Village	Micloşoara ○
Main road	
Secondary road	
Railway	
International boundary	
Transylvania boundary	
County boundary	
National Park	

Turda Gorge: easily accessible hiking in a sheer-sided gorge
page 260

Saxon fortified church at Bierta one of the largest fortified churches in Transylvania and a UNESCO World Heritage Site
page 208

Corvin Castle: with pointed turrets and towering buttresses, this magnificent icon is the archetypal Transylvanian castle
page 225

Roman ruins at Sarmizegetusa: ruins of the capital city of Roman Dacia, a UNESCO World Heritage Site
page 226

Retezat National Park: wild, rugged mountain scenery with some of the most stunning hiking in Romania
page 227

Sibiu: beautifully preserved Saxon city and European Capital of Culture 2007
page 193

N

Bradt

Şeş Mountains

ZALĂU

Dej

Gherla

Someşul Mic

Someş

CLUJ-NAPOCA

Gilău Mountains

L. Tarniţei
L. Gilău

Apuseni Mountains & Nature Park

L. Fântânele

Someşul Rece

Muntele Mare Mountains

Turda

Câmpia Turzii

Luduş

Iernu

Ocna Mureş

Aiud

Mediaş

Brad

Teiuş

Copş Mică

ALBA IULIA

Sebeş

Târnava Mare

DEVA

Uroi

Orăştie

Căpâlna

Cugir

SIBIU

Simeria

Hunedoara

Corvin

Cisnădie

Tăln

Ava

Călan

Costeşti-Cetăţuie

Costeşti-Bildaru

Grădiştea de Munte-Cioclovina Natural Park

Luncani Piatra Roşie

Cindrel Mountains

L. Oaşa

L. Negovanu

Sarmizegetusa

Castle Colt

Petrila

Băniţa

PETROŞNI

Aninoasa

Vulcan

Retezat National Park

Uricani

Lupeni

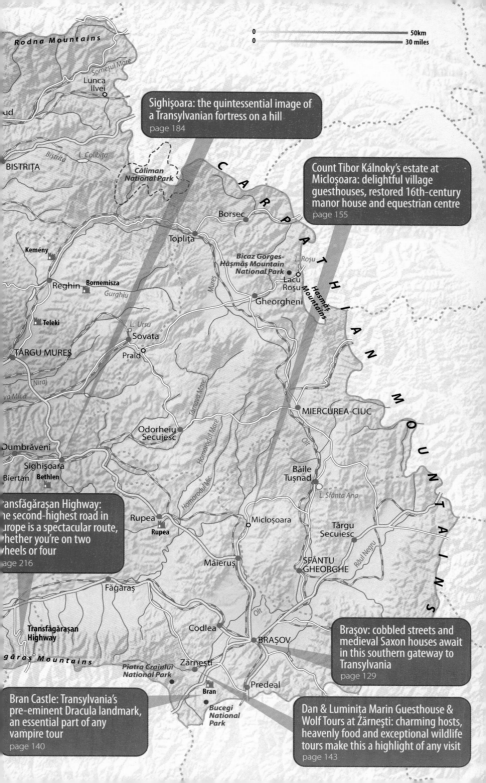

Sighişoara: the quintessential image of a Transylvanian fortress on a hill page 184

Count Tibor Kálnoky's estate at Micloşoara: delightful village guesthouses, restored 16th-century manor house and equestrian centre page 155

Transfăgărăşan Highway: the second-highest road in Europe is a spectacular route, whether you're on two wheels or four page 216

Braşov: cobbled streets and medieval Saxon houses await in this southern gateway to Transylvania page 129

Bran Castle: Transylvania's pre-eminent Dracula landmark, an essential part of any vampire tour page 140

Dan & Luminiţa Marin Guesthouse & Wolf Tours at Zărneşti: charming hosts, heavenly food and exceptional wildlife tours make this a highlight of any visit page 143

Transylvania
Don't miss...

Saxon fortress towns and churches

One of the largest and most impressive fortified churches stands in Biertan, which is listed as a UNESCO World Heritage Site. A true fortress, the site contains ringed double-walled fortifications and a clock tower (SS) page 208

Lost, unspoiled landscapes

From pastoral grasslands filled with wild flowers to craggy peaks like the Ceahlău Massif, the Transylvanian countryside is ideal for exploring on foot or by car (CIP/S) page 112

Spectacular cultural festivals

Bursting with dance, music and local delicacies, folk and harvest festivals occur throughout the year. Braşov's Junii Pageant is the city's largest, in which seven brightly costumed groups parade through the town on horseback (RA) page 96

Majestic castles and palaces

An iconic image of Transylvania, Corvin Castle in Hunedoara is the archetypal fortress, and one of the many impressive historical sites in the region (GM-R/S) page 225

Rural homestays

Experience true Transylvanian hospitality in one of the many private guesthouses and homestays, such as Count Kálnoky's estate in Covasna County or the Marin's guesthouse in Ţârneşti — Prince Charles himself owns guesthouses in Viscri and Valea Zălanului/Zalánpatak (pictured here) (SB/TC) page 85

Transylvania in colour

left   The Art Nouveau-style Palace of Culture in Târgu Mureş is a vivid explosion of colour: don't miss the striking stained-glass windows (LM) page 180

below left   Detail of the clock face and figures on the Sighişoara clock tower (RA) page 188

bottom left   The colourful historic centre of Sighişoara, looking towards the Church on the Hill (PW/A) page 189

bottom right   The Bridge of Liars in Sibiu's old town, one of the most beautifully preserved historic town centres in Transylvania and 2007 European Capital of Culture (RY/JAI/C) page 201

above left   One of the vividly lavish Roma palaces near Cluj-Napoca (LM) page 249

above right   Catherine's Gate guarding the medieval old town of Braşov (LM) page 135

below   The fortified Saxon town of Mediaş, the walls of which were once built, maintained and defended by craftsmen, hence the names Stonecutters' and Goldsmiths' towers (ACL/D) page 211

left   No single image evokes the Dracula legend quite like the imposing Bran Castle — though its historical links to Vlad the Impaler are far more tenuous (W/D) page 140

below   Vlad III Ţepeş birthplace in Sighişoara — tourists think it's Vlad but it's actually his father. Vlad was often called *drăculea*, meaning 'son of Dracul' (LM) page 184

bottom left   The many faces of Dracula — you're sure to find one to take home (SS) page 50

bottom right   Built in the 13th century on a rocky crag above Lacul Vidraru, Poienari Citadel was one of Vlad III Ţepeş's favourite castle residences (CaP/S) page 216

AUTHOR

Born and educated in the UK, **Lucy Mallows** worked for 12 years in Budapest as a reporter. Recently, she moved to Brighton where she works as a freelance photojournalist and translator. She first visited Transylvania in 1997, but her links with Romania go back to the late 1980s when she worked as a volunteer for Operation Romanian Villages, and to an early childhood fairytale *The Lost Princess*, written in 1924 by Queen Marie of Romania.

Lucy Mallows is also the author of the Bradt guides to Bratislava and Slovakia.

UPDATER

Rudolf Abraham (*www.rudolfabraham.co.uk*) is an award-winning travel writer and photographer specialising in southeast Europe. He is the author of several books, including guides to Croatia, Montenegro, Patagonia and Northumberland, and is the co-author of the Bradt guide to Istria.

AUTHOR'S STORY

Bradt is the only UK travel guide publisher to devote an entire guidebook to the Transylvania region and it is typical of their pioneering, ground-breaking attitude that they are the first to recognise that Transylvania has more than enough fascinating historical and cultural features, sporting hotspots and natural wonders to merit a book of its very own.

I wanted to write a travel guide that could lead travellers around a region that has an incredibly complicated history and blend of cultures and faiths, with Romanians, Hungarians, Saxons and Roma all struggling together and apart during the brutal Ceauşescu dictatorship. It is also quite a difficult region to visit; the infrastructure is not always in place and the roads are often diabolical. For an English-speaking visitor, there is a confusion of languages to wrestle with: Romanian, Hungarian, German, Romani and a complicated geographical demographic. However, Transylvania is an immensely rewarding country to visit, there is so much to discover and enjoy: romantic castles, Saxon fortress churches, secluded villages with ancient traditions and folk crafts, haystacks and hay-laden horse-drawn carts, gorgeous countryside, forests, rolling hills, more bears than anywhere else in Europe and welcoming, hospitable people offering delicious dishes and a wide range of lethal alcoholic drinks.

I haven't even mentioned Dracula yet! Although the Count's inspiration, Vlad III Ţepeş (the Impaler) was, in fact, a prince of Wallachia, a region to the south of Transylvania, Irish author Bram Stoker and later Hollywood placed him firmly in the more atmospheric setting of Transylvania and there are many places where his bloodthirsty name is evoked.

Bradt's unique brief gave me the chance to express personal feelings about the region (and Transylvania always elicits strong reactions). I hope this guidebook helps readers gain a deeper understanding of the region and a love for this unique, complicated and exciting part of Europe.

PUBLISHER'S FOREWORD   *Adrian Phillips, Publishing Director*

Transylvania is a cauldron for the popular imagination; so blurred is the line between the real and the imagined that many people don't realise the region exists at all. I've wanted to visit ever since seeing statues of freedom-fighting Transylvanian princes in Budapest, and reading about their fierce struggles against the Habsburgs. These chaps were every bit as dashing and colourful as characters from a novel. Transylvania is a place that cherishes its traditions, and where a past-century way of life is not just a cliché of the tourist postcard. Lucy Mallows delves into all its corners with the passion and commitment that makes us proud to call her a Bradt author.

Second edition January 2013   First published August 2008

Bradt Travel Guides Ltd
IDC House, The Vale, Chalfont St Peter, Bucks SL9 9RZ, England
www.bradtguides.com

Print edition published in the USA by The Globe Pequot Press Inc,
PO Box 480, Guilford, Connecticut 06437-0480

Text copyright © 2013 (Lucy Mallows)
Maps copyright © 2013 Bradt Travel Guides Ltd
Photographs copyright © 2013 Individual photographers (see below)
Project Managers: Anna Moores and Kelly Randell

ISBN: 978 1 84162 419 8
e-ISBN: 978 1 84162 747 2 (e-pub)
e-ISBN: 978 1 84162 648 2 (mobi)

British Library Cataloguing in Publication Data
A catalogue record for this book is available from the British Library

Photographs Lucy Mallows (LM); Rudolf Abraham (RA); Alamy: Paul Williams (PW/A); Serban Bonciocat/Transylvania Castle (SB/TC); Corbis: Russell Young/JAI (RY/JAI/C); Dreamstime: Adrian Catalin Lazar (ACL/D), Rechitan Sorin (RS/D), Warmcolours (W/D); FLPA: Jasper Doest/Minden Pictures (JD/MP/FLPA), Gianpiero Ferrari (GF/FLPA), Mike Lane (ML/FLPA), Michael Weber/Imagebroker (MW/I/FLPA); Dinu Mendrea (DM); Radu Mendrea (RM); Mihai Moiceanu (MM); Shutterstock: Emi Cristea (EC/S), Gabriela Insuratelu (GI/S), Brandus Dan Lucian (BDL/S), Gaman Mihai-Radu (GM-R/S), Claudiu Paizan (ClP/D), Catalin Petolea (CaP/S), Rechitan Sorin (RS/S), Dan Tautan (DT/S); Stephen Spinder/www.spinderartphoto.com (SSp); SuperStock (SS)
Front cover Bran Castle (DM)
Back cover A Roma fiddler in traditional dress (SSp)
Title page Golden eagle (ML/FLPA); Ancient street in Sighişoara with its colourful array of houses (GI/S); Harvesting hay (SS)

Maps David McCutcheon FBCart.S, country map based on source material from ITMB Publishing (*www.itmb.ca*), Dimap Bt, Budapest & Micromapper SRL, Cluj-Napoca
Colour map Relief map bases by Nick Rowland FRGS

Typeset from the author's disc by Wakewing
Printed and bound in India by Jellyfish

Acknowledgements

There are so many people to thank for their input, knowledge, experience and enthusiasm, I hope I haven't forgotten anybody. A massive *mulțumesc* goes out to Adeline Lörinczi in Mediaș; Alina Alexa, Andreea Bell and Georgiana Branescu in Brașov, Andrea Rost in Mălâncrav; Caroline Fernolend in Viscri; Erik László Szoboszlai in Sovata; Erika Stanciu, Ovidiu Bodean and Florin Emilian Tomuș in Retezat. Much support came from Anca Calugar in Saschiz, Andrea Fodor and Mike Wallace in Budapest, Dragoș Minea in Sibiu, Monica Cosma and Corina Vasiu in Biertan, Zorița Beisan in Bucium, Florin and Loredana Delinescu in Sarmizegetusa, Françoise Heidebroek in Roșia Montana, Ioana Alexandroaiei in Bucharest and Denisa Alexandroaiei in Brussels.

Danut and Luminița Marin in Zărnești, Tibor Kálnoky in Micloșoara and Gregor and Zsolna Roy Chowdhury in Zăbala all provided a valuable and real insight into the history and culture of their regions of Transylvania.

From Micloșoara, I am indebted to a host of knowledgeable Transylvania fans: Sabina & Robert ffrench Blake, Nathaniel and Katie Page, Barbara, Elfie and John Knowles, Ewen Cameron, Gill Graham Man, Richard Moon and Roy and Helen Pugh for their suggestions, advice and general enthusiasm. Dr John Akeroyd led a wonderful wild flower walk through the gorgeous countryside around the Olt River valley, and we even survived the bolting wild horse incident!

Many others have been generous with their knowledge and time: Alan Ogden, Jim Turnbull, Andy Hockley in Miercurea-Ciuc, Colin Shaw in Bod, Mike Morton, Gavin Bell, Julian Ross at Lunca Ilvei, Isabela Tusa in Deva Town Hall, Istvan Vincze-Kecskes in Sâncraiu, Jenő Ujváry in Târgu Mureș and József Kuszálik in Cluj-Napoca. A special thank you to fellow Bradt authors Tim Burford and Neil Taylor who were generous with their knowledge and time. Thanks are also due to those who answered my endless questions; László Potozky, Sue Prince and Oliver Brind, Maria Iordache in London, Mária Portik in Sovata, Marina Cionca in Brașov and Simion Alb in New York. At Bradt, I'd like to thank Kelly Randell, Anna Moores, Adrian Phillips, Hilary Bradt and all the team for their help and enthusiasm. Big hugs and thanks to my mum for introducing me to the vivid imagination of Queen Marie of Romania and to Ágnes Szarka for her tireless control of a wayward Dacia Logan.

Rudolf Abraham would like to thank Dan and Lumița Marin in Zărnești; Caroline Fernolend, Vice President of the Mihai Eminescu Trust; Tibor Kálnoky in Micloșoara; Gavin Bell in Brașov; Andrea Bettina Rost; Casa Luxemburg and Pensiunea Podul Minciunilor in Sibiu; and Lucy for allowing me to update her excellent book.

CONTRIBUTORS Flora: Dr John Akeroyd; wildlife: Danuț Marin; recipes: Luminița Marin; politics: Nathaniel Page.

Contents

	Introduction	**VI**

PART ONE   GENERAL INFORMATION   1

Chapter 1   **Background Information**   **3**
Geography 3, Climate 5, Natural history and
conservation 6, History 16, Government 30,
Economy 30, People 32, Language 36, Religion 38,
Education 41, Culture 42

Chapter 2   **Practical Information**   **48**
When to visit 48, Transylvania highlights 48,
Itineraries 49, Tour operators 52, Tourist offices 56, Red
tape 57, Embassies and consulates 58, Getting there and
away 58, Health 65, Safety 68, Women travellers 69,
Travelling with children 70, Disabled travellers 70,
Gay travellers 70, What to take 71, Money 72,
Budgeting 74, Getting around 76, Accommodation 83,
Eating and drinking 87, Public holidays and feast
days 94, Shopping 103, Arts and entertainment 105,
Castles, fortresses, palaces and ruins 107, Spas 108,
Sports and activities 109, Media and communications 113,
Maps 116, Business 117, Buying property 118,
Public toilets 121, Cultural etiquette 121, Travelling
positively 124

PART TWO   THE GUIDE   127

Chapter 3   **Braşov County**   **128**
Braşov 129, Places to visit *en route* from Bucharest to
Braşov 137, Entering Braşov County and Transylvania 139

Chapter 4   **Covasna County**   **151**
Sfântu Gheorghe 151, Around Sfântu Gheorghe 154

Chapter 5   **Harghita County**   **162**
Miercurea-Ciuc 162, Around Miercurea-Ciuc 166,
From Praid to Bicaz Gorges 172, From Gheorgheni to
Borsec 173

Chapter 6	**Mureş County**	**175**
	Târgu Mureş 175, Heading east 181, Heading north 182, Sighişoara 184, Around Sighişoara 189	
Chapter 7	**Sibiu County**	**193**
	Sibiu 193, Heading south and west 202, Heading north 206, Heading east 212	
Chapter 8	**Hunedoara County**	**218**
	Deva 218, Around Deva 222	
Chapter 9	**Alba County**	**232**
	Alba Iulia 232, Around Alba Iulia 236, Heading north from Alba Iulia 243	
Chapter 10	**Cluj County**	**247**
	Cluj-Napoca 249, Heading west 254, Heading north 257, Heading southeast 259	
Chapter 11	**Bistriţa-Năsăud County**	**262**
	Bistriţa 262, Around Bistriţa 267	
Chapter 12	**Sălaj County**	**271**
	Zalău 271, Around Zalău 273	
Appendix 1	**Language**	**275**
Appendix 2	**Further Information**	**284**
Index		**292**

LIST OF MAPS

Alba County	233	Poiana Braşov	147
Alba Iulia	235	Railway network	77
Apuseni range (including Apuseni		Retezat range (including	
Nature Park)	242	Retezat National Park)	228–9
Bistriţa	264	Road network	80
Bistriţa-Năsăud County	263	Romania	4
Braşov	132–3	Routes to & from Bucharest	138
Braşov County	129	Sălaj County	272
Bucegi range, The	141	Saxon villages with fortress	
Cluj County	247	churches	210–11
Cluj-Napoca	248–9	Sfântu Gheorghe	154
Covasna County	152	Sibiu	196–7
Deva	220	Sibiu County	194
Făgăraş range	214–15	Sighişoara	186
Harghita County	163	Târgu Mureş	178
Hunedoara County	219	Transylvania colour section ii–iii	
Miercurea-Ciuc	164	Transylvanian counties	5
Mureş County	176	Zalău	272

Introduction

Transylvania! The name is so evocative it demands an exclamation mark, although perhaps it should be a question mark – Transylvania? What is it? Where is it? Is it a real place? Wasn't it invented by Bram Stoker and developed by Hollywood?

As a place of the imagination, Transylvania is filled with forest-covered mountains, sinister castles on rocky crags, counts with pallid skin and pointed teeth, wolves, bears, werewolves, eagles, shifty-looking peasants, haystacks, and even Dr Frank N Furter, the 'sweet transvestite from transsexual Transylvania' in Richard O'Brien's *Rocky Horror Show* – an image of rural Romania that would have right-wing politicians like Gigi Becali frothing at the mouth.

'Transylvania had been a familiar name as long as I could remember. It was the very essence and symbol of remote, leafy, half-mythical strangeness; and, on the spot, it seemed remoter still, and more fraught with charms.' So wrote Patrick Leigh Fermor of his romantic walk across this strange and beautiful land in 1934. Like many of his observations about Romania, it is still strikingly appropriate today, although to the Dracula myth we can add the enduring weirdness of those Transylvanian Romanian songbirds, the Cheeky Girls. Bram Stoker, the Irish novelist who never visited, is responsible for its image of towering castles, dark forests and Count Dracula rising above them, but the real Transylvania is more interesting and complex than the strangest of fictions.

'Transylvania – the very name seemed a one-word poem' was a more apt summary from the Irish travelogue maestro Dervla Murphy, whose journey on foot across the country in the early 1990s, just after its violent revolution, inspired me throughout my travels across sunlit, flower-filled alpine meadows, through wild untamed forests, along rushing brooks and through what the botanist Dr John Akeroyd called 'the very last example of an untouched medieval landscape in Europe'. Transylvania is so much more than bloodthirsty counts – after all, Vlad III Țepeș, the inspiration for Stoker's *Dracula*, was the ruler of Wallachia, not Transylvania. He might have been born in Sighişoara, Transylvania's most perfect turreted symbol, but he spent most of his brutal days in other parts of Romania.

Transylvania is packed with romantic palaces, rocky ruins, imposing fortresses and forbidding citadels. There are more Saxon fortified churches than you can shake a stick at and dozens of lost-in-time villages where all visitors will hear is Hungarian spoken and the only transport is a horse-drawn cart, laden with the day's hay harvest. Transylvania is the perfect escape from the hectic, stressed-out Western world. It's impossible to rush; the roads will see to that. You have to take your time, go with the flow and admire the scenery *en route*. The distances are vast and the infrastructure is still getting its act together. The service in some restaurants and hotels can still seem locked in the surly 1970s, but many enterprising locals are working hard to improve the tourist industry. Transylvanian noblemen and women are returning to their family seats and restoring them as luxurious yet traditional guesthouses and many ecotourism groups strive to ensure that Transylvania's natural splendours are not spoiled in a hasty surge towards Mammon. Besides the cultural, architectural and historical treasures of the hidden villages and stunning cities such as Sighişoara, Sibiu, Braşov, Alba Iulia, Târgu Mureş and Cluj-Napoca, Transylvania's countryside is stuffed to the brim with destinations for sports enthusiasts, from skiers to hikers and cyclists to wind-surfers, and is an unspoiled paradise for nature lovers, bear trackers, birdwatchers and environmentalists.

The region is still extremely affordable, and is getting easier to navigate by the month. The local cuisine is delicious, hearty peasant fare and often the gorgeous fruit and vegetables are organic and locally produced. Transylvanians like a drink too, from herbal teas to refreshing beers to the fiery spirits such as ţuică. Transylvania has something to offer everyone – not just vampires.

A NOTE ON THE USE OF LANGUAGES IN THIS GUIDE Transylvania's diversity of languages is a fascinating yet often frustrating aspect of its cultural heritage. Due to the movement of peoples across the region, many places are identified by two or three different names. In this guide, references to place names and geographical sights are first in Romanian (RO) and then Hungarian (HU) and/or German (GER). Cultural sights are identified first in English then followed by one or more other languages in this order: (RO/HU/GER). All other references are in Romanian unless otherwise indicated.

Below are a few quick geographical references for maps (English–Romanian):

Lacu/lacul	lake	*Vârf*	peak
Râu	river	*Platou*	plateau
Munte	mountain		

See also *Hiking vocabulary* (page 230) and *Appendix I* (page 275).

Bradt Travel Guides

www.bradtguides.com

Africa

Access Africa: Safaris for People	
with Limited Mobility	£16.99
Africa Overland	£16.99
Algeria	£15.99
Angola	£17.99
Botswana	£16.99
Burkina Faso	£17.99
Cameroon	£15.99
Cape Verde	£15.99
Congo	£16.99
Eritrea	£15.99
Ethiopia	£17.99
Ethiopia Highlights	£15.99
Ghana	£15.99
Kenya Highlights	£15.99
Madagascar	£16.99
Madagascar Highlights	£15.99
Malawi	£15.99
Mali	£14.99
Mauritius, Rodrigues &	
Réunion	£15.99
Mozambique	£15.99
Namibia	£15.99
Niger	£14.99
Nigeria	£17.99
North Africa: Roman Coast	£15.99
Rwanda	£15.99
São Tomé & Príncipe	£14.99
Seychelles	£16.99
Sierra Leone	£16.99
Somaliland	£15.99
South Africa Highlights	£15.99
Sudan	£15.99
Tanzania, Northern	£14.99
Tanzania	£17.99
Uganda	£16.99
Zambia	£18.99
Zanzibar	£14.99
Zimbabwe	£15.99

The Americas and the Caribbean

Alaska	£15.99
Amazon Highlights	£15.99
Argentina	£16.99
Bahia	£14.99
Cayman Islands	£14.99
Chile Highlights	£15.99
Colombia	£17.99
Dominica	£15.99
Grenada, Carriacou &	
Petite Martinique	£15.99
Guyana	£15.99
Nova Scotia	£14.99
Panama	£14.99
Paraguay	£15.99
Turks & Caicos Islands	£14.99
Uruguay	£15.99
USA by Rail	£15.99
Venezuela	£16.99
Yukon	£14.99

British Isles

Britain from the Rails	£14.99
Bus-Pass Britain	£15.99

Eccentric Britain	£15.99
Eccentric Cambridge	£9.99
Eccentric London	£14.99
Eccentric Oxford	£9.99
Sacred Britain	£16.99
Slow: Cornwall	£14.99
Slow: Cotswolds	£14.99
Slow: Devon & Exmoor	£14.99
Slow: Dorset	£14.99
Slow: Norfolk & Suffolk	£14.99
Slow: Northumberland	£14.99
Slow: North Yorkshire	£14.99
Slow: Sussex & South	
Downs National Park	£14.99

Europe

Abruzzo	£14.99
Albania	£16.99
Armenia	£16.99
Azores	£14.99
Baltic Cities	£14.99
Belarus	£15.99
Bosnia & Herzegovina	£14.99
Bratislava	£9.99
Budapest	£9.99
Croatia	£13.99
Cross-Channel France:	
Nord-Pas de Calais	£13.99
Cyprus see North Cyprus	
Dresden	£7.99
Estonia	£14.99
Faroe Islands	£15.99
Flanders	£15.99
Georgia	£15.99
Greece: The Peloponnese	£14.99
Helsinki	£7.99
Hungary	£15.99
Iceland	£15.99
Kosovo	£15.99
Lapland	£15.99
Lille	£9.99
Lithuania	£14.99
Luxembourg	£14.99
Macedonia	£16.99
Malta & Gozo	£12.99
Montenegro	£14.99
North Cyprus	£13.99
Serbia	£15.99
Slovakia	£14.99
Slovenia	£13.99
Spitsbergen	£16.99
Switzerland Without	
a Car	£14.99
Transylvania	£14.99
Ukraine	£15.99

Middle East, Asia and Australasia

Bangladesh	£17.99
Borneo	£17.99
Eastern Turkey	£16.99
Iran	£15.99
Iraq: Then & Now	£15.99
Israel	£15.99
Jordan	£16.99

Kazakhstan	£16.99
Kyrgyzstan	£16.99
Lake Baikal	£15.99
Lebanon	£15.99
Maldives	£15.99
Mongolia	£16.99
North Korea	£14.99
Oman	£15.99
Palestine	£15.99
Shangri-La:	
A Travel Guide to the	
Himalayan Dream	£14.99
Sri Lanka	£15.99
Syria	£15.99
Taiwan	£16.99
Tibet	£17.99
Yemen	£14.99

Wildlife

Antarctica: A Guide to the	
Wildlife	£15.99
Arctic: A Guide to Coastal	
Wildlife	£16.99
Australian Wildlife	£14.99
Central & Eastern	
European Wildlife	£15.99
Chinese Wildlife	£16.99
East African Wildlife	£19.99
Galápagos Wildlife	£16.99
Madagascar Wildlife	£16.99
New Zealand Wildlife	£14.99
North Atlantic Wildlife	£16.99
Pantanal Wildlife	£16.99
Peruvian Wildlife	£15.99
Southern African	
Wildlife	£19.99
Sri Lankan Wildlife	£15.99

Pictorials and other guides

100 Alien Invaders	£16.99
100 Animals to See	
Before They Die	£16.99
100 Bizarre Animals	£16.99
Eccentric Australia	£12.99
Northern Lights	£6.99
Swimming with Dolphins,	
Tracking Gorillas	£15.99
Through the Northwest	
Passage	£17.99
Tips on Tipping	£6.99
Total Solar Eclipse	
2012 & 2013	£6.99
Wildlife and Conservation	
Volunteering: The	
Complete Guide	£13.99
Your Child Abroad	£10.95

Travel literature

Fakirs, Feluccas and Femmes	
Fatales	£9.99
The Marsh Lions	£9.99
Two Year Mountain	£9.99
Up the Creek	£9.99

Part One

GENERAL INFORMATION

Country name România (Romania)

Region name Transylvania (Ardeal/Erdély)

Location Romania is situated in central Europe, south of Hungary, north of Bulgaria, east of Serbia and west of Moldova and the Black Sea. Transylvania is situated right in the heart of Romania.

Size/area (km) Romania 237,500km^2, of which 57,800km^2 is Transylvania

Territory Transylvania is made up of ten modern counties (*judeţ*): Alba, Bistriţa-Năsăud, Braşov, Cluj, Covasna, Harghita, Hunedoara, Mureş, Sălaj and Sibiu

Population Romania 19,042,936 (February 2012). Transylvania's population is 7,221,733 with a large Romanian majority (74.69%). There are also sizeable Hungarian (19.60%), Roma (3.39%), German (0.73%), Serb (0.11%) and other (1.48%) communities. Eight Transylvanian counties have Romanian majorities, and two (Covasna and Harghita) are mostly Hungarian.

President Traian Băsescu (re-elected 6 December 2009)

Prime Minister Victor Ponta (elected 7 May 2012)

Capital Bucureşti (Bucharest), population 1.7 million

Languages Romanian 91% (official), Hungarian 6.7%, Romani 1.1%, other 1.2%

Nationalities Romanian 88.6%, Hungarian (including Székely) 6.5%, Roma 3.3%, Ukrainian 0.3%, German 0.2%, Russian 0.1%, Turkish 0.1%, other 0.5%

Religion Eastern Orthodox 86.7%, Roman Catholic 4.7%, Protestant 3.2%, Greek Catholic 0.9%, Unitarian 0.3%, Evangelical 0.1%, other 4.1%

Currency Romanian new leu (plural lei) (RON) 1 leu = 100 bani. Banknotes with a value of 1 leu and 5, 10, 50, 100, 200 and 500 lei; coins with a value of 1, 2, 5, 10 and 50 bani.

Exchange rate £1 = 5.69RON, US$1 = 3.59RON, €1 = 4.49RON (September 2012)

International telephone code Romania +40, Bucharest +40 021

Time Transylvanian time is EET (East European Time), two hours ahead of GMT (Greenwich Mean Time), seven hours ahead of New York (Eastern Standard Time) and ten hours ahead of Los Angeles (Pacific Standard Time).

Electrical voltage 220V/50Hz; two-pin plugs

Flag Three equal vertical bands of (from hoist side) blue (sky and water), yellow (crops, wheat) and red (blood)

National anthem *Deşteaptă-te, române* ('Awake, O Romanian!'), music by Anton Pann

Tourist board website www.romaniatourism.com

Public holidays and feast days 1–2 January (New Year's Day celebrations), April/May (Orthodox Easter), Easter Monday, 1 May (Labour Day), 1 December (National Day commemorating the union of Transylvania with Wallachia and Moldavia in 1918 (in Alba Iulia), 24–25 December (Christmas)

1

Background Information

GEOGRAPHY

Covering an area of 237,500km², Romania is the second-largest country in central Europe after Poland. Romania is situated in the southeastern Balkan region of central Europe and is bordered clockwise by the Ukraine, Moldova, the Black Sea, Bulgaria, Serbia and Hungary. Romania is situated between 43°37'07" and 48°15'06" latitudes north and 20°15'44" and 29°41'24" longitudes east.

The historical region of Transylvania covers ten present-day counties (*judeţ* in Romanian, abbreviated in addresses as '*jud*'), occupying 57,800km² right in the heart of Romania. The ten counties, surrounded on all sides by Romanian lands, are Alba, Bistriţa-Năsăud, Braşov, Cluj, Covasna, Harghita, Hunedoara, Mureş, Sălaj and Sibiu. The most populous cities are Cluj-Napoca (309,136), Braşov (227,961), Sibiu (137,026) and Târgu Mureş (127,849).

Some guidebook authors and historians, usually Hungarian, include the western part of Romania – Banat, Crişana and even Maramureş – in their description of Transylvania, covering a territory of 102,000km²; however this is not Transylvania in its strictest sense – the 'land beyond the forest'. This begins at the Piatra Cramluj (King's Pass, Királyhágó in Hungarian), a mountain pass between Oradea and Cluj-Napoca where the vast flat plains of eastern Hungary and Crişana give way to the romantic forest-covered Apuseni Mountains and wild, untamed countryside.

Transylvania's borders are easily defined by, appropriately, mountains. The swooping crescent-shaped loop of the Carpathians encloses the eastern and southern edges of Transylvania. In the south, the mountains are known as the Transylvanian Alps. Forming the northwest border is a branch of the Carpathians, the Apuseni Mountains, through which the Piatra Cramluj breaks a passage.

The Carpathians once formed Europe's longest volcanic range, and one extinct volcanic crater remains in Harghita County, now forming the beautiful Lacul Sfânta Ana.

Major mountain passes offered entry into Transylvania in medieval times and can be visited today. Three passes of note are the Piatra Cramluj to the west and in Hungary, Prislop Pass in the Rodna Mountains between Bistriţa-Năsăud County and Maramureş heading for the Ukraine, and the Tihuţa Pass (Bram Stoker's Borgó Pass) on the border of Bistriţa-Năsăud County and Suceava leading towards Moldova.

The Apuseni Mountains are lower than the Carpathians and comprise mostly limestone, with many gorges and caves. Romania has an estimated 12,000 caves, only half of which have been explored. The Carpathians are spiked with a series of massifs including the dramatic Bucegi, where many ski resorts are dotted; Piatra Craiului, home to an excellent national park; Retezat, another superb national park; Făgăraş, site of Ceauşescu's only road construction of worth, the Transfăgărăşan Highway; and the stunning Bicaz Gorge in the northeast region.

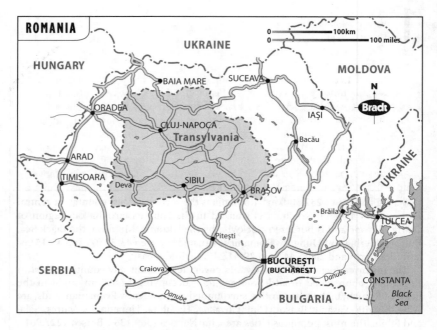

The Făgăraş Mountains hold Romania's highest peak, Moldoveanu (2,544m) on the southern border of Transylvania where Braşov and Arges counties meet. The Transfăgăraşan Highway leaves Transylvania heading south to Romania's capital, Bucharest and is mentioned in the Sibiu County chapter (see page 216) as a possible, and highly scenic route for leaving Transylvania.

Likewise, places of interest on the Braşov–Bucharest highway: the Bucegi Natural Park, Sinaia and Peleş Castle, the Prahova Valley and Snagov Island, are also covered in the Braşov County chapter (see page 137) for drivers and individual travellers who use Bucharest as their air or rail gateway to Transylvania.

Transylvania is criss-crossed by many waterways. The Mureş River crosses right through Transylvania, rising in the Giurgeu range of the Eastern Carpathians and flowing through Târgu Mureş heading southwest to Deva before flowing into the Tisza River at Szeged in southern Hungary. The Olt River, known as Alutus in Roman times, rises in the Haşmaşu Mountains of the Eastern Carpathians and flows southwest through the town of Făgăraş before heading south at Avrig to flow into the Danube and make for the Black Sea.

The Târnava River flows through Saxon fortress village country, formed from two tributaries, the Greater (Târnava Mare) and Smaller (Târnava Mică) and joins the Mureş River near Teiuş. Visitors can find some really beautiful lakes in Transylvania. The most stunning are Lacul Fântănele in Cluj County, Lacul Colibiţa in Bistriţa-Năsăud and Lacu Roşu by the Bicaz Gorge in Harghita County where the extinct volcano-turned-lake Lacul Sfânta Ana can also be found.

The Transylvanian Plateau, 300–500m (1,000–1,600ft) high, is drained by the Mureş, Someş, Criş and Olt rivers, as well as other tributaries of the Danube. This core of historical Transylvania roughly corresponds with nine counties of modern Romania. Other areas to the west and north, which also united with Romania in 1918 (inside the border established by peace treaties in 1919–20), have since that time been widely considered part of Transylvania.

Within the sheltered Carpathian bowl, Transylvania is not all the forest-filled mountains, rocky crags and terrifying fortresses of Bram Stoker's imagination, but more the Câmpia Transilvaniei or Transylvanian Plain: lush rolling hills, fertile flower-filled meadows and numerous lakes and rivers.

A third of Romania is covered by mountains, with unspoilt forestland of beech, hornbeam, ash, lime, spruce, oak and fir below alpine meadows providing home to Europe's richest wildlife including bears, wolves, deer, lynx and chamois. Another third is dominated by lower, rolling hills and plateaux where orchards and vineyards blossom and thrive in the long springs and summers. The final third is covered by fertile plains where cereals, particularly corn, and vegetables are grown. Traditional agricultural methods have maintained the meadows, orchards, vineyards and plains in a lush paradise for rare wild flower enthusiasts and natural world lovers. Visitors from England remark upon the resemblance of parts of Transylvania to great parklands such as Richmond, where oak trees dot meadow grazing areas and a host of rare plants find a safe home. The unspoilt, lost-in-time landscape recalls a kind of *Cider with Rosie* nostalgia for the lost landscapes of the Cotswolds and noble park estates in England before World War II.

CLIMATE

Romania has a temperate-continental climate, with four distinct seasons. The spring is pleasant with cool mornings and nights and warm days. Summer is usually pretty hot and steamy with long, sun-drenched days. The hottest areas in summer are the

TRANSYLVANIAN COUNTIES

lowlands in southern and eastern Romania where 40°C is often reached in July and August. In recent years the summers have been significantly more sweltering. When I was in Braşov in June, the temperature reached a breathless 45°C and Bucharest was said to have been even hotter. During the summer, the landscape is occasionally blasted by incredibly violent thunderstorms with dramatic displays of lightning and sudden bursts of torrential rain. Then the sun reappears and it's boiling hot all over again. When it gets unbearable, Transylvanians head for the mountains where the air is fresher and temperatures are cooler. Autumns are dry and cool, with meadows and trees producing beautifully coloured foliage, making the landscape look like a pastoral painting. Winters can be bitterly cold and snow covered especially in the mountains where temperatures can drop to below −4°F (−20°C). A bitter, icy wind called the *crivaţ* sears through from Siberia, while spooky fog often envelops the countryside, especially at night, making driving difficult and visibility a problem. Many horse and carts are hard to spot and they travel at a snail's pace on major highways, so be very careful if venturing out in a hired car. Heavy snow may fall throughout the country between December and mid March, although this does not occur every year. The ski resorts around Braşov can usually guarantee good skiing conditions from November throughout the winter. Another problem comes when sudden storms cause flash flooding – the lands around Sibiu and southern parts of Transylvania were covered with floodwater in June 2007, and there was severe flooding in several areas of Romania in 2010 and 2012.

For weather forecasts, look at www.accuweather.com and click on 'world' at the top of the page.

NATURAL HISTORY AND CONSERVATION

TRANSYLVANIAN FLORA (*Dr John Akeroyd: botanist, conservationist and specialist on European flora;* e *jrakeroyd@dsl.pipex.com*) Transylvania's botanical richness echoes its historical, cultural and ethnic diversity. The plateau (Câmpia Transilvaniei), locally hilly and dissected by rivers, is bordered to the south by the Transylvanian Alps, with the high Făgăraş Mountains reaching 2,544m on Mt Moldoveanu, to the west by the low Apuseni Mountains, and to the east by the Eastern Carpathians. Because of its location within the Carpathians and rich traditional farming culture, Transylvania retains high biodiversity and intact ecological systems. The cool dark forests and the colourful and often plentiful wild flowers are among the many pleasures for the visitor to this unspoiled region.

GIANT HAYSTACKS

Visitors to Transylvania will return home with one abiding image: hayricks and horse and carts covered with enormous piles of hay balancing precariously. The traditional hayrick (*căpiţă de fân*) is built according to age-old methods and usually by the grandmother in the family. A central wooden pole is fixed on a bed of dry leaves and the cut, drying grass is built up around the pole while granny stands on top packing the layers down. It's highly skilful work and the shape of the haystack varies throughout Transylvania: sometimes it's pear-shaped, sometimes quite thin and pointed, sometimes a chunky pyramid, but always with a sloping watertight top layer. The hay gradually dries in the autumn sun and then the ricks are toppled onto carts and transported to barns for winter livestock fodder.

Traditional agriculture survives, especially in hillier country – non-intensive crop cultivation, hay-meadows and pastures, interspersed with semi-natural woodland, scrub and grassland. Thus one sees vegetation ranging from moist and dry lowland grassland, oak–hornbeam woods, through extensive beech and conifer woods on the lower and middle mountain slopes, to high-altitude alpine grassland, heath, cliffs and rocks. The Carpathians possess some of Europe's largest undisturbed forests, and Transylvania not only has high geographical and ecological diversity but is also a transition between western and central Europe, the Eurasian steppes and Mediterranean vegetation and flora.

The forests of Transylvania are a mixture of beech, spruce, fir and sometimes oak. They are particularly lovely in autumn. Romanian forests have the highest regeneration rate in Europe. Historically much of the region was wooded, with a mosaic of woodland, scrub and grassland on steeper, unstable or dry slopes. However, human clearance for farming has greatly reduced the woodland cover over large areas of central and northern Transylvania, and semi-natural grasslands too have retreated. Much of the landscape retains woods of hornbeam (*Carpinus betulus*) and oaks, mostly sessile oak (*Quercus petraea*) and pedunculate oak (*Quercus robor*). Beech (*Fagus sylvatica*) is often intermixed with hornbeam, especially on limestone and along ridges and on slopes, sometimes with small-leaved lime (*Tilia cordata*). The margins of these beech–oak–hornbeam forests, still widely present in southern Transylvania, often have a fringe of the striking yellow- and violet-flowered endemic cow-wheat (*Melampyrum bihariense*), more or less restricted to Romania. The woodland flora is sparse but includes spring-flowering plants such as wood anemone (*Anemone nemorosa*), coralroot (*Dentaria bulbifera*), *Helleborus purpurascens* and spring pea (*Lathyrus vernus*), and orchids in early summer. A few woods of downy oak (*Quercus pubescens*) occur on dry slopes.

Woodland along streams and rivers is dominated by alders, willows and black poplar (*Populus nigra*), sometimes festooned with wild hops. Wood margins often have scrub dominated by blackthorn (*Prunus spinosa*), with hawthorn, wild pear, privet, dogwood, spindle and elder. As farmers abandon some agricultural land, scrub spreads and develops into woodland. Wood-pasture too is widespread, for example in the Saxon villages and the adjacent Székely Lands to the east and north, with great oaks or other trees growing as spaced individuals in grassland. A fine historic example lies just outside Sighişoara, on the plateau known as the Breite, where hundreds of veteran oaks grow in a clearing surrounded by dense woodland. The grassland is not wild flower-rich but has heath plants such as dwarf brooms, and scarcer species of damper grassland such as great burnet (*Sanguisorba officinalis*). Unfortunately the Breite, despite being a nature reserve, has been inadequately grazed and hornbeam scrub is invading formerly open grassland between the trees. Some other wood-pastures have been felled or over-grazed, but large stands survive on the fringes of the Carpathians.

The spectacular wooded mountain scenery has many good plant habitats. In the foothills and lower slopes of the Eastern and Transylvanian Carpathians up to 1,400m, the dominant trees are oak and beech. In lower woods grow endemic Transylvanian hepatica (*Hepatica transilvanica*), the candelabra-like martagon lily (*Lilium martagon*) and ancient relict species such as *Ligularia sibirica*, alongside the commoner oxslip (*Primula elatior*) and, in wet places, marsh marigold (*Caltha palustris*) and brook thistle (*Cirsium rivulare*). From 1,000m, beech grows in 'mountain forest' with sycamore (*Acer pseudoplatanus*), silver fir (*Abies alba*), and Norway spruce (*Picea abies*), which forms dense stands. Spruce in its native habitat is no spiky 'Christmas tree', but a tall, elegant spire of drooping branches.

Our Lady's bedstraw (*Galium verum*; *sânziene* in Romanian) is a perennial with tiny yellow flowers smelling of honey on tall, thin stems to about 60cm (2ft) high. A member of the bedstraw family and related to sweet woodruff, it is also known as yellow bedstraw, cheese renning and maid's hair (because the yellow flowers were stuffed into ladies' caps in order to dye their hair blonde). Found in the wild on dry, sandy grasslands, the plant has a bitter taste and the name comes from the Greek '*gala*', meaning 'milk'. The flowers were used instead of rennet to coagulate milk. It has been used to colour butter and cheese yellow. A concoction of this was believed to refresh the feet. Because its scent increases as it dries, it was often used as stuffing in pillows and mattresses, particularly for women about to give birth, as it was believed to ensure a safe and easy childbirth. In medieval times it was called Our Lady's bedstraw because it was believed that it provided part of the bedding in the stable at Bethlehem. The plant is also used to treat urinary and kidney problems, epilepsy, hysteria, skin disease and bleeding. It is also a good treatment for scurvy, cystitis, jaundice, sores and tonsillitis.

From 1,600m to 1,800m, at and above the timberline, shrubby juniper (*Juniperus communis*), mountain pine (*Pinus mugo*) and Carpathian alpenrose (*Rhododendron myrtifolium*) gradually replaces the spruces. In the Transylvanian Alps, heather-like *Brukenthalia spiculifolia*, named after Baron Samuel von Brukenthal, the distinguished 18th-century Governor of Transylvania, is locally abundant. These shrubs are interspersed with grassland, mostly managed as pasture. Above 2,200m is semi-natural alpine grassland with sedges and small rushes, and low alpenrose, bilberry (*Vaccinium myrtilus*) and dwarf willows. Late snow-patches have a flora of least willow (*Salix herbacea*), dwarf snowbell (*Soldanella pusilla*), white-flowered alpine buttercups and other alpine flowers. Grassland, rocks and screes are home to attractive flowers such as gentians, Carpathian bellflower (*Campanula carpatica*), edelweiss (*Leontopodium alpinum*), saxifrages and primulas.

Lime-rich rocks support special plants. The great ridge of Piatra Craiului National Park, southwest of Braşov, has woods, scrub and meadows, and an important gorge and rock flora. This includes narrowly distributed endemic plants such as two showy pinks, *Dianthus spiculifolius*, endemic to the Romanian Carpathians, and *Dianthus callizonus*, found only on Piatra Craiului. The mountain hay-meadows, a mixture of dry and damp grassland, around adjacent villages have beautiful wild flowers such as rosy vanilla orchid (*Nigritella rubra*) and globe orchid (*Traunsteinera globosa*), globeflower (*Trollius europaeus*), blue bellflowers and gentians, purple knapweeds and the famous medicinal herb arnica (*Arnica montana*). Retezat, Romania's first national park (1935), in far southeast Transylvania, has a similar range of habitats to Craiului and holds over 650 flowering plants, the richest flora on limestone. This is one of several Transylvanian sites for lady's slipper-orchid (*Cypripedium calceolus*), the over-exploited medicinal herb yellow gentian (*Gentiana lutea*) and rare alpines.

Traditionally managed wild flower-rich grassland is the jewel in Transylvania's floral crown, a manifestation of the sheer richness of plant diversity – and perhaps the best hay-meadows in Europe. These meadows are a living link with the past, and show how plant and animal diversity can thrive alongside agriculture. Their conservation requires sensitive farming, employing modern techniques but maintaining the careful traditional husbandry that nurtured the landscape for centuries. The best areas of lowland 'meadow-steppe' grasslands are probably in Maramureş and the Saxon villages, but there are plenty of examples along the Carpathians. The flora is a mix of western and central European plants, with a

NATIONAL AND NATURAL PARKS

Transylvania has four national parks (there are eight more in the rest of Romania), two biosphere reserves (Retezat in Hunedoara County and Rodna in the north of Bistriţa-Năsăud County), with a third at the Danube Delta, and three of the country's nine natural or nature parks. Romania also has 543 natural reserves, protected areas mostly in the Carpathians; and eight RAMSAR sites (Wetlands of International Importance). The first national park was created in 1935 in the Retezat Mountains and used for some time by Ceauşescu as a private hunting ground.

CĂLIMANI NATIONAL PARK (*www.calimani.ro*) On the border of Mureş, Harghita, Bistriţa-Năsăud and Suceava counties in the far northeast of Transylvania, the park comprises the largest massif in the Eastern Carpathians. This volcanic area is noted for its rare plants, bears, wolves, lynx and pine martens. Area: 240km².

BICAZ GORGES-HĂŞMAŞ MOUNTAIN NATIONAL PARK (*www.cheilebicazului-hasmas.ro*) The park (Parcul National Cheile Bicazului-Hăşmaş) incorporates picturesque Lacu Roşu and fantastic gorge scenery. Area: 66km².

PIATRA CRAIULUI NATIONAL PARK (*www.pcrai.ro*) One of Romania's richest parks for wildlife, known for its unusual honey-coloured bears, wolves, stags and lynx. Declared a national park in 1990, the scenery is magnificent. Area: 148km².

RETEZAT NATIONAL PARK (*www.retezat.ro*) This fabulous park, one of the PAN Parks group (*www.panparks.org*), protects more than 300 species of flora and 50 species of mammal including bears, wolves, lynx, foxes, deer and chamois. The rare monk eagle has also been spotted here. The park was declared a UNESCO Biosphere Reserve in 1979. Area: 380km².

Three natural parks in Transylvania are currently being considered for upgrading to national park status:

APUSENI NATURE PARK (*www.parcapuseni.ro*) Recognised as a geological reserve in 1938, the park protects the core area of the Apuseni limestone plateau, with rocky habitats and montane meadows. In the centre of the park is a karst plateau with an extensive cave system beneath. Area: 758km².

BUCEGI NATURAL PARK The dramatic Bucegi Mountains are the most accessible and visited in the country. The natural park seeks to limit the impact of this popularity on the environment, which contains abundant wild flowers including edelweiss. Area: 327km².

GRĂDIŞTEA MUNCELULUI CIOCLOVINA NATURAL PARK Surrounding the Roman ruins at Sarmizegetusa and other Dacian relics in the Grădiştea Mountains east of Haţeg. Area: 100km².

significant steppic element. Grasses share the sward with a wealth of wild flowers, including 20–30 or more clovers, vetches and other peaflowers, notably sainfoin (*Onobrychis viciifolia*) and stately Hungarian clover (*Trifolium pannonicum*), its scented sulphur-yellow flowers the shape and size of bantam eggs. The drier grasslands have an astonishing range of plants, including steppic gems such as yellow flax (*Linum flavum*) and Mediterranean plants such as tassel hyacinth (*Muscari comosa*).

The meadow-steppe species list runs into hundreds, among them the elegant lily-like *Anthericum ramosum* and *Ornithogalum pyramidale*, yellow- and white-flowered ox-eye daisy (*Leucanthemum vulgare*), frothy cream dropwort (*Filipendula vulgaris*), yellow *Cerinthe minor* and Our Lady's bedstraw (*Galium verum*), countless massed heads of the pale- and deep-yellow hay-rattle (*Rhinanthus rumelicus*), rich blue *Salvia pratensis*, pinkish-purple *Polygala major* and crimson Charterhouse pink (*Dianthus carthusianorum*). In the Apuseni and Carpathian foothills, mountain grassland plants such as arnica, globeflower, sticky catchfly (*Lychnis viscaria*) and alpine forms of kidney-vetch (*Anthyllis vulneraria*) join the sward. South-facing grasslands in Transylvania are rich in Eurasian steppe species, adapted to habitats hot and dry in summer but cold and snowy in winter. From spring to early summer, before they turn greyish with drought, these grasslands reveal a burst of colour: spring pheasant's-eye (*Adonis vernalis*), eastern sea-kale (*Crambe tataria*), burning bush (*Dictamnus albus*), red viper's bugloss (*Echium russicum*), purple-flowered *Iris aphylla*, pink steppe almond (*Prunus tenella*) and violet-blue nodding sage (*Salvia nutans*).

Reserves protect pockets of a vegetation and flora both attractive and increasingly diminished in eastern Europe: for example at Zau de Câmpie in Mureş County, the only place in Transylvania where the magnificent red-flowered *Paeonia tenuifolia* grows; and in Cluj County the species-rich Fânaţele Clujului ('Meadows of Cluj') and Suatu, which protects rare joint-pine *Ephedra distachya* and the only population of the endemic Transylvanian milk-vetch *Astragalus peterfii*. The Saxon villages district in the south of Transylvania has south-facing slopes and hummocks covered with this type of flora, especially from around Saschiz and Mihai Viteazu to the south of Viscri, and about Mălâncrav and Criş. These dry grasslands and scrub, set among dense oak–hornbeam woods, hold a representative selection of Transylvanian endemics, including the tall, branched yellow-flowered scabious (*Cephalaria radiate*) and the violet-flowered Transylvanian sage (*Salvia transilvanica*).

A spectacular flower of the hills and lower mountains is pheasant's-eye narcissus (*Narcissus poeticus* ssp. *radiiflorus*), which in May gives massed displays, notably at Dumbrava Vadului near Braşov, a site that attracts many visitors. Along woodland margins and streams in July and August blooms *Telekia speciosa*, a robust yellow daisy named after Sámuel Teleki de Szék (1739–1822), Székely nobleman and Chancellor of Transylvania, who presented his library to Târgu Mureş in 1802. This noble plant attracts a host of butterflies. A humbler wayside flower, chicory (*Cichorium intibus*), with pale blue dandelion flowers, tints roadsides and fields, and the cabbage family splashes the landscape with yellow from spring onwards, replaced in August by masses of white wild carrot (*Daucus carota*). Cornfield weeds too, almost lost from western Europe, persist in many places – the yellow allysum-like gold-of-pleasure (*Camelina sativa*), deep-blue cornflower (*Centaurea cyanus*) and larkspur (*Consolida regalis*), and scarlet common poppy (*Papaver rhoeas*). In the villages, even mauve burdocks and purple thistles have a stately air.

June and July are the best months for flowers, although plenty persist into autumn. Even September produces late gentians and, in damper meadows, sheets of lilac meadow saffron (*Colchicum autumnale*). On higher ground, lilac-mauve Banat Crocus (*Crocus banaticus*) can be found.

TRANSYLVANIA – THE WILDERNESS AT OUR DOOR (*Dan Marin: wildlife guide, and joint winner of the* Wanderlust *Paul Morrison Guide of the Year 2007*) A combination of very good forest management, traditional and wildlife-friendly farming activities makes Transylvania one of the best places in the whole of Europe for wildlife. Large numbers of wolf, bear and lynx still inhabit the forests that surround this place. Natural selection has ensured that there is a very good and healthy population of red and roe deer and wild boar. The variety of habitats – flood plains, river margins, hay-meadows, forested hills and high mountains – are good homes for an impressive number of species of butterflies, birds, mammals, reptiles and amphibians.

Wild plants and animals have always been very important in the traditional life of Transylvania. The folklore (traditions, stories, beliefs, superstitions) related to them is fascinating, with national festivities dedicated for instance to one flower, Our Lady's bedstraw. There are also folk tales that give the wolf a positive significance, which is something unique throughout Europe.

There is a good network of protected areas all across Transylvania. I will name a few of them, together with some of their highlights, in terms of the wildlife you might find there.

Piatra Craiului National Park is located in the southeastern part of Transylvania. The Piatra Craiului Mountains are considered by many to be the most beautiful and spectacular mountains in all Romania. The park includes a very well-preserved forested area as well as two traditional Romanian mountain villages. An important wildlife research programme, the Carpathian Large Carnivore Project, has done some very important work on the human–wildlife interaction in the area.

The symbol of these mountains is an exquisite flower, the alpine pink (*Dianthus callizonus*), that grows near or right on the ridge. Wild flowers, especially orchids, are a delightful sight on walks in different parts of the park. If you don't see large mammals like wolf and bear, you will almost surely find their tracks or other signs on the trails that cross the forests here. Spending a few hours may be rewarded with good sightings of birds like the wallcreeper, alpine swift, crag martin, black stork, black and three-toed woodpecker as well as raptors. The small ponds or puddles in the horse-carts' wheel tracks are good places to find the yellow-bellied toad (*Bombina variegata*).

Retezat National Park is in southwestern Transylvania. This was the first established national park in Romania (1935). Some 140 species of butterflies can be found here: the scarce swallowtail, clouded apollo and meadow fritillary as well as nine endemic species. There is a significant area that was declared an Important Bird Area (IBA), with birds like horned lark, golden eagle and white-backed woodpecker. A total of 15 species of bats have been recorded, among them the threatened species *Rhinolophus ferrumequinum*. The higher parts of the Retezat Mountains host an important population of chamois.

Bicaz Gorges-Hăşmaş National Park is in northeastern Transylvania. The Bicaz Gorge (Cheile Bicazului) and Lacu Roşu are just two of the landscape highlights of this national park. Three species of newt live here: *Triturus alpestris*, *Triturus montandoni* and *Triturus cristatus*. There is often rain in this region, which may not be great for walks, but it is great for salamanders. Birdlife includes capercaillie, Ural and eagle owl, wallcreeper and rock bunting. Beech martens share the forests here with bear, wolf and lynx.

ANIMAL–BIRD–FISH VOCABULARY

	Romanian	Hungarian
Animal	*animal*	*állat (ah-lot)*
Cow	*vacă*	*tehén (teh-hain)*
Pig	*porc*	*disznó (deece-noh)*
Goat	*capră*	*kecske (ketch-keh)*
Sheep	*oaie*	*birka/juh (beer-kah, yoo-kh)*
Chicken/hen	*puişor/găină*	*csirke/tyúk (cheer-keh, tchook)*
Bear	*urs*	*medve (med-veh)*
Wolf	*lup*	*farkas (far-kosh)*
Dog	*câine*	*kutya (coo-chah)*
Lynx	*linx*	*hiúz (hee-ooze)*
Cat/kitten	*pisică/pisicuţă*	*macska/cica (motch-ko, seet-sah)*
Eagle	*vultur*	*sas (shosh)*
Bird	*pasăre*	*madár*
Mammal	*mamifer*	*emlős*
Fish	*peşte*	*hal*
Butterfly	*fluture*	*pillangó*
Insect	*insectă*	*rovar*
Bee	*albină*	*méh*
Wasp	*viespe*	*darázs*
Reptile	*reptilă*	*hüllő*
Frog/toad	*broască/* *broască râioasă*	*béka/varangy*

Apuseni Natural Park forms the western borders of historic Transylvania. The park has an impressive network of little-known caves, gorges, underground lakes and waterfalls as well as beautiful alpine meadows. A few endemic invertebrates are found in some of the caves here as well as a good number of different bats. The clear streams have trout, Mediterranean barbell (*Barbus meridionalis petenyi*) and many others. The lesser-spotted, short-toed and golden eagles have been recorded in the region and the black woodpecker, dipper and ring ouzel are also found. Mammals are well represented and lucky visitors may spot wildcat, wild boar, wolf or otter.

Călimani National Park is in the northeast of Transylvania. A former volcano crater, 10km in diameter, huge expanses of different types of forest and a population of black grouse are the emblems for this important protected area. Sand lizards (*Lacerta agilis*) and smooth snakes (*Coronella austriaca*) are two of the reptiles that can be found here. Bear, wolf, red and roe deer and beech marten inhabit the forests of the park. Birds include the alpine accentor, black redstart and Tengmalm's owl.

What is really remarkable is that this rich and wild flora and fauna is equally and harmoniously distributed throughout the whole area. In fact, interestingly, places that are not included in any protected areas are sometimes better than national or natural parks. For the forested areas this is because there is less human activity. Most of the time there is almost no tourism at all, only seasonal sheep grazing and logging. For example, the vast forests between the **Piatra Craiului National Park** and the **Făgăraş Mountains** where there are no significant human settlements between the two mountain ranges, just the 'homes' of different wild animals and birds. Traditional farming methods result in lush hay-meadows and rich arable land.

Each stroll through the wonderful Transylvanian countryside can result in exciting moments: impressive stork nests on top of the chimneys; the unmistakable call of a corncrake from the grasses; and bear footprints right in the middle of a mountain village, especially in autumn when they come over for the ripe apples.

Also of note are the **47 IBAs** (Important Bird Areas) in Transylvania (there are 130 in Romania as a whole). They usually include a few different types of habitats, so although they are mainly interesting for their birdlife, sights of other interesting wildlife are almost guaranteed. For instance, the wetlands at Mandra or Rotbav in Braşov County offer potential sightings of beavers – a successful reintroduction programme was carried out in this area – besides the chance of spotting black stork, bee-eaters or little bittern.

The **Avrig-Scoreiu area** is a good place to find the corncrake, Syrian woodpecker or barred warbler. The Făgăraş Mountains (the Transylvanian Alps) are very close to this region and the fauna found here includes bear, wolf, chamois and marmot up or near the ridge.

The **Dealurile Homoroadelor** (Homoroade Hills) covers different areas and habitats (wetlands, forests, meadows) in Mureş, Covasna, Harghita and Braşov counties. This area includes one of the best wetland areas in Transylvania and the birdlife found here includes bitterns, lesser-spotted eagle and white-winged black tern.

In conclusion, I would quote the late James Roberts, author of the comprehensive *Romania: A Birdwatching and Wildlife Guide*. One of his remarks, after living in the country for a long time was 'the country as a whole is a quite wonderful wildlife habitat'.

Danuţ Marin has lived in Zărneşti (Braşov County) all his life. He left school at 14 to work in the local munitions factory. At the age of 30, he studied on a course to qualify as a wildlife guide and now works in the Piatra Craiului National Park. He

THE BROWN BEAR

Extinct in the UK since the 10th century, the brown bear (*Ursus arctos*) is virtually extinct in western Europe. It is estimated that only eight to ten bears are left in France. However, in Romania there are an estimated 5,500 brown bears still roaming the forests, half of the entire bear population of Europe. The bears live in the mountains, but their tracks may also be found close to towns and sometimes right in the heart of rural villages when they go hunting for food and particularly sweet snacks. The best place to spot bears is in the Carpathians, especially in the counties of Mureş, Harghita, Covasna and Braşov. Brown bears can live for 20–30 years in the wild, although most die in their first few years of life. In captivity, brown bears have been known to live for up to 50 years. Individual bears may be active at any time of the day but generally forage in the morning and evening and then rest in dense cover during the day, and may excavate shallow depressions where they like to lie down. The seasonal movements of the brown bears have been observed and some bears travel hundreds of kilometres during the autumn to reach areas where there are many orchards and a profusion of berry-producing bushes. Bears have a very sweet tooth and have been known to raid the bins in the suburbs of Braşov, especially in Valea Cetăţii (Răcădău) district to the south of the centre, sniffing out sugary drink bottles and leftover sweet goods.

and his wife Luminiţa run a guesthouse in Zărneşti (see page 143) where visitors can try traditional home cooking, stay in beautifully renovated rooms and explore the surrounding countryside under Dan's expert guidance. For the last eight years, Dan has been heavily involved in the Rowan Romanian Foundation where he carries out cultural and social programmes for psychiatric hospital patients and Roma communities (see page 126). As well as showing the country's mostly undiscovered wildlife gems and supporting ecotourism projects, he helps to open visitors' eyes to the realities of Romanian life.

ENVIRONMENTAL ISSUES Transylvania's natural environment suffered greatly under the communist regime. The area around Copşa Mică is a manmade disaster. For decades, Copşa Mică's factory belched noxious smoke and dust which covered every building in the town with a thick black coating. The whole town has been cleaned up and looks a lot better, but the land is polluted and families who grow their own vegetables take a great risk. Five decades of communist rule and reckless industrial expansion have left their mark on otherwise glorious landscapes. Right next door to Hunedoara's photogenic castle is a gigantic, hideous steel plant, acquired in 2004 by Mittal Steel.

At Roşia Montana, the Canadian gold-mining company Gabriel Resources (*www. gabrielresources.com*) wants to build a massive gold mine above a historic mining village. To make way for a vast quarry, the mining company proposes to remove five mountains and plans a 600ha cyanide tailings lake forcing 2,000 people to relocate. Rather ironically, their website states that 'the Rosia Montana region has been characterised by economic decline and environmental degradation'. In return, the company has funded archaeological digs, offered to build a new village elsewhere and promised to rescue the area from poverty. It also intends to landscape the site once the mine is tapped out. They estimate that the first gold will be extracted in 2015.

Local and national opposition (*www.rosiamontana.org*) to Gabriel Resources is strong, involving widespread campaigns by MindBomb. People are concerned about the threat cyanide waste poses to their health. They point out that the pit will be active for only about 20 years, but their unique archaeological heritage – an 8km network of galleries cut by Roman miners, remarkable tombs and other vestiges of Roman civilisation – will be destroyed for ever. They believe that most of the mine's profits will go abroad and they do not trust Gabriel to recreate their beautiful mountains, forests and pastures.

Further opposition comes from Hungarian conservationists who fear another environmental disaster like the 2000 Baia Mare (northwest Romania) gold mine where a dam burst spilling 100,000m³ of cyanide-contaminated water into neighbouring Hungary's Tisza and Danube rivers killing thousands of fish, birds and other wildlife in Romania, Hungary and Serbia and polluting the land for decades.

Walking in some national parks and places of outstanding natural beauty, I was dismayed to see plastic fizzy drink bottles and beer cans dumped in huge piles. Dan Marin explained that in Piatra Craiului National Park, the authorities have had difficulties making the rubbish bins bear-proof because bears are attracted by the sweet aromas emanating from old bottles and cans. The suburbs of Braşov have big problems with bears arriving from the surrounding mountains and raiding the rubbish. 'If the bins are strong enough to stop the bears, the visitors can't open them either,' said Marin.

Sadly, this argument doesn't hold water in the Turda Gorge, another spectacularly beautiful area, where there are no bears, but no bins either and the gorge is littered with beer cans and cola bottles lazily dumped by the scenic footpath.

Environmental contacts in Transylvania

AER Association of Ecotourism in Romania OP 1 CP 210, Braşov 500500; **f** 0368 441 084; **m** 0724 970 238; www.eco-romania.ro. Contact Bogdan Papuc, Communication & Marketing Officer (**e** bogdan.papuc@eco-romania.ro) or Colin Shaw, Tourism Adviser AER (**m** 0724 348 272; **e** roving@deltanet.ro).Works in partnership with many organisations to develop & promote ecotourism in Romania.

ANTREC Bl-d Marasti 59, 011464 Bucharest; **** 021 222 8001; **e** office@antrec.ro; www. antrec.ro. A rural tourism organisation, which lists accommodation in villages throughout Romania & guarantees a minimum standard. Well established in parts of the Saxon Lands, Székely Lands, Moţ Land, Huedin (Kalotaszeg) micro region & Rimetea (Torockó).

CERI Carpathian Eco-Region Initiative www. carpates.org. Covers 7 countries & is a coalition of NGOs & research institutes working towards a common vision for conservation & sustainable development of the Carpathians.

Fundaţia ADEPT Contact Cristi Gherghiceanu or Nat Page: Str Principala 166, Saschiz, jud Mureş; **** 0265 711 635; **m** 0748 200 088; www.fundatia-adept.org. Fundaţia ADEPT Ltd is a non-profit organisation promoting agricultural development & environmental protection in Transylvania (ADEPT). Their objectives are the protection of natural & cultural heritage, linked to economic regeneration of the area, so that each supports the other. This is summed up by the *triple bottom line* concept: conservation of biodiversity, sustainable use of natural resources & equitable sharing of benefits. For more information see the Mureş County chapter, page 192.

Fundaţia Mihai Eminescu Trust www. mihaieminescutrust.org. Dedicated to the conservation & regeneration of villages & communes in Transylvania & Maramureş, 2 of the most unspoiled regions in Europe. During Ceauşescu's dictatorship, the Mihai Eminescu Trust gave dissidents a lifeline to civilisation. By alerting the West to his plan to bulldoze Romania's rural architecture it helped save hundreds of towns & villages from destruction. In the post-communist era, much of Romania's countryside has come under new threat from agricultural collapse, the abandonment of houses & a lack of awareness of the value of this endangered heritage. The trust concentrates on the Saxon villages of Transylvania, a special case because of the age & richness of their culture & the emergency caused by the mass emigration of the Saxon inhabitants to Germany in 1990. Village councillor Caroline Fernolend works as a project co-ordinator from her home in Viscri, house No 13 (*office* **m** 0788 342 322; **e** dwk@ zappmobile.ro).

Kálnoky Conservation Trust Micloşoara 186, jud Covasna; **m** 0742 202 586; **e** k@ transylvaniancastle.com; www.kalnoky.org. The KCT identifies, encourages & supports projects that incorporate 3 objectives: restoration & preservation of constructed heritage, conservation & protection of natural heritage, & development & promotion of cultural activities. Present projects include the restoration of the watermill at Băţanii Mici/ Kisbacon, restoration of the dilapidated hunting manor at Micloşoara/Miklóvár as well as protection & promotion of the Vârghiş/Vargyás Gorge.

Milvus Group Str Crinului 22, Târgu Mureş 540343; postal address OP3 CP39 Târgu Mureş 540620; **f** 0265 264 726; **e** office@milvus.ro; www.milvus.ro. Involved with birds & other wildlife all over Romania. The Association for Bird & Nature Protection 'Milvus Group' is a non-profit NGO, acting in the fields of education, research & advice, in order to make Romania a better place for birds, wildlife & people. A few enthusiastic young birdwatchers founded the Milvus in autumn 1991. Soon after, they joined the Romanian Ornithological Society, becoming its branch in Târgu Mureş.

Opération Villages Roumains Started in 1988 by a Belgian charity, which established twin-town links between settlements in Romania & western Europe as a means to stop Ceauşescu's plans to demolish villages. The website www.hdd.dds.nl is now more of a travel site but has some useful links.

PAN Parks www.panparks.org. Founded by the WWF in partnership with the Dutch leisure company Molecaten. The PAN (Protected Area Network) Parks initiative brings all stakeholders of Europe's wilderness areas together. The PAN Parks logo represents a reliable & respected trademark for conservation management & sustainable development. It is a trademark for outstanding nature & high-quality tourism facilities, well balanced with the needs of wilderness protection & community development. The PAN Parks

Foundation co-operates with protected area managements & sustainable tourism businesses in order to make it possible for people to support, preserve & enjoy Europe's wilderness. Retezat National Park (*www.retezat.ro*) was verified as a PAN Park in 2004 (*www.panparks.org/visit/our-parks/retezat-national-park*). Gavin Bell, PAN Parks communication (e *gbell@panparks.org*).

Pro Patrimonio Foundation Str Plantelor 8–10, Scara A, et 1, apt 4, 023974 Bucharest, Sector 2; contact Programme Director Irina Prodan; ☎ 0213 184 771; e *propatrimonio@clicknet.ro*; www.propatrimonio.org. An NGO based in Bucharest, whose mission is to identify, preserve & advocate for the historic & natural heritage of Romania. It aims to restore, rescue & revitalise endangered buildings & sites for the benefit of future generations. The foundation also aims at integrating the buildings it restores in the economic & social fabric of the country & the local communities by stimulating traditional crafts & skills, educating the local population in the awareness & protection of the natural & historic heritage, developing tourism related to cultural sites' itineraries, & stimulating the local economy. Its projects have included restoring house No 18 in Viscri in conjunction with Caroline Fernolend (Mihai Eminescu Trust).

REPF – Romanian Environmental Partnership Foundation www.repf.ro. Based in Miercurea-Ciuc, the foundation supports community-based environmental improvement projects through grant-making & capacity building & through its own operational programmes. The activities of the foundation are developed based on the principles of sustainable development. László Potozky, Director REPF (e *laszlop@repf.ro*).

Transylvania Authentica (TA) is a project that seeks to establish ways in which to ensure the survival of Transylvania's incredibly rich agrarian culture & its traditional foods & agricultural products by bringing together the region's smaller producers & manufacturers. Underlying this is a wish to demonstrate the economic value of landscapes & areas of outstanding natural beauty & how local communities can benefit from the preservation of the status quo. A meeting in Nov 2007 brought together projects based in Transylvania willing to contribute to the creation of a brand or 'TA award' covering 3 types of product: local food products, local craft products & local ecotourism products. Transylvania Authentica has been developed by the Romanian Environmental Partnership Foundation & the Prince's Charities Foundation, at the suggestion of the Prince of Wales. Transylvania Authentica is a certification mark that can be awarded to businesses that demonstrate benefits to the environment, heritage & culture of Transylvania. The certification mark is owned by REPF & registered with the Romanian State Office for Inventions & Trade Marks. Its use is governed by clear criteria & is protected by law. For more information, please contact the Project Manager, Ajnacska Gál at REPF (e *ta@repf.ro*), Enikő Bandi at REPF (e *enikob@repf.ro*) or László Potozky, Director REPF (e *laszlop@repf.ro*).

HISTORY

HISTORICAL NAMES Transylvania was mentioned in a medieval Latin document in 1075 as Ultra Silva, meaning 'beyond the woods'. The name was later amended to Trans-Silvania with the same meaning.

The German name Siebenbürgen, meaning 'seven fortresses', refers to the seven Saxon-built cities in Transylvania: Braşov (Kronstadt), Sighişoara (Schassburg), Mediaş (Mediasch), Sibiu (Hermannstadt), Sebeş (Mühlbach), Bistriţa (Bistritz) and Cluj-Napoca (Klausenburg).

The Hungarian name Erdély has connections with *erdő*, meaning 'forest', a term first mentioned in its medieval Latin form in the 12th-century document, *Gesta Hungarorum*.

The Romanian name Ardeal, referred to as 'Ardeliu' in a 1432 document, and the Romani name Ardyalo are possibly borrowed from the Hungarian Erdély.

INTRODUCTION TO TRANSYLVANIAN HISTORY Throughout history, the territory of present-day Transylvania has been home to many different races and cultures.

Over the centuries, various migrating people invaded Romania. Transylvania was successively under Roman, Magyar, Habsburg, Ottoman and Wallachian rule, while remaining an autonomous province. As a political entity, Transylvania is mentioned from the 11th century as part of the Kingdom of Hungary. It then became an autonomous principality under Ottoman sovereignty in 1571, in 1711 part of the Habsburg monarchy (Austro-Hungary after 1867) and part of the Kingdom of Romania after World War I. Cluj-Napoca is considered by many to be the region's historic capital, although Transylvania was also ruled from Alba Iulia during its vassalage to the Ottoman Empire, and the seat of the Transylvanian Diet was moved to Sibiu for some time in the 19th century.

The puffer-fish shape that we today call 'Romania' has been around only since 1918, when the historical provinces of Wallachia, Moldavia and Transylvania were finally united to form a single state. As everything that went on in the central European region was so convoluted and interconnected, when talking about Transylvanian history, it is important to mention briefly some of the significant historical events in the other territories as well.

ROMANIAN ORIGINS

THE DACO-ROMAN CONTINUITY THEORY VERSUS THE 'OTHER THEORY'

There is no written or architectural evidence concerning the existence – or non-existence – of proto-Romanians in the lands north of the Danube during the millennium after Rome's withdrawal from Dacia. This has fuelled an age-old argument between Romanian and (often) Hungarian historians over the origins of the Romanians.

One theory states that after the Romans left, the whole population of Dacia shifted south of the Danube and that the deserted region was settled by nomadic, migratory people of Slavic, Germanic and Asian origin. Proponents of this theory argue that most of the Dacian population was exterminated when the Romans occupied Dacia. According to this theory, the Romanians developed in the Balkans, south of the Danube, from Romanised tribes who in the 10th century were called Vlachs by Byzantine and Bulgarian historians. These Vlachs then crossed the Danube and settled in the region that is now Romania. In the 13th century, some of them crossed the Alps to settle in Transylvania in response to the Hungarian king's policy of colonisation by foreigners.

The Continuity Theory, favoured by Romanian historians, is that they are the descendants of Latin-speaking Dacian peasants who remained in Transylvania after the Roman exodus and also Slavs who lived hidden away in Transylvania's dense forests, mountains and valleys, surviving there throughout the Dark Ages. Romanian historians explain the absence of hard evidence for their claims by pointing out that the region lacked organised administration until the 12th century and by suggesting that the Mongols destroyed any existing records when they plundered the area in 1241. This theory argues that when Aurelian's Roman legion left, the wealthy urban population along with magistrates and merchants also left. The Daco-Roman peasants and shepherds stayed behind. Fans of this theory say it explains how there has been a continuous Daco-Roman presence in Transylvania and the rest of the Carpathian Danubian region and that this population, together with Romanised Dacians, evolved into proto-Romanians and finally the Romanians today.

Ancient history – Transylvania before Christ Man first appeared in the territory that we now call 'Transylvania' during the Pleistocene Epoch about 600,000 years ago. Once the glaciers had disappeared, a humid climate prevailed in the area and thick forests covered the terrain.

Beginning about 5500BC, during the Neolithic Age, Indo-European people lived in the region. The Indo-Europeans gave way to Thracian tribes, who in later centuries inhabited the lands extending from the Carpathian Mountains southward to the Adriatic and Aegean seas. Roman geographer Pliny the Elder stated that 'Getae' was the Greek and 'Dacian' the Latin name for the same branch of Thracian tribes.

Around 2000BC, the Geto-Dacians appeared in Transylvania. The Greek historian Herodotus called the Geto-Dacians 'the noblest as well as the most just of the Thracian tribes'. They worshipped a god called Zalmoxis, a healing thunder god who was master of the cloudy sky. Bands of Celtic warriors penetrated Transylvania after 300BC and the Celts and Geto-Dacians lived in close proximity. Over the years, the tribes gradually managed to form a cohesive unit and formed a short-lived Dacian Empire under one leader, **Burebista** (82–44BC). The capital, Sarmizegetusa Regia, was at Grădiştea de Munte (see page 222) in Hunedoara County. From AD87–106, Geto-Dacian ruler **Decebal** established a new state, constructed a system of fortresses and outfitted an army.

When **Trajan** became Roman emperor in AD98, he was determined to stamp out the Geto-Dacian menace and take over their gold and silver mines. In AD101, Trajan launched his first campaign and forced Decebal into a peace treaty. Within a few years, Decebal broke the treaty and in AD105, Trajan began a second campaign. This time, the Roman legions penetrated to the heart of Transylvania and stormed the Geto-Dacian capital Sarmizegetusa Regia. Decebal and his officers committed suicide, drinking hemlock before the Romans could capture them. The Romans commemorated the victory by building Trajan's Column in Rome, just north of the Forum.

The Roman Empire After defeat by the Emperor Trajan in AD106, the Geto-Dacian Kingdom became the Roman province of Dacia and remained a part of the Roman Empire for some 200 years. Visitors can still see statues in many Transylvanian towns (Târgu Mureş, Sighişoara, Cluj-Napoca), showing the founders of Rome, Romulus and Remus, fed by the she-wolf.

The Romans built mines (an extensive system of Roman galleries can be explored at Roşia Montana, see page 239), roads and forts. Vulgar Latin became the language of administration and commerce. Colonists from other Roman provinces were brought in to settle the land, and cities such as Apulum (now Alba Iulia) and Napoca (Cluj-Napoca) were founded. The Roman capital, Ulpia Traiana Augusta is, confusingly, near a village called Sarmizegetusa, located 40km southwest of Sarmizegetusa Regia (see page 222). The Dacians rebelled frequently and in AD271, the Emperor Aurelian, also faced with rebellion on the Rhine and in Syria, was forced to abandon the region.

The age of the great migrations During the first millennium, waves of migratory peoples – Goths, Huns, Gepids, Avars, Slavs, Bulgars, Cumans, Petchenegs and others – crossed the region. The former Dacia Trajana province was controlled by the Visigoths and Carpi (free Dacians) until they were in turn displaced and subdued by the Huns in the 450s, under the leadership of Attila. After the disintegration of Attila's empire, the Gepids then Avars followed. The migration period brought Dacia linguistic and religious changes. The Dacians assimilated many Slavic words into their vocabulary. At the beginning of the 9th century Transylvania, along with eastern Pannonia, was incorporated into the Bulgarian Empire, followed by Magyar tribes linking it to the Kingdom of Hungary.

Magyars and Saxons arrive in Transylvania
In AD896, the Magyars – the last of the migrating tribes to establish a state in Europe – settled in the Carpathian Basin. A century later, Hungary's first Christian king, **Szent István I** (975–1038) integrated Transylvania into his Hungarian kingdom. The Hungarians constructed fortresses, founded a Roman Catholic bishopric and began converting Transylvania's indigenous people.

In the 11th–12th centuries, the Cumans, a Turkic people from the northern Caucasus, frequently attacked the eastern flanks of the Hungarian kingdom. Around 1150, King Géza II of Hungary invited German-speaking people from Flanders, Luxembourg and the Moselle Valley, known collectively as 'Saxons', to colonise and defend the sparsely populated Transylvanian Plateau. In 1211, Teutonic Knights returning from Palestine founded the town of Braşov and a settlement at Feldioara, 20km north of Braşov (see page 130) before a conflict with the king (András II) prompted their departure for the Baltic region in 1225. In 1241, the Tatars (Mongol hordes) invaded Transylvania from across the north and east Carpathians. They routed King Béla IV's forces, laid waste to Transylvania and central Hungary, and killed much of the population. When the Tatars suddenly withdrew in 1242, **King Béla IV** launched a vigorous reconstruction and defence programme. He invited more foreigners to settle in Transylvania and other devastated regions of the kingdom, granted loyal noblemen lands and ordered them to build stone fortresses. The foreign settlers included more Saxons, who constructed the Siebenbürgen (seven fortress towns) of Transylvania, and the Székely people, an ethnic Magyar group. Successive Hungarian kings repaid their loyalty by granting them land, commerce and tax privileges and relative autonomy. Nobility, however, was restricted to Roman Catholics.

The Ottoman invasions
In the 14th century, the Ottoman Turks expanded their empire from Anatolia to the Balkans. They crossed the Bosporus in 1352 and in 1389, crushed the Serbs at Kosovo Polje. In the late 14th century, the Ottoman Empire's expansion threat reached the Danube. Transylvania along with the principalities of Moldavia and Wallachia became for several centuries the bastion of the Christian world's defence against the Islamic advancement. A mixture of Romanian, Moldavian and Hungarian princes – Mircea cel Bătrân, Iancu of Hunedoara, Vlad III Ţepeş, Ştefan cel Mare (Ştefan III of Moldavia), Radu of Afumaţi, and Petru IV Rareş of Moldavia (1487–1546) – battled and often won against the armies of famous sultans Bayazid I Ilderim (The Lightning), Mohammed II (Conqueror of Constantinople) and Suleiman the Magnificent. In the 15th century however, the Ottoman Empire imposed its suzerainty upon the three principalities, allowing them a certain amount of autonomy.

15th-century noble rule
In 1437, a huge peasant uprising, known as the **Bobâlna Revolt** (Bobâlna is 18km west of Dej in Cluj County) broke out in Transylvania under the landowner Antal Budai-Nagy. Budai-Nagy died on the battlefield and the leaders of the revolt were executed at Turda, urban privileges were taken away from Cluj and its inhabitants declared peasants.

The uprising led to the creation of the political system based on Unio Trium Nationum (Union of Three Nations), which dictated that Transylvanian society was ruled by three privileged groups: the mostly Magyar nobility, the Saxon burghers and the Székely.

In the Union of Three Nations, the nobles pledged to defend their privileges against any power except that of Hungary's king. The document declared the Magyars, Saxons and Székelys the only recognised nationalities in Transylvania and all other nationalities there, including the Romanians, were merely 'tolerated'.

A key figure to emerge in Transylvania in the first half of the 15th century was **Ioan de Hunedoara/János Hunyadi** (1387–1456, see *Hunedoara*, page 224). His subsequent military exploits against the Ottoman Empire brought him further status as the Governor of Hungary in 1446 and papal recognition as the Prince of Transylvania in 1448. In 1456, he defeated the Turks near Belgrade but died of the plague shortly after. Ioan was called the 'White Knight' and was the father of **Mátyás Hunyadi/Matei Corvin** (ruled 1458–90), one of the most legendary and admired kings of Hungary. Mátyás was called Matthias Corvinus and Matthias the Just for his enlightened rule and influence in bringing the Renaissance to the region.

In one of his final acts, Ioan de Hunedoara installed **Vlad III Țepeș** (the Impaler) (1430–76) on Wallachia's throne. As Prince (Voivode) of Wallachia, Vlad reigned on three separate occasions: 1448, 1456–62 and 1476. These days, Vlad is best known for the exceedingly cruel punishments he imposed during his reign and for serving as the main inspiration for the lead vampire character in Bram Stoker's novel *Dracula* (see page 190).

Peasant revolts In 1514, greedy noblemen and an ill-planned crusade sparked a widespread peasant revolt in Hungary and Transylvania. Well-armed peasants under György Dózsa (Gheorghe Doja) sacked estates across the country. The peasants were defeated at Timișoara. Dózsa and the other rebel leaders were tortured and executed. The governor János Szapolyai (1487–1540) brutally put down the peasants and brought in laws that condemned the serfs to eternal bondage. The 1517 Werbőczy Code (Tripartium) was a feudal version of apartheid.

The Ottomans stormed Belgrade in 1521, thrashed a weak Hungarian army at Mohács in 1526, and conquered Buda in 1541. They installed a *pasha* to rule over central Hungary. Transylvania became an autonomous principality under Ottoman rule and the Habsburgs assumed control over fragments of northern and western Hungary.

After Buda's fall, Transylvania, although still a vassal state of the Ottoman Porte, entered a period of broad autonomy. Local *voivodes* (princes) governed Transylvania from 1540–1690. The Transylvanian Diet became a parliament and the nobles revived the Union of Three Nations, which still excluded the Romanians from political power. **István Báthory** (1533–86), Voivode of Transylvania from 1571–86 was considered by historians to be one of the greatest of the elected kings of Poland. **Mihai Viteazul** (Michael the Brave) (1558–1601) was the Prince of Wallachia (1593–1601), Transylvania (1599–1600) and Moldavia (1600). His reign coincided with the Thirteen Years War, one of the numerous wars that took place between the Habsburg and Ottoman armies. In October 1599, Mihai obtained an important victory against András Báthory in the Battle of Șelimbăr, giving him control of Transylvania. In 1600, Mihai united the three principalities of Transylvania, Moldavia and Wallachia, although this unification lasted for less than six months. Mihai was assassinated by mercenaries under the command of the Habsburg general Giorgio Basta in August 1601.

Religious movements The Protestant Reformation spread rapidly in Transylvania after Hungary's collapse, and the region became one of Europe's

MIHAI VITEAZUL – THREE CROWNS AT ONCE

Michael the Brave (1558–1601) is regarded as one of Romania's greatest national heroes and the first man to acquire the crowns of Transylvania, Wallachia and Moldavia at the same time. Born Mihai Pătraşcu into a poor peasant family, his rise to fame and fortune was remarkably swift. As a young man, he travelled and traded in the Balkan Peninsula and he married a rich noblewoman. Mihai was a skilful military commander, but he was also a shrewd politician. After returning from the Balkans, he was elected to the Wallachian Prince's Council. When the council unsuccessfully conspired against the prince, Mihai was the only one to avoid retribution and the sultan named him ruler of Wallachia (1593–1601). In 1598, the Transylvanian prince Zsigmond handed over the throne to Rudolf Habsburg. When Zsigmond changed his mind and transferred the crown to András Báthory instead, Rudolf asked Mihai for help to get his crown back. Mihai in turn asked the Székelys to provide the military muscle and he defeated Báthory's army at Sibiu, killing Báthory as he tried to flee. In 1599, the victorious Mihai arrived in Alba Iulia to accept power on behalf of the Habsburg emperor. Mihai, however, wanted more power and territories. In 1600, he invaded Moldavia and for one year held all three crowns at once. The Transylvanian nobles were not happy about this and joined forces with the Habsburgs to defeat Mihai at Turda. The Austrian general Giorgio Basta ordered Mihai's death, and he was assassinated on 9 August 1601.

Protestant strongholds. Transylvania's Saxons adopted Lutheranism, and many Hungarians converted to Calvinism. However, the Protestants, who printed and distributed catechisms in the Romanian language, failed to lure many Romanians from Orthodoxy. In 1568, the Diet of Turda granted freedom of worship and equal rights for Transylvania's four 'accepted' (*receptae*) religions: Roman Catholic, Lutheran, Calvinist and Unitarian. The law was one of the first of its kind in Europe, but the religious equality it proclaimed was limited. Orthodox Romanians were free to worship but their Church was not recognised as an accepted religion, only 'tolerated' (*tolerata*). Hungarian historians, however, consider the Diet of Turda to be the first legal guarantee of religious freedom in Christian Europe.

17th-century struggles The 17th century was marked by the struggle between the Ottoman and the Habsburg empires, and by the end of the century the Habsburg Empire had replaced the Ottomans in dominating Transylvania. In Transylvania, Basta's army had persecuted Protestants and illegally expropriated their estates until István Bocskay (1557–1607) got the Turks to help drive the Austrians out. In 1605, as a reward for his part in driving Basta out of Transylvania, the Hungarian Diet assembled at Mediaş and elected him Prince of Transylvania. After Bocskay's death and the reign of the tyrant **Gabriel Báthory** (1589–1613), the Porte compelled the Transylvanians to accept **Gábor Bethlen** (1580–1629) as *voivode*. Transylvania experienced a golden age under Bethlen's enlightened despotism. He promoted agriculture, trade and industry, sank new mines, sent students abroad to Protestant universities and prohibited landlords from denying an education to children of serfs. After Bethlen died, however, the Transylvanian Diet abolished most of his reforms. Soon György Rákóczi I (1593–1648), Voivode of Transylvania from 1630, championed Protestantism, fought for and won religious freedom in Hungary and made his principality virtually an independent state. Rákóczi and Bethlen both sent Transylvanian forces to fight with the Protestants in the Thirty Years War (1618–48) and Transylvania gained mention as a sovereign state in the Peace of Westphalia. Transylvania's golden age ended after György Rákóczi II (1621–60). Rákóczi II launched an ill-fated attack on Poland without the prior approval of the Porte or Transylvania's Diet. A Turkish and Tatar army turned on Rákóczi's troops and took Transylvania.

Transylvania under the Habsburgs In 1683, Jan Sobieski's Polish army crushed an Ottoman army besieging Vienna, and Christian forces began to drive the Turks from Europe. In 1688, the Transylvanian Diet renounced Ottoman suzerainty and accepted Habsburg protection. Eleven years later, after the 1699 Treaty of Karlovitz, the Porte officially recognised Austria's sovereignty over Transylvania. The Habsburgs began to impose their rule on the formerly autonomous Transylvania, strengthening the central government and administration and promoting the Roman Catholic Church. In addition, they tried to persuade Romanian Orthodox clergymen to join the Greek Catholic Church in union with Rome.

SAMUEL VON BRUKENTHAL – THE ENLIGHTENED GOVERNOR

Samuel von Brukenthal (1721(Nocrich)–1803(Sibiu)) was the Habsburg governor of the Grand Principality of Transylvania from 1774–87. He was a baron of the Holy Roman Empire and a personal adviser to and favourite of Empress Maria Theresa.

Brukenthal came from Transylvanian Saxon lesser nobility. He studied law, political administration and philosophy at Halle and Jena universities and was trained in the spirit of the European Enlightenment. An esteemed scholar and qualified diplomat, Brukenthal worked his way up the Viennese Imperial Court and finally he became 'aulic' chancellor of Transylvania. At this time he began his considerable collection of paintings, rare books and coins as well as archaeological and mineral items. In 1773, Brukenthal's fine art collection was mentioned in the *Almanach von Wien* where it was considered one of the most valuable private collections to be found in Vienna at that time. In 1774, Bruckenthal returned to Sibiu as he was appointed Governor of Transylvania and built up a palace in a late Baroque style on the model of the Viennese palaces. The luxurious rooms of the palace, the art galleries and the print room, the library, the musical evenings and literary soirées organised by Brukenthal represented a spiritual nucleus for Transylvania. The German physician Samuel Hahnemann (1755–1843) invented and developed his ideas on homeopathy in the basement of one of the old buildings connected to the palace (see page 200). It is now the Museum of Pharmacology. In an enlightened will, Brukenthal bequeathed his palace to be used as a public museum. The Sibiu Brukenthal National Museum, formed around the collections he gathered, and expanded from a public exhibit, first opened in 1817. Brukenthal's country house at Avrig (see page 213) has the most easterly Baroque garden in Europe. Brukenthal is remembered with a heather-like shrub named after him (see page 8). The Brukenthal Foundation (*www.brukenthal.org/en*), which started in Munich, is trying to save Avrig's English Garden Park, threatened by neglect and inadequate funding.

The 18th century – the age of empire As the Turkish Empire crumbled throughout the region, the Russian and Habsburg empires moved in to fill the gap. In 1703, people from all levels of Transylvanian society joined forces to battle against the Habsburgs. In 1704, the rebels elected a Hungarian nobleman Ferenc Rákóczi II as Prince of Transylvania. During the Rákóczi uprisings, the Saxons sided with the Habsburgs while the Romanians in Transylvania remained neutral. From 1711 onward, the princes of Transylvania were replaced with Austrian governors and in 1765 Transylvania was declared a grand principality. In 1761, Empress Maria Theresa agreed to recognise officially the Transylvanian Orthodox Church. During the reign of Maria Theresa, a second significant ethnic German minority, the Swabians, arrived and are still very much present in Crişana to the west of Transylvania.

The reign of Joseph II (1780–90) Before ascending to the throne, Emperor Joseph II (1741–90) made three tours of Transylvania and saw for himself the serfs' wretched existence. As emperor he launched an energetic reform programme. Steeped in the teachings of the French Enlightenment, he practised 'enlightened despotism' or reform from above designed to pre-empt revolution from below. He brought the empire under strict central control, launched an education programme, and instituted religious tolerance, including full civil rights for Orthodox Christians. In 1781, Joseph II issued an edict of religious tolerance, began the dissolution of the monasteries and embarked on the abolition of serfdom. However, this was too late to stop the **Peasant Revolt** of Horea, Cloşca and Crişan (see *Chapter 9, Alba County*, page 232), which began on 2 November 1784, at Zărand north of Arad and soon spread throughout the Apuseni Mountains. The leaders were Horea (born Vasile Ursu Nicola in 1731), Cloşca (born Ion Oargă in 1747) and Crişan (born Marcu Giurgiu in 1733). Their main demands were related to the feudal serfdom and the lack of political equality between Romanians and other ethnic groups in Transylvania. Battles were fought at Câmpeni, Abrud and Roşia and the peasants managed to defeat the Austrian Imperial Army at Brad on 27 November 1784. The revolt was crushed on 28 February 1785 at Dealul Furcilor (Forks' Hill); Alba Iulia and the leaders were captured. Horea and Cloşca were executed on a breaking wheel; Crişan hanged himself the night before his execution. In a bid to strike at the rebellion's root causes, Joseph II annulled Transylvania's constitution, dissolved the Union of Three Nations, and decreed German the official language of the empire. Hungary's nobles and Catholic clergy resisted Joseph's reforms, and the peasants soon grew dissatisfied with taxes, conscription, and forced requisition of military supplies. Faced with broad discontent, Joseph rescinded many of his initiatives towards the end of his life. Joseph II's Germanisation decree triggered a chain reaction of national movements throughout the empire. Hungarians appealed for unification of Hungary and Transylvania and Magyarisation of minority peoples. Threatened by both Germanisation and Magyarisation, the Romanians and other minority nations experienced a cultural awakening. In 1791, two Romanian bishops, one Orthodox and one Unitarian, petitioned Emperor Leopold II (1790–92) to grant Romanians political and civil rights, to place Orthodox and Uniate clergy on an equal footing, and to apportion a share of government posts for Romanian appointees. The bishops supported their petition by arguing that Romanians were descendants of the Romans and the aboriginal inhabitants of Transylvania.

The 19th century Leopold's successor, Francis I (1792–1835), whose almost abnormal aversion to change and fear of revolution brought the empire four decades of political stagnation, virtually ignored Transylvania's constitution and refused to convoke the Transylvanian Diet for 23 years. When the Diet finally reconvened in 1834, the language issue re-emerged. In 1843, the Hungarian Diet passed a law making Hungarian the official language of the Hungarian (and therefore Transylvania) Kingdom. In 1847, the Transylvanian Diet enacted a law requiring the government to use Magyar. Transylvania's Romanians protested in vain.

The 1848 revolution In early 1848, revolution erupted in Europe and the year was marked by a great struggle between the Hungarians, the Romanians and the Habsburg Empire. Battles broke out in November with both Romanian and Saxon troops under Austrian command battling Hungarians led by the Polish general József Bem. He carried out a sweeping offensive through Transylvania, and Avram Iancu (see box, page 241) managed to retreat to the harsh terrain of the Apuseni Mountains, mounting a guerrilla campaign on Bem's forces. In June 1849, after the intervention by the armies of Tsar Nicholas I of Russia, Bem's army was defeated decisively at the Battle of Timişoara on 9 August 1849.

Unification of Transylvania and Hungary Having quashed the revolution, Austria imposed strict conditions on Transylvania. In 1863, Franz Joseph (1830–1916) convened the Transylvanian Diet, boycotted by Hungarian deputies. The rump Diet passed laws that underscored Transylvania's autonomy and equal status for the Romanian, Hungarian and German languages. Transylvania's Romanians at last joined the Magyars, Székelys and Saxons as the fourth Transylvanian 'nation', and the Romanian Orthodox Church became a received religion. Franz Joseph later permitted Transylvania's Orthodox Church to separate from the Serbian Patriarchate. Romanian literary figures soon founded the **Association for the Cultivation of Romanian Language and Literature**, which became a focal point of Romanian cultural life in Transylvania.

The Ausgleich (Compromise) of 1867 establishing the Austro-Hungarian Empire ended the special status of Transylvania and it was re-incorporated into the Kingdom of Hungary. Emperor Franz Joseph abolished the Union of Three Nations and granted the Romanians citizenship, although the existence of the Romanians as a nation was not acknowledged. The Hungarian government intensified its policy of persecution and forced Magyarisation of the majority Romanian population. In response, in 1881 the Transylvanian Romanians set up the Romanian National Party and conducted a sustained national struggle.

Romania under Carol I Ion Brătianu, the leader of Romania's Liberals, nominated Prince Charles of southern Germany's Hohenzollern-Sigmaringen family to be Prince Carol I of Romania. Carol I (1866–1914) worked to provide Romania with efficient administration. In July 1866, the principality gained a new constitution that limited naturalisation to Christians, a measure aimed at denying civil rights to Jews. The Romanian Orthodox Church became the official state religion.

An almost obsessive distrust of Russia prompted Carol I to sign a secret alliance treaty with Austria-Hungary, Germany and Italy in 1883. Charles's kingdom became one of the Central Powers. Romania's alliance with Austria-Hungary did little to ease the strain in relations between the two countries that Hungary was creating with its efforts to Magyarise Transylvania's Romanian majority. Romanian nationalism smouldered in Transylvania during the period of the Dual Monarchy. The National Party advocated restoration of Transylvania's historic autonomy.

World War I After the 1907 peasant uprising, foreign events shaped Romania's political agenda. In 1908, Austria annexed Bosnia, a clear indication that Vienna sought to destroy Serbia. A year later Ion Brătianu, son of the former Liberal Party leader, became Romania's prime minister.

On 28 June 1914, **Gavrilo Princip**, a Bosnian Serb, assassinated **Archduke Franz Ferdinand**, the heir to the Austrian throne and the Dual Monarchy's most ardent supporter of the rights of Transylvania's Romanians.

In 1914, Romania entered the Great War on the German and Austro-Hungarian monarchy side. In 1916, however, Romania signed a secret agreement with the Allied forces of Britain, France, Italy and Russia, hoping to receive Transylvania and large chunks of the Banat and eastern Hungary if they were victorious. In August 1916, Romanian troops invaded Transylvania, although they were repelled by the Triple Entente (German and Austro-Hungarian Empire) forces.

At the end of 1918, Romania invaded and gained control of Transylvania and the region officially became part of Romania on **1 December 1918**, a date that is today celebrated as the country's national holiday and in thousands of street names. At the 1919 Paris Peace Conference, the Treaty of Versailles was signed on 28 June officially ending the war. On 4 June 1920, at the Grand Trianon Palace at Versailles, a further treaty was signed and Romania was officially awarded Transylvania, Bucovina, Bessarabia and part of the Banat: a total of 102,000km² and 5.3 million people.

Trouble between the wars In 1922, King Ferdinand I and Queen Marie were crowned at Alba Iulia. Between the two world wars political life in Romania was dominated by power struggles between the National Peasants' Party led by Iuliu Maniu and the Liberal Party led by Ion Brătianu.

In 1929, when the New York Stock Exchange crashed, world grain prices collapsed, and Romania was plunged into an **agricultural crisis**. In the early 1930s, the Iron Guard, a fascist band of thugs and anti-Semites, began attracting followers with calls for war against Jews and communists. Peasants flocked to the Iron Guard's ranks, seeking scapegoats for their misery during the agrarian crisis, and the Iron Guard soon became the Balkans' largest fascist party. Corneliu Zelea Codreanu, the Iron Guard's leader, dubbed himself Capitanul, a title similar to Hitler's Der Führer and Benito Mussolini's Il Duce.

After an Iron Guard assassinated Premier Ion Duca of the National Liberal Party in 1933, Romania's governments turned over in rapid succession, exacerbating general discontent. Iron Guards fought with opponents in the streets and railway workers went on strike. The government viciously suppressed the strikers and imprisoned Gheorghe Gheorghiu-Dej and other communists who would later rise to important political positions.

World War II At the outbreak of World War II, Romania tried to remain neutral, but after losing huge chunks of land to Hungary and the Soviet Union in the Molotov–Ribbentrop Pact (in August 1940), the second Vienna Award gave the northern half of Transylvania to Hungary. The Anglophile military leader General Ion Antonescu formed a new government in September 1940 and in 1941 finally declared war on the Soviet Union.

Hoping to regain northern Transylvania, Romania mustered more combat troops for the Nazi war effort than all of Germany's other allies combined. During the war, about 260,000 Jews were killed in Bessarabia, Bukovina and in the camps across the Dniester; Hungary's Nazi government killed or deported about 120,000 of Transylvania's 150,000 Jews in 1944. In 1944, Romania suddenly changed sides and turned on the German troops, reclaiming northern Transylvania at the Treaty of Paris in 1947. In 1946, parliamentary elections saw massive gains for the Communist Party, which formed a government with Petru Groza at the helm. King Mihai was forced to abdicate and flee the country in 1947. Romania was proclaimed a people's republic.

Postwar Romania (1944–85) With the king gone, communist control became total, when in February 1948 all remaining political parties merged to form the **Romanian Workers' Party**, which became the sole power. In 1953, Gheorghe Gheorghiu-Dej was named as General Secretary of the Party, and effectively became leader of the country. Gheorghe Gheorghiu was an activist railway worker who added Dej to his surname in memory of the Transylvanian town where he had been imprisoned. The 1950s were dominated by collectivisation, political repression and complete subordination to Moscow.

In 1956, fearing the Hungarian uprising might incite his nation's own Hungarian population to revolt, Gheorghiu-Dej advocated swift Soviet intervention, and the Soviet Union reinforced its military presence in Romania, particularly along the Hungarian border. After the revolution of 1956, Gheorghiu-Dej worked closely with Hungary's new leader, János Kádár. Kádár renounced Hungary's claims to Transylvania and denounced Hungarians there who had supported the revolution as nationalists and irredentists. In Transylvania, the Romanian authorities merged Hungarian and Romanian universities at Cluj and consolidated middle schools.

The Ceauşescu era Gheorghiu-Dej died of cancer in 1965, and was replaced by **Nicolae Ceauşescu**. Ceauşescu used Romania's already sour relationship with Moscow to his advantage and flirted with the West. Life was relatively good throughout the 1970s for many Romanians and on the back of this, Ceauşescu was able to build a personality cult to solidify his power, which by the late 1970s had become absolute. In 1973, Ceauşescu's wife, Elena, became a member of the Politburo, and in 1974 voters 'elected' Ceauşescu president of the republic. Romania's intensified persecution of Transylvania's Hungarians further aggravated relations with Hungary and Ceauşescu's bleak human rights record eroded much of the credibility Romania had won in the late 1960s through its defiance of Moscow.

Halfway through the Sixth Five-Year Plan (1976–80), the economy faltered. Coal, electricity and natural gas production fell short of planned targets, creating chaos throughout the economy. Ceauşescu's obsessive drive to pay off the foreign debt at virtually any cost caused the average Romanian terrible hardship. The government cut imports, slashed domestic electricity usage, imposed stiff penalties against hoarding, and squeezed its farms, factories, and refineries for exports. The regime's demand for food exports resulted in severe shortages of bread, meat, fruits and vegetables. The authorities limited families to one 40-watt bulb per apartment, set temperature restrictions for apartments and enforced these restrictions through control squads.

On 4 March 1977, a large earthquake killed more than 1,500 people in Bucharest. Romania became increasingly isolated during the 1980s as Ceauşescu embarked on an ambitious project to modernise the country.

The extent of nepotism in the Ceauşescu regime was unparalleled in eastern Europe. In 1989, at least 27 Ceauşescu relatives held influential positions in the party and state apparatus.

In the Stalinist tradition, Ceauşescu exploited a ruthlessly efficient secret police, the Securitate (Departamentul Securității Statului) to nullify all challenges to his authority. In relation to the country's population, the secret police service was the largest in eastern Europe and penetrated all strata of society.

Concerned for the fate of the large number of ethnic Germans who wanted to leave Romania, West German chancellor Helmut Schmidt travelled to Bucharest and negotiated a programme to purchase emigration papers for them. During the 1978–88 period, West Germany 'repatriated' some 11,000 'Saxons' annually, paying approximately US$5,000 for each exit visa. Ceauşescu cynically called the payments compensation for the education that the Saxons had received from the state.

The regime's attempts to assimilate the Transylvanian Hungarian community were particularly controversial and inflamed relations with Budapest. The Transylvanian Hungarian community comprised nearly two million people, making it the largest national minority in non-Soviet Europe. Potentially the greatest threat to the Hungarian community, however, was Ceauşescu's programme to 'systematise' the countryside. Conceived in the early 1970s, ostensibly to gain productive farmland by eliminating 'non-viable' villages, systematisation threatened to destroy half of the country's 13,000 villages, including many ancient ethnic Hungarian settlements.

Ceauşescu's assimilation campaign forced large numbers of ethnic Hungarians to flee their homeland, triggering large anti-Ceauşescu demonstrations in Budapest. In retaliation, Ceauşescu closed the Hungarian Consulate in Cluj-Napoca, the cultural centre of the Hungarian community in Transylvania. In early 1989, Hungary filed an official complaint with the United Nations Human Rights Commission in Geneva, accusing Romania of gross violations of basic human rights. In November 1989, Ceauşescu was re-elected for another five-year term.

In December 1989, **László Tökés**, a young Hungarian pastor in Timişoara who had been persecuted for months by the Securitate for his sermons criticising the lack of freedom in Romania, was threatened with eviction.

The 1989 revolution In early December 1989, protests against the persecution of László Tökés became political and were put down with violence. However, news of communist regimes collapsing elsewhere in eastern Europe added impetus to the protests. On 21 December, 100,000 workers were bussed into Bucharest to display their support for Ceauşescu at a massive staged rally. He was forced to interrupt his address from the Central Committee building after a few brave students unfurled anti-Ceauşescu banners and the crowd started chanting. Live television coverage was stopped and the screens went blank: a symbolic moment considered by many to be the exact time when Ceauşescu lost control.

On the morning of 22 December, protesters stormed the building, Ceauşescu and Elena boarded a helicopter and fled the capital. They were captured several hours later at Câmpulung, about 100km northwest of Bucharest. The Ceauşescus' attempts to bribe their captors failed and for three days they were hauled about in an armoured personnel carrier. Meanwhile, confused battles among various military and Securitate factions raged in the streets. Fighting was especially heavy near the Bucharest television station, which had become the nerve centre of the revolt. More than 1,000 people were killed.

A hastily convened military tribunal in Târgovişte tried Nicolae and Elena Ceauşescu for 'crimes against the people' and sentenced them to death by firing squad. On Christmas Day, a jubilant Romania celebrated news of the Ceauşescus' executions and sang long-banned traditional carols.

On 26 December, the National Salvation Front (NSF) headed by Ion Iliescu, appointed a new government.

1990–PRESENT DAY: ROMANIA'S TRANSITION (*Nat Page: Director, ADEPT Foundation, and a specialist on sustainable rural development in Romania;* e *npage@*

copac.org.uk) It was an ethnic Hungarian priest in Timişoara who in many ways lit the spark of the December 1989 revolution. Hungary indirectly supported the Romanian armed forces, who were supporting the revolution, sent food and medicines, and was the first state to recognise the National Salvation Front (NSF) as the legitimate government of Romania. At the same time, in January 1990, the NSF declared that it would guarantee the individual and collective rights of national minorities. This reduced the tension between Romania and Hungary, which had always been based mainly on the position of the Hungarian minority in Transylvania. (Hungarians constitute 7–8% (1.6–two million) of the total population of Romania: this translates to 21–26% of the 7.7 million inhabitants of Transylvania.) However, this period of reduced tension was short-lived, its ending marked by the bloody ethnic clash between Romanians and ethnic Hungarians in Târgu Mureş in March 1990 which left several people dead and hundreds injured.

1990–92 In early 1990 the first free elections for over 40 years took place and more than 200 political parties took part. The ruling NSF won, the Romanian public reassured by their promises of gradual reform. The main opposition parties were the National Liberal Party (PNL) and the Peasants' Party (PNŢCD), both of which had been important parties between the two world wars, and the Democratic Union of Hungarians in Romania Party (UDMR), which usually receives about 6% of the vote in any elections because that is the size of the Hungarian minority in Romania, who vote along ethnic lines.

Important reforms began under Prime Minister Petre Roman and his Westernised ministerial team, but received a setback with the 1990 and 1991 *mineriads*, the descent on Bucharest by train-loads of coal miners, angered by reforms. These *mineriads* may have been carried out with Iliescu's encouragement: he is even now facing legal investigation for his role in this event in which people lost their lives. Ion Raţiu, a PNŢCD leader, member of a famous reformist family from Turda near Cluj, distinguished himself by his bravery, in parliament, on this occasion.

Soon after this, Petre Roman was sacked from government. Together with other reformists he broke away from the NSF and created a new party, the Democratic Party (PD), which, after shedding Petre Roman, has gained ascendancy. Meanwhile Iliescu's party changed its name several times, currently the Social Democratic Party (PSDR), which is now the main left-wing opposition party.

1992–96 During this period, Iliescu's party won again. Romania's reform process was more or less stalled. The PSDR enjoyed especially strong support in the countryside – rural voters were grateful for the restitution of land to private farmers but feared rapid change, while the urban electorate favoured the reformist Western-oriented Democratic Convention (CD), a coalition of reformist parties. Iliescu was forced to form a coalition government with extreme left and right nationalist parties: the Romanian National Unity Party (PUNR), the Greater Romania Party (PRM), headed by the controversial populist-nationalist Corneliu Vadim Tudor, and the Socialist Workers' Party (PSM). The PUNR was at its most popular at this stage, led by the then Mayor of Cluj-Napoca Gheorghe Funar, a xenophobic nationalist and anti-Hungarian who stirred up controversy in Cluj-Napoca, where the population is nearly 20% Hungarian.

1996–2000 This period was another largely lost opportunity for Romania. The Democratic Convention won the elections, under President Emil Constantinescu, and invited the PD and the Hungarian UDMR to join the coalition, which survived three different prime ministers in four years. However, reforms were only patchy. One of the reforms was the return of forests to private owners: nice in theory, but it led to disastrous unsustainable felling of forests in Romania.

2000–04 President Iliescu was returned to power, with Prime Minister Adrian Nastase. The presidential election was remarkable for the fact that the run-off second round was between Iliescu and the populist-nationalist Corneliu Vadim Tudor, whose victory would have sent shudders through the EU. On the surface, this was a stable and successfully reformist government: a period of consistent economic growth, during which Romania joined NATO and signed an accession treaty to join the EU. But underneath, the interests of the old guard were still catered for, and corruption continued. Nastase himself, demoted in his party (now the PSDR), was investigated for corruption, as were other cabinet ministers.

2004–12 A tough-talking iconoclastic former merchant navy captain **Traian Băsescu** (who had replaced Roman as head of the PD) was narrowly elected as president in 2004. He appointed as prime minister PNL leader Călin Popescu-Tăriceanu, charismatic and Westernised, to head a coalition government including the PNL, PD, UDMR and 18 ethnic minority representatives. Thanks largely to the rough tactics of Băsescu, the old pre-revolutionary interests were weakened and progress made in the fight against corruption, as well as in modernising the judicial system. He was suspended again in July 2012 and reinstated in August.

During 2007, there was increasing tension between the PD and PNL. Tăriceanu's PNL Party split, with some senior figures establishing a pro-Băsescu Democratic Liberal Party (PD-L) which fused with PD in March 2008. This left Tăriceanu with a minority government, shared with the UDMR, but still an effective one that is bringing Romania into line with the EU. Traian Băsescu was suspended by the Romanian Parliament in April 2007 on charges of unconstitutional conduct, but was later reinstated.

The government's overriding objective was **EU accession**, which took place on 1 January 2007. The government also maintained strong relations with the US and NATO. Romania became a member of NATO in 2004, and in 2005 signed an agreement allowing US troops to train and be positioned at several Romanian military facilities. There have been strong suggestions that Romania, among other central European countries, has been used as an 'extraordinary rendition' destination.

After accession, and until the EU parliamentary elections of November 2007, Romanian MEP seats were distributed according to party representation in the national parliament. This gave Corneliu Vadim Tudor's anti-Hungarian, anti-Semitic and anti-Roma PRM party five seats out of Romania's 35, an image that most Romanians including the government found embarrassing. Of the 30% turnout in the EU parliamentary elections, Băsescu's PD won 29% of the vote, Iliescu's PSD 22% and the PNL only 13% (the vote was split by the appearance of the breakaway PLD) and the UDMR 5% (the ethnic Hungarian vote was also split owing to the appearance of another Hungarian party). Significantly, the nationalist PRM did not achieve any seats. Another extremist politician who adds colour to Romania's political scene is **Gheorghe 'Gigi' Becali**, the owner of Steaua Bucharest, Romania's main football club. Becali's great wealth originated from a successful career as a shepherd. Becali has led the New Generation–Christian Democrat Party (PNG-CD) since 2004.

The PSD won the November 2008 elections with a vote of around 33.9%, with Băsescu forming a coalition with the Liberal Democrats after the election and installing Emil Bloc as Prime Minister.

The global financial crisis since 2008 has had a cruel impact on the Romanian economy, forcing the government to take out a massive IMF loan in 2011. Thousands of jobs were cut, and the recent property boom took a major downturn.

Bloc resigned in February 2012 following violent protests against the drastic cuts introduced to counteract the downturn in the economy. He was succeeded by Mihai Răzvan Ungureanu, former foreign minister and director of the foreign intelligence service. Ungureanu replaced some of the ministers associated with the spending cuts, but has pledged to continue austerity measures on which the IMF loan depends. Victor Ponta replaced him on 7 May 2012.

GOVERNMENT

Romania is a parliamentary republic based on a bicameral parliament: the Chamber of Deputies and the Senate. All members of the legislature are directly elected from Romania's 41 counties.

The head of state is the president, who is directly elected, by universal suffrage, for a maximum of two consecutive five-year terms; the president is currently Traian Băsescu, who has been in office since 2004. Traian Băsescu is a former sea captain and Mayor of Bucharest.

The head of the government is the prime minister who is appointed by the president; the prime minister is currently Victor Ponta.

ECONOMY

Transylvania is rich in mineral resources, especially gold, iron, lead, copper, manganese, lignite, salt, sulphur and natural gas. The industry is based on iron and steel, chemical and textiles, while many in the countryside live from stock raising, agriculture, wine production and fruit growing. Timber is another valuable resource. Agriculture includes corn, wheat, barley, sugar beet, sunflower seeds and oil, potatoes and grapes.

Industry is based on mining, timber, construction materials, metallurgy, chemicals, petroleum refining, food processing, textiles and footwear, light machinery and auto assembly.

Transylvania accounts for approximately 35% of Romania's GDP, and has a GDP per capita around 10% higher than the national average. Romania had a GDP per capita of approximately €6,400 in 2011, the second lowest in the EU.

Despite the 2001–02 global slowdown, the strong domestic activity in agriculture, construction and consumption maintained GDP growth above 4%. However, the macroeconomic gains were slow to stimulate the creation of a middle class and address Romania's widespread poverty, while corruption and red tape continue to handicap the business environment. The global financial crisis of 2008 hit Romania hard, with GDP only creeping back to around 2007 levels in 2011–12.

The average salary is €340 a month, although this figure is deceptively high due to a small number of much higher earners – in reality, an average net monthly salary is more likely to be closer to €230. This is still a very low wage compared with the West and many people I have met complained bitterly that they could not afford to run a car.

THE ECONOMY AND THE EU Romania joined the European Union on 1 January 2007, and the IMF praised the country's reform efforts in preparation for EU accession.

After the brutal transition from communism to a market economy in 1989, life was very hard for the average Romanian. The industrial base was largely obsolete and when all the tractors and farm equipment from the state-owned co-operative farms were sold off on the black market, Transylvanians had to return to traditional methods of farming, using horses and oxen to pull the ploughs, transport hay and other crops and also as a vital means of transport. It seemed like the people were going back in time to the medieval ways of living, but, in the countryside, the Transylvanian people have always been expert at living close to nature and understanding its seasons and changes. People in this region still have smallholdings, drive horse-drawn carts, grow all their own fruit and vegetables and keep chickens, geese and hopefully a pig, to be slaughtered for the Christmas feast.

Unfortunately, the EU doesn't always come bringing gifts, and shepherds in the mountains fear their way of life will have to change forever. 'The most important thing here is the human–wildlife interaction, how the shepherds can maintain their way of life. The big teeth of the EU are more dangerous than those of the wolves,' said Zărneşti guide Dan Marin. EU officials scramble up mountains to inspect ancient shepherd camps, where people have found shelter and made cheese for centuries, and then declare that they must have proper washing and milking facilities installed. 'But they don't even have electricity up in the mountains. The EU doesn't say how to improve facilities, they just say if you don't change we'll close you down,' explained Marin.

The EU also wants to put a stop to the shepherds' migration when 5,000–10,000 sheep walk to the Danube then return in a three-year cycle. The EU made a bizarre condition that the shepherds must have a good map and GPS satellite navigation, 'when they managed without for 2,000 years, walking as far as Albania, Bulgaria and Greece!' said Marin. A new EU rule could also bring an end to a great Christmas tradition as the annual pig killing must be done with a high-voltage electric shock. Officials have also been heading deep into the countryside and fining 96-year-old ladies for 'growing drugs' when in fact they are planting hemp for the fibres.

Poverty is still widespread in the region, but the locals have shown they are very resilient and good at adapting to whatever life throws their way. The country emerged in 2000 from a punishing three-year recession thanks to strong demand in EU export markets.

Romania hopes to join the EU Schengen bloc, under which border controls are abolished between the signatory countries, although at the time of going to press this had not yet been approved. The Romanian government also announced plans to join the eurozone by 2014. To simplify future adjustments to ATMs at the adoption of the euro, when the new leu (RON) was adopted in July 2005 the new banknotes were the same size as euro banknotes. The old leu notes were much wider.

For information on banks, exchanging currency, ATMs and travellers' cheques, see *Chapter 2*, page 72.

CHALLENGES FOR THE FUTURE IN TRANSYLVANIA

Roşia Montana The proposed gold mine for Transylvania in the Apuseni Mountains is a significant ecological issue which continues to haunt the present government. The Hungarian government is opposed to it, on ecological and cultural grounds (failures in cyanide dams of other mines in Romania have already damaged Hungary through polluting the Danube, and the threat from Roşia Montana is much greater). Interestingly, the Nationalist Romanian Senator Gheorghe Funar and the Hungarian UDMR party have joined forces to sign a declaration against the use of cyanide in mining in Romania. At the time of going to press, this massive project is still in the balance.

The 'Bechtel' US-backed motorway This major route is being built from the northern part of Romania's border with Hungary (Borş-Oradea) to Braşov – albeit much more slowly than originally envisioned. There are suggestions that this route is as much a strategic NATO route as a public–commercial highway, and concerns that it will cut through some protected landscapes. But it is popular with local people and the route will speed up communication enormously between Braşov-Sighişoara, Târgu Mureş, Cluj-Oradea and Hungary, and take heavy traffic off the minor roads.

Nature protection Some 15% of Romanian territory has been nominated for Natura 2000 (the EU's system of protected areas), most of it in Transylvania. It will be a great challenge to manage these areas in a way that protects biodiversity and brings benefit to local people: responsible tourism contributing to local economies will be a necessary part of this solution. The control of illegal and unsustainable deforestation, especially in the rich mountain areas of the Carpathians, is an important issue in the prevention of floods as well as of biodiversity loss and climate change. Heavy flooding, accompanied by landslides, has afflicted Romania over the past few years, and is certainly made worse by deforestation.

Agricultural reform This is a massive challenge for Romania. Romania must try to bring its agriculture into line with the EU, absorbing massive rural development payments, but hopefully this can be achieved without destroying Romania's – and especially Transylvania's – remarkable rural heritage. There is some hope that this can be achieved, especially since EU rural development policies are emphasising broader, social interests rather than simply the increased profitability of farming.

Population migrations Already two million people, nearly 10% of Romania's population, have gone abroad to work in other EU states, especially Spain and Italy, which are similar in climate and language. Many of these are young, active Romanians whom their country can ill-afford to lose. There is a real labour shortage in the building sector, for example, because of higher wages in other countries. But there are also a large number of criminal Romanians, often ethnic Roma, who have moved abroad for easy pickings. The problems of economic migration will continue, from countryside to cities and from Romania abroad, until the economy and wage levels come to match those of western Europe.

PEOPLE

In the population of Transylvania there are four distinct nationalities: Saxons in the south, and mixed with them the Wallachs, who are the descendants of the Dacians; Magyars in the west, and Székelys in the east and north. I am going among the latter, who claim to be descended from Attila and the Huns. This may be so, for when the Magyars conquered the country in the eleventh century they found the Huns settled in it.

From Jonathan Harker's journal, Chapter 1, Dracula, by Bram Stoker

The country's name, România, comes from Român, a derivative of the Latin word 'Romanus' (Roman). **Romanians** calling themselves Român/Rumân date from as early as the 16th century in texts by many authors, among them Italian humanists travelling in Transylvania, Moldavia and Wallachia. The oldest surviving text written in the Romanian language is a letter from 1521 called *Neacşu's Letter from Câmpulung* which notifies the Mayor of Braşov about an imminent attack by Ottoman Turks. This document contains the first mention of the word 'Rumanian' (the spelling then).

There are two historical theories concerning the ancestry of the modern Romanian nation (see *History*, page 16). As is sadly often the case, politicians on both sides have corrupted the two theories for political gain and often it is impossible to see the wood for the trees. The name 'Vlachs' is an exonym that was used by Slavs when referring to all Romanised natives of the Balkans. These days it refers to the Romanised populations of the Balkans who speak Daco-Romanian, Aromanian, Istro-Romanian and Megleno-Romanian.

Led by Prince Árpád, **Magyar** tribes arrived in the Carpathian Basin in AD896. A fearsome tribe of horsemen, they are thought to have arrived from a region beyond the Urals, though the exact geographic origins have never been proved.

In 1820, the Székely explorer Sándor Kőrösi Csoma (born 1784 in Chiuruş, Covasna County) set off for Tibet hoping to discover the origins of the Magyars. He compiled the first Tibetan–English dictionary.

Magyars are the largest minority in Transylvania with a particularly strong community that preserves its traditions, language and culture. In Hungarian, Magyar refers to the people and language. Although Transylvania was a matter of dispute between Romanians and Hungarians over the centuries (see *History*, page 24) and despite some politicians' fiery rhetoric, the two cultures always managed to rub along together, albeit often in separate communities. Ceauşescu targeted Hungarians and made life particularly difficult for minorities. Playing the nationalist card, his 'official' version of Romanian history played down the role of Hungarians, education was almost exclusively in the Romanian language, and ethnic Hungarians were excluded from many important positions. The damaged relationship between Budapest and Bucharest was only repaired after Ceauşescu was removed and in 1995 a treaty was signed on basic relations between the two countries with Romania guaranteeing the respect of all minorities. Since 1 January 2007, both countries are now EU members and travel across the border is easy.

The Hungarian minority of Romania is the largest ethnic minority in the country, consisting of over 1.2 million people and making up 6.5% of the total population, according to a 2011 census. For historic reasons, most ethnic Hungarians in Romania live in Transylvania, where they make up about 19% of the population. Hungarians form a large majority of the population in Harghita and Covasna counties and a large percentage in Mureş (37.8%), Sălaj (23.2%) and Cluj (15.7%) counties.

The **Székely** people (pronounced 'say-kay') or Szekler in German, Secui in Romanian and Sicul in Latin, are a Hungarian-speaking ethnic group, who live mostly in Harghita, Covasna and Mureş counties and there is a small settlement at Feldioara, 15km north of Braşov on route E60. Their region is known informally as Székelyföld or Székely Land. With a population of some 665,000, the Székely people account for about 45% of the 1,237,746 ethnic Hungarians living in Romania (see box, page 168).

The Székely people claim to be descended from Attila's Huns and feel that they have played a special role in the history of the Hungarian kingdom. In Bram Stoker's *Dracula*, the Count regards himself as a Székely, and presents them as a nation separate from the Hungarians, saying 'We Székelys have a right to be proud, for in our veins flows the blood of many brave races who fought as the lion fights, for lordship.'

The **Moți** (pronounced 'mot-zee'), as they are known, are a distinctive tribe of people from the Apuseni Mountains. They are shepherding folk who have lived in the region since the time of the Roman Empire. The Moți architecture and style of dress are equally eye-catching with tall steeple-shaped thatched roofs on their cottages and barns and tall flower pot-shaped hats for the shepherd men. Famous Moți men include Avram Iancu and Horea, Cloșca and Crișan, the trio of leaders of the 1784 peasants' revolt.

Although official figures say half a million, educated estimates say nearer to two million **Roma** now live in Romania; many are still nomadic. In Zărnești, there are four different Roma communities. Two communities have a leader called a *bulibasha*. There is also a Roma emperor, president and king. The Roma emperor Florin Cioabă lives in a huge palace near Sibiu. His daughter Luminița Mihai Cioabă published a well-received book of poetry, *Negustorul de Ploaie* (*The Rain Merchant*).

People in the West sometimes confuse Romanian with Romani, which is the language of the European Gypsies, or Roma. The similarity is coincidental: the English word for the European Gypsy stems from an Indian/Sanskrit root.

Some, however, have become extremely wealthy and the *bulibashas* often live in 20-roomed mansions with elaborate silver roofing and turrets, which house their extended families. Romanian culture has been enhanced by the Romanis and they are respected for their music in a land where music-making is very important.

Romania has produced some of the greatest Roma musicians and bands in the world and presently Fanfare Ciocărlia is a great ambassador.

In November 2007, the EU decided to hold an unprecedented meeting with Roma people from all over Europe. It was a response to the challenge posed by what has become the biggest ethnic minority in the ever-enlarging EU. Europe is home to approximately ten million Roma who remain the poorest of the poor, often migrating abroad in search of work. In autumn 2007, the murder of an Italian woman sparked off a wave of hostility against the Roma and dozens of expulsions from Italy. A huge number of Roma had gone to Italy and Spain in search of work. However, all over Romania, alarm bells are ringing about a growing labour shortage. A factory near Sibiu even had to hire 100 metalworkers from India. Some employers argued that the Roma were either lazy or lacked the right skills, while the Roma claimed they faced discrimination.

In Zărnești, Dan Marin explained how people (visitors and locals alike) either see Roma as a problem (unemployed and lazy troublemakers) or idealise them as romantic travellers, living beyond the confines of society. Marin offers a chance (see page 143) to visit a *bulibasha* and see how they live. Magda Matache, executive director for Romani Criss, a Roma human rights group, said that at least 40% of the Roma population is unemployed. 'Although a lot of improvements have been made in the education system, the level of illiteracy in the Roma community is still high and 35–40% of Roma children don't have access to school. Roma families will not send their children to school because they don't see the importance of it, as after they finish school they won't get a job, they won't get equal treatment,' said Matache.

Jews arrived in Romania during the Roman Empire and more arrived in the 8th and 9th centuries after the collapse of the Jewish Khazar Empire.

More arrived in the 14th, 15th and 17th centuries from all parts of Europe, seeking a refuge after expulsion. They contributed a great deal to the country's culture, society and economy but were refused citizenship until 1878 when the powers at the Congress of Berlin forced Romania to grant equal rights.

The Jewish community reached its peak in the 1920s when some 800,000 lived in Romania, one of the few parts of the world where they were allowed to own land.

The 1907 revolt was fiercely anti-Semitic and was followed by the rise of the Iron Guard and other nationalist parties. Antipathy towards Jews spread unchecked and during World War II, out of 166,000 Jews rounded up and deported to concentration camps only 26,000 survived. The Jewish population was devastated.

After 1948, Stalin encouraged anti-Semitism and the Romanian regime restricted Jewish religious observances and harassed and imprisoned Jews who wanted to emigrate to Israel. Despite this pressure, however, a third of Romania's Jews had emigrated by 1951.

In 1952, Stalin turned again on Romania's Jews and Romania's communist leader Gheorghiu-Dej profited from mounting anti-Semitic Soviet policy by persuading Stalin to purge the Jewish Communist Foreign Minister Ana Pauker, who was charged with 'cosmopolitanism'. Ceauşescu continued where Gheorghiu-Dej left off and sold Jews to Israel for US$3,000 for each exit visa. At least 300,000 had left by 1989. Today only about 8,000 Jews remain, with more than half in the capital. There are around 800 working synagogues. Jewish heritage sites are scattered throughout the country: places of particular interest in Transylvania are found in Braşov, Cluj-Napoca and Târgu Mureş.

Saxons (Saşi/Erdélyi szászok/Siebenürger Sachsen) arrived in the 12th century to settle in Transylvania, mainly in modern-day Mureş, Sibiu and Braşov counties. They were invited to colonise the territory by Hungary's King Géza II (ruled 1141–62).

For decades, the Saxons' main task was to defend the sparsely populated southeastern border of the Kingdom of Hungary and many of their fortified churches (see box, page 47) remain to this day and can be visited to see the remarkable architectural and decorative skills of the craftsmen and master builders. Although the settlers came mostly from the western regions of the Holy Roman Empire – Luxembourg, Flanders and the Moselle Valley – and spoke Franconian dialects, they were known collectively as Saxons because of the many Germans working for the Hungarian chancellery. The Saxons held a privileged status with the Hungarians and Székely people of Transylvania. King Géza II granted them land, autonomy and tax benefits. The Saxons developed a strong and wealthy community that flourished during the Middle Ages. In German, Transylvania is known as Siebenburgen, from the seven fortified church towns: Sibiu, Sighişoara, Mediaş, Sebeş, Braşov, Bistriţa and Cluj-Napoca.

Along with the largely Hungarian Transylvanian nobility and the Székely people, the Saxons were members of the Unio Trium Nationum (Union of Three Nations) signed in 1438, an agreement which safeguarded political rights for the three groups and excluded the Romanian peasantry.

From a population of 800,000 Transylvanian Saxons and Swabians, only about 20,000 remain today; most of them fled communist repression or left seeking a better life in Germany after 1989. In World War II, the Russians deported many Saxons to Siberia. In the 1980s there was a secret arrangement to allow Saxons to leave and go to Germany. After much financial wrangling, they had to pay approximately US$5,000 and it became like selling Germans back to Germany. Nevertheless, many consider themselves Transylvanian and dream of going home. Viscri was once a thriving Saxon village, now only a few such villages remain. Now 60% of the population is Roma because they were given Saxon houses in the 1980s when the Saxons left for Germany as the communists tried to settle the Roma down in one place, making them easier to control.

In the 17th century, **Armenians** settled in Bistriţa (Bistriţa-Năsăud County), Frumoasa and Gheorgheni (both in Harghita County) after Prince Mihály Apafi I let them stay when they were fleeing from Tatar hordes. The Armenians from

Bistriţa went on to build the town of Gherla, north of Cluj-Napoca on the Bistriţa road and the town became the headquarters for the Armenian Catholic Church. The Armenians were skilful cattle traders and the town soon became rich. The people gradually assimilated into the dominant Magyar Transylvanian culture and society in the surrounding area, although they have kept their religion and traditions to this day, despite the population dwindling to fewer than 90 souls. The Armenian Catholic Pilgrimage takes place at the Baroque Armenian cathedral (1748–98) when Armenians come to Transylvania from all parts of the globe (see page 258).

LANGUAGE

ROMANIAN (*limba română*) The language originated from Vulgar Latin spoken by Dacia's Roman conquerors in AD106, but has since acquired about a fifth of its vocabulary from Hungarian, German, Turkish, Greek and Slavic influences. It is the closest of the Romance languages to the original Latin tongue. Any knowledge of French, Italian, Portuguese or Latin can help in understanding Romanian.

As a result of its geographical isolation, Romanian was probably the first language to split from Latin and until modern times was not influenced by other Romance languages, perhaps explaining why it is one of the most uniform languages in Europe. It is more conservative than other Romance languages in form and shape.

Romanian has declensions, but whereas Latin had seven cases, Romanian has only five; however, the nominative and accusative are morphologically identical as are the genitive and dative. The vocative is not used that often as it is the form when addressing people, as in the national anthem *Deşteaptă-te, române* ('Awake, O Romanian!').

There is also a neuter gender beside the masculine and feminine genders.

All the Romanian dialects are believed to have been unified in a common Romanian language sometime before the 7th century, when the area was influenced by the Byzantine Empire and Romanian became influenced by Slavonic languages. The Aromanian language, with few Slavonic words, is spoken by people living in the southern Balkans, Albania, Macedonia and Bulgaria and as an emigrant community living in Dobruja. They are the second most populous group of Vlachs, after modern-day Romanians.

Variations in the Daco-Romanian dialect (spoken throughout Romania and Moldova) are very small. The use of this uniform Daco-Romanian dialect extends well beyond the borders of the Romanian state: a Romanian-speaker from Moldova speaks the same language as a Romanian-speaker from the Serbian Banat.

HUNGARIAN A notoriously tongue-twisting and tricky-to-learn Finno-Ugric language, Hungarian is used in eastern Transylvania and widely heard in some cities like Miercurea-Ciuc, Tàrgu Mureş and Cluj-Napoca. Hungarian is widely used as a second language in counties such as Covasna and Harghita.

In the past, Romania had a sizeable German minority population, although nowadays the number of native German speakers is dwindling. However, the **German** language is still studied widely in Romania as a foreign language, and, due to the residing German cultural influence, it is used as a second (or third) official language in many parts of Transylvania.

ROMANI This is the language of the central and east European Roma. The term 'Gypsy' is considered derogatory. Where the term 'Gypsy' is used in this guide it is in association with music and traditions and used by Roma themselves as a marketing tool or in the titles of books and music CDs. The similarity between the names 'Romani' and 'Romanian' is purely coincidental. Romani is an Indo-Aryan language with many dialects throughout Europe. In Romania, Balkan Romani is spoken. Presently, there are independent groups working towards standardising the language, including groups from Romania, Serbia, Montenegro and Sweden. In Romania, the country with the largest identifiable Roma population, there is a unified teaching system of the Romani language for all dialects spoken in the country. This is primarily a result of the work of Gheorghe Sarău, who created Romani textbooks for teaching Roma children in their own language.

Visitors to Transylvania who are worried about upsetting ethnic sensibilities should remember that any attempt at the local tongue will be appreciated. A few words of Romanian, Hungarian and German can go a long way and a hearty *Noroc!*, *Egészségére!* (pronounced 'egg-ace-shaig-ir-re') or *Prost!* when presented with yet another *ţuică* goes down well in any language.

RELIGION

Romania is a very religious country and the mixed population practises a variety of faiths including Romanian Orthodox, Roman Catholic, Lutheran, Calvinist, Greek Catholic (Romanian Church united with Rome), Pentecostal and Protestant. The Unitarian Church is particular to Transylvania. There are also Jewish and 'newer' religions such as Mormon, Hare Krishna and Baha'i.

In Transylvania, religion and ethnicity are intertwined. If somebody says he or she is Roman Catholic or Calvinist then it is almost 100% certain that the person is Hungarian; if somebody says he or she is Orthodox then you can be virtually sure that person is Romanian. The Unitarian religion is small but mainly Hungarian. The Lutherans are Saxon.

Transylvania has so many religions because of the 1568 Turda Declaration, which allowed all Christian-based religions to practise freely and they flourished in an atmosphere of tolerance.

For information on Romanian saints and other beliefs, see page 123.

HISTORY OF RELIGIOUS MOVEMENTS IN TRANSYLVANIA Christianity arrived in Transylvania with the Roman soldiers in the AD106 conquest of Dacia, although some historians claim that St Andrew came evangelising earlier. After the conversion of the emperor Constantine in the 4th century, Romania was swayed more by the Greek Orthodox Church in Constantinople than by Rome and continued to follow the Orthodox path after the Great Schism (1054) between Western and Eastern Christianity. Romania also continued to use Church Slavonic for the liturgy until as late as 1863 when Romanian replaced Church Slavonic as the exclusive language of the Romanian Orthodox Church. From the mid 16th century, the Reformation swept through Transylvania and large numbers converted to Protestant denominations, namely Calvinist among the

CHURCHES WITH ELABORATE CEILINGS AND FRESCOES

BRAȘOV The Black Church (Biserică Neagra) is the largest church in Transylvania and the most easterly Gothic church in Europe. The church is crammed with panels, carvings, frescoes and more than 200 Turkish carpets (see page 135).

CLUJ-NAPOCA (Cluj County) St Michael's Church is the second-largest Gothic church in Transylvania and its soaring arches are spectacular (see page 252).

CRASNA (Sălaj County) has a 14th-century church with beautiful painted panels dating from the 17th century and depicting animals (see page 274).

DÂRJIU (Harghita County) has a fortified Unitarian church with frescoes showing the legend of St László. It is a UNESCO World Heritage Site (see page 170).

DENSUȘ (Hunedoara County) has a church dating from the 13th century and is possibly the oldest church in Romania. It has interesting frescoes (see page 226).

FILDU DE SUS (Sălaj County) has an 18th-century Romanian wooden church with beautiful frescoes depicting biblical scenes (see page 274).

Hungarians and Lutheran among the Saxons. Later on, a significant Unitarian minority developed, mostly among the Székely people. These days, the Lutheran churches, which catered for Saxon minorities, are emptying out as the Saxons return to Germany.

In the 1970s, the communist leaders realised that Soviet-style atheism wouldn't catch on and they decided to manipulate religion as a tool for nationalism. The Orthodox believers were closely monitored, but the Catholics and Unitarians of Transylvania were particularly oppressed. There are few Jewish people left in Romania, decimated by the Holocaust and emigration to Israel. The majority of Romania's Roma community is Orthodox Christian. Nowadays, religion plays a large part in daily life; in the 2002 census, 86.7% of the total population declared themselves Romanian Orthodox. In 1999, Romania was the first Eastern Orthodox country to host a visit from Pope John Paul II. Populist-nationalist politician Gigi Becali pushes religion in his homophobic, sinister diatribes. President Traian Băsescu recently approved a law requiring religious denominations to find 20,000 members before they can receive official recognition.

The **Romanian Orthodox Church** is by far the largest denomination in Romania. In Transylvania, for centuries the Orthodox religion was considered inferior to Western Christianity. The Turda Declaration referred to Orthodox as a 'tolerated' religion. After the unification of Transylvania with Moldavia and Wallachia in 1918, the Orthodox religion became the state religion in Transylvania. After this many Orthodox churches were built in the centre of towns such as Târgu Mureş, Sfântu Gheorghe, Alba Iulia, Cluj-Napoca, and usually right next to and dwarfing the Roman Catholic church in an attempt to assert national identity. During the Ceauşescu era, the authorities 'tolerated' the Romanian Orthodox Church and many important positions in the Orthodox hierarchy were filled by party nominees. The Church remained submissive to the regime, even in the face of repeated attacks on the most basic religious values and continued violations

GHELINŢA (Covasna County) has an architectural treasure of Székely Land, the Catholic church built in the 13th century in Romanesque style with Renaissance floral panels and frescoes depicting St László (see page 157).

HUEDIN (Cluj County) has a 13th-century Calvinist church built in Romanesque style with Renaissance panelling by Lörinc Umling showing exotic animals such as elephants (see page 254).

MUGENI (Harghita County) has a 14th-century Cavlinist church with frescoes showing the legend of St László (see page 170).

SIBIU (Sibiu County) has a 14th-century Gothic cathedral with superb frescoes by Johannes Rosenau (see page 200).

TÂRGU MUREŞ (Mureş County) has a Calvinist church built in the 17th century in the Castle grounds (see page 180).

ZĂBALA (Covasna County) has a 15th-century fortified Calvinist church with a ceiling decorated with floral motifs (see page 158).

of Church rights. Church leaders praised the 'religious freedom' that the state guaranteed and were known to collaborate with the Securitate in silencing clergymen who spoke out against the demolition of churches. Orthodox churches are very striking in appearance with vaguely oriental yet totally plain exteriors but inside a riot of colour and gilt with every possible surface covered with icons. As in Russian Orthodox churches, there are no chairs and the congregation stands throughout the service. Orthodox churches are very dark and atmospheric with the intoxicating scent of myrrh and burning candle wax.

The **Roman Catholic Church** makes up the second-largest religious group in Transylvania. After 1948, the Department of Cults took the official position that 'no religious community and none of its officials may have relations with religious communities abroad'. These regulations were designed to abolish papal authority over Catholics in Romania. The fact that most members of the Roman Catholic community were ethnic Hungarians probably contributed to the Church's tenuous position. In the early 1980s, there were indications that tensions between the Vatican and the regime over bishopric appointments were easing. Pope John Paul II successfully appointed an apostolic administrator for the Bucharest archbishopric. By the 1990s, however, the Romanian government had not officially recognised the appointment, and the issues of inadequate church facilities, restrictions on the training of priests, and insufficient printing of religious materials remained unresolved.

The **Lutheran Church**'s congregation has, for centuries, come from Transylvanian Saxons. In the 16th century, the printer and publisher Ioannes Honterus (1498–1549) worked hard to introduce the teachings of Martin Luther to Transylvania. There is a statue of Honterus in his birthplace, Braşov. Martin Luther inspired the Protestant Reformation when he nailed his 95 Theses to the door of the Wittenberg Castle Church in 1517. The 95 Theses were points for debate that criticised the Church and the Pope, particularly the practice of selling indulgences and the Catholic Church's policy on purgatory.

The **Reformed (Calvinist) Church** has an entirely Hungarian congregation. In 1564, the Aiud Synod broke with Martin Luther and began to follow the teachings of John Calvin (1509–64), a French Protestant theologian. Many Transylvanian princes and the Hungarian upper and middle classes converted to Calvinism, while Saxons preferred to stick with Luther. In 1622, Transylvanian prince Gábor Bethlén set up a Calvinist college in Alba Iulia and it became a centre for Calvinist intellectual life. Approximately half of all ethnic Hungarians in Transylvania (700,000) follow the Reformed Church teachings.

The **Unitarian Church** was introduced to Transylvania in Cluj in 1556 by the (previously) Calvinist minister Dávid Ferenc (1510–79) and by 1568 it was already accepted as one of the four official churches of Transylvania. Unitarianism had its origins among the Italian and Spanish humanists and some of the more extreme Anabaptists and its leader Faustus Socinus (1539–1604) who came to Cluj in 1578 before moving on to Krakow in 1580. Unitarianism derives its name from its main creed that 'God is one', and the rejection of the doctrine of the Trinity as well as of other basic doctrines such as the divinity of Christ, his atonement for the sins of the world and thus the possibility of salvation. Unitarians do not have a dogmatic approach and they are conspicuous for their devotion to reason in matters of religion and to civil and religious liberty and their tolerance of all sincere forms of religious faith.

Unitarianism spread worldwide, and by the 1830s had mutated to become the religion, for instance, of the Boston/Harvard establishment with an emphasis on scientific progress and material success. In Romania, there are now around 75,000 Unitarians, almost all among the Hungarian and Székely communities.

Many great minds throughout the world have been persuaded by Unitarian ideas. Charles Dickens, Charles Darwin, Sir Isaac Newton, George Stephenson, Alexander Graham Bell, Robert Burns and Béla Bartók were all Unitarians.

EDUCATION

Along with the aim of political socialisation, a chief goal of the communists was the 'democratisation' of education, which meant compulsory primary education for all members of society and implied greater access to higher education for peasants and workers.

According to the Law on Education adopted in 1995, the **Romanian Educational System** is regulated by the Ministry of Education and Research (Ministerul Educaţiei şi Cercetării – MEC). Kindergarten is optional between the ages of three and six.

Schooling begins at the age of seven and is compulsory until grade X, which usually corresponds to the age of 16 or 17.

Primary (*şcoala primară*) is from grade I to IV, and secondary education is divided into *gimnaziu* from grade V to VIII and *liceu* from grade IX to XIII.

Higher education (*studii superioare*) is still in the process of being organised according to the Bologna process principles which aim at the construction of the European higher education area.

Since the 1989 revolution, the educational system has been in a continual process of reformation that has been both praised and criticised in equal measures.

Apart from the official educational system and recent additions of private schools, there is also an informal, semi-legal private tutoring system (*meditaţii*), which is used by students when preparing for notoriously difficult exams. Tutoring was also used during the communist regime when great emphasis was placed on academic achievement.

The system gives the following diplomas: *Absolvire* (elementary school graduation, after the *Teste Naţionale* exam), *Bacalaureat* (high school graduation, after the *Bacalaureat* exam), *Licenţă* (university undergraduate programme graduation, after an exam and thesis), *Masterat* (Master's degree, after an exam and thesis) and *Doctorat* (PhD following the production of a thesis).

In 2004, nearly five million Romanians were enrolled in school: 14% of the population at primary and secondary level and 3% at university level.

During the Ceauşescu period, there was nothing on television except party propaganda and nationalistic music, and many Romanians were driven to literature as their only form of entertainment. Romanians are a very literate people and you will see people absorbed in weighty tomes on the train, bus, or in cafés. Literacy is defined as the percentage of the population aged 15 and over who can read and write. In Romania, 97.3% of the total population is literate. 98.4% of males are literate and 96.3% of females are literate.

There are many universities in Transylvania, situated in great cities of learning such as Alba Iulia, Braşov, Cluj-Napoca, Sibiu and Târgu Mureş.

The **Babeş-Bolyai University, Cluj-Napoca** (*www.ubbcluj.ro*) has over 43,000 students, making it the largest and most diverse university in Romania. It offers both undergraduate and graduate courses in fields ranging from literature and history to computer science and biology. Cluj-Napoca has six state (and several private) universities; consequently, the student population of the city is the largest in Romania.

The **Technical University of Cluj-Napoca** (*www.utcluj.ro*) designed the first ATM Metropolitan Area Network in Romania. The site presents the faculties, staff and alumni and offers information to current and prospective students, presents research groups and features live images.

The **Lucian Blaga University** in Sibiu (*www.ulbsibiu.ro/en/*) was founded in 1995, and includes faculties of theology, law, arts, engineering, economics and medicine.

The **Transilvania University of Braşov** (*www.unitbv.ro*) has four colleges: the medical college, technical college, the university of education and philology and the college of forestry economics and computer science.

The **1 December 1918 University** in Alba Iulia (*www.uab.ro*) came into existence in 1991, and is situated inside the star-shaped citadel in the higher town.

The **University of Medicine and Pharmacy** in Târgu Mureş (*www.umftgm.ro*) celebrated 60 years of learning in 2005.

CULTURE

The multi-cultural land of Transylvania has given birth to many colourful, often eccentric, characters. The stunning landscape has provided lyrical inspiration for poets and painters, while the turbulent history and unusual mix of nationalities and religions has given authors plenty to chew on.

Craftsmen and women find motifs for woodcarving, embroidery and ceramics in the natural world while Transylvanian architectural influences have reached far beyond the Carpathian Mountains.

At the beginning of the 20th century, Hungarian composers Béla Bartók and Zoltán Kodály set out on a journey around Transylvania, noting down over a period of seven years the folk melodies preserved previously only by the oral tradition.

The skills of Roma musicians from Transylvania are famous the world over (see page 288 for details of CDs).

Romanian cinema is also enjoying a renaissance and the annual Transylvanian Film Festival in Cluj-Napoca is a huge draw with famous stars of the silver screen in attendance (see page 254).

CINEMA Cristian Mungiu's *4 Months, 3 Weeks and 2 Days* (*4 luni, 3 săptămâni şi 2 zile*) won the best film prize at the 20th annual European Film Awards in Berlin (December 2007). The low-budget production, a harrowing film about illegal abortion in communist-era Romania, had already taken the top award at the 2007 Cannes Film Festival. Mungiu also took the best director award for the film. It was the first Romanian film to win the prestigious award. More recent films by Mungiu include *Tales from the Golden Age* (2009) and *Beyond the Hills* (2012). The French (with Roma and Algerian heritage) film director Tony Gatlif makes many excellent films usually featuring Roma actors and the locations are usually in Romania. Gatlif's film *Transylvania* (2006) is well worth watching, along with *Gadjo Dilo* (1997), *Latcho Drom* (1993) and *Mondo* (1996), to see realistic portrayals of Roma society set against a brilliant soundtrack.

Seven locations in Romania were used and many scenes in *Cold Mountain* (2003), the late Anthony Minghella's tale of the American Civil War, were shot in the Piatra Craiului National Park, near Zărneşti. The gorge provided a stunning final venue for the film. Hollywood stars Jude Law, Renée Zellweger and Nicole Kidman relaxed at Poiana Braşov ski resort after shooting the film. British comedian Sacha Baron Cohen filmed his idea of Kazakhstan for *Borat: Cultural*

Learnings of America for make Benefit Glorious Nation of Kazakhstan (2006) in Glod, 10km southwest of Sinaia on route 71. The locals were very upset when the film came out because they had been told the film would be a documentary about poverty in the region. Kevin Costner also filmed the mini-series *Hatfields & McCoys* (2011) near Braşov.

LITERATURE At the beginning of the 14th century, printing presses were set up in Bucharest, Târgovişte, Iaşi, Râmnicu, Buzău and in Transylvania at Blaj, Alba Iulia and Braşov. A sustained activity of printing texts in the Romanian language began in 1559 when Deacon Coresi printed *Catehismul* at his own printing house in Braşov.

The origins of Romanian cultural literature date back to the 17th–18th centuries. The string of scholars concerned to assert the Latin origin and identity of the Romanian nation continued with the representatives of the Transylvanian School including Samuil Micu (1745–1806), Gheorghe Sincai (1754–1816), Petru Maior (1756–1821), and Ion Budai Deleanu (1760–1820), the author of a strange, heroic-comic poem *Tiganiada* (the *Gypsies' Saga*). The philosopher Emil Cioran (1911–95) was born in Răşinari, near Sibiu, in a village he considered 'paradise on Earth'. Aged ten, he started high school in Sibiu and left the rural life. Cioran studied literature and philosophy in Bucharest and graduated in 1932 receiving a Humboldt scholarship to study in Germany. Cioran admired the Iron Guard and Hitler but renounced his extreme views in later life.

Albert Wass was a right-wing Transylvanian Hungarian novelist who went to the US in 1945. He has now been published in English and is often quoted by right-wing Hungarians who dream of recovering the lost territories of Erdély. Áron Tamási (1897–1966) was a Székely writer who wrote of village life in the Harghita Mountains. Balázs Orbán (1829–90) was called the 'greatest Székely'. The writer, historian, politician and traveller wrote a massive tome *Székelyföld leírása* (*Description of Székely Land*), the definitive work on the region.

VISUAL ARTS The religious paintings of the frescoes and panels found on the ceilings and pews of churches throughout Transylvania are quite striking.

The 18th- and 19th-century tradition of painted glass icons is another form of folk art typical of Transylvania, in which glass-painting techniques, possibly from Bohemia and the Tyrol, were applied to the custom of painting Orthodox icons. The resulting genre blends strict Orthodox iconography with the world of folk superstition – a world, which is not always in keeping with the teachings of the Church. The best glass icon painting collections can be found at Sibiel near Sibiu and Cincu near Făgăraş.

There are few Saxons left in Transylvania, but in recent years traditional festivals, such as the Kronenfest in Mălăncrăv (see page 209) have been being resurrected with great enthusiasm and large numbers participate in the events, including music and dance.

Today most of the painted furniture based on a once highly influential Saxon tradition and the highly decorative stove tiles (see *Mediaş*, page 211 and *Cisnădioara*, page 202) are for export. A shop in Sibiu sells fine examples of painted furniture (see *Shopping*, page 103). Many of the old Saxon village houses have survived untouched and in recent years many western Europeans have purchased them, although they need a lot of renovation work. Renaissance art influenced the patterns used in furniture paintings, such as the tulip motifs painted on wooden storage chests. Many villages have local wood sculptors who blend tradition with

ROMA MUSIC TRADITIONS

Roma musicians, performing from early childhood alongside their fathers, grandfathers and uncles, play at Romanian, Hungarian and Roma weddings and events. See page 288 for some CD suggestions. Here are some names to watch out for:

FANFARE CIOCĂRLIA From the village of Zece Prăjini in northeastern Romania, this celebrated brass band captures the energy and passion of Roma music and probably represents the most famous of Romania's Roma bands. They have released eight albums and performed worldwide to critical acclaim.

PĂLATCA BAND Probably the most well-known band in central Transylvania, led by members of the Codoban family in the village of Pălatca in Cluj County, 30km east of Cluj-Napoca just north of route 16 to Reghin.

SÁNDOR 'NETI' FODOR Neti Fodor (1922–2004) was the most respected Roma fiddler of the Kalotaszeg region.

THE MÁCSINGÓ FAMILY One of the important musical Roma families from central Transylvania based in the villages of Báré (Bărăi near Palatca) and Deva. György Mácsingó leads the band.

ÖKRÖS ENSEMBLE Csaba Ökrös is a talented fiddler and his traditional ensemble is one of the best Budapest *táncház* (dance house) groups. They often work together with village musicians from Transylvania.

SOPORU BAND Soporu are one of the best Roma groups from the Câmpia Transilvaniei (Transylvanian Plain), led by Dandoricb Ciurcui.

SZÁSZCSÁVÁS BAND Szászcsávás (Ceuaş in Târnava Mică Valley, south of Târgu Mureş) is a predominantly Hungarian village in the Kis-Küküllő region of Transylvania. Their Roma band, led by István 'Dumnezu' Jámbor, is one of the best in the region.

modern fashions to create useful kitchen utensils such as bowls and spoons, as well as decorative objects.

In regions with large Hungarian populations, visitors should see the Calvinist churches for their panelled ceilings, made up of square *kazeta* (cassettes or panels) painted in the 18th century along with the pews and galleries in a naïve style similar to the embroidery. The Kalotaszeg region is a good place to find these churches. Corund is a village in Harghita County filled with ceramic workshops and outlets that line both sides of the one main road leading through the settlement.

In the Székely Lands, many variations of the carved wooden *székely kapu* (gate) decorate the landscape, using many motifs and colours from nature and also pre-Christian Székely symbols such as the moon, sun and stars.

The Hungarian architect Károly Kós (1883–1977) often incorporated elements from its folk art into his work. Kalotaszeg is one of the best places in Transylvania to see old traditions. Many ethnic Hungarian-owned houses in this region still preserve the *tisztaszoba* (clean room), a kind of parlour used only to store and display family possessions such as painted furniture, decorated plates and ceramic bowls. The clean room also contains a *vetett ágy* (made-up bed) with a huge collection of embroidered pillows. The ethnic Hungarian Székely are found mainly in Harghita County, Covasna and parts of Mureş. They do not wear their folk costumes as often as those in Sic or Kalotaszeg, but dress up mainly for festivals and events. To see an unspoiled Székely village visit Inlăceni, 5km southwest of Corund, where there are no modern buildings and where it feels as if time has stopped still.

FOLK MUSIC These days, the best place to hear folk music is at a folk dancing club or one of the many festivals. Transylvanian folk music is still played at weddings and weekly dance houses. The Romanian and Hungarian melodies can be quite similar. The traditional ensemble consists of a string trio of a violin, a viola and a double bass. In parts of Transylvania, the cimbalom is also used. The first violinist or *primás* plays the melody and leads the musicians from one song to another, while the viola and bass provide the accompaniment and rhythm section for the band.

Muzsikás are Hungary's leading *táncház* (dance house) group and the leading ambassadors for Transylvanian music. Singer Márta Sebestyén joined Muzsikás in 1979. She knew founding member Péter Éri from her previous band, the Sebő group, then appeared first on Muzsikás's *Nem úgy van most, mint volt régen (Now It Isn't So, Like It Was Long Ago)* album in 1981. She was a permanent member until 1985, but in the 1980s, her solo career rocketed so that the record labels showed 'Muzsikás and Márta Sebestyén'. Sebestyén told me, 'My mother attended a school in Békestarhos which had a revolutionary musical idea.' Talented peasant children were picked out and taught by Kodály in a manor house. Unfortunately, the experiment was stopped in 1955. She showed a photo of her mother playing piano to Kodály and said, 'As a child I heard so many stories of Kodály *bácsi* (uncle), I really thought he was an elderly relative.' Hungarian composers Béla Bartók (1881–1945) and Zoltán Kodály (1882–1967) both spent long periods in Transylvania noting down the traditional folk melodies and incorporating the motifs in their music. In 1907, Bartók and Kodály set out for Transylvania, where they recorded and catalogued thousands of melodies. Through the project they discovered a rich vein of inspiration for their own compositions. Bartók declared that a genuine peasant melody was 'quite as much a masterpiece in miniature as a Bach fugue or a Mozart sonata'. Bartók gathered much musical material in the region surrounding Hunedoara and also collected carved furniture and handicrafts from the village of Izvoru Crişului (Körösfő) which are now displayed at his home-museum in Budapest (District II, Csalán utca 29). The Ardealul Ensemble, like Muzsikás, are based in Budapest but play the music of Transylvania.

The village of Sic (Szék) in Cluj County is a totally Hungarian village, filled with folk music, which visitors can often hear as they walk along the street.

Other villages with folk music include Sângeorz-Băi (Oláhszentgyörgy), Sopuru de Câmpie (Mezőszopor), Suatu (Magyarszovát) and Vaida-Cămăraş (Vajdakamarás).

As for popular music, Transylvania's most famous musical export is the twin-sister group of Monica and Gabriela Irimia from Cluj-Napoca, better known as the Cheeky Girls. In January 2004, their first single in the UK, 'The Cheeky Song (Touch my Bum)' was voted worst pop record of all time in a Channel 4 poll.

ARCHITECTURE The architects of the National Romantic school, led by Károly Kós (1883–1977) were strongly influenced by Transylvanian village architecture, as well as by that of the Finns, one of the ancient Magyars' distant relations. The Cockerel Church in Cluj-Napoca and the National Székely Museum in Sfântu Gheorghe are two of Károly Kós's most interesting works. I found a wonderful book by Kós in one of Budapest's many second-hand bookshops. Printed as a special edition in 1934 in Cluj-Napoca, the book *Erdély* contains a detailed history of the region (in Hungarian), church floor plans and 60 gorgeous linocuts of the most interesting buildings, usually churches. There is, apparently, an English-language translation of this book, but without the linocuts.

For details of folk and open-air architectural museums in Transylvania, see page 106.

The Turks destroyed many of Transylvania's architectural treasures during the occupation, but there are still many glorious buildings to discover.

All architectural styles – Romanesque, Gothic, Renaissance, Baroque and Art Nouveau – can be seen in the buildings throughout the region. The peculiar church at Densuş is considered the oldest in the country and has elements of **Romanesque** architecture although it is quite unique in style. Spread around Transylvania, built in the middle of the plain or on a hilltop, dominating the surrounding village, the fortified Saxon churches which started appearing in the 13th century feature watchtowers, windows for shooting or throwing fuel oil over the besiegers, secret passages and water ditches betraying the brutality of medieval life. The most striking examples are found at Biertan, Bazna, Câlnic, Cârţa, Cisnădioara, Copşa Mare, Homorod, Hosman, Moşna, Prejmer, Valea Viilor and Viscri. There are also smaller fortified churches in Székely Land such as Ghelinţa. Only a few of the intricately decorated altarpieces which once adorned the medieval churches still survive in the Saxon Lutheran churches at Biertan, Sebeş and Hălchiu just north of Braşov, which all feature beautiful triptychs.

Renaissance buildings are found in Cluj-Napoca and Alba Iulia. The magnificent Corvin Castle at Hunedoara and Bran Castle were built during the **Gothic** period. Corvin Castle looks like how we would imagine a Transylvanian castle to be with pointed turrets, imposing battlements and buttresses and a huge moat, whereas Bran Castle is more squared off and chunky. The Gothic influence was widespread in the Saxon lands, especially in medieval town centres such as Sighişoara's citadel Old Town. The stunning Saint Michael's Church in Cluj-Napoca displays soaring Gothic arches while Braşov's Black Church dominates the city with its sturdy form and pointed spire. The ruins of Gothic castles at Câlnic, Deva, Râşnov, Rupea and Slimnic are impressive.

The **Romanian wooden churches** also date from the 18th–19th centuries. Striking examples can be found in Târgu Mureş and at Fildu de Sus southwest of Cluj-Napoca. The spires are narrow and tall and the interiors are usually decorated with frescoes of biblical scenes painted in the naïve folk style. A few Romanian stone churches were also built in this period – the churches at Sâmbăta de Sus and Făgăraş are good examples.

During the 18th century, the **Baroque** style became dominant in Transylvanian towns, once more changing the urban landscape. The style came about through the Habsburg influence and can be seen at the elegant Bánffy Palace at Bonţida near Cluj-Napoca. The fanciful Upper and Lower Karl Gates at Alba Iulia, built to mark Habsburg emperor Karl VI's victory over the Ottomans, are typical of Viennese Baroque. Baroque-style palaces also appeared in Braşov, the Tholdalagi Palace in Târgu Mureş and Sibiu's Brukenthal Palace. Teleki Castle at Gorneşti and Wesselényi Castle in Jibou were also built in the Baroque style. In the 18th century, the Baroque town of Gherla was created with many townhouses constructed for wealthy Armenian

UNESCO WORLD HERITAGE SITES

There are three UNESCO World Heritage Sites in Transylvania (and another four in the rest of Romania), situated at Sighişoara, in the Saxon fortified church region and in the Orăştie mountain region.

Sighişoara's historic centre was inscribed on the UNESCO list in 1999; the other two inscriptions are spread over regions.

There are seven villages with fortified churches in Transylvania, inscribed in 1993, and extended in 1999. The seven villages are: Câlnic/Kelling (Alba County, southeast of Sebeş), Valea Viilor/Wurmloch (Sibiu County, south of Copşa Mică), Biertan/Birthalm (Sibiu County), Saschiz/Keisd (Mureş County), Viscri/Weisskirch (Braşov County) and Prejmer/Tartlau (Braşov County, northeast of Braşov). Dârjiu/Székelyderzs (Harghita County, east of Saschiz) is the odd one out on the list because it is a Székely Unitarian church while the rest are Saxon.

There are six sites featured as a collective site on UNESCO's list. The Dacian fortresses of the Orăştie Mountains (1999) are spread over a fairly wide area with five sites in Hunedoara County and one in Alba County.

Sarmizegetusa Regia was the capital of the Dacian Kingdom, found in the village of Grădiştea de Munte, south of Orăştioara de Sus.

Six citadels appear on UNESCO's list: the Dacian citadels of Costeşti-Cetaţuia, Costeşti-Bildaru, Sarmizegetusa Regia, Luncani-Piatra Roşie, Băniţa are in Hunedoara County; the Dacian citadel of Capâlna is in Alba County and east of Orăştie, and the Roman ruins of Ulpia Traiana Augusta at Sarmizegetusa are 40km west of Sarmizegetusa Regia and not on UNESCO's list.

merchants. At the beginning of the 20th century, **Art Nouveau** shaped the face of Târgu Mureş and the Palace of Culture is a vivid explosion of colour and design. At this time, Transylvania was still part of the Hungarian Kingdom and the major Art Nouveau architects were commissioned to design buildings. The Budapest duo Marcell Komor and Jakab Dezső designed the Palace of Culture and the stunning Art Nouveau stained-glass windows came from the workshops of Budapest master of colour Miksa Róth. Kós's architectural successor was László Debreczeni who worked to restore numerous Transylvanian village churches including the Unitarian church at Ocland in Harghita County, 20km northeast of Rupea and the Calvinist church at Căpuşu Mic, 30km west of Cluj-Napoca.

2

Practical Information

WHEN TO VISIT

Romanian winters are cold, especially in the mountains and high plateaux of Transylvania. If you want to ski, the resorts south of Braşov, such as Poiana Braşov, Predeal and Buneşti, can virtually guarantee snow-covered slopes from November to mid March.

April and May are generally considered good months to visit Transylvania to see the spring flowers and avoid the searing heat of summer, especially towards the south of the region, which can last from June to August. If you don't like the heat, head for the hills, as the mountainous regions of Harghita, Bistriţa-Năsăud and around the Făgăraş peaks are wonderfully refreshing and blessed with clean, fresh air. Cities such as Braşov, Sibiu and Cluj-Napoca can be stifling in summer, although Cluj-Napoca is a major student city and empties of youth during the summer break.

Autumn is a lovely season in Transylvania. The colours of the leaves turn the landscape into a beautiful painting. There are many festivals connected with the harvest and much pastoral merrymaking before the long, hard winter sets in.

Spring and autumn are best for tackling strenuous hiking routes and give good opportunities for wildlife-watching, bird spotting and nature trails.

TRANSYLVANIA HIGHLIGHTS

Oh, where to begin? Transylvania is so stuffed with attractions of all types of adventurous, cultural, historical and natural interest that there really is something for everybody. Those wanting to ski will find slopes that suit all from the beginner or families with young children to those wanting to ski off-piste or try cross-country skis on rugged mountain plateaux. Those who would like to hike, cycle or just ramble through stunning countryside, track bear, lynx or fox, watch birds or admire wild flowers in the unspoiled landscape can find many places where they can wander undisturbed on a journey back in time. Culture vultures will enjoy discovering the Saxon villages, each guarded by a magnificent fortress church, and beautifully restored historic town centres crammed with museums, galleries, bars and restaurants. Horror fans can pursue the legend of Dracula and his inspiration Vlad III Ţepeş. Spa holidays are becoming increasingly popular and Transylvania is home to a number of fun resorts.

As getting around Transylvania is still quite tricky and time consuming, it might be a good idea to pinpoint your interests, but here is a general overview of things to think about including on an itinerary. It wouldn't be possible to visit all 20 places in two weeks or do them justice, but be sure to catch at least half a dozen of these.

A PERSONAL TOP 20

- **Sighişoara** The most eye-catching Saxon fortress town, a UNESCO World Heritage Site and birthplace of Vlad III Ţepeş (see page 184).
- **Biertan** One of the most easily accessible Saxon fortress church villages, with places to stay, eat, walk and ride horses (see page 207).
- **Sibiu** European Capital of Culture 2007 and full of fascinating museums, buildings, cafés and restaurants (see page 193).
- **Sovata Băi** A relaxing spa resort with top-notch hotels, facilities and therapeutic wallowing in the salty Lacul Ursu (see page 181).
- **Zărneşti Wolf Tours** Visit the Marin family at their lovely guesthouse and spend the days walking and wildlife-watching in the Piatra Craiului National Park with *Wanderlust*'s Guide of the Year 2007 (see page 143).
- **Count Tibor Kálnoky's estate at Micloşoara** Stay in beautifully restored guesthouses and go on fascinating day trips around the region (see page 155).
- **The Mikes Estate at Zăbala** Go bear-watching and explore remote parts of the Carpathian Mountains while staying at a luxurious boutique hotel (see page 158).
- **Turda Salt Mine** A fascinating journey underground in the historic town of Turda (see page 259).
- **Turda Gorge** A great place for a hike in beautiful countryside (see page 260).
- **Bicaz Gorges and Lacu Roşu** Incredible crags and a sinister lake (see page 172).
- **Braşov** An exciting modern city with a medieval heart, surrounded by mountains and hiking regions (see page 129).
- **Deva funicular** Take a space-age ride up the 'Hill of the Djinn' in this lively town (see page 221).
- **Retezat National Park** Hike up to the scenic dam and see wildlife and wild flowers (see page 227).
- **Lacul Fântânele** A tranquil and scenic spot in glorious surroundings of the ethnic Hungarian Kalotaszeg region (see page 256).
- **Prejmer** The most impressive of all Saxon fortress churches with a fascinating history enclosed within mighty walls (see page 148).
- **The Apuseni Mountains** With the Padiş Plateau, the Scarişoara Ice Cave and the contentious Roşia Montana gold mines (see page 241).
- **Mămăligă, Ciuc beer and ţuică** Don't miss out on Transylvania's culinary delights: polenta, a huge range of fresh fruit and vegetables, great beer and the fiery spirits (see page 87).
- **Folk music** Visit the village of Sic (Szék) for Magyar folk music or hunt down Roma musicians in clubs and restaurants all over Transylvania (see page 45).
- **Negreni annual fair** (and girl fairs all over) The many open-air festivals with music, folk crafts, eating, drinking and general merrymaking (see page 254).
- **Transylvania film festival**, Cluj-Napoca, a great place to spot the latest cinematic talents (see page 254).

ITINERARIES

A LONG WEEKEND Fly to Cluj-Napoca or Sibiu on one of the low-cost airlines. In Cluj, spend a leisurely morning exploring the town, admiring the view of the rooftops from the citadel hill, gazing in awe at the stunning Gothic interior of St Michael's Church and the controversial statue of Hungarian king Matthias Corvinus – his birthplace is also nearby. Enjoy a sustaining lunch in one of the many student pubs in this young vibrant city and walk off the calories on a promenade around Cluj's lovely botanical garden. In the evening, tuck in to a meal in a traditional

Those wishing to visit all the places connected with the creepy Count would have to cover a lot of ground, and many sites outside Transylvania. Vlad III Țepeș (1431–76), the real person behind Bram Stoker's literary creation, spent more time in Wallachia than in Transylvania and his capital was at Târgoviște, 100km south of Bran, the Transylvanian venue that, besides Sighișoara, exploits the Vlad/ Dracula legend the most. However, Transylvania and the surrounding Carpathian Mountains contain many great places to visit that have links with the bloodthirsty, toothy Count.

The main places on a vampire-chasing tour:

BISTRIȚA Golden Krone Hotel. In Bram Stoker's novel *Dracula*, Jonathan Harker stayed here in 'Bistritz' *en route* to the Count's castle (see page 262).

BRAN CASTLE Always associated with Dracula but Vlad probably only stayed here once (see page 140).

BUCHAREST Palatui și Biserica Curtea Veche. Vlad III Țepeș built the Old Court Palace and church here on the site of a 14th-century fortress. Metro M1 or 2 to Piața Unirii. The Count Dracula Club restaurant has rooms with macabre themes. The 'Count' often mingles with guests. See www.count-dracula.ro.

CLUJ-NAPOCA Jonathan Harker stayed here too, at the Hotel Royale. Cluj is called 'Klausenburgh' in the novel (see page 249).

DOMENIUL DRACULA DANEȘ Hotel/country club just outside Sighișoara at Daneș on the Mediaș road, route 14 (see page 189).

restaurant before taking in a performance at the brightly coloured Romanian National Theatre and Opera House.

The following day, take a trip to the historic town of Turda where you will be stunned by the incredible museum down the salt mine. A refreshing walk through the scenic Turda Gorge is a great way to get some exercise and a taste of the Transylvanian countryside.

Alternatively, fly to Sibiu and spend the day wandering the streets of the beautifully restored historic centre. Don't forget to visit the superb Brukenthal Museum to see displays of wooden religious sculptures before enjoying a pizza and salad on one of the many pavement café terraces. The following day, don't miss the opportunity to whizz along the E68 highway to Brașov, one of Transylvania's most impressive Saxon cities. Explore the medieval pedestrianised centre before taking a cable car up Tâmpa hill for a delightful meal with a view in the restaurant.

ONE WEEK Explore the fortified church villages of the former Saxon population. Fly to Cluj-Napoca or Sibiu and stay locally in one of the traditional guesthouses in Biertan, Viscri, Saschiz or Mălâncrav, exploring the villages on foot, by bicycle or even on horseback. Alternatively, book a week's all-in holiday at Tibor Kálnoky's estate in Micloșoara and let the locals do all the planning, guiding, cooking and driving.

POIENARI CASTLE On the Transfăgărașan Highway, route 7C. Vlad III Țepeș spent a lot of time here. Climb 1,426 steps to reach the castle, a romantic ruin on a crag (see page 216).

SIGHIȘOARA Home to Vlad's dad and birthplace of Vlad Țepeș in 1431. A plaque on the wall announces that 'Vlad Dracul' (Vlad the Dragon, the Impaler's father) lived here from 1431–35 (see page 184).

SNAGOV ISLAND 35km north of Bucharest on route 1/E60, the headless body of Vlad Țepeș is said to be buried in a monastery on the island (see page 137).

TÂRGOVIȘTE Not in Transylvania but Vlad the Impaler's capital during the second of his three reigns, from 1456–62, and the scene of many impaling sessions.

TIHUȚA PASS Bistrița-Năsăud County, the 'Borgo Pass' from Bram Stoker's novel, and setting for the Castel Dracula Hotel, built in 1983 (see page 267).

TURDA The Castelul Prințul și Dracula/Hunter Prince and Dracula Castle is a bizarre, over-imaginative Dracula theme hotel with cave-like walls and a massive banqueting hall with hunting trophies, skulls and gory murals (see page 260).

DRACULA THEME PARKS There were three proposed sites: Sighișoara in an ancient oak forest, Bran Castle and Snagov Island. Locals opposed all three with even Prince Charles getting in on the act in Sighișoara. In 2002, the minister for tourism visited the proposed site at Bran and said, 'The only tourism we want to concentrate on is ski, beach and Dracula.'

TWO WEEKS Fly to Bucharest and hire a car. Drive up to Transylvania through the wine-growing Prahova Valley. Visit one of Vlad the Impaler's supposed old haunts at Bran Castle before calling in on Dan and Luminița Marin for a few nights at their Zărnești guesthouse, some real home cooking and some invigorating and inspiring walks in the unspoiled mountains of the Piatra Craiului National Park. Make Brașov your next base and catch up on culture in this beautiful Saxon city. Follow the E60 highway to Târgu Mureș, taking in the gorgeous town of Sighișoara on the way. You may want to stay longer in Sighișoara, so remember that this popular touri' destination can be overrun with crowds during the summer months and forw' planning is advised. Check out a few Saxon fortified church villages (Sas' Viscri, Biertan) before heading for Târgu Mureș. You might want a breath now, so visit Sovata and wallow in the warm, salty Lacul Ursu before catchir' breath down Praid's gigantic salt mine and picking up some folk pottery ir' Corund. Târgu Mureș has some incredible buildings and you shouldn't' stained-glass windows in the Art Nouveau creation, Palace of Culture continues to Cluj-Napoca (see above) but you might fancy a spot of h' Apuseni Mountains or a lakeside rest at Lacul Fântânele in the Kalot' of gentle rolling hills and traditional Hungarian villages. Culture vul' two more easily accessible highlights in southwest Transylvania: at ' citadel of Alba Iulia and the mighty Corvin Castle at Hunedoara, of Transylvania.

TOUR OPERATORS

Nature treks, village tourism, Dracula tours, train journeys, package ski holidays and flights to Transylvania are popping up all over the place as travellers discover the treasures hidden deep in the heart of one of the EU's newest members. Tour operators in the UK and USA are mad about Transylvania, with just the name alone being a PR person's dream ticket. In addition to those below, see also the beginning of each county chapter for local travel agents and tours.

UK

Adventures Abroad Delamere Close, Beighton, Sheffield S20 2QE; 0114 247 3400; www. adventures-abroad.com; telephone lines ⊕ 09.00–17.00 Mon–Fri. Offering several tours, which include Romania.

Charity Challenge Northway Hse, 1379 High Rd, London N20 9LP; 020 8557 0000; www. charitychallenge.com. The UK's leading adventure travel company specialising in fundraising expeditions. Trek Transylvania takes place Aug. See *Travelling positively*, page 125.

Exodus 0845 287 2315; e sales@exodus. co.uk; www.exodus.co.uk. Hiking & conservation tours, including culture & wildlife in the Carpathians with accommodation at local guesthouses. Prices start from £1,069 for 8 days, excluding flights.

Explore 01252 760000; e res@explore.co.uk; www.explore.co.uk; telephone lines ⊕ 08.30–20.00 Mon–Thu, 08.30–19.00 Fri, 09.00–16.30 Sat. Explore offers a 5-day Transylvanian Backwaters tour & an 8-day Trekking in the Transylvanian Alps tour.

Hands Up Holidays 020 7193 1062; e info@ handsupholidays.com; www.handsupholidays. com. Romania/Transylvania tour combined with

volunteering on the Black Sea coast. Prices start from £1,300.

Mihai Eminescu Trust (MET) 63 Hillgate Pl, London W8 7SS; 020 7229 7618. The MET Guesthouses; 020 7603 1113; e guesthouses@ mihaieminescutrust.org; www.mihaieminescutrust. org. Accommodation in guesthouses in traditional Saxon villages, horseriding & walking tours, including the Saxon Greenway route (www. drumulasezarilorsasesti.ro). Bookings should be made in advance via email.

Regent Holidays Mezzanine Suite, Froomsgate Hse, Rupert St, Bristol BS1 2QJ; 0117 921 1711; e regent@regent-holidays.co.uk; www.regent-holidays.co.uk. Independent operator specialising in Eastern European destinations, including a Dracula tour.

Responsible Travel 01273 600030; e amelia@ responsibletravel.com; www.responsibletravel. com. Based in Brighton, Responsible Travel is an online travel directory for travellers who want authentic holidays that benefit the local people. Ecotourism specialists offer cultural, wildlife, conservation & family tours, horseriding holidays, & hiking tours of Transylvania.

Sunvil Discovery 020 8758 4722; www.sunvil. co.uk; telephone lines ⊕ 09.00–17.30 Mon–Fri,

09.00–13.00 Sat. Offering a cultural & bear-watching itinerary in Transylvania. Sunvil calls Romania 'the most beautiful & interesting of the Eastern European states'.

Titan HiTours Crossoak Lane, Redhill RH1 5EX; \0800 988 5823; www.titanhitours.co.uk; telephone lines ⏲ 08.30–19.00 Mon/Tue, 08.30–18.00 Wed–Fri, 09.00–17.00 Sat. Offering a 7-day Romania/Transylvania discovery tour.

Transylvania Live UK – Expert in Transylvania UK free line \0808 101 6781; Romania \+40 364 405 641; e sales@visit-transylvania.co.uk; www.visit-transylvania.co.uk. Anglo-Romanian tour operator, with a responsible travel policy, based in London & Transylvania with cultural, natural, sightseeing tours, on foot, by motorbike, bike, helicopter or on skis.

Transylvania Uncovered 1 Atkinson Court, Fell Foot, Newby Bridge LA12 8NW; \0845 300 0247; office \015395 31258; e mike.morton@travelcounsellors.com, travel@beyondtheforest.com; www.beyondtheforest.com. Mike Morton runs one of the best specialist tour companies to all parts of Transylvania with tailor-made trips & organised tours, including Count Tibor Kálnoky's estate (see page 155) & the Mihai Eminescu Trust guesthouses. The brochure will have you drooling with anticipation before you've even left your living room.

Walks Worldwide Long Barn South, Sutton Manor Farm, Bishop's Sutton SO24 0AA; \0845 301 4737 or +44 1962 737565 (from outside UK); e sales@walksworldwide.com; www.walksworldwide.com. Offering 5 Transylvania/Romania hiking tours including Apuseni, a Transylanian Alps 'Haute Route' & a Grand Tour of the Carpathians.

World Expeditions 81 Craven Gardens, Wimbledon, London SW19 8LU; \020 8545 9030; e enquiries@worldexpeditions.co.uk; www.worldexpeditions.com. Offering a 6-day Transylvanian castles & mountains tour.

WILDLIFE SPECIALISTS IN THE UK

Avian Adventures \01384 372013; www.avianadventures.co.uk. Birdwatching tours in Transylvania & the Carpathian Mountains, led by Bernie Forbes & Shena Maskell.

Naturetrek David & Maryanne Mills; Cheriton Mill, Cheriton, nr Alresford SO24 0NG; \01962 733051; e info@naturetrek.co.uk; www.naturetrek.co.uk. Wildlife & wildflowers tours of Transylvania & the Carpathians, as well as the Danube Delta.

Probirder e gerard@probirder.com; www.probirder.com. Based in Budapest, British wildlife/bird expert Gerard Gorman is the author of Bradt's *Central and Eastern European Wildlife* guide (July 2008), & his team has been leading tours to Romania for over 20 years, including Large Carnivores in Transylvania & the Danube Delta in Summer.

Sunbird Steve Rooke, 26B The Market Sq, Potton, Sandy SG19 2NP; \01767 262522; e sunbird@sunbirdtours.co.uk; www.sunbirdtours.co.uk. Offering a trip to the Danube Delta in 2012.

Travelling Naturalist Jamie McMillan, PO Box 3141, Dorchester DT1 2XD; \01305 267994; e Jamie@naturalist.co.uk; www.naturalist.co.uk. Trips to the Danube Delta in spring & autumn.

US AND CANADA

Adventures Abroad 1124 Fir Av #101, Blaine, WA 98230; \+1 800 665 3998; e info@adventures-abroad.com; www.adventures-abroad.com; telephone lines ⏲ 09.00–17.00 Mon–Fri, Pacific Time. Several tours combining Romania & surrounding countries, & one 8-day Romania tour.

Quest Tours & Adventures PO Box 1060, Fairview, OR 97024; \+1 800 621 8687; e monica@romtour.com; www.romtour.com. Dracula tours, a 2-day Touch of Transylvania tour & other package tours.

Wilderness Travel 1102 Ninth St, Berkeley, CA 94710; \+1 800 368 2794; www.wildernesstravel.com. Offering a 12-day Mountains & Legends of Romania tour.

SKI TOURS

Balkan Holidays Sofia Hse, 19 Conduit St, London W1S 2BH; \0845 130 1114; www.balkanholidays.co.uk; reservation department ⏲ 09.00–19.00 Mon–Fri, 09.00–17.00 Sat. Ski & Black Sea coast packages.

LOCAL TRAVEL AGENTS/TOUR GUIDES I would definitely recommend going on an organised tour to get a real taste of the country. The long distances, reckless driving styles and poor road surfaces make going it alone in a hire car pretty tiring and time consuming. It's great to have a local do the driving, leaving you free to admire the stunning views. The guesthouses also provide meals, which means you don't have to spend valuable time searching for meal options, which can still be a pretty hit-and-miss affair, especially if you're vegetarian or have special dietary needs. Local tour guides are also highly experienced and knowledgeable about their beautiful country, its flora and fauna, history and traditions. It's an excellent introduction to Transylvania, and, if you've been before, a chance to let someone else do the hard work while you relax, enjoy and explore deeper into the heart and soul of the region.

For more on specialised guesthouses and organisations such as the Kálnoky and Mikes noble estates (Covasna), ADEPT Foundation in Saxon Villages/Sighișoara-Tärnava Mare Protected Area (Mureș), Dan Marin in Zărnești (Brașov), Françoise Heidebroek in Roșia Montana (Alba), Istvăn Vincze-Kecskés in Sâncraiu (Cluj), Christoph Promberger in Șinca Nouă (Brașov) and the Mihai Eminescu Trust in the traditional Saxon villages (Sibiu, Brașov and Mureș counties), see the relevant chapters.

Absolute Carpathian Contact Simona Munteanu, ☎ 368 413 524; m 0788 578 796; e book@absolute-nature.ro; www.absolute-nature.ro. Formed by campaigners from the Carpathian Large Carnivore Project, offering package & tailor-made tours with a focus on wildlife-watching, climbing, abseiling, paragliding & cycling in the mountains.

ADEPT Foundation Str Principala 166, Saschiz, jud Mureș; ☎ 0265 711 635; www.fundatia-adept.org. Organises small group botanical, natural history, walking & cultural tours with accommodation in local guesthouses. For more information, see box text, *The tourist information centre at Saschiz*, page 192.

Adventure Transylvania Diversis Travel Ltd, Str Petőfi Sándor 24, Satu Mare; m 0727 394 727; e Info@AdventureTransylvania.com; www.adventuretransylvania.com. Tour company based in Satu Mare since 1991 & offers tours for horseriding, hiking, mountain biking, kayaking, Dracula hunting or a combination of all these activities.

Apuseni Experience 1 Decembrie Square 4–6, floor 1, room 8, Oradea; m 0745 602 301, 0747 962 482; e contact@apuseniexperience. ro; www.apuseniexperience.ro. Young, learned guides share their enthusiasm about the Apuseni Mountains on a variety of ecotours.

Caliman Club Holidays Str Florilor 1, Bistrița; ☎f 0263 235 046; m 0744 600 148; e calimanclub@gmail.com; www.caliman.ro. Ready-made or tailor-made tours focusing on mountain hiking, biking, rafting, kayaking & skiing. With its own outdoor centre at Lacul Colibița (see page 267).

Centre for Mountain Ecology Contact Michael Orleanu, Moieciu de Sus 125, Moieciu 507134, jud Brașov; m 0745 978 023; e orleanu@gmail. com; www.cem.ro. Offering full guesthouse accommodation, theme-based hiking (geology, geography, botany, forestry, ethnography, history), birdwatching, wildlife-watching (large carnivores), mountain hiking, tour-skiing, snow-shoe tours, photo tours, rural cultural tours, cave exploration & mountain-bike tours in the region.

Daksa Eco-equestrian Centre Contact Mugur Pop, Str Actorului 13/A, 400441 Cluj-Napoca, jud Cluj; ☎ 0364 105 194; m 0744 100 645; e hello@ridingadventures.ro; www.ridingadventures.ro. Horseback adventures in the Apuseni Mountains, cultural trips.

Davincze Tours Sâncraiu 291, jud Cluj; ☎ 0264 257 580; e davincze@clicknet.ro; www. davincze.ro. István Vincze-Kecskés runs a small guesthouse & organises many traditional activities for tourists in this Hungarian village of Sâncraiu (Kalotaszentkirály). See more in the Cluj County chapter, page 256.

DiscoveRomania Contact Laura Vesa, Str Paul Richter 1, ap 1, Brașov 500025; ☎f 0268 472 718; m 0722 746 262; e office@discoveromania.ro; www.discoveromania.ro. Offers small group holidays designed to deeply immerse visitors in the nature & culture: cultural insight journeys, active tours that involve hiking & biking in Transylvania & beyond, ecotours exploring the Carpathian Mountains & special-interest tours involving Roma communities or joining traditional folk festivals.

Equus Silvania Contact Christoph Promberger, Șinca Nouă 507210, jud Brașov; ☎ 0268 228 601; e christoph@equus-silvania.com; www.equus-silvania.com. With their own guesthouse, cabin, stables, 28 horses & 3 ponies, guests welcome all year round. See the Braşov County chapter, page 144.

Focus Eco Center Contact Zoltán Hajdu, Str Crinului 22, Târgu Mureş; ☏0265 262 170; m 0744 774 897; www.focuseco.ro. A member of the European Centre for Eco-Agro Tourism (ECEAT), based in Amsterdam, which has a network throughout Europe & a list of B&Bs in Transylvania.

Green Mountain Holidays Mănăstireni 277; 407370, jud Cluj; ☏0264 418 691; m 0744 637 227; e gmh@cluj.astral.ro; www. greenmountainholidays.ro. Belgian–Romanian tour operator based near Huedin, specialising in ecotourism, hiking, cycling, caving, skiing, kayaking, steam-train rides, individual & customised trips in the Apuseni Mountains.

Inter Pares Contact Radu Zaharie, Str Cristian 19a, Sibiu 550073, jud Sibiu; ☏0269 228 610; e office@inter-pares.ro; www.inter-pares.ro. Tour operator in Sibiu offering trekking, cycling, mountain biking, skiing, winter trekking, rafting on timber rafts, canoeing & cultural activity programmes in English & German.

Kálnoky Guesthouse & Estate Contact Count Tibor Kálnoky, Kálnoky Panzió, Sat Micloşoara nr 186, jud Covasna; m 0742 202 586; f 0267 314 088; e k@transylvaniancastle.com; www. transylvaniancastle.com; ☺ all year. The perfect introduction to Transylvanian village life with sensitively restored traditional guestrooms, Hungarian home cooking, guide-led nature & culture walks. For more information see the Covasna County chapter, page 155. The Kálnoky Estate now also manages The Prince of Wales's guesthouse in Viscri & has also taken over Julian Ross's Ştefan cel Mare Equestrian Centre, offering trail-riding & carriage-driving tours through the Transylvanian countryside using locally-bred horses, including Semigreu, Shagya Arabian & Hutzul breeds.

MC Transylvania ☏f 0265 260 881; m 0751 254 118; e jmc@mctransylvania.com; www. mctransylvania.com. French perfectionist Jean Michel Corbet has 15 years' experience taking western Europeans to Transylvania. He specialises in tailor-made trips & the ever-popular Dracula tours, hiking, music & other trips.

Mikes Estate Mikes Kastély, 527190 Zăbala, jud Covasna; ☏0267 375 547; m 0720 069 816; www. zabola.com. Stay in a beautifully renovated boutique hotel in the estate's Machine House surrounded by

a 34ha park with opportunities for bear tracking, nature trails & visits to local shepherds. Discover the Székely region & its unique cultural heritage on tailor-made tours. As the motto says, it's 'Transylvania's best kept secret'. For more information see the Covasna County chapter, page 158.

Outdoor Holidays Contact Dan Şendriuc, Aleea Rotunda 4, Bl H6, ap 26, Bucharest Sector 3, 032705; ☏021 643 2402; m 0722 647 399; e office@ outdoorholiday.com; www.outdoorholiday.com. Romanian company offering a variety of hiking & mountain-biking trips with varying degrees of difficulty & many opportunities to see wildlife.

Professional Team Str Parcul Mic 5, Bl 105, ap 10, Oras Braşov; ☏f 0368 806 360; m 0745 999 412; e contact@professionalteam.ro; www. professionalteam.ro. Ecological education camps for young people aged 10 & over in the Piatra Craiului National Park focused on learning about the plants, animals, local history & traditions. In English & Romanian. Trainers are from the Zărneşti Mountain Rescue Team & the Romanian Ski-Climbing Federation.

Retro Travel Agency Str Potaissa 11–13, Cluj-Napoca; ☏0264 450 452; e office@retrotravel.ro; www.retrotravel.ro. Based in Cluj-Napoca, this travel agency offers UNESCO site tours, a Dracula tour & many mountain-hiking tours.

Rina Tours & Travel Splaiul Unirii 4, Building B3, Bucharest; ☏021 318 6184; e office@rinatours. ro; www. rinatours.ro. Bucharest-based agency offering Monasteries, Danube Delta & Dracula tours, as well as bespoke itineraries.

Roving Romania m 0724 348 272; e rovingrom@gmail.com; www.roving-romania. co.uk. An Englishman based in Braşov, Colin Shaw takes visitors all over Transylvania in a Land Rover, reaching fascinating & otherwise inaccessible destinations. He has been running tours in Romania for 15 years. Tours are 100% tailor-made in discussion with clients & focus on nature, wildlife, mountains, rural culture & local history. Colin often uses local English-speaking guides for specialist activities.

Step by Step Agency Str Lungă 175, Braşov; m 0744 327 686; f 0268 418 441; e contact@ mountainguide.ro; www.mountainguide.ro. Iulian Cozma is a professional mountain guide based in Braşov & takes visitors hiking, trekking & ski touring in the Făgăraş, Retezat, Bucegi & Piatra Craiului ranges.

2

Tioc Nature & Study Travel Contact Tiberiu Tioc, Aleea Genistilor 25, Sc. C, ap 61, Sibiu; m 0743 025 154; e contact@tioc-reisen.ro; www.tioc-reisen.ro. Offering programmes in the Retezat National Park & Transylvania with tours for nature lovers, birdwatchers & active types.

Transylvanian Wolf Contact Dan Marin, Str Mitropolit Ioan Metianu nr 108, Zărneşti 505800, jud Braşov; m 0744 319 708; e transylvanian_ wolf@yahoo.com; www.transylvanianwolf.ro. Guided tours with *Wanderlust* award-winning guide exploring traditional rural areas, Roma music & dance evenings, birdwatching, wildlife tracking, guesthouse accommodation & delicious home-cooked meals. For more information see the Braşov County chapter, page 143.

Ursita Inn Contact Françoise Heidebroek, Hanul Ursita, Valea Negrilesei 860, Bucium Poieni, jud Alba; m 0723 230 790; e fhe@ursita.ro; www.ursita.ro. Belgian Françoise Heidebroek has converted an old farmhouse into a 10-room

guesthouse in an old gold-mining village in the heart of the Apuseni Mountains. For more information see the Alba County chapter, page 239.

Via Transylvania Str Inainte 1510, Siria; m 0755 365 778; www.viatransylvania.com. Tailor-made & special interest holidays in Transylvania.

Visit Romania's Natural Protected Areas Contact Mihai Zotta (Romanian National Forest Administration – Protected Area Unit); m 0743 022 112; e office@rnp.rosilva.ro or mzotta@pcrai.ro; www.rosilva.ro. Guided tours in national parks, wildlife watching, including large carnivores & birds, horseriding, cycling, boating & sailing with accommodation in forest lodges or village guesthouses.

Visit Transylvania Str Stefan cel Mare 337, Ghimbav, jud Braşov; ☏ 0268 258 344; m 0726 236 784; e office@visittransilvania.ro; www.visittransilvania.ro. Customised itineraries including hiking, castles, Dracula & UNESCO tours.

TOURIST OFFICES

In 2005, **ANT (National Authority for Tourism)** announced that six million foreigners came annually to Romania, mostly from Hungary, Moldova, Germany, Austria and France. Visitor numbers peaked in 2008, with over eight million foreign visitors – a figure no doubt helped by Sibiu's status as 2007 European Capital of Culture, which ANT capitalised on to promote the Transylvanian counties of Alba, Mureş and Braşov. The current official tourism slogan, 'Romania. Explore the Carpathian Garden', is a particularly appropriate tagline for this land of unspoiled mountains and forests, scattered with sleepy villages, wooden churches and other wonders.

ANT operates under the auspices of the Ministry of Romanian Ministry of Small and Medium Enterprise, Trade and Tourism and has offices abroad.

OVERSEAS

🏛 **France** 7 Rue Gaillon, 75002 Paris; ☏ +33 1 40 20 99 33; e info@GuideRoumanie.com; www.GuideRoumanie.com

🏛 **Germany** Reinhardtstr 47, 10117 Berlin; ☏ +49 30 400 55 904; e info@rumaenien-tourismus.de; www.rumaenien-tourismus.de.

🏛 **Spain** Calle Alcantara 49-51; 28006 Madrid; ☏ +34 91 401 4268; e oficina@RumaniaTour.com; www.RumaniaTour.com

🏛 **UK** 12 Harley St, London W1G 9PG; ☏ 020 7224 3692; e romaniatravel@btconnect.com; www.RomaniaTourism.com

🏛 **USA** 355 Lexington Av, 8th Floor, New York, NY 10017; ☏ +1 212 545 8484; e info@RomaniaTourism.com; www.RomaniaTourism.com

IN TRANSYLVANIA

🏛 **Alba Iulia** Tourist Information Centre, B-dul Ferdinand 14; ☏ +40 258 813 736; e idan@apulum.ro

🏛 **Braşov** Tourist Information Centre, Piaţa Sfatului 30; ☏ +40 268 419 078; e turism@brasovcity.ro, infoturismbrasov@yahoo.com

🏛 **Bucharest** Piata Universitatii underpass, Bucharest; ☏ +40 021 305 5574, int 1003; e turism@bucuresti-primaria.ro; http://en.seebucharest.ro

🏛 **Cluj-Napoca** B-dul Eroilor 6-8; ☏ +40 264 452 249; e info-tourism@primariaclujnapoca.ro; www.visitcluj.ro

🏛 **Miercurea-Ciuc** CFR Office, Str Florilor 12; ☏ +40 266 317 007; e csikinfo@szereda.ro

☑ Odorheiu Secuiesc/Székelyudvarhely
Tourist Information Centre; Piaţa Márton Áron 2;
☏ +40 266 217 427; e office@tourinfo.ro; www.
tourinfo.ro
☑ Poiana-Braşov Fundatura Rosiorilor 2;
☏ +40 268 547 755; e office@omtravel.ro; www.
poianabrasov.org
☑ Predeal Str Intrarea Garii 1; ☏ +40 268 455
330; e contact@predeal.ro; www.predeal.ro
☑ Sibiu Piata Mare 7; ☏ +40 269 208 913;
e turism@sibiu.ro; www.sibiu.ro
☑ Târgu Mureş Str Enescu nr 2; ☏ +40 365 404
934; e turism@cjmures.ro; www.cjmures.ro

ROMANIAN TOURIST ASSOCIATIONS
☑ AGMR (Romanian Mountain Guides Association) www.agmr.go.ro
☑ ANAT (National Association of Travel Agencies in Romania) www.anat.ro. Has a good list of travel agencies in Transylvanian towns.
☑ ANTREC (National Association of Rural Ecological and Cultural Tourism) www.antrec. ro. See page 15.
☑ OPTBR (Organisation of Spa Owners in Romania) www.spas.ro
☑ Romanian 'Bed and Breakfast' Association www.bed-and-breakfast.ro

RED TAPE

The EU accession has opened up Romania to European travellers and visitors from the UK and all EU countries no longer require visas, making travel arrangements much simpler. Romania became a member of the European Union on 1 January 2007 and had hoped to join the EU Schengen bloc by 2012, though currently this is opposed by the Netherlands and Finland pending further reforms of Romania's justice system. The practice of free movement within an area without internal border controls was first set out by the Schengen Agreement in 1985. The subsequent Schengen Convention in 1995 abolished controls on internal borders between the signatory countries.

ENTRY REQUIREMENTS UK and other EU citizens, together with citizens of Canada, the US, Australia, New Zealand and Japan, do not need a visa to enter Romania as a tourist for stays of up to 90 days. EU citizens may enter the country with their National Identity Card; all other visitors require a valid passport. Passports need to be valid for at least six months from the date of entry.

Holders of passports not exempt from visa requirements must obtain a visa from a Romanian embassy outside Romania before travelling, and on arrival will also need to show that they have a return ticket, and at least US$100 for each day that they intend to stay in the country. You can check whether you are exempt from visa requirements at www.romaniatourism.com/entry-requirements.html.

Anyone who intends to take up temporary residence in Romania (for business, teaching, press activities, church or humanitarian aid projects) is requested to present themselves to the nearest Romanian passport office within 15 days of their arrival in the country. The passport office will register status and issue a residency permit, valid for a maximum of one year. This can be extended at the end of this period. Spouses and children of those applying to regularise their status in Romania must also apply at the passport office in person. Heavy fines have been introduced for foreigners who do not have the correct visa or whose visa has expired. In addition to fines, an exclusion order may be imposed preventing a foreigner from returning to Romania for a specific period of time.

CUSTOMS REGULATIONS Romanian customs regulations are in line with those of most European countries. A traveller can enter and leave Romania with up to €10,000 in cash or travellers' cheques. Amounts of more than €10,000 should be declared at customs. Import allowances are 200 cigarettes or 40 cigars, four litres of wine or two litres of spirits (or two litres of wine and one litre of spirits), a reasonable quantity of gifts and medicines for personal use. More information on customs regulations is available at www.customs.ro.

The **VAT/tax refund** applies to visitors from countries outside the EU. A 24% sales tax (raised from 19% in 2010) is included in the prices posted in shops, hotels and restaurants. Hotels charge an additional tax (0.5–5% depending on the class of hotel). Keep your original receipts and ask for a store-identified VAT refund form. VAT refund offices (Birou de Restituire TVA) can be found at any Romanian border crossing point (air, rail, road).

EMBASSIES AND CONSULATES

OVERSEAS

Australia 4 Dalman Crescent, O'Malley, ACT 2606, Canberra; +61 2 6286 2343; e embassy@roemb.com.au; http://canberra.mae.ro

Belgium Rue Gabrielle 105, 1180 Brussels; +32 2 345 2680; e secretariat@roumanieamb.be; http://bruxelles.mae.ro

Canada 655 Rideau St, Ottawa, Ontario, K1N 6A3; +1 613 789 3709; e romania@romanian-embassy.com; http://ottawa.mae.ro

France 5 Rue de l'Exposition 75343, Paris 75007; +33 1 47 05 10 46; e secretariat@amb.roumanie.fr; http://paris.mae.ro

Germany Dorotheenstr 62–66, 10117 Berlin; +49 30 2123 9202; e office@rumaenische-botschaft.de; http://berlin.mae.ro

Hungary 1146 Budapest, Thököly út 72; +36 1 384 8394; e postmaster@roembbud.axelero.net; http://budapesta.mae.ro

Ireland 26 Waterloo Rd, Ballsbridge, Dublin 4, +353 1 668 1085; e ambrom@eircom.net; http://dublin.mae.ro

UK Arundel Hse, 4 Palace Green, London W8 4QD; 020 7937 9666; e roemb@roemb.co.uk; http://londra.mae.ro

UK Consular & Visa Section MEIC Hse, 344 Kensington High St, London W14 8NS; 020 7602 9833; e consulara@roemb.co.uk

US 1607 23rd St NW, Washington, DC 20008; +1 202 232 4846 (Consular Section +1 202 232 4749); e office@roembus.org (consular section consular@roembus.org); www.roembus.org

IN ROMANIA

Australia 8th Floor, Vladimira Popovica 38–40, 11070, Belgrade (Serbia); +381-11 33 03 400; Honorary Consulate: Str Titu Maiorescu, 34E, Villa 7, Pipera-Voluntari, 077190, Bucharest; +40 21 319 0229; e austral.consulat@gmail.com

Belgium B-dul Dacia 58, Sector 2, Bucharest; +40 21 210 2969; e ambabuc@clicknet.ro

Canada Str Tuberozelor 1–3, Sector 1, Bucharest 011411; +40 21 307 5000; e bucst@international.gc.ca

Hungary Str Dimitrie Gerotă 63-65, Sector 2, Bucharest 70202; +40 21 620 4300; e mission.buc@kum.hu

UK 24 Jules Michelet, Sector 1, 010463 Bucharest; +40 21 201 7200; e Press.Bucharest@fco.gov.uk, consular@bucharest-mail.fco.gov.uk

US B-dul Dr. Liviu Librescu, 4–6, Sector 1, Bucharest; +40 21 200 3300; e visasabucharest@state.gov; http://romania.usembassy.gov

See also www.mae.ro/en/foreign-missions.

GETTING THERE AND AWAY

Romania has 35 international road crossings – of these 11 are open only to citizens of the relevant neighbouring countries. There are 17 rail crossings from the surrounding five countries (Ukraine, Moldova, Bulgaria, Serbia and Hungary) into Romania.

Transylvania is situated right in the heart of Romania, surrounded by Romanian counties on all sides of its regional borders. Transylvania has a natural horseshoe-shaped border of the Carpathian Mountains on three sides and the Apuseni Mountains to the northwest.

Until recently, travellers have been of the more adventurous nature, taking part in special hiking tours, nature study trips and wildlife-watching tours, to name a few. The ski resorts of Poiana Braşov, Predeal, Buşteni and Sinaia are growing in popularity after positive exposure in the UK press.

BY AIR Transylvania has three international airports (Cluj-Napoca, Sibiu and Târgu Mureş) although many travellers use Bucharest's two airports: Otopeni's Henri Coanda (usually scheduled and national carriers) and Aurel Vlaicu, usually known as Băneasa (mainly low-cost airlines), as a convenient gateway to Transylvania.

A new international airport will be built near Braşov (northwest of the city centre at Ghimbav) and will be a major boost for business and tourism in the area. The airport was originally scheduled for completion in late 2009 at a cost of €100 million, but, as of the time of writing, the project was still developing.

You'd do well to choose the Romanian national carrier, **Tarom**. According to the latest performance and punctuality figures from the Association of European Airlines (AEA), Tarom boasts one of the top on-time departure records and the lowest number of cancelled flights.

Discount travel websites such as www.cheapflights.co.uk, www.expedia.com and www.lastminute.co.uk can offer bargain flight prices.

If you travel by plane and feel bad about climate change, www.climatecare. org has a carbon calculator that allows travellers to offset their greenhouse gas emissions by contributing to energy-saving projects in the developing world. Bear in mind that Romania has an excellent railway network and is linked to all European cities.

From the UK

✈ **British Airways** ✆0870 850 9850; www. ba.com. British Airways fly twice daily from London Heathrow to Bucharest (return tickets start from £240 off-season & £300 peak-season), & daily to Cluj-Napoca via Munich. Flight time London to Bucharest is 3hrs 15mins; to Târgu Mureş is 4hrs 40mins.

✈ **Blue Air** ✆+40 21 208 8686, in UK ✆0871 744 0104; www.blueairweb.com. The low-cost Romanian airline flies daily except Wed from London Luton to Bucharest Otopeni with prices starting from €140 return including taxes. It also has 5 flights a week from London to Bacau, & 3 flights a week from Stuttgart to Sibiu. All 3 routes operate Mar–Oct.

✈ **German Wings** www.germanwings.com. Flies from London Heathrow to Bucharest via Cologne-Bonn (making it a fairly long flight).

✈ **Lufthansa** www.lufthansa.com. Lufthansa flies London Heathrow to Sibiu & Cluj-Napoca via Munich.

✈ **Tarom** 27 New Cavendish St, London W1G 9UE; ✆020 7224 3693; www.tarom.ro. The Romanian national carrier has daily, punctual flights from London Heathrow to Bucharest Otopeni. Tarom flies Bucharest to Cluj-Napoca several times every day & from Cluj-Napoca to Barcelona, Bologna, Frankfurt, London, Madrid, Milan & Vienna.

✈ **Wizzair** www.wizzair.com. Wizzair flies London Luton to Cluj-Napoca daily except Sat, & from London Luton to Târgu Mureş. The airline also flies London Luton to Bucharest Otopeni (daily) & Timisoara (3 times weekly), & from Arad to Milan (twice weekly). Wizzair also flies from Cluj-Napoca & Târgu Mureş to Barcelona, Budapest Ferihegy 1, Dortmund & Rome Fiumicino, Milan, Paris & other destinations; & from Bucharest Otopeni to Barcelona, Brussels, Dortmund, Paris, Rome Ciampino, Valencia Manises, Venice Treviso & many other airports. Tour operators advise those passengers flying to Bucharest with Wizzair to spend the first (& often the last) night of the trip in Bucharest. Be warned that local transfer companies may charge waiting time in the event of significant delays.

From Europe Bucharest is no more than two hours by plane from most cities in western Europe. Other cities in Transylvania including Cluj, Sibiu and Târgu Mureş are connected with destinations in Austria, Germany, Italy and Hungary by flights with Austrian Airlines, Carpatair and Tarom.

✈ **Austrian Airlines** \0870 124 2625; www. austrian.com. Flies daily except Sat Vienna to Sibiu, & several times daily Vienna to Bucharest.

✈ **Blue Air** \+40 21 208 8686; www. blueairweb.com. The low-cost Romanian airline flies from Brussels, Paris, Stuttgart, Rome, Barcelona & Madrid to Bucharest.

✈ **Brussels Airlines** www.brusselsairlines.com. Flies from Brussels to Bucharest Otopeni.

✈ **Carpatair** \+40 256 300 900 or 0800 8300 900 (toll free, in Romania only); www. carpatair.ro. The main private Romanian airline based in Timişoara & offering domestic flights to Bucharest, Sibiu & more Romanian cities. International flights from Timişoara to Ancona, Bari, Milan Bergamo, Bologna, Düsseldorf,

Florence, Munich, Rome, Stuttgart, Venice & Verona. A possible London Stansted to Timişoara flight is still in discussion.

✈ **German Wings** www.germanwings.com. Flies from Bucharest Otopeni to Cologne Bonn, Vienna, Munich, Rome, Lisbon & other airports.

✈ **KLM** www.klm.com. Flies daily Amsterdam to Bucharest.

✈ **Lufthansa** www.lufthansa.com. Flies to Cluj-Napoca & Sibiu from Munich, & from Bucharest to Frankfurt, Dusseldorf & Munich.

✈ **Tarom** www.tarom.ro. Flies from Bucharest & Cluj-Napoca to Budapest, Düsseldorf, Frankfurt, Milan, Munich, Paris, Rome, Stuttgart, Vienna & other cities.

From the Irish Republic The only non-stop Dublin–Bucharest flight is with Aer Lingus.

✈ **Aer Lingus** \0818 365 000; www.aerlingus. com. Flies Dublin to Bucharest on Mon & Fri.

✈ **Air France** \01 814 4060; www.airfrance.ie. Flies daily Dublin to Bucharest, connecting in Paris.

✈ **British Airways** \1800 626 747; www.

ba.com. Flies Cork to Bucharest & Dublin to Bucharest, in combination with Aer Lingus, connecting at London Heathrow.

From the US and Canada At present, no airlines fly direct from the US or Canada to Transylvania, but there are connections between Bucharest and some cities in North America, usually via London, Paris or Frankfurt. Another possibility is to fly to Budapest and then take either a bus, train or plane to Cluj-Napoca.

✈ **Air France** \1800 667 2747; www.airfrance. ca. Flies to Bucharest from Canadian cities, connecting in Paris.

✈ **Alitalia** \1800 361 8336; www.alitalia.ca. Flies from Canada to Bucharest connecting in New York & Milan or Rome.

✈ **Austrian Air** \1800 843 0002; www.aua. com. Offers daily connections via Vienna to Bucharest & Sibiu from several cities in the US & Canada.

✈ **British Airways** \1800 247 9297; www. ba.com. Flies from many US & Canadian cities to Bucharest via London.

✈ **Delta** www.delta.com. Flies from US cities to Bucharest often via London, Paris or Amsterdam.

✈ **Lufthansa** \1800 645 3880; www.lufthansa-usa.com. Flies from the US & Canada to Frankfurt & transferring to Bucharest, Sibiu or Cluj-Napoca.

✈ **Tarom** www.tarom.ro. Tarom flies to North America connecting in London & Frankfurt.

From Australia and New Zealand

✈ **Zuji** www.zuji.com.au (a good flight-finding website). Offers Sydney to Bucharest Otopeni

connecting in Singapore & Paris for AU$3,277 (£1,458).

Main airports

Bucharest Otopeni-Henri Coandă International Airport (OTP) (*www. otp-airport.ro*) The airport is 16km north of central Bucharest (*25 mins*) on route 1/E60 highway from Bucharest to Ploiesti and on to Braşov. It is smart and modern, with a brand new second terminal having opened in March 2012, and has a snack bar, restaurant, left luggage, first aid, facilities for those with limited mobility, post office, bank with ATM and nine car-hire company offices all in a row (on the upper floor between arrivals and departures; see below for further details). Since May 2004, it has been officially known as Henri Coandă International Airport.

Transfer to and from the airport An express bus service (No 783) runs every 15 minutes 05.30–20.00 and every 30 minutes 20.30–23.00 Monday–Friday, and every 30 minutes 05.30–23.00 Saturday/Sunday. The journey to Bucharest takes about 45 minutes. Tickets cost 7RON for two journeys. Route 783 will take you to Băneasa airport, and Piaţa Victoriei I which links up with the M1 circular red metro line and also the M2 north–south blue metro line. Route 783 continues to Piaţa Universităţii and then to the terminus at Piaţa Unirii, right in the heart of Bucharest where it also links up with the M1 and M2 metro lines.

Taxis, minibuses and limousines are available 24/7. Fly Taxi no longer have a monopoly as they once did.

Car-hire companies at Otopeni-Henri Coandă International Airport

🚗 **Absolut** ✆+40 21 319 5473; m +40 722 349 360; e office@rentacar.com.ro; www.rentacar. com.ro. From an office in Bucharest, Absolut offers car-hire services throughout Transylvania.

🚗 **Cars4Rent Ltd** No office at Otopeni but will deliver; m +40 723 347 192 or +40 788 303 923; e office@cars4rent.ro; www.cars4rent.ro. Cars4Rent also has locations at Băneasa Airport, Bucharest centre, Braşov, Sinaia, Poiana Braşov,

Sighişoara & Sibiu. Cars4Rent gives a good personal service & provides the Dacia/Renault Logan 1.5l from €17–25 a day. It runs on diesel & is both economical & comfortable.

🚗 **Eurocars** m +40 727 373 799; e office@ eurocars.ro; www.eurocars.ro. From an office in Bucharest, Eurocars offers transfers from the airport to any city in Transylvania, plus minibus rental.

Alternatively, you can try just turning up at the airport, during office hours, and calling in at one of the following nine offices, situated all in a cluster on the first floor between departures and arrivals. Somebody will be able to give you a good deal.

🚗 **Autogeneral** m +40 723 405 340; e rentacar.autogeneral@yahoo.com; www. autogeneral.ro

🚗 **Avis** ✆+40 21 210 4344; e reservations@ avis.ro; www.avis.ro

🚗 **Bavaria Rent** m +40 730 333 707; e email@bavariarent.ro; www.bavariarent.ro

🚗 **Budget** ✆+40 21 204 1667; e reservations@ budgetro.ro; www.budgetro.ro

🚗 **D&V Touring** ✆+40 21 201 4611; e office@ dvtouring.ro; www.dvtouring.ro

🚗 **Europcar** ✆+40 21 201 4937; m +40 740 044 964; e europcar@dataserv.ro; www.europcar. com

🚗 **Hertz** ✆+40 21 335 7533; e reservations@ hertz.com.ro; www.hertz.com.ro

🚗 **Rentauto Romania** ✆+40 21 316 5856; e reservation@rentauto-romania.ro; www. rentauto-romania.ro

🚗 **Sixt** ✆+40 21 350 4860; e office@sixt-nk.ro; www.sixt-nk.ro

See *Getting around*, page 79, for average rental prices.

Where to stay near Otopeni Airport For early flights, possible flight delays, or a good base in northern Bucharest, there are two hotels just two minutes from the airport:

🏠 **Hotel Rin Airport** (253 rooms, 2 apts) Otopeni, Calea Bucureștilor 255A; ☎ +40 21 350 4110; e reservations.rinairport@rinhotels.ro; www.rinhotel.ro. The 4-star Rin Airport hotel offers smart rooms & a large spa with pool, sauna, jacuzzi & fitness centre. B/fast €8. **$$$$**

🏠 **Hotel Rin Express** (150 rooms) Otopeni, Calea Bucureștilor 255A; ☎ +40 21 350 4110; e reservations.rinexpress@rinhotels.ro;

www.rinhotel.ro. Slightly cheaper, but still smart & convenient, with everything you need for a stopover. It's also popular with Bucharest families for Sat night weddings & knees-ups that take over the entire restaurant. If you arrive after an 8hr drive from the other side of Transylvania, tired & famished, you may find the receptionists less than sympathetic about your rumbling tummies. Free airport transfers. B/fast €6. **$$$**

Bucharest's second airport: Băneasa – Aurel Vlaicu (BBU) (40 Sos. Bucharest–Ploiești, Bucharest 1; ☎ +40 21 232 0020, tower information ☎ +40 21 633 0912; www.baneasa-airport.com)

Situated 8km north of central Bucharest on the Bucharest–Ploiești 1/E60 highway leading to Brașov, the gateway to Transylvania. Before 1989, Băneasa Airport was Tarom's domestic hub, while Otopeni Airport was used as an international hub. After 2000, Tarom moved all its activities to Otopeni (renamed Henri Coandă International Airport). Today, Băneasa Airport is becoming an increasingly important hub for business aviation and for budget flights. Formed in 1994, Romanian Airport Services began operations in 1995 just two months after Băneasa Airport gained international status. It was renovated in the summer of 2007 but still resembles a crowded, chaotic bus station at rush hour. I was there at 05.00 one Sunday morning in September and several fights nearly broke out in the 'non-queue'. Be prepared to push and shove with the best of them.

Transfer to and from the airport Buses 131 and 301 run from the airport to Piața Romana 04.30–11.30, and the 783 express service between Otopeni and downtown Bucharest stops at Băneasa. Bucharest city transport tickets (a single ticket costs 1RON) can be purchased at RATB (Bucharest surface transport company) kiosks opposite the airport exit. For taxis, use a reliable company (for further details, see the list of taxi companies in *Getting around*, page 81).

Car-hire companies at Băneasa Airport

🚗 **Bavaria** m +40 730 333 708; e email@ bavariarent.ro; www.bavariarent.ro

🚗 **Cars4Rent Ltd** m +40 723 347 192 or +40 788 303 923; e office@cars4rent.ro; www. cars4rent.ro

Alternatively, you could contact one of the car-hire companies at Otopeni Airport via their websites before leaving home and they will deliver the car to Băneasa Airport in time for your arrival (for further details, see above).

Airports in Transylvania

✈ **Brașov International Airport** www. airportbrasov.ro. An international airport with an annual capacity of one million passengers was scheduled to open by the end of 2009 at Ghimbav, 10km west of Brașov (route 1/E68 to Sibiu), though delays have meant that, at the time of writing, construction had not yet started.

✈ **Cluj-Napoca Someșeni Airport (CLJ)** Str Traian Vuia 149; ☎ +40 264 416 702; e office@ airportcluj.ro; www.airportcluj.ro. For more information on the airport, transfers & car hire, see the Cluj County chapter, page 250.

✈ **Sibiu Airport (SBZ)** Sos Alba Iulia 73; ☎ +40 269 253 135 or +40 269 253 135; www.sibiuairport.

ro. Sibiu International Airport is situated 5km west of Sibiu city centre on highway 1/7/E68/E81. For more information on the airport, transfers & car hire, see the Sibiu County chapter, page 195.

✈ Transilvania-Târgu Mureş Vidrasău Airport (TGM) Târgu Mureş–Ludus road, Vidrasău, 547612 Mureş County; ☏ +40 265 328 259 or +40 265 232 728; f +40 265 328 257; e office@targumuresairport.ro; www. targumuresairport.ro. For more information on the airport, transfers & car hire, see the Mureş County chapter, page 177.

BY TRAIN It's more expensive to travel to Transylvania by train (*tren*), but you can stop off *en route*, take your time, admire the view and feel good about decreasing your carbon footprint.

The shortest train journey London–Bucharest takes about 36 hours, but you can choose from a variety of routes. Begin in style with the Eurostar (*www.eurostar. com*) from London's glorious St Pancras International to Paris, then go via Munich, Vienna and Budapest. You could also try getting off the Eurostar in Brussels, stocking up on chocolate and beer, then choo-chooing via Cologne, Munich, Vienna and Budapest.

From Budapest the train to Bucharest stops in Cluj-Napoca so you could get off there. It's a lovely, historic version of the trip as the railway leaves the flat plains of Hungary and crosses into Transylvania in wild, forested hill country alongside a rushing river.

A possible journey from London to Bucharest could be to take the Eurostar to Paris, then the overnight train to Vienna, a day connection to Budapest followed by an overnight couchette ride to Cluj-Napoca. A standard second-class ticket should cost around £360. Remember to always make reservations for sleepers.

Bucharest's Gară de Nord (*Piaţa Gară de Nord 1;* ☏ *+40 21 223 2060; reservations can be made on* ☏ *9521 or 9522*) The station has two halls where same-day tickets can be purchased (allow time for queues). Looking towards the station, the hall on the right sells first- and second-class domestic tickets while the left-hand hall (*casa internaţionale*) sells international tickets and also first-class domestic tickets. International tickets must be bought in advance; take your passport.

From the airport, take a taxi or bus 783 (from Otopeni or Băneasa) or bus 131 or 301 (from Băneasa) to Piaţa Victoriei and then take the red metro 1 for one stop westwards to Gară de Nord. For domestic train schedules see the website www.infofer. ro. (See *Getting around*, page 76, for further information on domestic rail tickets and trains. See the relevant city sections for information on their railway stations.)

For all advance tickets bought more than 24 hours before travel, go to the **Agenţie de Voiaj CFR office** (*Str Domnita Anastasia 10–14;* ☏ *+40 21 313 2643; www.cfr. ro;* ⊕ *07.30–19.30 Mon–Fri, 09.00–13.30 Sat*). Remember that a seat reservation is compulsory when travelling with an Interrail or Eurail pass, and advisable on main routes anyway. You can also buy advance tickets online at https://bilete.cfrcalatori.ro.

Travelling by train from other European countries to Romania takes from six to eight hours (Budapest to Cluj-Napoca) to about 46 hours (London to Bucharest). Most train tickets allow several stopovers *en route* so train travel can be an affordable and relaxing way to include Romania in a European trip. For trains from Hungary to Romania see the website www.elvira.hu. For trains from Germany to Romania, contact Deutsche Bahn's UK office (☏ *+44 871 880 8066; www.bahn.com*).

Romanian National Railways (CFR) (*www.cfr.ro*) CFR operate services from Bucharest to many European cities. First- and second-class sleepers are available for journeys longer than ten hours and for overnight trains.

Train reservations can be made through **Wasteels** (☏ *+40 21 300 2730;* ⊕ *08.00–19.00 Mon–Fri, 08.00–14.00 Sat*), which has an agency on the platform in the Gară de Nord and can help with seat reservations (€1 for a seat, €8 for a couchette for services within Romania).

Rail passes

InterRail offers two types of ticket: a **Global Pass** (valid in all participating countries, currently 30) and a **One-Country Pass**. For more information and advance bookings see www.raileurope.co.uk and www.interrailnet.com.

Passes can also be bought from the Rail Europe Travel Centre (*193 Piccadilly, London W1;* ☏ *0844 848 4064; www.raileurope.co.uk*), along with details of international train schedules. Note that bookings made at the Travel Centre are subject to an £8 booking fee.

For details of the One-Country Pass for Romania giving rail travel of between three and eight days in a month see below.

InterRail One-Country Pass

Adults aged 26 and over pay €77 (€118 first class) for a three days in one month standard ticket; €95 (€146 first class) for four days; €127 (€195 first class) for six days; and €149 (€228 first class) for eight days.

Youth tickets (age 12–25) cost €51 for three days in one month; €62 for four days; €83 for six days; and €97 for eight days; for first-class tickets, you'll need to buy an adult pass.

Tickets for children (age 4–11) cost €39 for three days in one month; €48 for four days; €64 for six days; and €75 for eight days. Under fours go free.

Other useful information

The **Man in Seat 61** (*www.seat61.com*) is a career railwayman with a website full of ideas on routes and more.

Transylvania Uncovered (*www.beyondtheforest.com*) can help with train tickets to and from Transylvania.

BY COACH OR BUS
International services

🚌 **Eurolines** 52 Grosvenor Gdns, London SW1W 0AU; ☏ 0870 514 3219; www.eurolines.com; & at Bucharest's Gară de Nord: ☏ +40 21 222 3302; 📠 +40 21 222 3301; ℮ gara.nord@eurolines.ro; www.eurolines.ro

🚌 **National Express** Ensign Court, 4 Vicarage Rd, Edgbaston, Birmingham B15 3ES; ☏ 0870 580 8080; www.nationalexpress.com

Both companies run regular services from the UK to Romania and other European cities. Travellers can book a Eurolines pass for travel in a 15- or 30-day consecutive period. Mini-passes are also available in several combinations, giving travellers freedom to visit three cities, though those booked from the UK don't include Romania. Purchasing a Eurolines pass also gets you a discount on a connecting bus journey in the UK. Their motto 'Europe at your own pace' is more reassuring than their previous one, 'for people with more sense of adventure than money'.

There are many bus routes that connect Bucharest and Transylvania's main cities with all European capitals.

Eurolines Pass youth (under 26 years) and adult fares

An adult pass valid for 15 days in low/mid/high season costs €210/245/350, a 15-day youth pass for the same seasons €180/210/295. An adult pass valid for 30 days in low/mid/high season costs €315/355/460, a 30-day youth pass, €245/275/380.

Low season covers 4 January–28 March and 26 October–6 December; mid season 30 March–23 June and 4 September–25 October; high season 24 June–7 September and 7 December–3 January. Dates vary slightly from year to year.

Domestic services Bucharest's bus system is very convoluted. The constantly changing companies, locations and schedules make the prospect of taking the train or hiring a car ever more attractive. The most popular routes out of Bucharest by bus are the maxi-taxis to Braşov via the ski resorts of Sinaia, Buşteni and Predeal. For information see www.cdy.ro and www.autogari.ro.

Main bus stations

Central Bus Station (Autogară Gară de Nord). Located 350m east of the main railway station, Gară de Nord.

Autogară Filaret Piaţa Garii Filaret 1, Sector 5; \+40 21 336 0692. Located 3km south of Piaţa Universitaţii; take bus 7 or 232 from Piaţa Unirii.

Autogară Militari Str Valea Cascadelor 1, Sector 6; \+40 21 434 1739; www. autogaramilitari.ro. Located 8km west of central Bucharest; take the M1/M3 to Păcii.

BY CAR It is possible to drive from the UK or continental Europe to Transylvania and do some sightseeing on the way. The journey from London to Bucharest (as the crow flies) is 2,103km (1,307 miles) while London to Târgu Mureş is around 2,200km (1,350 miles). Border crossing between Romania and its western neighbours is just a formality. When renting a car in Europe please check with the car-rental company about its policy regarding taking the car across national borders (for example, some Budapest car-hire firms will not agree to their cars being driven into Romania). Insurance can be purchased at any Romanian border crossing point. Documents required by Romanian customs are the vehicle's registration, proof of insurance and a valid driving licence from the driver's home country. You will need to purchase motorway windscreen stickers for toll payments, particularly in Austria and Hungary. See www.viamichelin.co.uk for route details.

From western Europe, drive to Budapest. To reach Transylvania, keep on route E60 eastbound from Budapest (E60 runs Budapest–Szolnok–Oradea–Cluj-Napoca–Târgu Mureş–Sighişoara–Braşov). For Sibiu and the rest of southwestern Transylvania, take the E81 southbound from Cluj-Napoca. Cluj-Napoca is 335km (208 miles) southeast from Budapest.

Car hire For local and international companies, see page 61 and the relevant city sections in *Part Two* of the guide.

HEALTH   *with Dr Felicity Nicholson*

The standard of public health in Transylvania is good. However, be sure to take out adequate health insurance before setting off.

No vaccinations are legally required but it is wise to be up to date with routine vaccinations such as **diphtheria**, **tetanus** and **polio**. **Hepatitis A** should also be considered – a viral infection which is spread by infected food and water. For those who are going to be working in hospitals or in close contact with children, **hepatitis B** vaccination is recommended which is a course of three vaccines taken over a minimum of 21 days for those aged 16 and over and over two months for those under 16. **Typhoid** vaccine may also be considered for longer stay travellers.

General standards of healthcare in the towns are satisfactory but in the countryside it can be a long journey before you reach a qualified medical worker. Romanian **doctors** are educated, well trained and highly competent, but they are woefully underpaid and the system is underfunded.

Emergency medical treatment is free, but you may have to pay for some medicines.

It is the custom in central Europe to tip the doctors and nurses because it is universally acknowledged that the state salary is ridiculously low. This is done by discreetly handing over an envelope containing lei or euros (between €20 and €100 or the equivalent in lei, depending on the severity of the problem). Foreigners who would like to tip can give it a go but the envelope may not be accepted.

During the communist era of careless factory practices, toxic chemicals penetrated deep into the soil. If in doubt, even in the countryside, don't risk drinking tap water. **Mineral water** (*apă minerală*) is widely available, cheap and tastes good. Don't risk tap water unless you're sure it is from a spring source and don't drink tap water in towns – I suffered a particularly nasty bout of giardiasis on one visit (I'm sure I caught it at the heavily polluted Copşa Mică railway station's medieval loos), and I've felt nervous about tap water ever since. In restaurants, it is common practice for the waiter to bring a bottle of water to your table and open it in front of the guest, which is reassuring if you're worried about a gippy tummy interrupting your hiking trip.

Stray dogs, deer and foxes roam the countryside and carry a risk of rabies. **Rabies** is endemic in Romania, but has largely been confined to the rural mountain areas. Visitors should be wary of, and try to avoid, contact with stray dogs and sheepdogs guarding flocks in the mountains. But remember rabies can be carried by any warm blooded mammal and not just dogs! If bitten, scratched or licked over an open wound visitors should scrub the wound immediately with soap and water, apply an antiseptic and seek medical assistance as soon as possible. If no pre-exposure rabies vaccine has been taken then treatment with the blood product Rabies Immunoglobulin (RIG) and five doses of vaccine over a month is necessary to prevent the disease. RIG is not always easy to come by but is an imperative part of post-exposure prevention unless you have had the pre-exposure course of vaccine in which case it is not needed. Pre-exposure rabies vaccine (three over a minimum of 21 days) is advised for all travellers but particularly if you are planning longer stays in more rural areas of Romania and is an absolute must if you are working with animals.

The **air content** is relatively good as there is not so much heavy industry in Romania, but almost everybody smokes heavily and the concept of non-smoking areas in restaurants has been slow to catch on.

Alcoholism is a problem with the availability of powerful, cheap *ţuică*, therefore it's sensible to watch your intake. The local **diet** is heavy on the meat and *mămăligă* (polenta), although obesity is nowhere near western European levels. **Mosquitoes** are irritating, with waterways in summer plagued by the little devils. Take a good supply of insect repellent and cream.

The sun is very strong in central Europe. Take a supply of suntan lotion and after-sun care. If you intend to go **hiking** or **cycling** in the countryside remember that a tick bite can cause the potentially deadly disease **encephalitis**. The TBE- (tick-borne encephalitis) infected tick population is now endemic in 27 European countries including Romania. Vaccination against tick-borne encephalitis is available in the UK (Ticovac and Ticovac Junior (ages one to 15) and comprises a series of two injections that can be done one to three months apart. If time is short and urgent immunisation is required then the vaccine can be given two weeks apart. A third dose should be given from five to 12 months to complete the primary course. Take advice from your doctor or a reputable travel clinic. Whether you are immunised or not you should make sure that you wear suitable clothing, such as long trousers tucked into boots and a hat and use tick repellents.

Ticks should ideally be removed as soon as possible as leaving ticks on the body increases the chance of infection. They should be removed with special tick tweezers that can be bought in good travel shops. Failing that you can use your fingernails by grasping the tick as close to your body as possible and pulling steadily and firmly away at right angles to your skin. The tick will then come away complete as long as you do not jerk or twist. If possible, douse the wound with alcohol (any spirit will do) or iodine. Irritants (eg: Olbas oil) or lit cigarettes are to be discouraged since they can cause the ticks to regurgitate and therefore increase the risk of disease. It is best to get a travelling companion to check you for ticks and if you are travelling with small children remember to check their heads, and particularly behind the ears. If you think you have been bitten by a tick then seek medical advice locally, as treatment following exposure may be available. Tell the doctor whether or not you have been immunised.

Lyme disease has been present in Europe for decades but in Romania has possibly been under diagnosed until recently. The risk of acquiring the disease is not especially high if you take precautions to avoid being bitten by ticks and to remove any promptly and carefully as described (see above).

If you are bitten, then look out for the following **symptoms**: a few days to a month after the tick bite, a red bump develops which then spreads into a bull's-eye pattern. Fever, chills, fatigue, muscle aches and a headache may accompany the rash. Early treatment will prevent the longer-term problems of joint pain and swelling (especially of the knees) and other neurological problems such as meningitis and Bell's palsy.

If you're treated with appropriate antibiotics in the early stages of the disease, you are likely to recover completely. In later stages, response to treatment may be slower, but the majority of people recover completely with appropriate treatment.

Tick Alert (*www.tickalert.org*) has more information.

THE EUROPEAN HEALTH INSURANCE CARD
Transylvania has an adequate, if underfunded, health service. Tourists with health insurance will be well cared for and those from EU countries need to carry an electronic card, the European Health Insurance Card (EHIC), which replaced the E111 form guaranteeing free healthcare. UK citizens should ask for this card at their local social security or sickness insurance offices. UK residents can apply for the **EHIC card online** at the Department of Health website (*www.dh.gov.uk/travellers*). The card is free so avoid those websites that charge for processing the application. The card is valid in EEA (European Economic Area) countries, but the kind of treatment you can access varies from country to country, according to their healthcare policies and their arrangements with the UK. Everyone travelling to Romania should take out travel insurance, even for a short weekend break. The UK Foreign and Commonwealth Office has a website for its 'Know Before You Go' campaign, giving advice on all aspects of travel, including health and safety (*www.fco.gov.uk*).

TRAVEL CLINICS AND HEALTH INFORMATION
A full list of current travel clinic websites worldwide is available on www.istm.org. For other journey preparation information, consult www.tripprep.com (registration needed). Information about symptoms and medication can be found on www.emedicine.com.

PHARMACIES For minor ailments, a visit to the nearest pharmacy (*farmacie*) may suffice. Pharmacies are found all over towns, some opening until late and some offering a 24-hour emergency service; the staff are well trained and often multilingual, especially if you know the Latin name for the problem.

International brands of headache, indigestion and diarrhoea tablets or throat lozenges, as well as sanitary towels, tampons, tissues and condoms are available and can be requested by name.

SPAS Those central Europeans in the know are wildly enthusiastic about the curative powers of spa waters. Transylvania offers a great wealth of curative springs, thermal spas, climatic health resorts and natural mineral waters. Romania boasts one-third of all Europe's mineral springs and 160 spa resorts (*băile*). See page 108 for more details and also see the relevant chapters for added information on each spa.

SAFETY

According to the Foreign Office, around 75,000 British nationals visit Romania every year and almost all visits are trouble-free. The main types of incident for which British nationals required consular assistance in Romania generally involves petty crime, lost or stolen passports and car theft.

Visitors should be alert to the risk of petty theft in large towns, especially in Bucharest, and to pickpockets and bag snatchers in crowded areas, particularly near exchange shops, on buses (especially to the airport), main railway stations and inside airport areas. There have been reports of policemen stopping foreign cars and demanding payment of fines in hard currency for spurious offences. Bogus policemen may also approach pedestrians and ask to check their documents as a way of stealing cash. If approached in this way, visitors should decline to pay any fine or hand over any documents but offer instead to go with them to the nearest police station or back to the hotel. British visitors have reported thefts of valuables including passports from hotel rooms. Items of value, including passports and credit cards, should be deposited in hotel safes.

Transylvania, especially in the rural areas, is a very safe place. In many villages where everyone knows everyone else, doors are left open and children run around until late at night. This is the place to find charming Old-World courtesy and good manners. People say *Buna zuia/Jó napot kivánok* ('Good day' in Romanian/Hungarian) to every single person in the street and elderly gentlemen tip their hats and greet ladies with respect.

Stray dogs are present throughout Romania and while aggressive in Bucharest, in the countryside they tend to be of a nervous disposition and easily shooed away. The ones to watch out for are sheepdogs when walking in the countryside. These are trained to protect the sheep from wolves – and tourists, as the local joke says – but it's not funny if one attacks and hikers should always carry a big stick.

Another omnipresent danger is Romanian drivers who view all road journeys as an extreme sport. If I thought that Slovak locals were risky on the road, they are not in the same league as Romanians (see *Getting around*, page 78) who have some of the worst road accident statistics in Europe. Tailgating, speeding and overtaking on bends and hills are widespread and the only way the local authorities in Cluj-Napoca could stop drivers from risking their own and everybody else's lives was to build a low concrete wall along the middle of the road. Speed traps, cameras and heavy speeding fines have been introduced on highways but signs by the side of the road list the gruesome statistics of how many deaths and injuries occurred during the previous month.

When driving a hire car, be constantly vigilant, not only for silver BMWs approaching from the opposite direction in your lane, but also for wild horses running rampant, cows meandering across the road, inebriated cyclists weaving into the middle lane and the occasional unlit hay wagon, grinding at a snail's pace along a winding country road, shrouded in darkness. The Romanian man at the car rental in Bucharest even warned, 'Be careful when driving, we are not very civilised on the road!'

POLICE The police have a bad reputation, for monolingual boorishness, taking bribes and generally giving drivers, particularly those in a hire car or with foreign registration plates, a hard time. My experience was quite the opposite. When driving through Huedin, I heard a loud bang, almost like an explosion under the car and stopped to check if anything was going on under the bonnet. Immediately, a middle-aged man rushed out from his yard to try to help. He called to two policemen who were parked over the road and they also ran over. All three spent half an hour investigating the mysterious noise. One of the policemen spoke perfect English and German. The origins of the noise were never revealed.

After a road accident, report to the nearest police station and fill in a claim form for the car-hire company's insurance. Carry a photocopy of your passport at all times.

IN AN EMERGENCY A new system was introduced in 2005 in which the three services (police, fire, ambulance) were combined and the universal telephone number is now ✆112.

You may also see the following signs:

Poliţie Rendőrség (police); ✆955
Ambulanţa Mentők (ambulance); ✆961
Pompieri Tűzoltók (fire brigade); ✆981

Mountain Rescue ✆0-SALVAMONT (0-725826668)

WOMEN TRAVELLERS

For all her efforts following World War I, Queen Marie of Romania was dubbed 'The only man in Romania', but – of course – she had used a lot of eyelash fluttering and feminine wiles to get her way.

For women travelling on their own in Transylvania the trip can be lonely without somebody to discuss the beauty of the view, but, taking the right precautions, it should not be dangerous. Entering a bar, women will get some strange looks anyway, as these are usually exclusively male domains.

In 1990, Dervla Murphy, then aged 59, cycled and walked around Transylvania a few months after the fall of Ceauşescu. In her evocative travelogue, *Transylvania and Beyond* she described how she set off walking across the countryside in the middle of the night, with nothing except some money, a few notebooks and minimal Romanian language skills after her rucksack was stolen from the train on the Hungarian–Romanian border near Arad. In the memorable opening passages, Murphy hurls herself into Transylvanian life and does not appear to encounter too much sexism, apart from many funny sideways glances when she enters a pub on her own and downs a *ţuică* with the best of them.

Transylvania is still pretty old-fashioned in attitude and macho posturing is widespread, particularly on the road. Men are surprised and bemused by the idea of a woman on holiday without a male guardian. Romanians are not backward about coming forward and love to ask questions. If you can communicate with the village's head grandma, be prepared for some pretty probing enquiries as to where your husband is, why he lets you travel alone, how you manage to drive a car and use a map without your lord and master, and who is at home feeding the chickens while you are off gallivanting.

You will often see women of all ages, but particularly grannies, hitchhiking. This will occur in regions where local buses are non-existent and while locals will be respected, tourists might be viewed as foolhardy, wealthy Westerners and could be taken advantage of. Hitchhiking should not be attempted by anyone on their own and only by two women with first-class local language skills.

TRAVELLING WITH CHILDREN

Transylvania can be a great place to travel with kids, with fairytale castles inhabited by vampires and endless unspoilt wildernesses and national parks teeming with wildlife providing suitably engaging distractions to counterbalance museum visits. Reduced ticket prices for children are available at most attractions.

DISABLED TRAVELLERS

Transylvania is not very wheelchair-friendly. Many towns have winding, cobbled streets, which can make for a bumpy, uncomfortable ride. The Carpathian mountain range surrounds Transylvania on three sides and, while an ideal destination for hikers and skiers, is not designed with wheelchairs in mind and some hotels do not even have a lift to their upper floors. Having said that, larger towns such as Sibiu and Braşov have sensitively restored centres with a pedestrian heart built of smooth concrete, but side/back streets are riddled with pot-holes and bumps to make getting around a tiresome procedure. Every bank and many hotels are supposed to have an entrance ramp and lifts to their upper floors, but many restaurants are situated in inaccessible cellars or up the side of a mountain. Conversely, almost all the spa hotels are designed for visitors with limited mobility and have a range of facilities and treatments.

In 2007, Bucharest introduced buses and trolleybuses with wheelchair access, although the steep metro escalators still need some skill to negotiate.

Boarding trams is only possible if someone strong hauls the wheelchair up the very steep steps and on board. People always come to assist, but it's hard going. Romanian trains are not equipped for wheelchairs, although you would never be short of willing helpers attempting to lift the chair up the vertiginous steps.

Look at Gordon Rattray's website (*www.able-travel.com*) for advice on travel for not only people with physical disabilities, but also for those with sensory problems and the elderly who worry about climbing hundreds of steps, the availability of bathrooms and the possibility on some tours of a sit down and a rest.

Other useful sites are www.globalaccessnews.com, www.tourismforall.org.uk and www.rollingrains.com.

GAY TRAVELLERS

If you are homosexual, then Transylvania is not the best destination for a fun, gay holiday. During the Ceauşescu period, many homosexuals were imprisoned and gay life was denied or firmly closeted. Homosexuality was decriminalised only in

2001, but the majority of the population is very religious and still finds the idea of it to be against nature. Gays, lesbians, bisexual and trans-gender people face daily prejudice and are forced to keep their private lives hidden. Gigi Becali, the right-wing, nationalist politician exploits the religious feelings of country folk and once offered a reward of millions to anyone who could 'root out homosexuality in Romania'. Becali leads the PNG Party and said about the Eurovision Song Contest, 'It's just a show for faggots and mafiosi.' The US appeared to be playing with fire when they appointed openly gay diplomat Michael Guest as US Ambassador to Romania who served from 2001–03. His same-sex partner even accompanied Guest to official functions. One wonders what the Bucharest cocktail party glitterati made of it. Mr Guest was, however, accepted by some members of society: when we were looking around the ancient Densuş Church in the Haţeg region, the severe-looking priest mentioned that Guest was instrumental in the US government's funding of the church's renovation.

Accept (*www.accept-romania.ro*) is the country's solitary gay organisation, registered in 1996. Another website with gay travel advice is www.gayromania.ro.

WHAT TO TAKE

A trip to rural Transylvania may seem like a journey back in time, but with few additions to your suitcase or the occasional trip to a larger city, should provide all the comforts of (a 21st-century) home.

The summer months are very hot and few hotels are air conditioned. This is less of a problem in mountain villages but cities such as Bucharest can be stifling. Bring along some **mosquito repellent**, especially if staying in the south and in Bucharest.

You may also want to bring along some **earplugs** if you are a light sleeper and are spending time in villages. Romanians love to party and any reasonable provincial will almost certainly have a celebratory knees-up on a Saturday night. I was amazed by the Biertan villagers' capacity for partying until the early hours in the local pub every night of the week. You won't get much rest so it's best to go with the flow. Watch the dancing, the singing and the traditions and you'll probably be asked to take part.

Take **eye patches** purloined from long-haul flights, as curtains can often be flimsy or non-existent and you don't want to wake up at dawn after another raucous shindig.

Many of the historic towns are best explored on foot, so pack some **comfortable shoes** and perhaps an **anorak** for the occasional, unexpected summer shower. Winters can be chilly and summers baking, so choose clothes accordingly. The mountains are significant skiing and hiking venues, so take sturdy **walking boots**, water and a whistle.

Take out comprehensive **travel insurance** before your trip to cover lost baggage, theft and medical emergencies, and bring photocopies of the documentation with you.

Although Romania is still a cash-based system, take a secreted credit/debit card for topping up at the many ATMs that litter the country. Travellers' cheques are notoriously difficult to cash. If you lose money, your family can send extra to Western Union offices, found throughout Transylvania.

By Romanian law, you are supposed to carry your passport or identity card at all times. Take extra **passport photos** for extended travel passes and make extra copies of your passport, driving licence and insurance documents to leave in the hotel safe. You'll need a passport for many transactions: mobile phone SIM cards, gym/spa membership and when checking into your hotel.

2

Bear in mind that Transylvanians brew up a lethal spirit, *ţuică*, sometimes called *palincă*, from all manner of fruit. The wines and beers are also highly drinkable (see pages 92 and 165). Pack a **penknife** with a corkscrew and bottle opener, but remember not to take such an implement in hand luggage on planes but in checked-in luggage only. Transylvanian cuisine is hearty and rib-sticking. Bearing all these factors in mind, it might be a good idea to pack extra supplies of headache and indigestion tablets.

ELECTRICITY Romania's electrical current is 220V/50Hz, accessible via the European two-pin plug. Plug adaptors for use with three-pronged plugs are generally available from the larger supermarkets and pharmacies in shopping malls. Light bulbs are usually the screw-in type.

MONEY

The Romanian currency is the leu (plural: lei) often written out in full after the figure or shown as RON (Romanian new leu).

The leu (which means 'lion') comes in the following denomination banknotes: 1 leu and 5, 10, 50, 100, 200 and 500 lei. Each leu is divided into 100 bani, available as coins of 1, 2, 5, 10 and 50 bani.

PAPER NOTES AND THE FAMOUS ROMANIANS ON THEM

1 LEU (*un leu*) Historian, professor, poet, playwright and politician Nicolae Iorga (1871–1940). The colour of the note is green and blue with a blue gentian flower next to the portrait of Iorga. The reverse shows the cathedral of Curtea de Argeş Monastery. The see-through part shows an eagle holding a cross in its beak. Co-founder of the Democratic National Party, Iorga bravely spoke out against fascism as World War II loomed. In 1940, he was tortured and shot in the back and his body dumped beside a road with a copy of the newspaper *Neamul românesc* (*The Romanian Nation*) that he wrote for, forced down his throat.

5 LEI (*cinci lei*) Composer, pianist, violinist and conductor George Enescu (1881–1955). The colour of the note is purple and pink with a musical note over a carnation flower. The reverse shows the Romanian Athenaeum concert hall. The see-through part depicts a musical note. Enescu composed *Romanian Rhapsodies* in 1903. He lived in Paris after World War II and is buried in Père Lachaise Cemetery.

10 LEI (*zece lei*) Artist Nicolae Grigorescu (1838–1907). The colour of the note is pink and light orange with a hollyhock flower and a paintbrush. The reverse shows a house from the Oltenia region and a scene from Grigorescu's painting *Rodica* depicting a peasant girl. The see-through part shows paintbrushes and an artist's palette. One of the founders of modern Romanian painting, Grigorescu lived for long periods in Paris and worked on landscapes and pastoral themes.

50 LEI (*cincizeci lei*) Inventor, aeroplane constructor and pilot Aurel Vlaicu (1882–1913). The colour of the note is yellow, light orange and light green with an edelweiss flower next to the portrait. The reverse shows a mountain eagle's head and Vlaicu's design for his plane *Vlaicu II*. The see-through part depicts an eagle's head.

The banknotes are new and each has a see-through clear plastic part in the shape of an image describing the profession of the famous Romanian depicted on the note.

On 1 July 2005, the leu was revalued at the rate of 10,000 'old' lei (ROL) for one new leu (RON), thus psychologically bringing the purchasing power of the leu back in line with those of other major Western currencies. The old lei (ROL) remained as legal tender alongside the new RON until 31 December 2006.

On 1 January 2007, the new leu (RON) became the only legal tender. However, in some rural areas, some shopkeepers still speak in 'old lei' terms and you may be a bit taken aback when you are charged 10,000 lei for a bottle of mineral water.

1 new leu (RON) = 10,000 old lei (ROL)
100 new lei (RON) = 1,000,000 old lei (ROL)

EXCHANGING CURRENCY AND TRAVELLERS' CHEQUES Although there are many exchange offices dotted around larger towns, the best place to change money is at a bank. Banca Transilvania is very good. Euros are the most readily accepted, and some hotels quote their room prices exclusively in euros.

Travellers' cheques are nigh on impossible to exchange although can be cashed in large banks, some hotels and selected exchange offices where most of them charge

The first Romanian to excel in flight was born near Orăştie, Transylvania, in the village of Binţinţi, which now bears his name. There is another Aurel Vlaicu village just south of Sighişoara and a third in Botoşani County near the Moldovan border. Vlaicu died when his ageing *Vlaicu II* plane crashed in 1913.

100 LEI (*una sută lei*) Playwright Ion Luca Caragiale (1852–1912). The colour of the note is blue and purple with a violet flower and theatrical mask next to the portrait. The reverse shows the old building of Bucharest's National Theatre. The see-through part depicts a theatrical mask. Caragiale's plays were wry social commentaries with acute observations of Romania's modernising process at the end of the 19th century.

200 LEI (*două sutei lei*) Poet, philosopher, translator and dramatist Lucian Blaga (1895–1961). This note is legal tender but rarely used. The colour of the note is yellow and light orange with three red poppies and a book of poetry next to the portrait. The reverse shows a rainbow behind a farmhouse and a sculpture of a man sitting head in hands. The see-through part shows an oil lamp and a sheet of paper. Born in Lancrăm near Sebeş in Alba County, Blaga was acclaimed for his originality of thought and commented on Romanian society between the wars.

500 LEI (*cinci sutei lei*) National poet Mihai Eminescu (1850–89). The colour of the note is greeny-purple with lime tree blossoms next to a quill and an ink pot. The reverse shows the *Timpul* newspaper and the façade of the university library in Iaşi. The see-through part depicts an egg-timer. The historian Iorga (1 leu note) considered Eminescu the godfather of the modern Romanian language. Eminescu is celebrated as the greatest and most representative Romanian poet.

considerable commissions. Romania is still a cash-based society and for travelling around it's good to keep a supply of notes in a money belt up your jumper.

CASH PASSPORT Travelex Cash Passport (*www.cashpassport.com*) is a convenient, safe alternative to carrying piles of cash or cheques. The system is based on a pre-paid travel card that allows holders 24-hour access to their money in any local currency. You load up the card with funds before your trip and draw the cash out as you go along from ATMs. When you've used up your funds, simply throw the card away.

CREDIT CARDS Major credit cards including American Express, MasterCard and Visa are accepted in large hotels, by some car-hire companies and stores in the main cities. However, credit cards are unlikely to prove useful in small towns or away from tourist areas.

DISCOUNT CARDS The International Student Discount Card (ISIC) or International Youth Travel Card (for students under 26) will entitle you to reductions on entry to many museums, galleries and other attractions, and on journeys on some public transport networks. Concessionary rates for pensioners apply – in theory – to EU nationals. However, deep in the Transylvanian countryside, explanations can get lost in translation. Show a passport and try an official-melting smile.

BANKS

$ **National Bank of Romania/Banca Naţională a României** www.bnr.ro. The bank was established in 1880.
$ **Banca Transilvania** www.bancatransilvania. ro. The website shows 424 BT branches & 638 ATMs throughout Romania.

$ **Banca Comerciala Carpatica** ☏ 0800 807 807, free throughout Romania; www.carpatica. ro. There are 207 ATMs; the website lists their locations.

Banks' usual opening hours are 09.00–17.00 Monday–Thursday, 09.00–15.00 Friday.

ATMs (Bancomat) are available at main banks, airports and shopping centres. Do not expect to find ATMs in remote areas or villages.

BUDGETING

You can still find great bargains in Transylvania, although larger cities such as Braşov, Sibiu and Cluj-Napoca have some more expensive, upmarket restaurants. However, you can also go to the other end of the scale and have a right royal blowout. Everyone will find something to suit their taste and purse, and your money will go further in shops, restaurants, hotels and on public transport than in the West.

It's actually pretty difficult to spend vast amounts of money in Transylvania. If you are booked into one of the noble Transylvanian families' estates, almost everything is included except snacks and drinks on days out in larger cities like Braşov and Sibiu. If you're on your own, petrol for the hire car and restaurant meals will be your greatest costs. Compared with Spain, Italy, the US and Canada, car hire in central Europe is pretty overpriced with daily rates starting at €29 (if booked for two weeks, shorter periods and weekends could be significantly more expensive). Petrol is not too pricey but the distances are vast and both time and fuel consuming.

Rail and minibus travel is economical, and most cafés and restaurants are reasonably priced. If you stay in the heart of the Transylvanian countryside, hike or cycle everywhere and eat at local restaurants, you'd have to work hard to spend your lei.

The following guide lists daily budgets for one person, based on two people sharing accommodation (and therefore paying slightly less on the room, but not the beer bill).

A GUIDE TO BUDGETING

Penny-pinching You can probably get by on a budget of around 80RON (£14/US$22/€18) for a hostel dorm, eating in one of the local cafés, entry to a few museums and rounded off by a meal with drinks in a modest pub.

Modest You'll spend about 124RON (£22/US$35/€27) a day if you want basic accommodation in a two-star hotel, cheered on by occasional treats, a ticket to a performance at one of the concert halls or a slap-up meal in a top city restaurant.

Luxury A daily allowance of 296RON (£53/US$83/€65) will allow a stay in a swanky boutique hotel in Braşov, Sibiu or Cluj-Napoca, some sightseeing, stops for coffee, cake and beer, a meal in a decent restaurant, late-night drinks in a club and a taxi back to base. The greatest expense will be on the accommodation as hotels have smartened up their acts a lot recently and the room prices have consequently risen significantly.

TIPPING Never assume you should tip a taxi driver. Wait until he has counted out the small change into your hand and then give 10% or round up the figure to the nearest 10RON if the service was good. In large hotels and restaurants frequented by tourists, tipping is common and anything between 10% and 20% is expected. In

SOME SAMPLE PRICES

(1RON = £0.18/US$0.28/€0.22)

Loaf of white bread (1kg)	1.5RON
One litre of milk	3RON
Bowl of soup in restaurant	7RON
Bottle of Ciuc lager (0.5l)	4RON
Bottle of Romanian wine	10–30RON
Bottle of mineral water (2l)	2.40RON
Cup of coffee in café	2–5RON
Train ticket Bucharest–Cluj (first class on Intercity)	153RON
One litre of petrol (benzină)	5.72RON
One litre of diesel fuel (motorină)	5.89RON
Museum/gallery entrance ticket	5–15RON
Use of computer at internet café	3RON per hour
Smart restaurant meal for two with main, salad, water and wine	40–60RON
Pizza in café	9–13RON
New Dacia Logan car	€6,500–10,500
Average Romanian monthly wage	€230–460

restaurants and cafés used by locals, a small service charge is often included in the bill but a further 10% can be added.

GETTING AROUND

Public transport in Transylvania is well intentioned and cheap, but the bus service can be patchy in isolated areas. Although Romania has the most dense train network in Europe, there are still mountainous districts where only logging railways reach. The network has some idiosyncrasies and when I was there in 1997, almost every train appeared to go via the nightmarish rail transport hub of Copşa Mică.

In many places, the public transport is so unreliable or missing altogether that anyone with a tractor is commandeered into becoming an impromptu bus driver. Many locals of all ages have to hitchhike and stand waving their arms wildly at bus stops (see *Hitchhiking*, page 82).

Most towns and villages can be accessed by public transport in one way or another. Sometimes bus is better than train and sometimes vice versa. However, public transport (where it exists) is efficient although very crowded. Many regions are best explored by hire car, or consider going on an organised tour and letting a local negotiate the bumpy, pot-holed roads.

BY AIR

Tarom (*www.tarom.ro*) Daily except Saturday flights from Bucharest Otopeni to Sibiu and weekday flights to Cluj-Napoca. Tarom flies from Bucharest Otopeni to Târgu Mureş four times per week.

Carpatair (*www.carpatair.ro*) Based in Timişoara, Carpatair flies all over Romania and links the Transylvanian city of Sibiu with Bucharest Otopeni.

BY TRAIN
Romania's railway network, CFR (*www.cfr.ro*), is the densest and one of the largest in Europe. It has trains servicing every town and city in the country, and the many villages.

The fastest trains in Transylvania are the Intercitys running on the Bucharest to Cluj-Napoca route. Only the Săgeata Albastră (Blue Arrow) Intercity trains linking Bucharest, Braşov, Cluj-Napoca and other cities, have loos appropriate for the 21st century.

There are four types of train in Romania:

- **Tren personal** or **tren de persoane** (marked 'P' on timetables) trains are grindingly slow and stop at every tiny village. However, they are very cheap.
- **Accelerat** (A) trains serve larger towns and cities, but are slow and not too clean. It's not worth buying a first-class supplement for these trains as the standard is uniform.
- **Rapid** (R) trains are cleaner than the Accelerat numbers. They only stop at major cities and are therefore slightly quicker. Reservations (*loc rezervat*) are obligatory.
- **Intercity** (IC) trains are the ones to choose. They are the only trains where it's safe to visit the loo without feeling like you might catch dysentery. IC trains are the fastest, linking most major cities, but they run infrequently so it needs some planning ahead to use them. IC trains are more expensive than the other three categories and you'll need to buy a *loc rezervat*.

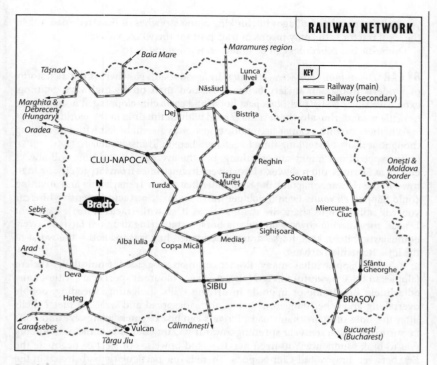

RAILWAY NETWORK

KEY
— Railway (main)
--- Railway (secondary)

Buying a train ticket Almost every city and large town has a CFR office; look for the sign 'CFR–Agenţia de Voiaj'.

A *bilet* is a basic second-class fare for a *personal* train; the *casa de bilete* is the ticket office. The *supliment* is the supplementary fare to upgrade to a faster train, to first class or to sleeping accommodation (*cuşetă*). The *loc rezervat* is the seat reservation.

See *Appendix 1, Language*, page 275, for more travel vocabulary, page 63 for details of Bucharest's Gară de Nord, and the relevant city sections in *Part Two* of the guide for their main railway stations. For train times and online booking see www.cfrcalatori.ro. It can be worth filling in the 'via' field to find alternative routes (for example, Cluj-Napoca–Sibiu has only one daily service listed, whereas searching the same journey via Mediaş gives several).

Sample 2012 train ticket prices Tickets are available from the Wasteels ticket office at Bucharest's Gară de Nord (*Bucharest office* ☏ *+40 21 300 2730; Braşov office* ☏ *0268 424 313*).

- Bucharest to Cluj-Napoca first class on Intercity (IC) train costs €35
- Cluj-Napoca to Mediaş second class on Intercity (IC) train costs €13
- Sibiu to Braşov second class on Rapid (R) train costs €10
- Braşov to Sighişoara second class on Rapid (R) costs €4

BY BUS OR COACH The Romanian bus network is not very reliable. Travel by train is almost always preferable and buses are not worth the effort unless the village you want to see has no rail link. Many villages have neither bus nor train services and you will see people of all ages hitchhiking along stretches of deserted road. Often the local tractor is the only means of transport for the whole village.

Domestic bus schedules can be found on www.autogari.ro.

BY CAR *Drum bun!* (*bon voyage!* – literally 'good road') Nowhere is the dichotomy of modern Romanian society better illustrated than on its highways. Shining, expensive silver BMWs whoosh past horse and carts clip-clopping at a snail's pace or cattle meandering alongside a main road with all the time in the world.

Whether you hire a car, or use public transport, you will be left with one abiding thought: it takes a long, long time to get anywhere in Transylvania.

The speed limit might say one thing, but the average driving time will always end up as 50km/h, often slower. I have given driving times from city to city, town to town in the relevant chapters, but remember that this is Transylvania and anything could happen *en route*. Even if you get the most luxurious and expensive hire car you will still have to share the road, such as it is, with tractors, lorries, ancient Dacias, meandering cows, wild bolting horses, staggering drunken farmers, over-enthusiastic hitchhikers, horse-drawn overloaded hay wagons and – the worst of the lot – Romanian drivers.

It would appear that many Romanian men upgraded from their ancient jalopies to huge powerful foreign (always silver-coloured) sports cars without any adjustment in attitude or upgrade in driving skills. Tailgating, speeding, double overtaking and other dangerous habits are widespread and wrecked metal shells litter the sides of many main roads. Drivers can be extremely aggressive and don't be surprised if you see a car speeding towards you on your side of the road forcing you to brake suddenly. You need nerves – and bowels – of steel to negotiate the E60 between Braşov and Cluj-Napoca. There is one particularly bad stretch in the Bogatii Nature Reserve where the steep mountainside has freshly widened hairpin bends. Local drivers use this stretch for overtaking and sometimes there are cars four abreast on a winding corner (see also *Safety*, page 68).

Drivers also need to be alert for horse-drawn carts and livestock, especially at night when they are not always clearly marked. Some villagers driving horse and carts wear fluorescent yellow waistcoats and some strap a fluorescent yellow triangle to the back of the cart. However, this is not the norm and many overloaded hay wagons are extremely hard to spot at night in villages where there are no street lamps and on winding country roads where it can be pitch black.

The government is responsible for the roads between the towns and predictably neglects some of the roads in counties with a large Hungarian population, such as Covasna and Mureş. The local council and town hall has to repair the roads in settlements with very little money from the government. Thus, you could be driving along on a relatively smooth highway, then turn off into a village and be faced with a dirt track and a virtual impasse. The roads were built for a 1970s capacity and now cannot cope with the huge increase in traffic. Cluj-Napoca sags under more than 11,000 cars a day.

In Mureş County, the road from Reghin to Lăpuşna is like a journey back in time – literally – as the road deteriorates from tarmac to cobbles to gravel to dirt track to non-negotiable mud as the settlements along the way become more and more destitute.

In Viscri, it takes about half an hour to rattle along the few kilometres between the main road and the village, passing through a desperately poor Roma settlement where tiny children run along beside the car pointing to their mouths and giving pleading looks. However, village councillor Caroline Fernolend said she didn't want the road repaired, as the historic village would be swamped with coach parties.

Nearby, another Saxon village, Biertan, has an excellent linking road and a few large coaches and buses park in the main square, but fortunately it is not overrun. The historic Saxon village of Mălâncrav is a nightmare to reach. Despite the road being repaired for about one-third of the distance, the smooth tarmac suddenly gives way to the usual monotony of pot-holes, sharp rocks and mud.

A good tip, not always possible on the deserted country roads, is to follow a local in his beaten-up ancient Dacia and copy the swerves as he dodges the pot-holes.

However, there is hope that things will improve – a good deal of repair work has been undertaken in recent years. The road between Sibiu and Braşov is now very fast, as is the E60 Bucharest–Braşov–Târgu Mureş–Cluj-Napoca highway, although this is a death trap where brand-new German- and Italian-made sports cars and SUVs swoosh impatiently past ancient jalopies and horse-drawn carts. There are many accidents on the *drum naţional* (major road) network and drivers should also be vigilant on route 1 between Cluj-Napoca and Sibiu. Secondary roads (*drum judeţean*) can be little more than dirt tracks which turn to muddy bogs in winter while forest/mountain roads (*drum forestier*) can be impassable in winter and after storms.

Transylvania has no motorways (*autostrada*), but the first four-lane super highway (*www.autostradatransilvania.ro*) is now in construction. The 415km stretch of the motorway will pass southeast to northwest across the whole of Transylvania, taking in the cities of Braşov, Făgăraş, Sighişoara, Târgu Mureş, Cluj-Napoca, Zalău and Oradea (Bihor County). Completion is scheduled for 2013, though work looks set to go on for longer.

Car hire Hire-car companies in Bucharest and the main towns in each of the ten counties of Transylvania all offer everything from tinny little Mitsubishi Colts to giant people carriers and swanky limousines. A Romanian driver in Micloşoara told me the old-style Dacia is very good because 'You can mend everything on it with a screwdriver and a piece of wire.' These old models are not available but the home-grown Dacia Logan, built by Renault in Romania (sometimes advertised on the web as a Renault Logan) is just as durable and perfect for Transylvanian roads. It seems to know the roads and pot-holes, and the suspension and high chassis make even the roughest mountain road pretty comfortable.

The Dacia Logan 1.5l uses diesel and is very economical. While neither petrol nor diesel vehicles are particularly environmentally friendly, there has been a growing drive to promote the use of diesel vehicles as environmentally less damaging, as they tend to have lower CO_2 emissions (see *www.ecotravel.org.uk*). When hiring a car in summer, make sure it has air conditioning.

Average prices for a two-week period
- Dacia Logan €25 a day
- VW Golf €35 a day
- Renault Clio sedan €30 a day
- Opel Astra €35 a day
- Audi A4 €55 a day

Petrol stations (benzarie) in Transylvania The main stations are:
- ARAL (German, but part owned by BP)
- LUKOIL (Russian)
- MOL (Hungarian)
- OMV (Austrian)

2

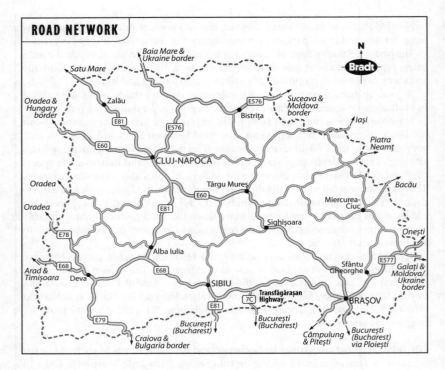

ROAD NETWORK

- PETROM (Romanian)
- ROMPETROL (Romanian)

Petrol and diesel prices (September 2012)

- Diesel (*motorină*) 6.28RON/litre
- Unleaded E95 (*Fără plumb* = lead free/*blei frei*) 6.58RON/litre
- 'Premium plus' petrol (*benzină*) 5.67RON/litre

The website www.gazonline.ro gives updates of fuel prices in every Romanian county.

Parking Parking in town centres is permitted in designated areas, marked *P cu plata*. Drivers must purchase a ticket directly from a parking attendant, from an automatic machine, from a news-stand or in a shop nearby that has the blue 'P' sign and the words *Aici găsti tichete*. Often the automatic machine is out of order and the old guy wandering around guarding the parking places is nowhere to be seen. In Sighișoara, a young guy was very efficient, popping up immediately; in Mediaș, Turda and Bistrița the ticket sellers had vanished into thin air. Sometimes you'll need to hunt down a shop selling parking tickets. This could be a newsagent, sweet shop, clothing boutique or camera shop. In Târgu Mureș a very kind lady in a secondhand clothes shop gave me a parking ticket, when I had no change, and let me pay later in the afternoon.

Tickets are charged per hour or per day.

Driving instructions Throughout Romania, the speed limits are 50km/h (31mph) in built-up areas, 90km/h (56mph) on country and side roads, 100km/h (62mph) on national European (E) and express routes and 130km/h (80mph) on motorways (less with a trailer). The Romanian Automobile Club (ACR) (✆ *9271*; *www.acr.ro*), provides technical assistance to all car owners. In order to enter Romania in their own cars, tourists are required to carry with them a driving licence, registration papers and a green card. US and Canadian driving licences are valid as are all EU international licences. The minimum age is 18. Driving is on the right-hand side of the road. Passengers in the front seat of a car must wear seatbelts at all times. Children under 12 years of age may not ride in the front seat. Unless otherwise indicated, by stop or yield sign, traffic coming from the right has the right of way. The use of mobile phones while driving is not allowed and the blood alcohol level is zero (and above 0.05% it is now a criminal offence). The best available road map is the DIMAP 1:250,000 Road Atlas, available in most bookshops or at MOL petrol stations.

Accidents and breakdowns If you have a road accident, call the police and make sure that you get a copy of the police report. The ACR (Romanian Automobile Club), based in Bucharest, has a 24-hour breakdown service (✆ *222 2222*), with English-speaking operators. The car-hire firm may give you a 24-hour contact number to use in case of emergencies. The first Romanian portal for road transport is at www.e-transport.ro.

AA UK ✆ 0870 600 0371 (international driving licence); 00 800 8877 6655 (European breakdown 24hr helpline); www.theaa.com

RAC UK ✆ 0800 015 6000 (European breakdown cover); www.rac.co.uk

Close encounters with Romanian police If you have a road accident, you must first call the police who will fill in the insurance form (for you or for the car-hire company). If stopped by the police for apparently no reason, remember that traffic officers cannot impose on-the-spot fines. All fine payments are made at a bank or local tax administration office. The officer can only write the ticket and will give instructions on how to pay/dispute the fine.

BY MINIBUS OR MAXI-TAXI

Minibuses (*microbuze* or *maxitaxiuri*) follow many of the same routes as buses and trains. Maxi-taxis can be crowded and cramped and in summer they are not recommended as there is rarely air conditioning. The drivers are often very reckless so a long journey can be tiring and bad for one's nerves. Maxi-taxis often pick up and put down by the local railway station, which makes connecting convenient. Prices are cheaper than trains and fares, payable on board, are usually €1 per 100km.

BY TAXI

Taxis get a very bad rap in Bucharest and, while my personal experiences have always been good, it does make sense to be on your guard. Avoid taxis with the telephone number '9403' on the side of the car, as these are dodgy independents impersonating trusted car companies. Three prices are displayed in taxis: *Pornire* is the basic price for choosing that taxi; *Pret km* means the price per kilometre. This should be 2–3.5RON per kilometre. Some dodgy firms have been known to charge as much as 8RON per kilometre, so pay attention. *Stationare* is the waiting price when stuck in traffic. Rates should be displayed on the side of the taxi, on the front door.

Trustworthy taxi companies in Bucharest include:

🚗 **Fly Taxi** ✆ 9440. They charge 3.5RON/km & your fare shouldn't cost more than €20.

🚗 **Prof Taxi** ✆ 9422
🚗 **Taxi 2000** ✆ 9494

If calling from a mobile phone, add the Bucharest dialling code 021. In Transylvania, taxis have a rather better reputation than in Bucharest, although the usual cautions still apply: stick to licensed taxis and make sure the fare is displayed. If unsure, ask your hotel to call a cab for you.

Marian Voinea (*Taxi Bucharest;* **m** *+40 722 933 297*) He was one of the taxi drivers at the airport waiting by the arrivals exit and the stop for the airport bus 783. Despite all the warnings I'd read about the dubious, lurking taxis, it was 40°C in the shade and I had a gigantic collection of bags. We agreed on a charge of €20 and Marian was charm itself, taking me all the way to a housing estate on the other side of Bucharest, searching for the right apartment among identical blocks, carrying my bags and turning up on time the next day to take me back to the airport (for the same fee of €20), through a traffic jam that took him one hour to negotiate.

HITCHHIKING Hitchhiking in Transylvania is called *autostop*. It's a common method of transport for locals of isolated villages where there may not be a bus service at all. It's also common to see a tractor pulling a cart laden with villagers, in a kind of impromptu bus service.

As in all European countries, women travellers should avoid hitching alone. Hitchers don't always stick out their thumbs. A common method is to wave one's right arm in a wild fashion, virtually flagging down the oncoming car. This can be quite disconcerting for car drivers who may think that an accident has happened when the person hitching is just trying to attract the driver's attention ahead of the other 20 people standing at the bus stop in the rain. Prospective hitchers often hold up a piece of cardboard with their destination as an abbreviated town name, eg:

BV – Braşov	MS – Mureş County	CJ – Cluj-Napoca
CV – Covasna	SB – Sibiu	BN – Bistriţa-Năsăud
HR – Harghita County	HD – Hunedoara County	SJ – Sălaj
TM – Târgu Mureş	AB – Alba Iulia	ZL – Zalău

ON FOOT Pedestrians should approach busy roads with care. Car drivers are unwilling to stop at zebra crossings, so step off the pavement at your own peril and never in front of an approaching car unless you're following a nun, a heavily pregnant lady or a tiny child.

In towns, the traffic lights have useful time counters attached to the pole up by the lights allowing both pedestrians and drivers full view of the number of seconds

THE BEST DRIVES IN TRANSYLVANIA

It's not all road rage and white van fever. Some stretches of road are deserted and a sheer joy to pootle along, gawping at the stunning scenery.

- Miercurea-Ciuc to Odorheiu Secuiesc (route 13A)
- From the main road (route 14 Sighişoara–Mediaş) to Biertan
- Gheorgheni to Bicaz-Chei (route 12C)
- Reghin to Lapuşna (too minor for a route number), the view is great, the road is terrible
- Transfăgărăşan Highway (route 7C)
- Predeal to Şinca Veche via Râşnov (route 73A)

GETTING AROUND BY HORSE AND CART

There are around 750,000 carts registered in Romania. However, a recent law (November 2007) banned horse-drawn carts and wagons from all main roads because they were blamed for 10% of all road traffic accidents in the country. Many believe it is not the horses and carts that cause accidents but nouveau-riche Romanian businessmen who have suddenly updated to a much more expensive, foreign-built car after decades of rattling along in an ancient Dacia, without learning how to drive such a powerful vehicle. Horse-and-cart drivers may be hard to spot at night, but many are now wearing reflective jackets. The horses are hardly to blame. From time to time a cart driver falls asleep at the reins, but even then the horses usually know where to go. If the police follow through on their threat to confiscate horses and carts found using the main roads, locals fear that many peasants will die through not being able to continue their livelihoods. Many horses have been abandoned since the law came into force and in March 2008, hundreds of stray horses were roaming the towns including 15 starving creatures found abandoned in central Bucharest. The horses are the victims of a disastrous law brought in to bring the country in line with EU transport regulations. Winter in Transylvania lasts seven months and horses are vital for everything from travel to ploughing to transporting timber down difficult thoroughfares from the mountainous forests to the plains to sell or use for heating. A significant proportion of Romania's population lives from subsistence farming. The new ban will be especially problematic in places where the main road runs right through the middle of the village. Local mayors are now busy trying to gather funds to build alternative side roads, but in some villages this is not viable as the villages are surrounded by steep mountain sides and the only possible entry point has already been taken.

left before the lights change from green to red via amber, or red to green (with no amber in between -- so run).

BY BICYCLE Romania's main highways are a confusing blend of ancient jalopies, horses and carts, meandering cows, wild horses, tipsy farm labourers, lorries, white vans, and expensive new German and Italian sports cars, almost always silver in colour. These all travel at differing speeds and with differing degrees of care and attention. Cycling on a main highway is not recommended, but off the larger roads it is an enjoyable way of exploring the countryside. Hire a good mountain bike (for bike tour companies, see page 53) with tough suspension for all those pot-holes which pepper the minor roads and be prepared for some strange looks from locals, for whom the cycling concept has not really caught on. There are no cycle paths in cities – yet. Taking your bike on a *personal* train is easy as it travels at the end of each carriage near the door. Stay with your bike at all times.

ACCOMMODATION

Transylvania has a blossoming tourist industry and an impressive range of accommodation to suit all budgets and interests. All towns offer endless varieties of old- and new-style hotels, pensions, apartments and hostels. Visitors can choose from an elegant family-run guesthouse to a rustic *cabana* in the mountains.

Communist retro-chic hunters can stay in one of Ceauşescu's personal villas or take a trip back in time to the beige 1970s décor of a Soviet-style hotel complex. Hikers in the mountains can find refuge at a *cabana* mountain lodge while skiers and spa lovers will find a range of prices and standards at large hotel complexes.

Prices have risen in recent years but Transylvania is still cheaper than almost anywhere in western Europe. Many hotels now post their prices exclusively in euros and prices range from €16 (70RON) for a basic 'sport hotel' to €120+ (525RON+) for a night in a luxurious business hotel.

HOTELS Many of the former state-run city-centre or resort hotels have either been refurbished or are undergoing major refurbishment programmes as international hotel groups take over and develop the facilities.

However, there are still many examples of old-style hotels with creaking smoke-filled lifts, dodgy plumbing and erratic hot water, but these are mainly in areas off the tourist-beaten track.

Cities such as Târgu Mureş, Cluj-Napoca, Sibiu and Braşov now have swanky business hotels with boutique interior décor, Wi-Fi in the rooms and lobbies, and superb-quality restaurants.

Service varies from indifferent and dour in the former state hotels and restaurants to a degree of genuine hospitality that is rarely found anywhere else.

MOTELS Transylvania's highways are littered with roadside motels. The E60 route from Braşov to Cluj-Napoca via Sighişoara and Târgu Mureş has many motels where you can enjoy anything from a restorative cup of coffee to a good night's sleep. For example, the Dumbrava at Rupea has 20 clean rooms while the Motel Tranzit at Mihai Viteazu is a good place for a snack and a drink. The gigantic Motel Darina near Târgu Mureş Airport (see page 177) is ideally placed for early or late flights but the restaurant is not very appealing for a longer stay. The National Tourist Office has a searchable accommodation guide on their website (*www.romaniatourism. com*) featuring 35 motels, although some venues on the list are more country club than roadside resthouse.

PENSIONS (*pensiune*) Since the fall of Ceauşescu in 1989 and the arrival of private enterprise there has been a boom in new, relatively small, private hotels and business hotels with the standards you would usually expect in the West. A good proportion of these have been built by Romanians who worked in Germany, Austria or Switzerland in the early 1990s and have now returned and invested their new-found knowledge and wealth into redeveloping the tourist industry.

PRIVATE GUESTHOUSES Descendants of ancient aristocratic Transylvanian families, namely the Kálnokys and Mikes noble families in Covasna County, are two of the shining examples here. Both have sensitively renovated their estates, in slightly different styles. Tibor Kálnoky (see page 155) blended a traditional 18th-century peasant-house ambience and features with modern interiors and superior bathrooms, whilst Gregor Roy Chowdhury's interior designer wife Zsolna Ugron (see page 158) created a designer boutique hotel within the walls of the Mikes Estate Machine House. Tibor Kálnoky's style of renovation even has royal approval and HRH Prince Charles asked Kálnoky to restore and manage his Saxon cottage in Viscri, now run as a small, private guesthouse (see page 149). A tempting feature of these private guesthouses is the home cooking, with the opportunity to taste Romanian, Székely, Moţ, Kalotaszeg and Saxon specialities you wouldn't find in a restaurant or café.

Based on the price of a double room in high season

$$$$$	340RON+	€74+
$$$$	264–340RON	€58–74
$$$	152–264RON	€33–58
$$	96–152RON	€21–33
$	>96RON	>€21

Many guesthouses combine accommodation with offering a variety of day trips. Dan Marin takes visitors on walks in the gorgeous Piatra Craiului National Park while his wife Luminiţa prepares divine traditional dishes. The Marins can also arrange traditional evenings with Roma music and dancing. This can also be tried in Sâncraiu where István Vincze-Keskés organises great parties in a village barn.

Julian Ross's riding stables have now been taken over by Count Kálnoky and Christoph Promberger has a stable and guesthouse near Braşov. The noble estates in Covasna County both offer an extensive range of trips, featuring birdwatching, bear trails, hiking and nature trails. Before 1989, tourist guests were forbidden in private homes and any prospective visitor had to sneak in during the night. Now, privately run guesthouses and cottages are springing up all over Transylvania and almost always have a very high standard of accommodation and family-style service.

RURAL TOURISM Since the 1989 revolution, many families in the countryside have offered rooms in their houses to let by tourists. The deal works both ways as the extra money helps locals in places where there is high unemployment and poor infrastructure, while the visitor has the opportunity to meet real people, discover a totally different way of life beyond the glossy travel brochure and make lasting friendships, built on a real understanding, appreciation and love for the Transylvanian countryside, its outstanding natural, animal and human assets. Those who stay with a family will be treated like a long-lost relative and will find that nothing is too much trouble for the host.

During the spring and summer, it's wise to book ahead, but in less busy seasons, you can just turn up in a village and look for a *camere de inchiriat* or *cazare de particular* sign.

Select your village wisely though, as sometimes the homes are situated along a bumpy, pot-holed road which, if you make the guesthouse your base, will add several hours' driving onto each day trip. Guesthouses in the Apuseni Mountains and some villages in the Saxon fortress church region (Mălâncrav and Viscri) are very inaccessible. Even the two noble estates (Kálnoky and Mikes) take a certain amount of hunting down and tiring drives along bumpy roads. All the more reason, therefore, to book an all-in holiday and go for the pick-up service from Bucharest Airport, letting an experienced local negotiate the pot-holes.

Those seeking accommodation in a real peasant house should try the Kálnoky Estate at Micloşoara and Viscri Guesthouse, Bucium, near Roşia Montana, Subcetate (Zetevăralja) south of Topliţa in Harghita County, Rimetea (Torockó), Sâncraiu (Kalotaszentkirály) and the Melinda Guesthouse at Băţanii Mici (Kisbacon).

ANTREC (*www.antrec.ro*, see page 15) is the largest rural tourism organisation while Opération Villages Roumains (*www.hdd.dds.nl*) was set up by a Belgian charity in 1988 to save villages from Ceauşescu's vicious demolition plans by twinning towns in Romania with those in western Europe. The website is mainly in Dutch but you can download a list of bed-and-breakfast accommodation from the English pages.

The European Centre for Eco-Agro Tourism (ECEAT), based in Amsterdam, has a network of members throughout Europe. In Transylvania, the contact person is Zoltán Hajdu in Târgu Mureş at the Focus Eco Centre (see page 55). The ADEPT non-profit foundation works with local people and has a list of guesthouses (see page 15) in the Saxon villages and Tărnava Mare Valley region.

The Mihai Eminescu Trust renovates traditional Saxon peasants' houses in villages such as Mălâncrav and Viscri and reservations can be made via email (see page 15).

Prices in private guesthouses can vary greatly with anything from 30RON to 90RON being the typical nightly charge, with gigantic breakfasts and often dinner included.

For contact details, see *Tour operators*, page 52.

CABANAS – MOUNTAIN REFUGES In the mountainous regions, there are more than 100 *cabanas*, otherwise known as hikers' huts. These can vary in standard from a basic wooden chalet with hard bunk beds and cold water to an alpine-style villa with all the comforts of home. Some are in very isolated spots accessible only by a long, steep climb on foot. Cabana Peştera in the Bucegi Mountains is reached by cable car from Buşteni while Cabana Bălea Lac and Complex Hotelier Capra are near the peaks of the Făgăraş Mountains, close to the Transfăgăraşan Highway. Specific regional hiking maps (see page 116), which you can pick up at bookstores and street stalls, pinpoint the locations of many *cabanas* that allegedly never turn a hiker away. In popular hiking regions and seasons, such as the Făgăraş range in spring and summer, it might be a good idea to book in advance through a local agency. Bed prices in a remote *cabana* start from 10RON, while it could be a bit more in a more luxurious hut.

HOSTELS The hostel network is not very developed in Transylvania, although there are some in the larger cities and tourist hotspots such as Sighişoara. A dormitory bed price starts from around 30RON with possibly a basic breakfast thrown in. Student accommodation is hard to find (even for students); however in places like Cluj-Napoca with a large student population it might be worth checking out, but only in July and August when the usual residents are away.

International Youth Hostel Federation 2nd Flr, Gate Hse, Fretherne Rd, Welwyn Garden City AL8 6RD; ☎01707 324170; f 01707 323980; e info@hihostels.com; www.hihostels.com

Youth Hostel Association Românìa P-ta Lucian Blaga 1, 1st Flr/AITASS, Cluj-Napoca; ☎+40 264 586 616; e office@hihostels-romania. ro; www.hihostels-romania.ro

CAMPSITES Campsites (*loc de campare*) are not particularly developed in Transylvania and many locals prefer to go 'wild camping' by pitching their tents in a particularly deserted spot. This is not officially allowed and for this you would need to have experience of the Romanian countryside, language skills and knowledge of the local flora and fauna would also be very advisable as there are many wild animals waiting to take advantage of a tasty, inexperienced human. Camping grounds often consist of wooden huts (*căsuţe*) with tightly packed bare mattresses and spartan facilities. Prices start at 3RON per person per night but often the sites are filled with locals using the place as a temporary home.

I had for breakfast more paprika, and a sort of porridge of maize flour which they said was 'mămăligă', and egg-plant stuffed with forcemeat, a very excellent dish, which they call 'impletata'. (*Mem., get recipe for this also.*)

From Jonathan Harker's journal, Chapter 1, Dracula, *by Bram Stoker*

TRANSYLVANIAN CUISINE Historian Nicolae Klepper writes in his book *Taste of Romania* that: 'the central characteristic of the Romanian cuisine is its great variety. It is a cuisine influenced by repeated waves of different cultures: the ancient Greeks, with whom Romanians traded; the Romans, who gave the country its name; the Saxons, who settled in southern Transylvania; the Turks, who for centuries dominated Romania; as well as Slavic and Magyar neighbours. All of these influences gradually blended into the varied and delicious Romanian culinary tradition.'

Romanian dishes take their inspiration from the land and the meals are hearty and filling, and excellent before a day's hike through the mountains.

Breakfast (*micul dejun*) This is often quite a simple affair enhanced with natural, local produce. Crusty bread (*pâine*) is accompanied by homemade jam (*gem*). If you stay with the Marins in Zărneşti, be sure to try Luminiţa's superb jams made from wild cherry, rose hip and divine elderberry, for which a recipe is given below (see box overleaf). Many small guesthouses offer their own yoghurt and the honey is more than often organic, from nearby orchard beehives. Lorries with many-coloured hives installed in the side of the truck tour the countryside pursuing the best blossoms. Many people like the acacia but the best is said to be *poliflora*, made from a variety of flowers. There may also be cheese (*brânză*), which could be a Cheddar-like *caşcaval* or *caş*, an unsalted feta-esque ewe's milk cheese, sometimes mixed with fresh dill and stuffed into fresh peppers. Peppers and the juiciest tomatoes you will ever taste are often served with a selection of salami and cold cuts at a traditional Hungarian breakfast, which is usually more savoury than sweet. If you're going on a long walk in the countryside, you might start the day with an omelette, which can sometimes be quite oily due to the addition of cubes of fatty bacon (*slănină*). This is washed down with orange juice, tea with lemon or milk, or thick black coffee. I stayed in a business hotel in Harghita County and noticed that the breakfast of choice for Moldavian businessmen was Red Bull and a ciggie. In *Dracula*, Jonathan Harker was served *mămăligă* (polenta) for breakfast and it's the Transylvanian equivalent of Scottish porridge, an excellent heart-warming start to the day, popular with shepherds who need something to keep them going up in the chilly hills.

Staying in a guesthouse with a local Romanian lady doing the cooking is a good way to get to grips with the heart and soul of the Transylvanian countryside. Our hosts served very sustaining breakfasts, with frankfurters, giant omelettes and even pork medallions on one occasion. If you are hungry around mid morning, even after that whopping day-starting meal, **snacks** (*gustări*) are varied and plentiful. In Târgu Mureş, I found the Hungarian favourite *lăngos*, giant frisbees of deep-fried dough, served with an imaginative selection of toppings: sour cream, grated cheese, ketchup or even cabbage. They usually cost 1.5RON. *Gogoşi* are sweet doughnuts. A rapidly expanding (much like your waistline after one of these) chain, Gogoaşa Înfuriată (Sizzling Doughnut) has branches in Cluj-Napoca and claims that these big fat babies are from a traditional Berliner recipe. The filling can be chocolate, vanilla crème, cherry jam or even crumbly *caş* cheese. They cost 1–2RON. Another sustaining snack, often served warm for dessert, is *papanaşi*, cheese dumplings rolled in breadcrumbs and sugar and slathered with cream and jam. At Lacu Roşu (with the appropriately spooky name in Hungarian: Gyilkos-tó – 'Murderer's Lake'), a young girl walked around in the pouring rain carrying a huge tray of *kürtös kalács*, a typical Magyar taste treat consisting of a hollow cylinder of sweet milk bread rolled in sugar, cinnamon, coconut or walnuts (3RON) and cooked by rolling around metal poles on a kind of barbecue. You can watch them doing it just outside the entrance to Praid Salt Mine in Harghita County.

Romanians love pretzels (*covrigi*), which are like pretzels we all know but magnified ten times and more bready, sprinkled with chunks of rock salt.

Lunch (*dejunul* or *masa de prânz*) This is usually the main meal of the day for most Romanians. Romanian cuisine, when served in restaurants, is pretty heavy and filling, a legacy of peasants living off the land and doing hard physical labour

TRANSYLVANIAN RECIPES

LUMINIŢA'S SECRET ELDERBERRY JAM RECIPE Elderberries are an excellent natural remedy, easing the symptoms of rheumatism and arthritis. Luminiţa's recipe makes a delicious jam which goes well with yoghurt as it is slightly crunchy. It's also great on fresh, crusty homemade bread.

Ingredients: 1kg elderberries, 1kg sugar, 50ml fresh lemon juice.

Remove the stalks from fresh and ripe berries, put the berries in a sieve and wash them under a strong water flow. Put the washed berries in a three- to four-litre pan (preferably a cast-iron one), in alternative layers with the sugar and lemon juice. Leave it covered until the next day to allow the fruit to let their juice. Boil it over a high flame to let the syrup thicken quickly.

Remove the pan from the heat and cover it with a moist dishcloth. When the jam has cooled, put it in jars, fasten the lids and keep them in a cool and dry place.

Tips: Sugar is boiled together with lemon juice so that it is transformed into more simple sugars (glucose and fructose).

Moisten the inner part of the lid and edge of the jar with rum.

Traditional medicinal use: rheumatic pains and gout, cleaning the kidneys, easing neuralgia.

MĂMĂLIGĂ RECIPE

Ingredients: 0.5l of water, salt, 1kg of cornmeal (*polenta, puliszka*), sour cream, sheep's cheese.

Boil half a litre of salted water. Add 1kg of cornmeal, pouring it gradually into the boiling water, stirring all the time. As you stir vigorously, the mixture will get stiffer. Stop adding the cornmeal once you get a firm consistency that will still pour, and continue on the lowest heat possible for about ten minutes with a lid half on as it will bubble and spit. Pour into small bowls or one large flattish dish and leave to set. Turn out the bowls onto a plate as individual portions. Serve with sour cream and a soft, salty curd cheese.

all day. Restaurant meals can still be a hit-and-miss affair, although they are improving by the hour. There is still an emphasis on meat which can be fatty and disheartening especially if you've just spotted a mountainous pile of aubergines in the market and fancy trying the divine *salată de vinete* (baked aubergine pulp mixed with garlic and oil).

For vegetarians, it can be hard work persuading your host that you actually prefer vegetables. As Dan Marin pointed out: 'In homestays, the families provide pork-rich meals because they want to give guests the very best from their larders. We have to explain to them that people from different cultures (western Europe) may prefer vegetables.' The author Alexandru O Teodoreanu, who wrote under the pen name Păstorel, enthused about Romanian cuisine and how it could be adapted for Western palates. Vegetarians can ask for something *fără carne* meaning 'without meat' or for *mâncare de post*, traditionally the dishes served during periods of fasting, still strictly observed by many in the religious population, when meat is avoided.

SALATĂ DE VINETE (AUBERGINE CREME) *Delicious on homemade bread or toast*
Ingredients: Two big aubergines, one onion, four tablespoons of sunflower oil, a pinch of pepper, salt.

Roast the aubergines, peel while still hot and then leave on a slanted cutting board to drain. Chop into small pieces, place in a bowl and then mix using a wooden spoon, with a little oil at a time, until it whitens and becomes foamy. Add finely chopped onions to taste, also pepper and salt. Serve in a shallow bowl and garnish with tomato slices and rounds of green pepper.

ZACUSCĂ *Great for a quick snack when spread on bread*
In Slavic languages, *zakuska* means 'snack' from the word *kus* or 'taste'.
Ingredients: 750g carrots, 0.5kg onions, 12 long red peppers, 1kg tomatoes, 25dl sunflower oil.

Finely shred the carrots, onions and red peppers. Crush up the tomatoes. Put the onions, carrots and peppers in a pan to simmer slowly in the sunflower oil. Then add the crushed tomato and simmer until the oil rises to the top. Skim off the oil. Add salt and pepper to taste.

CIORBĂ RUSEASCĂ FĂRĂ CARNE (Russian soup without meat)
Ingredients: 3l water, one carrot, one parsley root, one big onion, one handful green beans, one small beetroot, a quarter of a small cabbage, two green peppers, one tablespoon butter, one tablespoon chopped parsley and dill, half a teaspoon flour, salt, 1 cup sour cream.

Finely chop the carrot, parsley root and onion. Add to the three litres of water and bring to the boil, adding the beans and the beetroot cut into julienne strips. Let it boil for half an hour, then add the cabbage and strips of peppers, salt and peeled, seeded and diced tomatoes. Make a roux with the flour and oil on a gentle heat, add some of the vegetable liquid then mix the roux back into the soup. When the vegetables are tender, add chopped parsley and dill. When serving, add a tablespoon of sour cream to each bowl.

For centuries, Transylvania has been a melting pot of cultures, sometimes simmering, sometimes boiling over and this is reflected best in the great love all the cultures share for food and drink. To get a real taste of Transylvanian cuisine, be it Romanian-, Hungarian-, Székely-, Saxon-, Jewish-, Roma- or Armenian-inspired, stay in a guesthouse and eat with the locals. You'll be amazed at all the wonderful dishes you never knew existed and certainly never found in restaurants: *salată de vinete, zacuscă* (see *Transylvanian recipes*, previous page), homemade yoghurts, jams, cordials, herbal tea concoctions and brandies.

A typical lunch might begin with hors d'oeuvres (*gustări*) with a range of salamis and cold cuts, gorgeous home-pickled *gogoșari* (peppers) and *castraveți* (baby cucumbers), excellent sources of vitamins for the winter. A personal favourite is *zacuscă*, a blend of tomatoes, peppers and carrots stewed in sunflower oil and served cold on thick chunks of bread or toast. Like most people in the region, Romanians and Hungarians really love their soups and have three different kinds: *supa, ciorbă* and *borș*. Here, *borș* is not beetroot broth but a soup made sour by the addition of *borș*, a fermented wheat bran, sauerkraut and lemon juice mixture added to the liquid. *Borș cu perișoare* is a sour meatball soup. *Ciorbă* soups are also sour but pleasantly so and *ciorbă țărănescă* is a wonderful vegetable soup which comes with or without meat but always with lashings of sour cream (*smântană*). *Ciorbă de burtă* (tripe soup) is very popular and not as scary as it sounds.

Mămăligă, made from stone-ground cornmeal (polenta) is the unofficial national dish and is as essential to Romanian cuisine as pasta is to Italian. For breakfast, it is eaten fried with a slice of bacon; at lunch, it is sprinkled with *caș* cheese and baked or served as an excellent accompaniment to *sarmale* (cabbage or sometimes vine leaves stuffed with minced pork) or *ghiveci* (a ratatouille-like stew of vegetables). At dinner, *mămăligă* can be served on its own or with sour cream, hard-boiled eggs, cheese or mushrooms sautéed in herbs and wine. For special celebrations, the super-rich *balmoș* is made by adding sour cream, milk, *caș* and *urdă* cheeses to the polenta mix while cooking.

A *tocană* (HU *tokány*) is a meaty stew seasoned with onions and spices, while those seeking the original version of *Székely káposzta* (Székely cabbage), a very popular dish in Budapest consisting of pork, sauerkraut and sour cream, could taste *Varză de la Cluj* (cabbage à la Cluj). There are also many versions of the Hungarian 'national dish' *gulyás/gulaș* (goulash) found all over the country. Those staying at Count Tibor Kálnoky's estate in Covasna County will have the opportunity to taste superb Hungarian home cooking, with excellent soups, meats, vegetables, fruit and puddings Magyar-style. At a Romanian guesthouse, we tried *mititei* (*mici*, or 'wee ones'), which are a cross between spicy rissoles and skinless sausages. Mutton and goat's meat is usually eaten in autumn when it is washed down with *muşt* (new wine). Throughout Romania, there are more than two dozen words for 'potato'

RESTAURANT PRICE CODES

Average price of main course

$$$$$	91RON+	€20+
$$$$	51–91RON	€11–20
$$$	30–51RON	€6.5–11
$$	15–30RON	€3–6.5
$	>15RON	>€3

according to region (*cartof, burgonya, krumpli, pityóka, picioici, barabule, krumpen, grumpen* and *pere de tere* were some I heard). A delicious speciality from the Sarmizegetusa region is *pup de crump*, a kind of plate-sized fried, grated potato and *brânză* patty served with a mug of thick drinking yoghurt.

Eating in small villages you can be almost certain that all the fruit and vegetables are organic, out of financial necessity rather than any environmental fashion. If you're desperate for vitamins, visit one of the open-air **fruit and vegetable markets**, found in every town. The range of seasonal vegetables is lip-smacking, with gorgeous tomatoes, peppers, aubergines, corn cobs and cabbages and even in winter, Transylvanian housewives are expert at pickling vegetables and making delicious jams and herbal teas from the rich pickings of the wild meadows and orchards. Just-picked apples, plums, walnuts and tomatoes are full of an intense flavour long forgotten in modern supermarkets in the West.

Transylvanian housewives use a lot of herbs in their kitchens: basil, caraway, dill, juniper, lovage, marjoram, rosemary, tarragon and thyme are all popular, used for flavouring dishes, vinegars and brandies.

These dishes have more in common with Balkan and Mediterranean cuisine than the northern central European stodge.

It's also common to find fish on the menu: *saramură de pește* is grilled carp seasoned with paprika and salt; *păstrăv afumat* is a delicacy, trout wrapped in fir tree branches and smoked; while it's even possible to try *sturion la grătar* (grilled sturgeon). Italian cuisine is incredibly popular all over the region and every town in Transylvania will have half a dozen pizzerias, often a good refuge for the vegetarian.

If you have any room for desserts (*deserturi*) or pastries (*patiserie*) after this feast, you'll find the locals have a reassuringly sweet tooth. Ice cream (*înghețată*) is available everywhere along with delicious fresh fruit in summer and autumn: apples, pears, peaches, plums, watermelons and grapes are juicy and sweet. *Plăcintă* (HU *palacsinta*) are pancakes although they are sometimes called *clătite*. *Galuști* (HU *gombóc*) are plum dumplings, everyone's favourite childhood memory dish while the fruit loaf *cozonac* is traditionally eaten at Christmas. In Zărnești, Luminița Marin makes a delicious *budincă*. She calls it a cake but it's almost more of a soufflé with apples, which is a treat for those on a gluten-free diet. Lunch is usually accompanied by a *spriț* (spritzer) of white wine and soda and the meal is rounded off with thick Turkish coffee.

Dinner (*cina*) This is usually eaten between 19.00 and 22.00 and can be anything from a snack to a plate of *mămăligă* and fried meat. Locals drink wine, beer, mineral water and fruit juices with the meal and often finish with a soothing herbal tea. *Să vă fie de bine!* (I hope you enjoyed it!)

Opening hours Bars and pubs open around lunchtime and stay open until at least 02.00 at weekends. Restaurants open for lunch at noon and take their last orders around 22.30. They don't usually close during the afternoon, but this can vary across Transylvania.

DRINKS Transylvanians have embraced the global cola culture wholeheartedly, but fortunately there are many local drinks waiting to be sampled, from fresh sparkling mineral waters to healthy herbal teas to Turkish coffee, beefy red wines, clean crisp lagers and the lethal fruit brandies that will simultaneously blow the top of your head off and put hairs on your chest. At the Marins' in Zărnești, I drank the most delicious homemade elderflower cordial (*socata*) mixed with spring water. Many different and highly drinkable brands of mineral water are available (0.80RON a litre) all over the country in large plastic bottles and some of the best names are Dorna, Borsec, Harghita, Izvorul Minunilor and Perla. Fruit juices are also well worth trying and one of the best places for this is the Fresh Healthy Drink Bar (see page 252) in Cluj-Napoca's Sora Shopping Centre where 300ml of orange, apple and carrot squeezed on the spot will immediately revitalise. Romania is not known for its beers, but there are in fact some excellent brews from Miercurea-Ciuc, Cluj-Napoca and Timişoara. Beer is usually served in a *halbă* (HU *korsó*) or half-litre mug (see page 165).

Although Romanian reds have had a good reputation in western European supermarkets since the early 1990s, excellent white wines also come from the Prahova Valley, just south of Braşov. Many restaurants only serve wine by the bottle, although this is changing. When serving the wine the waiter will occasionally ask if you would like a splash of sparkling mineral water to be added to your wine to make a *spriţ* (spritzer) which is very popular during the summer. Mulled wine (*vin fiert*) with sugar and cinnamon is great on cold winter days. For something stronger, try *ţuică fiarta* (hot plum brandy with sugar and peppercorns). Drinks are not usually served with ice unless specifically requested. Coffee (*cafea*) is drunk enthusiastically throughout the country and it is often the thick Turkish variety. In the past, tea (*ceai*) was not usually drunk in cafés, but now it's coming into fashion; check out the wonderful Demmer's Tea House in Braşov and Flowers Tea House in Cluj-Napoca (see page 252). Tea is offered in every guesthouse, bed and breakfast or private home. In Romania and Hungary, herbal teas are used widely. These are made from dried herbs and grasses and in Micloşoara I had a local herbal tea blend of linden blossom, St John's Wort (a natural anti-depressant) and peppermint, which simultaneously aids digestion and cheers you up. In Zărneşti, Luminiţa Marin has a huge basket of dried plants and flowers ready to boil up a hot infusion also comprising linden blossom, St John's Wort, blueberry, yarrow (good for stomach complaints), mint or comfrey (soothing sore throats and stomachs, and known as 'knitbone' for its healing properties).

Transylvanian wine

Music and wine are the most direct and sincere manifestation of the feelings.

George Enescu, Romania's greatest composer

In Transylvania, there are vineyards whose fame dates back to the Roman Empire. There are many viticultural areas, the most important of which is the Târnave region where we find Blaj, Jidvei, Mediaş, Târnăveni and Zagăr. There are also wine-growing regions in Alba, Sebeş, Apold and Lechinţa. Within the walls of the medieval citadel of Alba Iulia, a chance discovery in 1968 revealed a number of tunnels which were perfect as cellars for the production of champagne, the storage of wine for ageing and wine-tasting rooms. In this region are found famous landmarks such as Ighiu, Cricău, Şard, Galda, Bucerdea Vinoasă, Sântimbru and Ţelna. It is said that Ţelna wine, regarded as superior to Tokay, was drunk at the wedding of King Mătyăs Corvinus. The varieties that dominate in the Alba region are Fetească Albă, Fetească Regală, Italian Riesling, Pinot Gris, Traminer and Muscat Ottonel. Whether dry or semi-sweet, their personality is impeccable.

Before World War II, the quality of Romanian wine was very high, but then the communist authorities pushed wine growers into collective farms and downgraded the vines to a low level to produce cheap plonk for the undiscerning Russian market. Fortunately, from the late 1990s onwards, the market began to get back on its feet and Romania is now the fifth-largest wine producer in Europe. Romania's climate and soil are hospitable to the production of many different types of wines, from dry, sparkling whites to rich, aromatic, purplish reds. And, since traditional Romanian fermentation methods do not employ chemicals, drinking these richly tasting wines seldom results in a hangover. Although we know the beefy Romanian reds from supermarkets in western Europe, around 75% of Romanian wine is white.

Jidvei (11.5%), a dry Riesling, has an unusual aftertaste, which to me was a bit like chlorinated swimming-pool water. However, I tried it only once and am prepared to be contradicted, especially if the argument requires another tasting session.

Wines from the Prahova Valley, just south of Transylvania, *en route* to Bucharest, are now highly valued. A good name to seek out is Halewood (*www.halewood. com.ro*). Halewood International, founded in 1978 by John Halewood, has been importing wines from Romania to the UK since 1987. Ten years later, the company founded its first Romanian subsidiary and today, after investing more than US$10 million, Halewood owns three subsidiaries in Romania with more than 400ha of vineyards in three areas: Dealu Mare, Podisul Transilvaniei and Murfatlar. Their Prahova Valley Pinot Noir and Cabernet Sauvignon blend (13%) is a beefy red with spicy notes while the Fetească Neagră (13%) private reserve from Dealurile Munteniei is full of rich, blackcurrant flavours. The Fetească Neagră variety dates from before the Phylloxera blight of the 1880s when most vines in the region were damaged for ever. The grape is called Fekete Leănyka (Black Maiden) in Hungarian and the variety is native to Transylvania.

Generally, a bottle of wine in a restaurant should not cost more than €4. Traditionally women drink semi-sweet or sweet wines. It is considered very masculine to drink dry white wine, though that should not prevent female visitors from sampling all the best vintages on offer. *Vin negru* or *vin roşu* is red wine, *vin alb* is white and *rozé* is rosé, while *sec* is dry, *demi-sec* is medium dry (pretty sweet actually), *dulce* is sweet and *spumos* is sparkling.

Ţuică and palincă

A traditional drink always presented to house guests on arrival or served with appetisers is *ţuică* (pronounced 'tsui-kuh'), a potent 30%-proof brandy usually made from plums but also from pears, apricots, bilberries, sour cherries and sometimes even caraway seeds. It varies in strength, dryness and bouquet according to the production area. *Palincă* (from the Hungarian *pálinka*) is also made from fruit, often plums, but distilled twice to produce a much stronger spirit, often hovering above 40% proof. Ceauşescu tried to ban *ţuică* but now every family in the countryside brews up its own version of the brain-tingling spirit. Memories of prohibition mean that nationalities are fiercely proud of their own brews. The Hungarians' claim to *palincă* prompted many jokes. In one, two villagers are talking: 'Have you heard?' says one. 'The Hungarians want our Transylvania again.' The other replies, 'Oh, let them have it, but don't include the plum trees. See if they still want it then.' Travelling around Transylvania, you will see young men sitting on the verge surrounded by a selection of copper distilling apparatus (HU *pálinkafőző*), bright copper tubes with a bulbous bit at the end for brewing up *palincă*. Author Alan Ogden coined the term 'getting palinkered' to refer to the stupefied sense of euphoria after a few shots of the stuff. Try it and feel the effects for yourself – you will most likely find it hard to avoid. There is a great shop in Sighişoara (see page 186) that sells *ţuică* and *palincă* in a cellar. Teo Coroian runs Teo's Distillery (www.delateo.ro). Teo is an IT engineer who works at night at a local cheese factory. He married into a family that had a long tradition of distilling plums, apples and pears and ageing them into fine brandies and fruit wines. Teo

2

credits his wife's father with teaching him the secrets passed down through three generations. According to Teo, *ţuică* is only made from plums and is 50% proof, but when I took a bottle of Teo's *ţuică* to friends in Bucharest, they insisted it was *palincă*. You can't win – everybody has a different version.

PUBLIC HOLIDAYS AND FEAST DAYS

NATIONAL AND PUBLIC HOLIDAYS Businesses and shops close for national holidays:

1 and 2 January	New Year's Day
April/May	Orthodox Easter, usually celebrated later than in western Europe. Easter Sunday dates: 5 May 2013, 20 April 2014, 12 April 2015.
1 May	Labour Day
1 December	Unification Day celebrating the union of Transylvania, Wallachia and Moldavia in 1918
24 December	Christmas Eve
25 December	Christmas Day

FESTIVALS AND EVENTS Transylvania is packed with festivals and events all year round. Many of them are traditional affairs, marking a saint's feast day and quite a number are based on folk traditions such as the welcoming of the sheep back from the mountain pasture in autumn or fairs held to find brides for lonely shepherds. There is also a good selection of contemporary cultural festivals such as the Transylvanian International Film Festival, held in Cluj-Napoca, and the Sibiu Jazz Festival. Most towns have their own folk festivals, with dancing, local costumes and food. These tend to be in the summer months leading up to the harvest festivals in September. The following is a selection of cultural events which are held annually in Transylvania.

January (Ianuarie)
Throughout Transylvania, especially around Făgăraş On 1 January, groups of young men wander through the villages wearing sheepskins, goatskins and sometimes bearskins, singing, dancing and banging drums, frightening away the winter. On New Year's Day morning, only men must enter the house, not women, because women entering is said to bring bad luck. People should drink red wine on New Year's Day to refresh the blood. Only pork meat should be eaten and never poultry. This is because when the pig snuffles in the earth it pushes forward, bringing financial benefits whereas the chicken scatters and scratches the earth backwards. On the morning of New Year's Day, children go around the village wishing everybody a Happy New Year with a *sorcova*, a green branch of an apple or pear tree decorated with coloured paper ribbons and flowers.

St John's Day (7 January) is when churches all over the country are packed with the faithful waiting to receive blessed water from priests.

In folk dialects, January is called *gerar* from the Romanian *ger* or 'frost'.

It is said that those who don't sneeze on this day will be alive the following year.

February (Februarie)
Apaţa, Prejmer and Bârsa Land The Farsâng takes place every February, before Lent. This Hungarian version of Mardi Gras is 200 years old, borrowed

by the Hungarians from neighbouring Saxons. During the celebration, young men who are eligible for military service wear masks to resemble bears, wolves, Gypsies, chimney sweeps, bridegrooms, brides, doctors, fortune tellers or fantastic characters and ride through town on horseback. The horses are decorated with ribbons, sticks and paper flowers, and the parade of men and horses goes through the village, knocking on gates and entering all houses to chase away evil spirits. A gathering is held in the village square and everyone eats pancakes.

Cluj-Napoca The Mátyás Festival of Renaissance and Baroque music is organised by the Hungarian Student Union (✆ *+40 264 595 700*).

Sighişoara The Sighişoara Blues Festival (*www.blues-festival.ro*) is a three-day music festival to shake off those winter blues.

Throughout Transylvania The 1 February is St Trif's Day (the madman), and represents the first great celebration of the grape-growing, fruit-growing and agricultural calendar. The old name for February is *făur*. A *făurar* is an old word for 'ironsmith'. The name *făur* implies not only the ironsmith who makes the tools used for the spring tilling of the fields, but also the frost which covers the ground.

March (Martie)
Rimitea In this village near Alba Iulia, the Immormantarea Farsangulu (Burial Carnival) is a pre-Lent event.

Şinca Nouă This tiny village in Braşov County hosts a spectacular pre-Lent festival.

Throughout Transylvania Mărţişor falls on 1 March, when all females are presented with a *mărţişor*; a brooch tied with red-and-white thread to symbolise the arrival of spring. On 8 March men give flowers to women all over the country for International Women's Day.

April (Aprilie)
Apaţa Near Micloşoara (Kálnoky) but in Braşov County, Apaţa hosts a Rooster Shoot when villagers denounce a fake rooster, then shoot it on the third Sunday in April.

Miercurea-Ciuc The Székely Pilgrimage is the largest traditional and religious festival of Székely people, held on Whit Sunday.

Sfântu Gheorghe A three-day St George's Day Festival is held on the last Sunday in April.

Throughout Transylvania April was the second month of the Roman calendar, which began on 1 March. In the Julian and Gregorian calendars it is the fourth month. The old name of April, *prier*, refers to meteorological omens. When the April weather was too cold for seeding, the month was called *traista-n băţ* (bag on a stick), a term associated with poverty. According to tradition, if the weather is beautiful in April, it will be cold and frosty in May, and vice versa.

St George's Eve (22 April) is the day when witches try to steal the milk and crops. It is also Armindeni, the 'bitter's day' or the 'drinker's day' named after the Prophet

Jeremiah and celebrating the beginning of summer. Armindeni is celebrated in the rest of Romania on 1 May.

On the weekend nearest to 23 April, many villages and towns hold St George's Day (*Sângiorz*) festivities to celebrate the first day of spring. On this day traditionally, the shepherds were chosen to look after the flock until St Dumitru's Day (26 October). On St George's Day, villagers used to rise before dawn and bathe in a river to make them healthy and strong. Girls would plant basil and keep the seeds in their mouths first so that the plants would be healthy and have a wonderful aroma. If St George's Day is foggy, the coming year will be financially rewarding.

In *Dracula*, St George's Day is given as 5 May, according to the old calendar, and Jonathan Harker is advised in Bistriţa not to travel when the innkeeper's wife says: 'It is the eve of St George's Day. Do you not know that to-night, when the clock strikes midnight, all the evil things in the world will have full sway?'

May (Mai)

Braşov The Days of Braşov and Junii Pageant is Braşov's biggest festival and begins in the first week after Orthodox Easter, with the parade moving through the centre of Braşov and continuing to the city's Schei district (late April/early May).

Carpathian Mountains The Stâna (Measurement of the Milk) Festival is held in villages all over the Carpathians after Easter.

Cluj-Napoca Wine festivals are held every weekend in May.

Gurghiu Mureş County holds many Girl Fairs (Tărgul Fetelor), of which Gurghiu is the best known.

Sibiu The Sibiu Jazz Festival (*http://sibiujazz.ro*) is a week-long jazz music festival in the middle of May, which has taken place since 1970.

Mayfeşt, Sibiu's Saxon Festival, takes place on 1 May.

Throughout Transylvania Orthodox Easter (Paşte) occurs usually between mid April and early May according to the Gregorian calendar.

1 May is a national holiday for Labour Day. May is known as *florar* or 'flower'.

June (Iunie)

Cluj-Napoca The Transylvania International Film Festival (*www.tiff.ro*) is held annually.

Fundata A fair of traditional folklore, originally held for people to get together and for shepherds to find wives.

Gherla Armenian Catholic Pilgrimage on St Gregory the Illuminator's name day.

Mălâncrav On the first Sunday after the Feast Day of Sts Peter and Paul (29 June), Kronenfest is a resurrected Saxon festival when the youngest bachelor climbs a 9m pole to beat an oak-leaf crown of leaves and flowers, releasing sweets for children. He then points his stick at the unmarried girls and dances with all of them.

Sibiu The International Theatre Festival (*www.sibfest.ro*) is held in the first week of June.

Şumuleu Ciuc (Csíksomlyó) Pentecostal Festival (Csíksomlyói búcsú), the largest Roman Catholic festival in central eastern Europe, is held at Whitsun, 50 days after Easter Sunday.

Târgu Mureş Carnival in Székely Land (last weekend in June) with folk dancing, music, beer and sausages.

Throughout Transylvania This month's name comes from the goddess Iuno, the protector of married women. In folk tradition, June is called *cireşar* meaning 'the month of the cherries' because fruits ripen at this time.

July (Iulie)

Avram Iancu (Alba County) Girl Fair, a traditional wife-finding festival at Mount Găiana in the Apuseni Mountains, is held on a Sunday before 20 July. The Fair on Mount Găiana (Târgul de fete de Mt Găiana) was a place where families who had marriageable girls and boys used to meet in order to arrange the weddings. Legend has it that fairies all over the world once decided to have a castle built in the Apuseni Mountains, so they brought along a magic hen that laid golden eggs. Once a year, the fairies would give those eggs to couples who really loved each other. On display are traditional costumes, traditional dances and songs from four districts: Hunedoara and the Moţ Lands as well as neighbouring Bihor and Arad counties. Details are available from the Alba Information Centre (☎+40 258 813 736).

Brâncoveneşti Near Reghin, Mureş County, Brâncoveneşti holds a Cherry Festival on the first Sunday in July.

Miercurea-Ciuc The Old Music Festival has been held since 1990, and takes place in the first week in July.

Ocna de Suş Near Praid, Harghita County. The third week in July sees a Székely Land dance camp (Székelyföld tánctábor).

Săcele Santilia is an age-old feast for shepherds celebrating the sun and fire god. It takes place in the town of Săcele, near Braşov, on 23–24 July, the first weekend after St Elie's Day. This pastoral day was closely connected to the life and activities of the shepherds of Săcele who used to cross huge swathes of land with their flocks.

Sighişoara Transylvania's most popular medieval arts festival is held in late July. Tourist Information Centre (☎+40 265 770 415).

Şumuleu Ciuc (Csíksomlyó) The Festival of One Thousand Székely Maidens (Ezer Székely Leány Találkozó) is held on the first Saturday in July. A festival of dance, music and folk costumes dating back to the 1920s. Tourist Information Centre (☎+40 266 317 007).

Târgu Mureş The Félsziget Festival (Festivalul Peninsula) is a DJ and rock festival held in late July. It's a mini-version of the Sziget (Island) Festival, a massive Woodstock-esque summer festival held on Budapest's Óbuda Island. Tourist Information Centre (☎+40 365 404 934).

Throughout Transylvania On 1 July Cosmandinul is held for the poor saint doctors Cosma and Damian who protect the people from illness. It is also Ana Foca Day, combining the names of two Christian saints, Ana and Foca, celebrated to protect the crops against the sun's crop-destroying heat and also against thunder and lightning. 8 July is St Pricopie's Day, the celebration of the wolf. If villagers ignore this day, St Pricopie will send thunder and lightning to destroy the crops. The Moți people from the Apuseni Mountains believe that those who don't respect St Pricopie's Day will be taken away by two powerful winds: Harcodan and Dornados.

August (August)

Fundata The Fundata Mountain Festival (Nedeia Muntelui) is held on the last Sunday in August, when livestock and crafts are exchanged and in the old days, marriages were arranged.

Bistrița The International Folk, Dance and Traditions Festival.

Făgăraș A folk arts and crafts fair is held 17–20 August, in downtown Făgăraș City at the Făgăraș citadel featuring folklore and crafts from the area. Craftsmen from all over the country show a large range of products including pottery and icons, wooden tables and traditional costumes.

Odorheiu Secuiesc/Székelyudvarhely Artisan Festival (Míves Emberek Sokadalma) with cultural events in an open-air fair. Tourist Information Centre (☏ +40 266 217 427).

MILK, MAIDENS AND HARVESTS

THE STÂNA (The Measurement of the Milk) This festival is held after Easter, usually in May. Shepherds strain curds, which are hung up to dry to make a ceremonial cheese known as *caș*. The curds are usually obtained from the most successful shepherd in the village. This title is given after each shepherd's flock has been milked and the yield quite literally measured. The festival marks the time of the year when the shepherds would leave for the mountains with their flock, though it has mostly become a thing of the past.

TÂRGUL FETELOR (The Girl Fair) Usually taking place around May Day, these fairs are held all over Mureș, Cluj and Alba counties. Girls of marriageable age were brought to the fair with part or all of their dowries (*zestre*) as a lure for similarly aged boys. Today the fair is merely a pageant and involves much younger girls and boys. The girl fair in the Apuseni Mountains takes place in July, while the Juni Festival in Brașov is a colourful procession of the town's bachelors in another rite of passage event. The costumes – hats, jackets, breeches and boots – are coloured and patterned according to which group the bachelor belongs.

ZILELE ORASULUI (Days of the Town/Village) These events are held all over Romania in autumn when towns and villages showcase the best they have on offer: enormous harvested vegetables, cakes and other snacks, handicrafts, combat skills or complicated local dances performed in traditional folk costumes. According to superstition, putting on a poor show at Zilele Orasului will mean a bad harvest the following year.

Prislop Pass, Bistriţa Hora de Prislop, is a wild dance festival held mid August when people from Transylvania, Maramureş and Moldavia come together for an almighty knees-up.

Roşia Montana The Hayfest (Fânfest) hosts more than 40 artists representing the best bluegrass music from around the globe. Fânfest is the indoor music festival of the year and also a mass protest meeting against the international mining development projects (see page 239). For more details see www.fanfest.ro.

Sighişoara Pro Etnika is the largest cultural gathering of ethnic minorities in Romania. For information on IBZ (\ +40 265 778 489).

Sibiu The Astra Museum holds the Festivalui National al Traditiilor Populare din Romania, an arts and crafts festival held over the first week of August.

The Medieval Festival happens during the last weekend of August during which time the knights of Transylvania meet for tournaments, princesses and witches strive to charm them, and actors, tumblers, musicians and dancers try to enchant the audience, each showing his/her own mastery. The city of Sibiu plays its medieval role very well, and this is why it was chosen as the European Capital of Culture for 2007.

Zărneşti The Edelweiss Festival (Floare de colţ) is held in the city of Zărneşti on 20 August, the first Sunday after St Mary's Day. The purpose of the festival is to promote the young artists in Zărneşti who keep musical traditions alive by showing traditional costumes from the area. The festival starts with a young horseriding parade in traditional costume.

Throughout Transylvania August is connected to *gusta*, 'taste', as fruit becomes ready for picking.

September (Septembrie)

Biertan Saxon Reunion is the largest gathering of Transylvanian Saxons with folk costumes and folk-dancing competitions. Contact the Democratic Forum of Germans from Sighişoara (\ +40 265 772 234).

Bran Sâmbra Oilor is the three-day welcome-home party for the sheep coming down from the mountains for winter, held late September/early October. The annual festival has more than 20 types of cheese, plum brandy, fruit and vegetable growers, and local barbecued meats. There is live folk music throughout the day and local artisans showing traditional crafts at the fair.

Braşov The International Arts Festival, and the International Chamber Music Festival, the latter organised by the Braşov Philharmonic Orchestra.

Praid The Stuffed Cabbage Festival is held annually in Praid, Harghita County, and is a unique event connected to the region. The idea of organising a festival of cabbages was proposed by Alexandru Mironov, formerly youth and sports minister. He suggested founding a gastronomic event, where local, regional and foreign participants compete in traditional cooking. The programme includes performances of folk dance, folk musicians and a classical music concert, held by the chapel of the famous salt mine in Praid.

Poiana Marului The Autumn Fair is held on 15 September, a traditional festival celebrating the harvest. Situated 14km from the town of Zărneşti, on the road to Sâmbata de Sus, the village of Poiana Marului is a good place to learn about the traditions of a typical southeastern Transylvanian village. Visitors taste traditional dishes and participate in the rural activities: milking the cows, scything, sowing, ploughing and harvesting – using traditional tools.

Rupea (Braşov County) The Fortress Festival is held from 24 September to 1 October on the plateau near Rupea Fortress. The annual Fortress Festival started in 1968 and features traditional customs from various regions of the country including parades in costumes and songs. The locals hang traditional hand-embroidered cloths in their windows.

After the parade, the representatives of the ancient fortress villages are received in the centre of the village by the mayor, and each of them presents the marks of the fortress they represent, for example a key, handmade tablecloths, etc. The festival ends with a march of all fortress representatives by torchlight, followed by a firework display.

Sibiu The Sibiu Philharmonic Orchestra hold an Opera Festival at the end of September.

The ASTRA Museum Annual Pottery Fair (Târgul Olarilor) is held from 2–3 September. The fair is one of the most prestigious events of the town, and was created to preserve and perpetuate the culture and value of traditional ceramics from pottery schools all over Romania.

Turda Turdafest is a fun agricultural fair with wine, onions, farm animals and lots of pastoral produce.

Throughout Transylvania September is referred to as *răpciune*, meaning 'the beginning of the cold period', and also *viniceriu*, because September is the month of grapes. Simeon of the Pillar's Day is 1 September. In folk beliefs, Simeon holds up the sky by sitting on a tall pillar. As the patron saint of winds he can cause earthquakes which garners the saint much respect. The weather on this day predicts the same for the rest of the autumn.

October (Octombrie)
Negreni (Cluj County) The annual open-air market/fair in the village of Negreni (Fekete tó/Black Lake) is a riot of colour, smells and sounds, held over the second weekend in October, and is one of the last great peasant fairs in eastern Europe. Book your accommodation months in advance, or stay in Cluj and approach from there.

Prejmer Harvest Day, held 6–7 October. Erntedankfest is a religious holiday for the Saxon population. The fortified church is decorated with fruit, food and ears of wheat. A loaf the size of a car tyre is placed on the altar and grapes, pumpkins and branches of apple trees adorn the church's interior.

After the religious ceremony, the villagers, dressed in their traditional costumes, walk from house to house and distribute fruit.

Sibiu The International Astra Film Festival (*www.astrafilm.ro*), held in September, hosts documentary film makers.

Throughout Transylvania October is known as *brumărel* in the folk tradition, as the hoarfrost (*brumă*) begins at this time. If the leaves turn yellow and fall early, the following year will be wealthy. Villagers respect St Luca's Day on 18 October as the Lucin protects the wolf packs born at this time of the year.

November (Noiembrie)
Alba Iulia Alba Iulia Folk Festival (Ziua de Maine).

Brașov Etnovember is a cluster of cultural events, a feast of shared joy and friendship, music, arts and crafts, taking place in Brașov annually on the third weekend of November. Also referred to as Mediateca Feast, it is known as a medieval festival but is in fact much more with dancing, concerts, craft markets and colourful processions. Contact Dr Marina Cionca (Transilvania University of Brașov), co-ordinator of the Mediateca Norbert Detaeye (m *+40 740 230 238 (English, French, German);* e *marina.cionca@rdslink.ro*), Antonia Czika at Hungarian weekly *Brassói Lapok* (m *+40 740 994 580 (English, Italian, Hungarian);* e *toni@ brassoilapok.ro*).

The Jazz and Blues Festival is also an international festival, hosted by 'Sica Alexandrescu' Theatre.

The Contemporary Drama Festival is held annually. It is host to Romania's most important theatre companies, together with those from France, Italy, the US, Belgium, Sweden, Brazil and many others.

Throughout Transylvania November is known as *brumar* from *brumă*, meaning 'hoarfrost'. St Andrew's Eve (29 November) is one of the most important nights in the folk calendar, known as Vampires' Night. A party called 'Guarding the Garlic' is held and young people gather in a house whose windows and doors have been rubbed with garlic. Every girl brings three cloves of garlic which are put in a vase that will be guarded by candlelight by an old woman. The young folk party until morning when the vase is taken out into the yard and they dance around it. The cloves are then given to all the partyers and then placed in front of icons as a protection against illness or evil spells. To protect against vampires on this day, people rub doors and window frames with garlic and turn pottery bowls to face the ground. The 30 November celebrates the feast of St Andrew, patron saint of wolves and protector against wolf attacks. On this day, people bless the salt and bury it under the stable door. It is dug up on St George's Day and given to the cattle.

December (Decembrie)
Alba Iulia Romania's National Day falls on 1 December and celebrates the union of Transylvania, Wallachia and Moldova in 1918. There is a religious service in Alba Iulia to acknowledge the place where the unification treaty was signed. In Bucharest, there is usually a military parade.

Throughout Transylvania December is known as *undrea*, from *Îndrea*, St Andrew's Day on 30 November, which ushers in the month. Naming a month after a feast day of the previous month recalls the ancient cycle of celebrations from the end of the autumn and the beginning of the winter, when the Dacian New Year was probably celebrated. St Nicholas's Day is celebrated on 6 December. Peasants believed that when the saint shakes his beard it starts snowing on this day. 24 December sees carol singers tramping around the chilly streets and 25 December, Christmas Day, is celebrated with pork (the pig is usually killed a week earlier). 31

2

December, New Year's Eve, is a rousing affair with open-air concerts in every town, regardless of the weather.

TRANSYLVANIAN EASTER

Romania celebrates religious events according to the Julian calendar but Easter is an exception and follows the Gregorian calendar, celebrating Easter about two weeks after western Europe. Easter is called **Paşte**. Before Easter, there are seven weeks of Lent when Orthodox Christians are not allowed to eat meat, cheese, milk or eggs and hold merry events such as weddings or baptism feasts. In the past, people would take special food and cakes to church on the Saturday before the Easter celebration for their deceased loved ones. In the countryside, housewives clean everything in the house and garden, wash the curtains and carpets, and buy food for the special dishes that they will cook two or three days before the holy night of Resurrection.

Palm Sunday is called **Florii** (Flowers Day). It is a very special day recalling how Jesus was welcomed on his arrival in Jerusalem. Villagers take fresh willow branches to church for a blessing then take them home and place them in front of the Orthodox icons, and eggs are painted, often in exquisite detail. Easter eggs have an important role in Transylvanian traditions. The painted eggs and the techniques used to paint them are mentioned by an Italian called Del Chiaro who described the life of the princely court in Bucharest during the reign of Constantin Brancoveanu (1689–1714).

On the last Thursday before Easter, village women would bake *pasca* and *cozonac*: traditional Romanian fruit cakes symbolising the face and body of Christ.

Orthodox Easter begins with Saturday's Holy Night and lasts for the next three days. It is said that the gates of heaven will open exactly on the night of the Resurrection and they will remain open for the next seven days. On this night, the whole family goes to church, the head of the family carrying a basket full of coloured eggs, *pasca*, *cozonac*, fresh cheese, dry basil, incense, a bottle of wine and candles.

After the religious ceremony, the priest comes out of the church and blesses the community and their baskets saying 'Christ has risen', and everyone responds in unison 'He has truly risen'. Families return home and enjoy a feast of roast lamb in the early hours of Sunday morning. Many families begin Easter Sunday morning by washing their face and hands with fresh water to which they have added a red-coloured egg and a silver coin, to bring wealth and good fortune. They breakfast on *cozonac*, *pasca* and dyed hard-boiled eggs. The eggs must be clinked top to top on the first day, top to bottom on the second and bottom to bottom on the third day. This custom guarantees that family members will meet again in the afterlife.

TRANSYLVANIAN CHRISTMAS TRADITIONS

In Romania, Christmas is called **Crăciun** and Father Christmas is known as **Moş Crăciun**. The colours of Christmas are black, red and white: black for the winter night, red for the costumes of the children when they go carol singing, and white for the snow that blankets the country. In Transylvania, families make stuffed cabbage which they eat on Christmas Eve and also the next day as it tastes even better when reheated. At 22.00 on Christmas Eve, the tree is decorated with walnuts, chestnuts, sweets and chocolates wrapped in coloured paper. Children then go from door to door in the village carol singing. They are led by one child carrying a *steaua*, or star, made of silver paper attached to a broomstick. They are sometimes accompanied by a fellow in an animal mask performing the wild *capră* (goat) dance in a kind of fertility rite. In return for their carols, the children receive *covrigi* (large pretzels), doughnuts, sweets, apples or money. After Midnight Mass, the children polish their best pair of boots and place them by the front door for Father Christmas to find and leave presents. In rural homes a pig is slaughtered on St Ignat's Day (20 December) and the meat is made into sausages, charcuterie and delicious smoked ham for the Christmas table. A traditional meal consists of many courses, starting with pig's head in aspic, sausages with pickles, a large variety of pork products, *ciorbă* (sour broth), *sarmale* (cabbage leaves stuffed with pork) and crowned by a gigantic roast pork. As at Easter, the rich fruit loaf *cozonac* is eaten as a traditional dessert, and cheesecake is also very popular with each region making its own version. This enormous repast is washed down with *ţuică* (brandy, usually made from plums), and wine, often red at this time of year.

NEW YEAR A *sorcova* is a small bouquet of branches entwined with coloured artificial flowers. Children go around the village on New Year's Day and tap their elders gently with the stick while wishing them a Happy New Year and a long life. According to tradition, they must tap 40 times as *sorcova* comes from the Slav word for 40 (*sorok*). The *sorcova* bouquet is made up of several fruit tree branches – cherry, apple, pear or plum – and the twigs are put into water on St Andrew's Day (30 November) in order to bud and blossom by the New Year. While tapping their elders, the children recite a verse which has roughly 40 words. In Hunedoara, children follow a similar custom on Christmas Eve when they go from house to house with a *pizără*, a handkerchief tied to a stick, and recite a verse.

SHOPPING

Opening hours in Transylvania are idiosyncratic, to say the least. The tradition is for shops to be open 09.00–18.00 on weekdays and 09.00–14.00 on Saturdays but there are plenty of exceptions to the rule. In large city centres and shopping malls, many are open 08.00–20.00 Monday–Saturday (sometimes until 22.00) while supermarkets are usually open 09.00–21.00. Most grocery shops and markets open from dawn until 20.00 or later. Some kiosks selling cigarettes, alcohol, soft drinks and newspapers stay open until 23.00.

Transylvanian shopkeepers are scrupulously honest and when they can't give you back even the smallest amount in change – 10 or 20 bani – they insist on paying in kind with a few sweeties or a paper tube of instant Nescafé. The first time it happened to me, in a tiny village shop in Mureş County on the deserted road to Lapuşna, I thought the lady was going to make me a cup of coffee as she suddenly asked in Hungarian, when handing over my purchases, whether I'd like a coffee!

For food and drink purchases, every village has a **Magazin Mixt**, a kind of general store for staples: milk, cheese, bread, sausage, beer, soft drinks, cigarettes and loo roll, sold in individual rolls for 30 bani each. **Honey** is sold by the side of the road, from the side of lorries which have multi-coloured hives built into the side. This is so the hives are mobile and can follow the best blossoms around the countryside, choosing from the acacia trees, orchards and meadows. A popular variety is called *poliflora*, from many different flowers. When the harvest is good and there's a glut of kitchen garden produce, grannies stand by the side of the road and offer garlic, onions and dried peppers strung up on wooden frames, heavenly tomatoes, pumpkins, beans, apples, walnuts, plums and high purple mountains of aubergines and knobbly green hummocks of watermelons. Every town has a large **central market**, often open air, where you can stock up on fruit and veg, bread and picnicking/snacking items.

You may also see large horse markets in fields by the side of a main road on the outskirts of towns such as Sighişoara, Târgu Mureş, Sibiu and Cluj-Napoca.

These are very exciting to visit although you will stick out like a sore thumb. There are cattle, sheep, chicken and other livestock markets and also the **annual Negreni fair** held in the second week of October to the west of Cluj-Napoca (see page 254).

You will probably want to take some *ţuică* or *palincă* home with which to impress your wealthy great uncle (or finish him off). The best shop for this is Teo's Distillery in Sighişoara (see page 186, Pensiunea Pivnita lui Teo Cetatea), where you can join in *ţuică* tastings and get professional advice on what to buy. If you want to try making it yourself, it's possible to buy copper distilling tubes from vendors by the side of the road, but I can't predict what problems might occur at the airport customs. It's also possible to buy delicious organic apple juice in Mălâncrav, on sale at the Biertan craft shop, Artefact Biertan (see page 207).

For **books** and **maps**, the university towns of Braşov, Cluj-Napoca and Sibiu will not disappoint. Cluj-Napoca has a particularly good university bookshop on the corner of Piaţa Unirii and a cluster of newspaper kiosks all around the same square, selling hiking maps, newspapers and magazines. Braşov has a lot of bookshops and also a few book, antique and junk shops on Strada Coresi and Strada Republicii. Some of the best things to take home are homemade **folk arts and crafts**. These can be bought *in situ* from the craftsman or from a shop specialising in local crafts. In Sibiu, the Galerile de Artă Populară on Piaţa Mică (see page 199) has a vast selection of clothes, ceramic pots, plates, jugs and bowls, clothes, ash trays and carved wooden items.

In Târgu Mureş and Cluj-Napoca, I saw very young boys and old ladies wandering along the pavement offering hand-carved wooden **spoons**. These are useful items to take home and remind oneself of the Transylvanian countryside while stirring the *mămăligă*.

Nearby in Biertan, Monica Cosma's folk gift shop (Artefact Biertan, see page 207) presents local artists and craftsmen and women with all kinds of **souvenirs**: delicately carved cow- and deer-bone jewellery, paintings and sketches of the countryside and Saxon fortress churches, wooden boxes, rugs and painted eggs.

In Rimetea, a little shop near the central square has a fine collection of handmade **ceramic** and **carved wooden items** while the Mecca for fans of ceramics has got to be Corund, in Harghita County, where the entire village consists of workshops and outlets selling ceramic pots, plates and vases.

You can't really return home from Transylvania without some **Dracula tat** for the horror-movie fans or Goth teenagers in the family. Stalls in the village beneath Bran Castle buckle under the weight of vampire-themed T-shirts, mugs, jigsaws and other ghoulish gifts. Sighişoara also has more than its fair share of Dracula merchandise although there are other more interesting and authentic souvenirs to be found lurking among Vlad's belongings. Look for the ADEPT shop and information centre at Saschiz near Sighişoara and you can purchase some excellent **homemade jam**.

If you hire a car and drive around Transylvania, you cannot fail to notice the constant series of **markets** that seem to spring up at the roadside overnight with stalls selling baskets, mugs, towels decorated with football teams' crests or large-breasted ladies in lurid colours and a huge number of overweight garden gnomes. I have never actually spotted one of these gnomes in a garden but they must be very popular as these old chaps are everywhere. There are other imaginative garden ornaments on offer at stalls near Sinaia and Cluj-Napoca, and I even saw life-sized statues of Dobermans, possibly for use as static guard dogs? I think I'd rather have a giant gnome.

MUSIC AND DANCE Transylvania has a rich musical heritage and at the beginning of the 20th century, composers Bartók and Kodály travelled around the countryside, documenting and recording folk music melodies. **Roma musicians** are famous the world over, with ensembles such as the Nadara Orchestra and the Hungarian group Muszikás, and world-class singers such as Márta Sebestyén, introducing Transylvanian music to a wider audience. The outstanding Taraf de Haïdouks from the south of Romania have taken the world music scene by storm. Opera houses and concert halls in cities such as Cluj-Napoca, Braşov, Sibiu and Târgu Mureş hold regular concerts. Churches are also great places to hear music, in particular Braşov's Black Church, where regular concerts are packed out. Cluj-Napoca has several **opera houses** where you can catch high-quality performances of *Madame Butterfly* or *The Nutcracker Suite*.

The main Transylvanian cities have year-round packed cultural programmes with many performances taking place in churches, cultural houses or beautiful turn-of-the-last-century theatres. **Piano recitals** or **chamber music** concerts often take place in historic mansions and the setting makes the effect even more atmospheric and evocative.

At one of the many cultural houses you can also take part in a '**dance house**' (HU *táncház*), a combination of folk dance lesson and performance.

Hungarian folk music and dancing has flourished since 1989 as the ethnic minority finds artistic expression for issues of identity. A good starting point for visitors interested in learning more or even giving it a whirl, is the Sfântu Gheorghe-based **Háromszék Dance Ensemble** (*www.hte.ro*) whose website in Hungarian, Romanian and English, gives helpful pointers. Other famous groups are the **Zurboló Dance Ensemble** (*www.zurbolo.ro*) from Cluj-Napoca and the **Harghita National Székely Folk Ensemble** (*www.harghitatanc.ro*), based in Miercurea-Ciuc. Unfortunately, their website is in Hungarian only and so inaccessible to a wider audience. **Dance classes**, often held in July and August all over Transylvania (Aiud, Ceuaş, Comandău, Gyimeş, Praid, Răscruci, Sâmbriaş, Sâncraiu, Sic and Voivodeni are some venues) are more often than not in Hungarian and so heavy going for those without language skills or a helpful interpreter. However, if you would like to give it a go, see the relevant chapters for more details. The website www.tanchaz.hu has information (in English too) on summer dance camps.

CINEMA Given Romanian **cinema**'s recent successes on the international screen, particularly at Cannes, it is a surprising fact that Romania has fewer cinema-goers and fewer cinemas per head than any other European country. Financial backing is also desperately needed for the industry, which has lower public investment than its neighbours. Even the Transylvanian Film Festival (*www.tiff.ro*), running annually since 2002 in Cluj-Napoca, has had to rely solely on private sponsors. You will probably be too exhausted after a day-long hike to go to the pictures or may be staying in an isolated village far from the shopping malls and multiplexes, but if you want to see a film, you can find a cinema (Romanian *cinema*) in all large towns. Pick up a copy of the free listings magazines *24-Fun* (*www.24fun.ro*), *Şapte Seri* (*www.sapteseri.ro*) or *Zile şi Nopţi* (*www.zilesinopti.ro*) to see what's on. Tickets at multiplex cinemas cost 13–35RON depending on the time, and most films are shown in the original language with subtitles.

CHURCHES AND MONASTERIES Transylvania is packed with **churches** of many different denominations. Whatever their official opening hours, visitors are unlikely to be turned away from **monasteries** within daylight hours or in many even at night because some offer accommodation. Church opening hours are erratic, especially ones that are not major tourist attractions. It is sometimes a case of being there when the cleaner comes or waiting for a service or asking at the parish office for the keys. Often a local living in a house near the church will have the keys and you should knock on the door and ask politely, 'May I look around the church?' (*Noi am dori să vizităm biserica/Szeretnénk megnézni a templomot* in Romanian/Hungarian) or 'Who keeps the keys?' (*Cine are cheia?/ Kinél van a kulcs?*)

MUSEUMS AND GALLERIES Transylvania has an unusually large number of **museums** and **galleries**, usually well put together (if a little dusty) and also often in beautiful old buildings or castles. Museums pop up unexpectedly all over the country, sometimes in the most unlikely places. A tiny village will have a house devoted to a writer who once lived there, or one who popped in for a visit. Museums are usually open 10.00–17.00 Tuesday– Sunday (in the bigger cities a few are open on Mondays).

Useful questions you might wish to ask: 'What time does the museum open?' ('*La ce oră se deschide muzeul?/Mikor nyit a múzeum?*'); 'How much does an entrance ticket cost?' ('*Cât costă biletul?/Mennyibe kerül a belépő?*')

Folk-Art collections and open-air museums Transylvania is an ideal destination for anybody interested in folk traditions and culture. There are three open-air museums and, for those who want to explore in more depth, the **Museum of the Romanian Peasant** in Bucharest has a fascinating collection of ceramics, textiles, carvings and icons. See the relevant chapters for more on the various museums and collections.

Open-air museums
- **Bran Village** Museum in Bran Castle grounds (see page 140).
- **Cluj-Napoca** Ethnographic Museum in two parts (see page 253).
- **Sibiu** ASTRA Open Air Museum (see page 202).

Folk art collections
- **Brașov** The Ethnographic Museum displays folk art from southeast Transylvania (see page 136).
- **Cristian** The Heimat Museum has an amazing collection of Saxon folk art in Sibiu County (see page 204).
- **Lupșa** The Pamfil Albu Ethnographic Museum has a rich collection of Moț culture from the mountainous parts of Alba County (see page 243).
- **Miercurea-Ciuc** The museum of Székely culture in Mikó Castle, Harghita County (see page 165).
- **Rimetea** (Torockó) The Folk (Néprajzi) Museum has a superb collection of craftsmen's tools. Also several private houses have collections of painted furniture which can be visited in this beautiful, traditional village in Alba County (see page 246).
- **Sfântu Gheorghe** The Székely National Museum has important collections of folk crafts, and also Székely gates and a preserved cottage in Covasna County (see page 153).
- **Zăbala** Ferenc Pozsony has a small, private museum of Csángó culture and painted wooden furniture from the Háromszék region of Covasna (see page 158).

In a fascinating combination of Eastern subtlety and Western pragmatism and pomp, Romanian architecture has stylised various influences for more than seven centuries. In addition to the German Gothic, the Austrian Baroque and the Italian Renaissance, there are original Romanian creations such as the 17th-century Brancovan and the 19th-century neo-Romanian styles.

Transylvania boasts dozens of **Saxon fortified churches** and strongholds. The **churches** encapsulate history, art and sociology in one venue and a good way to tour the churches is by bicycle or on a hiking trip. These make great destinations for a walk in the fresh air, a dose of culture and a glimpse into Transylvania's rich history, all in one. Tourists fight their way through forests of stalls selling Dracula souvenirs in their hunt for Bran Castle and also Hunedoara's magnificent Corvin Castle with its towers that retain the spirit of the medieval court and the exterior that sums up the magic of Transylvania, all contained in one romantic fairytale picture. Lăzarea Castle, in Harghita County, preserves the memories of old princely families. Several hundred years of influence from the powerful Habsburg Empire brought the Viennese Baroque to the Transylvanian cities of Cluj-Napoca and Sibiu, with sumptuous palaces adorned with tall windows and gilded decoration.

Here are some of the architectural treasures to look out for:

CASTLES
- **Aiud** Medieval castle in the centre of town (see page 244).
- **Alba Iulia star-shaped fortress** With seven bastions, subtle yet spectacular in a stellar shape, it was built between 1716 and 1735 by Giovanni Morando Visconti, using the Vauban method and is the largest of its kind in southeast Europe (see page 235).
- **Bánffy Castle** (Cluj County) Was formerly known as the 'Versailles of Transylvania' and is undergoing restoration work (see page 257).
- **Bran Castle** Prince Vlad III Țepeș may have spent only two nights imprisoned here, but that doesn't stop the Dracula industry mushrooming beneath the castle's precipitous walls (see page 140).
- **Corvin Castle** (Hunedoara County) The archetypal Transylvanian castle: all pointed turrets, buttresses and a deep, wide moat (see page 225).
- **Făgăraş Fortress** During the rule of Transylvanian prince Gábor Bethlen (1613–29), the town became an economic role model for the southern regions of the realm. Bethlen rebuilt the fortress entirely. Făgăraş became the residence of the wives of Transylvanian princes, similar to Hungary's Veszprém, the 'city of queens' (see page 145).
- **Lăzarea Castle** (Harghita County) Built as a residence by the Lázár family in 1532 (see page 174).
- **Sighişoara Clock Tower** Like Bran and Corvin, this is one of the most popular images of Transylvania. The walled fortress on a hill is a favourite destination for visitors (see page 188).

RUINS
- **Câlnic** Southeast of Sebeş, built by Saxon nobles, is a UNESCO World Heritage Site (see page 237).
- **Deva Citadel** Built in the 13th century, the citadel stands on a hill dominating the city of Deva, known as the 'Hill of the Djinn' (see page 221).

- **Ocskay Castle** These ruins sit on top of the impressive Uroi Hill near Orăştie (see page 222).
- **Orăştie** Five ruined Dacian citadels, now on the UNESCO World Heritage Site list (see page 222).
- **Peleş Castle** Near Sinaia, Peleş is the most beautiful residence of Romania's former royal family. Designed to resemble a grand hunting lodge, German neo-Renaissance is blended with Italian Renaissance (see page 138).
- **Pelişor Castle** Next to Peleş Castle, Pelişor was built between 1899 and 1902 by the Czech architect Karel Liman. Queen Marie contributed much to the style of the interior décor (see page 138).
- **Poienari Citadel** By the Transfăgăraşan Highway. If you leave Transylvania by this scenic route, don't miss out on Vlad III Ţepeş's genuine castles. Built in the 13th century and repaired by Vlad, it is now a ruin with a spectacular view, after climbing 1,426 steps (see page 216).
- **Râşnov Castle** Built around 1215 by Teutonic Knights and conquered only once in its history, by Gabriel Báthory (see page 140).
- **Rupea** (Braşov County) Called Kőhalom in Hungarian, meaning 'a pile of stones', it was built and extended between the 14th and 17th centuries (see page 149).
- **Slimnic** Just north of Sibiu on the Mediaş road is a Gothic castle, built in 1765 (see page 206).

PALACES
- **Avrig** (Sibiu County) Has the most easterly Baroque garden (see page 213).
- **Bánffy Palace** (Cluj-Napoca) Built in Baroque style by the architect J E Blaumann between 1774 and 1785, on what is now Piaţa Unirii (see page 257).
- **Brukenthal Palace** (Sibiu) One of the most important Baroque monuments in Romania. Built in several stages between 1778 and 1788, it was the official residence of Baron Samuel von Brukenthal, Governor of Transylvania. It now houses the Brukenthal Museum (see page 199).
- **Palace of Culture** (Târgu Mureş) Built between 1911 and 1913 by Marcell Komor and Dezső Jakab. The Hall of Mirrors contains stunning stained-glass windows by Miksa Róth's workshop (see page 180).

SPAS

Spas were started by the Romans and are an impressive feature of Europe's watery resort landscape. Today, Romania has 70 natural spas, 13 of which are in Transylvania. These resorts provide relief for many medical disorders and illnesses, including rheumatism; endocrine, kidney, liver, respiratory, heart, stomach and nervous diseases; and nutrition, metabolism and gynaecological disorders.

Romania is home to more than one-third of Europe's mineral and thermal springs. Natural factors are complemented – under attentive medical care – by physiotherapy, acupuncture, electrotherapy and herbal medicines.

For spa packages, look at www.balneoturism.ro. This website (in Romanian) gives prices per night at hotels in most of the spa resorts – the price of a double room per night with breakfast ranges from 150RON to 250RON.

A selection of the best therapeutic spas
- **Băile Tuşnad** (Harghita County) Băile Tuşnad mountain spa is beneficial for those suffering from nervous complaints and gastric problems. The cure

involves about a two-week stay when guests drink the waters, which come in an amazing variety: alkaline, chlorinated, carbonated gases, and sodium-, iodine-, magnesium-, sulphate- or iron-rich.

- **Balvanoş** (Covasna County) Near Băile Tuşnad and located in the curvature of the Carpathians. The surrounding volcanic rock gives out carbon dioxide and hydrogen sulphide which are used for treating the stomach and intestines.
- **Borsec** (Harghita County) Good for digestive problems and the endocrine system.
- **Covasna** Famous for its mineral waters and carbon dioxide-rich *mofettes* (fumaroles). Cardiovascular and circulatory problems are treated here. Nearby in the Covasna Valley, at Balta Dracului (Devil's Pond) there is a nature reserve.
- **Praid** (Harghita County) Thermal waters and aerosols from the old salt mine.
- **Sângeorz-Băi** Near Năsăud (Bistriţa-Năsăud County), for digestive, hepatic and nutritional diseases. Also acupuncture, electrotherapy, massage, hydrotherapy and *mofette* treatments available.
- **Sovata** The best place for gynaecological problems in the salty outdoor Lacul Ursu. Sovata's salt waters are also recommended for the treatment of locomotive system diseases, cardiovascular, digestive and endocrine diseases, and also post-traumatic conditions.

In addition, guests can bathe in hot springs or **sapropelic muds** (containing black clay and shale), breathe in foul, eggy fumes at *mofettes* (see page 161), or indulge in a new generation of complementary therapies such as ultrasound and aerosol treatment, ultraviolet light baths, acupuncture and electrotherapy.

SPORTS AND ACTIVITIES

Romanians have always excelled in sports; footballer Gheorghe Hagi, who in September 2007 resigned as coach of Steaua Bucureşti, was known as the 'Maradona of the Carpathians'; giant NBA basketball star Gheorghe Mureşan hails from Cluj County; gymnast Nadia Comăneci won hearts the world over with her impish smile and the first perfect 10 score at the 1976 Montreal Olympics; while Ilie Năstase and Ion Ţiriac brought their personalities to the tennis court. Transylvanian sports stars are less well known: Gabriela Szabó, the Olympic athlete, hails from Bistriţa.

Ion Ţiriac, a former doubles partner for Năstase and former manager of Boris Becker and famous for his magnificent moustache, comes from Braşov and after retiring from tennis he founded Banca Ţiriac in 1990 as the first private bank in post-communist Romania. He is now one of the richest businessman in the country.

Comăneci hails from Oneşti, east of the Carpathians, but the world-famous gymnastics coach who first spotted her is Béla Károlyi, an ethnic Hungarian from Cluj-Napoca. Together with his wife Márta, Károlyi coached both the Romanian and US Olympic teams to medal success, although their brutal training methods were controversial. The most successful Transylvanian sporting hero is Gabriela Szabó (*www.gabiszabo.com*), an ethnic Hungarian from Bistriţa who at the 2000 Sydney Olympics won gold in the 5,000m and bronze in the 1,500m and also a silver in the 1,500m at the 1996 Atlanta Olympics. Szabó has also triumphed at three world championships, winning gold in 1997, 1999 and 2001. Szabó's coach and now husband, Zsolt Gyöngyössy, is also of Hungarian descent. Romania won a total of eight medals in the 2008 Beijing Olympics, four of them gold, with 38-year-old Romanian athlete Constantina Diţă Tomescu setting a world record as the oldest Olympic women's marathon winner.

BIRDWATCHING The bird migration season in spring lasts from March to May; in autumn it is August to October. There are many birdwatching tours that twitchers can arrange, either from home or in Transylvania. Gerard Gorman, author of Bradt's *Central and Eastern European Wildlife* guide, runs birdwatching trips throughout the region (see page 53). Tibor Kálnoky (see page 155) is an enthusiastic and knowledgeable birdwatcher and a stay at his estate includes several birding trails.

In Zărneşti, Dan Marin (see page 143), joint winner of the *Wanderlust* Paul Morrison Guide of the Year 2007 award, also takes visitors around the Piatra Craiului National Park on well-informed rambles (see page 11 for Dan's section on wildlife), while the Retezat National Park reception centres have a lot of information on the local flora and fauna. For further information, see *Tour operators*, page 52.

CAMPING Get up close and personal with Transylvania's natural beauty by spending a few nights camping beside one of the many rivers or magnificent mountains. The best period for pitching a tent is from late spring to mid summer. The Romanian Tourist Office (*www.romaniatourism.com*) publishes a map detailing 49 campsites and 127 motels. See page 86 for details of campsites.

CAVING Romania has an extensive network of some 11,000 caves (*peştera*). Some are open to visits by members of the public, others are reserved exclusively for speleologists. In the Apuseni Mountains, the Peştera Ghetarul de la Scărişoara (Scărişoara Glacier Cave) is one of Alba County's most spectacular sights (⊕ *10.00–16.00 Tue–Sun; adult/child 4.50/3RON*). In Cluj County, there are the following caves: Peştera Mare, Peştera Piatra Ponorului and Peştera Vârfurosu. In Cluj-Napoca, the Emil Racoviţă Institute of Speleology Museum (see page 252) details the life and work of Romanian biologist Racoviţă (1868–1947), who studied more than 1,000 caves. The Institute gives advice on which caves to visit and when, and can arrange guided tours of Romania's longest cave, the Peştera

BASKETBALL'S BIGGEST STAR

Gheorghe Dumitru Mureşan, known as **Ghiţă**, was born in Tritenii, just east of Turda in Cluj County in 1971. He has now retired from professional basketball, but standing 2.31m (7' 7") tall in his socks, he was probably the tallest man ever to play in the USA's NBA. His parents are both average size and Ghiţă's great height is the result of a pituitary disorder. Ghiţă grew up in a poor family and played college basketball for Cluj University. He played professionally in the French league during the 1992–93 season and was an instant hit with fans. The NBA took interest in him and he was drafted by the Washington Bullets in the 1993 NBA Draft. He played in the NBA from 1993–2000, showing signs of a promising career that was unfortunately derailed by injuries. After returning to France and playing for the start of the 1995–96 season, Ghiţă was named the NBA's Most Improved Player. He joined the New Jersey Nets for the final 31 games of his career. After retiring from the NBA, Mureşan returned to the French league for three more years before returning to settle in New Jersey with his family. He usually wore number 77, referring to his height. After his distinguished basketball career, Mureşan dabbled in acting, playing the title character in the 1998 film *My Giant*, which also starred comedian Billy Crystal.

Vantului (Wind Cave) in the Pădurea Craiului Mountains (in Bihor County), usually closed to the public.

Romania's biggest negative drop (540m) is recorded in the Aven under Coltii Grindului (the Sand Bank's Fangs) in the Piatra Craiului Massif. Two tour companies, Green Mountain Holidays (*www.greenmountainholidays.ro*) and Apuseni Experience (*www.apuseniexperience.ro*) offer week-long, all-in caving holidays (for further details, see page 54).

CLIMBING Rock-climbing enthusiasts should head for the main rock-climbing gateways at Bușteni, and Zărnești in Brașov County or Petroșani in Hunedoara County. Near Zărnești, rock climbers scale sheer cliffs in the Piatra Craiului National Park while the Bicaz Gorge on the eastern border of Harghita County has some spectacular rock formations and challenging climbs.

CYCLING AND MOUNTAIN BIKING Transylvania is ideal for mountain-bike tours and it's incredible that these have only taken off in recent years. In spring and summer, some excellent places for biking include Păltiniș southwest of Sibiu in the Cindrel Mountains, up high on the Bucegi mountain plateau, in the scenic environs of Lacul Colibița, or around the Apuseni Mountains and the Huedin micro-region. In Poiana Brașov, the Vila Club Rossignol, situated near the cable-car station, rents out bikes as well as ski equipment.

Local tour operators such as Absolute Carpathians, Green Mountain Holidays and Inter Pares organise cycling tours of the countryside. Caliman Club Holidays even has its own outdoor centre and organises a one-week cycling tour of the Saxon fortified church villages of Transylvania (for further details, see page 54).

FISHING Fishing is permitted in any lake or river in Romania from 1 June to 31 March. The sport is popular around Transylvania and especially good in the Apuseni Mountains where the catch includes carp, mullet, pike and pike-perch. Lacul Fântânele, north of the Apuseni Mountains, is a spectacularly beautiful and peaceful place to sit by the water. Trophy-sized catfish, carp, pike and sturgeon thrive in the hundreds of lakes and rivers that dot the countryside.

FOOTBALL Romanians are mad about football. The national side were the fourth team to qualify for Euro 2008. Romania were in the same group (C) – the toughest – as Italy, France and Holland, eventually finishing third. At home there are 18 clubs jostling for position in the top division Liga 1 (*www.lpf.ro*). The 2010–11 season champions were Oțelul Galați (*www.otelul-galati.ro*), with their first league title, while in the 2009–10 season it was Transylvania's own **CFR Cluj** (*www.cfr1907.ro*). At the time of writing, **CFR Cluj** were at the top of the pile again. **Steaua București** are Romania's most successful team, linked historically to the army. They have won the title 23 times and are owned by right-wing religious nationalist politician Gigi Becali who fell out with manager Gheorghe Hagi, Romania's most popular player of all time, in September 2007, after a run of poor results. Becali's meddling makes Chelsea FC's owner Roman Abramovitch look like a pussycat.

The third Bucharest team in Liga 1 is **Rapid București**. Another great Transylvanian team, **Gloria 1922 Bistrița**, have the nickname '*Vampirii Albaștri*' (Blue Vampires). From watching Romanian television for many months, I discovered that one of the most popular footballers in the country is the wonderfully photogenic (and talented) Adrian Mutu, formerly of Chelsea and Juventus, and now Italy's AC Cesena.

GOLF The only golf course in Transylvania is at Pianu de Jos, west of Sebeş in Alba County. The private **Golf Club Paul Tomita** (*Pianu de Jos, jud Alba;* m *+40 750 990 200;* e *office@golfclubpaultomita.ro; www.golfclubpaultomita.ro*) was named after Professor Paul Tomita, King Mihai of Romania's golfing instructors. The 18-hole golf course was inaugurated on 12 May 1995 and its aim was to promote the sport of golf throughout Romania.

A nine-hole course can be found at Breaza on the E60 highway south of Sinaia in Prahova County. The **Lac de Verde Golf Club** (*Str Caraiman 57, jud Prahova;* \+40 244 343 525; *www.lacdeverde.ro*) has an adjoining country club with restaurant, spa, tennis courts and health club. There's another nine-hole course, **Tite Golfresort** (*Str Gh. Lazar 30–32, Timişoara;* \+40 356 402 231; *www.titegolfresort.com*) near Timişoara.

HIKING *Să trăieşti!* Cheers! (The hikers' greeting.) As much as 31% of Romania's territory is mountainous. The Carpathians form a huge horseshoe-shaped border for Transylvania on three sides. Within this arc are innumerable places of unspoiled natural beauty: peaks, gorges, lakes, forests, caves, mud volcanoes and marshes. Transylvania has something for every kind of walker, from the serious hiker who wants to cover as much difficult terrain as possible to those who like to take it easy and admire the flora and fauna of Transylvania's uplands. The hiking season begins in earnest in June, as before that unpredictable weather conditions make heading for the hills a risky business. A well-marked network of hiking routes can be found in the Ceahlău Massif near the Bicaz Gorge in northeast Transylvania. The Bucegi, Făgăraş and Apuseni mountains also have well-marked hiking routes and a network of *cabana* mountain huts (see *Accommodation*, page 86) to spend the night in. The website http://alpinet.org/main/poteci/cabane_ro_t_index-cabane.html has a list, mostly in Romanian, of all the *cabanas* in the country.

HORSERIDING A trip to Transylvania is a journey back in time and the unspoiled countryside is best appreciated on horseback. In Romania, working horses still outnumber motor vehicles and the pace of life is more in tune with nature and the seasons than in western Europe. Englishman Julian Ross ran a riding centre in **Lunca Ilvei** which has now been taken over by Count Tibor Kálnoky, and more experienced riders can enjoy the best trail riding in Europe and also experience an authentic living culture. Christoph Promberger and his wife Barbara run the

---

SAFETY IN THE MOUNTAINS

Salvamont (*www.salvamont.org*) provides emergency rescue. It is a voluntary organisation with 20 stations around Romania. Its members are skilled climbers, guides, skiers and medics. They are an invaluable source of weather warnings and practical advice. Salvamont's HQ is in Braşov.

Dial \ 0-SALVAMONT (the equivalent numbers on the dialling pad: 0-725826668) for help.

Braşov Str Varga 23, Braşov; m 0725 826 449
Buşteni Primărie, B-dul Libertăţii 91, Buşteni; \0244 320 048
Sibiu Str Nicolae Bălcescu 9; \0269 216 477; m 0745 140 144
Sinaia Primărie, B-dul Carol II; \0244 313 131
Zărneşti Str Metropolit Ion Meţianu 17; m 0722 737 911

Equus Silvania (*www.equus-silvania.com*) riding centre in Şinca Nouă, 50km west of Braşov. It's a German–Romanian venture combining Western standards and animal treatment with Transylvanian traditions, lifestyle and cuisine. Situated 20km north is the **Horseriding Inn Merlelor** (*www.merlelor.com*) at Hălmeag, where visitors can see the largest Lippizaner stud farm in the country and ride around 1,800km² of unrestricted countryside. Merlelor also offers students and voluntary workers board and lodging in return for work on the stud farm (see page 145).

HUNTING Hunting is big business in Transylvania and popular with local people. The **Hunter Company** (*www.huntercompany.net*) will take care of permits, licences and importing of firearms. There are many restrictions on how and where hunters can shoot, but for those who must kill Transylvania's beautiful wildlife, they can choose from deer, boar, bear, duck, geese, rabbits, quail and pheasant. The list of animals available for slaughter is deeply depressing – wouldn't a Dracula tour be more satisfying for the bloodthirsty?

PARAGLIDING On a sunny morning in September we saw paragliders setting up in the Retezat Mountains south of Haţeg. One of the popular launching spots is from Uroi Hill, north of Simeria (E68) in Hunedoara County. Try contacting a company like **Eagle Air Sport** (*www.paragliding.ro*). **Wing Club** (*www.wingclub. go.ro*) is based in Miercurea-Ciuc and ideally placed for the Harghita Mountains.

RAFTING The most popular rafting rivers are the Criş and Olt. **Outdoor Experience** (*www.whitewater.ro*) have rafting trips on the Mureş River, on the Crişul Repede west of Cluj-Napoca and on the Bistriţa River in northern Transylvania.

SKIING AND SNOWBOARDING If the resorts of the Prahova Valley and Bucegi Mountains become too crowded and you prefer wild skiing, then head for Lacul Bâlea, an unmarked ski area in the Făgăraş Mountains above the Transfăgăraşan Highway. There is a *cabana* (Cabana Bâlea Lac) near the highway route 7C. Skiers can find great snow here as late as June.

Transylvania has several excellent mountain resorts offering slopes for the novice to the experienced. Many of these resorts offer a multitude of other activities including cross-country skiing, snowboarding and tubing. The major ski resorts in Transylvania are at Poiana Braşov and Predeal in Braşov County, Păltiniş in Sibiu County and Straja in Hunedoara County.

In Poiana Braşov, the Vila Club Rossignol, situated near the cable-car station, rents out ski equipment. Just south of Transylvania's border are two popular ski resorts at Azuga-Buşteni and Sinaia, from where cable cars lead up to the towering massif of the Bucegi Mountains.

MEDIA AND COMMUNICATIONS

PRINT Tabloids and sports papers are now the most popular types of newspapers in Romania.

In Cluj-Napoca, I bought a copy of the *Dracula* (1.5RON) tabloid. It contained 16 pages packed with stories about satanic rites, superstitions, astrology, varicose veins and recipes for meals containing potatoes (a jolly good read). In Sfântu-Gheorghe, I bought a copy of the 12-page daily *Háromszék* (0.60RON), the local Hungarian-language newspaper (*www.3szek.ro*). It has a lot of community news for the Székely region, plus long wordy articles on local history and small ads for plots of land and farm machinery.

Romania's newspaper market thrived after the 1989 revolution, but many newspapers subsequently closed because of rising costs. The 1991 constitution upholds freedom of expression, but prohibits 'defamation of the country'. In 2007, the media rights body Reporters Without Borders praised reforms to the criminal code; journalists can no longer be jailed on defamation charges. *Adevărul* (*www.adevarul.ro*) is a daily paper with serious news, sports, lifestyle pages plus articles on Romanians living in Spain and Italy. *Libertatea* (*www.libertatea.ro*) is a red top-type tabloid, packed with juicy titbits about politicians and celebrities. *Libertatea* comes from the Swiss Ringier stable which also publishes the business weekly *Capital* (*www.capital.ro*) and the sports daily *Pro Sport* (*www.prosport.ro*). *Jurnalul Naţional* (*www.jurnalul.ro*) is a daily with English-language pages on its online version.

For entertainment listings all over Transylvania, there are many A5-sized free magazines. *Şapte Seri* (*www.sapteseri.ro*) or *Seven Evenings*, publishes different issues in different cities and regions and has details of events, concerts, bars, clubs, restaurants, sports and hotels in Cluj-Napoca, Târgu Mureş, Sibiu and Braşov. It is in Romanian but with a few pages in English and relatively easy to work out from the context if you're looking for a particular event. *Zile şi Nopţi* (*www.zilesinopti. ro*) or *Days and Nights* is available every two weeks in different editions in different cities and regions. It is in Romanian but clearly set out with information on clubs, bars, restaurants, cinemas, concerts and theatre. There are at least two others with the same format: *24-Fun* (*www.24fun.ro*) and *Where are YOO! going Today?*

English-language press *Nine O'Clock* (*www.nineoclock.ro*) is a daily paper which was started in 1991 by a group of Romanian journalists who specialised in foreign politics and who wanted to build a bridge between cultures. The name comes from the time in the morning when Romanian businessmen traditionally read the newspapers while drinking their first cup of coffee. The online version is an excellent source of information but it is best about Bucharest. *Business Review* (*http://business-review.ro*) is a business weekly.

TELEVISION During the Ceauşescu era, state television, the only choice, broadcasted for two hours a day. State television offered one hour of news featuring the latest co-operative farm and factory successes, and an hour of stirring music. After two hours, the television closed down for the night with the words, 'Goodnight comrades, there's another hard-working day tomorrow'. People living in the countryside made sophisticated aerials to get Bulgarian television with some music. 'We couldn't understand the language, but at least the music was a little light relief', said a local in Bran.

Now, Romania has one of the most dynamic media markets in southeast Europe and television is the preferred medium for most Romanians. There are hundreds of cable stations and channels springing up every week, but the state-owned **Romania 1** and the private stations **Pro TV** and **Antena 1** still account for the lion's share of viewers. There are a large number of smaller, private stations, some of them part of local networks. The state broadcaster, **TVR**, operates a second national network, **TVR 2**, and a pan-European satellite channel. Most households in Bucharest have cable television. There are hundreds of cable distributors offering access to Romanian, European and other stations. Pay television channels have a small but significant audience.

RADIO The first private radio stations appeared in 1990, and there are now more than 100 operating. State-owned and run **Radio Romania** (*www.srr.ro*) operates four national networks and regional and local stations. The **BBC World Service** is available on 88FM in the capital and **Radio Romania International** (*www.rri.ro*) has news in English on its website. Travelling around the countryside by hire car, you will find a huge selection of radio stations in different languages, especially between 85FM and 105FM. Disco music and golden oldies from the 1960s, 1970s and 1980s blast out from every tinny speaker and radio. **Magic Radio** (*www.magicfm.ro*) is inoffensive and quite entertaining. **Europa FM** (*www.europafm.ro*) is a commercial radio station broadcasting on 90Mhz in Bistriţa, 107.7 in Deva and 106.20 in Sibiu. **Paprika 95.1FM** (*www.paprikaradio.ro*) has news from Cluj in Hungarian.

TELEPHONE AND FAX Cheap local calls can be made from any phone, but you'll need a Romtelecom phonecard to use a public phone booth; buy a card from a tobacconist or post office.

To dial a phone number abroad, dial 00 then the country code, shown below.

Australia	☏61	Germany	☏49	Poland	☏48
Austria	☏43	Greece	☏30	Romania	☏40
Belgium	☏32	Hungary	☏36	Spain	☏34
Canada	☏1	Ireland	☏353	UK	☏44
France	☏33	Italy	☏39	USA	☏1

Transylvanian city codes Calling numbers in Romania from abroad, first dial Romania's country code (+40) then the local code minus the first zero, then the telephone number.

Useful and emergency telephone numbers The standardised number for police, fire and ambulance is now ☏112.

Mountain rescue Salvamont (*www.salvamont.org*) has 20 rescue stations around Romania. The mobile number 0-SALVAMONT corresponds to the numbers on the phone dialling pad, ie: 0-725826668 (see *Safety in the Mountains* box, page 112).

Cellphones/mobiles The mobile phone providers Orange, Vodafone (formerly Connex-Vodafone), Cosmote România (*www.cosmote.ro*) and Zapp Mobile cover virtually all of Romania. There are more than 21 million mobile phone subscribers in the country. To call a mobile number in Transylvania dial all the numbers including the first zero; from outside the country dial +40 and omit the first zero. Mobile phone owners from the US may find that their phones don't work on the tri-band GSM system. The best method is to purchase a new SIM card with a Romanian number. **Orange** (*www.orange.ro*) and **Vodafone** (*www.vodafone.ro*) shops are in virtually every town throughout the country. From personal experience, getting an Orange SIM card with a Romanian mobile number was a very convenient way of making cheap phone calls and sending text messages. A non-subscription package with pre-paid credit cost under 10RON with credit given in euros, top-up cards for varying prices cost from €10. **Zapp** (*www.zapp.ro*) is currently aimed at business people and companies and offers internet access in the absence of public Wi-Fi networks. Customers can have a dial-up connection, cheap international calls and a wide choice of television channels via cable. The coverage and quality of signal have improved consistently in recent years, and coverage now reaches more than 90% of the urban population.

POST OFFICES (*poşta*) Most main town post offices (Poşta Română – look for a red sign or post box with a yellow PO bugle symbol; *www.posta-romana.ro*) open 07.00–20.00 Monday–Friday, 08.00–13.00 Saturday. You can also buy a stamp (*timbru*, plural *timbre*) from some tobacconists and street kiosks. Poste restante is available in large towns; simply write *Poştal no 1, poşte restante*, followed by the name of the town. Sending a parcel is a highly complicated procedure and not recommended for those with limited time.

INTERNET Internet cafés have sprouted up in larger Transylvanian towns (Sibiu, Cluj-Napoca, Braşov and Târgu Mureş); expect to pay around 3RON (€1) per hour.

Many hotels offer either Wi-Fi connections in rooms (for a fee) or some have free Wi-Fi zones in their cafés and lobbies.

MAPS

Maps (*harta*) of Transylvania are improving but some map makers such as Romania Digitala are forsaking paper and heading straight for GPS maps and information on the Garmin Nuvi group of satellite navigation systems.

However, **Fundaţia ADEPT** (see page 15) are working hard to map certain regions for nature- and Saxon village-loving tourists.

Fundaţia ADEPT recently published a really excellent tourist map (*harta turistică*) of the Sighişoara-Târnava Mare region (1:50,000). Look for it in the Saschiz Fundaţia ADEPT information centre and shop.

The **Association of Ecotourism in Romania** has produced a new series of maps in association with Bogdan Florescu, focusing on Ecotourism destinations including Retezat and Piatra Craiuliu. They can be ordered through the Discover Eco-Romania website (*www.eco-romania.ro*).

Hungarian cartographers **Dimap** (*www.dimap.hu*) produce good maps of the national parks and hiking districts and has an online shop.

Stanfords (*www.stanfords.co.uk*) stock Dimaps, as do The Map Shop (*www. themapshop.co.uk*), including the detailed hiking maps (listed under Szarvas Andras rather than Dimap); or if going to Transylvania via Budapest pop into the Budapest shop Térképvilág ('map world'). Dimap produces a 'Transylvania' (1:400,000) map as does Freytag & Berndt.

Micromapper (*www.micromapper.ro*) produces some of the best interactive web maps as well as paper maps.

For drivers, **Cartographia** (*www.cartographiaonline.com*) in Budapest offer a detailed spiral-bound Auto Atlas România (1:300,000), which is invaluable for exploring the smaller roads of Transylvania. Dimap also produce a road atlas (1:250,000) for Romania.

Canadian cartographers **ITMB** (*www.itmb.ca*) publish a full-country Romania map (1:850,000), available online.

There are also maps on sale in **newspaper kiosks** in towns such as Cluj-Napoca and Târgu Mureş.

Local tourist offices (ANT) around Transylvania often have free town maps and also maps dedicated to the locations of campsites and *cabanas*. For bookshops, see the relevant town sections in *Part Two* of the guide.

Before you set off, check out Stanfords, in London's Covent Garden, specialising in maps and travel books, and which has branches in Bristol and Manchester. The Map Shop has a huge selection of maps online and in its Upton upon Severn store.

In Brussels, I recommend the superb map and guidebook shop L'Anticyclone des Açores, which stocks the Erdély (Transylvania) map I found in Budapest published by Dimap, with incredible detail and the Romanian and Hungarian names of every single tiny hamlet throughout the region.

MAP SHOPS

Dimap Báthory utca 104, 1196 Budapest; +36 1 377 7908; e dimap@hu.inter.net; www.dimap. hu. Shop online only.
L'Anticyclone des Açores Rue Fossé aux Loups 34, 1000 Brussels 34; +32 2 217 5246; ⏲ 11.00–18.00 Mon–Sat
Stanfords 12–14 Long Acre, London WC2E 9LP; e sales@stanfords.co.uk; www.stanfords.co.uk; ⏲ 09.00–19.30 Mon, Wed, Fri, 09.30–19.30 Tue,

09.00–20.00 Thu, 10.00–19.00 Sat, 12.00–18.00 Sun
Térképvilág Szugló utca 83–83, 1141 Budapest; e dimap@hu.inter.net; ⏲ 10.00–18.00 Mon–Fri
The Map Shop 15 High St, Upton upon Severn WR8 0SP; 01684 593146; e themapshop@ btinternet.com; www.themapshop.co.uk; ⏲ Mon–Sat 09.00–17.30. They are particularly strong on hiking maps.

BUSINESS

Business hours are normally 09.00–17.00 with a lunch break between 13.00 and 14.00. Don't expect to find any government workers still at their desks after 15.00 on a Friday afternoon. Banks operate 09.00–17.00 Monday–Thursday, 09.00–15.00 Friday.

The Ottoman influence has left Romanian business people super skilled in the arts of trading and negotiations. Be prepared to haggle in the market and use your charms to negotiate a good deal.

Timekeeping is not as strict as in western Europe, as people understand the difficulties of getting from place to place, because of poor roads, traffic jams or cows meandering across the highway.

Romanian business folk all appear to smoke like chimneys and drink strong Turkish coffee and sickly energy drinks from as early as 09.00.

If you are already confident enough to do business in Romanian, you'll know that there are four ways of saying 'you' (*tu, dumneata, voi, dumneavoastră*). This socio-linguistic minefield (*see Appendix 1, Language*, page 275) is best avoided by all except those who are fluent.

Many Romanians speak English, German or French and some have Hungarian as their native tongue.

Don't even think of arranging a business meeting during the holiday months of July and August and also be aware that most companies shut down between 24 December and 3 January.

USEFUL CONTACTS/WEBSITES

American Chamber of Commerce Floor 4, Str Ion Câmpineanu 11, Union International Centre, Bucharest; +40 21 312 4834; e amcham@ amcham.ro; www.amcham.ro
British Romanian Chamber of Commerce Room 107, Floor 1, IPCT Bldg, Str Tudor Arghezi 21; Bucharest; m +40 752 003 066; e astefan@ brcconline.eu; http://brcconline.eu

Cluj Chamber of Commerce and Industry Str Horea 3, Cluj-Napoca; +40 364 730 980; e office@ccicj.ro; www.ccicj.ro
European Commission Representation in Bucharest Str Vasile Lascăr 31, Bucharest; +40 21 203 5400; e comm-rep-ro@ec.europa. eu; http://ec.europa.eu/romania/index_ro.htm

Romanian Chamber of Commerce and Industry B-dul Octavian Goga 2, Sector 3, 030982 Bucharest; +40 21 319 0114; www.ccir.ro

Romanian Chamber of Commerce Brussels Representation 51 Rue D'Arlon, 1040 Brussels; +32 2 230 2395; e ccir.bruxelles@skynet.be; www.ccir.ro

The Romanian Government www.gov.ro

The Ministry of the Economy and Finance www.minind.ro

The Ministry of Foreign Affairs www.mae.ro

The Ministry of Regional Development and Tourism www.rndlpl.ro

The Bucharest Stock Exchange (Bursa de Valori Bucureşti) www.bvb.ro

BUYING PROPERTY

Transylvania is a mystery to many people: some don't realise that it's a real place outside Bram Stoker's and Hollywood's imaginations. Hidden for decades behind the Iron Curtain and famous for having several creepy castles haunted by Count Dracula, it is now an EU member state and one of Europe's property hotspots.

Until recently, Transylvania was not served by low-cost airlines, and there were no large British tour operators active in the region. So whereas the Bulgarian coast has been bought up by Brits with the same fervour when they swarmed through Tuscany and the Costa del Sol, Transylvania has been spared a large influx of property buyers and the prices are thus still affordable. Property prices vary greatly with anything from a run-down cottage in the wilds for €9,000 (£7,400) to a new villa located near Braşov or Sibiu for €350,000 (£250,000) to your very own vampire's castle for a few million.

Of the three former principalities that make up modern-day Romania (Wallachia, Moldavia and Transylvania), Transylvania, protected from the outside

BRAN CASTLE – TRANSYLVANIA'S HOTTEST PROPERTY

Bran Castle (*www.bran-castle.com*), a 14th-century fortress and now creepy vampire-inspired museum, has never shied away from cashing in on its (albeit very tenuous) link with Vlad III Ţepeş, the 'Impaler', the inspiration for Bram Stoker's 1897 novel *Dracula*.

In May 2006, the former residence of Queen Victoria's granddaughter, Queen Marie of Romania, was returned to the family by 70-year-old New York architect Archduke Dominic von Habsburg on condition that it remained a state-run museum for the next three years. In 1947, the castle was appropriated by Romania's communist regime, but 60 years on, after a lengthy legal wrangle, it was handed back to von Habsburg, a descendant of its previous owner, Princess Ileana of Romania.

Von Habsburg decided that, rather than co-habiting with Vlad's imposing spirit, he would prefer to sell it back again to the state as a refurbished tourist venue. Castle Dracula is one of Transylvania's top attractions, pulling in 450,000 visitors a year. Adults now pay 25RON (€5.70) a time to visit the museum, which is maintained in appearance as a royal residence, and a new buyer is virtually guaranteed a long-term money-spinner. The government has first option to buy the 57-room medieval castle, but it could still return to private hands, although they'd have to have good circulation. Bran Castle's rooms and towers surround an inner courtyard. Other rooms are connected through underground passages. There is no central heating inside the chilly castle walls, just a few electric radiators in some of the rooms. Plus maintenance and restoration bills could be a pain in the neck. There's always something that needs repairing although for a building

world on almost all sides by the Carpathian Mountains, is the one that's taking off as a property jewel to be dug up by anyone seeking rural bliss.

Romania is still an emerging market and as such there are dangers. It also does not have an evolved body of property law so potential buyers must be on their guard.

There are no restrictions to foreigners owning property in Romania. To acquire the freehold title to land, however, a foreign citizen needs to either set up a Romanian company or associate with a Romanian national in the transaction. However, now Romania is now part of the EU this rule is expected to change at some point.

Be aware that, until 1989, almost all property was owned by the former Communist Party and should have since been returned to its rightful owners or their heirs. If you have bought property that comes under dispute you might lose it, so make sure your lawyer has checked the title deeds. You will also have to check that there are no outstanding debts to settle on a property, as you will inherit them. Purchasing a new-build property should avoid this problem.

If you decide to rent out your Transylvanian cottage, you will be liable for a uniform 16% tax on your rental income, although since January 2007, there is no longer a capital gains tax. This tax, formerly at 16%, was replaced by a sales tax representing approximately 2–3% of the property value. For property purchased from companies, VAT is charged at 19%. If buying through a Romanian company, the reverse charge principle is applied to VAT.

Along with the problems, however, come many benefits and the new Bucharest–Braşov–Cluj–Oradea–Budapest motorway under construction will cut straight through Transylvania, increasing the region's profile and profitability. Many low-cost airlines now fly to Cluj-Napoca, Sibiu and Târgu Mureş, and Bucharest is only

dating from 1377 it's in pretty good condition. It would cost a fortune to convert it into a private home, but, as with many historic properties in Transylvania, it is still a very good investment.

In keeping with its colourful past, the castle sits on top of a 61m (200ft)-high crag overlooking the village of Bran, 30km southwest of Braşov. Bran is jam-packed with souvenir stalls selling Dracula tat: mugs, T-shirts, baseball caps, etc, all featuring Vlad's face with its piercing eyes. Vlad actually only spent one or two nights at Bran, but this appears to be no barrier to the booming tourist industry. The huge asking price is partially explained by the presence of a rich collection of Romanian and foreign furniture and *objets d'art* dating from the 14th–19th centuries. Three hectares of forest and three smaller buildings are included in the sale. Braşov Council was given 30 days to consider a possible purchase, after which the castle would be offered to a private buyer, with plenty to get his or her teeth into.

During a parliamentary debate in September 2007, opposition MP Dumitru Ioan Puchianu said the return of the castle had been illegal because of procedural errors.

He said von Habsburg, whose family was thrown out of the castle after World War II, should not be allowed to sell it. In response, Mr von Habsburg – who said he had never given up hope of getting the castle back and that he was finally going home – issued a letter through his lawyers threatening to sue for damages of some US$200m if the MPs stripped him of his right to sell the castle. The letter read, 'I live once more with the feeling of dread in which I once lived, as a child, when my family and I were forced out of our home and thrown out into the streets in mid-winter.'

three hours' drive from Braşov, its ski resorts and the Prahova Valley, the vineyard-filled gateway to Transylvania.

There are also problems associated with a market in which poor eastern Europeans are selling to rich Westerners. Many Romanians consider Westerners to be both very rich and very naïve. EU membership and the arrival of large multi-national companies sent the property market in attractive Transylvanian cities such as Sibiu, Braşov and Cluj-Napoca spiralling upwards, but in the more remote rural areas there is no market at all, few benchmarks and no agents. Country folk are often desperately poor and are catching on to the fact that their romantic farmhouses might be worth something.

For all its jaw-dropping beauty, Transylvania is not an easy real estate option. Don't just check out a few tempting websites and snap up the first crumbling cottage you fall in love with. The trick is to go there and look for yourself – and make more than one trip.

It costs very little to make several reconnaissance trips and, as a first venture, a tailor-made tour via Mike Morton's Transylvania Uncovered (see page 53) could be the best way to get a feel of the place and the lie of the land.

Traditional village houses, and especially those off the main roads, are usually too cheap to be worth an agent's while, so you won't find them on most agency websites. Villagers distrust agencies and prefer to sell direct, so you need to choose your village then make enquiries; try putting out feelers in the local pub.

The Saxon villages, especially those with the magnificent fortified churches, are very appealing to British buyers. Here there is no transparent market, and a good idea is to consult Edward Russell, the sole British real estate agent from Homes in Romania (for further details see below).

For a ruined farmhouse in a less famous village, you might find a few thousand euros would be more than enough. Choose a more famous UNECSO-listed village such as Viscri and you'll find property prices three times as high.

Another problem in Transylvania is infrastructure. Outside the big towns, you have access to electricity and also, perhaps, to a telephone line, but there are no water mains or sewers, so you would need to dig your own well and sink your own cesspit.

The restoration will provide plenty of causes to tear your hair out, and you'll need to find a good network of trustworthy neighbours, builders, painters and decorators. After restoration you'll have to find tenants and can expect to charge upwards of €100 (£70) a month. It is not a good idea to leave a property empty as there are many people roaming the countryside looking for inviting, empty places to inhabit. You should find a friendly local who will keep an eye on your place for around €50 (£35) a month.

I would recommend you get a copy of Alex I Pintea's *An Insider's Guide: Buying Property in Romania*. However, this handbook was published in November 2006 before Romania joined the EU, so many legalities could have changed since then. Head for Transylvania with your mind and eyes wide open and you will not be disappointed. Who knows, you might end up living in your own rural paradise by this time next year.

USEFUL CONTACTS

Anglo-Romanian Development www.anglo-romaniandevelopment.co.uk

Arc Property Alastair Norman is a big fan of Transylvania; ☏020 7385 0840; www.arc-property.co.uk

Count Tibor Kálnoky m +40 742 202 586; www.transylvaniancastle.com

Edward Russell Homes in Romania; ☏01223 238 330; e info@homesinromania.co.uk; www.homesinromania.co.uk

Romanian Properties Ltd www.romanianpropertiesltd.co.uk
Romtrade Consult ☎ +40 266 240 408; www.romtradeconsult.com

Transylvanian Holiday Homes Cristian Gontariu **m** +40 745 960 032; www.transylvanianholidayhomes.com

PUBLIC TOILETS

Transylvania's main roads are dotted with motels, but the loos are rather aromatic and paper non-existent. The best places to spend a leu are petrol stations (Shell, OMV, MOL, Rompetrol, Petrom), particularly the MOL stations, where the services are often excellent with drinks, sandwiches, maps and flowers on offer. The public conveniences will be clean and well equipped and by law all petrol stations are obliged to provide a public loo free of charge. In the country, behind a bush will often be the only (and certainly most salubrious) option. In villages, the best solution is to pop into a pub or café for a coffee and hope that their services include a toilet, although these are not always available.

Try to avoid toilets on trains or in railway stations altogether, as they will not enhance your journey's experience. If you must go, take your own supply of loo paper. In the countryside, the local shops sell individual loo rolls for a few *bani*. Only the Săgeata Albastră (Blue Arrow) Intercity trains have restrooms appropriate for the 21st century.

Doors are marked in Romanian/Hungarian *femei/női* (ladies) and *bărbați/férfi* (gents). Try asking *Unde este toaletă/Hol van a WC* ('where is the toilet?'). WC is pronounced 'vay-tsay').

CULTURAL ETIQUETTE

In Chapter 2 of Bram Stoker's 1897 novel *Dracula*, the eponymous Count says: 'We are in Transylvania; and Transylvania is not England. Our ways are not your ways, and there shall be to you many strange things.'

GREETINGS In Romanian, there is a complicated system of addressing people, using a formal or informal method. The informal for 'you' is *tu*, but the formal is the tongue-twisting *dumneavoastră*, which takes the second-person plural verb conjugation. Also, when talking *about*, rather than *to* somebody formally, there are special forms.

There is also the form *dumneata* (you), less polite than *dumneavoastră* but more formal than *tu*. When referring to females use *dumneaei*, for males use *dumnealui* and for the plural 'them' use *dumnealor*.

If all of this seems too much of a linguistic minefield, choose instead a few appropriate phrases from the *Language* appendix (see page 275). Men can charm the ladies easily by saying *Sarut mâna*, which means 'I kiss your hand'. If the lady is Hungarian-speaking, try *Kezét csókolom* (pronounced 'kez-ate cho-ko-lom'), which also means 'I kiss your hand'.

When entering a shop, lift, or intimate café, it is good manners to always say (in Romanian/Hungarian) *Buna ziua/Jó napot* (Good day!), and *La revedere/Viszontlátásra* (Goodbye).

SPELLING A–Z Stalin forced Romania to change the 'â' to an 'î' to make the language appear more Slavic, although he let a few exceptions (Româna, Brâncuşi, etc) stay as they were. In 1994, the Romanian Academy decreed that 'î' should change back to its original 'ă', so that, for example, Tîrgu Mureş is now officially Târgu Mureş, Cîmpulung is now Câmpulung. However, often when the word begins with an 'Î', this rule does not apply.

DRUGS Romania is a 'zero tolerance' country. Do not take any illegal drugs into the country. The penalties are draconian with up to seven years for being a user and almost life for distributing. Do not try to bribe officials either. EU law enforcers are even touring the countryside fining grannies who grow hemp (for material and rope).

LIQUIDS Don't expect your glass to be topped up until you have finished the last drop. Be wary if your host fills up your glass when it is half full – it means he/she wants to kill you!

Traditionally, your inner power and strength is derived from alcohol which explains why many Transylvanians drink in large quantities and at all times of the day. On the street, if someone crosses your path carrying a bucket of water it will bring good luck. This could happen quite frequently if you are staying in a small village.

HOSPITALITY Romanians are friendly and open and foreigners are usually made very welcome. Chatting with visitors is very common for Romanians and they will find a way to communicate with you even if they cannot speak your language and often ask very probing questions. Older people appreciate old-fashioned politeness. Try the greetings explained above. Handshaking is the most common form of greeting. When a Romanian man is introduced to a woman, he will probably kiss her hand, strictly avoiding her eyes.

On arrival, never shake hands or kiss across the threshold as it is considered bad luck.

Take off your shoes when you enter the house; you'll be offered a pair of grandpa's old slippers or some beach sandals to wear indoors. A spider in the house means that a guest is coming; the bigger the spider the more important the guest.

If the guest says 'No, thank you' to the host's offerings of food or drink, this is often taken as a polite refusal by a guest who really wants to say 'Yes' but needs his/ her arm twisting. To avoid ţuică, if you have not acquired a taste for it, try saying you are driving or on medication. When visiting someone at home take a small gift. The best gifts are flowers or chocolates for women, or a bottle of wine or a spirit from your home country for men. Be careful to take an odd number of flowers as an even number has funereal echoes. It is not considered impolite to question guests on their views on politics, religion, history, homosexuality or financial matters, so don't be surprised by a serious probing.

PHOTOGRAPHY People's attitudes to having their photograph taken will always vary from place to place and from person to person. While many people are perfectly happy to be photographed – and may even ask you specifically to take their photo – it is worth remembering that Transylvania remains a fairly conservative region, and some will object to being photographed. It is always polite to ask someone before pointing a camera in their face; the chances are, if you ask and they don't mind, you'll get a better and much more engaging photo anyway. Military, police and other 'sensitive' buildings should be considered off-limits for photography.

GAY RIGHTS See page 70.

ROMANIAN SAINTS AND BELIEFS A holiday in the world of the Romanian village will provide you with an opportunity to encounter captivating folk customs. Besides the saints' days of local churches and yearly fairs, many of these ancient customs are celebrated with great ceremony, and visitors are always invited to take part.

Traditional belief says that on **24 June**, around the time of the summer solstice, **herbs** have the maximum potency to heal and that whoever gathers them will have good fortune for the whole of the year. This is the festival which, celebrating the middle of summer, is called Sânziene in Transylvania. Sânziana is also an alternative name for a yellow-flowered plant (Our Lady's bedstraw, *Galium verum*, see box in *Chapter 1*, page 8) which grows in forests and glades on the plain, as well as in the mountains. The yellow flowers are woven into wreaths and hung on doors to ward off evil and in commemoration of the souls of the departed. Wreaths are also placed on the horns of cattle to drive away ghosts and malevolent spirits.

Water plays a very important role in society's rituals. Sprinkling with water is common in a number of them. One of the most beautiful customs takes place on **6 January**, the Holy Theophany of the Lord, which celebrates the Baptism of Christ the Saviour. The water is blessed at the church and then there is a procession through the village, in which the priest blesses the walls of the houses and barns, sprinkling them with a bunch of basil dipped in holy water. In another old custom on the feast of the Holy Theophany priests cast a wooden cross into moving water – rivers, the Danube, even the Black Sea. The young men then jump into the water, competing to see who will be the first to retrieve the cross and return it to the priest.

Trees also have a privileged place in traditional beliefs. The fir features in both wedding and funeral ceremonies. Those who die young are interred with a ritual

SUPERSTITIONS

I read that every known superstition in the world is gathered into the horseshoe of the Carpathians, as if it were the centre of some sort of imaginative whirlpool.
From Jonathan Harker's journal, Chapter 1, Dracula, by Bram Stoker

Romanians are very superstitious. 'Myths are part of rural traditions and the soul of the country,' said Dan Marin. In Romania, the luckiest colour is **red**. Horses wear red tassels with two uses: first as decoration but second to protect against the 'evil eye'. Some people have the evil eye without knowing. If you meet somebody with the evil eye you must touch something red or say 'I swear on red.' Red is a positive colour and keeps evil away. Many people in the country and town wear red jumpers, red anoraks and a lot of red clothes wherever possible. Black is the colour of death. In stables, when there are baby piglets, the farmer must praise the runt with the words 'May the evil eye not touch you,' spit three times then say some special words.

Wolves are a central figure for keeping evil away and a positive animal, unlike in the West. 'We live under the wolf,' said Dan Marin. 'Dacian' means 'wolf warrior'.

Many towns have a statue, donated by Italy, in the main square of a wolf suckling Romulus and Remus to show the Daco–Roman link. In Transylvania, the wolf statues make a howling sound when the wind passes through them. Look in the main squares in Sighişoara, Târgu Mureş and Cluj-Napoca. After a great victory in Dacia, they erected a column in Rome to Trajan in AD113 depicting battle scenes.

chant, in which it is said that the fir tree will spread its branches to lead them into the next world. When I stayed at their Zărnesti guesthouse near Braşov, Dan and Luminiţa Marin offered tastes of a whole cheese encased in pine tree bark, which gave the chunky cheesy tube a wonderful pine flavour.

Basil is a very popular herb. Romanians consider it holy and keep it in their houses under the icon and on the windowsill. Bunches of basil flowers are taken to church. It is said that you should keep basil about you for luck. Young girls who take basil from the church and wind it into the strands of their hair are said to become more attractive and marry sooner.

On **14 September**, Romanians celebrate the Exaltation of the Precious and Life-Giving Cross. Traditional belief holds that fruit and plants gathered on this day have the gift of healing any illness. The Day of the Cross marks the beginning of the grape harvest, when the vines and the wine cellars are blessed.

On **30 November**, the feast of St Andrew is celebrated. On the eve of St Andrew's Day, maidens bake a special kind of bread, which they eat with trepidation, for it is said that, in their dreams that night, it has the power to reveal to them the man they will marry.

Peasants also used to call 30 November the **Night of the Wolf**. The wolf was an animal worshipped by the Dacians. On St Andrew's Eve, ghosts take on the shape of wolves and it was thought that the Moţi people living in the Apuseni Mountains also changed into real wolves on this night. Folk belief holds that anyone bitten by a wolf on St Andrew's Day will become a werewolf.

Garlic possesses the power to protect against wolves and vampires. If you rub garlic on your body, then on the door, the door handle, the window frames and sill, and the cattle stalls, you will be protected. To protect against vampires, wear a small silver cross, carry garlic flowers and a small silver dagger is also good.

TRAVELLING POSITIVELY

Nicolae Ceauşescu sucked the lifeblood out of Transylvania with more vicious enthusiasm than any vampire. The ruthless megalomaniac's excesses, which lasted for almost a quarter of a century, drained the country of its physical, spiritual and national resources. With his warped ideas about modernising the country and paying off the massive national debt, he made ordinary Romanians live in terribly difficult conditions. The weakest members of society, the sick, elderly and unwanted minorities such as the Roma, suffered the most. Ceauşescu's regime rationed electricity, relentlessly persecuted the ethnic Hungarians of Transylvania and, like all communist regimes in central Europe, damaged the environment with greedy, short-sighted factory projects and wasteful collective farms. After the 1989 revolution, many charitable organisations were set up with local or foreign initiatives to restore society to something resembling normality, improve the environment, give advice and support to addicts, or help the long-neglected orphanages where many children were infected with HIV through a bizarre and tragically misguided theory about blood transfusions. The region still needs a lot of help and advice. Many of the charities are faith-based and as such have quite strict criteria for acceptance.

CHARITIES

Accept www.accept-romania.ro. The only gay & lesbian organisation in Romania, campaigns against discrimination & homophobia, deeply entrenched in this highly religious, superstitious country, particularly in isolated rural areas. Projects include HIV education & prevention & challenging negative social attitudes towards LGBT people in Romania.

APT Foundation www.weteachenglish.go.ro. Based in Târgu Mureş, gives English-language classes as a form of Christian outreach.

Asociatia Atelier Sacelean www.facebook.com. Based in Braşov, organises extra-curricular activities such as courses & spare-time activities for children & teenagers who are in danger of abandoning school & for children who have abandoned or have never been to school.

Asociata Un Pas Spre Viitor (A Step to the Future) www.upsv.org. Based in Braşov, an association also made up of children & young people who have lived in Romanian orphanages. The non-profit organisation's objective is to create a social integration centre in order to help the children & the young people when they turn 18 & have to leave the orphanage & face the world outside.

Blue Cross Romania www.healthyblue.org. Based in Sibiu, a member of the International Blue Cross. It was created in 1990 as a humanitarian & Christian association, which provides help or support to alcohol or drug addicts. It is also providing help for children whose parents are alcoholics or drug addicts & also for family members.

Bonus Pastor Foundation www.bonuspastor.ro. Based in Cluj-Napoca, gives Christian support for addicts & treatment for the medical & psychological dimensions of addiction. The foundation helps those who suffer from alcohol, drug & other addictions, recovering people & their families. The need is huge as 15% of Romania's adult population is estimated to have a problem with alcohol. The 'Good Shepherd' Foundation is an NGO with a Reformed Christian background, operating since 1993 primarily in the regions of Cluj, Târgu Mureş & Odorheiu Secuiesc.

Casa Mea www.casamea.org. Based in Braşov, a non-profit, non-faith-based corporation dedicated to providing loving group homes for orphaned & abandoned children in developing countries. Casa Mea embraces any orphaned or abandoned child regardless of age, sex, race, nationality or creed.

Charity Challenge www.charitychallenge.com. A UK-based adventure travel company specialising exclusively in the organisation, leadership & administration of inspirational fundraising expeditions. It's Trek Transylvania challenges usually take place in Aug, & consist of a 6-day trek through the Transylvanian Alps, climbing to heights of 2,400m, visiting Bran Castle, staying in locally owned village pensions & visiting an orphanage supported by Charity Challenge. The cost of the trip has 2 versions: self-funder & minimum sponsorship (the latter is £1,995).

Community Aid Network Braşov www.canbv.ro. A good portal to many community project sites all over Transylvania.

Fast Charity www.fastcharity.ro. The Foundation for Social Assistance & Youth based in Săcele, Braşov County, is an NGO established in 1998 with the purpose of making a difference in the lives of the Romanian children. Their mission is to support the underprivileged people from Romania in their fight against poverty & discrimination. The charity works with UK charity STEPS Romania (*www.romanian-children.co.uk*).

Habitat for Humanity Romania www.habitat.ro. A non-profit ecumenical Christian housing organisation, working in Romania since 1996. Working through locally run affiliates, HFH builds & renovates simple, decent, healthy & affordable housing & the houses then are sold to those in need at no profit & with no interest charged.

Impreuna Community Arts Network www.impreuna.arts.ro. Consists of more than 700 members from Romania & abroad: educators, psychologists, carers, doctors, nurses, teachers specialised in helping children with special needs as well as parents of children with special needs. They all use combined arts techniques to improve the quality of life for people with special needs.

New Horizons www.noi-orizonturi.ro. An American-led charity based in Lupeni, Hunedoara County. New Horizons works to develop the capabilities of children through experimental education & religious traditions.

Pro Sovata www.roemeensekinderhulp.nl. A charity based in the Netherlands, raising funds to help poor families in Romania. The charity, working in Romania for 18 years, organises an annual children's summer holiday in the Netherlands for 42 children during which time they live with foster families. The charity also delivers relief goods packages, made by Dutch families, to Sovata during the difficult winter period. In 2007, they shipped more than 2,300 boxes & €40,000 for food tickets for more than 1,300 Sovata families. The main project is the **Tinkerbell Family Children's Home**, open since 2004 & offering places for 20 abandoned children looked after in a family set-up by 2 families. Pro Sovata are currently looking for more 'fixed' sponsors on a monthly basis to secure

www.stuffyourrucksack.com is a website set up by television's Kate Humble which enables travellers to give direct help to small charities, schools or other organisations in the country they are visiting. Maybe a local school needs books, a map or pencils, or an orphanage needs children's clothes or toys – all things that can easily be 'stuffed in a rucksack' before departure. The charities get exactly what they need and travellers have the chance to meet local people and see how and where their gifts will be used. The website describes organisations that need your help and lists the items they most need. Check what's needed in Romania, contact the organisation to say you're coming and bring not only the much-needed goods but an extra dimension to your travels and the knowledge that in a small way you have made a difference.

the future of the project. The organisation in the Netherlands is called **Stichting Roemeense Kinderhulp** (*The Secretary, Achtersloot 9/b, 3401 NR Ijsselstein, the Netherlands*), in Romania **Pro Sovata** (*Str Lunga 46D, Sovata, jud Mureş*).

Romanian Angel Appeal Foundation www.raa.ro. Established in 1990 in London & Los Angeles. Through its projects, RAA focuses on improving the medical, social & psychological services offered to people in need, especially children & young people affected by HIV/AIDS, by providing direct services, developing education programmes for specialists active in the field (physicians, nurses, psychologists, social workers) & implementing education & prevention campaigns.

Romani Criss Str Buzesti 19, Sector 1, Bucharest 011011; +40 21 310 7070; e office@romanicriss. org; www.romanicriss.org. Romani Criss (Roma Centre for Social Intervention & Studies) is an NGO that defends & promotes the rights of Roma in Romania. The founding members of the organisation are Roma Ethnic Federation (FER), Research Centre of Roma/Gypsies from the René Descartes University in Paris & the Sociology Institute of the Romanian Academy. Since its inception in 1993, the organisation has addressed the problems faced by the Roma population from a human rights perspective, by using specific tools such as conflict resolution, mediation, litigation & advocacy. Romani Criss provides legal assistance in cases of abuse & works to combat & prevent racial discrimination against Roma in all areas of public life, including the fields of education, employment, housing & health.

Rowan Romania Foundation http://

transylvanianwolf.ro/wp/community-work Contact: Danuţ Marin; Fundaţia Rowan România, Zărneşti, Braşov County, CIF 16495283; m +40 744 319 708; e transylvanian_wolf@yahoo. com. A legally registered charity in Romania currently running different programmes for the benefit of the patients at the long-stay psychiatric hospital in Zărneşti (Braşov County) as well as cultural & social programmes with the Roma communities in the same town. To support this charity, send donations to the (£) bank account No RO69RNCB0061009173520004; Swift: RNCB RO BU at Banca Comerciala Braşov, Sucursala III, Zărneşti, Braşov County.

SOS Children's Villages Terrington Hse, 13–15 Hills Rd, Cambridge CB2 1NL; 01223 365 589; e info@ soschildrensvillages.org.uk; www.sponsorachild.org. uk. The Romanian communist government in the 1980s believed blood transfusions kept people healthy & administered them unnecessarily to children in orphanages. Instead of boosting the immune system, some of the transfusions were contaminated with HIV & many nurses reused needles, further causing the spread of the disease. Today, Romania has the highest rate of HIV/AIDS among children in Europe. AIDS orphans are often stigmatised. Fortunately, almost all children are now receiving treatment & Romania has the world's largest paediatric AIDS clinic.

STEPS Romania www.romanian-children.co.uk. A UK-based charity. Projects include building a welfare centre for very poor Roma children & families in Săcele, near Braşov, working in conjunction with Fast Charity.

For a list of useful environmental contacts in Transylvania, see page 15.

Part Two

THE GUIDE

3

Braşov County

Situated in the central part of Romania, at the southeast corner of Transylvania, Braşov County (5,363km²) straddles the Olt River and is packed with tourist spots and stunning scenery. The southern part of Braşov County has the municipality of Braşov as its geographical centre. In Braşov County, the Olt River meadow meets the mountainous massifs such as the Postăvaru, Bucegi, Făgăraş, Piatra Craiului and Piatra Mare rising up to 2,500m above sea level.

Braşov is a region of great variety. The landscape alternates from the green of the rich vegetation in thick forestland to the austere grey of the rocks then to the mountain pastures which are filled with multi-coloured wild flower carpets. The mountains are covered by oak, beech and fir trees providing a safe habitat for a wealth of mammals – the chamois, Carpathian stag, roebuck, brown bear, wolf, lynx, wild boar, fox and hare.

Traditionally, the Romanian population was concentrated in the west and southwest of the county, the Hungarians settled in the eastern part and the Germans lived in the north and around the city of Braşov.

Braşov is one of the most prosperous regions in Romania. There is quite high unemployment but compared with cities such as Târgu Mureş and Cluj-Napoca, Braşov has an atmosphere of prosperity and wealth. During the communist era, Braşov was heavily industrialised and some very large industrial complexes still remain as blots on the landscape. The predominant industries in the county are mechanical engineering and cars, chemicals, construction materials and food. Around the towns of Făgăraş and Victoria there are big chemical complexes which cause concern for environmentalists.

Two large foreign investments are in resorts. The Cold Mountain luxury housing and holiday resort opened in April 2008 between Râşnov and Bran, while the American resort of Poiana Braşov is a multi-million dollar project by developers from South Carolina.

Braşov County is packed with numerous historical, architectural, cultural and art monuments. There are many architectural gems, among them several fine examples of the fortified Saxon churches at Prejmer and Viscri. There is an excellent selection of castles to visit: Râşnov, Făgăraş and the immensely popular Bran Castle, sitting on a crag drawing tourists and Dracula hunters alike

There are also many natural attractions such as Poiana Narciselor (Narcissus Meadow), a 39ha flora reserve near Făgăraş, the Hărman-Dealul Lempeş marshes just north of Braşov with their unique micro-climate and flora, and the stunning Piatra Craiului National Park (*www.pcrai.ro*) with its spectacular gorges and deserted meadows. The county contains some of the most popular ski resorts in the country at Poiana Braşov and Predeal, making Braşov a county with something for everyone.

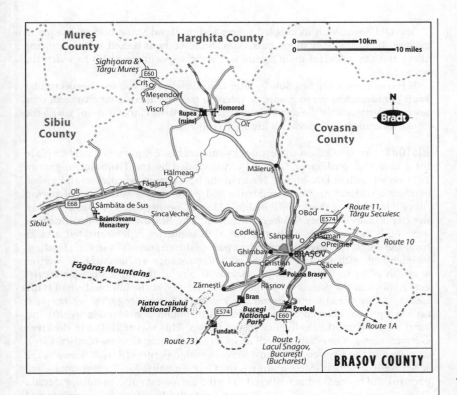

BRAȘOV   *Telephone code 0268, sometimes 0368*

The lively city of Brașov is located in the heart of Bârsa Land, guarded on three sides by the Tampa Hill, Dealul Cetății (Citadel Hill) and Warthe Hill. Brașov (pronounced 'brash-ov') is known as Brassó in Hungarian and Kronstadt in German. In medieval Latin the city was called Brassovia or Corona. Brașov is the southern gateway to Transylvania and the first major settlement visitors will come across if arriving by hire car, train or bus from Bucharest.

From the 1950s onwards, the communists brutally industrialised the city, bringing in workers from the rest of Romania and forcing many German and Jewish inhabitants to leave the city in droves. As a result, the city has more economic problems than other cities in Transylvania and the unemployment rate in Brașov County is the second highest among counties in Transylvania. However, visitors would never suspect that when visiting Brașov as it has an atmosphere of success and prosperity; the Old Town centre has been beautifully restored and the walls look clean and strong. Brașov attracts many tourists as the Old Town retains much of its medieval charm. Some people claim that the Pied Piper led the children from Hamelin and re-emerged right in the main square. However, others say they appeared in the Almaș (Vârghiș) cave near Baraolt in Covasna County (see box, page 157). Brașov does have one definite fairytale link as the city was used as a location for the Harry Potter films. With a population of about 300,000, Brașov is the perfect base from which to tour Saxon Transylvania and to explore the spectacular nature, mountains, ski resorts, castles and fortress churches that surround the town.

The Old Town, with its cobbled streets and medieval Saxon houses, is a joy to explore. There are many shops, bars, cafés and restaurants tucked away in enticing alleys and the colourful main square is a perfect spot from which to watch the world go by.

If you're in town the first Sunday after Easter, make sure you see the spectacular **Junii parade**, when seven groups of riders in traditional costume charge all over town on horseback for the day, yelling 'Hristos a înviat!' ('Christ is risen!'), with the crowd shouting back 'Adevărat a înviat!' ('Truly risen!').

HISTORY Surrounded on three sides by mountains, Braşov was a perfect place for a medieval settlement. The old city, founded by the Teutonic Knights in 1211 on an ancient Dacian site, is one of the best-preserved cities in all Europe, exuding a distinct medieval ambience and popular as a backdrop for period films. The city was first mentioned in 1235 as Corona, when Saxons settled in the city. Braşov's history has been turbulent. The Braşov defence fortifications were built between the 15th and the 17th centuries, after repeated attacks from the south and east. A significant part of the citadel walls is still standing. Resplendent with Gothic, Baroque and Renaissance architecture, as well as a wealth of historical attractions, Braşov is one of the most popular tourist destinations in the country. The location of the city, at the intersection of trade routes linking the Ottoman Empire and western Europe, together with certain tax exemptions, allowed Saxon merchants to obtain considerable wealth and exert a strong political influence in the region. This was reflected in the city's German name, Kronstadt, as well as in its Latin name, Corona (Crown City), displayed in the city's coat of arms: a crown with oak roots. Braşov is one of the seven walled citadels (Siebenbürgen, the German name for Transylvania – see page 16) and home to what is alleged to be the narrowest street in Europe, Strada Sforii (Rope Street), which is just over 1m wide. Fortifications were erected around the city and continually expanded, with several towers maintained by different craft guilds, according to medieval custom. Stroll around the Old Town Hall Square (Piaţa Sfatului) where you can admire colourfully painted and ornately trimmed Baroque structures.

GETTING THERE, AWAY AND AROUND

By air **Braşov International Airport**, originally planned to open in 2009 at Ghimbav, 5km west of Braşov, is now estimated to open in 2014. Until then, the closest airports are located in **Sibiu** (SBZ), 156km west of Braşov; **Târgu Mureş** (TGM), 174km north; **Cluj-Napoca**, 198km northwest of Braşov; or **Bucharest** (OTP or BBU), 173km south of Braşov.

The Bucharest–Braşov–Cluj–Oradea–Budapest motorway has been delayed and will probably not be ready before 2014.

By rail

Brasov Railway Station (Gară Braşov) (*Bd Garii 5;* \ *0268 410 233*) The train station is located 4km north of the centre. Bus No 4 runs from the train station to Piaţa Unirii in the city centre.

There are three direct **international trains** from/to Budapest. One of them continues to Vienna and another to Bratislava and Prague. Trains to other western European cities run via Budapest.

There are **daily trains** to and from Bucharest connecting Braşov to Cluj-Napoca, Sibiu, Sighişoara, Târgu Mureş and several other cities in Romania.

There is a daily **Intercity** (Express) service between Bucharest and Braşov; the journey takes 2½ hours. To check the latest train schedules for domestic routes visit www.cfrcalatori.ro.

Train schedule information and reservations up to 24 hours in advance are available from **Agenţia de Voiaj CFR** (*Str 15 Noiembrie 43;* ✆*0268 477 018*). Tickets for same-day travel can only be purchased at the station.

Public transport Several bus and trolleybus routes connect Braşov's main areas and tourist attractions. Take bus No 20 from Piaţa Revoluţiei in the city centre to the ski resort of Poiana Braşov.

🚌 **Autogară No 1** (Braşov's main bus station) Bd Garii 5, next to the railway station; ✆0268 427 267. Fast minibuses (every 2hrs) connect Braşov with Târgu Mureş (2.5hrs) & other destinations.
🚌 **Autogară No 2** Str Avram Iancu 114. Many buses & microbuses leave for local destinations from here.

🚌 **Autogară West** (Bartolomeu) By the Dealul Bartolomeu on Calea Făgăraşului, just west of Autogară No 2. Many microbuses depart from here for local destinations.

Taxi companies
🚕 **Martax** ✆0268 313 040
🚕 **Rey** ✆0268 411 111

🚕 **RO Taxi** ✆0268 319 999
🚕 **TOD Taxi** ✆0268 321 111

Car hire
🚗 **Ecoline** Str Alexandru Vlahuta 10; m 0743 839 859; e office@ecoline.ro; www.ecoline.ro

🚗 **Thrifty** Bd Eroilor 19 (Hotel Capitol/near Aro Palace Hotel); m 0740 002 000; e office@thrifty.ro; www.thrifty.ro; ⏰ 09.00–19.00 daily

TOURIST INFORMATION
🛈 **Information Centre** Centrul de Informare Turistică Braşov; Piaţa Sfatului 30; ✆0268 419 078; e turism@brasovcity.ro; www.brasovcity.ro or www.brasovcounty.ro; ⏰ 09.00–17.00 daily. Situated in the Old Town Hall building right in the heart of

Council Square (Piaţa Sfatului), the information centre offers accommodation advice & booking, help with transport & entertainment ideas. There is also another office in front of the railway station with the same opening times & email.

Also see www.brasovtravelguide.ro.

🏠 WHERE TO STAY
🏠 **Bella Muzica Hotel** (2 sgl, 16 dbl, 5 suites) Piaţa Sfatului 19; ✆0268 477 956; e hotel@bellamuzica.ro; www.bellamuzica.ro. In a 400-year-old building just off the main square, the rooms are small but tasteful in a rustic style. **$$$$**
🏠 **Casa Rozelor** (3 apts) Str Michael Weiss 20; ✆0268 475 212; m 0747 490 727; www.casarozelor.ro. In a 15th-century granary with interiors designed by the artist Mihai Alexandru. Behind the Bistro De L'Arte providing b/fasts. Kitchen facilities, cable TV & internet in each 60m² apt. **$$$$**
🏠 **Casa Wagner** (12 dbl) Piaţa Sfatului 5; ✆0268 411 253; e office@casa-wagner.eu; www.casa-wagner.com. Great hotel on the main square

situated in a German bank dating back to 1477. Every room is different & the décor is lovely with exposed beams. **$$$**
🏠 **Pensiunea Luiza** (15 rooms) Str Lunga; ✆0268 546 910; e receptie@pensiunealuiza.ro; www.pensiunealuiza.ro. A small 3-star north of the city centre. **$$$**
🏠 **Casa Cristina** (7 dbl, 1 suite) Str Curcanilor 62A; m 0722 322 021; e rezervare@casacristina.ro; www.casacristina.ro. Situated in the Schei district, this family-run pension has great, reasonably priced B&B accommodation. **$$–$**
🏠 **Aro Sport** (10 sgl, 34 dbl) Str Sf Ioan 3; ✆0268 478 800; www.aro-palace.ro. A 1-star

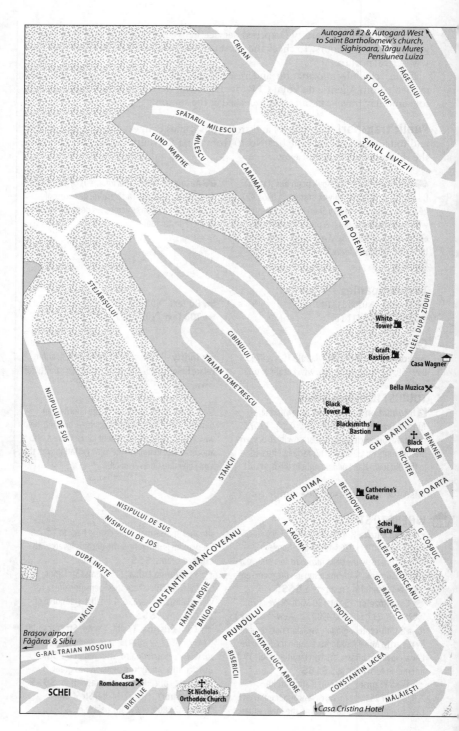

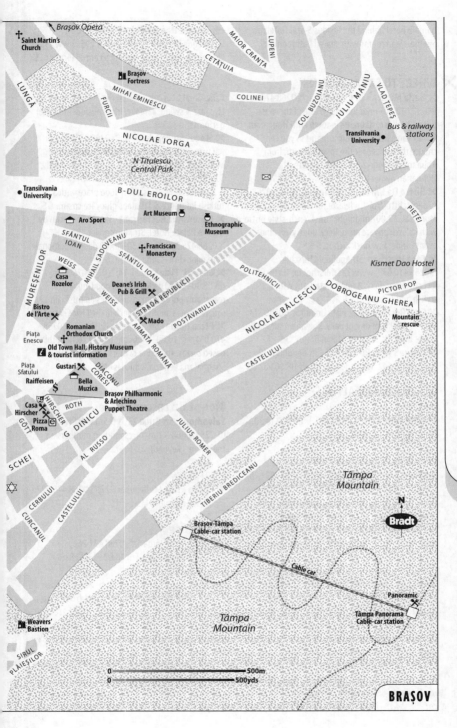

bargain hotel behind the luxious 5-star Hotel Aro. Simple, clean rooms with shared bathrooms. **$**

✕ WHERE TO EAT AND DRINK

✕ Bella Muzica Str Gh Bariţiu 2; ☎0268 477 946; ⊕ 12.00–midnight daily. One of the most popular cellar restaurants in town with Hungarian & Mexican cuisine & a music menu so you can choose the tunes over the sound system, from Abba to Gheorghe Zamfir. Named after the Hungarian owner Béla. **$$$**

✕ Bistro De L'Arte Piaţa Enescu 11 bis; ☎0268 473 994; http://bistrodelarte.ro; ⊕ 09.00–01.00 Mon–Sat, 12.00–midnight Sun. French-style bistro with its own private art gallery, poetry evenings, events under low brick arches. **$$$**

✕ Casa Hirscher Str Apollonia Hirscher 2; ☎0268 410 533; www.casahirscher.ro; ⊕ 09.00–last customer daily. A good restaurant with a stylish hotel above. **$$$**

✕ Casa Românesca Piaţa Unirii 15; ☎0268 513 877; ⊕ 12.00–midnight daily. Romanian cuisine & dishes from the Schei quarter of Braşov. **$$**

✕ Deane's Irish Pub & Grill Str Republicii 19; ☎0268 474 542; www.deanes.ro; ⊕ 08.00–02.00

⌂ Kismet Dao Hostel (5 dorms, 3 dbl) Str Neagoe Basarab 8; ☎0268 514 296; www.kismetdao.com. Cheap beds in a central location. **$**

daily. Great Irish cuisine & all the legendary drinks. Live jazz & swing, karaoke, Irish music & theatrical performances. **$$**

✕ Mado Str Republicii 10; ☎0268 475 385; www.madobrasov.ro; ⊕ 08.00–midnight Mon–Thu, 08.00–02.00 Fri/Sat, 10.00–midnight Sun. This pedestrian street is lined with cafés & restaurants & Mado is a fast-food place with a Turkish influence & fabulous gluey ice cream. **$$**

✕ Panoramic Restaurant Tâmpa Peak, run by the Aro Palace Hotel, Str Mureşenilor 12; ☎0268 475 349; ⊕ 09.30–19.00 daily. Traditional Romanian dishes atop Tâmpa. **$$**

✕ Gustari Piaţa Sfatului 14; ☎0268 475 365; ⊕ 08.30–23.00 daily. Offering good-quality, reasonably priced Romanian dishes on the main square (there's another branch in the Civic Centre). **$**

✕ Pizza Roma Str Apollonia Hirsher 2; ☎0268 470 011; ⊕ 10.00–midnight daily. Excellent thin-based pizzas. The same owners run the nearby Spaghetaria Venezia, which is also good. **$**

OTHER PRACTICALITIES

Bank
$ Raiffeisen Piaţa Sfatului 18; ⊕ 09.00–18.30 Mon–Fri, 10.00–14.00 Sat

Internet
▣ CyberCafé Str Republicii 58; m 0729 589 618; ⊕ 11.00–21.00 Mon–Fri, 12.30–21.00 Sat/Sun (Mar–Nov until 22.00). A great coffee shop with internet (*3RON/hr*). Staff always on hand to assist customers with all their needs (xerox, CD burner, card reader, colour printer, etc) & a large selection of hot & alcoholic drinks.

Mountain rescue
Salvamont Str Varga 23; ☎0-SALVAMONT (0-725826668 – the corresponding numbers on the phone's keypad)

Pharmacy
✚ Farma Plus Str Republicii 27; ☎0268 475 627; ⊕ 08.00–midnight Mon–Fri

Post office
✉ Str Nicolae Iorga 1; ☎0268 471 260; ⊕ 07.00–20.00 Mon–Fri, 08.00–13.00 Sat

WHAT TO SEE AND DO The Saxons built massive stone walls and seven bastions around the city that can still be seen today, as well as elaborately trimmed buildings, ornate churches and one of the finest central squares in the country. Located at the heart of old medieval Braşov and lined with beautiful red-roofed merchant houses, **Council Square** (Piaţa Sfatului), known to the Saxons as the Marktplatz, is a good place to rest and soak in the beautiful scenery. The vibrant pedestrian street **Strada Republicii** leads north from the square and is lined with terrace cafés and restaurants. In the centre of the square stands the Old Town Hall (1420), now home to Brasov's **History Museum** (*Piaţa Sfatului 30;* ☎ *0268472 363; www.istoriebv. ro;* ⊕ *Mar–Nov 10.00–18.00 Tue–Sun, Dec–Apr 09.00–17.00 Tue–Sun; admission* *adult/child 7/2RON*) while the southeast corner is dominated by the town's most famous landmark, the **Black Church**. In the centre of Piaţa Sfatului, the **Old Town Hall** (Casa Sfatului) was built in the 13th century. The house served as a meeting place for the town councillors, known then as centurions. Crowning the building is the Trumpeter's Tower, used during the Middle Ages as a watchtower to warn the citadel inhabitants of approaching danger. Just south of the main square is the **Black Church** (*Biserica Neagră, Curtea Johannes Honterus 2;* ✆ *0268 511 824;* ☉ *15 Jun–15 Sep 10.00–17.00 Mon–Sat, 16 Sep–14 Jun 10.00–15.30 Mon–Sat; admission adult/child 6/2RON; concerts Jun & Sep at 18.00 on Tue, 6RON, Jul/Aug at 18.00 on Tue, Thu, Sat 6RON*), the largest Gothic church in Romania and also boasting the largest church bell in the country, weighing in at seven tons. Its name derives from damage caused by the Great Fire of 1689, when flames and smoke blackened its walls. The interior houses one of the largest organs in eastern Europe, a 4,000-pipe organ dating from 1839. Instead of an ornate frescoed interior or walls hung with paintings, it is decorated with 119 antique Anatolian carpets donated by tradesmen over the centuries. Built between 1385 and 1477 on the site of an earlier church destroyed by Mongol invasions in 1242, the construction of the Marienkirche, as it was called in German, was hampered by extensive damage caused by Turkish raids in 1421. After the 1689 fire, restoration took almost 100 years.

From the time of the first Saxon settlers' arrival in the early 12th century, invading Mongols and Turks repeatedly attacked and destroyed the old settlements of Bartholoma and Corona. The Saxons had to build **defence fortifications** around their town. Most work was done between 1400 and 1650, when the outer and inner walls were erected, together with massive defence towers and gates. Part of the defensive wall, once 12m high, 2m thick and 3km long, can still be seen today, though most was taken down in the 19th century to make room for the city's expansion. Of the **original seven bastions**, several have survived, including the recently restored **Graft Bastion** (*Bastionul Graft, Aleea După Ziduri;* ☉ *10.00–17.00 daily; admission adult/child 7/2RON*), located in the middle of the citadel's northwest wing and showing displays of medieval artefacts. On the west side of the wall, walk along picturesque **Aleea După Ziduri** ('Behind the Walls' Street) to catch a glimpse of the 15th-century **White Tower** (*Turnul Alb, Aleea După Ziduri;* ☉ *10.00–18.00 Tue–Sun; admission adult/child 7/2RON*) with 200 steps up to a great view of the city, and **Black Tower** (*Turnul Negru, same as for Turnul Alb*), built in 1494 on a rock on Starja Hill. The Black Tower provides great photo opportunities to capture the Black Church. The **Blacksmiths' Bastion** (Bastionul Fierarilor), one of the original seven built and guarded by the city's guilds, is located at the southern end of Strada După Ziduri. The bastion hosts the **Braşov Archives**, including the oldest letter written in Romanian dating from 1521 by a merchant named Neascu. Follow the city wall southeast along Sirul Beethoven to the fairytale **Catherine's Gate** (Ecaterina Poarta). Built in 1559 and once the main entrance to medieval Kronstadt, it is the only original city gate to have survived intact to this day. Nearby is the Classicist **Schei Gate**, built in 1827–28 by Emperor Franz I, which was the entrance to the **Schei district** where during the 13th–17th centuries Romanians had to live as they were forbidden from owning property inside the city walls. Romanians could only use the Schei Gate and had to pay a toll to enter.

The **Weavers' Bastion** (*Bastionul Tesatorilor, Str George Cosbuc 9;* ✆ *0268 472 368;* ☉ *10.00–17.30 Tue–Sun; admission adult/child 7/1.50RON*) dates from 1522 and now hosts an exhibition of medieval weapons that can be visited on the way up to **Tâmpa Mountain** (Muntele Tâmpa), to the southeast of the centre. You can't miss Tâmpa as it is 'decorated' with gigantic white 'Braşov' lettering à la

'Hollywood'. It is possible to hike to the top of Tâmpa or take a cable car to the site where the original defensive fortress was built. When Vlad Ţepeş attacked Braşov in 1458–60, he destroyed the citadel and had 40 merchants impaled at the summit of the mountain. Walking to the top takes about an hour; follow the red triangles from the cable-car station or the yellow triangles from **Aleea Tiberiu Brediceanu**. The **cable car** (*Telecabina Tâmpa, Aleea Tiberiu Brediceanu;* \ *0268 478 657;* ⊕ *09.30–17.00 Tue–Fri, 09.30–19.00 Sat/Sun; price 15RON return*) carries 20 people a time up 320m on a 573m route. The Panoramic Restaurant (see page 134) is a great place for a meal with a view. Strategically located on a hill north of town beyond the Parc Central, **Braşov Fortress** (*Cetăţuia de pe Strajă, Dealul Cetăţii;* \ *0268 417 614;* ⊕ *11.00–midnight daily*) was part of Braşov's outer fortification system. Built in wood in 1524, it was replaced with a stone structure in the 16th century, only to be abandoned in the 17th century.

Dominating the Schei quarter, the **Saint Nicholas Orthodox Church** (*Biserica Sfântul Nicolae, Piaţa Unirii 1–2;* ⊕ *08.00–18.00 daily*) was first built in wood in 1392, replaced with a stone structure in 1495 and expanded in the 18th century. With a mix of Byzantine, Baroque and Gothic styles, it features a slender tower and four corner towers and is an architectural masterpiece. The interior features beautiful frescoes by Mişu Pop.

Braşov has many important religious buildings including the **Franciscan Monastery** (*Mănăstirea Franciscanilor, Str Sfântu Ioan 7*), built by the Lutherans in 1725; the **Romanian Orthodox Church** (*Catedrala Ortodoxă Adormirea Maicii Domnului, Piaţa Sfatului 3*), built in a Byzantine style in 1896; **Saint Bartholomew's Church** (*Biserica Sfântul Bartolomeu, Str Lunga 247*), the oldest monument in town dating from 1223; and, on Citadel Hill stands **Saint Martin's Church** (*Biserica Sfântul Martin, Str Dealul de Jos 12*), with its present form dating from 1792.

Jews have lived in Braşov since 1807, when Rabbi Aaron Ben Jehuda was given permission to live in the city, a privilege until then granted only to Saxons. The Jewish community of Braşov was officially founded 19 years later, followed by the first Jewish school in 1864 and the construction of the **synagogue** (*Str Poarta Schei 27;* ⊕ *10.00–16.00 Mon–Fri; admission 5RON*) in 1899, with Art Nouveau elements added to the façade 16 years later. The Jewish population of Braşov expanded rapidly to 1,280 people in 1910 and 4,000 in 1940. Today, the community has about 230 members, after many families emigrated to Israel between World War II and 1989. The **Art Museum** (*Muzeul de Arta, Bd Eroilor 21A;* \ *0268 477 286; www.muzeulartabv.ro;* ⊕ *Apr–Sep 10.00–18.00 Tue–Sun, Oct–Mar 09.00–17.00 Tue–Sun; admission adult/child 4/1RON*) features a national gallery of canvases with anonymous Transylvanian painters of the 18th century, up to the who's who of Romanian 20th-century artists, including Theodor Pallady, Nicolae Grigorescu, Stefan Luchian and Horia Bernea. The **Ethnographic Museum** (*Muzeul de Etnografie, Bd Eroilor 21A;* \ *0268 476 243;* ℮ *muzeul@etnobrasov.ro; www.etnobrasov.ro;* ⊕ *Mar–Nov 10.00–18.00 Tue–Sun, Dec–Apr 09.00–17.00 Tue–Sun; admission adult/child 5/1.5RON*) is dedicated to folk art, costumes and crafts from southeast Transylvania. It has two more exhibition sites at Săcele and Rupea.

Opera, ballet and music

📺 **Arlechino Puppet Theatre** (Teatrul de Papusi Arlechino) Str Apollonia Hirscher 10; \0268 475 243; www.teatrularlechino.ro

📺 **Brasov Opera** Str Bisericii Române 51; \0268 415 990; www.opera-brasov.ro

📺 **Brasov Philharmonic** (Filarmonica Braşov) Str Apollonia Hircher 10; \0268 473 058; www.filarmonicabrasov.ro

If you are heading for Transylvania by **hire car** from Bucharest airport, it is really not worth the angst of heading south into Bucharest; the traffic is terrible, the roads are tricky to negotiate and it is very time consuming – you can't just pop in and out. It is better to turn right out of Otopeni or Băneasa and get straight onto the E60/ route 1 heading north towards Ploiești. The drive to Brașov is 173km and could take as long as three hours. If you are taking the **train**, you will have to go into Bucharest by bus and then find the Gară de Nord railway station (see *Chapter 2*, *Getting there and away*, page 58 and *Getting around*, page 76). Trains are better than buses and minibuses but a hire car is best and really worth the expense as you can explore many hidden treasures not covered by public transport services. If you need a break *en route* to Brașov, here are some suggestions.

LACUL SNAGOV The lake is situated 20km north of Otopeni Airport on E60/route 1 towards Ploiești; turn right and it's at Ciolpani (signposted for Lacul Snagov). Delightful and peaceful, the lake has a surface area of 5.75km² and is surrounded by holiday homes and beaches. According to legend Vlad III the Impaler, the inspiration for Bram Stoker's *Dracula*, was buried in the crypt in Snagov Monastery on an island accessible only by boat. A wooden church was built by Mircea cel Bătrân in the 11th century and replaced 400 years later by a stone monastery which sank into the lake. Vlad the Impaler liked the site and built fortifications around the monastery in 1456. Vlad was allegedly murdered nearby and his head chopped off and sent to Istanbul as a trophy. In 1935, the grave was exhumed and a decapitated body found, giving credibility to the rumour that it was indeed Dracula. However, in the entertaining Dracula-chasing novel *The Historian*, Elizabeth Kostova writes that the body found after exhumation still had its head on and couldn't have been Dracula, thereby serving her narrative that Dracula was still alive.

PRAHOVA VALLEY The Prahova Valley (Valea Prahovei) follows the Prahova River between the Bucegi and Baiului mountains, part of the Carpathians, about 100km north of Bucharest. Geographically, the Prahova River separates the Eastern Carpathians from the Southern range and, historically, the valley was an important passageway between the principalities of Wallachia and Transylvania. The E60/ route 1 highway leads right through the valley on a scenic journey after the flat, dull plains between Bucharest and Ploiești. The road clings to the side of a steep hillside and it may be your first, terrifying encounter with Romanian drivers who view motoring as an extreme sport. The winter mountain resorts of Sinaia, Bușteni and Azuga are in Prahova Valley, and in Prahova County, south of the Transylvanian border. When you reach the resort of Predeal, you cross imperceptibly into Brașov County and the start of Transylvania.

Prahova Valley is also the name of a leading Romanian wine brand, launched onto the UK market in October 2000 by leading UK agent Halewood International. Blending New-World style with Old-World traditions, Prahova Valley combines the best of both with its modern approach to winemaking coupled with top-quality grapes from prime vineyard sites. The range includes Chardonnay, Pinot Noir, Cabernet Sauvignon and Merlot, which sell for around £3.49. There is also a Reserve range which focuses on red varieties: Pinot Noir, Merlot, Cabernet Sauvignon and Fetească Neagră.

Sinaia Known as the 'Pearl of the Carpathians', the **winter resort** of Sinaia is located in the Prahova Valley, in the Bucegi Mountains. Sinaia has a sub-alpine climate with

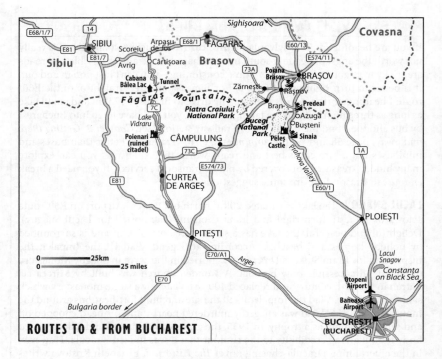

ROUTES TO & FROM BUCHAREST

an average January temperature of +4°C and an average snow depth of 50cm. Cable cars sway up the mountains to the pistes. The early December snow usually lasts until April and the region has some of the best ski slopes in the country at an altitude of 2,000m. Sinaia takes its name from the 17th-century monastery built here by a Romanian nobleman after undertaking a pilgrimage to Mount Sinai, Egypt. Sinaia was first mentioned as a mountain resort in 1869, when the first hotel was constructed. In 1873, King Carol I of Romania built Peleş Castle on a hillside above the town and used it as a royal summer residence. Before World War II and the abdication of the royal family, Sinaia was a summer retreat for Romania's aristocracy.

Sinaia is 121km north of Bucharest. To get to Sinaia and the castles of Peleş and Pelişor (see below) by **car** follow the E60 route 2 44km south of Braşov. By **train** on the Bucharest–Oradea route, the journey time from Gară de Nord is one hour 40 minutes. Sinaia's railway station is an amazing building, like a huge piece of beige-and-white wedding cake.

Peleş and Pelişor castles (*http://peles.ro;* ⊕ *Winter 11.00–17.00 Wed, 09.00– 17.00 Thu–Sun, summer (Peleş) 11.00–17.00 Tue, 09.00–17.00 Wed–Sun, (Pelişor) 11.00–19.00 Thu, 09.00–17.00 Fri–Sun; admission adult/child 20/5RON, groups are 20–35 people for Peleş, 10–20 for Pelişor*) A lovely tree-lined road leads to the fairytale **Peleş Castle** (Castelul Peleş). Located above Sinaia, the palace was built in 1875 by King Carol I as his royal summer palace. It was the first castle in Europe to feature electric lighting, an electric lift, and central heating in all 170 rooms. The electric current was generated by the castle's own electrical plant, located by the Peleş creek. Peleş Castle's interior was decorated by Carol's wife Elisabeta, who was also a novelist with the pen name Carmen Sylva. The castle's exterior is quite striking with a mock-Tudor half-timbered effect beneath spiky towers. Ceauşescu liked to stay in the castle's little sister, **Pelişor** (Castelul Peleşor), 100m uphill. English-born Queen Marie of Romania (1865–1938) decorated the interior in an Art Nouveau style and later died at Pelişor (see box, page 142). The exterior also features the half-timbered style but the turrets are distinctly Transylvanian and chunky. Both palaces can be visited on guided tours. The **Foişor Park** above Pelişor can also be visited (⊕ *09.00–16.00 Wed–Sun*) although the castle cannot. Peleş and Pelişor have been turned into museums with their interiors sensitively preserved.

Bucegi Natural Park The Bucegi Mountains loom over Sinaia as giant rocky peaks. The highest peak, **Omu**, reaches 2,505m. They are part of the Southern Carpathian group of the Carpathian Mountains. The Bucegi Mountains owe their reputation to the spectacular landscapes and the accessibility of their routes. Well known for hiking, winter sports and climbing, these mountains are high compact blocks, edged by steep slopes, which dominate the Prahova Valley and resorts of Sinaia, Buşteni, Azuga and Predeal. At a higher elevation is the Bucegi Plateau, where wind and rain have turned the rocks into spectacular figures such as Sfinxul (sphinx), a rock with a human face and enigmatic smile, and Babele (the old ladies). Visit the Centre for Mountain Ecology (see page 54) for local tours. By **car** travel via the E60/route 1 and resorts of Sinaia, Buşteni, Azuga and Moieciu de Sus from the west (see *Fundata*, page 142).

Buşteni and Azuga Situated in the Prahova Valley, 37km south of Braşov and 6km north of Sinaia on the E60/Route 1, at an 880m altitude, **Buşteni health resort** is a popular destination. Dominated by the impressive peaks of Caraiman (2,384m) and Costila (2,489m) and lying next to the Prahova River, Buşteni is a picturesque place to stop for a breather *en route* to Transylvania. Buşteni is a crowded, bustling tourist centre filled with houses that wouldn't look out of place in *The Addams Family*. A cable car climbs from the Hotel Silva to Cabana Babele (*www.babele. ro*) on the top of the Bucegi range at 2,206m. A second cable car from the top of Caraiman links Buşteni with the Peştera Hotel and an unusual monastery in a cave.

Azuga is a few kilometres further north along the E60/route 1 and sits at an elevation of 1,110m at the foot of the Bucegi Mountains. Sorica, the longest ski run in Romania, is here and is accessible by chairlift. On top of the Caraiman Massif, visitors will spot the 40m-tall steel memorial cross erected between 1926 and 1928, in honour of the country's World War I heroes. The road through Azuga is lined with stalls selling baskets, towels and all manner of gift and souvenir ideas.

ENTERING BRAŞOV COUNTY AND TRANSYLVANIA

PREDEAL SKI RESORT Continuing along the E60 from Sinaia, Buşteni and Azuga, we enter Braşov County and the beginning of Transylvania at Predeal, the northernmost resort in the Prahova Valley, 25km south of Braşov and 16km north of Sinaia. Predeal (Predeál/Schanzpass) is the highest town in Romania at an elevation of 1,033m. It is surrounded by five massifs – Postăvarul, Piatra Mare, Bucegi, Baiului and Fitifoi – and is a good base for mountain hikes and skiing down the Clabucet and Cioplea slopes. The name comes from the Romanian *pre deal* meaning 'on the hill'.

Tourist information
☑ **Predeal Tourist Information Centre** Str
Intrarea Gării 1; ☏0268 455 330; ⊕ 08.00–16.00
Mon–Fri, 09.00–14.00 Sat/Sun

⌂ Where to stay, eat and drink

⌂ **Predeal Comfort Suites** (16 sgl, 4 dbl, 16 apts) Str Trei Brazi 33; ☎ 0268 455 795; e office@ predeal-hotel.ro; www.predeal-hotel.ro. A new, luxury complex overlooking the town, with a spa, sauna, gym & conference rooms. The Le Cedre restaurant (**$$$$**) serves excellent Romanian & Lebanese dishes. **$$$$$**

⌂ **Vila Vitalis** (12 dbl) Str Unirii 7; ☎/f 0268 457 019; e vitalis.ro@gmail.com; www.vilavitalis.ro. 2 rooms have balconies. **$$$**

⌂ **Vila Andra** (12 dbl) Str Libertăţii 39; m 0722 425 330; e rezervare@vilele-andra-predeal.ro; www.vilele-andra-predeal.ro. A large family house with clean rooms & terraces offering a fantastic view. **$**

RÂŞNOV From Predeal, drivers can either continue on the E60/route 1 towards Săcele and Braşov or turn left onto the 73A road through the mountains towards Râşnov and Bran Castle. This is a lovely winding drive ascending an aromatic pine-and-birch-covered mountain with a clutch of good hotels before descending to the flat plains around Râşnov where your journey will probably be interrupted by cows, wild horses and flocks of sheep meandering across the road. The only low point is the profusion of litter along the way. You can also take a **bus** from Braşov, from the bus stop in front of the railway station or from Autogară No 2. By **car**, it's 14km southwest of Braşov on the E574/route 73 towards Piteşti.

The hilltop fortress in Râşnov (Barcarozsnyó/Rosenau) was built as a refuge by Saxon settlers in the Middle Ages, to protect themselves against frequent raids by Tatars and Turks. The citadel was built around the year 1215 by Teutonic Knights and was conquered only once in its history, in 1600 by Gabriel Báthory. The **fortress** (☎ 0268 230 255; ☉ 09.00–18.00 *daily; admission adult/child 10/5RON*) sits on a rocky outcrop overlooking the town and there is a Hollywood-style 'Râşnov' sign similar to that in Braşov and also in Deva. Visitors will see a 143m-deep well. A legend tells of how, during a particularly long siege of the fortress, the citizens of Râşnov were concerned about the lack of available fresh drinking water. Two captured Turkish soldiers were ordered to dig a well in the centre of the fortress. The two men were assured that they would be given their freedom once the well was completed. It took them 32 years to finish digging and the cruel locals didn't keep their promise and killed them once they'd finished.

BRAN Saxons built **Bran Castle** (Castelul Bran/Törcsvár/Törzburg) on a cliff above the plains in 1377 to protect the gateway to Transylvania at the Bran Pass. The imposing construction with its solid, squared-off walls and reddish-brown roofs looks like a typical Transylvanian castle and it attracts a huge number of tourists who often come for the Dracula link. It is promoted as Dracula's Castle, but Vlad III Ţepeş, the real person behind the Dracula myth, spent only a few nights at the castle, probably when he was imprisoned by the royal Hunyadi family. The Gothic portals, narrow staircases carved into the stone, secret stairs and passageways, vaulted halls and arches make Bran an atmospheric and impressive destination. In the 1920s, Bran became home to Queen Marie of Romania (1875–1938) and she decorated the interior, importing much of the furniture from western Europe. The castle is now a **museum** (☎ 0268 238 333; *www.bran-castle.com*; ☉ *summer 12.00–18.00 Mon, 09.00–18.00 Tue–Sun, winter 12.00–16.00 Mon, 09.00–16.00 Tue–Sun; admission adult/child 25/5RON*) showing period furniture, carpets and a collection of weapons. In the grounds, an **ethnological museum** (same ticket as for museum) displays the way of life and architecture of the surrounding area. Beneath the castle is a vast collection of stalls selling mainly Dracula tat – T-shirts, mugs and jigsaws – in a heady ambience of candyfloss and burgers. Bran town is almost entirely made

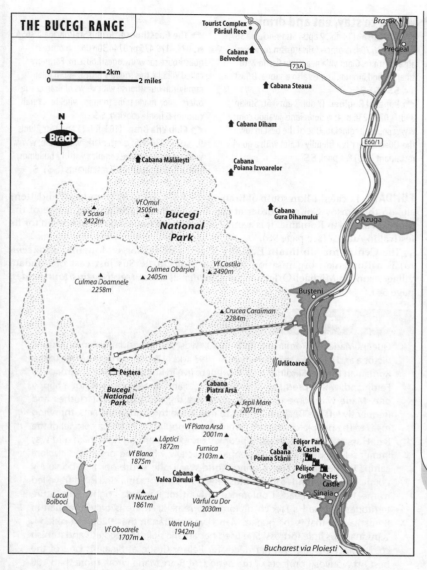

THE BUCEGI RANGE

0 ▬▬▬ 2km
0 ▬▬▬▬ 2 miles

N

Bradt

Brașov

Predeal

Tourist Complex
Pârâul Rece

Cabana
Belvedere

73A

♦ Cabana Steaua

E60/1

♦ Cabana Diham

Cabana
Poiana Izvoarelor

♦ Cabana Mălăiești

Cabana
Gura Dihamului

Azuga

Vf Omul
2505m

*Bucegi
National
Park*

V Scara
2422m

Culmea Obârșiei
▲ 2405m

Vf Costila
▲ 2490m

Culmea Doamnele
2258m

Bușteni

▲ Crucea Caraiman
2284m

*Bucegi
National
Park*

♦ Urlătoarea

⌂ Peștera

Cabana
Piatra Arsă

▲ Jepii Mare
2071m

Vf Piatra Arsă
2001m ▲

▲ Lăptici
1872m

Furnica
2103m ▲

Foișor Park
& Castle

Vf Blana
1875m

Cabana
Poiana Stânii

Pelișor
Castle

Peleș
Castle

Cabana
Valea Darului

Sinaia

*Lacul
Bolboci*

Vf Nucetul
1861m

Vârful cu Dor
2030m

Vf Oboarele
1707m ▲

Vânt Urișul
1942m
▲

Bucharest via Ploiești ↘

up of pensions and families letting out part of their homes to visitors. (See box, *Chapter 2, Bran Castle – Transylvania's hottest property*, page 118, for the latest Bran Castle news.)

Get there via **bus** from Brașov Railway Station, or by **car** on the E574/route 73, 25km southwest of Brașov.

Tourist information

Ⓩ Antrec Str Principală 509; ☏ 0268 236 340; www.antrec.ro; ⏱ 09.00–17.00 Mon–Fri, 09.00–13.00 Sat

Where to stay, eat and drink

Vila Alisa (14 dbl, 2 apts) Str Principală 387; 0268 236 704; e office@alisaturism.ro; www. alisaturism.ro. Giant villa near Bran Castle with smart, wood interior. There's also a sauna. B/fast inc. **$$–$$$**

Popasul Reginei (7 dbl, 3 apts) Str Stoian 398; 0268 236 834; e dobreianis@yahoo.com; www.popasulreginei.ro. One of the best in town, the 'Queen's Rest' is a friendly chalet with a good restaurant (**$$**) & a pool. **$$**

The Guesthouse (6 dbl) Str Principală 365A; m 0745 179 475 or 0744 306 062; e office@ guesthouse.ro; www.guesthouse.ro. Formerly called Villa Jo, this friendly British–Romanian family-run guesthouse with views of Bran Castle offers tailor-made tours (nature, wildlife & rural culture) & home cooking. **$$**

Club Vila Bran (103 dbl, 11 apts) Str Alunis 9; 0268 236 866; e rezervari@vilabran.ro; www. vilabran.ro. A massive complex with 12 buildings, cheap & clean rooms & 2 restaurants (**$$**). **$**

FUNDATA Located 14km south of Bran on the E574, Fundata (Fundáta/Fundatten) sits on the Braşov County border at the Giuvala Pass (1,290m) and is one of the highest villages in Romania. It is a small collection of houses but best known for its festival in August (see page 98).

The **Centre for Mountain Ecology** (Centru de Ecologie Montană; *www.cem. ro*) is a Romanian organisation based in Moieciu de Sus just east of Fundata village, run by Michael Orleanu (*see Chapter 2, Local travel agents/tour guides*, page 54).

QUEEN MARIE OF ROMANIA

Queen Marie of Romania (1875–1938) was the granddaughter of Queen Victoria and caused a scandal when, in 1893 aged 17, she married the heir to the Romanian throne, Ferdinand I, and went to live in Romania. Marie's marriage to Ferdinand, which produced three daughters and three sons, was not a happy one. Marie was something of a rebel, she dressed in peasant clothes and frequently left the Bucharest court to ride alone through the streets, throwing roses to the people during the carnival and appointing herself a colonel of the Red Hussars. She was an early 'people's princess', learning Romanian and was immensely popular with the people, especially when she organised cholera camps in the Balkan war. During World War I, she wrote her first book, *My Country*, to raise funds for the British Red Cross in Romania. She even travelled to the 1919 Paris Peace Conference to fight for Romania's rights and future territories. This led a French diplomat to remark, 'There is only one man in Romania and that is the queen.' Marie lived at Bran in the 1920s and called it 'a pugnacious little fortress'. She used her artistic skills to decorate and furnish cold, empty castles, and her décor for Pelişor Castle at Sinaia is one of the best Art Nouveau projects of the period. At Bran, Marie wrote more than 100 diaries, an autobiography and 15 books for adults and children, including the enchanting fairy tale *The Lost Princess* (see page 285). Marie died in a strange event, worthy of one of her tales. Her two sons, Carol and Nicholas, argued over Carol's mistress, Magda Lupescu, and they settled the quarrel with a duel. Marie was hurt in an attempt to intervene in the duel and she died from her injuries at Pelişor Castle. Marie's body is buried at Curtea de Argeş on the Transfăgăraşan Highway. Her heart was entombed in a gold casket at Bran for many years, but it is now in the National History Museum in Bucharest. The box in which the casket was placed can still be seen at Bran.

ZĂRNEŞTI   To reach Zărneşti (Zernest/Molkendorf), **from Fundata**, turn left and continue for about 8km. By **car from Braşov**, follow the signs to Piteşti. When you arrive in Râşnov, 15km away from Braşov, there is a sign for Zărneşti. Turn right and after about 8km along a lovely country road, you reach Zărneşti. By **bus from Braşov**, 18 buses leave daily from the Autogară West, journey time one hour.

Zărneşti – a long winding town that seems to stretch for many kilometres – is an unprepossessing sort of town but it is fast becoming an important and popular stop on any ecotourist's agenda owing to the efforts of one man. Danuţ 'Dan' Marin was the joint winner of *Wanderlust's* Paul Morrison Guide of the Year 2007, a richly deserved award for his efforts, together with his wife Luminiţa, to promote the local natural attributes as well as working for the community. Together, Dan and Luminiţa run a guesthouse called Transylvanian Wolf (see below for contact details), which they bought in 2003. The spacious rooms have log-burning ceramic stoves and modern bathrooms. A visit to their Zărneşti home gives a thoroughly satisfying glimpse into the society, nature, culture, history and legends of the region. Dan is an extremely knowledgeable host and guide, and, after a fantastic breakfast, leads walking tours of the surrounding region, including the Piatra Craiului National Park, the village of Vulcan and the difficult-to-reach village of Măgura. He is informative on the flora and fauna and reads animal footprints, follows shepherds' trails, spots distant soaring birds and recounts myths and legends for the guests. Dan can also arrange bear-watching trips to one of the hides in the area. He also speaks impeccable accent-free English, which is amazing considering he is entirely self-taught from a book, as well as French. Dan's charming and hospitable wife, Luminiţa, prepares delicious Romanian, Transylvanian and Roma dishes, lighter Western-style dishes and caters for special dietary needs. She also gives classes in the art of local cuisine and brews all manner of healing herbal teas. A recipe for her delicious elderberry jam is on page 88. On a walk with Dan, visitors can meet a shepherd in his isolated mountain hut and assist with the cheese making, a tradition now under threat from the EU bureaucrats. Groups of eight can take part in a special Roma music and dance evening, meet the *bulibasha* (Roma leader) and gain a real understanding of their way of life and culture, beyond the usual tourist-trip stereotypes. This is a genuine highlight of any visit to Transylvania, whether in search of culture, food or wildlife. Read Dan's account of Transylvanian wildlife on page 11.

Tour operator

Carpathian Tours   In the village of Măgura, run by Hermann & Katharina Kurmes, a German–Romanian couple, a geologist & a botanist. Their chalet (see below) in the isolated village of Măgura is very comfortable & 25% of the accommodation price is donated to local ecology projects & the setting up of the Bucegi Natural Park.

Where to stay, eat and drink

🏠 **Vila Hermani**   (12 dbl) Sat Măgura 130, 507133 Moieciu; m 0745 512 096; www.cntours.ro. Hermann is a Transylvanian Saxon, born in 1954 in the village of Vulcan near Braşov. In 1977, he emigrated to Germany. In the 1990s, he returned to his homeland with his wife Katharina & their children. In 2004, they opened Vila Hermani offering rooms with en-suite facilities, wildlife & birdwatching, cross-country skiing, snowshoe rental, rides on horse-drawn carriages & sleighs. To get there by car, follow directions for Zărneşti, then drive in the direction of Gura Râului & Prăpastie to a forest road, which you follow along a winding road to Măgura. If you arrive by train or plane, there is a pick-up service from Braşov. **$$$$**

🏠 **Transylvanian Wolf**   (4 dbl) Str Mitropolit Ioan Metianu nr 108, Zărneşti 505800, jud Braşov; m 0744 319 708; e transylvanian_wolf@yahoo.

co.uk; www.transylvanianwolf.ro. Dbl **$$**, b/fast inc, or dbl **$$$** b/fast, packed lunch & fabulous

traditional dinner. Sgl room supplement +€10. See above for further information.

PIATRA CRAIULUI NATIONAL PARK Piatra Craiului (King's Stone) is one of the country's most popular mountains especially with hikers and nature lovers. It is a beautiful limestone ridge, about 25km long, from where you have superb views over the surrounding country. The shimmering huge white limestone ridge can be seen from far away and has the largest biodiversity in the country. The wildlife is very diverse with chamois on the high cliffs and brown bear, wild boar, red and roe deer, foxes, wolves, pine martens, red squirrels and even lynx in the mixed (coniferous and deciduous) forests. Because of the limestone and traditional farming activities there is an abundance and variety of wild flowers, especially orchids. The gorges are a good place to see wallcreepers and alpine swifts, also three-toed and white-backed woodpeckers and Ural owls in the forested parts. There is even a pair of black storks nesting close to the visitors' centre.

In 1938, when the natural reserve was set up, it was only on a 440ha site. This territory increased in 1972 to 900ha and now the core conservation area (core area) covers 4,879ha and the buffer zone stretches on for a further 9,894ha. The Piatra Craiului National Park stretches over the counties of Braşov and Argeş, including the towns of Zărneşti, Moieciu, Măgura, Peştera, Bran, Rucar and Dâmbovicioara. The park is best reached from Zărneşti heading north across a wide plain where visitors will come across the visitors' centre, built in an organic shape like a mountain and with traditional black shingles covering the roof. At the time of writing, the centre had not yet opened. The park has six shelters to be used in case of bad weather or ill health. They are Diana (formerly 'Consomol', 1,480m), Şpirlea (1,410m), Ascuţit (2,156m), Şaua Grindului (1,610m), Şaua Funduri (1,951m) and Curmătura (1,440m).

To reach Piatra Craiului follow details for Zărneşti (above), then head west out of town. The park is a one-hour walk from Zărneşti, which is a good place to hitch a ride with a car or a local's horse and cart.

Information

⛑ Park Administration Str Toplitei 150, Zărneşti; ☎0268 223 165; e office@pcrai.ro; www.pcrai.ro

⛑ Zărneşti Mountain Rescue Team Str Metropolit Ion Meţianu 17; m 0725 826 668
⛑ Zărneşti Police ☎0268 220 810

FROM ZĂRNEŞTI TO FĂGĂRAŞ The road from Zărneşti heading northwest towards Făgăraş follows the most glorious route (73A), one of my personal favourite drives (see box, page 82). In the picturesque valley is the village of **Şinca Nouă**, where it is possible to stay and ride horses at Christoph Promberger's modern guesthouse and stables (see below).

 Where to stay

⌂ Equus Silvania (9 dbl) Contact Christoph Promberger, Şinca Nouă 507210, jud Braşov; ☎0268 228 601; e christoph@equus-silvania. com; www.equus-silvania.com. With their own stables in idyllic, pastoral surroundings, 28 horses

& 3 ponies, guests are welcome all year round for riding, trekking, bear-spotting tours or guided 6-day riding tours through the Carpathian foothills. **$$**

FĂGĂRAŞ From Zărneşti, hire-car drivers will count themselves very fortunate as it's possible to take one of the loveliest, most deserted scenic routes in Transylvania and drive north via Poiana Mărului and Şinca Veche to link up with the E68 Braşov–Sibiu highway at Sércaia and turn left for Făgăraş. Făgăraş (Fogaras/Fogarasch) lies on the Olt River, 72km west of Braşov. By **car** on E68/route 1 Braşov to Sibiu road, 60km west of Braşov, it's a journey time of 1½ hours. By **bus**, microbuses depart from Casa de Cultura and the station for Braşov and Sibiu, tickets 15RON, journey time one hour. From Braşov, 11 **trains** depart daily for Făgăraş, journey time 1–1½ hours. Although the city has become almost totally Romanian after Saxon and Hungarian emigration, the diverse background is still obvious. The name is supposed to have come from the Romanian word for beech (*fag*). Another source of the name could be from the Hungarian *fa* (wood) and *garas* (farthing, cent), with a legend telling how money made of wood was used to pay the peasants who built the fortress around 1310. During the rule of Transylvanian prince Gábor Bethlen (1613–29), the city became an economic role model city in the southern regions of the realm. Bethlen rebuilt the fortress. Făgăraş was the site of several Transylvanian Diets, mostly during the reign of Prince Michael I Apafi (1632–90). In the 20th century, the fortress was used as a stronghold by the communist regime. During the 1950s, it was a prison for dissidents. Since 1989, the castle has been restored and is currently used as a **museum and library** (*Valeriu Literat Făgăraş;* \ *0268 211 862;* ☉ *Jun–Sep 08.00–18.00 Tue–Fri, 08.00–16.00 Sat/Sun, Oct–May 08.00–18.00 Tue–Sun; admission 5RON*), which shows local history and sculptures by local artist Virgil Fulicea.

Făgăraş Fortress is the most impressive monument of the town, and the core around which the town was actually built. The citadel was ranked among the strongest in Transylvania, standing in the way of Turkish and Tatar invasions. Its massive walls, towers and tall roofs are arranged in the shape of a trapezium with four corners guarded by four large bastions. For the Transfăgăraşan Highway and Făgăraş Mountains see the Sibiu County chapter, page 216.

HĂLMEAG Located 12km northeast of Făgăraş, Hălmeag (Sarkány)/Schirkanyen) is the largest Lippizaner stud in Romania, with 45 horses and foals. Visitors can ride the horses over 1,800km² of unrestricted country with no fences or paved roads. Riders will meet shepherds herding goats, sheep, cows and buffalo.

To reach Hălmeag by **bus**, see Făgăraş, alight at Şercaia, 15km east of Făgăraş, but then there's a 4km walk north. By **car**, turn off the E68/route 1 at Şercaia and head north.

BRÂNCOVEANU MONASTERY AT SÂMBĂTA DE SUS Situated 21km southwest of Făgăraş is the elegant Brâncoveanu Monastery (Manastirea Brâncoveanu), built in 1696 to the orders of Romanian prince Constantin Brâncoveanu (1688–1714). The monastery was constructed from bricks and stone with a door carved from oak. The interior was decorated with icons painted on glass and wood and the ceiling was adorned with neo-Byzantine fresco paintings. The **museum** now contains one of the richest collections of 18th- and 19th-century paintings on glass, icons painted on wood, priestly and bishops' vestments, and a unique collection of old books, parchments, letters and religious objects.

SAXON FORTIFIED CHURCHES ON THE WAY TO BRAŞOV
Cristian (Kereszténfalva/Neustadt) (*Contact Erhard Porr; Bd Piaţa Libertăţii 14;* \ *0268 257 191*) This early **Gothic basilica** was built in the late 13th century. It has a massive bell tower in the western part of the edifice, defended by a horseshoe-shaped bastion. It also had a moat, like those in Prejmer and Hărman. There is

another village called Cristian (Grossau) with a fortified church near Sibiu (see page 204).

Cristian is located 8km southwest of Braşov. By **car**, follow the E574 from Braşov towards Râşnov; **microbuses** leave every hour from Autogară West for Cristian, journey time 15 minutes.

Codlea (*Contact Klaus Untch;* m *0744 127 047*) Situated right in the centre of the town, the fortress in Codlea (Feketehalom/Zeiden) contains storerooms surrounding a Romanesque church built in the early 13th century. In the 15th century, the church was transformed into a Gothic hall-type church with a neo-Gothic altarpiece by Johann Bartel from Braşov dating from 1904.

Codlea is on the E68/route 1 from Braşov to Sibiu, 12km west of Braşov. Dozens of **microbuses** (from Autogară West) and **trains** (from main railway station) leave Braşov daily. Buses take 18 minutes, trains take 15–33 minutes, depending on type.

Ghimbav (*Contact Klaus Untch;* m *0744 127 047*) An early Gothic basilica was constructed during the 13th century in Ghimbav (Vidombák/ Weidenbach). The late Romanesque bell tower is in the west of the church, surrounded by a polygonal precinct. Most of the storerooms have been demolished. The Classicist altarpiece was created in 1848 by Heinrich Pop from Braşov. Ghimbav is halfway between Braşov and Codlea.

Vulcan (*Contact Daniel Klaus; Str Principală 3;* \ *0268 256 477*) In Vulcan (Szászvolkány/Wolkendorf), only the chancel arch has been preserved from the original 13th-century church. The bell tower was built between 1793 and 1794. The storerooms can still be seen inside the fortifications.

To reach Vulcan, take the E574 heading southwest out of Braşov towards Râşnov and turn right at Cristian. There is no bus service to Vulcan. **Microbuses** leave on the hour every hour from Autogară West for Cristian, journey time 15 minutes. Then it's 5km further west.

POIANA BRAŞOV Located at an altitude of 1,030m at the foot of Mount Postăvarul, Poiana Braşov (*www.poiana-brasov.com*) is accessible via **bus** No 20 from Braşov's Livada Postei bus station. By **car**, drive for 12km (*15mins*) heading southwest on route DN1 out of Braşov. The town is the best-equipped **ski resort** in the country with excellent ski slopes, mainly for beginners and intermediates. The ski area

POIANA SLOPES

Piste (pârtia) name	Difficulty	Length	Height
Camelia	beginner	450m	30m
Pine Tree (Bradul)	beginner	458m	77m
Red Way (Drumul Rosu)	beginner	3,821m	630m
Stadion	beginner	300m	32m
Kanzel 1, 2	intermediate	350m	134m
Slalom Poiana	intermediate	575m	217m
Sulinar	intermediate	2441m	645m
CableCar (Sub teleferic)	advanced	1,000m	300m
Ruia 1, 2	advanced	540m	200m
Wolf (Lupului)	advanced	2,860m	775m

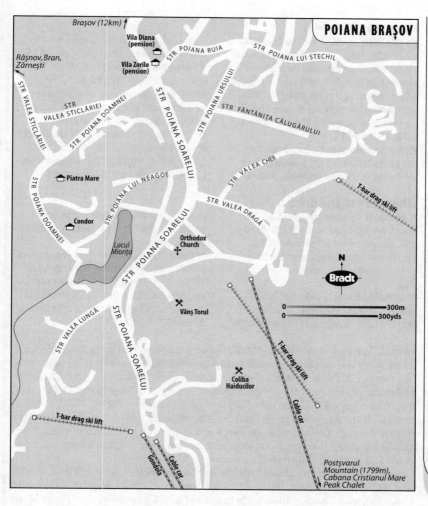

Brașov (12km) ↑

Vila Diana (pension)

Str Poiana Ruia

Str Poiana Lui Stechil

Râșnov, Bran, Zărnești

Vila Zorile (pension)

Str Poiana Ursului

Str Valea Sticlăriei

Str Poiana Doamnei

Str Valea Sticlăriei

Str Poiana Soarelui

Str Fântânița Călugărului

Piatra Mare

Str Poiana Lui Neagoe

Str Valea Chei

Str Poiana Doamnei

Condor

Str Poiana Soarelui

Str Valea Dragă

T-bar drag ski lift

Lacul Miorița

Orthodox Church

N

Bradt

Vânș Torul

0 — 300m
0 — 300yds

Str Valea Lungă

Str Poiana Soarelui

T-bar drag ski lift

Coliba Haiducilor

Cable car

T-bar drag ski lift

Gondola

Cable car

Postșvarul Mountain (1799m), Cabana Cristianul Mare Peak Chalet

offers easy progression to the main pistes with the added advantage of skiing back to the village on a long blue run. For non-skiers there is a great range of activities and excursions available including horseriding, archery, climbing and paragliding. The early December snow usually lasts until April.

The first chalet was built on Mount Postăvarul in 1883 and Romania's first ski competition was held here in 1906. The winter resort has many sports facilities (12 pistes, two cable cars, one gondola and eight drag lifts) as well as numerous hotels (from two to four star), and pensions. The resort is an excellent destination for families with young children, who can learn to ski on the gentle nursery Bradul slope with instruction in either English or German. Beginners soon progress onto the main ski area and, by the end of the week, most will be skiing all the way back to the village on the long, confidence-building blue run from the top of Christianul Mare. Advanced skiers will also find some challenges at Poiana Brașov. The Lupului (Wolf) black run is almost 3km long with an 800m altitude difference. Other, gentler slopes are ideal for mastering the basics of snowboarding.

🏠 Where to stay

🏠 **Vila Zorile** (6 dbl, 11 apts) Str Poiana Ruia 6; ☎0268 262 286; e office@vila-zorile.ro; www. vila-zorile.ro. Situated near Vila Diana & boasting a Hansel & Gretel-style wooden exterior. Jude Law & Nicole Kidman were guests during the filming of *Cold Mountain*. Vila Zorile was also voted one of the top 66 hotels in the country. With a day bar, b/fast hall & sauna. **$$$$$**

🏠 **Hotel Condor** (21 dbl, 2 apts) Zona hotel Piatra Mare; ☎0268 262 121; e gabriela.rusu@ hotelcondor.ro; www.hotelcondor.ro. A smart

4-star hotel in the centre of the resort near the lake, with spacious rooms, sauna & gym. **$$$$**

🏠 **Hotel Piatra Mare** (11 sgl, 136 dbl, 38 suites, 1 penthouse) Poiana Brașov; ☎0268 262 170; e office@piatramare.ro; www.piatramare. ro. Gigantic hotel with luxurious rooms, jacuzzi, sauna, pool & gym. With 3 restaurants: Emerald, Crystal & Topaz ($$$) & a non-stop bar. **$$$$**

🏠 **Vila Diana** (8 dbl, 1 apt) Str Poiana Ruia 6C; ☎0268 262 040; f 0268 262 037. A more modest, friendly villa to the north of the resort. **$$**

✖ Where to eat and drink

✖ **Vânătorul** Poiana Brașov; ☎0268 262 354; www.restaurant-vanatorul.ro; ⊕ 12.00–02.00 daily. Situated near the Orthodox church, the 'Hunter' restaurant provides a great selection of game, including venison, boar & even bear meat. **$$$**

✖ **Coliba Haiducilor** (Haiduc Hut) Drumul Sulinar; ☎0268 262 137; www.colibahaiducilor. com; ⊕ 11.00–midnight daily. Situated near the

chairlift, the 'Outlaws' Hut' offers rustic dishes in a setting decorated with animal skins, guns & dried peppers. **$$**

✖ **Cabana Cristianul Mare Peak Chalet** At an altitude of 1,690m up Mount Postăvarul; ☎0268 186 545; ⊕ 11.00–21.00 daily. This ski chalet directly below the cable-car station at the top of the mountain is a good place to fill up on fast food & beer. **$**

SĂCELE Situated 9km southeast of Brașov on the E60/route 1 is the town of Săcele, which every July comes alive to celebrate **Săcele Santilia**, an age-old shepherd's feast (*see Chapter 2, Public holidays and feast days*, page 97). Săcele lies in the valley of Tärlung at an altitude of 600–700m at the foot of the Piatra Mare Massif (1,843m). In the 11th century, Săcele was called Septem villae valacheles (Seven Vlach Villages) because of the surrounding settlements. The most established residents were the *mocani* (local shepherds) who were very successful with thousands of sheep. They herded the sheep over great distances and there is even a village by the Black Sea called Săcele, founded by travelling *mocani*.

To see the town from above, take the **Bunloc chairlift** (☎ 0268 339 932; ⊕ Jun–Sep 08.00–16.00 Mon–Fri, 09.30–17.30 Sat/Sun; adult/child 1-way 8/5RON, return 13/8RON), which rises from 660m in Săcele to 1,170m near the peak of Piatra Mare.

SAXON FORTIFIED CHURCHES NORTHEAST OF BRAȘOV

Hărman The church in Hărman (Szászhermángy/Hönigberg) was built in the Roman style between 1500 and 1520 with 5m-thick and 12m-high walls. It has an inner church erected in the Roman style by Cistercian monks between 1280 and 1290 and later rebuilt in the Gothic style. A strong peasant citadel was built around the church between 1500 and 1520 and there was a moat around its ellipse-shaped interior. Visitors can see a collection of carved grotesque heads and there is a funeral chapel with Gothic murals from 1460 with the Last Judgement as the theme.

Get there by **car** via the E574; Hărman is 6km northeast of Brașov on route E574; by **bus** from Brașov city bus terminal 3 at Str Harmanului 47A.

Prejmer (☎ 0268 362 052; ⊕ 09.00–15.00 Tue–Sat; admission 7RON) To the north and west of Bran there are more than 500 Saxon villages, many with fortified churches. The largest of these is at Prejmer (Prázsmár/Tartlau) with 272 individual storage chambers arranged within an impressive ring-shaped defensive wall. This is a real fortress, with double walls and dungeons. Inside the fortifications there is a church, built by the Teutonic Knights in the 13th century. The honeycomb-like interior of the surrounding wall contains one small room for every family in the village, each numbered to avoid confusion, where they could find shelter if their village was attacked. There are also larger storage rooms for food. Prejmer is on the UNESCO World Heritage Site list, and there is a small museum (same opening times and price as the church) with Saxon folk costumes.

You can take the **train** (15km) from Braşov on the Sfântu Gheorghe line. Get off at the Ilieni stop, closer to the church than Prejmer station. By **car**, drive northeast out of Braşov on the E574, turn right at Hărman onto route 10. **Buses** from Braşov city bus terminal 3 at Str Harmanului 47A.

Sânpetru
(*Contact Gudrun Kraus;* \ *0268 360 730*) The first 14th-century, early Gothic church in Sânpetru (Barcaszentpéter/Petersberg) was demolished in 1794 and a new Classicist church built in its place. A strong precinct strengthened with towers encircles the church and a second defensive wall has bastions. A chapel in the northern corner has 15th-century murals.

Sânpetru is located a few kilometres west of Hărman on a minor road, or by frequent **buses** from Braşov's Autogară West (*12mins*).

Bod
(*Contact Manfred Copony;* m *0721 982 431*) In 1802, the church in Bod (Botfalu/Brenndorf) was destroyed in an earthquake and only the bell tower remains from the medieval building. A new church was built in 1804 and a few parts of the polygonal defensive wall are still standing.

Bod is 6km north of Hărman. Many **microbuses** leave the Autogară West daily, journey time 28 minutes.

RUPEA AND HOMOROD
If driving from Braşov to Sighişoara on the busy E60/route 13 highway, you will see a castle ruin on top of a hill at **Rupea** (Kőhalom/Reps), around 60km northwest of Braşov. The fortress was first mentioned in 1324 and it has two defensive walls guarding a lower court. The town has an attractive Gothic hall church with a Baroque altarpiece.

The main road bypasses **Homorod** (Homoród/Hamruden), but you might like to make a small detour to see the 13th-century fortified church (*contact Thomas Johann; casa No 37A;* \ *0268 286 556*). The church was transformed in 1784 with a choir attached to the southern façade. Wall paintings are still in evidence from the Romanesque period.

VISCRI
The unmistakably Saxon village of Viscri (Szászbuda/Deutschweisskirch) lies northwest of Rupea and is only accessible by car. Turn left off the main Braşov–Sighişoara road (E60) at Buneşti and rattle along a bumpy, unpaved road for 7km. You will pass through a Roma settlement where little children run alongside the car, pointing desperately at their mouths. This sad sight is off-putting, but the village is worth visiting to see the eggshell blue and turquoise Saxon houses lining the main square and the beautiful, imposing fortified church. The **church** (*admission adults 4RON, groups of 10 or more adults 2RON, children free*) is on UNESCO's list and it dates back to 1100 when Székely settlers first arrived. Saxon colonists took over the church in 1185, added fortifications and towers in 1525, and a second defence wall in the 18th century. It is possible to wander around the church and bastions where there are some dusty exhibits of agricultural and household tools.

⌂ Where to stay Prince Charles visited and liked Viscri so much he bought a Saxon house with three double bedrooms, two bathrooms and a kitchen. The house is available for holiday lets (*dbl* **$$–$$$** *B&B*, **$$$** *all-inclusive 1- or 2-week-long holidays*). The house is managed by Count Tibor Kálnoky (see page 156 for contact details). Count Kálnoky's Transylvanian holidays offer transfers, 'Food & Culture' tours and guided hikes centred on Viscri (*www.transylvaniancastle.com/Viscri.html*). It is possible to book a two-centre holiday, staying at Viscri and Micloşoara.

⌂ **Viscri 125** (10 dbl) Viscri 125; m 0723 579 489; e contact@viscri125.ro; www.viscri125. ro. Beautifully renovated house offering accommodation as well as cookery classes & other workshops. **$$$**

The **Mihai Eminescu Trust** has a house comprising two separate buildings, which accommodate four people (*see page 52 for contact details;* **$$$**). The Eminescu Trust can arrange accommodation in a traditional house in Viscri with meals. Contact **Gross Gerhild** (e *gerhild06@yahoo.com*; m *0742 077 506*). For further details on the Mihai Eminescu Trust contact Vice-President **Caroline Fernolend** (*Str Cojocarilor 10, Sighisoara*; e *cfernolend@mihaieminescutrust.org*; m *0740 145 397*). It is hoped that what is one of the few remaining, genuine Saxon villages will not in the future become overrun by countless coach parties.

SAXON FORTIFIED CHURCHES NORTH OF VISCRI

Meşendorf (*Contact Martin Werner; casa No 71*) The village of Meşendorf (GER Meschendorf) was first mentioned in 1289; however, the settlement was destroyed four times by fire, in 1469, 1641, 1755 and 1804. The church was first built in the 14th century as a very simple early Gothic building. A high sandstone wall, a defence corridor and two three-storey defence towers as well as a steep pyramidal roof were built in 1495. Restoration works were begun in 1701, and in 1888 parts of the circular outside wall and of the inside wall tower were taken down. The triptych altarpiece dates from 1653.

To reach Meşendorf by **car**, turn left off the main Braşov–Sighişoara road at Criţ.

Criţ (*Contact Stefan Depner; casa No 81*) The fortified church stands on a hill to the west of the village of Criţ (GER Deutschkreuz). A medieval church was demolished and a new church built between 1810 and 1813 in the Classicist style. The **Mihai Eminescu Trust** have a guesthouse in Criţ (see page 52 for contact details) which sleeps four (**$$$** *with b/fast & 3 meals*). There are several more fortified churches in the vicinity (Roadeş, Caţa, Buneşti, Drăuşeni), so Criţ would make a good base for further exploration. By **car**, follow the E60 and turn left after Buneşti.

4

Covasna County

Covasna County's (3,710km²) borders consist of mountains from the Eastern Carpathian range. Most settlements can be found in the valleys and depressions located along the different rivers crossing the county. The main river is the Olt and the county town Sfântu Gheorghe is situated on its banks. Covasna County is a land of spas and *mofettes* – dry 'saunas' where patients sit or stand in empty 'pools' and underground gases swirl about their bodies healing certain medical problems (see page 161). Surrounded by low-altitude volcanic mountains covered with beech and fir forests, Covasna County has a rich ozone and ionised climate. Around the important watering-hole town of Covasna alone there are more than 1,000 springs of table water, some of them with a flow of 10,000 litres per hour. Rich in carbonic acid, these table waters are very varied in taste and curative effects. The ionised air, the radioactive *mofettes* situated within a 40km radius and carbo-gaseous waters created the fame of Covasna Spa as the most complex cure spa in Europe. There are also many other smaller spas offering treatment for dermatological, rheumatic, orthopaedic, cardiological, nutritional, endocrinal, gynaecological and male reproductive problems. Covasna County is also the county of the old fortified churches, peasant fortresses, and wooden Székely gates with dovecots and pillars carved in wood. Covasna contains much of the historical Háromszék region, populated with ethnic Hungarians and Székelys. In 2011, it had a population of 206,261 comprising 74% Hungarian, 22% Romanian and 4% Roma. Covasna County has the second-largest percentage of ethnic Hungarians in Romania, just behind the neighbouring county of Harghita. The Hungarians of Covasna County are mostly Székely. The Vârghiş Valley is home to some 60 caves, including the cave where the Pied Piper of Hamelin is said to have reappeared leading a crowd of blue-eyed, blonde-haired Saxon children.

The fauna is very rich here especially in the Bretcu zone, but also throughout the county. The hunting of bear, wolf, Carpathian stag, roebuck, wood grouse and hare is common and several excellent guesthouses, namely at the noble estates at Micloşoara and Zăbala, arrange wildlife tours, animal tracking and spotting as well as flora and fauna discovery trips. The county is criss-crossed with numerous rivers and the Reci, Olt and Râul Negru lakes are excellent places for anglers and wildlife spotters.

The predominant industries in the county are wood, textiles, electrical components, food and beverages.

SFÂNTU GHEORGHE   *Telephone code 0267*

Sfântu Gheorghe (pronounced 'SFUN-too-gay-OR-gay') translates as 'Saint George'. In Hungarian the name is Sepsiszentgyörgy (pronounced 'SHEP-she-sent-djurdj'). It's a sleepy, industrial town and the centre is marred by many grey tower blocks

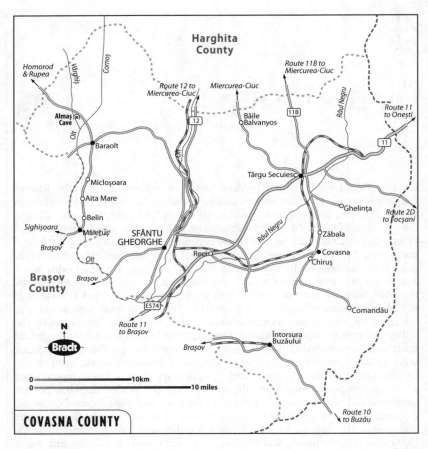

from the architecturally uninspiring 1960s. The city lies on the Olt River in a valley between the Baraolt and Bodoc mountains.

The town is 75% Hungarian, with most of them Székely, and the street signs could be confusing as they are an arbitrary mix of Hungarian and Romanian; sometimes you'll see *utca*, sometimes *strada* ('street' in Hungarian and Romanian respectively). Also, I saw Szabadság tér and Piaţa Libertăţii (Freedom Square – the city's main park). The local newspaper, *Háromszék* (see *Chapter 2, Media and communications*, page 113) is in Hungarian and there is an energetic Hungarian State Theatre, the only other in Romania being in Cluj-Napoca. There's not a huge amount to see here, but if you're a fan of Károly Kós architecture, you will find several important buildings among all the bland concrete.

HISTORY Sfântu Gheorghe was first mentioned in 1332, making it one of the oldest cities in Transylvania. The city takes its name from Saint George, the patron of the local church. Historically it was called Sankt Georgen in German. As part of the Kingdom of Hungary, the city was an economic and administrative centre for the Hungarian county of Háromszék (see box, page 155), which nowadays spreads over Covasna and Braşov counties. From the 15th century, Sfântu Gheorghe became an important centre for the Székely people in the region known to them as Székelyföld,

above left	A familiar rural sight in Richiş, Sibiu County — a horse and cart on the way home, piled high with hay (LM) page 209
above right	The archetypal image of the Transylvanian countryside (SS) page 6
below left	Work until the cows come home — the evening parade in Micloşoara (LM) page 154
below right	A shepherd keeps warm in winter, Sic (SSp) page 257

above left   A traditional Saxon house in the lovely village of Biertan (LM) page 207

above right   Lavishly detailed and gaily coloured fabrics in Sâncraiu (SS) page 43

left   Two young girls pose in classically patterned Romanian folk costumes (SSp) page 32

below   A group of dancers in traditional dress practise in Cluj-Napoca (SSp) page 45

above Local honey from the surrounding mountains and meadows for sale in the market in Zărneşti (RA) page 143

right A colourful group of ladies get a ride home on a rural country road (SSp) page 83

below A Roma fiddler — Roma musicians are famous the world over (SSp) page 44

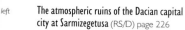

left   The atmospheric ruins of the Dacian capital city at Sarmizegetusa (RS/D) page 226

below left   Vibrant church frescoes in the Orthodox cathedral in Sfântu Gheorghe, Covasna County (LM) page 154

below right   The ancient church in Densuş is one of the oldest Orthodox churches in Europe, possibly dating from the 6th century — its architecture is a unique mixture of styles (SS) page 226

bottom   The honeycomb-like interior wall of Prejmer fortified church contained one small room for every family in the village — numbered to avoid confusion, these rooms would provide shelter in the event of an attack (RA) page 148

right With its shingle onion dome and beautiful interior, the wooden Church of Sfântul Mihail (Saint Michael) is a delightful detour in Târgu Mureş (LM) page 180

below The simple spire of Drumul Carului Church in the Bucegi Mountains stands out from a blanket of snow (RM) page 139

bottom Designed to resemble a grand hunting lodge, Peleş Castle is the most beautiful residence of Romania's former royal family (EC/S) page 138

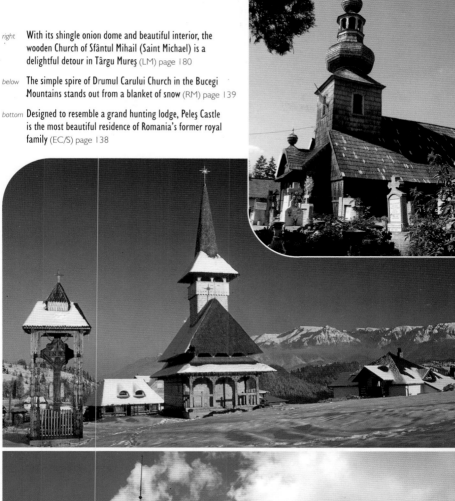

above Cabana Caraiman in the Bucegi
Mountains — one of the many *cabanas*
that cater to hikers and trekkers
(SS) page 86

left Turda Salt Mine — descend into its depths
for a surreal experience
(SS) page 259

below The first established national park in
Romania and a UNESCO Biosphere
Reserve, Retezat National Park protects
more than 300 species of flora and 50
species of mammal (MM) page 227

right   The region surrounding Pasul Tihuţa (page 267) has the largest number of brown bears (*Ursus arctos*) in Europe (MW/I/FLPA) page 13

below left   There is excellent birdwatching in Transylvania — spot golden eagles (*Aquila chrysaetos*) catching updraughts in Apuseni Nature Park (ML/FLPA) page 12

below right   The distinctive colouring of the scarce swallowtail butterfly (*Iphiclides podalirius*) (GF/FLPA) page 11

bottom   Unlike in many Western cultures, the wolf (*Canis lupus*) enjoys a high status in Romanian folkloric tradition as a protector against evil; wolves were also worshipped by the Dacians (JD/MP/FLPA) page 123

above   You don't have to go far to find incredible hiking and trekking in the Carpathian Mountains (DT/S) page 112

left   The Transfăgărașan Highway is the most exciting road in Europe for those on two wheels or four — just keep an eye out for horses and carts around those bends! (RS/S) page 216

below   Skiers take advantage of the soft powder in Poiana Brașov — Transylvania is a great skiing destination for all levels and styles (BDL/S) page 146

and it is home to the Székely National Museum. Turkish attacks during 1658–71 left the city in ruins and a plague in 1717 wiped out much of the population. In the late 19th century, Sfântu Gheorghe saw the development of both textile and cigarette factories. The city hosts two market fairs each year and St George's Day in April is always a big knees-up.

GETTING THERE AND AWAY The **railway** and **bus** stations are 2km southeast of the centre along Boulevard 1 Decembrie 1918. There are 16 trains daily to Braşov and three to Covasna. Train schedule information is available from **Agenţia de Voiaj CFR** (*Str Mikó Imre 13;* ☏ *0267 311 680;* ⏰ *08.00–15.00 Mon–Fri*), which sells train tickets.

Microbuses and **maxi-taxis** leave the bus station, 50m north of the railway station. They pass along Strada 1 Decembrie 1918, with stops clearly marked.

TOURIST INFORMATION
 Tourinfo Str 1 Decembrie 1918 2; ☏ 0267 316 474; e sepsinfo@sepsi.ro; www.sepsiszentgyorgy. ro or www.covasna.info.ro; ⏰ 07.30–15.30 Mon– Wed, 07.30–17.30 Thu, 07.30–14.00 Fri. Can book homestays in nearby villages & spas.

🏠 WHERE TO STAY
🏠 **Ferdinand Panzio** (5 dbl) Str 1 Decembrie 1918 10B/7; m 0745 304 114; e fp@zoltur.ro; http://ferdinandpension.zoltur.ro. Renovated 19th-century building in a quiet, central location. **$$$**

🏠 **Sugáskert** (24 dbl, 5 apts) Str 1 Decembrie 1918 12; ☏ 0267 312 171; www.sugaskert.ro. A smart, 3-star hotel right in the centre with a good restaurant ($$) serving Transylvanian specialities. **$$$**

🏠 **Bodoc Hotel** (10 sgl, 55 dbl, 8 suites) Str 1 Decembrie 1918 1; ☏ 0267 311 291; e bodochotel@planet.ro; http://bodochotel. proturism.ro. Large 10-storey tower-block hotel near the park, with simple rooms & a good restaurant ($$). **$$**

✗ WHERE TO EAT AND DRINK
✗ **Pizzeria Bella Italia Pta** Mihai Viteazu 2; ⏰ 13.00–23.00 Mon, 10.00–23.00 Tue–Sun. Popular pizzeria with free Wi-Fi. **$**

OTHER PRACTICALITIES
Bank
$ **Raiffeisen** Str 1 Decembrie 1918 33–37; www. raiffeisen.ro; ⏰ 09.00–17.30 Mon–Fri. With a 24hr ATM (Visa, MasterCard).

Bookshop
Corvina könyvház Str Ciucului/Csíki utca 1; ☏ 0267 313 067; e corvine_sf@nextra.ro; www. corvina.ro; ⏰ 08.00–19.00 Mon–Fri, 09.00–13.00 Sat. Good selection of maps of the surrounding area, books in Hungarian & a few in English.

Pharmacy
✚ **Hipocrate** Str 1 Decembrie 1918 15; ☏ 0267 324 300; ⏰ 07.30–20.00 Mon–Fri, 07.30–16.00 Sat

Post office
✉ Str 1 Decembrie 1918 18; ⏰ 07.00–20.00 Mon–Fri, 08.00–13.00 Sa

WHAT TO SEE AND DO The **Székely National Museum** (*Str Károly Kós 10;* ☏ *0267 312 442; www.sznm.ro;* ⏰ *09.00–17.00 Tue–Sun; admission adult/child 5/2RON*), just south of the city park, is housed in a beautiful building with traditional pointed turrets designed by the architect **Károly Kós** (see page 45) between 1911 and 1912.

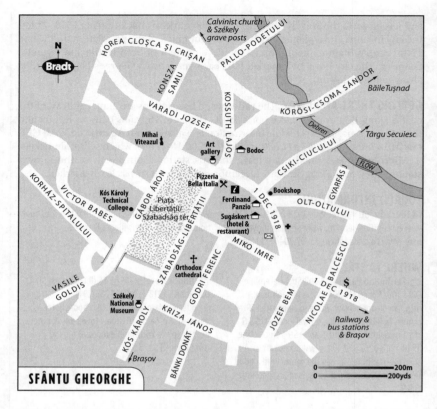

SFÂNTU GHEORGHE

The museum displays many Székely items and crafts, and much material on the 1848 uprising against the Habsburgs. The museum garden has two Székely *kapu* (gates) and a recreated peasant's cottage from Armăşeni (HU Csíkménaság). There is no information in English. Behind the park, **Piaţa Libertăţii** (Szabadság tér), the technical college, was also created by Kós and there's another house he designed by the Hotel Bodoc at Strada Kossuth 19. At the north end of the park, an **art gallery** (⊙ *09.00–16.00 Tue–Fri, 10.00–14.00 Sat/Sun*) displays paintings by Transylvanian artists such as Imre Nagy in a yellow building with a tall clock tower. The square north of the park has an impressive statue group featuring Mihai Viteazul and five soldiers. Heading north along Strada Kossuth is the fortified **Calvinist church** on Piaţa Kalvíny. The church's Gothic style dates from 1547. The cemetery behind the church has good examples of wooden **Székely grave posts** (*kopjafák*). The **Orthodox cathedral**, hidden behind concrete blocks just east of the park has, like the one in Târgu Mureş, an ugly grey concrete exterior but the interior is an explosion of colour, gold, icons and incense.

AROUND SFÂNTU GHEORGHE

MICLOŞOARA Micloşoara, known usually by its Hungarian name, Miklósvár, is a Székely village where you will mostly likely hear only Hungarian spoken in the street. Brush up on your *Jó napot* ('Good day', see *Appendix 1, Language*, page 282) expressions because the courteous villagers greet anyone and everyone in the street and, in the warmer months, everyone sits outside their houses to watch the daily promenade home of the cattle (at 20.00) along the main street. It is a wonderful rural sight and each cow knows instinctively which yard to turn into. Micloşoara sits on a slope and at the lower end is the **Miki Kocsma** (*pub;* ⏰ *allegedly non-stop but usually from 17.00 until late*), doubling up as a corner shop, where visitors and farmers alike can enjoy a cool bottle of beer and watch the carts piled high with hay trundle past pulled by docile horses or oxen. Further along the road is the 16th-century manor house under restoration and belonging to Count Tibor Kálnoky, whose **guesthouse** is the main reason why so many people now visit this lost-in-time backwater village. The urbane Kálnoky is a 40-something Székely entrepreneur and descendant of a noble family, who settled in the misty, myth-laden region in the 13th century and lived there until communism forced the family to flee. Kálnoky, who grew up in France and Germany and studied to be a vet, moved back to the ancestral home after communism ended in 1989. In the last few years he has created one of Romania's most successful tourist ventures out of his ancestral hunting manor and has counted Prince Charles among his guests. Prince Charles also asked Kálnoky to manage his Saxon guesthouse in Viscri (see page 149). The Count's guesthouse complex, in two venues in the village, opened in 2001 and is one of the best places to stay in Transylvania. Guests can make the place their base (staying a minimum of three nights in high season) and explore the countryside by hire car, but it is highly recommended to stay on an all-inclusive package and let knowledgeable locals take you to secret places you'd never find alone, and also negotiate the dubious road surfaces and Romanian road hogs. Day trips are organised for every day of the week and after a huge breakfast, guests visit the Seven Stairs Waterfall, go bear- or birdwatching, visit Saxon fortress towns, see volcanic lakes, go on a fossil trail, and ride on a horse and cart to what botanist Dr John Akeroyd (see page 6) calls the 'very last example of an untouched medieval landscape', where a rustic picnic will sustain travellers until dinner.

In early 2008, Kálnoky took over the operations of the Ştefan cel Mare Equestrian Centre, previously in Bistriţa-Năsăud County, as the centre's founder, Julian Ross had to return to the UK for health reasons. At **Count Kálnoky's Equestrian Centre Transylvania**, as it is now known (*www.riding-holiday.ro*), visitors can ride seven of Ross's locally bred horses as well as Kálnoky's Shagya Arab and Lipizzaner breeds through the glorious 'Woodlands' (Erdővidék) region of Covasna County. See the website for a one-week riding holiday based at the riding centre at Valea Crişului/Sepsikőröspatak. The delicious Hungarian dishes and organic fruit and vegetables

HÁROMSZÉK – THE THREE SEATS

Sfântu Gheorghe is situated at the heart of the old Magyar region of Háromszék. A *szék* ('seat', literally 'chair') was the old name for regions in the Hungarian Kingdom from the 12th century until 1874. In Hungary and Felvidék (Slovakia) there were *vármegye* (literally 'castle counties'), which were administrative counties built up around a *vár* (castle). The western part of Transylvania had *vármegye* but in the Székely and Saxon territories they had *szék*. They kept the *szék* instead of *vármegye* as the society was completely different from that in Hungary. In Transylvania, they had more independence, especially for the Székelys and Saxons. The capital of Háromszék was Sfântu Gheorghe/Sepsiszentgyörgy. Its area covered 3,889km² in 1910 and was a combination of three Székely seats: Kézdiszék, Orbaiszék and Sepsiszék.

are all prepared by a collection of charming Hungarian-speaking ladies and in the warmer months are enjoyed under an arbour in the fragrant garden. If it gets chilly, guests can retire to the 17th-century wine cellar or sit in front of a roaring fire, sampling some of the excellent vintages, before retiring to rooms decorated with authentic Transylvanian furniture, huge fairytale beds with pure wool mattresses and discreet Western-style bathrooms. There is even a sauna incorporated in a vast, ancient bread oven.

Getting there and away By **car**, from Braşov drive north on the E60/route 13 towards Sighişoara and fork right after 33km just before the village of Măieruş. Turn right in the heart of the village and cross a bridge over the Olt River. The road deteriorates into a dirt track which you follow until it meets a main tarmac road. Turn left and drive north for 13km through the villages of Belin and Aita Mare before reaching Micloşoara. After the church, go down the hill and you'll see a large wooden gate in front of a large white house at No 186. Turn sharp right and park in the courtyard at the back. For an additional fee there is a **pick-up service** from Bucharest, Târgu Mureş or Cluj-Napoca airports or Braşov railway station.

Where to stay, eat and drink

Kálnoky Guesthouse & Estate
(8 dbl, 1 apt) Contact Count Tibor Kálnoky & his staff; Kálnoky Panzió, Sat Micloşoara 186, Covasna County; **m** 0742 202 586; **f** 0267 314 088; **e** k@ transylvaniancastle.com; www.transylvaniancastle. com. See above for details. **$$–$$$**

BĂILE BÁLVÁNYOS (*www.balvanyos.eu*) Băile Bálványos (Bálványosfürdő/ Bálványos) is a **spa resort** in the mountains at the northern border of Covasna County at an altitude of almost 800m on the southern slopes of the Bodoc Mountains, about 40km from Sfântu Gheorghe. The spa is located on a scenic tree-covered mountainside near the ruins of the 13th-century Cetăţile Păgânilor Citadel. The spa is one of several hydrothermal and volcanic features of the region. It lies 10km from Lacul Sfânta Ana formed from an extinct volcanic crater, just over the border in Harghita County (see page 166) and unique in this region of Europe. Nearby is an unusual geological feature, a precipice created by sulphur–hydrogen emanations, known locally as 'the Birds' Cemetery'. The spa has been known for its health properties for centuries, but was only used as a spa after 1938 when a spa resort (now the Best Western) was built. The **Festivalul Pomana Porcului**, celebrating and promoting all things porcine, takes place in Băile Balvanyos in February.

Getting there and away Băile Bálványos is located on a minor mountain road reached by **car** by travelling north from Sfântu Gheorghe on route 12 and turning right after 28km at Bixad. Follow a winding mountain road for 12km, the drive is very time-consuming and could take as long as 1½ hours. Alternatively, a longer route from Miercurea-Ciuc leads south also on route 12 for 35km and turns left at Bixad following the 12km mountain road. There is no public transport.

Where to stay

Best Western Bálványos (10 sgl, 66 dbl, 2 suites) 525400 Balvanyos; \0267 360 700; **e** bestwestern@easynet.ro; www. bestwesternhotels.ro. A luxury hotel above the village, with a superb restaurant ($$), bar & its own spa with a sauna. **$$$$**

Balvanos Panzio (7 dbl, 3 tpl) Balvanyos 77; \0267 365 277; **e** balvanyospanzio@istvana.ro; www. www.balvanyospanzio.ro. Also has 3 apts, 5 bungalows, a restaurant & a campsite. **$$**

THE PIED PIPER RE-EMERGES

In Transylvania there's a tribe,
Of alien people who ascribe,
The outlandish ways and dress,
On which their neighbours lay such stress,
To their fathers and mothers having risen,
Out of some subterranean prison,
Into which they had been trepanned,
Long time ago, in a mighty land,
But how or why they don't understand.

Robert Browning *The Pied Piper of Hamelin*

The Pied Piper was a rat catcher. In 1284, the German town of Hamelin was suffering from an infestation and a man dressed in colourful stripy clothes appeared, saying he could solve the rat problem. He used a musical pipe to lure the rats into the Weser River. When the townspeople refused to pay him, he played his pipe again and this time lured 130 boys and girls who followed him out of the town. The children disappeared into a cave and were never seen again. However, according to Transylvanian legends, the children re-emerged from the Almaş Cave in the gorge of the Vârghiş River near Baraolt, 25km north of Micloşoara (one of the day trips from Count Kálnoky's guesthouse (see above), visits the 7.3km cave system, populated by colonies of bats – not vampire bats). The children were the ancestors of the Saxons and the legend explains why there were so many blonde-haired, blue-eyed German speakers following traditional customs, who lived isolated hundreds of miles from Germany.

TÂRGU SECUIESC Târgu Secuiesc (Kézdivásárhely/Szekler Neumarkt) is a sleepy Székely town and a major trading centre. The Romanian name means 'Székely Market', and in Hungarian *vásárhely* means 'marketplace'. It was first mentioned in 1407 and 20 years later, Hungarian king Zsigmond granted it the title of free royal town, allowing it to hold fairs. As a typically Székely town, it has an unusual layout comprising a kind of grid system with the buildings in the main square separated by 73 alleys. The houses have beautiful Art Nouveau wrought-iron gates. The dusty streets are tree lined and the locals are very friendly and eager to help or strike up a conversation – in Hungarian. During the 1848 uprising against the Habsburgs, local foundry owner Áron Gábor helped the struggle by melting down the Székely Land church bells and casting cannons from them. These became known as Áron Gábor's famous Cannons of Brass. Between October 1848 and June 1849, Gábor's workshop cast 68 cannons, using more than 400 bells. There is a statue of Gábor in the town's main square.

Getting there and away Situated 56km northeast of Braşov on the E574/route 11. Three **coaches** or **microbuses** leave from Braşov's bus stations No 1, No 2 and West. Arriving from Băile Balvanyos by **car**, the road is very scenic and outside Turia village, with its elegant manor house, passes under a huge Székely gate.

GHELINŢA Ghelinţa (Gelence/Gälänz), situated 11km southeast of Târgu Secuiesc, is home to a very significant 13th-century **Catholic church**. It is the most easterly and oldest Catholic church in the Carpathian Basin. It was built in the Romanesque style on the foundations of an ancient Cistercian monastery. Over the centuries, its style was altered, incorporating many Gothic elements including an elegant fan-vaulted ceiling in the sanctuary. There the panelled ceiling consisting of 103 painted 'cassettes' (*kazetta*) was created in 1628 with Renaissance-style floral motifs. The interior walls are decorated with beautiful frescoes dating back to the 1330s and displaying the legend of Saint László (see *Turda*, page 259), who is seen chasing a Cuman on horseback. To visit the church, try asking the locals for the elderly lady bell ringer (*harangozó*) who keeps the keys. (See *Chapter 2, Arts and entertainment*, page 106, for church-visiting phrases.)

There are eight buses (weekdays only) from Târgu Secuiesc to Ghelinţa (30mins) and one on Saturdays.

ZĂBALA In Hungarian, the word *zabola* (or *zabla*) means a 'bridle-bit', the straps of leather put around a horse's head to allow the rider to control it. In the course of various battles with the Tatars, the villages north and south of Zăbala (Zabola) were destroyed by the Tatars. However, the inhabitants of Zăbala managed to hold the Tatars in check and survived, almost as if they had reined in the Tatars' horses. Outside the village lies the Tatárhalom (Tatar Hill). Some historians think the Tatars that were killed in action were buried there.

Zăbala village has several fine examples of *Székely kapu* (gate) and also there is a small **Csángó Ethnographic Museum** (*Csángó Néprajzi Múzeum, Str Gării/Vasút utca 789;* \ *0267 375 566;* e *csangomuzeum@gmail.com; www.csangomuzeum.ro;* ☉ *10.00–18.00 daily*), founded by Dr Ferenc Pozsony, who teaches at the University of Cluj-Napoca. The Csángó are a Hungarian ethnic group who live in Moldavia. They are famous for their folk music, folk costumes and beautiful weaving work.

Getting there and away By **car** from Braşov, drive for 56km northeast on the E574 towards Târgu Secuiesc, turn right just after Sântionlunca towards Covasna and Zăbala (*1hr*). Half a dozen buses leave Braşov for Zăbala with a change at Covasna (*4hrs*) and Târgu Secuiesc (*2½hrs*).

Mikes Estate (*The Zabola Estate of the Count Mikes Family; 527190 Zăbala; for contact details, see page 55;* **$$$$–$$$$$**) After Ghelinţa continue south on a very minor road to find the village of Zăbala and another elegant Székely nobleman's estate hidden away in 34ha of parkland in the foothills of the Eastern Carpathians. An imposing metal gateway with an intercom system gives way to a long beech tree-lined avenue, leading to the Machine House of the estate, the first of several buildings to be restored and home to Katalin Roy Chowdhury (Countess Mikes, pronounced 'meak-esh'), her son Gregor, his wife Zsolna and the Countess's younger son Alexander. The Machine House also has six double guestrooms, beautifully restored by Zsolna and turned into a boutique hotel.

Zăbala is the oldest ancestral home of the noble Székely Mikes family. It was first mentioned in 1629. In 1946, the communists seized the property and the Mikes family was forced to flee to Austria. After 45 harrowing years of communism, a new generation returned to Transylvania. Katalin Roy Chowdhury de Ulpur, born Countess Mikes de Zabola, managed to get the property back from the Romanian state. Her late husband Shuvendu Basu Roy Chowdhury of Ulpur, a Bengali aristocrat, supported her fight. When Ceauşescu was deposed, land was slowly returned to its original owners but it still took years of legal battles before the countess could return to her near-derelict home in 2005.

SZÉKELY GATES IN COVASNA COUNTY

A typical piece of Székely folk art is the Székely gate (*Székely kapu*), a gate with a separate entrance for pedestrians and for the horse and cart, decorated with woodcarvings featuring floral motifs. Here are some of the towns and villages in Covasna County where you will be sure of spotting a gate or two:

TOWNS Sfântu Gheorghe (Sepsiszentgyörgy), Covasna (Kovászna), Întorsura Buzăului (Bodzaforduló), Târgu Secuiesc (Kézdivásárhely), Baraolt (Barót).

SMALLER VILLAGES Aita Mare (Nagyajta), Araci (Árapatak), Arcuş (Árkos), Bățanii Mari (Nagybacon), Bodoc (Sepsibodok), Cernat (Csernáton), Chichiş (Kökös), Estelnic (Esztelnek), Filia (Erdőfüle), Ilieni (Illyefalva), Lemnia (Lemhény), Ozun (Uzon), Reci (Réty), Sânzieni (Kézdiszentlélek), Valea Crişului (Sepsikőröspatak), Zagon (Zágon), Zăbala (Zabola).

Her sons Gregor and Alexander are working on rebuilding not only the estate but also the economical background of it, together with Gregor's wife Zsolna (born Ugron de Ábranfalva) who has Székely family roots related to the estate.

There are many fine old buildings still to be renovated in the parkland, which also has a 2ha lake. The Swiss House was shipped from Berne via the Paris Exhibition of 1889 and also the Prater fairground in Vienna. There is also a large sanatorium building and a secret underground tunnel. In the future, a new villa will offer ten rooms to guests. The boutique hotel in the Machine House has roaring open fires and huge rooms with wooden floors, including a romantic 'red room' with a free-standing bath. During a visit to this isolated paradise, guests have the opportunity to choose from a variety of activities, both in winter and summer. It is possible to visit Székely shepherds in the mountains and experience their daily lives, while enjoying a rustic meal prepared by them of grilled meats and homemade cheese. Mountain climbing, hiking to the high-altitude village of Comandău (1,100m), bear watching and wildlife treks are all available. Meals are prepared from family Transylvanian cookbooks using organic fruit and vegetables from the 0.8ha kitchen garden.

COVASNA The 'spa of a thousand springs', Covasna (Kovászna/Kowasna) is a town totally dedicated since the 1880s to **health treatments** using natural mineral spring water and *mofettes* (see box, page 161). The town is modern and filled with concrete housing blocks, and patients wander about in their pyjamas and dressing gowns. In the centre of the town is a **public watering hole**, a covered fountain sunk in the ground emitting a powerful eggy aroma. This is called the *pokolsăr* in Hungarian, or 'mud from hell' – it certainly smells diabolical. Locals and patients fill up plastic bottles with the sulphurous mineral water to take home and 'enjoy' at their leisure. The hotels offer treatments for cardiovascular, neurological and skin disorders.

Getting there and away By **car** from Braşov, drive for 56km northeast on the E574 towards Târgu Secuiesc, turn just after Sântionlunca towards Covasna (*1hr*). It is possible to take a short cut by turning off the main road at Reci, but it is a bone-rattling ride. Three daily **buses** leave Braşov Autogară West for Covasna.

⌂ Where to stay

⌂ Covasna Hotel (19 sgl, 99 dbl, 3 suites) B-dul 1 Decembrie 1918 1–2; \0267 340 401. A 1960s-style block houses a 3-star treatment complex with spas, a *mofette* & treatment facilities. **$$**

⌂ Hotel Turist (20 dbl, 2 tpl) B-dul 1 Decembrie 1918 4; \0267 340 573; e office@hotel-turist-covasna.ro; http://hotel-turist-covasna.ro. A 70s-style place in a central location. **$$**

⌂ Pensiunea Sruetti (18 dbl/tpl) Brazilor 2; \0267 340 918; e sruetticovasna@gmail.com; www.sruetti.co.nr. Good value place with simple rooms, a restaurant & a large terrace. **$$**

COMANDĂU Comandău (Komandó) village is the highest-altitude Székely village, at 1,100m. It was once an old Habsburg border army base and is also the site for one of Transylvania's few preserved steam narrow-gauge forest railways.

Romania is one of very few European countries that still have working (not just tourist ride) **steam narrow-gauge railways**. Over 65% of Romania's land surface consists of hills and mountains, much of which is heavily forested and there is a thriving timber industry. Many of these tracks are the remains of forest logging railways and 50 years ago you could find narrow-gauge steam engines labouring up steep inclines towing strings of wagons, returning later in the day with heavy loads of timber. As recently as 1960, more than 6,000km of forest logging railway existed in Romania and even in the mid 1980s over 20 lines were in regular use. Today, much has given way to the internal combustion engine. In 1999, only two of the forest railways (CFFs) were in regular use, one at Vişeu de Sus in the far north near the Ukrainian border, and one with a unique inclined plane at Comandău. Contact Mike Morton at Transylvania Uncovered (for contact details see page 53) for steam-locomotive tours.

Getting there and away Comandău is 15km south of Covasna on a very minor road. The Mikes Estate organises hiking trips from Zăbala for those in good physical condition.

CHIURUŞ The village of Chiuruş (Csomakőrös) was originally called Kőrös in Hungarian, similar to its name in Romanian, but in 1904 'Csoma' was added to the Hungarian name in honour of its most famous son, **Sándor Kőrösi Csoma** (1784–1842), the great Székely Orientalist who walked most of the way to Tibet to search for the origins of the Hungarian people. He studied the Tibetan language and wrote the first Tibetan–English dictionary.

The Hungarian Who Walked to Heaven by Edward Fox (see *Appendix 2, Further Information*, page 285) recounts the fascinating and unusual life of Kőrösi Csoma, whom Fox calls Alexander Csoma de Koros, who set off on a 30-year odyssey in search of his and the Magyar identities and ended up in Ladakh, where, through a bizarre sequence of events, he found himself decoding the mysteries of Tibetan culture for the British government.

Kőrösi Csoma appears to have been a very strange character and it is interesting to learn how penny pinching and obsessed with money he was. He lived in such abstemious, spartan conditions and put himself through such misery and hardship, living and working in a dark cell with a Buddhist monk, in pursuit of his dream, that you have to admire his courage and determination, even if he does seem a little weird. The entire village is dedicated to him with several statues, the main street and cultural centre named after him, and several memorial houses in his honour.

Getting there and away By **car** from Braşov, drive for 56km northeast on the E574 to Târgu Secuiesc, turn right in town heading for Covasna (*1hr*). Chiuruş

MOFETTES – A DRY BATH IN HOT AIR

Daring visitors can try a *mofette* or 'dry sauna' at Baile Balvanyoş, Băile Tuşnad, Covasna, Borsec and Harghita-Băi. Guests stand or sit gingerly in a deep, octagonal 'pool' lined with slatted benches. The vents in the sides of the 'pool' give out gases, which come from an extinct volcano and some of the noxious gases are sulphurous, giving off a powerful aroma of bad eggs. The idea is that the gases are absorbed into the body through the skin and have a beneficial effect on the cardiovascular system, the locomotive system and some skin conditions. However, patients have to try this cure under medical supervision, as inhalation of the gases can prove fatal. A visit to a *mofette* must be for a very short, limited time. Patients must always be on their guard that the gas does not rise higher than knee level, and any movement must be slow and deliberate to avoid stirring up the gases. Even talking can disturb the gases and then patients might accidentally breathe them in. Small children should not go into *mofettes*, nor should people who are very short in height, intoxicated, ill or alone. Perhaps it's a new one for the extreme sports fans …

is a few kilometres south on a very minor road. Three daily **buses** leave Braşov Autogară West for Covasna from where you have to change for Chiuruş.

5

Harghita County

Harghita County (6,639km²) is a very mountainous county in the Eastern Carpathians, made up of the Ciuc and Harghita mountains as well as volcanic plateaux, foothills and the more densely populated river valleys. The volcanic mountains are known for their superb hot mineral springs and the county has excellent spa resorts and bottles some of Romania's best mineral waters from some of its 2,000 springs of table waters. Harghita is one of the coldest regions in Romania, although summers can be quite warm. Two of the most important rivers in Romania, the Mureş and the Olt, originate in Harghita County. The stunning natural scenery includes Sfânta Ana Lake, created from a volcanic crater, the strange mountain lake Lacu Roşu and a dramatic canyon formed by Bicaz stream. Near the town of Vlăhiţa is a gorgeous narcissus meadow covering 30ha which blossoms in late May with a spectacular density of 180–200 flowers/m².

The karst rocks have created many grottos and caves. Among them are the Sugó Cave near Voşlăbeni and the Bears' Grotto and Ice Cave near Borsec Spa. The village of Praid boasts a gigantic salt mine, with a sanatorium and a huge space underground, which makes an unusual tourist destination. Harghita County has the highest percentage of ethnic Hungarians, mostly Székely, in Romania. Hungarians account for 84.8% of Harghita's population, Romanians 13% and Roma 1.8%. The Székelys form a majority in most of the county's municipalities with a few Romanian enclaves such as Topliţa.

The county's main industries are wood, food and beverages, textiles and leather processing.

MIERCUREA-CIUC *Telephone code 0266 (or 0366)*

With a population of a little over 41,000 people, around 80% of them Székely, Miercurea-Ciuc (Csíkszereda/Szeklerburg) is a lively if somewhat dusty, ramshackle town, capital of both Harghita County and the historic Csík region. The centre of town is marred by a collection of ugly communist-constructed monstrosities, dull office buildings and ten-storey housing blocks, but there are some sights worth hunting down among all the concrete. The pedestrian street Strada Petőfi is a pleasant place to while away an afternoon at one of the many pavement cafés and you must not forget to try a Ciuc beer (see page 165), the best brew in the country. On the beer bottle's label, note Mikó Castle which itself contains an excellent museum and a huge collection of Székely gates in the fields behind it. See below for details.

HISTORY The city's main sight, the Mikó Castle (Castelul Mikó/Mikó-vár), was built in 1623–30 in a late Renaissance style at the request of Ferenc Mikó Hídvégi,

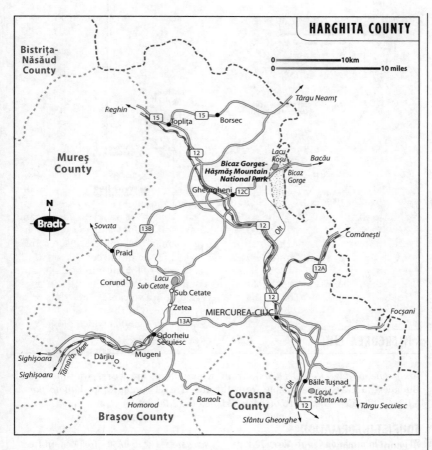

personal adviser to Gábor Bethlen, the Prince of Transylvania at the time. In 1661, the Turkish–Tatar troops of Ali Pasha invaded the Csík region and destroyed the castle, leaving it in ruins. It was rebuilt only later during the time of Gubernium at the order of the Austrian general Stephan Steinville between 1714 and 1716. The fortress had an important role in the eastern defence of the Habsburg monarchy as it housed the imperial troops until 1764 when the Székely border guard was established. From 1764 until 1849, the castle was the headquarters of the first Székely infantry.

GETTING THERE AND AWAY Miercurea-Ciuc is 67km north of Sfântu Gheorghe (Covasna County) on the second-class main road No 12.

The **railway** and **bus** stations are situated 50m apart to the west of the centre near Strada Florilor/Virá utca.

Train schedule information is available from **Agenția de Voiaj CFR** (*Str Kossuth 12;* \ *0266 311 924;* ⏰ *08.00–20.00 Mon–Fri*), which sells advance tickets: 11 trains to Gheorgheni, 10 trains to Brașov, three to Bucharest and the Korona Express international train to Budapest.

Buses and **microbuses** leave the bus station (*Str Brașovului 1;* \ *0266 324 334*) daily for Gheorgheni (*1¾hrs*), Odorheiu Secuiesc (*1¾hrs*), Sfântu Gheorghe

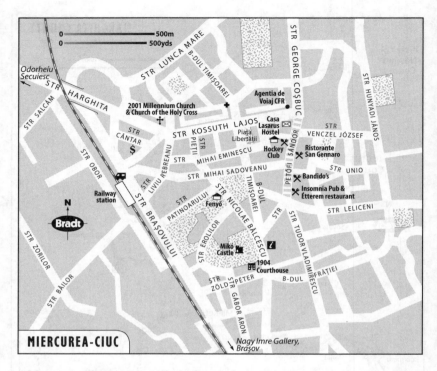

MIERCUREA-CIUC

(*only one a day, 19.00, 1¾hrs*), from where there are buses to Braşov and Budapest. Tickets are available from the **Itas Travel Agency** (*Str Vanatorilor 7;* ☎0266 311 555; ⏰ *08.00–16.00 Mon–Fri, 08.00–12.00 Sat*).

TOURIST INFORMATION

ℹ️ Tourist Information Centre Room 20, Piaţa Cetăţii 1; ☎0266 317 007; e csikinfo@szereda.ro; www.szereda.ro; ⏰ 07.30–16.00 Mon–Fri. Free maps & accommodation information.

WHERE TO STAY

🏠 Hotel Fenyő (88 dbl, 3 suites) Str N Bălcescu 11; ☎0266 311 493; e reserve@ hunguest-fenyo.ro; www.hunguest-fenyo.ro. In a bright, white 8-storey block, the 3-star Fenyő is the best in town with local flavours at the Melissa Room restaurant (**$$**), business facilities & a wellness centre. **$$$**

🏠 Casa Lasarus Hostel (36 beds, mostly in quadruple dorms) Str Gál Sándor 9; ☎0266 310 497; e lasarus@lasarushostel.ro; www.lasarushostel. ro. Excellent bargain hostel with kitchen facilities. You can also pay for 4 beds & take the whole room. Discount €10 pp for longer stays. **$**

WHERE TO EAT AND DRINK

✕ Bandido's Str Petőfi 25; ☎0266 314 749; http://bandidospizza.ro; ⏰ 10.00–midnight daily. A Mexican restaurant with a large selection of pizzas & pasta. **$**

✕ Hockey Club restaurant & pizzeria Str Petőfi 4A; ☎0266 371 605; ⏰ 09.00–midnight Mon–Thu, 09.00–01.00 Fri, 10.00–01.00 Sat,

10.00–midnight Sun. A good place to watch sports or sit in the courtyard & enjoy a Ciuc beer. **$**

✕ Insomnia pub & Étterem restaurant Str Petőfi 35; ☎0366 104 974; ⏰ 09.00–midnight Mon–Thu, 09.00–05.00 Fri–Sun. A trendy, newish place with local dishes, good soups & pasta in a smart cocktail bar setting. **$**

✕ Ristorante San Gennaro Str Petőfi 15; ☎0266 206 500; ⏰ 09.00–midnight daily. Possibly the best restaurant in the county, certainly the best pizza I ate in Romania. Authentic Italian thin crusts (12") with a huge variety of toppings.

The terrace is under siege from tiny Roma children who beg for a crust & the waitress spends her day chasing them away. Hungarian poet & revolutionary Sándor Petőfi stayed in the building on 23 July 1849. $

OTHER PRACTICALITIES
Bank
$ **Banca Transilvania** Str Kossuth 18; ☎0266 310 203; ⏰ 09.00–18.00 Mon–Fri, 09.30–12.30 Sat

Interesting blog
'**Csíkszereda Musings**' http://szekely.blogspot.com/

Pharmacy
✚ **B-dul Timişoarei 31** ⏰ 08.00–20.00 Mon–Fri, 09.00–14.00 Sat, 09.00–13.00 Sun

Post office
✉ Str Kossuth 3; ⏰ 07.00–20.00 Mon–Fri, 08.00–13.00 Sat

WHAT TO SEE AND DO Besides the **Mikó Castle** (*Csíki Székely Múzeum/Muzeul Seciuesc al Ciucului/Székely Museum of Ciuc; Piaţa Cetăţii 2;* ☎ *0266 311 727;* ℮ *info@csikimuzeum.ro; www.csszm.ro;* ⏰ *closed for restoration in 2012, but previously 09.00–17.00 Tue–Sun; admission adult/child 5/2.5RON*), there is not a great deal to see in Miercurea-Ciuc.

In 1970, after a large-scale restoration project the castle became the home of the **Székely Museum of Csik**, founded in 1930 and showing weapons, dolls in folk costume, zoological and sociological items, Franciscan typography and bookbinding. There is also an **extensive art gallery** within the sturdy walls. The overgrown meadow behind the castle is home to a *skanzen* (outdoor village museum) with a small group

BEST BREWS

CIUC PREMIUM (5.0%) The best lager in Romania, and served widely, either bottled or on tap. Brewed with fresh spring water from the Harghita Mountains. The Miercurea-Ciuc (*www.ciucpremium.ro*) brewery is now owned by Heineken Breweries in Bucharest. Ciuc (pronounced *chook* in Romanian) can be requested by name and if you're in a Hungarian-speaking pub, try asking for a 'cheeky shirt' (*Csiki sört*) and see what you get. It should be a foaming half-litre mug of Ciuc.

URSUS PREMIUM (5.0%) This Bere Cluj comes from a brewery founded in 1878 and is called the *regele berii* (King of Beer). Ursus Breweries (Cluj-Napoca, http://ursus.ro) are official partners of the Romanian rugby team.

CIUCAŞ (4.5%) Made by Ursus Breweries (now a member of the South African SAB Miller group) from an original recipe from Braşov (1892).

TIMIŞOREANA (5.0%) Anno 1718, made by Ursus Breweries in Timişoara. This beer has a good fruity flavour.

STEJAR (7.0%) A strong lager from Ursus Breweries in Cluj-Napoca. Made with natural ingredients and too potent as a lunchtime refreshment.

BERGENBIER (4.8%) A watery lager from Bucharest with connections to football.

of traditional Csík cottages and about a dozen Székely gates. Across the road from the castle is the city hall built in 1886, originally the county hall of the old Hungarian royal county. Beside the castle is the 1904 Courthouse.

The **Nagy Imre Gallery** has an important collection of paintings by this Romanian artist (*Nagy Imre 175;* *0266 313 963; www.csszm.ro;* ⊕ *May–Oct 09.00–17.00 Tue–Sun; admission adult/child 5/2.5RON*). However, you might want to time your visit to coincide with the city's most sparkling event, the **Whitsun Pilgrimage** to Şumuleu/Csíksomlyó, a Franciscan church situated 2km to the east of the city. A large meadow nearby has been the site of an annual Roman Catholic pilgrimage to visit the weeping Madonna in the church since the 15th century. The event attracts half a million people from the Székely, Csík and even Csángó regions every year and is held on Whit Sunday (HU Pünkösd).

The latest significant addition to the architectural landscape is the controversial **2001 Millennium Church**, designed by Hungarian architect Imre Makovecz (*www.makovecz.hu*) and located next to the Baroque **Church of the Holy Cross**.

AROUND MIERCUREA-CIUC

BĂILE TUŞNAD Situated in the beautiful wooded Olt River valley, 28km southeast of Miercurea-Ciuc on route 12 is the peaceful **spa resort** town of Băile Tuşnad (Tusnádfürdő). The town and the surrounding area are famous for their spas and mineral waters. It has been a spa resort since the days of the Austro-Hungarian Empire but has recently seen the construction of several modern hotels, which rather spoils the view.

Getting there and away One direct **bus** and several **trains** (*1½hrs*) wind their way from Sfântu Gheorghe to Miercurea-Ciuc. It's better by car because then you can explore the Sfânta Ana volcanic lake (see below).

Tourist information
 Molnar Tur Str Oltului 78; m 0744 612 397; www.tusnadfurdo.ro. Accommodation details & local tours.

Where to stay, eat and drink
🏠 **Hotel Ciucaş** (78 dbl, 16 suites) Aleea Sf Ana 1; \\ 0266 335 004; e contact@hotelciucas. ro; www.hotelciucas.ro. A large, modern hotel in lovely forest surroundings with a good restaurant ($$) & great gym with sauna, jacuzzi, massage, electrotherapy. HB available. *Dbl* $$$, *suite* $$$$, *b/fast inc.*

LACUL SFÂNTA ANA (⊕ *09.00–20.00 daily; car admission 15RON, to park and walk 7RON*) Driving from Băile Tuşnad, continue south along route 12 to the village of Bixad where you turn left for Lacul Sfânta Ana (Szent Anna-tó) at the summit of the extinct volcano Mount Ciomat (950m). It is the only intact volcanic lake in Europe and called after a small chapel of Saint Ana near the watery crater, which was known as Puciosul.

Nearby is a rare **Tinovul Mohoş peat bog**, found in a secondary crater with glacial relics such as *Drosera* insectivorous plants having existed here since the Ice Age. To protect the environment, visitors walk on specially constructed wooden walkway bridges over the 800m-diameter bog. Visitors can also see remarkable **sulphur caves**, which give an unforgettable sensory experience. In the summer,

Csík (Ciuc in Romanian) was the name of a historic administrative county (*comitatus*) of the Kingdom of Hungary. The capital of the county was Csíkszereda (Miercurea-Ciuc). Csík County was situated in the Carpathian Mountains, around the sources and upper reaches of the Olt and Mureş rivers. In 1910, its territory covered 4,859km². The Csík region was a combination of three settlements (*szék* or seats) of the Székely: Csíkszék, Gyergyószék and Kászonszék. Csík County was formed in 1876, when the administrative structure of Transylvania was changed. In 1918, the county became part of the Kingdom of Romania, confirmed by the Treaty of Trianon in 1920. Its territory lies in the present-day Romanian counties of Harghita and Neamţ, a county beyond Transylvania's border.

the meadows up near Lacul Sfânta Ana are filled with tents as a huge collection of locals, particularly Székely, come to spend a few days swimming and boating in the lake and having barbecues. The road downhill to the lake (19.5ha) is guarded by an officious, elderly gentleman, who leaps out of his hut to demand a fee to reach the water's edge. It is possible to hire a boat (*barca*) for 1RON per hour. It was very encouraging – and unusual – to see park wardens walking around with bin bags clearing up all the detritus just before closing time.

Getting there and away Buses and trains from Sfântu Gheorghe to Miercurea-Ciuc stop at Bixad, but from there it's a long uphill **walk** (15km) to the lake. You could try hitching but most cars are jam-packed with numerous family members. A **hire car** is the best method.

ODORHEIU SECUIESC Even more Hungarian (96%) than Miercurea-Ciuc/ Csíkszereda and filled with 19th-century buildings rather than concrete blocks, Odorheiu Secuiesc (Székelyudvarhely/Odorhellen) is often called the 'most Hungarian town' in Transylvania. Known to locals as 'Udvarhely', which literally means 'court place', the town was the former seat of the *comitatus*, and one of the historical centres of the Székely Land. It was first mentioned in papal registers in 1333. In 1492, a **fortress** was constructed, rebuilt and strengthened in 1565 by John II Sigismund Zápolya to control the Székelys who then joined up with Wallachian prince Mihai Viteazul during his Transylvanian campaign and destroyed the fortress in 1599. Because of constant attacks and reconstructions, the building is now known as the 'Székely-attacked fortress'. Visitors can stroll around its gardens and inner walls. While Miercurea-Ciuc is known as the capital of the Csík region, Odorheiu Secuiesc is known as the heart of Székely culture. The town has an old-fashioned, Mitteleuropa ambience but is actually pretty prosperous thanks to the textile, leather and furniture industries. The town has been a centre of learning for centuries. In 1670, the Calvinist College was founded and one of its former students was **Balázs Orbán**, known as 'The Greatest Székely' (see box, page 168). In 2004, a **statue park** was opened at the northwest end of the main square, **Piaţa Primeriei/Városháza tér**, by Hungarian politician Viktor Orbán and mayor Jenő Szász. One of the statues called *Vándor Székely Hazatalál* (*The Wandering Székely Finds His Homeland*) caused controversy as it was interpreted as representing far right-wing poet Albert Wass (see page 43), who was sentenced to death *in absentia* for alleged war crimes. The other 12 statues show architect Károly Kós, statesman

István Bethlen, politican Miklós Wesselényi, *voivode* Gábor Bethlen, Father György (Cardinal Martinuzzi), King Saint László, Prince Csaba, Hungarian regent János Hunyadi (Ioan de Hunedoara), Hungarian governor István Báthory, Ferenc II Rákóczi, Polish general Józef Bem and writer József Nyírő.

Getting there and away The road between Miercurea-Ciuc and Odorheiu Secuiesc is a really lovely drive (*1hr*) and passes through many villages with Székely gates. The village of **Satu Mare/Máréfalva**, a few kilometres east of Odorheiu Secuiesc, has some particularly impressive painted gates. The landscape is beautiful and a little reminiscent of the Scottish Lowlands. The **railway station** is 500m north of the centre along Str Bethlen Gábor. Three trains leave daily in the direction of Sighişoara. The **bus station** is a little nearer the centre (*Str Târgului 10;* \ *0266 217 979*) and many buses leave for Sighişoara, Sovata, Miercurea-Ciuc and Târgu Mureş. Daily buses leave for Budapest. By **car**, Odorheiu Secuiesc is halfway between the Sovata resort and Miercurea-Ciuc on the scenic route 13B and 13A.

Tourist information

Z Tourist information Piaţa Márton Áron 6; \ 0266 217 427; e www.tourinfo.ro; ⊕ Apr–Oct 08.00–20.00 Mon–Fri, 09.00–16.00 Sat; Nov–Mar 08.00–17.00 Mon–Fri. Information about accommodation, events & sights.

THE SZÉKELY

The origin of the Székely people (RO Secui, GER Szekler) has always created debates among historians. The Székely speak Hungarian and their culture and customs are similar to Hungarian culture. There are about 700,000 Székelys and they live mainly in the counties of Hargita, Covasna and Mureş, also known as 'Székely Land'.

Some claim that Székelys are descendants of **Attila the Hun** and this theory is reflected in many Székely legends. Other theories suggest that the Székelys have Avar or Turkic ancestry. Other historians believe that they are simply Magyars like the Hungarians since their language is identical, their cultural differences stemming from the fact that they were more isolated than the Hungarians living in Hungary and therefore they preserved the ancient traditions brought from Asia.

For this reason, Hungarians tend to idealise the Székely and consider them the 'real' Hungarians. Urban Hungarians, particularly in Budapest, are a little nervous of the Székely, calling them 'wily' (*furfangos*). Having survived Ceauşescu's brutal regime, the Transylvanian Hungarians, including the Székely, are tougher and better at using the system. The belief in Hun ancestry is strongly present in Székely legends. According to these legends, after Attila's death, a war broke out between his sons Aladár and Csaba. In the final battle Csaba was defeated and his army had to withdraw, ending up in the eastern part of Transylvania. Csaba went further east to get help from Greece, but he never returned. There is a saying among Székelys: 'We will see him again when Prince Csaba returns from Greece.' **Csaba** is considered to be the father of the Székely, there are many statues of him (for further information on the one in Odorheiu Secuiesc, see previous page).

Attila's favourite wife, Réka, who was the mother of Aladár and Csaba, is also featured in the folk tales. In Târgu Mureş, in the Palace of Culture some of

Where to stay, eat and drink

 Hotel Korona (5 dbl, 1 trpl) Varosháza tér 12/2; \0266 218 061; e office@koronapanzio.ro; www.koronapanzio.ro. On the main square with a great beer garden, restaurant ($) & pancake bar (☉ *10.00–23.00 daily*), the 'Crown' has clean rooms, free internet & solarium. You can also stay in the Korona's traditional peasant house nearby in Sub Cetate (see below). **$$**

ZETEA AND SUBCETATE Just northeast of Odorheiu Secuiesc are two villages – Zetea (Zetelaka) and Subcetate (Zeteváralja/Burgberg) – with traditional peasant houses where you can stay and really get to the heart of Székely culture as the locals arrange many activities such as baking bread, milking cows, shoeing horses, weaving, carving, rope making and musical evenings. Both villages would make a good base if you want to hike to the peak of the Harghita-Mădăraş Mountain (1,800m) where there is a mountain refuge (*cabana*) (m *0740 354 012;* e *office@ madarasi.ro; www.madarasi.ro; en-suite dbl or dorm* **$**).

To reach the villages by **car**, go to Odorheiu Secuiesc and then take the road leading northeast towards Satu Mare and Vlăhiţa. Fork left at Brădeşti and drive for several kilometres. From Odorheiu Secuiesc there are several weekday **buses** to Subcetate (*30mins*).

 Where to stay In **Zetea**, around 70 families offer rural tourism homestays, but one of the best is a lovely peasant house run by Olga Lajosné Sándor.

the stories connected with the Hun legends are pictured in the stained-glass windows (see page 180).

A typical piece of Székely folk art is the **Székely *kapu*** (Székely gate), a gate with a separate entrance for pedestrians and for the horse and cart, decorated with woodcarvings. These gates express the Székely identity and the social status of their owner. There is an impressive collection of Székely gates in the Székely Museum in Miercurea-Ciuc's Mikó Castle (see page 165). When travelling in the Székely Land, you can see many of these typical gates, showing that the tradition is very much alive even today.

Runic scripts (*rovásírás*) are also very typical of the Székely culture. The Székely runic scripts are a variation of runic scripts, which were used by the Kazars (an ethnic group with Turk origins) in middle Asia and they were used until the 16th century. The most important memorial using runic scripts is in the fortified **Church of Dârjiu**, dating from 1431 (see page 170)

The most comprehensive description of the Székely Land and traditions was written between 1859 and 1868 by **Balázs Orbán** in his *Description of Székely Land*.

There is a small number of scholars who believe that Székelys are related to Scythians who joined the Magyars on their trek westward and assimilated into the proto-Hungarian culture. There are others who have suggested that the Székely are simply Magyars, like other Hungarians, and their cultural differences stem from centuries of relative isolation in the mountains. Other scholars believe in a two-fold Hungarian migration to the Carpathian Basin (including the Transylvanian and the Pannonian Plain, now in Hungary), with a first group, the Székelys, arriving in Transylvania some time before the main Magyar conquest in AD896.

Olga kulcsosház (7 dbl) Zsögöd utca 732; \0266 241 221; m 0744 615 423; e olga@ erdelyivendeglatas.com; www.erdelyivendeglatas. com. A *kulcsosház* is literally a 'keyhouse': guests get a *kulcs* or key & can come & go as they please. Roma music evenings can be arranged for a fee of €70/group. **$–$$**

A few kilometres further north and into the Harghita foothills is **Subcetate** where the Korona Panzió has a traditional peasant's house.

Korona Tájház (1 sgl, 7 dbl) Contact through the Hotel Korona in Odorheiu Secuiesc (see page 16). The house is 500m from the 140ha reservoir, ideal for swimming, sunbathing & angling. All rooms are furnished in authentic Székely peasant style with original furniture & decoration. Guests can use the laundry, kitchen & outdoor barbecue. There is also a large oven suitable for baking bread or even roasting a pig. **$**

MUGENI
Located 8km southwest of Odorheiu Secuiesc on the second-class main road heading towards Cristuru Secuiesc is the village of Mugeni (Bögöz). Six buses leave daily from Odorheiu Secuiesc for Cristuru Secuiesc; get off after 8km in Mugeni. Find here the 14th-century Calvanist church with **frescoes** depicting gory scenes of Saint László's battle against the Cumans. To visit the church, enquire at the parish office at No 268. See page 106 for some church-visiting phrases.

DÂRJIU
The 13th-century **fortified Unitarian Church** in Dârjiu (Székelyderzs) is one of seven Transylvanian churches featuring on UNESCO's World Heritage List, inscribed in 1993 and extended in 1999.

As in Ghelinţa and Mugeni, the beautiful church at Dârjiu has scenes from the legend of Saint László. There is a strong cult of Saint László in Székely Land (see also *Turda*, page 259) where he is immortalised in beautiful frescoes on the walls of the churches. One of the stories you will see illustrated most often depicts a clash between the then Prince László and a party of Cuman raiders. A Cuman had carried off a Hungarian girl and László was unable to catch up with them. The young lady boldly took matters into her own hands, dragging the Cuman off his horse at full gallop. László then defeated the pagan raider in a sword battle. Colourful and gory scenes decorate the walls of the church.

Getting there and away
By **car**, Dârjiu is 5km south of Mugeni on a very poorly maintained road, Dârjiu is perhaps best approached from the E60/route 13 highway from Braşov to Sighişoara; turn right at Mihai Viteazu, 8km before Saschiz, and drive for 13km. Two **buses** a day connect Odorheiu Secuiesc and Dârjiu, but taking public transport turns it into a whole day's outing.

CORUND
Corund (Korond) is a village devoted totally to **ceramics**. The one main road leading through the village is lined with workshops and open stalls selling pots, plates, vases, bowls, cooking equipment and decorative objects, in fact anything and everything that can be made by craftsmen experienced in the art of pottery and porcelain. The pottery is often coloured green, brown and yellow, with a cobalt blue introduced by the Saxons. The motifs feature the natural world – usually birds, animals and flowers. Another motif is the 'Tree of Life' which is also the name of a local association (HU *Életfa*), of 22 ethnic Hungarian potters (*www.korondifazekasokszovetsege.ro*). The association, founded in 2006, guarantees the authenticity of the ceramics and promotes the potters and their creations. The centre of the village has a monument to the Hungarian language with medal-

like plaques featuring famous authors. Just outside the village on the way from Odorheiu Secuiesc to Praid, scores of Roma woman stand at the roadside offering buckets overflowing with chanterelle mushrooms.

Getting there and away By **car**, Corund is 24km north of Odorheiu Secuiesc on route 13B; the drive is very scenic. **Microbuses** leave Odorheiu Secuiesc for Sovata, stopping in Corund (*40mins*).

Tourist information

🛈 Corund Tours/Csavargó Corundtrans Piac utca 88t; \0266 249 000; www.csavargo.ro; ⏱ 08.00–12.00 & 16.00–18.00 Mon–Fri, 08.00–12.00 & 18.00–20.00 Sat. The office can also provide transport details, such as buses from Odorheiu Secuiesc to Budapest, which run to & fro daily.

PRAID The small town of Praid (Parajd), situated in the heart of Țara Sarelui (Sóvidék/Salt Country) contains an unusual and unpredictably fun destination – a salt mine. **Praid Salt Mine** (*Salina Praid/Parajdi Sóbánya; Str Gării 44;* \ *0266 240 200;* e *office@salinapraid.ro; www.salinapraid.ro;* ⏱ *08.00–15.50 daily; admission adult/child 20/12RON; the bus departs once there are 25 people on board, visitors spend 1hr max in the mine*) makes a great day trip, especially on rainy days. The information reads that it's not suitable for pregnant women or those suffering from high blood pressure or claustrophobia. However, I can personally testify that once past the bizarre ride on a rickety town bus which heads off down a dark, foreboding 1.5km tunnel, it is not claustrophobic at all. The tunnel opens out into the largest underground space I have ever seen. Located 120m beneath the surface, the vast, high, cavernous chambers are like giant, black-walled, marble-floored playgrounds. Children run around screaming and shouting, playing badminton, billiards, handball and ping-pong. The air is sterile and rich in salts and calcium and there is a therapy centre, café, library, ecumenical chapel, exhibition hall and even internet club. Salt has been mined here for centuries at seams 3km deep underground. Around 3,000 people visit daily. In 2012, the baths were undergoing renovation and are due to re-open in 2013. I should warn potential visitors that the 'queue' for the bus back up to the surface is totally chaotic and an aggressive crush – that's when the claustrophobia sets in! There are also quite a number of steps to descend and climb. Salt-mine fans, see also *Turda*, page 259.

Once back on the surface, Praid is filled with cafés, restaurants and small stalls offering snacks, postcards, black leather cowboy hats to blend in with the locals, salt, and badminton racquets (which you can't buy down the mine). There is also a **small thermal saltwater pool and** *strand* or 'beach' (*Băile Hidrotermale Praid;* ⏱ *Jun–Sep 09.00–18.00 daily; admission adult/child 10/5RON*) where you can sit in warm water outdoors and the calcium, sodium, sulphur and magnesium will soothe aching joints and muscles.

Getting there and away By **car**, Praid is a scenic drive 36km north of Odorheiu Secuiesc on route 13B. **Microbuses** leave Odorheiu Secuiesc for Sovata, stopping in Praid (*1hr*).

Where to stay, eat and drink

🏠 Pensiunea Praid (10 dbl) Str Principală 1085; \0266 240 471; e office@pensiuneapraid. ro; www.pensiuneapraid.ro. A good place to stay if you are considering a longer cure at the salt mine (season tickets available) or salt pool. The usual cure length is adults 16–18 days, children 10–12

days. Praid Pension has a gym, jacuzzi, sauna & internet. Each room has its own kitchen. **$$**
✘ **Casa Telegdy** Str Principală 1173; ✆0266 240 217; ⊕ 10.00–22.00 daily. Opposite the salt mine exit. A popular place to get one's strength back after all that running around down the mine. Traditional dishes & friendly service in the house where the famous engineer Károly Telegdy lived (1904–95). **$**

FROM PRAID TO BICAZ GORGES

It takes two hours to drive from Praid along route 13B, changing to 12C at Gheorgheni/ Gyergyószentmiklós. After Gheorgheni, the road through the mountains is stunning and the final destination of Bicaz Gorges-Hăşmăş Mountain National Park (Parcul National Cheile Bicazului-Hăşmăş) is well worth the journey. Two-thirds of the way there, the road meanders through low hills passing sweet little wooden chalets near **Statiunea Bucin**, then moves onto a flat plain passing through **Gheorgheni**, a Székely town that is home to the largest Armenian community in Romania (see *Gherla*, page 258). The **Tarisznyás Márton Museum** (*Str Rákóczi Ferenc 1;* ✆ *0266 365 229;* e *muzeum@tmmuzeum.ro; www.tmmuzeum.ro;* ⊕ *May–Oct 09.00–17.00 Tue– Fri, 10.00–17.00 Sat/Sun, Oct–Apr 09.00–17.00 Tue–Fri, Sat/Sun by appointment; admission adult/child 4/2RON*), housed in a former Armenian merchant's inn, contains an interesting collection of folk costumes and artefacts. The museum is in front of an Armenian Catholic church built in 1733 with elegant Baroque ornamentation.

From Gheorgheni, the road is pretty spectacular, winding through the forest, sometimes on the side of the mountain with vertiginous drops below and great views. There is also an excellent general store on the road leading out of Gheorgheni, good for stocking up on snacks and picnic items.

BICAZ GORGES-HĂŞMĂŞ MOUNTAIN NATIONAL PARK The 6,575ha territory of the park falls into two counties, Harghita and Neamţ (the latter beyond the Transylvanian border), and is divided into two zones: the special conservation zone and the protection zone beyond. The national park contains many interesting sights for hikers, nature lovers, botanists and geologists. It is also interesting from the point of view of its landscapes, and biological diversity generated by the great variety of geo-climactic conditions. The towering **Bicaz Gorges** (Cheile Bicazului) are famous for their 300m-high limestone rocks overhanging narrow roads and precipitous passes. At the same time, **Lacu Roşu** (see box below), formed through the natural damming of the Bicaz River's waters in a landslide in 1838, is a beautiful, if somewhat creepy sight.

The park is located in the Hăşmăş Mountains – situated in the central group of Oriental Carpathians, also known as the Moldo – the Transylvanian Carpathians.

There are many tourist **trekking** routes well marked in the national park with different symbols such as a red horizontal stripe, a red cross, a blue triangle, a yellow vertical stripe or a blue-filled circle, signifying the different routes.

Getting there and away Straddling the northeastern border of Transylvania, the national park is reached on the 13B/12C road from Sovata (*2½hrs*). Several **trains** and three **buses** leave from Miercurea-Ciuc for Gheorgheni, but then there is only one daily bus from there to the national park.

Information

🅻 **Park Administration** Str Principala 44/A, Izvorul Muresului; ✆f 0266 336 540; e pnbicaz@ mciuc.rosilva.ro; www.cheilebicazului-hasmas.ro

Lacu Roşu/Gyilkos-tó Lacu Roşu (Red Lake, in Hungarian Gyilkos-tó, or 'Murderer's Lake') is a natural dam lake situated in the Hăşmăş Mountains. The lake was formed in the 19th century, after a landslide blocked the waterflow. To this day, stumps of tree trunks, the remains of a submerged forest, poke out of the water and give an eerie atmosphere, especially when mist frequently descends on the water. Many stalls cluster around the lake and there are several restaurants and hotels if you want to stay longer and explore the park.

Information
Eco-Info-Centre ⊕ 10.00–18.00 Tue–Sun. Located by the lake's car park on the main road, the centre gives information on trekking routes in the region.

Boating ⊕ May–Oct 09.00–19.30 daily; 15RON for 1–2 people for 30mins. If you dare!

Where to stay
Lacu Roşu Hotel (4 sgl, 30 dbl, 2 apts) 535502 Lacu Roşu; ☏ 0266 380 008 or 0266 380 020; e gyilkostohotel@gmail.com; www.

hotellacurosu.ro. A comfortable modern hotel in beautiful surroundings with a restaurant ($) & café-bar. **$$–$$$**

FROM GHEORGHENI TO BORSEC

LĂZAREA If you turn left at Gheorgheni and head north towards the spa town of Borsec, instead of carrying straight on for the Bicaz Gorges-Hăşmăş National Park you will come after 5km to Lăzarea (Gyergyószárhegy), where a monastery with a white tower visible from the road sits on the side of a steep hill above the village. By **car**, Lăzarea is on route 12 between Gheorgheni and Topliţa, and by **train**, the

---

THE LEGEND OF MURDERER'S LAKE

There are many legends surrounding the formation and colour of Lacu Roşu. One tale tells of a beautiful young girl named Eszter who lived in the nearby village of Ditrău. One Sunday, while waiting by the spring Eszter was kidnapped by an evil man. Eszter cried to the sky for help. The mountain answered with a thunderous storm, which brought heavy rains and swept rocks down its slopes. The rocks crushed both Eszter and the kidnapper and blocked a river below, thus forming the lake. Another legend claims that the valley where the lake now lies was once a fertile grazing land inhabited by some shepherds. While looking over their sheep a storm arose which caused a landslide. The shepherds and their sheep were buried beneath the fallen karst rocks, which also blocked the valley of the river. The red colour of the lake came from the blood of the shepherds and the sheep.

The most plausible explanation is that heavy rain in the summer of 1838 stimulated a landslide from the face of Murderer's Mountain. The landslide produced a dam, forming the lake. The lake's distinctive red shade is the result of the red earth flowing into the river, although some claim it is from the blood of a group of picnickers who were crushed in the landslide. Today, the Red Lake is one of Romania's most popular tourist attractions. Its environment has been left untouched, thus providing an excellent escape. The lake itself is L-shaped and relatively small. Its maximum depth of 10m makes it ideal for rowing or fishing.

town is one stop after Gheorgheni on the Miercurea-Ciuc to Topliţa line. There is one daily **bus** from Miercurea-Ciuc to Lăzarea. The **Lăzarea Castle** (*Castelul Lázár; Aleea Bastionului 67;* \ *0266 364 030;* ⊕ *09.00–17.00 Tue–Sun; admission 5RON*), constructed in 1532 by the Lázár family, is just below the Franciscan Monastery; the Renaissance Hall and fresco-filled façade are under restoration.

BORSEC Borsec (Borszék) was one of the most elegant **spas** of the Austro-Hungarian Empire and has a wonderful location (at 900m) with clean mountain air, a favourable climate and delicious mineral water. The resort is surrounded by an overcoat of coniferous forests, protecting it from cold winds. The forest purifies the air and lessens any sudden temperature variations. Borsec owes its fame to its curative mineral waters. Natural cures (the microclimate, the air cures and healing water cures), and physiotherapy procedures claim to heal or ameliorate nutritional or metabolic illnesses. The name comes from the Hungarian *borvizszék*, meaning from 'mineral water chair', the *chairs* being the old administrative districts (see box, page 155) in Székely Land. The resort is adorned with 72 Swiss-style chalet villas, constructed in the 1920s but sadly many of them are now in a poor, run-down state. The reputation of Borsec's mineral water dates back to the 16th century. Documents from this epoch prove that the mineral water from Borsec was transported by carts in wooden casks to the royal court in Alba Iulia in 1594. Owing to the curative effect and empirical experience the mineral waters from Borsec were bottled in sealed pitchers which were then put into sacks and were transported on horseback to Transylvania, Moldavia, Wallachia and Hungary, beginning in the 18th century. Bottling began in 1806 and now Borsec accounts for a quarter of the Romanian mineral water consumption.

Getting there and away Borsec is situated 28km from Topliţa, 130km from Târgu Mureş and 220km from Braşov. By **car**, the road between Topliţa and Borsec is very scenic, crossing the Giurgeu Mountains at Creanga Pass. Take the train to Topliţa then change to a local bus or maxi-taxi.

6

Mureş County

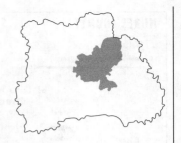

Mureş County (6,696km²) has a population of 531,380 inhabitants (Romanians, Magyars, Roma and Germans). Lying in the central part of the country, following the course of the Mureş River, the county is in a mostly flat region within the loop of the Carpathians. There are plateaux and hills and the Călimani and Gurghiu mountains to the north and east respectively. The Mureş River basin and its tributaries, such as the Târnava Mare and Târnava Mică, form a watery network all over the county. The climate is characterised by long and cold winters and hot summers.

Whereas Odorheiu Secuiesc is considered the cultural capital of the Székely Land, the county town Târgu Mureş is definitely the Székely capital of trade and commerce. Its name in Romanian (Târgu), the *vásárhely* of Márosvásárhely in Hungarian and Szeklerneumarkt, the 'new market of the Székely' in German, signify a marketplace that has existed since the Middle Ages. The Mureş River valley north of the capital is flanked with important castles and manor houses belonging to Transylvanian nobility and the south of the county has a fine collection of Saxon fortified churches. To the east is the Ţara Sarelui/Sóvidék (Salt Country), where the spa resort of Sovata sits on the banks of the atmospheric thermal, saltwater Lacul Ursu (Bear Lake). Mureş County has many ethnographic and folk treasures in its villages. Traditional feasts and customs such as the 'Wetting of Wives' in Hodac (before Whitsun), the Girls' Fair in Gurghiu (May), the Cherries Fair in Brâncoveneşti (July) and the Fish Fair in Zau de Câmpie (July) are great spectacles. The county's economy is based on natural resources: natural gas, salt, mineral springs, wood and stone for building materials. Agriculture is the second most important sector of the county's economy and farmland covers more than 60% of the county.

TÂRGU MUREŞ   *Telephone code 0265, sometimes 0365*

Târgu Mureş (Márosvásárhely/Neumarkt am Mieresch) is a vibrant market town, very much a Romanian and Hungarian mix and getting the best out of both cultures. Târgu Mureş is called 'the city of roses' because of its gardens full of the many-coloured flowers. At first glance, the city appears a little dusty and ragged at the edges, less wealthy than the renovated Saxon cities of Braşov and Sibiu, and a little 'Wild West' in ambience. This impression increases with the sight of many moustachioed Roma gentlemen strolling along the main street wearing huge black cowboy hats and black leather waistcoats, smoking and joking with their mates. Elderly Roma ladies in brightly coloured long skirts sell wooden spoons and children run about giggling. Unlike western Europe, however, the streets are free of litter and there are many flower beds, which combined with the gaily painted Art Nouveau buildings and cosmopolitan terrace-café atmosphere make Târgu Mureş a lively and memorable place to visit. Pop music from the 1980s blasts out from

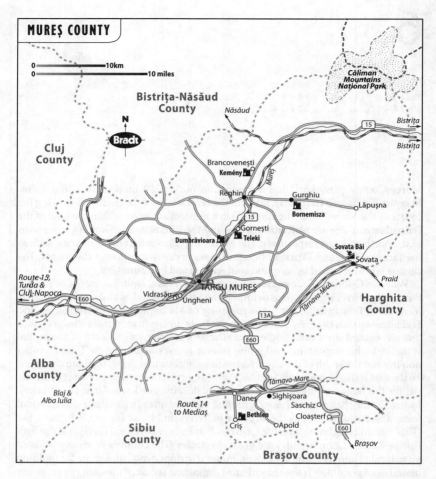

radios in the many pizzerias and the city does seem a little stranded in the past, despite many brand-new shopping centres to the west of the centre. Though I was delighted to count about ten local lads wearing Chelsea replica football shirts with No 7 (Shevchenko, the Ukrainian wizard) on the back!

HISTORY The settlement was mentioned in documents in 1322 as Novum Forum Siculorum, meaning 'new market town', with a population of mostly Hungarian origin and it became the main economic centre in the area. Merchants and guild members got involved in economic activities in the feudal age. During this time, the spiritual life of the region developed and the county town became an important economic and cultural nucleus.

A famous school was founded in 1557 and important scientists studied and taught here, including the mathematician Farkas Bolyai and his son and student János, the founder of non-Euclidean geometry. After 1754, the Royal Table, the supreme court of Transylvania operated in the city and young revolutionaries such as Avram Iancu and Alexandru Papiu Ilarian formed their ideas here. Transylvanian nobleman Samuel Teleki founded the documentary library in Târgu Mureş and it became a public library in 1802. It bears his name and the initial collection of 40,000 books has now swelled to more than 200,000. During the Ceauşescu era, Târgu Mureş was a 'closed city' and only Romanians were allowed to settle here in an effort to dilute the Hungarian community. Today the population is 53% Romanian, 38% Hungarian and 9% Roma. Despite the present easy-going climate, Târgu Mureş witnessed ethnic tensions during the 1980s which boiled over in 1990, when there were violent clashes between Hungarian students, protesting about Hungarian-language facilities at the local university, and Romanians who raided the local Hungarian political party offices. The rabble attacked the Hungarian playwright András Sütő (1927–2006), who was blinded in one eye. These days, the atmosphere is much less confrontational and I heard Hungarian spoken in the street and in shops. Being a town of flowers, in Târgu Mureş time is measured by a floral clock in Piaţa Trandafirilor.

GETTING THERE, AWAY AND AROUND
By air
Transilvania-Târgu Mureş Vidrasău Airport (TGM) (*Târgu Mureş–Ludus road, Vidrasău, 547612 Mureş County;* \ *0265 328 259;* f *0265 328 257;* e *office@ targumuresairport.ro; www.targumuresairport.ro*) The airport at Vidrasău is situated 15km southwest of central Târgu Mureş on route 15/E60. **Wizzair** flies direct from Târgu Mureş to London Luton. **Tarom** has flights to Bucharest. Beyond the scrum of the baggage collection are a cluster of hire-car offices, though opening hours often don't coincide with Wizzair's outrageously early departures. A **shuttle bus** leaves Târgu Mureş for the airport from outside the Tarom office on Piaţa Trandafirilor (*Piaţa Trandafirilor 6–8;* \ *0265 236 200*) two hours before flight departure times – though you're unlikely to find any information on this apart from asking in the Tourist Office. If you're uncertain, book a **taxi** through your hotel. Early morning taxis between the centre of town and the airport cost 30–35RON.

By rail and bus
The main railway station and bus station are to the southwest of the centre.

The **railway station** is at Piaţa Gării, off B-dul Gheorghe Doja. For rail information, contact **Agenţia de Voiaj CFR** (*Piaţa Teatrului 1;* \ *0265 266 203;* ⊕ *08.00–19.00 Mon–Fri*), who sell advance tickets. There are six trains daily to Miercurea-Ciuc (*5hrs*), two trains daily to Sibiu (*5hrs*), one train to Cluj (*2½hrs*), two to Bucharest (*9hrs*) and one to Budapest (*8hrs*).

The **bus station** is further south along B-dul Gheorghe Doja 52, behind the Hotel Voiajor. Many buses and microbuses leave for Sighişoara (*every hour, 1½hrs*), Cluj (*5 daily, 3hrs*), two to Sibiu (*3hrs*), five to Bistriţa (*2½hrs*) and many to the Csík and Székely regions. If you're arriving by bus, try to get dropped off in town rather than having to walk back from the bus station – minibuses from Sighişoara, for example, will drop off near the top of B-Dul Decembrie 1918, by Piaţa Victoriei.

Taxi companies
🚕 **Cornisa** \ 0265 204 943
🚕 **Royal Taxi** \ 0265 204 942

Car hire
🚕 **Caruno** Târgu Mureş airport; m 0757 656 700; e office@caruno.eu; www.caruno.eu. Offering free drop offs at Cluj-Napoca & Sibiu airports. Dacia Logan from €20 per day for 7 days excluding VAT.

🚕 **Hertz** Târgu Mureş airport; \ 0265 328 122; e rotgm51@hertz.com.ro; www.hertz.com.ro.

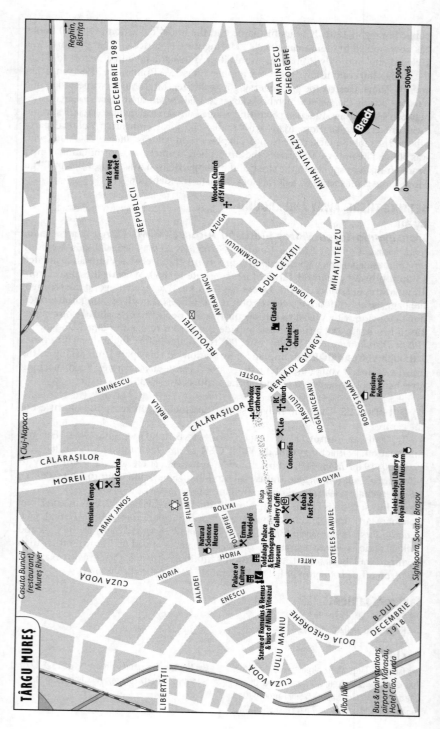

TÂRGU MUREŞ

Casuta Bunicii (restaurant), Mureş River
Cluj-Napoca
Reghin, Bistriţa

22 DECEMBRIE 1989

REPUBLICII

Fruit & veg market

Wooden Church of Sf Mihail

AZUGA

COZMINULUI

MARINESCU GHEORGHE

N

Bradt

0   500m
0   500yds

B-DUL CETĂŢII

Citadel

MIHAI VITEAZU

N IORGA

AVRAM IANCU

REVOLUŢIEI

EMINESCU

Calvanist church

BERNÁDY GYÖRGY

BRĂILA

CĂLĂRAŞILOR

POŞTEI

Orthodox cathedral

RC church

Leo

TÂRGULUI

KOGĂLNICEANU

BORSOS TAMÁS

Pensiune Helveţia

CĂLĂRAŞILOR

MOREII

Pensiune Tempo

Laci Csarda

Concordia

BOLYAI

ARANY JANOS

A FILIMON

BOLYAI

Natural Sciences Museum

POLIGRFIEI

HORIA

Emma Vendeglö

Piata Trandafirilor

Gallery Caffé

Kebab Fast Food

BOLYAI

Teleki-Bolyai Library & Bolyai Memorial Museum

CUZA VODA

HORIA

BALADEI

Toldalagi Palace & Ethnography Museum

KOTELES SAMUEL

ARTEI

ENESCU

Palace of Culture

IULIU MANIU

Statue of Romulus & Remus & bust of Mihai Viteazul

CUZA VODA

DOJA GHEORGHE

B-DUL DECEMBRIE 1918

Sighişoara, Sovata, Braşov

Alba Iulia

Bus & train stations, airport at Vidrasău, Hotel Ciao, Turda

LIBERTĂŢII

178

Oltea B-dul 1 Decembrie 1918 291D; ☎0265 255 350; m 0744 801 135; www.rentacar.targu-mures.ro. Offices in town & at the airport. A Ford Fiesta costs €30 a day for 7 days.

TOURIST INFORMATION
Tourist Information Centre Str Enescu 2 (on corner of Palace of Culture bldg); ☎0365 404 934; e turism@cjmures.ro; www.cjmures.ro/turism; ⊕ Jun–Aug 08.00–16.00 Mon/Sat, 08.00–18.00 Tue–Fri, Sep–May 08.00–16.00 Mon, 08.00–18.00 Tue–Fri. Very helpful with information, accommodation ideas & entertainment options.

WHERE TO STAY
Hotel Concordia (30 dbl, 4 suites) Piaţa Trandafirilor 45; ☎0265 260 602; e rezervari@hotelconcordia.ro; www.hotelconcordia.ro. Super-stylish hotel with snazzy rooms, pool, sauna, jacuzzi, Wi-Fi & zebra-print sofas in the lobby, & restaurant ($$$) in a converted turn-of-the-last-century building. $$$$
Hotel Ciao (32 dbl, 2 sgl) Str Gheorghe Doja 143; ☎0265 250 750; e office@hotel-ciao.ro; www.hotel-ciao.ro. Modern 3-star located next to the bus & train stations. If you really need to stay in this area & they're full, try **Hotel Perla** (*www.hotel-perla.ro*, $$$$). $$$

Pensiune Helveţia (9 dbl, 2 suites) Str Borsos Tamás 13; ☎0265 216 954; e office@villahelvetia.ro; www.villahelvetia.ro. Friendly Swiss-owned 3-star pension with a restaurant ($$), Arosa Bar, wine cellar & terrace. $$$
Pensiune Tempo (10 dbl, 1 suite) Str Morii 27; ☎0265 213 552; e office@tempo.ro; www.tempo.ro. Perhaps the nicest place to stay in town, with friendly & efficient staff & just a short walk from Piaţa Trandafirilor. It's also within easy staggering distance of its excellent & hugely popular restaurant, Laci Csarda (see below). $$$

WHERE TO EAT AND DRINK
Casuta Bunicii Str Matei Corvin 2; ☎0265 307 011; www.lacupola.ro; ⊕ 08.00–midnight daily. Hearty dishes below Pensiunea La Cupola ($$$). $$
Gallery Caffé Piaţa Trandafirilor 17; ☎0265 250 590; www.gallery-caffe.ro; ⊕ 09.00–midnight Mon–Fri, 10.00–midnight Sat/Sun. Coffee, cocktails & smoothies in a vaulted, cellar-like interior with small exhibitions of local artwork & photography on the walls. Wi-Fi access. $$
Laci Csarda Str Morii 27; ☎0265 213 552; www.tempo.ro; ⊕ 10.00–midnight daily. Next to Pensiune Tempo, this is a standout restaurant serving traditional Transylvanian dishes to the wild accompaniment of live Roma musicians. $$

Emma Vendéglő Str Horea 6; ☎0265 263 021; www.emmacatering.ro; ⊕ 08.00–20.00 Mon–Fri, 11.00–20.00 Sat. Dinky little bistro with Hungarian home cooking lunch menus (11RON). $
Kebab Fast Food Str Bolyai 10; ☎0265 268 510; ⊕ 06.30–22.00 Mon–Sat. Wooden café interior with great kebabs & juice, run by the Emma bistro (above). $
Restaurantul Leo Piaţa Trandafirilor 43; ☎0265 214 999; www.leocatering.ro; ⊕ 10.00–22.00 Mon–Fri, 11.00–22.00 Sat/Sun. Packed-out place with covered terrace, blaring pop music & giant pizzas, as well as other dishes. $

OTHER PRACTICALITIES
Bank
$ **OTP** Piaţa Trandafirilor 50; www.otpbank.ro; ⊕ 08.30–17.30 Mon–Fri

Internet
Gallery Caffe (see above).

Pharmacy
✚ **Atlas** Piaţa Trandafirilor 55; ⊕ 08.00–20.00 Mon–Fri, 09.00–13.00 Sat

Post office
✉ Str Revoluţiei 1; ⊕ 07.00–20.00 Mon–Fri, 08.00–13.00 Sat

WHAT TO SEE AND DO The colourful main square, the **Square of Roses** (Piaţa Trandafirilor) stretches for a long way in a northeasterly direction towards the black-and-white neo-Byzantine **Orthodox cathedral** (1925–34) built right opposite and dwarfing the Baroque **Roman Catholic church** (1728–64). The Orthodox cathedral is like the one in Sfântu Gheorghe: grey and dull outside, a riot of colour and gilt inside. On the left of the entrance is a painting showing cruel Magyars beating up poor Romanian peasants. The church and the impressive statue of Avram Iancu in front were the reply to the Hungarian imperialist buildings towards the southern end of the square. At the beginning of the 20th century, the influential Hungarian mayor Dr György Bernády (1864–1935) shaped the cityscape and many elegant Art Nouveau villas sprouted around the Piaţa Trandafirilor. The jewels in the crown were the **Palace of Culture** (*Palatul Culturii/Kultúrpalota; Piaţa Trandafirilor;* ⊕ *09.00–18.00 Tue–Sun; admission adult/child 6/1.5RON*), built in 1913, and its neighbouring **Old Town Hall** (1907), which is now government offices and guarded by a young man dressed in a uniform. Try to persuade him to let you see the entrance hall as it is very beautiful with shallow arches, marble floors and columns. In the little garden at the front is a **statue of Romulus and Remus** feeding from a she-wolf as well as an impressive **bust of Mihai Viteazul**. Both buildings are the work of Budapest architects Dezső Jakab and Marcell Komor, inspired by the British Arts and Crafts movement. The polychromatic roof tiles were created in the Zsolnay ceramics workshop in Pécs, Hungary, but the real treasures are found inside, in the Hall of Mirrors; not a fairground novelty but a stunning hall filled with fantastic stained-glass windows from the workshop of Miksa Róth, the Budapest genius of colour and glass. The windows illustrate ancient Hungarian legends and Székely folk ballads (see box, page 168). Upstairs is an art gallery with some pleasant pastoral paintings from the 19th–20th centuries and there is a small concert hall with a huge 4,463-pipe organ. The interior is dark, all gilt and floral wallpaper, totally over the top and overwhelming.

The **Toldalagi Palace** is a Baroque building dating from 1772 and now housing the **Ethnography Museum** (*Muzeul de Etnografie şI Artă Populară; Piaţa Trandafirilor 11;* ☎ *0265 250 169; www.muzeumures.ro;* ⊕ *09.00–16.00 Tue–Fri, 09.00–13.00 Sat/ Sun, but closed in 2012 while the heating system was replaced*). Walk along Strada Horea to find the **Natural Sciences Museum** (*Str Horea 24;* ☎ *0365 430 390; www. muzeumures.ro;* ⊕ *09.00–16.00 Tue–Fri, 09.00–14.00 Sat, 09.00–13.00 Sun; admission adult/child 5/2RON*). It is possible to make a short detour along Strada Aurel Filmon to see the elegant, beige and white **synagogue** (1899), serving the 100 remaining Jews from the pre-World War II population of 5,500. Crossing over the main square and heading uphill in a leafy quarter, is the **Bolyai Memorial Museum** (*Str Bolyai 17;* ☎ *0265 261 857; www.telekiteka.ro;* ⊕ *10.00–17.00 Tue–Fri, 10.00–13.00 Sat/Sun; admission adult/child 5/2RON*) and **Teleki-Bolyai Library** with a vast collection of 40,000 volumes amassed by Count Sámuel Teleki. Outside the museum, statues of Farkas Bolyai and his son János rest under a tree. Head in a northeasterly direction, through tree-lined suburban streets and family houses up to the **citadel** where fairs and barbecues are often held. The citadel surrounds a **Calvinist church**, built in 1430 for the Dominican monks. Further north, along Strada Avram Iancu, then second right heading east for 100m is the **Wooden Church of Sf Mihail** (1793–94) sitting in a large churchyard with a shingle onion dome and a beautiful interior. Romanians seek out this church because the national poet and hero Mihai Eminescu slept in the porch in 1866 when there was no room at any of the taverns. Further north towards the railway line, the **fruit and vegetable market** (*Piaţa 22 Decembrie 1989*) is a great place to meet the locals. Farmers sell their fruit and vegetables, as well as homemade Romanian cheeses such as *caş, telemea* and *urdă*.

SOVATA BĂI Sovata and Sovata Băi (resort) are located in a beautiful wooded valley in the heart of the **Ţara Sarelui/Sóvidék** (Salt Country). Around 20 million years ago, the region was covered by the sea, which left a deep seam of salt (see *Praid*, page 171 and *Turda*, page 259) eroded over the centuries by water until 1875, when there was a downpour on 27 May and a sinkhole formed in a hay-meadow which became full of water and collapsed, forming the saltwater **Lacul Ursu** (*Bear Lake* ⊕ *09.00–13.00 & 15.00–17.00 daily; admission adult/child 12/8RON*). The **Mini-Tren** (train) Sovata leaves every 15 minutes from the Lacul Ursu entrance for a 20- to 25-minute tour around the resort. Tickets cost 10RON, children under three travel free. The saline solution (250gm/l) is as full of salt as the waters in the Dead Sea and very buoyant and relaxing. The water is said to be excellent as a treatment for gynaecological problems. Around the lake, spa hotels, restaurants and elegant early 20th-century villas cluster. The green hills shelter many more salty lakes: Negru (Black), the oldest among them and formed in 1710 by the implosion of a salt-pit; Aluniş; Mierlei (Blackbird); Şerpilor (Snake), now dried up; Roşu (Red); Verde (Green); and Lacul Paraschiva, the only freshwater lake. There are many footpaths and marked trails around the lakes, which make for pleasant walks. Beyond the Red Lake is a strange Salt Mount (Muntale de Sare), a cliff made of rock salt with unusual formations.

Getting there and away Sovata is situated 45km due east of Târgu Mureş but reached on a longer route. First head south on the E60 towards Sighişoara. After 20km at Bălăuseri, turn left onto route 13A and drive for 40km through small villages and beautiful farming land to reach Sovata. From there you have to keep your eyes peeled for signs to Sovata Băi, the lake resort and hotels. By **bus**, around 17 microbuses leave Târgu Mureş bus station for Sovata every day (*1½hrs*). There are also several buses from Odoheiu Secuiesc and Miercurea-Ciuc.

Tourist information

🇮 **Tourist Information Centre** Salt Lake Travel, Str Bradului 2/A; \0265 577 421; e office@sovatatravel.ro; www.sovatatravel.ro; ⊕ Sep–May 09.00–17.00 Mon–Fri, Jun 09.00–17.00 Mon–Fri, 09.00–13.00 Sat, Jul/Aug 10.00–21.00 Mon–Sat, 10.00–14.00 Sun. Advice on accommodation, plane, train & bus tickets.

Where to stay

🏠 **Danubius Hotel Sovata** (168 dbl, 2 disabled on each floor) Str Trandafirilor 111; \0265 570 151; e sovatahotel@szovata.ro; www.danubiusgroup.com. Treat yourself. This is the best hotel in the resort by far & the only one worth staying in. The 6-storey white concrete block has a very good restaurant with huge buffet for b/fast & dinner (**$$**), charming waitresses & excellent receptionists. The 4-star rooms have the most glorious view of the lake & surrounding hills. The smoky foyer bar has free Wi-Fi access. The hotel has a extensive range of treatments & holiday packages, a small pool (⊕ *07.00–21.00 daily*), warm salt pool, sauna & guests have free access to Lacul Ursu. **$$$–$$$$$**

🏠 **Hotel Brădet** (96 dbl, 2 suites) Str Vulturului 68; \0265 570 506; e sovatahotel@szovata.ro; www.danubiusgroup.com. Brădet & Făget (see below) are also Danubius-run but much cheaper & with fewer facilities, & less English spoken. A 2-star hotel with a wooden 1970s lobby that has to be seen. Treatments for gynaecological, dermatological & locomotive problems. Restaurant (**$**) & café. **$–$$$**

🏠 **Hotel Făget** Str Vulturului 39; \0265 570 651; e sovatahotel@szovata.ro; www.danubiusgroup.com. A 2-star hotel offering similar treatments to the Brădet. **$–$$$**

🏠 **Villa Anna** (1 dbl, 6 tpl, 2 apts) Str Stâna de Vale 5; m 0742 523 337; e rezervari@vilaanna.ro;

www.vilaanna.ro. For something a little more low key & homely, this small guesthouse is only 1.5km from Lacul Ursu & offers accommodation in 2 buildings, with shared kitchen facilities in each. $

✕ Where to eat and drink

✕ **Boema Sovata Restaurant** Str Bradului 36; 📞0265 571 102; ⏰ 08.00–22.00. Traditional Romanian & Székely dishes with live music & a pleasant terrace. $

✕ **Vila Sovata Restaurant** Str Trandafirilor 84; 📞0265 577 501; ⏰ 08.00–22.00. Located in an atmospheric, wooden Transylvanian villa with typical turrets, the restaurant offers traditional dishes. $

Other practicalities

Bank
$ **Banca Comerciala Romană** Str Trandafirilor 111; ⏰ 08.30–17.00 Mon–Fri, 08.30–12.30 Sat. ATM accepts Visa, MasterCard, Cirrus.

Internet
🖵 **Danubius Hotel Sovata** (see above & free for guests). One PC, 5RON/hr.

Pharmacy
✚ Str Trandafirilor 82; ⏰ 08.00–20.00 Mon–Fri, 09.00–20.00 Sat/Sun

Post office
✉ Str Trandafirilor 74; ⏰ 07.00–20.00 Mon–Fri, 08.00–13.00 Sat

HEADING NORTH

CASTLES ALONG THE MUREŞ RIVER VALLEY The Mureş River valley leads north out of Târgu Mureş to Reghin. Route 15 follows the course of the river through a series of villages, graced with manor houses and castles belonging to noble Transylvanian families, making it the Romanian equivalent of France's Loire Valley. Most of the 14 medieval castles in the Mureş Valley are in deplorable condition, and few can be visited as they are used as children's homes, hospitals or colleges, but here are the best.

Dumbrăvioara Castle At 15km north of Târgu Mureş, the castle is the final resting place of two Transylvanian aristocrats with the same name. The **Teleki Mausoleum** (1772) holds the bones of Count Sámuel Teleki (1739–1822), one-time chancellor of Transylvania and founder of Târgu Mureş's Teleki Library (see page 180). The other Sámuel Teleki was an African explorer who discovered Lake Turkana in Kenya. To visit the mausoleum, ask at the parish office by the Calvinist church.

To reach the castle, turn right off route 15 heading towards Sângeru de Pădure. The mausoleum is on a hill. **Buses** run from Târgu Mureş every half-hour.

Teleki Castle At **Gorneşti** (Gernyeszeg), this 18th-century castle was built in a Baroque style with Transylvanian traditional elements. In the fashion of the time, it incorporated 52 rooms and 365 windows to signify the weeks and days of the year. These days, it is used as a sanatorium although it is still possible to walk around, if you ask nicely. The surrounding park is very attractive, although the former Japanese, French and English gardens with their statues are in a poor condition.

The castle is situated 15km north on route 15 from Târgu Mureş to Reghin. Buses run from Târgu Mureş every half-hour.

Bornemisza Castle At Reghin, turn right off route 15 and travel along the Gurghiu River valley to reach the town of **Gurghiu** (Gorgenyszentimre/Görgen), 13km east of Reghin. **Buses** run regularly from Târgu Mureş to Reghin; change there for Gurghiu, where Bornemisza Castle is located. The castle was once used by the Habsburg crown prince Rudolf as a hunting lodge. A restoration project began in 2010 (*www.castelintransilvania.ro*).

Lăpuşna If your car is tough, it is possible to continue along the Gurghiu River valley all the way to Lăpuşna (45km east of Reghin), at the end of the road in the Gurghiului Mountains. The road's condition gets steadily worse and worse corresponding to the surroundings travelling gradually back in time. It's a lovely, albeit bone-rattling, ride and the scenery is glorious. The road alongside a rushing brook is lined with cherry and walnut trees, deep red roses, purple clematis and vines heavy with grapes. People wander along the road wearing straw hats balancing long hoes on their shoulders. Elderly men stand at the roadside holding long scythes and watch the passing cars, looking rather menacingly like the Grim Reaper waiting for his next arrival! At Lăpuşna, there is a **crumbling castle**, not open to the public, and a **wooden church**.

Kemény Castle Beyond Reghin, at **Brancoveneşti** (Marosvécs/Wetsch), this 16th-century castle is the most representative castle situated in the Mureş Valley. It functions now as a psychiatric hospital, but its beautiful exterior is worth the journey. The castle is situated 10km north of Reghin on route 15 towards Topliţa. **Buses** from Reghin.

REGHIN Upstream from Târgu Mureş, at the confluence of the Mureş and Gurghiu rivers, Reghin is known as Szászrégen in Hungarian ('Saxon Reghin') and Sachsisch-Regen in German, acknowledging the large population of Saxons living in the region. At the beginning of the 20th century, there were still many Saxons left, but nowadays there are hardly any. The town came into being around 1218, when Saxons built a settlement on the ruins of a Dacian fortress. In the 18th–19th centuries, the town became a centre of a Romanian national renaissance, initiated by the scholar Petru Maior. Today, Reghin is still a hotbed of culture and known as the 'Violin Town' and also 'New Cremona', inspired by the many violin makers working in the town. Reghin is also famous for its unique string factory.

Getting there and away Reghin is situated 30km north of Târgu Mures on route 15. Many **buses** travel between the two towns. By **car**, if you are visiting Reghin from Sovata and have time to spare, there is a lovely 40km 'short cut' cross-country route 153 (*50mins*), passing through many isolated villages. At **Câmpu Cetăţii**, there are five fishing lakes and a fish restaurant (Halászcsarda). At **Eremitu**, many women wear traditional dress, long pleated skirts and waistcoats; the men wear high straw hats. There are lots of horse-drawn carts, haystacks and logging lorries. At **Chiheru de Jos**, the cobbled road is in a very bad state. Roads in villages are the local council's responsibility, whereas inter-city roads are the state's.

CĂLIMAN MOUNTAINS NATIONAL PARK In the far northeast of Transylvania, on the border of Mureş and Suceava counties with tiny bits of Harghita and Bistriţa-Năsăud poking into the park, Căliman comprises the largest volcanic massif in the Eastern Carpathians. The park is a protected area because of the numerous species of plants and 236 invertebrate species that live there. Almost 76% of its 24ha territory is covered with forest, a mix of spruce, fir and zâmbru (*Pinus cembra*), a rare coniferous tree.

Getting there and away The park is pretty difficult to approach from Transylvania. The only good road is from Vatra Dornei (80km east of Bistriţa on the E576, beyond the Tihuţa Pass, see page 267) in Suceava County. Hikers can reach the park by heading north for 10km from Răstoliţa (on the Reghin–Topliţa road 15) towards Lacul Răstoliţa or from Stânceni, 15km further east on the same road.

Information

🏢 **Călimani National Park Administration** Str   ✆/f 0230 371 104; e office@calimani.ro; www.
22 Decembrie 5, Vatra Dornei (Suceava County);   calimani.ro

SIGHIŞOARA *Telephone code 0265, sometimes 0365*

Situated 40km southwest of Târgu Mureş, Sighişoara (Segesvár/Schassburg) is the archetypal Transylvanian town, just how we imagine it. The 12th-century Saxon citadel town does not disappoint and everything looks like a Dracula film set, from the dusty lower town to the steep climb up to the citadel itself adorned by a fairytale clock tower, covered wooden steps up to the Gothic church on the hill and ancient medieval houses lurching into narrow cobble-stoned streets.

Sighişoara is a living museum, a mix of a modern town and a Disney fantasy with a touch of Gothic horror thrown in for good measure. It has a great atmosphere that even the countless cheesy Dracula souvenir shops cannot diminish. The town is a UNESCO World Heritage Site and a miss-at-your-peril item on the Transylvanian tour agenda.

Sighişoara is like taking a trip back in time to the medieval age, to an era crowded with vampires, evil counts, wolves, peasants riding through the untamed countryside on horse-drawn carts and tipsy old men tottering along the narrow, winding streets.

Visitors who arrive by train will first encounter the unusual black-and-white **Orthodox Cathedral of the Holy Trinity** (Sf Treime) by the river, which stands out, built in 1934–37 in quite a different style and colour to all other buildings in the town. A modern building painted luminous orange now sits next to the cathedral and draws attention with its incongruity.

Walking through the ancient cobbled streets, sloping to the middle where ancient shallow drains ran, you can admire the crumbling **burghers' houses** in the walled citadel district, each one a little shabby with pastel green, custard or plum paint peeling from beneath the shuttered windows, but still evocative of a more magical time. You can imagine yourself on a film set for a creepy Transylvanian thriller and it is easy to fantasise that at any moment Dracula himself might come swooping down from the belfry to sink his teeth into your neck. This image becomes more real when you turn a narrow corner and come face to face with a plaque announcing that Vlad Dracul lived in the very same building from 1431 until 1435. The walls of the citadel include nine surviving towers, the most impressive being the **Clock Tower**, once home to the City Hall and whose spire dominates the Sighişoara skyline. Visitors reach the citadel's inner treasures through an arch in the tower, climbing up a steep, cobbled path to step back in time. The tower contains a fascinating **history museum** (see page 188), with displays on many levels and at the top, visitors can peer into the workings of the clock through its open back. The intricate machinery has been ticking away since the Middle Ages and the carved wooden figures rotate, showing the position of the planets.

After the climb, visitors will be rewarded with a glorious view over the reddish-brown curving rooftops of the town. A timeless ambience hangs over the old city. The different guilds (carpenters, blacksmiths, tailors and tin-workers, etc) were each charged with building a dungeon in the towers, thus each of the remaining nine is very different in character. A covered wooden stairway leads to the **Gothic church** on the hill. Down in the more modern part of town (Str Târnavei, north of the citadel near the river) is a huge open-air market with gigantic mountains of aubergines and watermelons, with men carrying white geese in sports holdalls and elderly ladies selling live chickens.

History Founded by Transylvanian Saxons during the 12th century, Sighişoara is one of the most beautiful and best-preserved medieval towns in Europe. Sighişoara's citadel was built in the 12th century, when it was known as Castrum Sex (Fort Six), and was further strengthened and extended in the 15th century. The Saxons built their walled town on the ruins of a former Roman fortress. In 1298, the town was mentioned as Schespurch, while in 1367 it was called Civitas de Seguswar. The name of Sighişoara was first noted in a written document issued in 1431 by Vlad II Dracul, the father of Vlad III Ţepeş, the Impaler we today know as Dracula.

In the 14th–15th centuries, Sighişoara's industrious burghers, craftsmen and tradesmen provided the funds for the construction of a strong defence system guarded by 14 towers and several bastions, and gun towers pointing in all directions. Each tower was built, maintained and defended by a craft guild. The most striking is the 14th-century Clock Tower. This tower controlled the main gate of the 1km-long defensive wall and stored the city's treasures. Although not the biggest or richest of the seven Saxon walled citadels in Transylvania (Siebenbürgen), Sighişoara has definitely become the most popular.

Getting there, away and around

By air The closest airports are at **Târgu Mureş** (TGM) 48km, **Cluj-Napoca** (CLJ) 145km and **Sibiu** (SBZ) 87km away.

By rail and bus The railway and bus stations are situated north of the centre over the Târnava Mare River.

The **railway station** (Gară Sighişoara) is at Strada Libertaţii 52 (✆ *0265 771 130*). There are daily trains to Budapest (*10hrs*), Vienna (*12hrs*) and Prague (*19hrs*). Daily trains connect Sighişoara to Bucharest (*5hrs*), Braşov (*2–3hrs*), Cluj-Napoca (*3hrs*), Sibiu (changing at either Mediaş or Copşa Mică – three to five hours because of the change).

The **bus station** is at Strada Libertatii 53 (✆ *0265 771 260*; ⊕ *04.30–18.00 daily*). Hourly buses to Târgu Mureş (*1½hrs*), three a day to Mediaş (*1hr*) and Sibiu (*2hrs*).

Parking It's possible to park along Piaţa Hermann Oberth or Strada 1 Decembrie 1918, but be sure to wait for the man handing out parking tickets; he's very thorough. Tickets cost 5RON per day.

Tourist information

🛈 **Tourist Information Centre** Str Octavian Goga 8; ✆0265 770 415; e office@sighisoara-
infotourism.com; www.sighisoara-infotourism.com; ⊕ 10.00–17.00 Mon–Sat

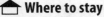 Where to stay

🏠 **Casa Cu Cerb** (2 sgl, 8 dbl) Str Şcolii 1; ✆0265 774 625; e info@casacucerb.ro; www.casacucerb.ro. The Stag House is in a historic 13th-century building
named after the mural, stag skull & antlers on the corner. The best restaurant (**$$**) in town is part of the local Slow Food movement. **$$$**

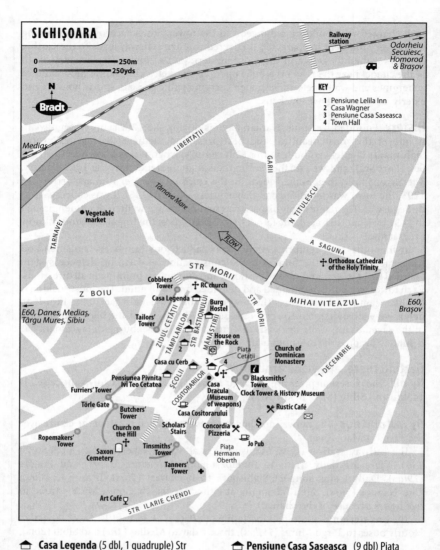

SIGHIȘOARA

0 ——— 250m
0 ——— 250yds

N

Bradt

Mediaș

KEY
1 Pensiune Lelila Inn
2 Casa Wagner
3 Pensiune Casa Saseasca
4 Town Hall

Railway station

Odorheiu Secuiesc, Homorod & Brașov

LIBERTATII

GARII

N TITULESCU

Târnava Mare

FLOW

A SAGUNA

Vegetable market

TARNAVEI

STR MORII

Orthodox Cathedral of the Holy Trinity

Z BOIU

Cobblers' Tower

RC church

Casa Legenda

Burg Hostel

MIHAI VITEAZUL

E60, Brașov

E60, Danes, Mediaș, Târgu Mureș, Sibiu

Tailors' Tower

ZIDUL CETATII

TAMPLARILOR

STR BASTIONULUI

MANASTIRII

STR MORII

House on the Rock

Piața Cetății

2

Casa cu Cerb

3 4

Church of Dominican Monastery

1 DECEMBRIE

SCOLII

COSITORARILOR

Pensiunea Pivnita Ivi Teo Cetatea

Casa Dracula (Museum of weapons)

Blacksmiths' Tower

Clock Tower & History Museum

Furriers' Tower

Törle Gate

Butchers' Tower

Casa Cositorarului

Rustic Café

Ropemakers' Tower

Church on the Hill

Scholars' Stairs

Concordia Pizzeria

Jo Pub

Saxon Cemetery

Tinsmiths' Tower

Piața Hermann Oberth

Tanners' Tower

Art Café

STR ILARIE CHENDI

Casa Legenda (5 dbl, 1 quadruple) Str Bastionului 8; m 0744 632 775; e contact@legenda.ro; www.legenda.ro. A charming pension just north of the citadel's main square. B/fast not inc. The annex, Grandma's House (Casa Bunicii), sleeps 4 & has its own kitchen (**$$**). **$$$**

Casa Wagner (3 sgl, 14 dbl, 5 suites) Piața Cetații 7; ☎ 0265 506 014; e office@casa-wagner.com; www.casa-wagner.com. In a 400-year-old building painted bright orange, a stylish pension with antique furnishings & an inner courtyard for dining at the great restaurant (**$$**). Wine cellar with live music. **$$$**

Pensiune Casa Saseasca (9 dbl) Piața Cetații 12; ☎ 0265 772 400; e office@casasaseasca.com; www.casasaseasca.com. Small pension in the heart of the citadel, on the main square, with hand-painted furniture & an inner courtyard. **$$$**

Pensiune Lelila Inn (5 dbl, 1 tpl) Str Tamplarilor 14; ☎ 0265 779 332; e office@sighisoara-pensiune.ro; www.sighisoara-pensiune.ro. Small, rustic-feeling pension between the Shoemakers' Tower & the Tailor's Tower. **$$$**

Pensiunea Pivnita lui Teo Cetatea (4 dbl) Str Scolii 14; ☎/f 0265 771 677; m 0722 496 263; e office@delateo.ro; www.

cazareincetateasighisoara.ro. A small pension in the heart of the citadel, selling excellent *ţuică*, *palincă* & local wines in the cellar shop (*www. pivnitaluiteo.com*). **$$$**

✕ Where to eat and drink

♀ **Art Café** Str Ilarie Chendi 26; www.artcafe.ro; ⏰ 08.00–midnight daily. No food, just an honest drinks bar with a cylindrical ceramic stove in one corner. Blues & jazz music. **$**

⬛ **Casa Cositorarului** Str Cositorarilor 9; www. casa-cositorarului.ro; ⏰ Sep–May 09.00–22.00 daily, Jun–Aug 09.00–midnight daily. Near the covered stairs is a calm refuge away from the Dracula hysteria of the main square. Good juice, coffee, cocktails, cakes & sandwiches. Also a guesthouse. **$**

⬛ **Jo Pub** Piaţa Hermann Oberth 1; ⏰ 10.00– midnight daily. On a large terrace just beneath the

⌂ **Burg Hostel** (9 dbl, 1 sgl, plus dorms) Str Bastionului 4–6; ☏ 0265 778 489; e burghostel@ ibz.ro; www.burghostel.ro. Dbls as well as dorms in a renovated 17th-century building between the main square & the Cobblers' Tower. **$**

Concordia, at the foot of the citadel hill. A good place for a postprandial coffee or ice cream. **$**

✕ **Pizzeria e Spaghetteria Concordia** Piaţa Hermann Oberth 1; m 0752 833 762; www. restaurant-concordia.ro; ⏰ 10.00–midnight daily. Very popular & convenient Italian joint with pizzas the size of manhole covers. **$**

✕ **Rustic Café** Str 1 Decembrie 1918 7; ⏰ 10.00–midnight daily. Friendly pub-café with brick walls, barrels & a big oven. Good *sarmale cu mămăliguţă şi smântână* (stuffed cabbage rolls with polenta & sour cream). **$**

Other practicalities

Bank
$ Banca Transilvania Str Hermann Oberth 15; ☏ 0265 772 719; ⏰ 09.00–18.00 Mon–Fri, 09.30–12.30 Sat. With an ATM outside.

Internet
▣ **House on the Rock** Piaţa Cetăţii 8; ☏ 0265 777 844; www.veritas.ro; café ⏰ 09.00–19.30 Mon-Sat. A Christian organisation runs a café, internet centre (with 5 computers; 5RON/hr) in their International Café (open for soups, sandwiches & other snacks 10.00–18.00 Mon–Sat)

on the main square up in the citadel. The café also sells local handicrafts.

Pharmacy
✚ **Pharmacy Genţiana** Piaţa Hermann Oberth 45; ⏰ 07.30–20.00 Mon–Fri, 08.00–20.00 Sat/ Sun

Post office
✉ **Central Post Office** Str Hermann Oberth 16–18; ☏ 0265 772 055; ⏰ 07.00–20.00 Mon–Fri

What to see and do The 'Pearl of the Târnava' is situated on the Târnava Mare River. It calls itself a 'museum town' and claims it is the only still inhabited medieval citadel in Europe.

For several centuries, Sighişoara was a military and political stronghold. During the 14th–16th centuries, the Saxon and Magyar guilds built towers along the citadel walls to protect **Sighişoara's Citadel** (Cetatea Sighisoarei) from Turkish raids. Laid out on two to four levels, the towers stored ammunition and food supplies and were provided with firing windows for cannons, shells and arrows. Of the original 14 towers and five artillery bastions, nine towers and two bastions have survived the test of time. Starting at the Clock Tower, Sighişoara's most lasting image, it is possible to follow the walls around anticlockwise; doing so, we first come to the **Blacksmiths' Tower** (Turnul Fierarilor), built in 1631 to protect the monastery church. Next, the **Cobblers' Tower** (Turnul Cizmarilor) was a defence tower first mentioned in 1521. Today it houses a local radio station and newspaper office. The **Tailors' Tower** (Turnul Croitorilor) has a double gateway and guarded the back entrance of the citadel. It was destroyed in the 1676 fire and later rebuilt.

The **Furriers' Tower** (Turnul Cojocarilor) forms with the octagonal **Butchers' Tower** (Turnul Măcelarilor) the **Törle Gate** with a typical medieval house underneath. The **Ropemakers' Tower** (Turnul Franghierilor) is the only inhabited tower. Traditionally the cemetery guard lives here.

Then we must turn around and go back down Strada Scării then head east towards the **Tinsmiths' Tower** (Turnul Cositorarilor), an unusual tower with a rectangular base, two pentagonal upper storeys, an octagonal higher level and a hexagonal roof. Next door the **Tanners' Tower** (Turnul Tăbăcarilor) is a very simple and often ignored square tower. The ninth tower is the stunning **Clock Tower** (Turnul cu Ceas) housing the **History Museum** (*Piaţa Muzeului 1;* \ *0265 771 108;* e *info@ muzeusighisoara.com; www.muzeusighisoara.com;* ☉ *summer 09.30–17.30 Tue–Fri, 10.00–17.30 Sat/Sun, winter 09.00–15.30 Tue–Fri, 10.00–17.30 Sat/Sun; admission adult/child 7/2.50RON*), the symbol of the city, built in the late 14th century and expanded in the 16th century. After a fire in 1676 when the town's gunpowder deposits located in the Tailors' Tower exploded, Austrian artists rebuilt the roof of the tower in its present Baroque style and colourful tiles were added in 1894. In the 17th century, in Switzerland, the same clock makers who made Prague's famous clock, created something similar for Sighişoara; a two-plate clock with figurines carved from linden wood was built into the top of the tower, with one dial looking over the **Orasul de Jos** (Lower Town), and the other facing the **cetate** (citadel).

The figurines, moved by the clock's mechanism, each represented a different character. On the citadel side, Peace holds an olive branch, accompanied by a drummer who beats the hours on his bronze drum. Above them are Justice with a set of scales and Law wielding a sword, accompanied by two angels representing Day and Night. At 06.00, the day angel appears and at 18.00, the night angel comes out carrying two burning candles. **The dial** overlooking the Lower Town features a set of seven figurines, each representing the pagan gods who personified the days of the week: Diana (Monday), Mars (Tuesday), Mercury (Wednesday), Jupiter (Thursday), Venus (Friday), Saturn (Saturday) and the Sun (Sunday). The spire of the tower ends in a small golden sphere. At the top, there is a meteorological cockerel which, turned by air currents, forecasts the weather.

Underneath the Clock Tower, three men appear each day at noon, dressed in medieval costume, bang a drum and announce in many languages: 'The gates of the citadel are open to you, have a nice day, nice to meet you'. In the past, **Citadel Square** (Piaţa Cetăţii) was the location for markets, public executions and witch trials. Now it is overwhelmed by Dracula souvenir shops and terrace cafés. The most striking near the Clock Tower is the **Casa Dracula**, a restaurant (*Str Cositorarilor 5;* \ *0265 771 596;* ☉ *10.00–midnight daily*) that houses a **Museum of Weapons** (*Colectia de Arme Medievale; see History Museum*) on the first floor. The front façade features an oft-photographed plaque telling how Vlad Dracul, son of Mircea cel Batran, lived here from 1431 to 1435.

The plaque reads:

În această casă a locuit	In this house lived
Între anii 1431–1435	between 1431–1435
Domnitorul Ţării Româneşti	governor of the 'Romanian Land'
VLAD DRACUL	VLAD DRACUL
fiul lui Mircea cel Bătrîn	son of Mircea the Elder

This actually refers to Vlad's dad, Vlad II Dracul, son of Mircea cel Bătrân (Mircea the Elder) who was given the title 'Dracul' because he was a member of the Order of the Dragon created by King Zsigmond. The word *dracul* means 'the devil' in modern Romanian but in Vlad's day also meant 'dragon' derived from the Latin word *draco*. His son, Vlad III, was called 'Drăculea', meaning 'son of Dracul' (see box overleaf).

Near the Clock Tower stands the late Gothic **Church of the Dominican Monastery** (Biserica Mănăstirii Dominicane), built in 1289 and the remaining half of a Dominican monastery demolished in 1888. As in Brașov's Black Church, here can also be found a collection of 16th- and 17th-century oriental carpets. Classical music concerts are often held here. In the square next to the church is a **bust of Vlad III Țepeș** looking pretty sinister. By the church is the **Town Hall** (Primăria), built around 1885 in a neo-Renaissance style. The **Roman Catholic church** (Biserica Romano Catolică) was built in 1894 on the ruins of a former Franciscan monastery. From here it's a pleasant walk following the citadel's walls towards the southern end of the hill to find the **Covered Stairs** (Scara Acoperită), also known as the Scholars' Stairs at the end of School Street (Strada Școlii) and leading up to an even higher hill and the Church on the Hill (Biserica din Deal). Built in 1642, the covered wooden stair passage was designed to protect schoolchildren and church-goers on their climb to the school and church during wintertime. Originally, the stairs had 300 steps but after 1849 the number was reduced to 175. At the top, the **Biserica din Deal** (⊕ *10.00–18.00 daily*) was first mentioned in a document in 1345, and its construction took more than 200 years. Initially a Catholic church, it became the main church for the Saxons of Sighișoara, who had shifted from Roman Catholicism to Lutheranism after the 1547 Reformation. Nearby is a beautiful, overgrown **Saxon Cemetery** (⊕ 08.00–20.00 daily).

Down in the **Lower Town** (Orasul de Jos) Piața Hermann Oberth is crammed full of places to eat and drink. Oberth (1894–1989) was one of the forefathers of astronautics and rocketry. He was born in Sibiu and raised in Sighișoara. He designed the V1 and V2 bombers that attacked Britain in World War II, then went to the USA to work for NASA.

AROUND SIGHIȘOARA

DANEȘ Situated 8km west of Sighișoara on route 14 to Mediaș, turn off to the left to find the little village of Daneș, notable only for its swanky country club Domeniul Dracula Daneș comprising three venues, an outdoor swimming pool and a large riding stables. The restaurant (**$$**) is full of local businessmen enjoying extended lunches.

 Where to stay and eat

⌂ **Centru ecvestru (Equestrian centre) Dracula Daneş** (16 dbl, 1 apt) Same contact details as Domeniul Dracula Daneş. With 5ha of land & a barbecue site. **$$$**

⌂ **Domeniul Dracula Daneş** (30 dbl, 1 apt) Str Principală 804; ☎ 0265 772 211; e info@dracul.ro; www.dracul.ro. **$$$**
⌂ **Dracul Inn** (21 dbl) Same contact details. A smaller cottage in the grounds with its own restaurant (**$$**). **$$–$$$**

CRIȘ Continue along the road (read 'dirt track') for 10km to the Daneș Country Club, and eventually reach Criș. Criș is the home of the 16th-century **Castle Bethlen**, built in the Renaissance style. The castle has a rectangular shape, the southwestern side having a *belle vue* looking out on an inner yard. Statues with soldiers have been mounted on the outer façade of the top floor. Criș is an idyllic village, a stream runs through its heart and the picturesque castle-church is on a wooded hill. The village is very photogenic with bright flowers and shaded spots, claret hollyhocks, purple clematis and house walls covered with grape vines.

SASCHIZ Heading west out of Sighişoara, on the hectic E60 highway, after 27km you will reach Saschiz (Szászkézd/Keisd) The **Saxon fortress** was built during the 14th–15th centuries and the fortified church dates from 1494. Near the church is a tower inspired by the Clock Tower in Sighişoara and one of the most beautiful examples of Saxon architecture in Transylvania. Its roof is covered with multi-coloured enamel tiles. It has four corner turrets and a pointed spire placed on a ball-shaped base. A few hundred years ago, Saschiz was the seat of a bishop and vied with Sighişoara for political superiority.

Saschiz is a good place to stop off *en route* to and from Sighişoara as it is the headquarters for the ADEPT Foundation (see box, page 192). The office sells maps (15RON), booklets (10RON) and jam made by local producers.

VLAD DRĂCULEA – THE MAN BEHIND THE MYTH

Bram Stoker and Hollywood have given us more than 150 versions of Dracula. Christopher Lee and, ironically, a Hungarian, Béla Lugosi from Lugoj, Timiş County, have played the vampire Count perhaps most memorably. The real person behind the fictional Count Dracula was even more cruel and bloodthirsty. Bram Stoker claimed *Dracula*, published in 1897, was, 'born of a nightmare following a supper of dressed crab'.

The real-life Dracula was born in 1431 in Sighişoara, the son of Vlad II Dracul, who had received the title 'Dracul' after being inducted into the Order of the Dragon (*draco*) by King Zsigmond. The boy was called Vlad III Drăculea, meaning 'son of Dracul'. The family moved to Târgovişte in 1436, to take up residence in the palace when Vlad senior became Voivode of Wallachia.

In 1442, in order to keep the Turks at bay, Dracul sent his son Vlad and his younger brother Radu, to Istanbul, as hostages of Sultan Murad II. Vlad was held there until 1448. This Turkish captivity played an important role in the young Vlad's upbringing. He learned much about the brutality of life and was particularly interested in the Turkish method of impaling prisoners on stakes.

Ioan de Hunedoara arranged the assassination of Vlad senior and Drăculea's elder brother, whom they tortured and buried alive. Ioan also arranged the release of Drăculea and Radu, to be pawns in the struggle between the newly emerging empire and the Ottomans. Vlad III Drăculea became the ruler of Wallachia in 1448, although the first term lasted only two months, again between 1456 and 1462, and finally in 1476.

During his reigns he committed many cruelties and thus established his reputation, earning him the posthumous moniker of 'Ţepeş' ('Impaler'). His preferred method involved binding victims spread-eagled then hammering a stake up through the rectum as far as the shoulder, then leaving them to die in agony, raised up for the crowd to watch.

Vlad's first major act of revenge was aimed at the *boyars* of Târgovişte for not being loyal to his father. He arrested all the *boyar* families who had participated at the princely feast for Easter Sunday. He impaled the older ones on stakes while forcing the others to march from the capital, Târgovişte to Poenari in the Argeş River valley on a gruelling 80km trek. Vlad then ordered

SAXON FORTIFIED CHURCHES AT APOLD AND CLOAŞTERF

Apold (*Contact Sebastian Bethge, Apold No 245;* m *0724 155 977; visits 09.00–17.00 daily; suggested donation 5RON*) Located 15km south of Sighişoara on a fairly good road, heading through Lower Town away from the river, Apold (GER Trappold) is home to a Gothic 'Hallenkirche' in the centre of the village on a hilltop. On the western side of the church is a defensive bell tower. The double defensive walls are fortified on the southwest side by a gate tower and in the north by two defensive warehouses. Many Gothic elements have been preserved, including the vestry doorway and niche frames. The folding triptych altar dates from 1821.

Cloaşterf (*Contact János Kerekes, Cloaşterf, casa No 99;* \ *0265 711 674*) Cloaşterf (GER Klosdorf) has a small but special fortified Church of St Nicholas with well-preserved typical elements of a late Gothic fortified church: pews, inner galleries and balconies. The fortified precinct is in the shape of an irregular square and is strengthened by corner towers. The bell tower was built in 1816–19.

the *boyars* to build him a fortress on the ruins of an older outpost. Many died in the process, and so Vlad managed to refresh the noble stock and at the same time create an impregnable fortress. The ruins can be visited today at the southern tip of Lacul Vidraru (see page 216).

Vlad started feuds with just about everybody. In 1457, he accused the Saxons of supporting claims to his Wallachian throne and burnt many of their villages. In 1460, he wiped out the forces of his rival Dan III and a month later attacked the Bârsa Land around Braşov and impaled thousands of villagers before marching off to Făgăraş to continue plotting against the Turks. To withstand Turkish raids, Vlad formed an alliance with his cousin, Ştefan cel Mare of Moldavia and the Hungarian kingdom. In 1462, he declared war on the Turks, attacking their camps and inflicting heavy casualties. He impaled 20,000 Turkish troops on a field of stakes and the remaining soldiers retreated in terror. When the Transylvanian Saxons traded with Germany and western Europe, they demonstrated negative feelings about Vlad. In 1462, he was arrested and held prisoner by the Hungarian king Matei Corvin at Visegrád, near Budapest until 1474. In 1474, Ştefan cel Mare won a battle against Matei at Baia and forced him to set Vlad free. Ştefan needed Vlad to fight the Ottomans once again. Vlad regained the throne of Wallachia in 1476, but the reign lasted for only two months. During Vlad's eight-year captivity, the throne had been held by his younger brother Radu 'the Handsome', who had been doing deals with the *boyars*.

There are several versions of the death of Vlad III Ţepeş. Some sources say he was killed in battle against the Ottomans near Bucharest in December 1476. Others say he was assassinated by disloyal Wallachian *boyars* while out hunting. Other accounts have Vlad falling in defeat, surrounded by the bodies of his few remaining loyal Moldavian guards. Still other reports claim that Vlad was struck down at the moment of victory by one of his own men. Vlad's body was decapitated by the Turks and his head was preserved in honey and sent to Istanbul where the sultan displayed it on a stake as proof that the Impaler was finally dead. Vlad's headless body was reportedly buried at a monastery on an island in Lacul Snagov (see page 137), although some doubt that he is actually still resting there. (See also box *Dracula destinations*, page 50.)

THE TOURIST INFORMATION CENTRE AT SASCHIZ

The ADEPT Foundation aims to bring local benefits from traditional farming and other rural activities, so that conservation of the landscape has local support and a viable future. The Foundation's **Tourist Information Centre (TIC) in Saschiz** (*Str Principală 166 (across the square from the Saxon church);* \ *0265 711 635;* f *0365 814 076;* e *info@fundait-adept.org; www.fundatia-adept.org;* ⏰ *all year 09.00–17.00 Mon–Fri, May–Oct also 09.00–18.00 Sat/Sun*) provides information on a network of reliable local farm guesthouses over a wide area, from Biertan in the west to Viscri in the east, plus a range of activities in the area. The TIC can take bookings, and can arrange activities, guided or not, to give a tourist an experience that gets under the surface and allows visitors to meet food producers and others. The TIC staff speak English, French and German. The Foundation has off-road vehicles based in Saschiz, which are part of the guided tour offer. The TIC sells local products, including the famous local jams, as well as very useful books and maps of the area, many of which are produced by the Foundation itself.

Activities include local exhibitions, visits to the historic local churches, 'Meet the Bees' (a detailed tour of bee-keeping and honey production, wearing full protection suits available at the TIC), traditional bread making, specialist botanical or birdwatching walks. More general activities can include lunch at a sheepfold with fresh cheese, sheep milking and cheese making, visiting a blacksmiths, basket and blanket weaving, traditional barrel making (from the tree to the barrel, all by hand), and meals in farmhouses where traditional farm activities and food preparation are explained and experienced at first hand.

The **Mihai Eminescu Trust** (for contact details, see page 52) has a guesthouse for two people in Cloașterf in the bellringer's house (**$** *with b/fast,* **$$–$$$** *with lunch & dinner*), set within the fortified walls.

Getting there and away From Sighişoara, **drive** to Saschiz on the E60 highway, and take the second right after Saschiz. Cloașterf is a further 3km along a very minor road.

7

Sibiu County

Sibiu County (5,432km²) is located in the south of Transylvania. Marking the southern border are the Carpathian Mountains made up of the mighty Făgăraş range with peaks higher than 2,500m and the Lotru and Cindrel ranges. The Olt River crosses the Făgăraş peaks, passing from Transylvania into Wallachia to the south. The Transfăgărăşan Highway also leads from Sibiu County through the mountains on probably one of the most spectacular and exciting drives in Romania, through Wallachia to Piteşti and eventually on to Bucharest. Sibiu is dominated by mountain territory covered by coniferous and deciduous forest, pasture-filled hills, hay fields and orchards, plains, rivers and lakes with both fresh and salt water. The variety of terrain makes it possible to find snow in the mountains for up to six months of the year, while down in the urban areas the weather can be warm and spring-like. The Păltiniş (1,450m) ski resort, 30km southwest of Sibiu, has hills drenched in crystal-clean air to soothe the nervous and respiratory system, and a good selection of services such as pistes, cable cars and après-ski. There are several spa resorts in the county, located in beautiful countryside. The majority of the population is Romanian, with Magyars, Germans, Transylvanian Saxons, Swabians and Roma making up the numbers. However, in the past, Sibiu County had a high proportion of Saxons and the large number of fortress churches, some of them UNESCO World Heritage Sites, as well as the magnificent Saxon city of Sibiu itself, testify to its historic wealth and power. Like Braşov, Sibiu feels like a confident European city and it's no surprise that in 2007, Sibiu was the first city in eastern Europe to be declared a European Capital of Culture (shared with Luxembourg). Sibiu County has one of the most dynamic economies in Romania and has one of the highest levels of foreign investment. The biggest natural resource in the county is natural gas, and the predominant industries are machine and car components, textiles and wood processing. During the communist era, there were two chemical industrial plants at Copşa Mică and the town is notorious for being one of the most polluted communities in Europe. After 1989, many of the industrial complexes were shut down and the authorities have made great efforts to clean up the area, but the pollution has penetrated deep into the soil and it will take decades to rectify, if ever. Keep your windows closed when driving through Copşa Mică as the aroma is pretty pungent.

SIBIU   *Telephone code 0269, sometimes 0369*

Sibiu (Nagyszeben/Hermannstadt) is one of the most visitor-friendly cities in Transylvania. The city has two levels: an 'Upper Town' containing most of Sibiu's historic sites located on pedestrian streets and three easily navigated squares, and the 'Lower Town', a charming tangle of old houses and cobbled streets. Connecting the Upper and Lower towns are dozens of tunnels, stairways and

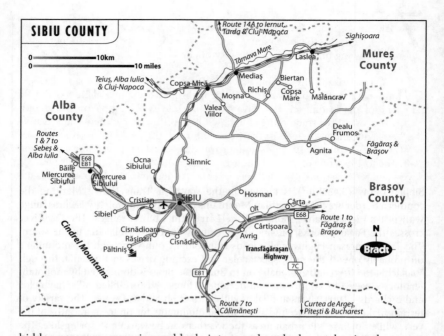

SIBIU COUNTY

0 —————10km
0 —————————10 miles

Route 14A to Iernut,
Turda & Cluj-Napoca

Sighişoara

Mureş
County

Târnava Mare
Laslea

Teiuş, Alba Iulia
& Cluj-Napoca
Copşa Mică
Mediaş
Biertan
Richiş
Moşna
Copşa
Mare
Mălâncrav

Valea
Viilor

Alba
County

Dealu
Frumos

Routes
1 & 7 to
Sebeş &
Alba Iulia

Agnita
Făgăraş &
Braşov

Ocna
Sibiului
Slimnic

Băile
Miercurea
Sibiului
Miercurea
Sibiului

E68
E81

SIBIU
Hosman

Braşov
County

Cristian
Olt
Cârţa

Sibiel
Cârţişoara
E68
Route 1 to
Făgăraş &
Braşov

Cisnădioara
Răşinari
Cisnădie
Avrig

Pălteniş
Transfăgărăşan
Highway

N

Bradt

Cindrel Mountains

E81

7C

Route 7 to
Călimăneşti

Curtea de Argeş,
Piteşti & Bucharest

hidden passages, emerging suddenly into sun-drenched, pastel-painted squares, which are fun to explore. In the Old Town, the magnificent Piaţa Mare marks the heart of the city and is home to shops, cafés, museums and the impressive tourist office. Piaţa Mică has beautiful painted 17th-century houses. With more than 100 attractions in the city alone, Sibiu contains the largest concentration of tourist attractions in Romania. In 2007, Sibiu was declared European Capital of Culture with a bizarre slogan 'Normal. Sibiu. Young since 1191', which confused some visitors with the 'normal' part, somewhat damning with faint praise. However, the emphasis on youth is an attempt to distance itself from the tired old Dracula themes and retreat into the dusty past. To prepare for the Culture Capital year, the city started a massive regeneration and renovation project and buffed up the buildings. The people of Sibiu like to speak of the 'old young city', to describe the disparity between the architecture, with its medieval city walls and towers, and the city's dynamic social life. 'Theatre, film, photography and jazz festivals are traditional in Sibiu,' explained Stela Matioc, programme co-ordinator for the Capital of Culture Office (*www.sibiu2007.ro*). Throughout the centuries, Romanians, Germans, Hungarians and Roma have existed side by side in Sibiu and a climate of cultural tolerance has developed, from which the city deservedly earns its cosmopolitan reputation. Since Romania's 2007 accession to the EU, Sibiu's economy has expanded significantly with Germany the largest trading partner. About 15,000 companies with German investment have been set up in the region, including numerous firms in the engineering sector, the textile and construction industries and the chemical and pharmaceutical sector. During 31 May–1 June 2007, European Commissioner for Multi-lingualism, Leonard Orban, visited Sibiu and said: 'Sibiu is a splendid city, fully deserving the title of European Capital of Culture. It is a city at the vanguard of multi-culturalism and multi-lingualism in the European Union.' A development from 1929, when Walter Starkie wrote, 'In contrast to the gay atmosphere of Cluj, Hermannstadt is sad and mysterious.' There's nothing gloomy about the city these days and in spring and summer, the pavement terrace cafés are packed with students and visitors wallowing in an exciting cultural milieu.

HISTORY In 1191, the city of Sibiu was founded on the site of the Roman village of Cibinium, named after the River Cibin flowing through the centre. Sibiu has always been one of the leading cities of Transylvania. Hard-working Saxon merchants made the most of the trade route along the Olt River gorge between Transylvania and Wallachia and at the end of the 14th century, at the peak of Saxon influence, Sibiu had approximately 19 guilds under royal charter, each representing a different craft. The fortress, one of the Siebenburgen, was protected by sturdy walls with 39 towers and four bastions. This defence system was enough to repel Turkish raids on three occasions. From 1703–91 under the Habsburgs and again from 1849–67, Sibiu was the seat of the Austrian governors of Transylvania. In 2000, the people of Sibiu elected a mayor with Saxon heritage. Klaus Werner Johannis of the Democratic Forum of Germans in Romania has remained popular ever since.

GETTING THERE, AWAY AND AROUND

By air Sibiu International Airport (SBZ) (*Şosea Alba Iulia 73;* \ *0269 253 135; www.sibiuairport.ro*) is situated 5km west of Sibiu city centre on highway 1/7/ E68/E81. Sibiu International Airport links with many European cities, especially those in Germany and Italy. **Carpatair**, Transylvania's largest airline, offers daily connections to Munich, Bergamo and Treviso, and connections three times a week to Bologna, Verona, Rome, Paris and Stuttgart. **Tarom**, Romania's national carrier, flies from Sibiu to Bucharest, Munich and Vienna, while **Blue Air** flies to Stuttgart, **Austrian Airlines** to Vienna and **Lufthansa** to Munich. **Trolleybus No 8** runs between the airport and the railway station.

By rail and bus Sibiu's railway and bus stations are situated to the northeast of the centre, 15 minutes' walk along the road G-ral Gh Magheru.

The **railway station** (Gară Sibiu) is at Piaţa 1 Decembrie 1918 6 (\ *0269 211 139*). Four trains daily to and from Bucharest (*5hrs*), one train daily to Budapest (*8hrs*) and several trains daily to Braşov (*3hrs*) and Cluj-Napoca (*3½hrs*). For Sighişoara (*2½hrs*), change at Mediaş. For the Sibiu timetable, see www.sibiu.ro/ mersultrenurilor.htm.

For rail information, contact **Agenţia de Voiaj CFR** (*Str Nicolae Bălcescu 6;* \ *0269 212 085;* ⊕ *10.00–18.00 Mon–Fri*). Train schedule information and reservations up to 24 hours in advance are available at this office. Tickets for same-day travel can only be purchased at the station.

The **bus station** (Autogară Sibiu) is also at Piaţa 1 Decembrie 1918 6 (\ *0269 217 757*). Daily buses and maxi-taxis run to Alba Iulia (*10 daily, 2hrs*), Braşov (*13 daily, 2½hrs*), Cluj-Napoca (*9 daily, 3½hrs*), Deva (*4 daily, 2½hrs*), Sighişoara (*4 daily, 2hrs*), Târgu Mureş (*13 daily, 2½hrs*).

Public transport Several bus and **trolleybus** routes connect Sibiu's main areas and tourist attractions. Bus and trolleybus tickets can be purchased at ticket kiosks in town and must be punched on board. Trolleybus No 1 and bus No A5 run from the railway station to Piaţa Unirii.

Taxis Taxis are still relatively inexpensive and widely available. The price/km is marked on the outside of the car.

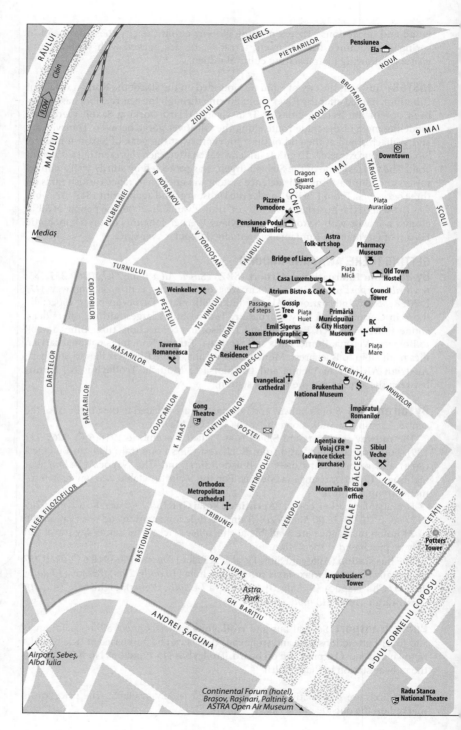

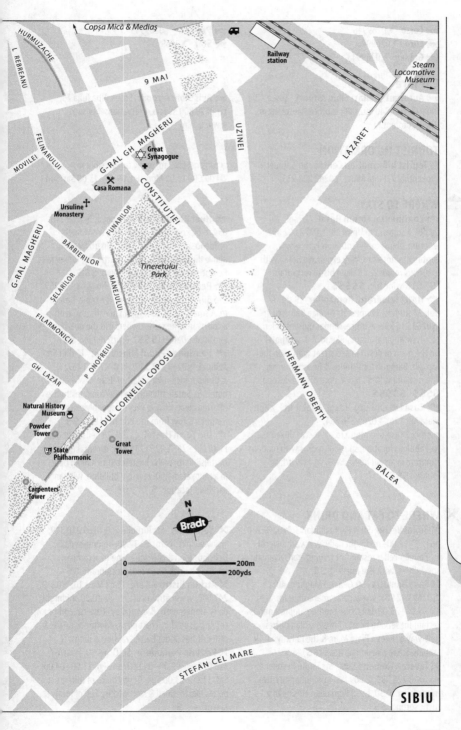

🚗 **Corso** ☎0269946
🚗 **Euro** ☎0269946
🚗 **Galaxy** ☎0269943

🚗 **Pro Taxi** ☎0269949
🚗 **Star** ☎0269953

Car hire
🚗 **Autorent (Dollar) Sibiu Airport** Şosea Alba Iulia 73; m 0740 002 000; e office@autorent.ro; www.autorent.ro

🚗 **Avis Sibiu Airport** Şosea Alba Iulia 73; m 0729 800 393; e reservations@avis.ro; www.avis.ro

TOURIST INFORMATION
🛈 **Tourist Information Centre** Str Samuel Brukenthal 2, Piaţa Mare; ☎0269 208 913;

e turism@sibiu.ro; www.turism.sibiu.ro; ⏰ 09.00–17.00 Mon–Fri, 09.00–13.00 Sat/Sun

🏠 WHERE TO STAY
🏠 **Continental Forum Hotel** (25 sgl, 93 dbl, 5 suites) Pta Unirii 10; ☎0372 692 692; e forum.sibiu@continentalhotels.ro; www.continentalhotels.ro. Very expensive hotel, with luxurious rooms & a Balkan bistro restaurant ($$$) & wine bar. **$$$$$**
🏠 **Hotel Împăratul Romanilor** (9 sgl, 37 dbl, 27 studios, 12 apts) Str Nicolae Bălcescu 4; ☎0269 216 500; e office@imparatulromanilor.ro; www.imparatulromanilor.ro. A 3-star hotel on the main pedestrianised street with over-the-top gilt, Baroque furnishings & Rococo mirrors. The restaurant ($$) has a more bizarre décor. **$$$$–$$$$$**
🏠 **Casa Luxemburg** (2 sgl, 2 dbl, 1 trpl, 2 apts) Piaţa Mică 16; ☎0269 216 854; e office@casaluxemburg.ro; www.casaluxemburg.ro. Fabulous location, spacious rooms with modern furniture in an old house, with Wi-Fi & b/fast lounge. **$$$**

🏠 **Huet Residence** Piaţa Huet 3; ☎0269 216 854; e office@huet-residence.ro; www.huet-residence.ro. Lovely rooms in a superb location, above the old town walls. Nice little café downstairs. Reception next to Casa Luxemburg. **$$$**
🏠 **Pensiunea Ela** (9 dbl) Str Nouă 43; ☎0269 215 197; e ela@ela-hotels.ro; www.ela-hotels.ro. A small, clean, family-run guesthouse with a courtyard. The same owners run the nearby Pensiunea Daniel ($$$). *B/fast not inc.* **$$**
🏠 **Pensiunea Podul Minciunilor** (6 dbl) Str Azilului; ☎0269 217 259; m 0747 053 457; e podul.minciunilor@ela-hotels.ro; www.ela-hotels.ro. Small, friendly, family-run guesthouse offering clean, cosy & very reasonably priced rooms a stone's throw from the Bridge of Lies. **$$**
🏠 **Old Town Hostel** (2 dbl, 28 beds in dorms) Piaţa Mica 26; ☎0269 216 445; e contact@hostelsibiu.ro; www.hostelsibiu.ro. Cheap beds in a renovated, 450-year-old building, with an excellent location. **$**

✕ WHERE TO EAT AND DRINK
✕ **Sibiul Veche** Str A Papiu Iliarian 3; ☎0269 210 461; ⏰ 12.00–midnight daily; www.sibiulvechi.ro. Popular cellar restaurant serving Transylvanian specialities, with live music. **$$$**
✕ **Casa Romana** Str General Magheru 40; ☎0369 442 966; www.casaromanasibiu.ro; ⏰ 08.00–23.00 daily. Outstanding, unpretentious restaurant serving hearty Transylvanian dishes, half-way between Piaţa Mare & the railway station. Small pension upstairs ($$). **$$**
✕ **Taverna Romaneasca** Str Târgul Pestelui 4; m 0728 728 333; ⏰ 09.00–midnight daily, live music from 19.30. Local Romanian cuisine in a rustic setting. **$$**

✕ **Weinkeller** Str Turnului 2; ☎0269 210 319; www.weinkeller.ro; ⏰ 12.00–midnight daily. Delicious food & the right wine to accompany meals in a brick-lined cellar restaurant. **$$**
✕ **Atrium Bistro & Café** Piaţa Mică 16; ☎0269 242 000; www.atriumcafe.ro; ⏰ 10.00–midnight daily. Underneath (& owned by) Casa Luxemburg, serving good thin-crust pizza, enormous salads & other dishes under barrel-vaulted ceilings. **$**
✕ **Pizzeria Pomodore** Str Ocnei 10; m 0767 425 071; ⏰ 09.00–04.00 Mon–Fri, 11.00–04.00 Sat, 11.00–23.00 Sun. Good choice of thin-crust pizzas, pasta, salad & sandwiches. Full of locals & taxi drivers. **$**

OTHER PRACTICALITIES

Bank
$ **Raiffeisen** Str Nicolae Balcescu 29; ⏰ 09.00–
18.30 Mon–Fri, 10.00–14.00 Sat

Internet
🖥 At downtown Str 9 Mai 24; ⏰ 08.00–02.00
Mon–Sat, 12.00–02.00 Sun. Free Wi-Fi; ask the
waitress for the password.

Mountain rescue
Salvamont Str Nicolae Bălcescu 9; ☎0269 216
477; m 0745 140 144

Pharmacy
➕ Constituției 24; ⏰ 08.00–21.00 Mon–Fri,
08.00–14.00 Sat

Post office
✉ **Main post office** Str Mitropoliei 14; ☎0269
323 179; ⏰ 07.00–20.00 Mon–Fri, 08.00–13.00
Sat

ENTERTAINMENT AND NIGHTLIFE Culture vultures will always find something of interest at Sibiu's many concert halls, theatres and galleries. The **State Philharmonic of Sibiu** (*Str Cetatii 3–5;* ☎ *0269 210 264;* e *filarmo@filarmonicasibiu.ro; www. filarmonicasibiu.ro*) has weekly classical music concerts taking place in Thalia Hall, which dates from 1787. The **Radu Stanca National Theatre** (*B-dul C Coposu 2;* ☎*0269 210 092;* e *info@sibfest.ro; www.sibfest.ro*) is one of Romania's leading theatres, dating back also to 1787. It attracts some of the best-known directors in the country and has five shows a week in Romanian and German. The **Gong Theatre** (*Str Alexandru Odobescu 4;* ☎ *0269 211 349*) specialises in puppetry, mime and unconventional shows for children and teenagers, in both Romanian and German. In May, Sibiu hosts an annual **Jazz Festival** (*http://sibiujazz.ro*), in late May/early June the International Theatre Festival (*www.sibfest.eu*), while in August and September, there are many more festivals and fairs celebrating folk crafts and culture.

SHOPPING A great shop for souvenirs, **Galerile de Artă Populară 'Astra'** can be found on Piața Mică (☎ *0269 432 250;* ⏰ *09.00–17.00 Tue–Sun*), selling carved wooden items, clothes, ceramics and postcards. **Gossip Tree** is a small shop at the top of the Passage of Steps selling clothing and jewellery by local and Romanian designers (m *0742 985 489;* ⏰ *10.00–20.00 Mon–Fri, 10.00–16.00 Sat*).

WHAT TO SEE AND DO Sibiu's Old Town displays the grandeur of its earlier days when rich and powerful guilds dominated regional trade. As with Sighişoara and Braşov, Sibiu has a definite Saxon ambience. Sections of the medieval wall still guard over the historic area, where narrow streets weave past steep-roofed, brightly coloured 17th-century buildings before opening into vast, church-dominated squares such as the **Great Square** (Piața Mare), **Little Square** (Piața Mică) and **Huet Square** (Piața Huet). Sibiu is a great city to explore on foot. **Strada Nicolae Bălcescu**, the main pedestrian street, leads south from Piăta Mare and is lined with cafés and bars that spread out their terraces in spring and summer to create an almost Mediterranean atmosphere. First mentioned in 1411 as a grain market, Piața Mare was witness to the town's lively merchant activity, assemblies and even public executions. The north side of Piața Mare is graced by the **Roman Catholic church** (Biserica Romano-Catolica), a beautiful Baroque structure with Classical decorations which was built between 1726 and 1738.

Piața Mare is dominated by the imposing **Baroque Palace** (1785) of former Austrian governor Samul Brukenthal. The building now houses the **Brukenthal National Museum** (*Muzeul Brukenthal Piața Mare 4–5;* ☎ *0269 217 691;* e *info@*

brukenthalmuseum.ro; www.brukenthalmuseum.ro; ☉ *summer 10.00–18.00 Tue–Sun, closed Mon and first Tue of each month, winter 10.00–18.00 Wed–Sun; admission adult/child 12/3RON, guide 100RON/hr*), Transylvania's finest art museum, founded in 1790 and opened to the public in 1817. The art collection includes paintings by Rubens and Van Dyck as well as works of German, Austrian and Romanian masters, and also featuring a 16th-century silverware collection, painted glass icons and 350 rare books, many dating to the days of the first printing press. Opposite the museum entrance is the excellent **tourist office**, a good starting point to ask for maps and advice. If you're planning to visit several museums, it's worth buying a One Day Ticket at the Brukenthal Museum (30RON). This includes entrance to the History Museum, Natural History Museum, Pharmacy Museum, the art galleries of the Brukenthal Museum itself and more. To the west of the square, the **City History Museum** (*Str Mitropolitei 2;* ☎ *0269 218 143; www.brukenthalmuseum.ro;* ☉ *summer 10.00–18.00 Tue–Sun, closed Mon and first Tue of each month, winter 10.00–18.00 Wed–Sun; admission adult/child 12/3RON*) is housed in the **Primăria Municipuilui** (1470) building, part of the 'Casa Altemberger' which is considered one of the most important ensembles of non-religious Gothic architecture in Transylvania, and was the Town Hall for some 400 years. The museum concentrates on the history of Sibiu and its surroundings.

The former **Council Tower** (*Turnul Sfatului;* ☉ *10.00–20.00 daily; admission 2RON*) links Piaţa Mare with its little sister Piaţa Mică. Throughout the centuries, the Council Tower served as a grain storehouse, a fire watchtower, a temporary prison and even as a museum of botany. The roof, originally built in pyramid form, has undergone various changes, culminating in the addition of four corner turrets in 1826. It's well worth the long climb to the top to see a great view of the square and surrounding rooftops. **Piaţa Mică**, the second fortified square, was home to the town's most prestigious master craftsmen, who lived in rows of arcaded houses along the north and east sides. Today, boutiques and cafés line the square, painted in bright pastel hues of pea green, plum and apricot. The square is also home to the **Museum of the History of Pharmacy** (*Piaţa Mică 26;* ☎ *0269 218 191;* ☉ *see Brukenthal Museum; admission adult/child 6/1.5RON*), located in a historic building dating from 1569, where one of the oldest pharmacies in present-day Romania was located. In the basement, Samuel Hahnemann invented homeopathy and developed his version of treatment. Some of his phials and plans are on display. The exhibition is laid out like a classical pharmacy, including two laboratories, a homeopathic sector and a documentation sector. It contains over 6,000 ancient medical instruments and dispensing tools from the time when Sibiu was home to more chemists than anywhere else in Transylvania. At the front, a reconstructed shop is decked out with wooden counters and stacks of glass jars recreating the atmosphere of an 18th-century apothecary. To the north of Piaţa Mică down a flight of steps is the **Goldsmiths' Square** (Piaţa Aurarilor), a peaceful and intimate square, surrounded by charming old houses with medieval 'eyelid' windows in the roofs, doorways and turrets. For many years, it was the main point of passage between the Little Square and the Lower Town, the two connected by a 15th-century stairway.

Piaţa Mică's southwestern neighbour, Piaţa Huet, is home to a mix of Gothic buildings topped by the **Evangelical cathedral** (*Biserica Evangelica;* ☉ *summer 10.00–18.00 Mon–Sun, winter 11.00–16.00 Sun*). This impressive structure with five pointed towers was built in 1520 on the site of an old Roman basilica. The simple, stark interior is in total contrast to that of the Catholic church. A gigantic fresco, painted in 1445 by Johannes of Rosenau, covers much of the chancel's north wall. The mural shows the Crucifixion and marks a transition in painting from late

Gothic style to Renaissance. On the south side, the choir loft boasts a beautiful fan-vaulted ceiling, home to a Baroque organ designed by a German master in 1671. Six thousand pipes were installed in 1914, making it the largest organ in Romania. The **Church Tower** can also be visited (☉ *10.00–17.00 Sat/Sun, 12.00–15.00 on demand Mon–Fri; admission 3RON*). The Evangelical Cathedral was undergoing extensive renovation work in 2012. Piața Huet is also home to the **Emil Sigerus Saxon Ethnographic Museum** (*Piața Mică 11;* ✆ *0269 202 422;* e *sigerus@muzeulastra.ro; http://muzeulastra.ro;* ☉ *summer 10.00–18.00 Tue–Sun, winter 09.00–17.00 Tue–Sun; admission adult/child 5/1RON*), located at the back of the Casa Hermes, with a collection of household items.

Traditionally, the **Upper Town** (Orasul de Sus) was the wealthier, more commercial part, while the Lower Town served as the manufacturing area. The beautiful **Passage of Steps** (Pasajul Sărilor) connects the Upper Town to the Lower Town. At one end of the passage stands the city's oldest building, which now hosts the oldest restaurant in Romania, the **Golden Barrel** (Butoiul de Aur). Nearby, the iron **Bridge of Liars** (Podul Minciunilor) was built in 1859 by Fredericus Hutte and was the first wrought-iron bridge in Romania. Legend tells how the name derived from the merchants' fiery disputes, which flared up around it and the passionate but transitory vows of young lovers who often met here. Situated at the northern corner of Piața Mică, the bridge provides memorable photo opportunities.

For hundreds of years, Sibiu was one of the most powerful and prosperous strongholds in Europe. Surrounded by imposing walls, Sibiu's original fortifications included 39 defensive towers, five bulwarks, four gates and five artillery batteries.

Although the entire network is remarkably well preserved, the best-maintained section is the most often attacked southeast side which had to be reinforced several times throughout the centuries. Three 15th-century towers have withstood the test of time: **Arquebusiers' Tower** (Turnul Archebuzierilor), later known as the Drapers' Tower, the **Carpenters' Tower** (Turnul Dulgherilor) and the **Potters' Tower** (Turnul Olarilor). The 16th-century **Great Tower** (Turnul Gros) was the site of Sibiu's first theatrical performance, staged in 1778.

Around Lower Town

The **Lower Town** (Orasul de Jos) comprises the area between the river and the hill, and developed around the earliest fortifications. The streets are long and quite wide by medieval city standards, with small city squares dotted along. The architecture is rather rustic, typically two-storey houses with tall roofs and gates opening passages to inner courts. Sibiu is home to some impressive places of worship. The **Orthodox Metropolitan Cathedral** (*Catedrala Ortodoxa Mitropolitana Sf Treime; Str Mitropoliei 33–35*) was constructed 1902–06 on the site of a former Greek church and has a style similar to that of the Hagia Sofia in Istanbul. The **Ursuline Monastery** (Manastirea Ursulinelor) at Strada General Gh Magheru 38 was built in 1474 on a former Dominican monastery. Although documents attest to the existence of Jews in Sibiu since the 12th century, the Jewish community of Sibiu was never very large. In 1940, the town had some 1,300 Jews, three synagogues, three rabbis, two cemeteries and two ritual baths managed by the Sephardic and Orthodox communities. Today, the handful of Jews who remain in Sibiu hold weekly and holiday services at the **Great Synagogue** (Str Constitutiei 19) built by architect Ferenc Szalay in 1899, with funds collected by Sibiu's small Jewish community. The synagogue boasts a beautiful neo-Gothic façade. To the east of the centre, the **Pulverturm** (Powder Tower) was converted into a theatre in 1788 and just beyond it the **Museum of Natural History** (*Str Cetății 1;* ✆ *0369 101 782; www.brukenthalmuseum.ro;* ☉ *10.00–18.00 Tue–Sun;*

admission adult/child 8/2RON) has a collection of more than one million exhibits including botanical, zoological and mineral items.

Located behind the railway station, the **Steam Locomotive Museum** (*Muzeul de Locomotive cu Aburi; Str Dorobantilor 22;* ✆ *0269 431 685;* ◷ *10.00–17.00 Tue–Sun; admission adult/child 5/1RON*) opened in 1994 and displays 23 standard-gauge steam engines, ten narrow-gauge steam engines, two snow-ploughing engines and two steam cranes made between 1885 and 1958. Seven of the locomotives are still in good working order and are used on a variety of special trains for enthusiasts. There is also a narrow-gauge steam locomotive based at the depot of the **narrow-gauge Sibiu-Agnita Railway**. To get there, follow the narrow-gauge lines east from the station.

In the 19th century, Sibiu developed as a centre for cultural and intellectual life and the first Congress of ASTRA, the Association for the Propagation of Romanian Culture in Transylvania, was held in 1861 on Strada Mitropoliei.

South of the Orthodox cathedral, at the southern end of Strada Mitropoliei is the **Astra Park**, where busts of famous Romanians hold court.

The **ASTRA Open Air Museum** (*Muzeul in aer liber ASTRA – Dumbrava Sibiului; Calea Rasinarilor 14;* ✆ *0269 202 447;* e *muzeuldumbrava@clicknet.ro; www. muzeulastra.ro;* ◷ *May–Oct 09.00–18.00 Tue–Sun, Nov–Apr 10.00–17.00 Tue–Sun; admission adult/child 15/3.5RON*) is 4km south of the city at Dumbrava in the middle of a dense forest and by a beautiful lake. At over 100ha, Astra is the second-largest open-air museum in the world. There are more than 300 buildings as well as watermills and windmills, giant wine presses, and village buildings from many parts of the country. There is a wonderful collection of wooden farmhouses as well as a wooden church and two traditional inns. To get there, from Piaţa Unirii take bus No 1 or the tram, which goes all the way to Răşinari. At peak times (*07.00–09.00 & 13.00–15.00*), the tram runs every 30 minutes, the rest of the day every hour.

HEADING SOUTH AND WEST

CISNĂDIE AND CISNĂDIOARA Situated 7km south of Sibiu, Cisnădie (Nagydisznód/Heltau) features one of the biggest German churches, while up on the hill, at Cisnădioara (GER Michelsberg), visitors can find one of the oldest buildings in the country, the local Romanesque church.

Cisnădie Cisnădie was mentioned for the first time in a document from the year 1204 under the name Rivetel. In the 12th century, Saxon colonists settled here and in 1323 the German name Heltau was first mentioned. Over the years, the village flourished, particularly the guilds of sicklesmiths and wool weavers. Weaving remained the traditional occupation of the townspeople until the 20th century, when large textile factories were built.

Two **buses** an hour leave from Sibiu's bus station. You can also reach Cisnădie by **car**, drive south out of Sibiu city centre and continue for 12km.

Tourist information
🚩 **Cisnădie Information Centre** Str Cetăţii 1; ✆ 0269 561 236; e info_cisnadie@sibiu-turism.ro; www.cisnadie.ro; ◷ 10.00–17.00 Mon–Fri

Cisnădioara The village is situated 5km west of Cisnădie and 12km south of Sibiu on a lovely country road lined with orchards and poplar trees. It makes a great walk.

Cisnădioara has a **Romanesque church** (⊕ *summer 10.00–17.00 Tue–Sun*) dating from 1223 on top of a 70m-high crag above the village, which frequently withstood Tatar attacks. The villagers often took cover in the citadel, which they defended by hurling down rocks, which had been carried into the citadel by aspiring husbands. Villagers believed that no young man was marriage-worthy until he had carried a heavy rock from the riverbed up the steep track.

 Where to stay

⌂ **Secret Transylvania** (4 dbl) Str Bisericii; ☏0269 562 119; m 0742 247 664; e admin@ secrettransylvania.co.uk; ww.secrettransylvania. co.uk. Offering accommodation in 2 restored village houses, self catering or fully inclusive holidays with excursions, including to the 'Ice Hotel' at Bâlea Lac (see page 217). **$$$**

RĂŞINARI Răşinari (Resinár/Städterdorf) is located 12km south of Sibiu on the road to Păltiniş and is famous in the region for the skills of its local carpenters and sheep farmers. The village has a beautiful painted Orthodox church built in 1752 and an **ethnographic museum** (*Str Grădiniţa de Copii 2;* ⊕ *10.00–17.00 Tue–Sun; admission adult/child 3/1RON*).

Tram No 1 runs from Sibiu to Răşinari through the Dumbrava forest. Take **bus No 1** from the railway station to the tram's departure point south of the city. Bus 22 runs four-times daily, from Sibiu railway station to Păltiniş.

Tourist information

🗹 **Răşinari Information Centre** Str Sibiului FN; ☏0269 557 200; e info_rasinari@sibiu-turism.ro; ⊕ 10.00–17.00 Mon–Fri

 Where to stay

⌂ **Pensiunea Melania** (6 dbl) Str Sub Costiţă 1540; m 0742 938 676; e contact@pensiunea-melania.ro; www.pensiunea-melania.ro. Small family-run guesthouse. B/fast & dinner available on request. **$$**

The website www.ruraltourism.ro lists some guesthouses for Răşinari.

PĂLTINIŞ Situated 20km south of Sibiu and built by the Transylvanian Carpathian Society (SKV) in 1894, Păltiniş (Szebenjuharos/Hohe Rinne) is the highest (1,440m) and oldest **tourist resort** in the country. A favourite for **ski enthusiasts**, Păltiniş, with its beautiful location, fresh air and numerous hiking opportunities, is also a draw for **summer hikers**. Marked trails make it easy to reach the main points on the surrounding mountains. Most of the trails are also suitable for mountain biking. Păltiniş usually has snow for six months a year. The skiing track on Oncesti Mountain has a chair lift, drag lift and a baby lift. Oncesti has two slopes: for beginners and medium-level skiers. At the Schit (Hermitage) near the wooden church is the grave of philosopher Constantin Noica (1907–87). The resort has four hotels, six chalets and 17 villas for tourists plus many restaurants, bars and shops. Păltiniş is a starting point for many tourist destinations in the Cindrel and Lotru mountains. The red spot trail leads northwest towards Cheile Cibinului (5km).The red cross trail fellows an unpaved road part of the way to Vf Batrâna (Old Woman Peak, 1,911m).The red stripe trail (25km) leads to the Cindrel peak (2,244m) and is a more difficult route but very rewarding.

Bus 22 leaves Sibiu railway station four-times daily and stops at Răşinari.

⌂ Where to stay

⌂ **Cindrelul Hotel** (35 dbl, 2 tpl, 2 suites) 550001 Păltiniş; ☏ 0269 574 057; e rezervari. cindrelul@apps.ro; www.apps.ro. Friendly chalet hotel, each room with a balcony. Good value restaurant ($). **$$$**

⌂ **Casa Turiştilor Hotel** (1 sgl, 52 dbl, 4 trpl) 550001 Păltiniş; ☏ 0269 574 035; e rezervari@ scpaltinis.ro; www.scpaltinis.ro. Wellness & fitness centre & a good restaurant ($) in this over-sized chalet hotel. **$$**

CRISTIAN Situated 10km west of Sibiu on route E68/81 heading towards Sebeş, Cristian (Kereszténysziget/Grossau) was settled by Saxons in the 14th century. The grand fortified church looms over the red-roofed, white-walled peasant houses (*contact Liane Hergetz, Str Libertăţii 10, by the entrance to the church*). The village itself is famous for its large **stork population**; look out for the huge nests on the tops of telegraph poles. The **Village (Heimat) Museum** (*Muzeul Sătesc; ⊕ 12.00–17.00 Tue–Sun; admission adult/child 5/1RON*) shows exhibits on local history.

Regular local **buses** leave Sibiu for Cristian; journey time 30 minutes.

THE MĂRGINIMEA SIBIULUI REGION The Mărginimea Sibiului (Borders of Sibiu) is a special region covering a territory of 1,200km² with 18 settlements in the foothills of the Cindrel Mountains. The inhabitants were legendary shepherds who preserved the traditional customs, folk costumes and original Romanian architecture. The region represents the soul of traditional rural Transylvania as depicted by Romanian craftsmen. The villagers in these 18 settlements preserve the ancient crafts such as woodcarving, weaving, painting icons on glass and colouring eggs. The fields are worked with animals and people travel on horse-drawn carts. The 18 villages are: Boiţa, Sadu, Râu Sadului, Tălmaciu, Talmacel, Răşinari, Poplaca, Gura Râului, Orlat, Făntănele, Sibiel, Vale, Sălişte, Gales, Tilisca, Rod, Poiana Sibiului and Jina. The website www.ruraltourism.ro has many suggestions for guesthouses, pensions and villas. One scene in Sălişte's **church frescoes**, dating from 1354, remains covered at all times. It depicts the devil surrounded by naked human bodies, a subject the villagers consider too obscene to be displayed. Tourists can take a peek upon request.

Local **trains** from Sibiu to Sebeş stop at Sibiel (25mins) and Sălişte (35mins).

SIBIEL Sibiel (Szibiel) is located 24km west of Sibiu, and just 5km south of Sălişte and is famous throughout Transylvania for its tradition of painting icons on glass, a craft that has been going on for 200 years. In 1968, Father Zosim Oancea, who spent 17 years in prison during the communist era for his beliefs, founded the **Icon Museum** (*Muzeul de Icoane pe Sticla; Sta Bisericii 329; ☏ 0269 552 536; e www.sibiel. net; www.sibiel.net; ⊕ winter 07.00–13.30 & 14.00–19.00, summer 08.00–13.30 & 14.00–20.00; admission adult/child 4/2RON*) and started to collect 18th- and 19th-century icons richly painted on glass. Today, the museum exhibits the largest collection of painted glass icons in Europe with more than 700, as well as furniture and ceramics.

Many local **trains** from Sibiu to Sebeş stop at Sibiel (25mins) and Sălişte (35mins). Travelling by **car**, take the E68/E81 west out of Sibiu, heading for Sebeş, turn left at Săcel for Sibiel, 5km south.

Tourist information

🛈 **Sibiel Information Centre** Principala 298; ☏ 0269 552 560; e info_sibiel@sibiu-turism.ro.

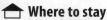

Where to stay

Pensiunea Mioritica Sibiel (6 dbl) Str Raului 197A; 📞 0269 552 640; 📱 0740 175 287; e coldeasv@ yahoo.com. A lovely family-run guesthouse by a stream with a garden filled with objects salvaged by the owner, including commie relics. A great base for hiking in the Cindrel & Lotru mountains. **$**

MIERCUREA SIBIULUI AND BĂILE MIERCUREA-SIBIULUI SPA
Miercurea Sibiului (Szerdahely/Reussmarkt) still has a market on Wednesday, the traditional day for such events and from where the name 'Miercurea' derives. See also Miercurea-Ciuc in Harghita County (page 162). In the town centre is a well-preserved **13th-century** church, fortified during the 15th century. Visitors can still see the storerooms where villagers kept supplies in times of Turkish raids.

Situated 7km further on towards Sebeş right on the Sibiu–Alba County border, **Băile Miercurea-Sibiului** is a small resort town, built around the healing mineral water springs, with some tourist *cabanas* and a run-down campsite.

Several **trains** daily leave Sibiu railway station for Miercurea Sibiului. If you're **driving**, Miercurea Sibiului is on the E68/E81 highway to Sebeş, 35km west of Sibiu. Băile Miercurea-Sibiului is 7km further on the same main road.

Where to stay

Comfort Hotel (33 dbl, 1 suite) Drum Naţionale 1 (E68) No 816; 📞 0269 533 033; e mail@comfort-hotel.ro; www.comfort-hotel.ro. Not the swankiest hotel in the world but adequate for a night or 2 if you want to explore the region. Good parking, 2 restaurants ($). **$$**

OCNA SIBIULUI
Actually called Salzburg in German (and Vízakna in Hungarian, which literally means a 'manhole'), Ocna Sibiului is a **resort** built around salty lakes. If you see 'ocna' in a town's name, it refers to a salt mine.

The first serious research into the curative effects of the **saline lakes** was made in 1820. After that, cabins were constructed around the lakes, trees planted and pavilions built for bathing in cold weather. The resort officially opened in 1858. The central pavilion and bathing house were built 1906–09 and can still be seen today. There are places for warm baths, mud packs and 'aerosol' treatments. The resort also has three lakes for swimming, named Horea, Cloşca and Crişan after the leaders of the peasant uprising in 1784. These lakes were formed when six old salt mines were flooded with water. Situated near the Sibiu–Copşa Mică railway line are more lakes, the most important being **Lacul Fără Fund** (Bottomless Lake), formed from the Francisc Grube Salt Mine (32m deep), abandoned in 1775. This has been declared a natural reserve because of its thermal strength and mineral content. Another lake, **Avram Iancu** (Abandoned Salt Mine) was created from the Fodina Maior mine (160m deep) abandoned in 1817. **Lacul Brâncoveana**, formed in 1699 from an abandoned salt mine, is the most saline with 310g/l salinity. Lacul Ocniţa and the lakes of the Flax, the Cats and the Mud are all very salty. The saline waters are effective in the treatment of rheumatism, locomotive and gynaecological problems. Therapies offered include hydrotherapy, electrotherapy, thermotherapy and balneo-therapy.

The Sibiu–Copşa Mică railway passes through Ocna Sibiului, with many **trains** daily. By **car**, head north towards Copşa Mică on route 14 and fork left for Ocna Sibiului just outside Sibiu's city limits.

Where to stay

Salinas Hotel (2 sgl, 19 dbl, 2 suites) Str Băilor 22–24; 📞 269 577 348; e rezervari@ ocnasibiului.ro; www.ocnasibiului.ro. A 3-star hotel with smart, clean rooms, the restaurant ($$) has Romanian, Italian & Chinese cuisine. **$$–$$$**

SLIMNIC (Szelindek/Stolzenburg) (*Contact Reverend Walter Gottfried Seidner; Str Lungă 73;* ☎ *0269 856 110;* ☉ *visiting possible anytime; donations welcome*) Located on the road to Copşa Mică, Slimnic is an impressive ruined **fortress church** on a hill above the village. Three naves divide the fortress into two courtyards. In the first is a bell tower with a chapel, in the second is a well surrounded by a defensive wall. The fortress twice came under siege and was destroyed in 1529 and 1706.

Travelling by **car**, take route 14, 16km north of Sibiu on the right.

COPŞA MICĂ The factory in Copşa Mică (Kiskapus/Kleinkopisch) was built in the late 1930s to process heavy metals, a giant smelting works that over the following decades belched out contaminants on a terrifying scale and turned the entire town black. The factory's current owners, the Greek firm Mytilineos Holdings, recently installed new filters to bring emissions into line with European standards. However, there is a poisonous legacy. Official statistics show life expectancy in the town is nine years shorter than the national average. The environmental organisation EcoTur carried out a survey in the area from 1999–2004 and found the soil contained 92 times above the permitted level of lead resulting in the vegetation having a lead content 22 times above the permitted level.

Another study into children aged between two and 12 years old found heightened levels of lead in their systems and evidence of arrested development. In 2006, 80 workers from the factory were treated for lead poisoning and for years hundreds of people have complained of bronchial problems.

Further evidence of a health impact came during an official investigation into the deaths of two horses. The national veterinary service found the hay fed to the horses had lead levels ten times higher than the legal limit, and the horses themselves were carrying high levels of lead and other heavy metals. There is a high risk that food grown locally is similarly toxic. In the market, traders emphasise that vegetables sold on their stalls were grown a long way from Copşa Mică.

A detailed environmental control programme has been agreed with the local authorities, part of a package of measures designed to bring Romanian industry in line with EU standards. The factory, Sometra, is adamant that its emissions record is now improving.

There is talk of a clean-up: hundreds of new trees have been planted and driving through (with the car windows closed to keep out the strong aroma), it is possible to see where the blackened house walls have been scrubbed to an off-white. The rusting remains of a decaying factory still blight the landscape and the toxins have penetrated at least 1m into the soil. Improvements will need to be measured over decades rather than years.

Getting there and away Copşa Mică is on route 14 between Sibiu and Mediaş. Copşa Mică is 42km north of Sibiu. There is nothing to visit in the town. Copşa Mică lies at a junction of two important rail lines, and if you are travelling by train (from Sibiu to Cluj-Napoca, for example), you may have to change trains; however, you are advised to do so at the more attractive town of Mediaş (see page 211), just a short distance further on the same line.

VALEA VIILOR The fortified Saxon church at Valea Viilor (Nagybaromlak/ Wurmloch) is one of the seven listed as a UNESCO World Heritage Site. The others are at Câlnic (Alba), Biertan (Sibiu), Saschiz (Mureş), Viscri (Braşov), Prejmer

(Braşov) and Dârjiu (Harghita). Dârjiu is the odd one out because it is a Székely Unitarian church while the rest are Saxon.

Valea Viilor is 47km north of Sibiu. By **car**, take route 14 to Copşa Mică then turn right signed for Valea Viilor.

The **fortified church** (*Contact Johanna Schneider,* \ *0269 515 266;* ⊕ *by appointment; donations welcome*) is situated in the centre of the village. The church has late Gothic elements dating from around 1500. The church hall has a tunnel vault with a late Gothic ribbed net. Towers were placed in the four compass points; the western tower was the gate tower and also a bell tower with impressive buttresses. The Baroque altar dating from 1779 has two tiers, statues of saints and painted panels. The existing organ dates from 1808. The fortress was inscribed onto UNESCO's list because of the sculptural character of its fortifications.

BIERTAN For those who want to take time and explore as many Saxon fortified churches as possible, Biertan (Beretthalom/Birthälm) is the best village to use as a base camp – the town of **Mediaş** is another possibility if you fancy something more urban – because it is the most accessible village and has the best road leading to it. It also has the best facilities, including several guesthouses, a post office, several grocery shops, a 'Magazin Mixt', a great folk art and crafts gift shop, a good restaurant, a wine factory open for tasting sessions and the rowdy, late-opening Ady Pub (unfortunately right opposite the bedroom windows of the Eminescu Trust guesthouse – take earplugs or join in)!

Biertan is situated between Mediaş and Sighişoara. By **car**, drive for 17km east from Mediaş and turn right at Dumbrăveni. Biertan is 9km south on a lovely road.

Where to stay and eat

🏠 **Casa Dornroschen** (8 dbl, 1 trpl, 1 quad) Piaţa 1 Decembrie 1918, Str Gheorghe Coşbuc 25; \0269 244 165; e office@biertan.net; www.biertan.net. Behind the fortress church, go up the alley beside the postcard kiosk to the left of the church by the main square. Geared towards German-speaking guests & nestling under the fortress walls, this guesthouse is not a bad bet. **$$$$**

🏠 **Guesthouse** (2 dbl) Run by the Mihai Eminescu Trust (see page 52). Next door to the Artefact Biertan gift shop (see below) is an unmarked guesthouse beside a courtyard attached to the gift shop building where meals are taken in the lovely basement kitchen & dining room, complete with all-wooden furniture. The rooms can be booked by email through the Mihai Eminescu Trust. Meals extra by arrangement with a

local lady who can prepare b/fast, lunch or dinner or any combination of the 3. **$$**

🏠 **Pension Unglerus** (14 dbl, 2 apt) Situated across Piaţa 1 Decembrie 1918, Str 1 Decembrie 1918 1; \0269 806 699; e office@biertan.ro; www.biertan.ro. Tastefully restored village house. Enquiries at the office or restaurant (see above). **$$**

✗ **Restaurant Unglerus** Str 1 Decembrie 1918 1; \0269 806 698; ⊕ 10.00–22.00 daily. A medieval-themed restaurant with huge chairs with studded leather backs, spears & shields all around. The walls feature huge paintings of knights in armour & scary ladies in wimples. The extensive menu has meat, fish, salads, good starters & a selection of quality beers & wines. There are more rooms above & below. It can get packed with coach parties, so pick your moment. **$$**

Shopping

Artefact Biertan On the corner by the main square; \0269 868 494; e artefact_biertan@ yahoo.com; ⊕ 30 Apr–31 Oct 10.00–19.00 Mon–Sat. This folk art gift shop, run by Monica Cosma is a great place to find souvenirs & presents

with handmade wooden boxes, paintings, jewellery made from delicately carved cow & deer bone, rings, painted eggs, egg timers, etc, all in a restored ancient building featuring a beautiful blue & white ceramic stove & wrought-iron chandeliers.

Visitors can also buy organic apple juice (*suc de mere*) from Mălâncrav (9RON).

Crama-Weinkeller-Winecellar On the road to Richiş, 15mins' walk; ⊕ 08.00–16.00 Mon–Fri. In a large factory, making wine from the surrounding region.

Postcard kiosk ⊕ 10.00–19.00 Sun–Fri. If there's no room at any inn, Bianca Iorga at the kiosk can give advice. She sells postcards, maps &

brochures in English. The large square spreads out beneath the steps up to the church & in summer, several coaches are parked there. However, the place is big enough to accommodate the traffic & it never feels overcrowded.

Shop 'Felix Em' Opposite the Artefact Biertan gift shop; ⊕ 06.45–21.00 Mon–Sat, 09.00–21.00 Sun. Selling bread, loo rolls, ice cream, beer, water & soft drinks.

Other practicalities

Post office

✉ Piaţa 1 Decembrie 1918; ⊕ 08.00–12.00 Mon–Fri

Information

Unglerus Tourist Agency ☎ 0269 806 699; www.biertan.ro. Local accommodation & tours can be arranged.

Biertan Church (⊕ *visiting Apr–Oct 10.00–19.00 daily; admission 5RON*) Biertan has one of the biggest fortress churches and once housed the Lutheran Bishop of Transylvania. It is a UNESCO World Heritage Site. The church was first mentioned in 1402 as a Gothic basilica, but it was completely demolished and the hall-shaped church with a chief nave and two side aisles that we see today was built 1500–25. The late Gothic and Renaissance stone masonry is well preserved with doorways, the pulpit and brackets. The wooden furniture, including the folding triptych, dates back to the beginning of the 16th century. Europa Nostra carried out restoration work (1978–91) and found parts of earlier paintings and inscriptions. The fortress has three concentric exterior walls, which can be explored and in the Mausoleum Tower are carved gravestones of priests and bishops. The building's territory is large, taking up almost 1ha and the church is protected by two circular fortified walls with a third one on the west-southwest side. The complex has seven towers. On the northeastern side is the Clock Tower, with firing windows and a wooden footbridge. The clock is still working and every day the crank is turned. On the southern side is the Catholic Tower where there is a chapel for the Transylvanian Saxons who didn't convert to Protestantism. On the southern side are two gate towers, with one known usually as the Bacon Tower because food was stored here during sieges. The Prison Tower was used to punish husbands who wanted a divorce. Legends say that feuding couples were held in this tower with one single bed, one table, one chair, one plate and one glass. The man and wife were held for a period of time here and the legend claims that because of this reconciliation tactic, there was only one divorce in 300 years. Personally, this method would drive me to something nasty and violent!

Since 1990, an **annual meeting of Transylvanian Saxons** takes place in Biertan on the first Saturday after 15 September. The ceremony is followed by a parade in folk costume, a craftsmen's market and a fair.

COPŞA MARE It is possible to **walk or drive** from Biertan to Copşa Mare (Nagykapus/Gross-Kopisch); it is 3km east of Biertan. The road goes up over a hill to the next valley. The good road peters out at the top of the hill and down towards Copşa Mare there is a dirt track with large, sharp pebbles. It is quite tricky to negotiate the road, especially when a horse-drawn cart suddenly appears from round a bend. In Copşa Mare itself there is no proper road either, just a dirt track. Little children run along behind the car, waving and shouting *Bună seara!* (Good evening).

Copşa Mare Church (*Contact Samuel Hertel or Stefan Schuster; Copşa Mare No 112 or No 237;* ✆ *0269 868 307; visiting by appointment; donations welcome*) is found on the western slope of a hill above the village. At the beginning of the 16th century, the earlier Gothic basilica was transformed and fortified with massive buttresses added to the choir. The vault is decorated with star-shaped ribs. Gothic and Renaissance details are preserved in the windows, doorways, niches and brackets. The folding triptych is Classical and dates from 1854.

RICHIŞ Richiş (Riomfalva/Reichesdorf) is situated at the crossing of three main streets through the village and by **car**, it is 6km south of Biertan on a minor but passable road. The **church** (*Contact Johann Schaas; Richiş No 87;* ✆ *0269 258 429;* ⊕ *visiting by appointment; donations welcome*) is a 14th-century Gothic basilica without a western tower. The choir is on the west side with a polygonal wall and two chapels on each side, a design also found in Evangelical churches in Cluj-Napoca and Cristian. Some of the furniture was made in the early 16th century. Various bosses and cantilevers contain natural and anthropomorphic elements. The theme of the 'green man', a motif in western European architecture, is also present. The Baroque altar was made by Johann Folbarth in 1775 and the organ dates from 1788.

MOŞNA The church in Moşna (GER Meschen) (*Contact Ilse Diplaş, who also offers accommodation, Moşna No 531;* ✆ *0269 862 154;* ⊕ *visiting by appointment; donations welcome*) was first built in 1283 as an early Gothic basilica. The structure seen today dates from the end of the 15th century and is the work of Andrea Lapicida, a stonemason from Sibiu. Lapicida created the ribbed vault of the nave, the choir and the vestry. The interior of the church is entirely filled with wooden scaffolding, but it is still possible to see the little panels decorated with flower patterns and delicate paintwork. A plaque on the wall tells how Prince Charles visited on 4 November 1998.

By **car**, Moşna is best reached via Mediaş, situated 10km south of Mediaş. It is also possible to get to Moşna from Richiş and Biertan. From Richiş, continue south for 3km then turn right and drive for a further 7km west.

MĂLÂNCRAV Mălâncrav (Almakerék/Malmkrog) has the highest proportion of remaining Saxons in any village in Transylvania. From an original population – before the general exodus – of 900, 170 Saxons remain. In summer, a traditional Saxon **Kronenfest** takes place and Saxons from the surrounding area all congregate for a big party with dancing and merrymaking (see page 96). The village has very original and **well-preserved houses** owing to the terrible condition of the 13km road leading to Mălâncrav.

The **Mihai Eminescu Trust** (MET, see page 52) has three houses in the village available for ecotourists to rent.

The **Lutheran Evangelical church** was built by the Apáfi family in the second half of the 14th century. The chancel of the church holds what is considered the most valuable set of **Gothic murals** in Transylvania. Close to the church, the noble Hungarian manor house has been restored by the MET and the ancient orchard, now organic, is owned and managed by the MET, providing delicious freshly pressed apple juice.

The **manor house** was built by the Hungarian Apáfi family, probably in the 15th century. It is very unusual to have a manor house in a Saxon village. Mălâncrav and only two or three other villages were governed by Hungarians. In the late 18th century, the Apáfi family died out, and the property passed to the Bethlen family. In the 19th century, a Hungarian commoner bought the house. The deeds

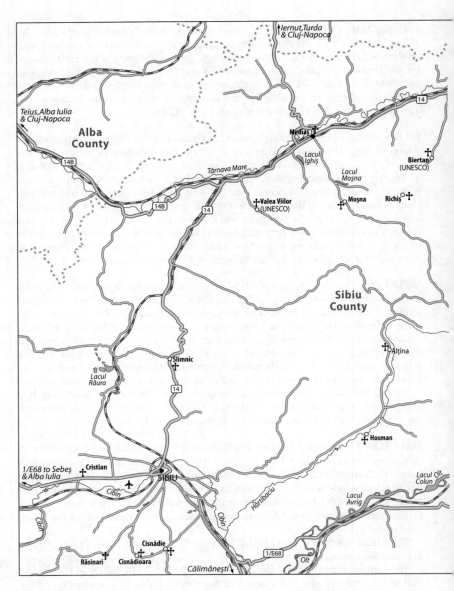

of the house record that in the 1920s it was sold by its last private owner to the Evangelical village community. The house was illegally confiscated and misused by the communists from 1947–89. In late 2000, the MET helped the Evangelical community to establish its legal rights to the house. In December 2000 the totally derelict and dilapidated building was sold to the MET.

Under the architect Jan Hülsemann and master builders Fritz Klutsch and Ernst Linzing, the manor house has been restored as much as possible to its original 18th-century plans.

It is possible to rent out the manor house; see page 52.

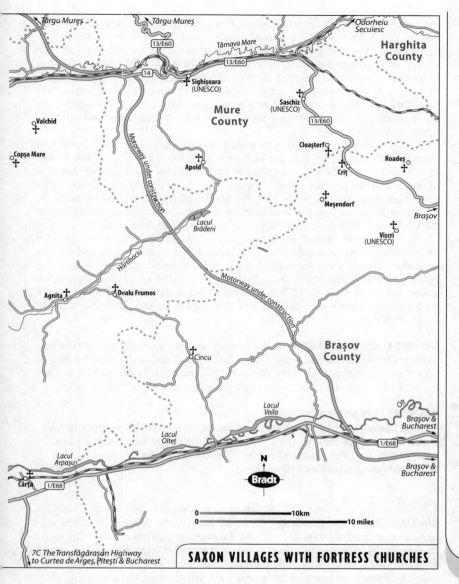

Map labels:

Târgu Mureş

Târgu Mureş

13/E60

Odorheiu Secuiesc

Harghita County

Târnava Mare

14

Sighişoara (UNESCO)

Saschiz (UNESCO)

13/E60

Mureş County

Cloaşterf

Roadeş

Valchid

Criţ

Copşa Mare

Apold

Meşendorf

Braşov

Lacul Brădeni

Viscri (UNESCO)

Hârtibaciu

Agnita

Dealu Frumos

Motorway under construction

Braşov County

Cincu

Lacul Voila

Lacul Olteţ

Olt

Braşov & Bucharest

Lacul Arpaşu

1/E68

Braşov & Bucharest

Cârţa

1/E68

N

Bradt

0   10km
0   10 miles

7C The Transfăgărăşan Highway to Curtea de Argeş, Piteşti & Bucharest

SAXON VILLAGES WITH FORTRESS CHURCHES

Mălâncrav is accessible by **car** – drive from Mediaş towards Sighişoara on route 14. After 27km, turn right at Laslea and follow the awful road for 13km south to Mălâncrav.

MEDIAŞ The town of Mediaş (Medgyes/Mediasch) has existed since 1267 as a Saxon village, although earlier settlements date back to the Stone Age. Mediaş was first mentioned during the Roman Age as Per Medias (the town at crossroads) and the seat of the third Roman legion (Media). Mediaş obtained urban status in 1359 as Civitas Medgyes. The fortifications of the Mediaş citadel were built in the 14th and 15th centuries, after repeated Ottoman invasions. Most of the citadel and the Old Town has been conserved, making Mediaş a great tourist destination, and it's easy to get to by train. Mediaş is one of the seven Siebenburgen and has an important role in the history of Transylvania. In the Middle Ages the city was known as an important centre of crafts and trade. In the 15th and 16th centuries, there were 33 craft guilds. Besides the significant economic role they played, they would also protect the city. The bastions of the walled city (the Goldsmiths' and Stonecutters' Towers are still standing today) were built, maintained and defended by the craftsmen themselves.

Transylvania's affairs were more than once debated at Mediaş, as the Diet was held there several times. In 1571, István Báthory was elected as a prince of Transylvania in Mediaş. In 1773, the city was visited by Joseph II, who was to become emperor of the Austro-Hungarian Empire. In 1848, the people of the city participated in the revolution under the leadership of Stefan Moldovan and Stefan Ludwig Roth. On 8 January 1919, the Saxon assembly of the town endorsed the decision taken in Alba Iulia on 1 December 1918 to unite Transylvania with Romania.

The **Evangelical Church of St Margaret** (⊕ *May–Sep 10.00–18.00, Oct–Apr 10.00–15.00; suggested donation 5RON*), known as 'the Castle' represented the core around which the citadel gradually developed. There is a remarkable series of 15th century frescoes inside the church, and note the coats of arms of the local guilds above you in the main aisle. The interior also has several impressive altarpieces, a 14th century font, a large collection of Anatolian rugs, and a Baroque organ by Johannes Hahn.

Getting there and away By **train**, Mediaş is on the main Braşov–Oradea line. There are frequent trains to Braşov (*3hrs*) and Sighişoara (*3hrs*), five trains daily to Cluj-Napoca (*75mins*) and four trains daily to Sibiu (*1hr*). By **car**, Mediaş is 55km north of Sibiu on route 14 and 35km west of Sighişoara on route 14.

 Where to stay and eat

➤ **Hotel Traube** (12 dbl, 1 apt, 2 business rooms) Piaţa Regele Ferdinand I 16; ☏ 0269 844 898; e receptie@hoteltraube.ro; www. hoteltraube.ro. In a quiet location just off the main square, this renovated, 200-year-old building has rooms with exposed wooden beams & a large restaurant (\$\$\$). **\$\$**

HEADING EAST

AGNITA (*Contact the parsonage, Str Nouă 14;* ☏ *0269 540 934;* ⊕ *visiting by appointment; donations welcome*) Agnita (Szentágota/Agnetheln) was originally a Romanesque basilica, transformed in the Gothic period into a hall-shaped church with late Gothic net ribbing. The Baroque altar dates from 1650 and resembles a triptych Gothic altar. Four defensive towers are still standing and give the structure a solid, chunky appearance.

Until 2004, trains operated on the State Railways' only remaining stretch of narrow-gauge track between Sibiu and Agnita. Although deemed unviable, it provided a lifeline to the many towns and villages along its route. Today, there is a move to restore the track bed and resume operation of regular trains.

The narrow-gauge railway from Sibiu to Sighişoara ceased to operate in two stages. The section from Sighişoara to Agnita closed in 1963. The track was torn up, and there is little evidence of its existence apart from station buildings along the old route, many of which are now private homes. The remaining section from Agnita to Sibiu continued to operate for a further 30 years. A British consortium is attempting to restore the line for the benefit of local town and village communities and also for tourism development, and the MET have undertaken a feasibility study for the project. The railway has been formally recognised as a historic monument in Romania.

For more information on the history of the line and proposed redevelopment, see the website www.spurfilm.eu. *Mocanita* (or 'coffee machine') is the affectionate name for a narrow-gauge steam locomotive, as the driving gear resembles a coffee grinder in action and the steam boiler is like an Italian-style espresso machine in noise and drama.

By **car**, Agnita can be approached from either the north or south. From the north, drive south from Sighişoara on a fairly good road for 43km. From the south, turn right off the main E68 highway from Făgăraş to Sibiu at Voila, 11km west of Făgăraş and drive for 36km.

DEALU FRUMOS (*Contact Johann Herberth;* \ *0269 513 685;* ⏲ *visiting by appointment; donations welcome*) Dealu Frumos (GER Schonberg) has one of the most beautiful fortified churches in the region. It appeared first as a low Romanesque basilica with three bays, a bell tower, a square choir and a semicircular apse. In the 15th century, during fortification, the apse was removed and a tower erected above the choir. The enclosure consists of a very regular square defensive wall with towers in the four corners.

Dealu Frumos is reached from the south; turn right off the main E68 highway from Făgăraş to Sibiu at Voila, 11km west of Făgăraş and drive for 28km. Dealu Frumos is 8km east of Agnita.

CÂRŢA (*Contact Reverend Michael Reger; Cârţa No 137;* \ *0269 204 912 ext 125;* ⏲ *visiting by appointment; donations welcome*) Situated on the River Olt, the village Cârţa (Kerc/Kerz)developed around the Cistercian monastery, established around 1203. Today only the choir and ruins of the basilica, as well as those of the eastern side of the monastery, are preserved. The parish house, still in use today, is located in the southern part of the monastery. The monument is remarkable for its valuable details of Cistercian architecture, including capitals, supports, portals, window frames, gathered columns, niches, and other shapes characteristic of this architecture. The church choir is used today as a Lutheran church, with its Baroque altar dating back to 1751. The monument represents an early example of Gothic architecture, which had a great influence on other Transylvanian monuments, such as Prejmer, Hărman, Hălmeag and Sic.

Slow *personal* **trains** between Braşov and Sibiu stop at Cârţa – look for the 'Halta Cârţa' stop 33km west of Făgăraş. By **car**, drive 33km west from Făgăraş on the E68 and turn right just after Apaşu de Jos.

AVRIG Avrig (Felek/Freck) is a small dusty town on the busy E68 Sibiu–Braşov highway that conceals a little treasure. The Baroque **Avrig Palace** was built by General Buccow in the 18th century and given to the Brukenthal family (see *Sibiu*, page 199). It was their summer residence for many years. The palace served as a state hospital and sanatorium during the communist period and fell into a bad state of repair. Avrig Palace is surrounded by the most easterly Baroque garden in Europe, which suffered damage through poor drainage during the communist period but is now being restored by the Brukenthal Foundation (*www.brukenthal.org*). The **gardens** (⏲ *08.00–22.00 daily; admission free, but donations welcome*) cover around 20ha, which can be explored along winding paths surrounded by lawns, trees and flower

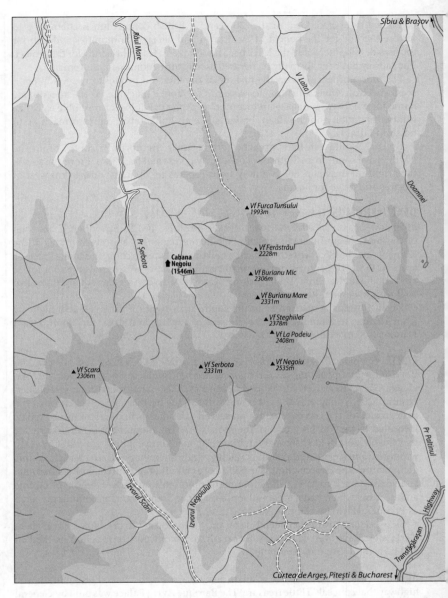

beds. A small bistro opened in 2012, and accommodation is offered with rooms overlooking the park. It is possible to make donations to the Brukenthal Foundation through their website (e *doerr@brukenthal.org* or *feyer@brukenthal.org* for further details).

Just outside Avrig is a **Traseul Cultural Brukenthal** (Cultural Walk; *4km, 1hr*) to Săcădate.

Avrig is on the E68, 30km east of Sibiu. Eight **trains** run daily from Braşov (*2–3hrs*), ten trains daily from Sibiu (*50mins*).

FĂGĂRAȘ RANGE

Transfăgărașan Highway

7C

Arpășelu

Ucea Mare

0 ━━━ 2km
0 ━━━━━━ 2 miles

N

Bradt

Cabana
Turnuri
(1520m)

Cabana
Bâlea Cascada

Cabana
Bâlea Lac
(2030m)

Ice Hotel

Lacul Bâlea
(2030m)

Cabana
Palținu
(2034m)

Tunel

Cabana
Podragu
(2136m)

Lacul
Podragu
(2034m)

Vf Moldoveanu
2544m

7C

Vf Arpașu Mare
2468m

Vf Arpașu Mică
2460m

Complex
Hotelier Capra
(1520m)

Capra

P Mircea

7C

HOSMAN Hosman (GER Holzmengen) is situated on the left bank of the Hârtibaciu River. The **fortified church** (*Contact Helmut Michaelis,* m *0747 282 821 in Hosman, or Winfried Ziegler in Sibiu* m *0745 493 986;* ⊕ *visiting hours by appointment; suggested donation 10RON*) was built on a hill situated in the southern part of the village A remaining portal from the Romanesque basilica is of special value. The Gothic gate with its painted statues of St Peter and Mark the Evangelist are particularly beautiful. Along with Sighișoara, Hosman has the only Saxon fortified church whose 300-year-old clock is still working. The church is surrounded by a double row of defensive walls, strengthened by several towers and a house. On the western façade, a clover-shaped window can still be seen, as well as a relief showing two figures. The Classical altar can also be dated to 1803, as can the decoration of the balcony and the organ. **Moara Veche** is an old mill in Hosman which has been carefully restored, and can be visited by arrangement (*Contact Gabriela Cotaru;* m *0748 800 049; www.moara-veche.ro (in Romanian only);* ⊕ *visiting hours by appointment; suggested donation 10RON*).

'**Transilvanian Brunch**' [sic] is an event which takes place between April and September on the last Saturday of the month at one of the villages in the Hărtibaciu region, promoting local food and culture (*contact Joachim Cotaru;* m *0748 800 049;* e *cotaru@gmail.com; http://brunch.dordeduca.ro*).

Hosman is 40km east of Sibiu on a minor road. There are several **buses** a day from Sibiu.

TRANSFĂGĂRAŞAN HIGHWAY
Route 7C, the second-highest road in Europe (highest point 2,034m), also known as the Transfăgăraşan Highway, crosses the Făgăraş Mountains travelling between Cârtişoara in the north to Curtea de Arges, but the road is only open from late June to October (sometimes September if it snows early). The highway is the most spectacular drive in the country and is possibly the only positive project constructed during the 1970s under Ceauşescu's demonic plans to conquer nature. The two-lane highway took soldiers nearly five years to build with construction possible only in the summer months and it opened to traffic in 1974. Building the highway came at a considerable cost in human lives – around 40 soldiers died during construction, according to official records. Romania's highest asphalt-covered road is an unforgettable experience for the passenger as well as the driver. In a 24 March 2008 article in *The Guardian*, *Uneasy Rider* author Mike Carter described the Transfăgăraşan Highway as 'the best biking road I've ever ridden', and in 2009, Jeremy Clarkson of BBC's *Top Gear* pronounced it 'the best road in the world!'

To reach the start of highway 7C, turn off the E68 Sibiu–Braşov main road just after Scoreiu. The mighty highway has no sign indicating that it begins here, so take the turning to the village of Cârtişoara on the plain beneath the snow-capped peaks. If you reach Arpaşu de Jos on the E68 you've gone past the turn. Cârtişoara is a pleasant village and in the Făgăraş foothills are many pensions and guesthouses.

After 12km of flat meadows, the road suddenly begins to climb a steep hill, surrounded by thick forest. If you are travelling in the autumn, be warned that there is no information at any stage as to whether the road and tunnel across the mountain peak are still open. Before setting out, check with the mountain rescue service **Salvamont** (see box, page 112) or ask a local about the weather conditions.

After a 22km climb, you reach the waterfalls and here the 360° views are stunning. There are a few stalls dotted about and it is possible to spend the night in the **Cabana Bâlea Cascada** (1,234m), a two-star *cabana* (✆ *0269 211 703;* e *info@balea-turism.ro; www.balea-turism.ro;* **$$**) which can accommodate 80 people. From here a **cable car** (⊕ *summer 09.00–17.00 daily; 20RON each way*) takes passengers up to **Lacul Bâlea** and the three-star **Cabana Bâlea Lac** (✆ *0269 523 517;* m *0745 072 602;* e *cabana.balealac@yahoo.com; http://balealac.ro;* **$$$$**).

After an 887m-long tunnel through rock under the Palţinu ridge, the highway descends along the **Argeş Valley**. After 27km, the road enters a forest, then re-emerges on the shores of the beautiful **Lacul Vidraru** and crosses a 165m-high dam built in 1968. At the southern tip of the lake, drivers will spot the ruined walls of **Poienari Citadel**, one of Vlad III Ţepeş's favourite castle residences. Poienari was built in the 13th century on a rocky crag above Lacul Vidraru by rulers of the

Wallachian region. In the decades following, the name and the residents changed a few times and eventually the castle was abandoned and left in ruins. However, in the 15th century, Vlad III Țepeș realised the potential for a castle perched high on a steep precipice of rock, and he repaired and consolidated the structure, making it one of his main fortresses. Although the castle was used for many years after Vlad's death in 1476, it was eventually abandoned again in the first half of the 16th century and, by the 17th century it lay in ruins. Owing to its size and location, the castle was very hard to attack, but in 1888, nature succeeded where man had failed and a landslide brought down a portion of the castle which crashed into the river far below. To reach the castle, visitors must climb 1,426 steps.

 Where to stay

🏠 **The Ice Hotel** (10 dbl, 3 dbl igloos) \0269 523 111; e bookings@hotelofice.ro; www. hotelofice.ro. Located near the cabana & offering an icy experience under furs in igloos, but only in the frozen winter months (usually Dec–Apr). *B/fast not inc.* **$$$**

🏠 **Transfăgărașan Pension** (14 dbl) \0269 856 295; m 0740 467 843; www.cartisoara.ro. Small pension between Cârtișoara & the Balea chalet; can also arrange transport & tours. B/fast inc. **$$**

The best route back to Bucharest From Poienari Citadel, car drivers and bikers may need to get back to Bucharest, to return the hire car or catch a plane home. Continue south for 30km along route 7C to Curtea de Argeș and then another 30km south, still on route 7C to Pitești, where one of Romania's few motorways (E70) leads in a southeast direction for 107km to Bucharest. However, in summer, this motorway is not a pleasant route and the Bucharest ring road linking the Bucharest–Pitești motorway to the Bucharest–Ploiești (E60/route 1) where the two airports, Otopeni and Baneasa are found, is always jammed. If you have time, a better and more scenic route is to cut across to Târgoviște (an interesting place for Vlad III the Impaler hunters). Follow route 7 as far as Găești then take route 72 north to Târgoviște. From there, it's possible to take route 72 for another 42km to Ploiești which is a drab industrial town located 40km north of Bucharest on the E60/route 1. The E60/route 1 then leads conveniently south for a short, straight drive to Otopeni and Baneasa airports.

8

Hunedoara County

Hunedoara County (7,063km²), in the southwest corner of Transylvania, is made up mostly of mountains, divided by the Mureş River which cuts straight across its rectangular form from east to west.

On the northern side of the Mureş are the Munţii Metaliferii, the lower peaks of the Apuseni Mountains. To the south are the mountains forming part of the Southern Carpathians: the Parâng, the Retezat-Godeanu, Orăştie and Sureanu, and Poiana Ruscă mountains. The Retezat Massif, a part of the Southern Carpathians, covers 800km² and has more than 30 peaks, including Peleaga at 2,509m and Papula at 2,502m, and a wonderful national park, founded in 1935 and later named a biosphere reserve.

In the Orăştie Mountains, at Grădiştea de Munte, visitors can find Sarmizegetusa Regia, the capital city of the Dacian kings, while 40km away southwest of Haţeg are the ruins of Ulpia Traiana Sarmizegetusa, the capital city of Roman Dacia, at a village confusingly called Sarmizegetusa.

Near the foothills of the Poiana Ruscă Mountains, the town of Hunedoara is graced by an archetypal Transylvanian castle, the 15th-century Corvin Castle, which now unfortunately has one of the ugliest steel factories in Europe as its neighbour, so plan your photographic angles carefully.

DEVA   *Telephone code 0254*

Deva (Déva/Diemrich, Schlossberg) often gets a bad press and has been called 'industrial and ugly'. You have to wonder if anyone hangs around long enough to see what a fun place Deva is in the evening, when the city centre is packed out with locals enjoying live music performances, popping into pizzerias with their mates, visiting the theatre or sipping beer and people-watching on the many café terraces. Of course, there are brutish, concrete housing estates from the 1970s but the visitor need visit only one or two main streets to see all the sights and have refreshments before heading off to Hunedoara Castle or the Retezat National Park. Like Braşov and Râşnov, Deva also has one of those 'Hollywood' town signs in giant white letters, placed on the most prominent hill overlooking the northwest, older part of town. From there, four main roads lead in parallel through the centre heading towards the southeast and the road to Hunedoara. These roads are Strada Mihai Eminescu, a mainly residential street; the pedestrianised Strada 1 Decembrie which changes suddenly into B-dul 22 Decembrie at Piaţa Victoriei; and B-dul Decebal. The fourth parallel road leads past the entrance to the railway and bus station to the northeast of the centre.

HISTORY There was a settlement in the Deva region as early as the Neolithic Age (4000–1800BC), according to archaeological finds. Geto-Dacians inhabited

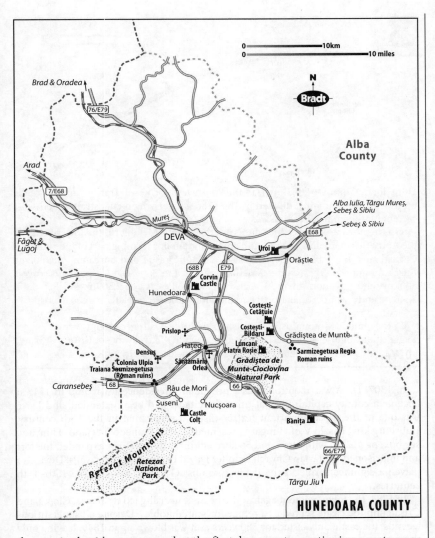

the area in the 6th century BC, but the first documents mentioning a *castrum* or fort date from 1269. The castle was built on a volcanic hill, resembling a cone with its top chopped off, known as the Hill of the Djinn, because of a legend telling of a mighty battle between the spirits (*djinns*) of the Retezat Mountains and those of the plain. A typically gloomy Hungarian folk ballad tells of how 12 stonemasons worked on the construction of Deva Castle (Cetatea Devei) on top of the hill overlooking the town. They felt they were cursed because whenever they built a wall during the day, it had collapsed by the following morning. They came to a decision that, in order to strengthen the walls, they would burn at the stake whichever stonemason's wife arrived first at the castle and her ashes would be mixed in with the building materials. The wife of the head stonemason, Kelemen Kőmives, appeared and stoically agreed to this idea. The castle was soon finished.

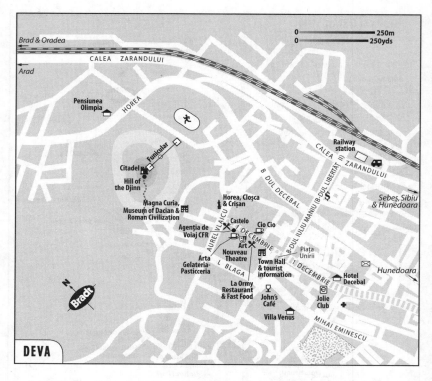

In 1307, Deva was mentioned as a principality residence town, and in 1317 it became a county capital. By that time, the citadel had been extended, and Deva was one of the most important fortresses in Transylvania. In the 15th century, Habsburg king László V of Hungary presented Ioan de Hunedoara (János Hunyadi; see box, page 224) with Deva and 56 surrounding villages. Ioan expanded the fort and imprisoned Unitarian Church founder Dávid Ferenc within its walls. Deva also played a significant role in the defence against Ottoman raids in the 15th–16th centuries.

In 1784, the town held out against the peasant uprising led by Horea, Cloşca and Crişan and the castle served as a refuge for scared nobles. Despite all superstitious legends, the castle only lasted for 580 years as it was blown up in 1849, leaving only the ramparts and barricades. Today, Deva boasts a private university and many high schools. Numerous ensembles and groups perform folk music and dances, chamber and classical music.

GETTING THERE AND AWAY Deva is located 123km west of Sibiu on route 7 and 178km southwest of Cluj-Napoca on the E81 highway to Sebeş. The **railway** and **bus stations** are located side by side to the northeast of the centre. Follow B-dul Libertăţii for 500m northeast from Piaţa Unirii in the heart of town. **Local buses** leave regularly for Hunedoara (*45mins*) and Orăştie (*30mins*). Deva is on a main railway line and several trains leave daily for Cluj-Napoca (*3½hrs*) and Sibiu (*3hrs*).

For rail information contact **Agenţia de Voiaj CFR** (*Str 1 Decembrie, Bloc A;* \0254 218 887; ⏰ 08.00–20.00 Mon–Fri) who can issue advance train ticket sales.

TOURIST INFORMATION

 Tourist Office Town Hall, Piața Unirii 14; ◷ 09.00–17.00 Mon–Fri. Not strictly the tourist office, but the only place offering any information.

County council ☏0254 211 624; www.cjhunedoara.ro

WHERE TO STAY

⌂ **Villa Venus** (9 dbl, 2 suites, 1 family room) Str Mihai Eminescu 16; ☏0254 212 243; e office@villavenus.ro; www.villavenus.ro. Boutique 5-star with luxurious surroundings, jacuzzi, internet, marble & presidential furnishings, but very eerie & expensive. **$$$$**

⌂ **Pensiunea Olimpia** (13 dbl) Str Horea 100A; ☏0254 219 030; m 0721 902 098; e cazare@pensiunedeva.ro; www.pensiunedeva.ro. A very good 3-star non-stop motel to the northwest of town, but actually a short-cut walk away via the funicular base station. Clean rooms, quiet & good buffet b/fast. Conveniently right opposite the Petrom petrol station for filling up & late-night snacks. Recommended. **$$–$$$**

⌂ **Hotel Decebal** (27 dbl, 3 apts) Str 1 Decembrie 37; ☏0254 212 413. A 2-star hotel with a cat & a budgie guarding the reception. Old-fashioned & quiet. **$$**

WHERE TO EAT AND DRINK

⊑ **Arta Gelateria-Pasticceria** Str 1 Decembrie 21; ◷ 08.00–22.00 Mon–Fri, 10.00–23.00 Sat/Sun. With gorgeous cakes. **$**

✗ **Castelo** Aurel Vlaicu 1; ☏0254 213 883; ◷ 08.00–23.00 daily. Very popular Italian restaurant near the foot of the citadel hill. **$**

⊑ **Cio Cio Cofetarie-Patiserie** Str 1 Decembrie 20; ◷ 07.00–20.00 Mon–Fri, 09.00–21.00 Sat/Sun. A friendly café & good spot for a break. **$**

♀ **John's Café** Str Eminescu 2; www.johnscafe.ro; ◷ 18.00–04.30 daily. An English-style pub, with a club in the basement. **$**

✗ **La Ormy Restaurant & Fast Food** Str 1 Decembrie 11–13; ◷ 09.00–20.00 daily. With a large covered terrace & serving special Romanian pancakes. Kind waiters. **$**

OTHER PRACTICALITIES

Bank
$ **Raiffeisen** B-dul Iuliu Maniu 18; ☏0254 703 500; ◷ 09.00–17.30 Mon–Fri

Internet
🖳 **Jolie Club** Str 1 Decembrie, next to Cinema Patria; ◷ 09.00–midnight Mon–Sat, 10.00–midnight Sun. A very brown café ($) with wicker chairs & cane tables, but there is free Wi-Fi.

Pharmacy
✚ **Farmacia Remedia** Piața Victoriei; ☏0254 224 488; ◷ 24hrs

Post office
✉ B-dul Decebal 16; ☏0254 212 222; ◷ 08.00–20.00 Mon–Fri, 08.00–14.00 Sat

WHAT TO SEE AND DO In the northwest part of town in a leafy park beneath the **Hill of the Djinn** and the **citadel** is the **Magna Curia**, a pretty pink building built in 1621 by the Transylvanian prince Gábor Bethlen. It is now home to the **Museum of Dacian and Roman Civilization** (*Muzeul Civilzatiei Dacice si Romane; B-Dul 1 December Nr 39;* ☏ *0254 216 750;* e *muzeucdr.deva@gmail.com; www.mcdr.ro;* ◷ *09.00–17.00 Tue–Sun; admission adult/child 3/1RON*), on the left side of the square and presently undergoing restoration work though still open to visitors. In front of the building are **three busts** on high pillars of the leaders of the 1784 peasants' revolt, Horea, Cloșca and Crișan. From the western end of the park it's possible to walk through a tunnel in the side of the hill and find a path leading up to the castle. If that seems too much like hard work, there's a **funicular** (*Cetate Deva Telecabina;* ☏ *0254 220 288;* ◷ *May–Sep 09.00–21.00 daily, Oct–Apr 08.00–20.00 daily; up & down adult/child 7/3RON*) which started climbing the hill in 2005 – its cabins are the only ones of their kind in Romania: very modern like spaceship pods. To find the base station, follow the foot of the hill in a northeasterly direction, through a leafy suburb towards the stadium. It's only about ten minutes' walk maximum and *en route* to the Pensiunea Olympia. The pedestrianised Strada 1 Decembrie leads from the National History Museum to the centre of town and is lined with cafés and bars. The **Art Nouveau theatre** halfway down the street on the right was created by Dezső Jakab and Marcell Komor who also designed the Palace of Culture in Târgu Mureş (see page 180).

AROUND DEVA

ORĂŞTIE Orăştie (Szászváros/Broos), 20km east of Deva, was an important military stronghold. In 1200, work began on the construction of a fortified church and for a time Orăştie was one of the most important Saxon towns in Transylvania. Orăştie was a feudal city in the 13th century. The rocky outcrop at **Uroi**, halfway between Orăştie and Deva, at Simeria, is a very popular hang-gliding jump-off point (see *Chapter 2, Sports and activities*, page 113).

DACIAN FORTRESSES OF THE ORĂŞTIE MOUNTAINS In 1999, six Dacian fortresses were listed as UNESCO World Heritage Sites. One, Căpâlna is in Alba County (see page 238); the other five are in Hunedoara County, south of the town of Orăştie. These fortresses were built from 100BC–AD100 and most are in good condition to this day. Archaeologists continue to work in the area and discover more about this ancient civilisation.

The five fortresses south of Orăştie are Sarmizegetusa Regia, the capital city of the Dacian state with two (Costeşti-Cetăţuia and Costeşti-Bildaru) fortresses just north and two (Piatra Roşie and Bănița) fortresses to the south.

Getting there and away Four fortress sites are clustered together. By **car**, from Orăştie head south on a very minor road towards Orăştie de Sus. After 17km Costeşti-Cetăţuia is reached. The second fortress, Costeşti-Bildaru, is 4km further south and Sarmizegetusa Regia another 7km south. From Sarmizegetusa, Piatra Roşie is located in a natural reserve and can only be reached **on foot**. The hike is approximately 5km.

Bănița is reached via the E79 highway, 39km southeast of Hațeg. Several **buses** leave Hațeg for Târgu Jiu daily.

Sarmizegetusa Regia This capital of pre-Roman Dacia is a complex of sanctuaries actually situated in the Orăştie Mountains on a 1,200m-high hill. Sarmizegetusa Regia included the city, the sacred zone and a civil settlement. The Great Round Sanctuary and the 'Sun of Andesite' are remarkable relics. The fortress, a quadrilateral formed by massive stone blocks, was constructed on five terraces, on an area of almost 30,000m².

The civilians lived around the fortress, down the mountain on manmade terraces. Dacian nobility had flowing water in their houses, brought through ceramic pipes. The Dacian capital reached its peak under King Decebal who fought two wars against the emperor Trajan of the Roman Empire in AD101–102 and AD105–106, the second culminating in the Battle of Sarmizegetusa and defeat for the Dacians. In AD106, Dacia's capital was conquered and destroyed by the Roman army who established a military garrison 40km from the ruined Dacian capital and called it Colonia Ulpia Traiana Augusta Dacica Sarmizegetusa.

Costeşti-Cetăţuia The hill of Cetăţuia with the **fortress** on its summit (561m) forms a superb observation point with a wide view over the surrounding countryside. The hill is positioned at a pass in the mountains where the valley of Grădiştei suddenly narrows. The defence mechanism was based on a three-tier system of fortifications: terraces made of earth, a 3m-wide stone wall flanked by three bastions and a double palisade on the southern side. Two sandstone block towers stand on the highest plateau and also traces of the garrison soldiers' living quarters can be seen here. Places of worship and water-storage tanks were found on the terraces.

Costeşti-Bildaru Situated on the Bildaru peaks (703m), the **fortress** includes two linked precincts with six strong towers. The first city occupies the higher plateau on the hill with a trapezium shape and four exterior towers at the corners. The settlement is surrounded by forest and the scenery is very beautiful.

Luncani Piatra Roşie Piatra Roşie was built to guard the entrance to the Strei River valley and the access route to the capital, Sarmizegetusa Regia. The hill Piatra Roşie (Red Rock, 831m) is a little isolated at the end of the Luncani Valley. The fortress was built of stone in a quadrilateral shape with four towers at the corners and a fifth tower in the middle of the east wall. A wooden building stood at the heart of the precinct and its stone foundations are well preserved. A tank was dug into the rock to store water. Outside the precinct are the remains of a sanctuary. Piatra Roşie is situated inside the boundaries of the **Grădiştea de Munte-Cioclovina Natural Park**, a small natural reserve that makes a good destination for walks and less strenuous hiking trips.

Băniţa Băniţa (Banica) is a little way from the other fortresses, situated 17km south of Piatra Roşie and just south of the main E79 highway between Haţeg and Petroşani. Archaeologists found the ruins of a Dacian citadel on the Piatra Cetăţii hill. The hill has very steep sides and can only be reached on the northern side where the slope was blocked by a Dacian wall made of stone blocks linked together with wooden beams. On the peak, three successive terraces were places for buildings, possibly living quarters or towers. Two sets of steps and three areas of foundations have been preserved and traces of the sanctuary were discovered.

HUNEDOARA It is a sad irony that one of Europe's most impressive, beautiful and typically Transylvanian castles should be found in one of Romania's least attractive towns. Hunedoara is a dreary, Soviet-style sprawl of concrete housing estates concentrated around processing plants for the metal and coal industry.

An iron ore-processing plant was founded in 1884. After World War II, the communists built a massive steel plant right next to the historic monument. Ceauşescu loved the idea that a stunning castle and symbol of the Hungarian nobility, connected to the Hunyadi 'Corvinus' family, should be spoiled with a hideous neighbour and emblem of Romania's industrial might. In fact, Ioan de Hunedoara/János Hunyadi, father of Matei Corvin, was of both Hungarian and Romanian descent, so it seemed like a case of cutting off one's nose to spite one's face (for more information on Matei Corvin's birthplace in Cluj-Napoca, see page 252). The Siderurgica *combinat* was one of the largest in the country. In 2004, the LNM Group, the world's second-largest and most global steel producer, announced that it had completed the US$43 million privatisation of Siderurgica. The LNM Group is headed by Indian-born, UK-based businessman Lakshmi Mittal, ranked at No 21 on Forbes's World's Richest Billionaires list.

You will find that frequent **buses** and **maxi-taxis** run between Deva's railway station and Corvin Castle (*30–40mins*). By **car**, Hunedoara is 18km south of Deva. Take the E68 heading south out of Deva and turn right after 6km, signposted for Hunedoara.

Where to stay

Hotel Rusco (100 dbl, 4 sgl, 2 apts) B-dul Dacia 10, Hunedoara; \0254 717 575; www. hotelrusca.ro. Large 3-star block in the centre of town. **$$**

Vila Tiffany (12 dbl, 2 sgl, 2 apts) Sta Dacia 28B, Hunedoara; \0254 714 500; www. vilatiffany.ro. Small central guesthouse with Wi-Fi & restaurant. **$$**

IOAN DE HUNEDOARA – THE WHITE KNIGHT

Known as Ioannes Corvinus in Latin and János Hunyadi in Hungarian and called the 'White Knight', Ioan de Hunedoara was a *voivode* (ruler) of Transylvania from 1441 to 1456. Ioan was the father of Matei Corvin (ruled 1458–90), one of the most legendary and admired kings of Hungary.

Ioan was born into a minor noble family in 1407 as the son of Voicu, a *boyar* from Wallachia and Elisabeth Morzsinay (Mărgean in Romanian), the daughter of a Romanian noble family.

Voicu took the family name of Hunyadi (de Hunedoara) when he received the estate around Hunedoara Castle from King Zsigmond, in 1409, and was given the title Count of Hunedoara. Rumour has it that Ioan was in fact Zsigmond's illegitimate son after a love affair with a Romanian peasant woman. Both Hungarians and Romanians like to claim János/Ioan and his son Mátyás/Matei (see *Cluj*, page 252) as their own. Ioan married Erzsébet Szilágyi, a high-ranking Hungarian noblewoman. Szilágy was the name of a county which overlaps with present-day Sălaj. The title 'Corvinus' was first used for his son Matei Corvin of Hungary, but is sometimes also applied to Ioan. The name Corvin (raven) has a legend attached to it. During a trip with his parents, the seven-year-old Ioan was playing with a precious gold ring belonging to his mother and father while they were sleeping. A raven swooped down and stole the ring. Little Ioan took a bow and arrow and shot the bird. King Zsigmond was so impressed with his skill he bestowed the crest of a raven with a ring in his beak to the family and the image can be seen in many places by Hunedoara Castle.

Thanks to his prowess in battle and military skills, Ioan rose through the ranks and soon became one of the wealthiest and most respected aristocrats in the country. He was particularly admired for his campaigns against the Ottoman Empire. However he also made many enemies. After the fall of Constantinople in 1453, Sultan Mehmet II rallied his troops with the intention of subjugating Hungary. The sultan's first objective was Belgrade. Ioan arrived at the Siege of Belgrade at the end of 1455 and in July 1456, a flotilla of boats assembled by Ioan destroyed the Ottoman fleet. After fierce fighting, the camp was captured, and Mehmet lifted the siege and fled to Istanbul. With his flight, a 70-year period of relative peace commenced on Hungary's southeastern border. However, three weeks after the siege's end, plague broke out and Ioan de Hunedoara died in 1456. He was buried in the Catholic cathedral at Alba Iulia flanked by his son László (died 1458) and elder brother, also called Ioan (died 1442).

What to see

Corvin Castle (*Str Corvineștilor 1–3,* \ *0254 711 423;* e *contact@castelulcorvinilor. ro; www.castelulcorvinilor.ro;* ⊕ *May–Aug 09.00–15.00 Mon, 09.00–18.00 Tue–Sun, Sep–Oct & Mar–Apr 09.00–15.00 Mon, 09.00–17.00 Tue–Sun, Nov–Feb 09.00–15.00 Mon, 09.00–16.00 Tue–Sun; admission adult/child 10/5RON, photo permit 5RON, video 10RON, guide 30RON, parking 5RON*) A truly magnificent sight and the highlight of any trip to southwest Transylvania. The late, great travelogue maestro Patrick Leigh Fermor called it 'fantastic and theatrical' and 'at first glance, totally unreal' and visitors from Budapest will immediately recognise it from a fairytale copy, the Vajdahunyadvár, built in the Hungarian capital's City Park (Városliget) for the nation's 1896 millennial celebrations. In 1409, Hungarian king Zsigmond of Luxembourg gave Voicu de Hunedoara/Vajk Hunyadi a castle at Hunedoara as a reward for his military expertise. Voicu passed the property on to his son, Ioan (see box opposite) who enlarged and strengthened the fortress, adding new precincts, seven protective towers, a chapel and an interior palace complete with a Council Hall and Knight's Hall. The wide stone bridge over a deep moat makes the approach to the castle, with its many towering battlements and pointed turrets, quite magical. Ioan died in conflict with the Ottoman Empire at the 1456 Battle of Belgrade. His wife **Erzsébet Szilágyi** added Renaissance features, constructing the Matthias loggia in the north wing and finishing the chapel and the Council Hall. Ioan and Erzsébet's son **Matei Corvin** further developed the castle, which remained in the family until 1508. One of a succession of 22 owners was Transylvanian prince **Gábor Bethlen** who added some Baroque elements. In the 18th century, the Habsburgs took control of Hunedoara's castle and the building was turned into the administrative headquarters for the mining industry and even a storage place (1724–1854) for iron products. In 1854, a great fire destroyed all the wooden interior structures and restoration work in 1868–74 replaced the shingle roof with tiles, some of the towers were elevated and a neo-Gothic façade was built by the Bethlen Palace. In 1974, the castle was made into a museum. More sensitive restoration works that took place in 1956–68 and again after 1997 have made Hunedoara's Corvin Castle an unmissable item in any Transylvania agenda.

HAȚEG Haţeg (Hatszeg/Wallenthal) is an attractive, if somewhat nondescript cattle-market town, situated in the Haţeg Basin and accessible on the main E79 road between Deva (41km north) and Petroşani (47km southeast). Three **buses** leave Deva for Haţeg on weekdays (*40mins*); there is no direct train route. The main town (population 15,000) is in an area that includes the wonderful Retezat National Park, several fascinating historic churches and the Roman ruins at Sarmizegetusa. Haţeg was an island in the Jurassic Period and in the 19th century the fossilised remains of many species of mini-dinosaur were found in the region. The **Haţeg Country Dinosaurs Geopark** (*http://geopark.go.ro*) is still in its early stages, but organisers hope that one of the newest dinosaur and fossilised reptile sites in the world will become a big draw for visitors to the region. Visitors will be able to walk freely around several sites and visit the places where dwarf dinosaurs were discovered.

PRISLOP Situated around 12km northwest of Haţeg, the 14th-century **Prislop Monastery** (Sfânta Mănăstire Prislop) holds one of the oldest convents in the country and, despite the large number of visitors milling about for an Orthodox festival (the 14 September Raising of the Holy Cross) when I was there, has an atmosphere of tranquillity and spirituality. Female visitors arriving in trousers must don a large, long skirt with an elasticated waist over their clothes before entering, to 'blend in' with the sisters. It's not one for the photo album! Nuns potter about the dinky red-brick church and the interior displays some beautiful frescoes. It's possible to follow a path up through the woods to a graveyard where the nuns are buried and many stand lost deep in prayer. Further along the side of a tree-covered mountain, the **Casa Sfântului** is a cave set into a rocky wall. Bear in mind it's quite tricky climbing the side of the rock in a long skirt. The name 'Prislop' means a 'place to pass in the mountains'.

Accessible only by **car**, drive north from Haţeg for 6km then turn left at Silvaşu de Sus and continue for another 6km. The carved wooden gateway by the car park is not Transylvanian, by the way: it's a gift from a religious community in Maramureş. In the autumn, look out for freshly fallen walnuts by the entrance.

Sântămăria Orlea Church At 3km south of Haţeg is a church in the village of Sântămăria Orlea, built in 1363 and reconstructed in 1782. Here, visitors can also see the Kenderffy family castle, now an orphanage and the strange and remarkably unwelcoming Hotel Restaurant Baron Kenderffy, whose Soviet-style 'guard-granny' managed to put the backs up of our normally relaxed Romanian hosts. Not worth the aggro.

A few local **buses** travel between Haţeg and Sântămăria Orlea on the route to Petrila. It's also quite pleasant to **walk** the 3km.

DENSUŞ At Densuş (Demsus) is a strange, **ancient church**, one of the oldest Orthodox churches in Europe and which is still used for religious services. Historians believe that the church dates from the 6th century and some have postulated that it was earlier a pagan temple to Mars, then after the Romans left, the Christians moved in and used stones from Sarmizegetusa to rebuild the church. Although historians in 1961 discovered that the church is much older, the first written documentation comes from around 1300.

The church is 30m long, 8m wide and 18m tall with a unique exterior shape. The walls were built of bricks with Roman inscriptions, capitals, tombstones, sewerage pipes, blocks, marble, columns and sculptures taken from the Colonia Ulpia Traiana. The altar table is made of a tombstone with the lettering deleted. Above, there are two lions that stand back to back. The mural paintings inside, on an ultramarine background, date from the 15th century, and the painter who made it added a simple signature 'Ştefan'. There are some violent depictions of Saint Thomas holding his skin on a stick. The elderly priest, Father Gherghel, explained that the Calvinists did not respect the Orthodox cross or icons and showed how they had destroyed the eyes on paintings of saints. After destroying the paintings they covered most of the walls with white paint. A few years ago, with the help of the then American ambassador in Bucharest, Michael Guest, the church received a US$20,000 donation from the US, money that was used to renovate many of its mural paintings.

Drive 10km southwest out of Haţeg on route 68 towards Băuţar. Turn right in the centre of Toteşti village. If the priest is not there, ask at house No 15 on the main road for the key guardian.

ULPIA TRAIANA SARMIZEGETUSA The **ruins** of the capital city of Roman Dacia on the Haţeg Plain at Sarmizegetusa are 40km west of Sarmizegetusa Regia.

Colonia Ulpia Traiana Augusta Dacica Sarmizegetusa (to give it its full title) was the biggest city in Roman Dacia, with a partly conserved forum, an amphitheatre and several temples. The city was destroyed by Goths, and the ruins of Ulpia Traiana Sarmizegetusa offer visitors an excellent portrayal of a Roman town with a forum, the

Augustals' Palace, thermal baths, an amphitheatre with seating for 6,000 spectators as well as many public and private buildings. In 1982 a **museum** (*Sarmizegetusa;* ☉ *08.00–20.00 daily; admission adult/child 5/2.5RON*) opened, exhibiting silver and bronze objects, pottery, statues, coins, headstones, medallions and mosaics. So far, only 3% of the total 32ha area has been explored by archaeologists from Britain, Belgium, Hungary and Romania.

One of the scientists working at the archaeological site, Florin Delinescu, and his wife Loredana run a small pension 'Ulpia Traiana' (see below) on the main street around the corner from the site entrance. Loredana cooks the most amazing lunches with delicious soups, and a speciality from the Sarmizegetusa region, *pup de crump*, a grated potato and *brânza* cheese fried pancake (like a cross between a Polish/Jewish *latka* and Swiss *rösti*, but much bigger) served with a mug of fresh drinking yoghurt.

Getting there and away Sarmizegetusa is 18km southwest of Hațeg on the main route 68 leading from Hațeg to the Iron Gate of Transylvania (Poarta de Fier a Transilvaniei), a narrow pass at 699m in the Munții Tarcului marking the southwest boundary of Transylvania. A gigantic mace statue marks the place where in 1442 some 15,000 Transylvanians under Ioan de Hunedoara's command defeated 80,000 Turks. The pass is 10km long and further along is the place where in AD106, the Dacians and Romans battled for the last time. It is also the place where the Dacian ruler Decebal committed suicide rather than suffer the humiliation of being paraded through Rome.

 Where to stay

⌂ Pension 'Ulpia Traiana (2 sgl, 3 dbl) Sarmizegetusa No 153; ☏0254 776 453; m 0744 984 613; e office@ulpiatraiana.webpro.ro; www.ulpiatraiana.webpro.ro. A delightful house with grape vines hanging from the wooden upstairs gallery. Home cooking & family atmosphere. **$**

SUSENI Just south of Râu de Mori is a small farming community with a **little church** dating from 1310. The interior has a rich collection of frescoes and a wooden icon wall guarding the sacred place behind where only the priest may go. The walls have been covered in unsightly graffiti since the 16th century and the church is at risk because there are no solid foundations. The church was renovated with donations from widows and poor people when the Ministry of Culture dipped out. At Densuș and Suseni, the priests give long-winded descriptions in Romanian, so it would be advisable to find an interpreter if you want to go deeper.

Castle Colț (Cetate din Colț) is 45 minutes' walk from Suseni. The ruins are the remains of a fortress that inspired Jules Verne in his novel *The Castle of the Carpathians*.

RETEZAT NATIONAL PARK Established in 1935, the Retezat National Park (380km^2) is the oldest in Romania. It covers some spectacular country and visitors will not only lose their breath from the hill climbing but also from the incredible views. Retezat is a natural park of extreme statistics and contains the largest number of mountain peaks higher than 2,000m in all Romania, more than 20 in all. Altitudes vary, from 794m at the park entrance in the Râu Mare Valley, to the Peleaga Peak (2,509m). Retezat also has more than 80 glacial lakes and Lacul Bucura (8.8ha) is the largest in the country. Lacul Zănoaga (29m deep) is the deepest glacial lake in Romania. The Retezat Mountains have some of the most beautiful landscapes in southeastern Europe. The massif is crossed by many

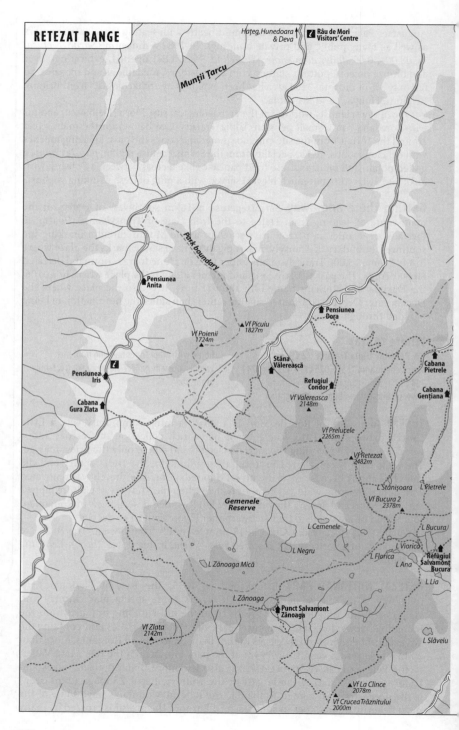

RETEZAT RANGE

Hațeg, Hunedoara & Deva

Râu de Mori Visitors' Centre

Munții Țarcu

Park boundary

Pensiunea Anita

Pensiunea Dora

▲ Vf Picuiu 1827m

Vf Poienii 1724m ▲

Pensiunea Iris

Stâna Vălereàscă

Cabana Pietrele

Refugiul Condor

Cabana Gențiana

Cabana Gura Zlata

Vf Valereasca 2148m ▲

Vf Prelucele 2265m ▲

▲ Vf Retezat 2482m

L' Stânișoara

L' Pietrele

Gemenele Reserve

Vf Bucura 2 2378m ▲

L Cemenele

L Bucura

L Viorica

L Negru

L Florica

Refugiul Salvamont Bucura

L Zănoaga Mică

L Ana

L Lia

L Zănoaga

Punct Salvamont Zănoaga

Vf Zlata 2142m ▲

L Slăveiu

▲ Vf La Clince 2078m

Vf Crucea Trăznitului 2000m

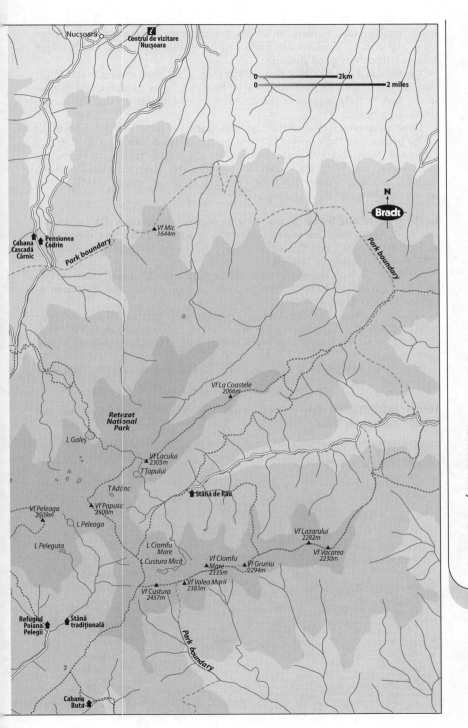

Nucşoara

Centrul de vizitare Nucşoara

0   2km
0   2 miles

N

Bradt

▲ Vf Mic
1644m

Park boundary

Cabana
Cascadă
Cârnic

Pensiunea
Codrin

Park boundary

Vf La Coastele
2066m

Retezat
National
Park

L Galeş

Vf Lacului
2305m

T Tapului

T Adânc

⬆ Stâna de Râu

Vf Peleaga
2509m

▲ Vf Papuşa
2508m

L Peleaga

Vf Lazarului
2282m

L Peleguţa

L Ciomfu
Mare

Vf Vacarea
2230m

L Custura Mică

Vf Ciomfu
▲ Mare
2335m

▲ Vf Gruniu
2294m

▲ Vf Valea Marii
2383m

Vf Custura
2457m

Refugiul
Poiana
Pelegii

⬆ **Stână**
tradiţională

Park boundary

Cabana
Buta

tourist trails on which hikers can admire the landscape and enjoy the wilderness. More experienced climbers can find some barely explored areas, Colții Pelegii being a particularly good challenge.

The flora in Retezat is very rich with at least 1,200 plant species found in the zone, a third of the total flora species in all Romania. There are many wild animals in the park, mainly because of the diverse habitats but also because the human impact is minimal.

Three communities exist on the edge of the park, and have land-use rights in the alpine pastures for their livestock. These are the Sălașu de Sus, Râu de Mori and Câmpu lui Neag. People in these communities still practise traditional agriculture and preserve some of the traditional lifestyle of the area. Retezat is ideal for hiking, walking, trekking, wildlife-watching, camping, climbing, skiing, Nordic skiing, mountain biking and birdwatching.

Getting there and away By **train**, for the north park entrances (Cârnic, Râușor and Gura Apei), there are two railway stations: Subcetate (fast and slow trains) and Ohaba de sub Piatră (slow trains only). Bucharest to Ohaba de sub Piatră (*7½–9½hrs*); to Subcetate (*7½hrs*).

For the south park entrances (Buta, Cheile Buții and Câmpușel), there are two stations: Petroșani and Lupeni, but there are no good connections. Bucharest to Petroșani (*6hrs*); Lupeni (*7–10hrs*).

Regular **minibuses** run from Petroșani to south park entrances (Buta and Cheile Buții) (*105mins*). In summer, regular minibuses run from Ohaba de sub Piatră to Cârnic (*45mins*). There is no regular public transport for the Gura Apei and Râușor park entrances.

By **car**, the best route is via Hațeg to Râu de Mori and south along the Râul Mare River valley.

Tourist information Two visitors' centres opened in 2005, one in **Nucșoara** and the other at **Râu de Mori**.

HIKING VOCABULARY

Peșteră	cave	Vârf, Pisc	peak
Colț	cliff	Câmpie	plain
Nori	cloud	Ploaie	rain
Stâncă	crag	Râpă	ravine
Câmp	field	Creastă, Coamă	ridge
Ceață [che-ah-tzah]	fog	Râu	river
Pădure or codru	forest	Piatră, Stâncă	rock
Chei	gorge	Stână	sheepfold
Deal, măgură	hill	Zapada	snow
Cabana	hut	Izvor	spring
Gheață	ice	Pârâu	stream
Lac	lake	Culme	summit
Mlaătină	marsh	Vale	valley
Poiană	meadow	Sat	village
Pas	pass	Vreme, Timp	weather
Pășune	pasture	Padure	wood
Potecă, traseu	path		

The Retezat National Park is a member of PAN Parks (*www.panparks.org*), a unique concept set up in the 1990s by the World Wildlife Fund and Dutch tour operator Molecaten to bring together nature conservation and sustainable tourism. It was created with the aim of raising awareness about European wildernesses. Most Europeans are unaware of the large number of wilderness areas on their own doorsteps. This vision gave birth to PAN Parks. Inspired by the FSC certificate, it aims to create an internationally recognised independent standard for protected areas and the development of sustainable tourism in and around them. The PAN Parks brand gives visitors a guarantee that their visit is supporting the future of Europe's wilderness. As of April 2012, there were ten certified PAN parks in Europe, plus one in Georgia and one in Russia. To be a PAN park, a national park must fit a series of principles and criteria. It must have a minimum size of 20,000ha and its management of both nature and visitors must be of the highest standard.

Nuçşoara Visitors' Centre 0254 779 968; e office@retezat.ro; www.retezat.ro; ⊕ in theory, all the time, somebody is always on duty in the centre, in the summer the official opening times are 08.00–14.00 daily. Nuçşoara is the bigger visitors' centre with an exhibition site & indoor rockery featuring some of the plants found on the hills, including many types of gentian, rhododendron & a famous symbol of the mountains, the edelweiss (*Leontopodium alpinum*). **Râu de Mori Visitors' Centre** Same contact details as for Nuçşoara. The centre has displays of folk crafts, local culture & an exhibition of black-&-white photos of the Retezat area.

There are also two tourism information points: one in the south, close to **Câmpu lui Neag** village and one in the **Râu Mare Valley** (*www.turismretezat.ro*).

Retezat Park Administration Str M Viteazu 10, Deva; Nucsoara, 284, Salasu de Sus, jud, Hunedoara; 0254 218 829; e office@retezat.ro; www.retezat.ro. To book into local pensions/cabins; f 0254 218 829; e grig@retezat.ro.

Where to stay and eat There are also campsites, cabins and refuges in and around the park, as well as 19 recommended guesthouses in the Râu Mare Valley and the Retezat parks zone. Tourists can use only designated campsites inside Retezat National Park. Accommodation can also be found in *cabanas* (mountain cabins).

Pensiunea Iris (8 dbl, 1 trpl) Râu Mare Valley; f 0254 772 344; e artmotel@geraico.ro; www.geraico.ro. Comfortable rooms – they're very proud of their system of colours instead of room numbers, a large, friendly restaurant ($$) with local dishes, wines & *ţuică's*. $$–$$$$

Anita Pension (11 dbl) Râu Mare Valley; contact Marius Constantinescu; 0254 776 620; m 0744 524 871; www.anita.ro. In a lovely villa by the rushing Râu Mare River with a spa, sauna, fitness room & massage salon. Good restaurant ($$) & bar. $$–$$$

9

Alba County

Alba County (6,242km²), known as Fehér ('white') in Hungarian, is a county in the west of Transylvania sandwiched between Cluj and Hunedoara counties. Mountains cover almost 60% of the county's territory. In the northwest are the Apuseni Mountains and in the southern bit that dangles down into a triangular shape between Hunedoara and Sibiu counties are the Sureanu and Cindrel mountains. In the east is the Transylvanian Plateau with deep, wide valleys. The three mountain groups are separated by the Mureş River valley which traverses the county in a diagonal direction. Other rivers include the tributaries of the Mureş: the Târnava, Sebeş and Arieş. The climate is varied, with moist, cold days in the mountains and drier and warmer conditions in the Mureş Valley, helping to establish Alba as a centre of the Romanian wine industry since the 1st century AD.

The population of Alba County is 90% Romanian and the county town Alba Iulia has a significant place in history as the Union of Transylvania with Romania took place here on 1 December 1918. Alba County has much to offer the visitor with numerous historic, cultural and architectural places of interest as well as natural attractions. For those interested in folk customs and traditions, Alba is a good place to find festivals such as the Girls' Fair on Mount Găiana in the Apuseni Mountains held every July. The predominant industries in the county are textiles, wood, mechanical and mined metals such as gold, silver and copper as well as construction materials such as marble and granite, and also salt.

ALBA IULIA   *Telephone code 0258*

Alba Iulia (Gyulafehérvár/Weissenberg) is another of those Transylvanian cities with two distinct parts. Alba Iulia's Old Town, situated inside a star-shaped citadel wall, is less than 1km from its Lower Town, but a world away. Inside the citadel, everything is calm, cultivated, like a trip back in time to an enlightened era, with wide, tree-lined roads and beautiful historic buildings. The Lower Town is modern, hectic and businesslike. Cars rush along the highway right through the town, passing tall unattractive office blocks and high-rise hotels from the 1970s. Alba Iulia has many interesting buildings but they are almost all exclusively within the citadel's walls. For eating, drinking and accommodation, however, you'll have to go down into the modern town, but it's only a five-minute walk away through the flouncy Viennese Baroque Lower Karl Gate, built to commemorate Habsburg emperor Karl VI's victory against the Ottoman army.

HISTORY In the 9th century, the city was mentioned under the name of Belgrad/ Belograd ('White Castle' in Slavic languages). The Hungarian *Gestas* chronicles mention a ruler named Geula/Gyula/Jula who in the 10th century discovered the

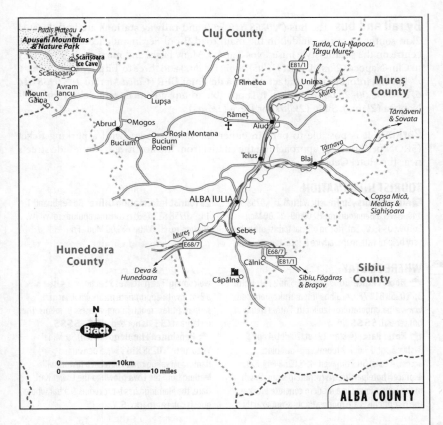

ALBA COUNTY

city and made it the capital of his dukedom. Following the establishment of the Catholic Transylvanian episcopacy after Stephen I of Hungary adopted Catholicism, the first cathedral was built in the 11th century and the city named Gyulafehérvár. The present cathedral was built sometime around the 12th–13th centuries. In 1442, Ioan de Hunedoara, Voivode of Transylvania, used the citadel to prepare for a major battle against the Ottomans. The cathedral was enlarged during his reign and served as his eternal resting place and his tomb. As Gyulafehérvár, Alba Iulia became the capital of the Principality of Transylvania in 1541–1690. During the reign of Prince Gábor Bethlen, the city reached a high point in its cultural history with the establishment of an academy. In November 1599, Mihai Viteazul, Voivode of Wallachia, entered Alba Iulia following his victory in the Battle of Şelimbăr and became Governor of Transylvania. On 1 December 1918, thousands of Romanians and Transylvanian Saxons gathered in Alba Iulia to hear the proclamation of the union of Transylvania with the Kingdom of Romania, now commemorated annually as the National Day. In 1922, Ferdinand of Romania was symbolically crowned King of Romania in Alba Iulia in an act which mirrored the achievement of Mihai Viteazul more than 300 years earlier.

GETTING THERE, AWAY AND AROUND
By air The closest airports are at **Târgu Mureş** (TGM) 137km, **Cluj-Napoca** (CLJ) 94km and **Sibiu** (SBZ) 73km away.

By rail and bus The bus (☎ *0258 812 967*) and **railway stations** are both located 2km southeast of the citadel on the main road B-dul Ferdinand, accessed from the centre on the shuttle-style buses Nos 3 and 4. Many buses and **maxi-taxis** leave daily to Cluj-Napoca (*2hrs*), Deva (*1½hrs*), Sibiu (*1½hrs*) and three to Târgu Mureş (*3½hrs*).

For rail information, contact **Agenţia de Voiaj CFR** (*Calea Moţilor 1;* ☎*0258 816 678;* ⏲ *08.00–20.00 Mon–Fri*). It is possible to buy advance train tickets for Cluj-Napoca (*2½hrs*), Sibiu (*2½hrs*) or Deva (*1½hrs*).

Parking It is possible to park in either the Lower Town, with a parking ticket (5RON per hour), or approaching the citadel from the northwest, in the side streets near the Hotel Cetate.

TOURIST INFORMATION

⌕ Albena Tours Str Frederic Mistral 2; ☎0258 812 140; www.albenatours.ro; ⏲ 09.00–17.00 Mon–Fri, 09.00–13.00 Sat. Not an official tourist office but very helpful with maps, advice & local tours.

⌕ Tourist Information Office Bd Ferdinand 1 14; ☎0258 813 736; e turism@apulum.ro; www.apulum.ro. ⏲ 09.00–16.00 Mon–Fri

WHERE TO STAY

⌂ Hotel Cetate (6 sgl, 86 dbl, 5 apts) Str Unirii 3; ☎0258 811 780; e alba@imparatulromanilor.ro; www.alba.imparatulromanilor.ro. Rather gaudy but central. **$$$$**

⌂ Hotel Parc (4-star: 12 sgl, 20 dbl, 4 apts; 3-star: 3 sgl, 27 dbl, 2 rooms with disabled access, 4 apts) Str Primăverii 4; ☎0258 811 723; e office@hotelparc.ro; www.hotelparc.ro. Down in the Lower Town, in a modern concrete block, the receptionists are monosyllabic & not exactly

welcoming. The hotel has 2 sections: a 4-star & a 3-star with appropriate prices. Pool, jacuzzi, saunas, fitness room, internet access in rooms. The restaurant (**$$**) is not bad. **$$$–$$$$**

⌂ Pensiunea Flamingo (7 dbl) Str Mihai Viteazul 6; ☎0258 816 354; e pensiunea_flamingo@yahoo.com. Found in a historic villa leading from the Lower Town to the Lower Karl Gate, the Flamingo has basic rooms & a bar where guests can eat snacks. **$**

WHERE TO EAT AND DRINK

✗ Marco Steak House Calea Moţilor 67; m 0728 162 962; www.marcosteakhouse.ro; ⏲ 10.30–midnight Mon–Fri, 14.30–midnight Sat/Sun. Rich local pork, beef, chicken & fish as well as pasta & other dishes under a wood-beamed ceiling, with a terrace outside. **$$**

⚲ Pub 13 Str Aleea Sf. Capistrano 1; m 0728 444 415; www.pub13.ro; ⏲ 12.00–midnight Sun–Thu, 12.00–02.00 Fri/Sat. Medieval-themed bar & restaurant built into the citadel walls. **$$**

⌑ Caffe Leonard B-dul 1 Decembrie 1918 7; ⏲ 09.00–21.00 Mon–Sat, 10.00–21.00 Sun. A pleasant café with good coffee & chocolate cake. **$**

⚲ Ciuc Terasa Mena Tineretului Park to the west of the citadel; ⏲ 08.00–midnight daily. A large pub & terrace, good for a sit down. **$**

✗ Hotel Parc Str Primăverii 4, ☎0258 811 723; ⏲ 07.00–23.00 Mon–Fri, 12.00–23.00 Sat/Sun. Fast food & main meals in a rather gloomy setting with yellowish walls. **$**

OTHER PRACTICALITIES
Bank

$ BRD Bank B-dul Ardealului 1 31B; ☎0258 806 640; ⏲ 09.00–17.00 Mon–Fri. With an ATM accepting Visa, MasterCard & Western Union transfers inside.

Internet

⎚ Shooter's Non-Stop B-dul Horea 42, behind the Euroil petrol station; ⏲ 24hrs. Pretty gruesome, filled with young boys playing violent computer games; the waitress removed my bottle of water & warned, 'They're all animals.' 20 machines; 2.50RON/hr.Alternatively, there's a Wi-Fi hotspot in the Hotel Parc.

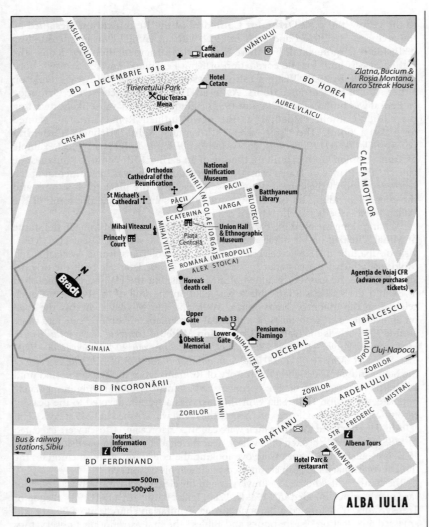

ALBA IULIA

Alba County   ALBA IULIA

9

Pharmacy

✚ **Farmacia Sic Volo** B-dul 1 Decembrie 1918
No XI ground floor; ⏲ 24hrs

Post office

✉ Romtelecom bldg, Str Brătianu 1; ⏲ 07.00–20.00 Mon–Fri

WHAT TO SEE AND DO The interesting sights are all clustered within the citadel walls and the tree-lined roads are dotted with maps, information posters and lots of helpful signs. The citadel fortress was built in 1716–35 by Giovanni Morando Visconti, in the shape of a star with seven points topped with bastions. The citadel is the largest constructed using the Vauban system in southeast Europe. The Marquis de Vauban (1633–1707) was a French military engineer to Louis XIV, who designed impregnable fortresses in around 300 cities, usually with geometric shapes such as pentagons and stars. Approaching the citadel through the **IV Gate**, decorated with the Austrian coat of arms, the bicephalous eagle, we come

235

to the yellow and pink **Orthodox Cathedral of the Reunification**, designed by the architect Ştefănescu and built in 1921 with an arched cloister surrounding it. Inside it is quite small but there is very rich ornamentation and icons. The cathedral was built for the coronation of King Ferdinand and his Scottish-born Queen Marie in 1922. Visitors can see fresco portraits of the royal couple on either side of the entrance doors. As in all Transylvanian cities, the Orthodox cathedral was built in the 1920s and 1930s right next to and, most likely, dwarfing the earlier Catholic cathedral, as the newly unified Romanian state wanted to make a point. The three-nave, 18th-century **Saint Michael's Cathedral** (⊕ *Apr–Oct 08.00–20.00 daily, Nov–Mar 08.00–16.00 daily*) is a typical example of Transylvanian Gothic, built on the site of an earlier 13th-century Romanesque church. The Prince of Transylvania, Ioan de Hunedoara, was instrumental in the reconstruction of the cathedral and also chose it as the place for his tomb and those of his brother and one of his sons. Visitors can also see the tomb of the Polish-born Isabella Jagiello, Queen of Hungary.

Walking along the pleasant, car-free road inside the citadel you come to the **statue of Mihai Viteazul** on his horse, created in 1968 by the sculptor Oscar Han. Mihai visited Alba Iulia in 1599 to celebrate the unification of Transylvania, Wallachia and Moldavia, which fell apart after his assassination a year later. He built the original church where the Orthodox cathedral now stands, but the Habsburgs demolished it. Behind the statue is a large black bas-relief on the wall of the **Princely Court**, celebrating the union of Transylvania, Wallachia and Moldavia. Across the road on an avenue lined with busts of influential Romanians, six on one side and more around the back, is the **National Unification Museum** (*Muzeul Naţional al Unirii; Str Ecaterina Varga;* ☏ *0258 813 300; http://mnuai.ro/muzeu;* ⊕ *Jun–Sep 10.00–19.00 Tue–Sun, Oct–May 10.00–17.00 Tue–Sun; admission adult/child 7/3.50RON*), one of the better museums detailing the history of Romania from the Dacian period until 1944. The ethnographic section occupies the basement of the building immediately opposite, the **Union Hall** (Sala Unirii), which has a section devoted to the peasant revolutionaries Horea, Cloşca and Crişan. The revolt was crushed in 1785 at Forks' Hill (Dealul Furcilor) and the three men were captured. Horea and Cloşca were executed in 1785, gruesomely broken on a wheel, near the citadel walls. An **obelisk** erected in 1937 just outside the **Upper Gate** overlooking the Lower Town commemorates the three revolutionaries. Crişan committed suicide in his prison cell.

The citadel is also home to a university and the elegant **Batthyaneum**, a library of rare manuscripts founded in 1794. In 1780, Ignac Batthyany (1741–98), Bishop of Transylvania, transformed a Baroque former Trinitarian church into a library and amassed a collection of rare books and Bibles. The first astronomical observatory was founded here in 1792. At the **Piaţa Centrală**, the area looks like a beautiful park and the buildings are elegant and so incongruous in Alba Iulia's modern concrete sprawl that it feels as if the entire citadel has crash-landed from another planet and been plonked down in the wrong city at the wrong period in history. The Lower Town can be reached by heading east and downhill through the Lower Gate, passing **Pub 13** (see above), a venue built into the citadel's outer walls. Their sign reads 'Be nice or leave', which is us told!

AROUND ALBA IULIA

SEBEŞ Situated 15km south of Alba Iulia on the main E81 highway, Sebeş (Szászsebes/Mülbach) is one of the seven Siebenburgen and a good place to stop for a break on the way to Sibiu, 60km further east along the same highway.

The other Siebenburgen citadels are Bistriţa (Beszterce/Bistrit), Braşov (Brassó/ Kronstadt), Cluj (Kolozsvár/Klausenburg), Mediaş (Medgyes/Mediasch), Sighişoara (Segesvár/Schassburg) and Sibiu (Nagyszeben/Hermannstadt).

The city was built in the late 12th century by Transylvanian Saxons, originating from the regions by the Rhine and Moselle rivers. The city walls were reinforced after the Tatar invasions of 1241–42, but the Ottoman troops occupied Sebeş in 1438. The Transylvanian Diet often met in Sebeş and the city had a significant role in Transylvania's medieval history. Guilds in Sebeş (armour makers, tinsmiths, blacksmiths, furriers, shoemakers, bakers, potters and drapers) had thriving businesses in Sebeş and from there traded with Wallachia, as well as with central and western European cities. After the union with Romania in 1918, the city's first mayor was Lionel Blaga, brother of the poet and philosopher Lucian Blaga (see box *Paper notes and the famous Romanians on them*, page 72) who was born in the nearby village of Lancrăm.

Construction of Sebeş citadel began in 1387 with major restoration work taking place in 1571 after the Turkish raids. Its walls are made of stone blocks and bricks surrounded by a rectangular precinct with eight towers. The 1.7km-long precinct wall with battlements, ramparts and openings used to pour hot tar over the assailants, is well preserved. As in Sighişoara, the local guilds were invited to build towers in the fortress walls, although only two, the Shoemakers' and the Tinsmiths', remain to this day.

The fortress is in the centre of town and at its heart the impressive tower of the **Lutheran church** (⊕ *10.00–13.00 & 15.00–17.00 Tue–Sat, 15.00–17.00 Sun*) dominates the surroundings. It is a remarkable accomplishment of medieval art and architecture. Construction started before 1241, and it was formerly conceived as a Romanesque basilica with three naves and a belfry. The two side towers were never completed. After the Tatar invasion in 1241, elements of early Gothic style were introduced during reconstruction. The church has the largest altar (13m high and 6m wide) of all churches in Transylvania and, as in most large Evangelical churches in Transylvania, Sebeş church displays Anatolian carpets offered to God by Saxon tradesmen as a token of their veneration, gratitude and respect.

Getting there and away Sebeş is on the main E81 highway between Alba Iulia and Sibiu. By **train** or **bus** is also convenient, but the railway and bus station are 20 minutes' walk east of the centre. Sebeş has regular bus connections with Sibiu (*1hr*) and regular trains. There are also trains to Deva (*1½hrs*). However, for Alba Iulia (*20–30mins*) and Cluj-Napoca (*2½hrs*), the regular bus service is better than the train where a change is needed at Vinţa de Jos.

CÂLNIC The little village of Câlnic is located 13km southeast of Sebeş (Kelnek/ Kelling) and has a remarkable **13th-century citadel** which features on UNESCO's World Heritage List. The fortress, initially conceived as a noble residence, was built by Count Chyl de Kelling. The large rectangular keep was surrounded by massive walls forming an oval precinct with a three-storey Sigfried Tower (1270–72) and two watchtowers. The defence system was completed with a moat. Until 1430, Câlnic fortress was a residence for Saxon counts. Finally it was sold to the peasant community of the village and they began reconstruction in the 14th century with a barbican to fortify the gate tower and a Lutheran chapel, which is used today for concerts and exhibitions. The key is available from the Lutheran parish office, to the left of the fortress.

Several **buses** travel daily from Sebeş (*30mins*). By **car**, from Sebeş, take the E81 towards Sibiu and turn right after 9km, signed for Câlnic.

CĂPÂLNA For those interested in the Dacian and Roman ruins listed as UNESCO World Heritage Sites (see box, page 47), the county of Hunedoara, to the south of Alba, is the place to go. However, Alba County contains one of the Dacian citadels inscribed on the list in 1999.

The limestone stronghold resembles those in the Oraştie Mountains (see page 222) and the village itself is famous for its folk dance tradition, especially the Maids' Dance.

By **car**, travel 16km south of Sebeş on route 67C towards the southern dangling tip of Alba County, the Tărtărău Pass (1,678m) and the Parâng Mountains.

BUCIUM AND BUCIUM POIENI Situated approximately 60km northwest of Alba Iulia on the main but winding route 74 towards the Apuseni Mountains, Bucium (Bucsony/Baumdorf) is the **traditional mining** *comuna* (commune) made up of six villages called Bucium.

Françoise Heidebroek, an enterprising Belgian lady who speaks fluent Romanian (French and English, too), has converted an old farm cottage 'Ursita' (destiny), redecorating it and enlarging it with local materials, and respecting local architectural techniques and traditions. The farm has two large main buildings and a grassy garden with plum and apple trees beside a rushing stream. The ten double bedrooms are decorated beautifully with locally made window frames and doors. The communal living room has a huge oven where open fires are laid each evening when the weather gets chilly and the kitchen is available for use by guests. One of Françoise's neighbours, Zoriţa Beisan, prepares huge breakfasts (of four-egg omelettes, homemade blueberry jam, thick peasant bread, soft white cheese, cucumbers and peppers) or dinners (superb soups, fried meat and potatoes, cucumber, pepper and tomato salad and fresh fruit) for an extra fee, if required. Ţuică is also offered at regular intervals! A large 60m² covered porch is an ideal spot to relax and gaze at the Apuseni Mountains and greenery all around. Visitors can hold barbecues and even take a dip in a pool in the rushing brook behind the house. **Ursita Inn** is a superb base for hikers and nature-lovers. Françoise and many locals protest against the proposed gold mining at Roşia Montana nearby through an NGO Alburnus Maior, led by a local farmer and with active participation from a number of foreign environmentalists including Heidebroek and Stephanie Roth. Françoise can explain the background to the issue and give details of how to explore the region. Bucium villagers are famous for their hospitality, their traditions and their good nature. Every occasion is used for a celebration: many Orthodox holidays, weddings and christenings, the sacrifice of the pig, the distillation of the *ţuică* and the warm welcome for guests. On these occasions the villagers wear their traditional gold-woven Bucium costume. Itinerant Roma bands play and the dances last till dawn.

Getting there and away By **car**, it can take around 75 minutes to reach Bucium from Alba Iulia. When you know the route a little better, some time can be cut from the journey, but within the villages, the roads can be tricky to navigate. However, the road from the main highway to Mogos has recently been asphalted, taking some time off the journey. By car, leave Alba Iulia from the Upper Town district and head northwest on route 74 through Meteş and Zlatna ('gold' in Slav languages), where lots of crumbling disused factories make a depressing sight. To the north of Zlatna, the road becomes more green and scenic and after 22km turn right for Mogos.

Bucium is about 8km further east on a winding road. Follow the signs to Hanul Ursita (Ursita Inn) on a steep, winding road through the village that sometimes looks as if you're entering a farmer's muddy courtyard.

 Where to stay

Ursita Inn (10 dbl) Contact Françoise Heidebroek, Hanul Ursita, 860 Valea Negrilesei, Bucium Poieni, Alba County; m 0723 230 790; e fhe@ursita.ro; http://ursita.ro. Note that mobile phones don't always work in the mountains! B/fast €3, dinner €5 per course. For more details, see previous page. **$$**

ROŞIA MONTANA A few kilometres cross country north of Bucium, Roşia Montana (Verespatek/Goldbach, Rothseifen) was a very important mine (Alburnus Maior) as long ago as the Roman Empire. The gold lured the Roman armies to this part of Europe and they exploited the land's riches to finance the empire. Trajan's Column in Rome was paid for by Apuseni gold. The still undiscovered 'Decebal's Treasure', is said to be buried here. It was also important for Hungarians in the Middle Ages. Much later, the Austro-Hungarian Empire intensively exploited the mines in Bucium and Roşia Montana. The villagers could rent small mining concessions and some of them made a fortune. Old mansions and churches bear witness to a more prosperous time. In 1948, the communists confiscated the gold and shut down the mines which they considered strategic and secret reserves. Ceauşescu's secret services suspected the villagers were continuing to work the mines and persecuted them. Some older people recall how the *duba* (black van) used to come and take away those accused of having hidden a few ounces of gold. In the 1970s, Ceauşescu started mining again and the man's relentless quest for wealth took off the top of the entire Cetate Massif. For the last few years, a Canadian mining company Gabriel Resources (*www.gabrielresources.com*) has been trying to reopen what would be the largest open-cast gold mine in Europe at Roşia Montana and also Bucium. The locals all oppose the plan and environmentalists and archaeologists all over the world are trying to save this important site, as the use of cyanide in the gold mining process could cause irreparable damage (see box overleaf). The village itself is very interesting, made up of low cottages with white walls and black roofs. Some houses bear a green Gabriel Resources placard, where the residents have sold their properties to the Canadian company and moved elsewhere. However, most people stay and fight. Banners for both sides cover the village's main square, Piaţa Veche. Some cottages display the sign 'Our house is not for sale!'

In the lower part of the village is the **Mining Museum** (⊕ 09.00–17.00 Mon–Fri; admission adult/child 5/2RON). Ignore the blue 'muzeu' sign on the left as you go up the hill but head to an open square 100m further uphill and look for the gates on the left. In the open-air part of the museum, visitors can see machines used to process gold ore in the 19th and 20th centuries. There are also Roman lamps, tombstones and waxed boards written in Latin used to record details of shifts. The 2,000-year-old Roman galleries can be explored down 150 steps and visitors can wander along 400m of the 8km-long system, the remains of a remarkable feat of engineering.

The **Golden Way** (Drumul Aurului) is a project implemented in partnership by the Environmental Association 'Floarca de Colt' (*www.aefc.org*) and the 'Alburnus Maior' (Roşia Montana's Latin name) Association with financial support from the Environmental Partnership Foundation. The project aims to develop alternative activities to Roşia Montana's mining industry in integrating into the Greenway network (*www.greenways.pl*). The project involves locals in activities that can bring alternative income and empowers them to develop private initiatives, especially

THERE'S GOLD IN THEM THAR HILLS

The Roşia Montana Gold Company, of which 80% is owned by the Canadian company Gabriel Resources, intends to build Europe's largest open-cast gold-mining project in the region. There is substantial opposition to the project, both at international and local level, mostly on account of the environmental risks. Opponents also worry about the cultural heritage (there are Roman mines at the site) and about the fact that the project involves the resettlement of more than 2,000 people. The environmental concerns are connected with the Baia Mare gold mine disaster, which is probably the worst industrial accident in Europe since the Chernobyl nuclear accident in 1986. In February 2000, the dam of an Australian-owned gold mine in Baia Mare (northwest Romania) overflowed and 100,000m³ of water contaminated with cyanide escaped. The cyanide solution is used in mining to separate gold from rock. The cyanide spill travelled down though the River Tisza in Hungary, reaching the Danube in northern Serbia. The pollution caused enormous destruction to wildlife, killing almost all the fish in the river all the way through Hungary and northern Serbia. It took years before the river recovered. The Baia Mare incident caused tensions between Romania and Hungary. The Roşia Montana project plans to use the same mining method (involving cyanide) as the one in Baia Mare and environmental groups think that the risks are just too high. Gabriel Resources claim that they use post-Baia Mare standards and that their opponents exaggerate the environmental risks. They also emphasise that the project would have a positive economic impact, creating jobs in this depressed area. However, the environmental groups point out that the lifetime of the project is only 16 years so it would not have a big impact on the long-term economic situation of the region.

At the time of writing, the licensing procedure for the project is still pending and riddled with legal battles. The environmental assessment study of the project was approved by the Romanian authorities, despite vehement protests from Hungary and many civil organisations. In July 2007, the Cluj Court suspended the urban certificate (one of the many permits required) for the project and in September of the same year the Ministry for Environment announced that the whole licensing procedure was suspended. There are also talks about a new draft legislation which would ban the use of cyanide in mining but its timing is unclear. Alburnus Major and MindBomb are two of the most active groups opposing the project, the former organising the 'Save Roşia Montana' campaign (*www.rosiamontana.org*), including in 2012 a short and extremely powerful video featuring Maia Morgenstern, one of Romania's greatest actresses. Also in 2012, MindBomb put posters up all over the country featuring a golden Kalashnikov bullet, with the words 'Each Romanian will get a piece of gold from Roşia Montana'. The award-winning documentary *New Eldorado* by Tibor Kocsis (*www.neweldoradofilm.com*) gives a good insight into the ecological and social problems of Roşia Montana.

ecotourism. The website (*www.drumulaurului.ro*) has details of accommodation and 'Discovery Walks'.

To reach Roşia Montana by **car**, turn right off the Abrud–Câmpeni road (route 74A) at Ignateşti onto route 742. A large sign reads 'Bine aţi venit! Roşia Montana', so you can't miss it. It's not possible to travel here by public transport.

AVRAM IANCU From Câmpeni, the road follows along the Arieş River valley to the west into the heart of Moţi country (see box, page 245). Following the river on a more minor road, visitors come to the village where Avram Iancu was born and which is now named after him. In the village, Iancu's former home is now a **museum** (*Str Inceşti; \ 0258 771 215; www.alba.djc.ro (listed under Obiective culturale);* ⊕ *10.00– 18.00 Tue–Sun; admission 5RON*), which has a collection of Moţ folk art.

Beyond the village, signs point west to the 1,487m-high peak of Hen Mountain (Muntele Găina), where the annual Girls' Fair is held (see page 97).

APUSENI MOUNTAINS AND NATURE PARK Located on the western border of Transylvania, the Apuseni Nature Park (*www.parcapuseni.ro*) falls into Alba, Cluj and Bihor counties, and some of the best approach routes are from Alba County. The name 'Apuseni' translates as 'of the sunset', thus 'western'. The park has been visited and studied since the time of the Austro-Hungarian Empire. The oldest tourist trails in the area date from the early 1900s and were described and marked by the traveller Gyula Czárán. The scientist and speleologist Emil Racoviţă

AVRAM IANCU – THE LITTLE KING OF THE MOUNTAINS

Avram Iancu was born in 1824 in Vidra de Sus, today named Avram Iancu in his honour. Iancu was a Transylvanian Romanian lawyer who played an important role in the local chapter of the 1848–49 revolutions against the Habsburg Empire and was particularly active in the Ţara Moţilor (Moţ Land) and the Apuseni Mountains. Iancu rallied the peasants in the support of the Habsburgs and earned the moniker *Crăişorul Munţilor* ('the little king of the mountains'). Born into a family of emancipated serf peasants Iancu graduated from Cluj's law school and became a legal clerk in Târgu Mureş. Iancu was outraged that Hungarian revolutionaries refused to debate the abolition of serfdom, which at the time still affected most of the Romanian population of Transylvania. Iancu organised protests in Câmpeni and Blaj, and like the Transylvanian Saxons, he looked to Vienna for progress and support. The new emperor Franz Joseph and the Austrian government granted the Romanians numerous liberties and rights. The territory was organised in *prefecturi* ('prefectures'), with Avram Iancu as a prefect in the Apuseni region. In 1849, Hungarians under Józef Bem carried out a sweeping offensive through Transylvania. Avram Iancu's remained the only resistance force. He retreated to the difficult terrain of the hills, mounting a guerrilla campaign on Bem's forces and blocking the route to Alba Iulia. When the Austrians took over, Iancu agreed to disarm. The Habsburgs abolished serfdom, but Iancu did not get to enjoy the changes. He was arrested in December 1849, and although the charge was overturned after local protests, he was censored throughout his life, had his library confiscated and was placed under constant surveillance. In 1852, Iancu was arrested a second time as the authorities thought that his presence would inflame local feeling. Soon after his release, Iancu visited Vienna and attempted to petition the emperor. He was prevented from doing so by the police, a public humiliation, which provoked a nervous breakdown from which he never recovered. He took to drink and became homeless, wandering through the Apuseni region playing a pipe. In 1872, Iancu died and according to his request, he was buried under Horea's tree in Ţebea, by legend the place where the Revolt of Horea, Cloşca and Crişan had started.

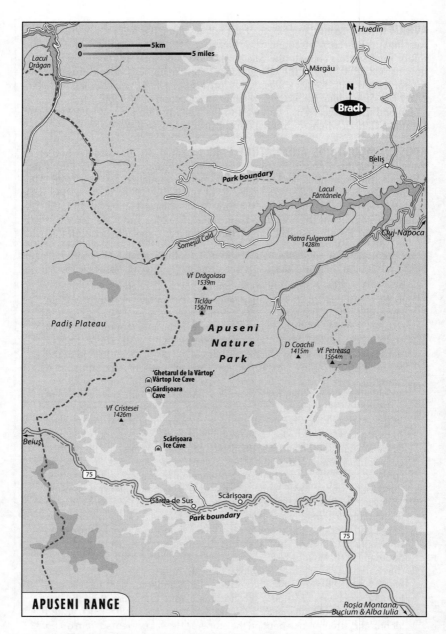

Map labels (reading across the image):

- Huedin
- Lacul Drăgan
- 0 — 5km
- 0 — 5 miles
- Mărgău
- N
- Bradt
- Beliş
- Park boundary
- Lacul Fântânele
- Someşul Cald
- Cluj-Napoca
- Piatra Fulgerată 1428m
- Vf Drăgoiasa 1539m
- Ticlău 1567m
- Padiş Plateau
- Apuseni Nature Park
- D Coachii 1415m
- Vf Petreasa 1564m
- 'Ghetarul de la Vârtop' Vârtop Ice Cave
- Gârdişoara Cave
- Vf Cristesei 1426m
- Beiuş
- Scărişoara Ice Cave
- 75
- Gârda de Sus
- Scărişoara
- Park boundary
- 75
- Roşia Montana, Bucium & Alba Iulia

APUSENI RANGE

formulated a plan to protect the park at the first Congress of Romanian Naturalists in 1928. The mountains are considered of middle height as the peaks reach only 1,400m, although the highest peak, Cucurbăta Mare, does reach 1,849m. There is a huge variety of natural attractions such as gorges, plateaux, mountain passes, caves, waterfalls and also the famous Scărişoara Ice Cave. The park is criss-crossed with well-marked hiking and ski trails.

Information **Mountain rescue teams** from Alba, Cluj and Bihor counties are active in the park area. In an emergency call ✆ 112 or ✆ 0-SALVAMONT (0-725826668).

Mountain and Cave Rescue is based in Oradea in Bihor County (*Str Sovata 34/A, 410290 Oradea, jud Bihor;* ✆f *0358 436 022;* m *0744 185 081;* e *salvamontbihor@ yahoo.com; http://salvamontbihor.ro*).

Two excellent companies offer tours: **Apuseni Experience** (see page 54) and **Green Mountain Holidays** (see page 55) offer all-in guided hiking holidays, designed to give a genuine taste of local life in the great outdoors.

SCĂRIŞOARA ICE CAVE Situated right up in the northwest corner of Alba County, deep in the Apuseni mountain forests, the Scărişoara Ice Cave (Peştera gheţarul) is the biggest ice cave in Romania and a unique phenomenon in southeast Europe. The exact date when the cave was discovered is unknown, but the German geographer Adolf Schmidl mentioned the cave in 1863 and made the first map. Scientists believe that the cave was created during the Ice Age, when the mountains were covered with ice and snow. Scărişoara is a truly impressive sight as visitors enter the underground glacier at a height of 1,165m through a large sinkhole and walk on 70,000m³ of 23m-thick ice, descending 48m to two chambers at the bottom of a great abyss. The most stunning ice structures are found in the second chamber, 'The Church', where the pillar formations reach more than 3m high and stalactites and stalagmites shimmer eerily all around.

The ice cave is accessible by **car**, approach Scarişoara from the south on route 75 from Câmpeni (35km) to Gărda de Sus. There is a minor road leading almost to Scărişoara, but the two-hour **hike** (red triangle trail) is very enjoyable. Note that the ice cave is not at Scărişoara village, which is 4km east of Gărda de Sus.

PADIŞ PLATEAU The Padis Plateau (Plateul Padiş), located right on the Alba–Bihor county border, is in the heart of a classic karst area and wonderfully scenic with streams disappearing underground and unexpectedly springing up. Many hollows offer access to the huge cave systems that lie beneath. Padiş is a five-hour hike northwest from Scărişoara along a track marked with blue stripes to the **Padiş Cabana** (*www.padis.ro; 65 beds in 2-,4- or 6-bed cabins;* **$**), which lies at the heart of the plateau – a paradise of caves, subterranean rivers and sinkholes.

Dodgy mountain roads lead to Padiş from the west (Bihor County) and east, but from Alba it's **on foot** only. Continue along the trail past Scărişoara on the blue triangle-marked route. The journey will take a full day's strenuous hiking.

LUPŞA From Câmpeni, head east for 14km on route 75 towards Turda, this time to find the small town of Lupşa (Nagylupsa/Wolfsdorf) and a great museum detailing the lives of the local Moţi people.

The **Moţ Ethnographic Museum** (*Muzeul Etnografic Pamfil Albu; www.alba. djc.ro;* ⊕ *14.00–18.00 Mon–Wed, 08.00–12.00 & 14.00–18.00 Thu–Sun; admission adult/child 5/2RON*) has a rich collection of Moţ culture with numerous tools, pots, jugs, folk costumes and even gold-panning equipment from the Arieş River valley. The museum is next to a little stone Orthodox church built in 1421 on a mound.

HEADING NORTH FROM ALBA IULIA

BLAJ Blaj (Balázsfalva/Blasendorf) is now a little faded around the edges but in the 19th century the town was the centre for Romanian nationalism and Romanian religious, political and cultural life. Today, it produces some excellent white wines, including the local Feteasca Regală.

Blaj was first mentioned in 1271 as Villa Herbordi, after a deed by Count Herbod. In 1313, the domain passed to Herbod's son Blasius Cserei who created a hamlet for his servants' 20 families. In 1737, the town, now called Blaj, was awarded town status. The first public school, teaching in Romanian, was established in Blaj in 1754. Blaj was also the first place to have Romanian written with a Latin alphabet instead of the traditional Cyrillic alphabet. As the founding venue for the Şcoala Ardeleană Society, Blaj was at the heart of the Romanian Age of Enlightenment and was called 'the Little Rome'.

The 15th-century **Bethlen Castle** hosts the **Town Museum** (*Parcul Avram Iancu 2;* \ *0258 711 714; www.alba.djc.ro;* ⊕ *10.00–17.00 Tue–Fri, 10.00–14.00 Sat/Sun; admission adult/child 2/1RON*), which has a collection of books and historical items.

Blaj is 40km northeast of Alba Iulia. By **car**, head north out of Alba Iulia on route 1 (E81) towards Teiuş and Turda. In the centre of Teiuş, turn right and continue for 20km east to Blaj. Regular **buses** leave Alba Iulia daily for Blaj (*70mins*). Many trains go from Blaj to Sighişoara (*2hrs*), Cluj-Napoca (*2hrs*) and to Alba Iulia (*40mins*) via Teiuş.

AIUD Aiud (Nagyenyed/Strassburg am Mieresch) has one of the oldest fortresses in Transylvania, although its name is often connected with a prison, which held Soviet spies during World War II and Iron Guard members after the communist takeover.

Aiud Citadel (Cetatea Aiudului) is located in the centre of town and was built during the 14th century in the form of a pentagon with two Hungarian churches inside: a 15th-century Calvinist church and a 19th-century Lutheran church.

The **Orthodox Cathedral** was built after the unification of Transylvania in 1918. Construction began in 1927 and continued for decades. The architecture was inspired by the former patriarchal basilica-turned-mosque Hagia Sofia in Istanbul, built in Byzantine style with high arches and elaborate painting.

Aiud is 27km north of Teiuş on route 1 (E81) between Alba Iulia and Turda. The town is located on the national road running Bucharest–Oradea–Budapest and most **coach** services running between the capitals stop in Aiud.

Aiud is an important **railway** hub and is served frequently by CFR national trains. It is located on the main line from Oradea to Bucharest via Cluj-Napoca; consequently, some 46 trains pass daily through Aiud with 18 trains daily to Cluj-Napoca (*2hrs*), 11 trains daily to Alba Iulia (*35mins*), four to Sighişoara (*2hrs*), six to Deva (*100mins*) and three to Târgu Mureş (*1½–2½hrs*) and Sibiu (*2½–3½hrs*).

RÂMEŢ Râmeţ Monastery is an Orthodox monastery thought to have been built in the 15th century with a church built 200 years earlier. It is one of the oldest Orthodox religious monuments in the country and features paintings made in 1376 by the craftsman Mihu from Crişul Alb. Its architecture is classically Romanian, resembling the painted monasteries of Moldavia such as Voroneţ. Râmeţ Monastery played an important role in preserving the Orthodox faith during oppression by the Catholic Habsburgs, particularly after 1700. In 1969, the monastery opened a **museum** exhibiting icons on wood, icons on glass, old service books and an important numismatic collection. Ask one of the 95 nuns or sisters in the monastery for the key to the museum (try in French if all else fails). There is also a **small shop** selling items of embroidery and weaving made by the

Situated in the Apuseni Mountains, Țara Moților (Land of the Moț), also known as Țara de Piatră (Land of Stone), is an ethno-geographic region situated around the basin of the Arieș and Crișul Alb rivers. In Transylvania, the Moț Land falls into Alba, Cluj and Hunedoara counties and part of the Apuseni Nature Park, while beyond the borders, there are Moți in Arad and Bihor counties. Some anthropologists claim that the people living in this region, the Moți, must be descendants of the Celts because of their blonde hair and blue eyes which occur much more frequently here than anywhere else in Romania. Other scholars believe that they are descendants of Slavs or of the Alans, originating from north of the Black Sea. Yet another group of scholars suggest that they are descendants of Germanic Gepid tribes. In total, 17 theories have been formulated about the origins with no single agreed answer. Many people like to believe they are the direct descendants of the Dacians, who fled to the hills when the Romans left. Moți live in scattered villages at altitudes up to about 1,400m, higher than any other permanent settlements in Romania. As the Moți are isolated hill people who keep to themselves, town-dwelling Romanians are a bit nervous of them and think they are wild people from the mountains. Moți wear unusual hats like upside-down flower pots. In Bucium, I saw a very dignified, young Moți shepherd with the typical hat, a cape thrown over his shoulders and a long walking staff. Moți are skilful shepherds and good at crafts.

nuns. They only make to order and the prices are high, but the work is delicate and of high quality.

Râmeț is located 36km northwest of Alba Iulia, 23km west of Aiud. There are three **buses** daily from Alba Iulia, but the road from Aiud west is pretty dire.

UNIREAC Situated 16km northeast of Aiud, Unirea (Felvinc/Oberwinz) is the centre of a Székely (see box, page 168) enclave called Aranyosszék (Golden Seat or Scaunul Arieșului in Romanian).

The Arieș River is called Aranyos (Golden) in Hungarian and the Transylvanian Székely people lived in the Arieș River valley, far from the rest of the Transylvanian Székelys in the far east of Transylvania in Harghita and Covasna counties. Free Székely guards were granted a part of the lands belonging to the king around the old Turda Castle as a reward for their courage in battles against the Tatars. They settled here in 21 villages in around 1270; the eastern Székely territories were populated a century earlier. There are about 10,000–15,000 Székely still living in the former territory of Aranyosszék although the territory is now more mixed with both Hungarians and Romanians.

Take the main route 1 (E81) between Alba Iulia and Turda (19km). Frequent **buses** pass through Unirea (*40mins*).

RIMETEA Rimetea (Torocó/Eisenmarkt), in the northeast tip of Alba County, is a little out of place in such a Romanian county as it is totally Hungarian. Many consider Rimetea (Torockó in Hungarian) one of the most beautiful Hungarian villages in the country. Torockó is a small, graceful village of uniform white houses in rows, nestling in the shadow of the dramatic 1,129m **Székelykő** (Székely Stone) outcrop. The stone mountain has a mystical significance for the Székelys and they say the sun rises twice in Torockó because it appears briefly at dawn before disappearing behind the rock and reappearing later over the village. To walk to the rock, take the red stripe path before the village on the left. A blue cross path leads to a **watermill** (*moară de apă*).

The village was actually founded by Saxons, who came to explore the region and process iron ore. The mix of German and Hungarian cultures created a beautiful, **colourful folk costume**, which many villagers still wear to this day. In the centre of the village, by the white **Unitarian church**, is a small **ethnographic museum** (*Néprajzi Múzeum; www.alba.djc.ro*; ⊕ *09.00–17.00 Tue–Sun; admission adult/ child 3/1RON*). Opposite is a sweet little **shop** (⊕ *10.00–16.00 Mon–Fri*) selling folk crafts in the local style. Turn left just before the museum and drive for 100m to find the tourist office on the right.

🏠 **Where to stay and eat** Alpin Tour (*Agenţia de Turism;* ✆ *0258 861 902*) offers accommodation with local families (*21RON pp per night, b/fast 13RON, lunch 21RON, dinner 16RON, or HB 60RON*). Gabriella Varga at Alpin Tour (e *alpin-gabriella@personal.ro*) can help non-Hungarian speakers.

There is no restaurant in the village so half board is advisable as it's a bumpy ride to the nearest metropolis.

Torockó Guesthouse Association (Torockói Vendégfogadók Egyesülete) Hse No 125, Rimetea/ Torockó; ✆ 0258 860 272 (Mária Király), 0258 861 211 ext 127 (Zsuzsa Tulit), 0258 861 211 ext 110 (Sára Vajda); e torocko@email.ro; www. torocko.hu. The village is geared up for Hungarian-speaking visitors & the locals are a bit freaked out at the thought of communicating in other languages. German or Romanian may help.

Another good website (in Hungarian) for accommodation is www.szekelyfoldiinfo. ro/Menu/Szallashelyek/Panziok/Torocko.html.

Getting there and away The village is best approached from Turda in Cluj County. Drive west out of Turda heading west towards Câmpeni on route 75. After 20km, turn left at Buru. Rimetea is 8km south. The road from Buru to Rimetea is in terrible condition with a 3km-stretch of pot-holes and sharp stones, but locals say the Rimetea–Aiud road is even worse. A **bus** travels twice a day between Rimetea and Aiud, but it's an uncomfortable ride.

10

Cluj County

About one third of Cluj County (6,674km²) is covered with mountains. Situated on the western border of Transylvania with only the Crișana region between it and Hungary, Cluj has a very mixed population of Romanians (76%), Hungarians (20%), Roma (3%) and also Germans, Ukrainians and Jews.

Geographically, the region is made up of the Apuseni Mountains, the Transylvanian Plain (Câmpia Transilvaniei/Mezőség) and the terrace of the Someș River. Hills and mountains, covering two-thirds of the county, dominate the relief. The lower hills (around 500m), part of the Transylvanian Plain, are bald, but the hills around the Somaș River valley are covered with lush forest. The hills below 600m are covered with oak forests and, at higher altitudes, Norway spruce and silver fur. Beech, elm, ash and hornbeam are also common below 1,000m.

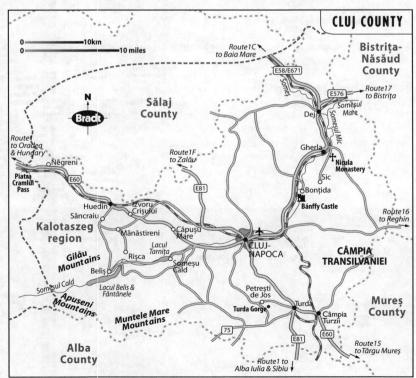

The varied vegetation and landscape provide habitats for many wild animals. On treks, visitors can spot fox, hare, roe deer and also sometimes brown bear, wolf, wild boar, elk and even lynx. The karst regions are ideal places to see reptiles such as lizards and snakes and on the higher ground birdwatchers have often seen golden eagles. The many rivers and lakes hold chub, brown trout, grayling and carp.

The beauty and natural wealth of the region has attracted humans since the Stone Age. Archaeological digs in the Cheile Baciului Gorge found the remains of settlements from the Neolithic period (484–425BC), the oldest discoveries in Romania. Nowadays, Cluj County attracts visitors from all over Europe with more than 600 architectural monuments in every European style from the Gothic, Baroque and Renaissance to the Art Nouveau and modern style. Cluj County has one of the most dynamic economies in Romania and is one of the most popular for foreign investment. The county town, Cluj-Napoca is one of Romania's most important IT and financial services centres. Cluj's main industries are wood processing, glass manufacture, pharmaceuticals and cosmetics, mechanical components and textiles.

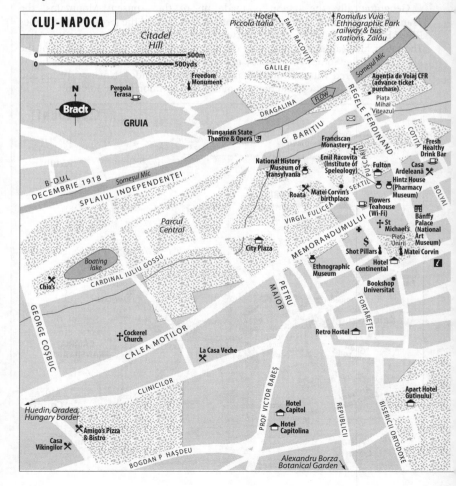

'There is an air of pride about Cluj,' wrote Walter Starkie in 1929. Cluj-Napoca (Kolozsvár/Klausenburg) is one of Transylvania's cultural and economic dynamos. Along with Braşov and Sibiu, Cluj-Napoca forms a triangle of go-getting metropolises, constantly renovating and reinventing themselves in the struggle to find a healthy balance between tradition and progress. At first glance, Cluj-Napoca is not as attractive as the two Saxon cities of Braşov and Sibiu, but it was the Hungarian provincial capital, known to the Magyars as Kolozsvár during the Austro-Hungarian Empire, and remains one of Romania's most visited towns. Cluj was one of the Siebenburgen, but it does not have an intact medieval Old Town heart like those in Sibiu, Sighişoara or Mediaş. The Baroque and Art Nouveau façades are a little faded but efforts are continuing to freshen up the city and a gaggle of swanky business hotels and international-themed restaurants have sprouted. The city also has a fabulous botanical garden to escape to when the summer heat becomes oppressive. The city has six state and several private universities, of which the Babeş-Bolyai University, with over 43,000 students, is the largest and most diverse university in Romania. If you visit during term time, you may find it hard to get a table in the numerous bars and terrace cafés. During the summer, however, the city empties out and the eternally dusty, car-packed streets are more easily navigated. Driving in Cluj-Napoca is not fun, but hiring a car in Cluj is easy and there are many small villages, lakes and mountains in the vicinity, which are best explored with your own wheels.

HISTORY Cluj-Napoca can trace its origins back to the 2nd century AD, when the Dacian settlement 'Napuca' was first mentioned. After the Romans conquered Dacia, they renamed the city 'Napoca' and gave it the title of 'municipum' in AD124.

The name Cluj comes from 'Castrum Clus', first used in the 12th century, meaning 'closed citadel' to refer to the citadel overlooking the town and the seven hills that surround it. In the 12th century, German settlers founded the town, which they called Klausenburg, on the previous Roman *municipum* site for the Hungarian king Géza II.

In the 16th century, Cluj was at the centre of the Hungarian Reformation, with first Calvinism, then the Unitarian faith. Before World War II, Cluj was a great centre of Hungarian cultural life and it has a special significance for Hungarians even now when the Magyar population has fallen to less than 20%. In 1974, Ceauşescu added 'Napoca' to Cluj's name to remind everyone of the Daco-Romanian origins. During the 1990s, the 'mad mayor' Gheorghe Funar tried to whip up anti-Hungarian sentiment. Former leader of the Romanian National Unity Party, Funar was Mayor of Cluj-Napoca from 1992–2004 and painted litterbins and park benches in the red, yellow and blue Romanian flag colours, especially those surrounding Saint Michael's Church and the statue of King Matei Corvin/Mátyás on his horse (they are back to normal now). Like his father Ioan de Hunedoara/János Hunyadi (see box, page 224), Matei/Mátyás has long been the subject of cultural haggling between Romanian and Hungarian historians, both eager to claim him as their own. These days, Funar doesn't do so much frothing at the mouth and there is little evidence of a supposed Romanian–Hungarian tension.

GETTING THERE, AWAY AND AROUND

By air Cluj-Napoca Someşeni Airport (CLJ) (*Str Traian Vuia 149;* \ *0264 416 702;* e *aercj@codec.ro; www.airportcluj.ro*) is 4km east of the city centre on the E576 towards Bistriţa. **Bus** No 8 runs from the airport to Piaţa Mihai Viteazul in the centre – just walk out of the terminal onto the main road and turn right to find the stop and a small office selling tickets (3.5RON). Don't forget to validate your ticket on the bus.

Operating as a military airport since the 1920s, Cluj Airport opened to international passengers and cargo in 1996 and in the same year the airport began a process of modernisation and extension. Since March 1998, Cluj-Napoca International Airport has hosted the scheduled Bucharest–Cluj-Napoca–Bucharest flight. Cluj-Napoca International Airport is Romania's third international airport with scheduled flights from several European cities, including London Luton, Budapest, Frankfurt-am-Main, Munich, Vienna, and a number of Italian cities. Low-cost airline **Wizzair** flies from Cluj-Napoca to Barcelona, Budapest Ferihegy 1, Dortmund, London Luton and Rome Fiumicino. Cluj-Napoca has upgraded its runway and equipment and is a good base for Sighişoara and the Székely Lands.

By rail The **railway station** (*Str Garii 1–3;* \ *0264 592 952*) is situated 20 minutes' walk north of the centre, over the Someş River and along Strada Horea.

Fast inter-city trains connect Cluj-Napoca with Bucharest (*8hrs*), Braşov (*5hrs*), Mediaş (*105mins*), Sighişoara (*3½hrs*), Sibiu (*4hrs*) and Târgu Mureş (*2½hrs*). There are also several international trains to and from Budapest (*8hrs*). Trains to other western European cities run via Budapest.

For rail information, contact **Agenţia de Voiaj CFR** (*Piaţa Mihai Viteazul 11;* \ *0264 432 001;* ☉ *08.00–20.00 Mon–Fri*), which has train schedule information and reservations for up to 24 hours in advance. Same-day travel tickets must be purchased at the station.

By bus The **bus station** (*Str Giordano Bruno 3–5;* \ *0264 435 275*) is five minutes' walk further northwest of the railway station and daily domestic services leave for Alba Iulia, Braşov Bistriţa, Bucharest, Hunedoara, Reghin, Sebeş, Sibiu and Târgu Mureş.

A **second bus station** is located to the east of town along B-dul 21 Decembrie at the junction with Anghel Salign.

Cluj **Eurolines bus station** is at B-dul 21 Decembrie 54–56, Hotel Victoria ground floor (\f *0264 431 961;* e *cluj@eurolines.ro; www.eurolines.ro*).

Public transport Several **bus** (*autobuz*), **tram** (*tramvai*) and **trolleybus** (*troilebuz*) routes connect Cluj-Napoca's main areas and tourist attractions. Public transport runs 05.00–23.15. Tickets must be bought at kiosks before boarding and validated on the vehicle.

Taxi companies
🚗 **Atlas** ☎969
🚗 **Diesel** ☎946
🚗 **Napoca (Diesel Taxi)** ☎953; www. taxipronapoca.ro

🚗 **Clima&Confort** ☎943; www. climasiconfortcluj.ro
🚗 **Nova** ☎949
🚗 **Pritax** ☎942
🚗 **Pro Rapid** ☎948

By car The European highways E60, E81, E576 and E871 all meet in Cluj-Napoca. The Transylvanian segment of the Bucharest–Budapest motorway (opening in 2014, possibly), will pass near Cluj-Napoca, placing the city on one of the most important road corridors in Europe, linking the Atlantic Ocean with the Black Sea.

Car hire
🚗 **SIXT** Cluj Airport; ☎0264 274 046; e cluj@sixt.ro; www.sixt.ro

🚗 **Thrifty** Cluj Airport; ☎0740 002 000; www. thrifty.ro

TOURIST INFORMATION
🛈 Listing Magazines The free listings magazines *Şapte Seri* (*www.sapteseri.ro*) & *Zile şi Nopţi* (*www.zilesinopti.ro*) have details of theatres, etc

🛈 Tourist Information Office Eroilor Boulevard 6–8; ☎0264 452 244; e info-tourism@primariaclujnapoca.ro; www.visitclujnapoca.ro; www.primariaclujnapoca.ro. .

🏠 WHERE TO STAY
🏠 **City Plaza** (42 dbl) Str Sindicatelor 9–13; ☎0264 450 101; e contact@cityhotels.ro; www.cityhotels.ro. Very upmarket 4-star business hotel with the superb Marco Polo restaurant ($$$), bar & lounge & conference facilities. **$$$$**
🏠 **Hotel Capitolina** (20 dbl, 6 suites) Str Victor Babes 35; ☎0264 450 490; e office@hotel-capitolina.ro; http://hotelcentralcluj.ro. Smart new hotel built in 2005, with sister hotels the Capitol & ApartHotel Gutinului for longer stays. **$$$$**
🏠 **Hotel Fulton** (17 dbl, 2 suites) Str Sextil Puscariu 10; ☎0264 597 766; e office@fulton.ro;

www.fulton.ro. Tastefully renovated building in a quiet, central location. *B/fast inc.* **$$$**
🏠 **Piccola Italia** (4 dbl, 5 trpl) Str Emil Racoviţă 20; ☎0263 536 110; e piccolaitaliacluj@yahoo.com; www.piccolaitalia.ro. Family-run guesthouse with a pleasant terrace, quite a hike out of the centre on a hill above town. *B/fast inc.* **$$**
🏠 **Retro Hostel** (4 dbl, 3 sgl, 2 trpl, dorms) Str Potaissa 11–13; ☎0264 450 452; e retro@retro.ro; www.retro.ro. Clean, friendly, popular budget accommodation just 500m from Babeş-Bolyai University. **$**

🍴 WHERE TO EAT AND DRINK
🍴 **Casa Ardeleană** Sora Shopping Centre; B-dul 21 Decembrie 1989 5; ☎0264 439 451; www. casaardeleana.com; ⏰ 12.00–midnight daily. Hearty, traditional Romanian cuisine. Live music on Mon. **$$**
🍴 **Chio's Restaurant** Str Arinilor 18, Parcul Central; ☎0264 596 395; www.chios.ro; ⏰ 11.00–midnight daily. Trendy restaurant in the middle of boating lake. **$$**

🍴 **La Casa Veche** Str Clinicilor 14; ☎0264 450 583; ⏰ 11.00–23.00 Mon–Sat, 11.00–22.00 Sun. Traditional Romanian dishes, just west of the city centre. **$$**
🍴 **Roata** Str Al. Ciura 6; ☎0264 592 022; ⏰ 12.00–23.00 Tue–Sat, 13.00–23.00 Sun/Mon. Good, hearty, traditional Romanian & Transylvanian dishes, with a terrace. **$$**

✖ **Amigo's Pizza & Bistro** Str Piezişă 23A; ☎0264 445 122; ⏱ 08.00–01.00 Mon–Thu, 08.00–02.00 Fri, 10.00–02.00 Sat, 12.00–02.00 Sun. Smart bar & restaurant in the student zone. $
✖ **Casa Vikingilor** Str Haşdeu 70;☎0264 595 280; www.casavikingilor.ro; ⏱ 24hrs. A very studenty & smoky pub serving pizza & other dishes. $
⊑ **Flowers Teahouse** Piaţa Unirii 24; ⏱ 08.00–22.00 Mon–Fri, 10.00–22.00 Sat/Sun. Lovely teahouse with plants, mosaics & Wi-Fi. $

⊑ **Fresh Healthy Drink Bar** Sora Shopping Centre; ⏱ 10.00–22.00 Mon–Sat, 10.00–20.00 Sun. Wonderful freshly squeezed orange, apple, carrot, grapefruit juices & banana-based smoothies. $
⊑ **Pergola Terasa** Dealul Cetatuia; ⏱ 10.00–02.00 daily. A terrace with a great view overlooking the city. Drinks & ice cream only. $

OTHER PRACTICALITIES
Bank
$ **Banca Transilvania** Piaţa Unirii 22; ⏱ 09.00–17.00 Mon–Fri, 09.30–12.30 Sat. With a 24hr ATM accepting Visa & MasterCard.

Pharmacy
✚ **Farmacia Terrafarm** Piaţa Unirii 26; ⏱ 08.00–20.00 Mon–Fri, 09.00–14.00 Sat. Homeopathic medicines.

Bookshop
Universitat Corner of Piaţa Unirii & Str Universităţii; ⏱ 08.00–20.00 Mon–Fri, 09.00–16.00 Sat

Post office
✉ **Main Post Office** Str Regele Ferdinand 33; ⏱ 07.00–20.00 Mon–Fri, 08.00–13.00 Sat

Internet
▣ **Flowers Teahouse** Piaţa Unirii 24. For further details, see above.

WHAT TO SEE AND DO Piaţa Unirii, the main square, resplendent with Gothic, Baroque, Renaissance and neo-Classical buildings and home to many shops and restaurants, is dominated by the 15th-century **St Michael's Church** (*Mass at 07.00, 08.45, 10.00, 11.30 & 18.00 Sun, 06.15 & 07.30 Mon–Fri, festivals 06.15, 07.30, 10.00 & 18.00*), one of the finest examples of Gothic architecture in Romania. The church was built (1350–1487) in four stages. The 24m altar is very Baroque and overwhelming and dates back to 1390. The interior is quite stunning with soaring Gothic arches, the highest in Romania after Braşov's Black Church. On the southern side of the church, an equestrian statue of the 15th-century ruler **Matei Corvin** has been a controversial figure ever since it was created by János Fadrusz in 1902, with Hungarians and Romanians haggling over plaques, heritage and anything else they can think of. Visit the house where Matei was born in 1458 (*Str Matei Corvin 6*) a low 15th-century building where two large black plaques, one in Hungarian and one in Romanian and English, read: 'The Romanian Matthias Corvinus is considered the greatest of all Hungarian kings.' The region is famous for its caves and the **Emil Racoviţa Institute of Speleology Museum** (*Str Sextil Puşcariu 8*) displays fossils and collections by Racoviţa who founded the Romanian Speleology Institute in 1920, though it was closed for renovation in 2012. A few narrow streets further north is the **National History Museum of Transylvania** (*Muzeul Naţional de Istorie a Transilvaniei; Str C Daicoviciu 2; www.istoria-transilvaniei.ro; closed for renovation in 2012*) with many floors of historical displays. On the eastern side of the Piaţa Muzeului, the **Franciscan monastery and church** (*Mănăstirea şi Biserica Franciscana; Str Victor Deleu 4; ⏱ 07.00–19.00 daily; admission free*) is one of the city's oldest buildings, built in the 13th century after the Tatar attacks and given to the Dominican order by Ioan de Hunedoara in 1455, then transferred to the Franciscans in 1728. Futher north, on the riverbank, is the **Hungarian State Theatre and Opera** (*Teatrul și Opera Maghiara din Cluj; Str Emil Isac 26–28; www. hungarianopera.ro*), where the Cheeky Girls learned their 'craft'.

Back in the main square, the eastern side of Piața Unirii houses the 18th-century Baroque **Bánffy Palace**, where the **Art Museum** (*Muzeul Național de Artă; Piața Unirii 30; www.macluj.ro; ⊕ May–Oct 12.00–19.00 Wed–Sun, Nov–Apr 10.00– 17.00 Wed–Sun; admission adult/child 4/2RON*) displays fine art and weaponry. In the southwest corner of the square stands the **Hotel Continental**, built in 1895 in an eclectic style combining Renaissance, Classical and Baroque elements. During World War II, the hotel served as the German military headquarters in Transylvania. Nearby, the **'Shot Pillars' Monument** of seven bulbous bronze columns stands on the pavement marking the spot where 13 people were killed and 26 wounded by bullets on 16 December 1989. The columns have symbolic bullet holes. Across the square, you can visit the **Hintz House**, which served as Cluj's first and longest-running pharmacy (1573–1949) and is now home to the **Pharmacy Museum** (*Muzeul Farmaceutic; Str Regele Ferdinand 1; ⊕ 10.00–16.00 Mon–Wed/ Fri, 12.00–1800 Thu; admission adult/child 5/3RON*), with a fascinating display of 2,300 medical instruments. It's a short walk along Strada Regele Ferdinand and across the Someș River to climb the steps up the **Citadel Hill** (Dealul Cetatuia) to reach the **Freedom Monument**, in memory of those who died in World War I. The name refers to an Austrian fortress built here in the 18th century to ensure control of the city, by keeping an eye on the residents' behaviour, rather than ensuring its defence. The hill is now crowned with the hulking white **Hotel Transilvania**.

To the west of the centre is **Central Park** with a large **boating lake** (⊕ 10.00– 20.00 daily; adult/child 6/3RON*) and green space by the river. Heading south towards the university zone, Strada Memorandumului contains the **Ethnographic Museum of Transylvania** (*Str Memorandumului 21; ☏ 0264 592 344; ✉ contact@ muzeul-etnografic.ro; www.muzeul-etnografic.ro; ⊕ 09.00–17.00 Tue–Fri; admission adult/child 4/2RON*) with a collection of more than 65,000 folk items. Founded in 1922, the museum offers an excellent introduction to Transylvanian folk art and traditions, with sections devoted to trades, lodging, pottery, food, textiles, costumes and customs. The museum also has an open-air section, the **Romulus Vuia Ethnographic Park** (*Str Taietura Turcului, located north of town on Hoia Hill, bus No 30 from Piața Unirii; ✉ contact@muzeul-etnografic.ro; www.muzeul-etnografic. ro; ⊕ 1 May–31 Oct 09.00–17.00 Tue–Sun, last admission 16.00; admission adult/ child 4/2RON*), founded in 1929 with three gorgeous 18th-century wooden churches, peasant houses and outbuildings for grinding gold ore, sheep rearing and tanning. Towards the university area in the south of the city, some of the **old city walls** can be seen at Piața Ștefan cel Mare and the **Tailors' Bastion** (Bastionul Croitorilor), at Piața Baba Novac, dates from 1550. The **Cluj Philharmonic** (*Str Mihail Kogălniceanu*) nearby was founded in 1955 and hosts frequent orchestral and chamber music concerts. Fans of Transylvanian architecture should continue west on Strada Moților to No 84 where the Calvinist church was built in 1913 by Károly Kós who designed the entire building and its fixtures and fittings. It is known as the **Cockerel Church** because of the motifs all over the building symbolising St Peter's three-fold denial of Christ before the cock crowed. On a hill to the south of the centre, the **Alexandru Borza Botanical Garden** (*Str Gheorghe Bilascu 42; ⊕ 08.00–19.00 daily; admission adult/child 5/2RON*) stretches over hills and valleys with several greenhouses, a Japanese garden and a huge collection of cacti. Back in the centre, to the east of Piața Unirii is another large square dominated by the imposing **Orthodox cathedral** (⊕ 06.00–13.00 & 17.00–20.00 Mon–Sat*), built in

1923–33 and guarded out the front by a tall **statue of Avram Iancu** teetering on a high pillar. The southern side of the square is decorated by the **Romanian National Theatre and Opera House** (*Piaţa Ştefan cel Mare 24;* \ *0264 597 175;* e *info@ operacluj.ro; www.operacluj.ro*), a bright yellow building which opened in 1919.

Romania's only international film festival, the **Transylvanian International Film Festival (TIFF)** (*www.tiff.ro*) began in 2002 and got off to a flying start with audiences of more than 9,000 piling in to see the 43 films shown. It has now expanded to occupy several cinemas in Cluj-Napoca and takes place annually during the first week of June, before moving to Sibiu.

Daksa Eco-equestrian Centre (*Contact Mugur Pop, Str Actorului 13/A, 400441 Cluj-Napoca, jud Cluj;* \ *0364 105 194;* m *0744 100 745;* e *hello@ridingadventures. ro; www.ridingadventures.ro*) offer horseriding tours from Cluj-Napoca into the Apuseni Mountains lasting several days.

HEADING WEST

From Cluj-Napoca it's a 42km drive to Huedin (Bánffyhunyad/Heynod), and the scenery along route 1 (E60) towards Oradea and the border with Hungary is lovely, with little grass-covered hills almost like waves rolling past, dotted with bushes. At **Căpuşa Mare**, there are many stalls alongside the road offering baskets and ceramic objects. At the turning to **Dumbrava**, many ladies stand holding buckets filled with sinister-looking mushrooms. Route 1 is not very restful, however, as many lorries thunder along to Hungary. The villagers in **Izvoru Crişului** (Körösfő) make a living from selling crafts by the roadside and the village resembles Corund (Harghita County) with its profusion of goods: baskets, straw hats, jugs, brown bowls, embroidered tablecloths, sheep fleeces and the ubiquitous sports towels. The **Calvinist church** (1764) on the hill above the village is one of the prettiest in the Kalotaszeg region.

HUEDIN My first entry into Transylvania was via Huedin and, after the **Piatra Cramlui** (Királyhágó or King's Pass) in the mountains, the train followed the rushing **Crişul Repede River** through forests and dramatic scenery. Huedin was also author/ fiddler Walter Starkie's first stop on his journey documented in *Raggle Taggle* (see page 285) and he noted: 'Transylvania is a country of contrasts, at one moment you wander through undulating plains. Then you are transported into mountainous country and deep ravines full of torrents and wild crags. It is a romantic scenery, full of melancholy.' I followed my initial journey in reverse and discovered that, although Huedin was founded in the Middle Ages, the centre is quite modern, with many buildings from the 1960s. The road leading west out of Huedin has around eight huge **Roma palaces** (see box, page 265), with shining tin roofs, turrets, balconies and towers; quite a sight in the sunshine, although many are unfinished. From 1330 until 1848, the landlords of the town, which was part of the Kingdom of Hungary, were the Bánffy family. Recently, Huedin has become known for many ecotourism initiatives.

Trains run from Cluj-Napoca, Braşov and Bucharest to Budapest all stop in Huedin. By **car**, it is on the main route 1 (E60) towards Oradea and Hungary.

NEGRENI On the second weekend of every October, the village of Negreni (Feketető/Black Lake) turns into a vast **open-air market and fair** when all the hotels and pensions are booked up long in advance as people arrive from all over Romania – and many from Hungary – to meet up with their mates, buy farming equipment, catch up on gossip, eat *mici* (spicy skinless sausages) and toast everyone's good health with endless shots of *ţuică*. Many traders turn up on the Thursday and Friday, and there is an animal market on the following Monday; however, the best day is Saturday, especially if you're looking for folk crafts, antiques or unusual, ancient musical instruments.

Negreni is 25km west of Huedin on route 1/E60. **Buses** and **trains** travel from Cluj-Napoca and are packed for the fair. Try hiring a **car**.

PIATRA CRAMLUI The pass is high in the mountains (582m), just after the village of Bucea, called Bucsa until 1899. It now marks the border between Cluj County in Transylvania and Bihor County in the Crişana region. In the past, the Crişul Repede River often flooded the road in spring, and in 1780, a new road was built leading uphill from Bucea. Habsburg emperor-in-waiting Josef II travelled this way before his coronation and the new road was linked to his name: Királyhágó or 'King's Pass'. A plaque reading 'Királyhágó' was put up in 2007 but removed after a few days. On the top of the mountain there is a great view towards Bihor County and Hungary (a sign reads '318km Budapeşta') in the west and back east over the rolling hills of Transylvania. The pass itself is not very photogenic, full of 1970s-style motels and truck-stop cafés. The Piatra Cramlui restaurant is open 24 hours, if you're desperate for a lorry-driver lunch. On the right, an illegible orange signpost points to a forest road leading to a little wooden **Orthodox church** dating from 1791 hidden away at Vânători. It makes a nice diversion (4.5km) by (sturdy) car or hiking.

THE KALOTASZEG REGION The Kalotaszeg area between Cluj-Napoca and Huedin includes around 50 villages in beautiful surroundings and has a large Hungarian population. It has a remarkable geography, history and ethnography. Authentic Hungarian culture is alive here and is part of everyday life, where old people still wear traditional costumes on Sundays and feast days and travel by horse and cart. The **local embroidery** is particularly famous. It consists of stylised leaves and flowers, in bold colours, usually red on a white background. This style is known as *irásos*, meaning 'drawn' or 'written', as the designs are drawn onto the cloth before being stitched. The **Hungarian Calvinist churches** are famous for their coffered ceilings made of beautifully painted square panels or 'cassettes' (*kazeta*) and also painted pews and galleries. The **cemeteries** deserve attention for their unique carved wooden headstones, originating from pre-Christian Hungarian traditions. The famous Hungarian composers Béla Bartók and Zoltán Kodály travelled around Kalotaszeg collecting thousands of old melodies which served as a rich vein of inspiration for their own compositions as well as preserving the local folk music.

A selection of beautiful Kalotaszeg villages and towns follows, with the Magyar names in brackets: Beliş (Jósikafalva), Călăţele (Kiskalota), Ciucea (Csucsa), Izvoru Crişului (Körösfő), Mărişel (Havasnagyfalu), Mărgău (Meregyó), Mănăstireni (Magyargyerőmonostor), Poieni (Kissebes), Măguri-Răcătău (Rekettyó), Rişca (Roska), Săcuieu (Székelyjó) and Sâncraiu (Kalotaszentkirály). Hungarian anthropologists consider this region a stronghold of Transylvanian Magyar rural culture and many Hungarians make regular cultural pilgrimages here from Budapest.

There is no regular **bus** service to these villages and many people ride on the back of impromptu tractor 'buses'. Hiring a **car** is the best way to explore these villages (see *Cluj-Napoca*, page 251).

SÂNCRAIU Situated 5km southwest of Huedin is Sâncraiu (Kalotaszentkirály), the unofficial 'capital' of the Kalotaszeg region. Kalotaszeg stretches out over glorious rolling hills south of Huedin and the E60 highway.

István Vincze-Kecskés (*Sâncraiu No 291;* \ *0264 257 580;* m *0745 637 352;* e *davincze@clicknet.ro; www.davincze.ro;* ☉ *09.00–18.00 Mon–Sat*) has a drop-in office next to the beautiful white 13th-century church, and provides information on the region and arranging accommodation in nearly 50 little **family-run pensions** in the region, including the Vincze family guesthouse (**$**). Each house has two or three rooms and staying with a family is a great way to see how people live. The food and drink is also of the highest quality. Vincze-Kecskés has a large barn for evening events such as a programme for groups of 20–50 with dinner, music, folk-dancing presentations and classes.

MĂNĂSTIRENI Situated a further 11km to the southeast of Sâncraiu, the village of Mănăstireni (Magyargyerőmonostor) has a lovely 13th-century walled **Calvinist church** with a painted ceiling from the 18th century. The steeple still bears the bullet holes from the Ottoman raids. **Green Mountain Holidays** (*Mănăstireni 277; 407370 jud Cluj;* \ *0364 144 742;* m *0744 637 227;* e *gmh@cluj.astral.ro; www. greenmountainholidays.ro*), an excellent Belgian–Romanian tour operator, are based in the village and specialise in ecotourism with hiking, cycling, skiing, kayaking, steam-train rides, individual and customised trips in Kalotaszeg and the Apuseni Mountains. Through Green Mountain Holidays it is possible to book an entire holiday chalet (sleeping up to four) for a do-it-yourself holiday in glorious countryside.

LACUL BELIŞ AND FÂNTÂNELE Lacul Fântănele is a continuation of Lacul Beliş to the west. The two-in-one lake was created artificially in the 1970s with the construction of a huge dam near Măguri.

During the 1848–49 uprising against the Habsburgs, 200 Hungarian soldiers were killed at the Battle of Mănăstireni. They were buried in a mass grave by a church that was submerged under the waters of Lacul Beliş. Between 1970 and 1974, during the construction of the Fântănele Dam, the old village of Beliş (Jósikafalva) was moved away from its original location in the valley to the nearby hills, but occasionally, in drought-ravaged summers, the spire of the village's church, lying at a depth of 25m under the lake's surface, can be seen rising from the depths.

The **drive** between Sâncraiu and Beliş is beautiful and particularly lovely after the village of Călăţele, where the road weaves among Christmas-tree forests with a bubbling brook to the right. The view of the lake from the road high above recalls an image of the Canadian wilderness. The road to the vertiginous dam at Someşul Cald passes on a high ridge of the Munţii Gilăului with two gorgeous valleys either side. Beside the road, a tap sprouts from the side of a cliff gushing forth spring water. A sign beside reads 'Good for health'. At Someşul Cald, the road crosses the River Someşul Cald at a narrow point between two smaller lakes: Tarniţei and Gilău. There are many delightful houses here and little triangular wooden chalets that reminded me of Moravia in the early 1980s.

⌂ **Where to stay and eat** There are several places to eat, drink and sleep at the lake. The restaurants **Nou** and **Veche** ('New' and 'Old') (☉ *08.00–22.00 daily*) have whacked-up prices (6.50RON for a bottle of iced tea, 6RON for a small bottle of water) but you can't argue with the view from the terrace. **The restaurant** (**$**) is also pretty expensive, but they have a monopoly on the area, and thus the best view.

⌂ **Hotel Bianca** (25 dbl, 5 apts) *407075 Fântănele, Comuna Răşca;* \ *0264 334 163.* Pretty basic rooms, tennis & billiards but a great hiking base. A little like a holiday home for ageing Communist Party members. Restaurant (**$$**) & café. **$$$**

Radu Hotel (25 dbl, 5 apts) 407075 Fântânele, Comuna Râşca; \0264 334 163. Run by the same people as Hotel Bianca with a restaurant ($), conference room, billiards, tennis & ping-pong. A bit cheaper than the Bianca. **$$$**

Pensiunea Fântânele (6 dbl, 3 sgl) Beliş-Fântânele; m 0745 471 344; e pietrealbe@gmail.com; www.pensiuneafantanele.ro. Most rooms have shared bathrooms, & there's a shared kitchen & dining room. **$-$$**

HEADING NORTH

CÂMPIA TRANSILVANIEI Câmpia Transilvaniei (HU Mezőség – 'fieldness') is the name of the countryside of rolling hills between Cluj-Napoca and Târgu Mureş. The population is a mix of Romanians and Hungarians and the Transylvanian folk culture is particularly rich.

Formerly known as the 'Versailles of Transylvania', **Bánffy Castle** (*Castelul Bánffy; Bonţida No 246;* \f *0264 439 858;* e *office@transylvaniatrust.ro; www. transylvaniatrust.ro or www.heritagetraining-banffycastle.org;* ☉ *09.00–19.00 daily*) at **Bonţida** was built in several stages, starting in the 16th century. The tall, square castle tower can be seen from the banks of the River Someş in Răscrui village on the road from Cluj-Napoca heading to Dej. Dénes Bánffy inherited the castle when he was 12. He spent his youth in Vienna at the court of Empress Maria Theresa, who sent him to Transylvania as a high dignitary in charge of the imperial stud farms. In 1747, Bánffy started the reconstruction of the castle. The new structures, designed in the spirit of the Viennese Imperial Baroque style consisted of a riding hall, stables and servants' quarters. The courtyard was decorated with more than 30 Baroque statues, representing characters from Ovid's *Metamorphoses*. In 1820, József Bánffy tore down the gate building and enlarged the courtyard, building a watermill in the vicinity. He also created an English-style park in the surroundings. In 1944, the estate was devastated when the retreating German troops plundered the castle, then set it on fire. The furniture, the library, the famous portrait gallery and the sculpture gallery are now preserved only in a few photographs. The last member of the Bánffy family to live at Bonţida was Miklós, author of *The Transylvania Trilogy* (see *Appendix 2, Further Information*, page 284). The dilapidated condition of the castle was officially confirmed in 1999, when it was added to the World Monuments Fund (*http://wmf.org*) list of 100 most endangered sites. The Transylvania Trust (*www.artnouveau.org/TTF*) is working to restore the castle to use as an educational and training centre for restoration. In 1963 the castle was used as a set for Romanian director Liviu Ciulei's film *Forest of the Hanged*, which won Best Director at Cannes.

Travelling by **car**, Bonţida is 33km from Cluj-Napoca on the E576 towards Dej. More than 15 **buses** leave Cluj-Napoca bus station daily for Bonţida (*30mins*). Eight *personal* **trains** leave Cluj-Napoca railway station daily (*38mins*).

SIC The surprisingly large village of Sic (Szék/Seckgen) plays an extremely important role in Transylvanian Hungarian folk culture. Sic village was once an important centre for salt mining and spread over several hills with a number of churches and municipal buildings. **Folk traditions** and **folk music** are lovingly preserved in Sic. The women in the predominantly Magyar (96%) village still wear folk costumes coloured red and black, colours originating from the Turkish occupation: red for blood and black for mourning when all the menfolk were wiped out. Above the full red and black skirts, they wear a tight leather waistcoat and a white headscarf. Visitors to Budapest might spot these Széki ladies, often near the main market hall (Nagy Vásárcsarnok) selling folk crafts. They arrive regularly on the eight-hour bus from Cluj. Sic is famous for its enthusiasm for folk music and visitors will hear tunes coming from the houses as they walk around. In the past, the three districts of the village each had its own dance house with quite distinct styles. These days, folk music dances are more for weddings and special events.

Seven **buses** travel daily from Gherla. By **car**, the route from Cluj-Napoca follows a high loop heading north to Gherla on the E576 and turning right onto the road signed for Țaga and then right again after 2km and heading south through the countryside to Sic.

Where to stay

Sóvirág Panzió (3 dbl, 7 twin bed, 2 apts) Sic/Szék; 📞0264 228 004; e sallai.janos@yahoo. com; www.soviragpanzio.ro. Located at the beginning of the village when approaching from Gherla, the Sóvirág has clean rooms with furniture painted with folk motifs such as red tulips on black & a large, rustic restaurant ($). **$$**

NICULA In 2002, **Nicula Monastery** celebrated 450 years since its first written mention in 1552. The village and surrounding forest get their name from a hermit Nicolae who lived around 1326. The monastery was initially constructed as a modest hermitage and as a place where the peasants could find refuge from marauding Tatars. In 1659, the building became a religious school and a place of pilgrimage to see the miraculous weeping icon of the Virgin Mary. In 1681, the Orthodox priest, Luca of Iclod, painted an icon of the Holy Virgin and in 1699, villagers were astonished to see the icon shed tears for 26 days. This event predicted a period of great suffering for the Transylvanians: natural disasters, occupation by foreign powers and religious tension, and consequently the monastery soon became famous throughout the country. On 15 August, the **Assumption of the Virgin Mary,** up to 300,000 people cram into the little village. Nicula village saw the inauguration of the first school of painting on glass in Transylvanian and many icon painters still live here. Nicula Monastery has one of the largest collections of icons on wood and glass and the tiny wooden church dating from 1650, brought from the hamlet of Năsal to replace an earlier wooden church (1552) which was destroyed by fire in 1973, has a good display of icons.

Travelling by **car**, follow the road to Sic, heading north to Gherla on the E576 and turning right onto the road signed for Țaga and then right again after 2km towards Sic. Nicula is the first village you pass through. Turn left in the village for the *mănăstire*.

GHERLA Gherla (Szamosújvár/Nauschloss, Armenierstadt) was once an important centre for the Armenian minority. In 1672, the Transylvanian prince Mihály Apafi I let Armenian refugees from the Tatar raids settle in Bistrița and they eventually moved to Gherla and built the town, then called Armenopolis. Many became successful cattle traders and the settlement was a wealthy urban centre. Carved Armenian family crests are still visible over many doorways and the town is unique in being the first planned town in eastern Europe with its streets on a grid system. The Baroque **Armenian-Catholic cathedral**, built between 1748 and 1804, adorns the town centre. Gherla is also famous for its **prison**, created in a 16th-century bastioned castle and used from 1650 onwards to keep prisoners. In the communist period, the prison was known as the harshest in the country and the word 'Gherla' in Romanian is synonymous with 'gaol'. It is called Hayakaghak in Armenian.

Gherla is 45km northeast of Cluj-Napoca. Frequent **buses** travel along the E576 highway to Bistrița.

DEJ Fans of Gothic architecture will not want to miss out Dej (Dés/Desch) on a tour of the region as it has one of the most beautiful 15th-century **Gothic Calvinist churches** in the country. In 1752, the most famous stone carver in Transylvania, Dávid Sipos, created the pulpit. Dej's **Municipal Museum** (*Muzeul Municipal Dej; Piaţa Bobâlna 2;* \ *0264 212 525; http://muzeulmunicipal.dej.ro;* ⊕ *10.00–16.00 Tue–Sun; admission adult/child 4/1RON*) shows exhibits concerned with medieval history, the 1848–49 uprising and the local salt mines.

Dej is 60km northeast of Cluj-Napoca, on the E576 highway that passes through Gherla, Dej and Beclean *en route* to Bitriţa. Frequent **buses** travel along the E576.

HEADING SOUTHEAST

TURDA Turda (Torda/Thorenburg) has a significant place in Transylvania's religious history as in 1568 the **Diet of Turda** granted freedom of worship and equal rights for Transylvania's four 'accepted' (*receptae*) faiths: Roman Catholic, Lutheran, Calvinist and Unitarian. However, at first glance, modern-day Turda doesn't have a lot going for it, besides the name, which would be every schoolboy's scatological giggle. Turda's town centre is a bit of a mess, a long, dusty main street surrounding Piaţa Republicii with many darkened shop windows and money-changing offices, but the town has several secret weapons and reasons why you should stay longer. The highlight of Turda is the **Turda Salt Mine** (*Salina Turda; Str Salinelor 54B;* \f *0264 311 690; www.salinaturda.eu;* ⊕ *09.00–17.00 daily; admission adult/child 15/8RON*), where visitors take a 90-minute guided tour around the chambers, although it is also possible to buy an English-language pamphlet and go it alone. The salt mine operated from 1231–1972 and a selection of chambers can be reached along a creepy 500m tunnel. The Franz Jozef gallery, dug in 1853–70 is a horizontal cave used for moving the salt to the surface. From 1948–92 the gallery was used as a cheese storehouse. The impressive Rudolf Mine is a trapezium-shaped extraction hall started in 1867. The ceiling is spiked with salt stalactites which grow to a length of 3m then snap off under the strain of their own weight. Be careful where you stand! The bell-shaped Terezia Mine is possibly the most beautiful with an underground lake and a cascade of salt crystals flowing from above like a frozen waterfall. The Gizela Mine holds a gallery and frequent art exhibitions and there is also an altar carved in salt so that the miners could attend religious services.

An annual festival, **Turda Fest** (*Asociaţia Turda Fest, Piaţa 1 Decembrie 1918 1;* \ *0264 317 555;* e *office@turdafest.ro; www.turdafest.ro*), takes place at the end of September and is the first agrarian festival in Romania designed for the whole family, incorporating multi-cultural activities from Transylvanian communities. Turda Fest also promotes tourism in Turda and the Apuseni Mountains. Events include hot-air balloon rides, folklore performances, a pageant and traditional costumes parade when surrounding villages present a traditionally decorated chariot and a traditional craft fair when artisans demonstrate their skills in woodcarving, painting, embroidery and leatherwork. Romanian cuisine is also on display and culinary treats can be tasted along with a showcase from the Slow Food delegation. Other novelties include record-breaking attempts at the world's longest onion string, or the longest *kürtös kalács* (a traditional Hungarian cylinder of sweet milkbread).

Turda is 32km southeast of Cluj-Napoca on the hectic E60/E81 highway. It is not on a railway line, but **buses** and **maxi-taxis** run regularly to Cluj-Napoca (*30mins*), Târgu Mureş (*1hr*) and Alba Iulia (*35mins*).

Transylvania has a deep-rooted shepherding culture and delicious cheeses are made on site, high in the mountains, although if the EU has its way, this might cease.

Brânză afumată	Smoked cheese
Brânză de vaci	Cottage cheese
Brânză topită	Processed cheese
Caş	Unsalted ewe's milk cheese, a bit like feta
Caşcaval	A hard dairy cheese, like Cheddar
Şvaiţer	Like a Swiss Emmental
Telemea	*Caş* that has been stored in brine
Urdă	A soft unfermented cheese, made from whey after making *caş*

In Zărneşti, I tasted a particular special log-shaped cheese wrapped in bark which infused the cheese with a delicious, unusual aroma.

Tourist information

⛨ Transylvania Live Contact Alin Todea; Str Republicii 28, Turda; ☏ 0364 405 641; e contact@ visit-transylvania.us; www.visit-transylvania.eu; office ☉ 09.00–16.00 Mon–Fri. This Anglo- Romanian company, based in both Turda & London, are experts in guided tours & tailor-made holidays in Transylvania.

 Where to stay and eat Turda also has another secret treasure, hidden away along a back street: the bizarre, over-imaginative Dracula-themed hotel with interior décor so over the top you have to admire its gumption.

⌂ Turda Castelul Prinţul şi Dracula/Hunter Prince & Dracula Castle (9 sgl, 2 dbl, 5 junior suites, 2 suites) Str Şuluţiu 4–6; ☏ 0264 316 850; f 0264 311 171; e contact@huntermail.eu; www.huntercastle.ro. Designed by owner Adrian Sărmăsan & his wife, every aspect of the 4-star rooms' & restaurant's interiors has been decorated down to the last light switch, with a unique style. The showers are like caves with stone walls, 1 room has its own sauna (€10/hr for other guests, when not occupied), & there are antiques & hunting trophies all over. The restaurant (☉ *07.00–midnight daily;* $$) has a huge, gory battle mural & it's like a medieval banqueting hall in a film directed by Fellini & Buñuel. There is a Gaudi-esque mosaic-strewn terrace garden & a cellar tavern underground. Even if you don't stay for a night, be sure to drop in for a meal or a coffee. It's an experience, to say the least! $$$$

TURDA GORGE Turda Gorge (Cheile Turzii) is just half an hour's drive north out of Turda on the E60 road towards Cluj-Napoca. Take the left turning opposite the church and head for Petreştii de Jos. Continue past a quarry along a road, which bends around to the left. In a small village, you'll see a yellow sign indicating 'Turzii gorges'. It is the most wonderful place for a Sunday **afternoon stroll** or a **strenuous hike**. The gorge is overshadowed by 300m-high, almost vertical, limestone cliffs where outlaws used to hide out in some of the 60 caves. The cliffs are ideal for **free climbing** and there are more than 100 routes with all levels of difficulty. The 1.5km-long gorge has a large variety of morphological features: caves, fossils, towers and arcades formed by the river's repeated attempts to penetrate the limestone walls. The canyon has a unique microclimate, providing a habitat for flora usually only found in central Asia or by the Mediterranean Sea. The only thing spoiling the view is the amount of litter lazily discarded by the rushing stream, beer cans and fizzy drink bottles being the worst offenders. English ramblers should be warned that oncoming hikers don't stop on the narrow slippery path through the gorge but charge straight ahead, gaze fixed firmly on the horizon. Be prepared to hurl yourself into the undergrowth rather than down the steep cliffside into the tributary of the Arieș River. By the car park there is a small **café** (⊕ *08.00–20.00 daily*) and a lawn out the front where some locals have pitched their tents. Reached across a footbridge made from two tree trunks, it's a good place to buy coffee, ice cream or beer. Gorge 'taxes' (*adult/child 5/2RON*) are paid to an old guy in a kagoul, sitting in a hut.

11

Bistrița-Năsăud County

The region (5,355km²) of Bistrița-Năsăud County is, according to Bram Stoker, 'In the midst of the Carpathian Mountains; one of the wildest and least known portions of Europe.' One-third of the county is covered with mountains from the Eastern Carpathian range. The Someşul Mare River crosses the county and on the Bistrița River there is a huge dam and Lacul Colibiţa, where an excellent sports centre and tour company has a vast range of tourism suggestions.

According to the 2011 census, Bistrița-Năsăud has a population of 277,861, of which 90% are Romanian, 5% Hungarian, 4% Roma and 0.2% German. The mountains and hills are home to a diverse range of flora. Along the river valleys, in river meadows and terraces situated in the southwest region, there are farmed fields where cereals and vegetables are the popular crops. The mountains are home to many protected animal species such as the Carpathian bear, Carpathian stag, black and white stork, hazel hen and black eagle. Edelweiss grows in the limestone areas of the Rodna Mountains and other protected species in the alpine zone include mountain marigold, yew tree, yellow gentian and mountain narcissus.

Bistrița-Năsăud County is popular with visitors who love the outdoor life, with many opportunities for sports, excursions on mountain bikes, horseriding or trekking.

Bistrița City and the Tihuţa Pass (Borgó Pass) is also popular with visitors exploring the Dracula myth, because Bram Stoker placed Dracula's castle near Bistrița and the city exploits this link to the max. The county lost out when the Dracula Land Park project folded, but plans to go it alone and develop a Transylvania Legend Land project with holiday homes, folk-craft tuition, horseriding, sports and folklore facilities as well as training in rural and mountain tourism. SC Coroana Tourism hopes to attract investment from western European and North American businesses.

BISTRIȚA   *Telephone code 0263, sometimes 0363*

Bistrița (Beszterce/Bistritz) is a charming, if rather isolated city, which only gets attention because of the Dracula link. Bram Stoker chose the Bărgău River valley to be the setting for Dracula's castle and Stoker's lead character Jonathan Harker stopped in Bistrița on his way to stay with the Count. However, Bistrița has a clutch of interesting sights, a good museum and a beautiful main square dominated by an elegant Saxon Evangelical church. Bistrița is one of the seven fortress towns or Siebenburgen, the German name for Transylvania, and has a population of around 80,000. The Saxon minority has almost disappeared since the early 1990s. Bistrița lies in northern Transylvania on the Bistrița River, in a region of hills covered with orchards. The city's industries are mainly mechanical engineering, electro-technical, textiles, wood processing and glassworks.

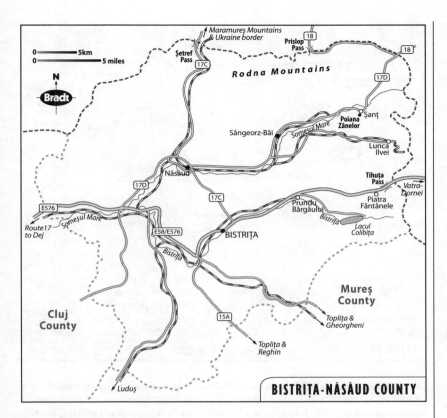

The city consists of two distinct parts: to the southwest is the medieval district surrounding the Piața Centrală and streets nearby; and the pedestrian Strada Liviu Rebreanu leads up in a northeasterly direction to the Orthodox church where there is a more modern district with housing estates, banks and many of the most popular hotels.

HISTORY Archaeological findings show that the area was inhabited during the Neolithic Age, the Bronze Age, the Iron Age and the ancient Dacian era. Bistrița is one of the oldest Transylvanian towns. Pecheneg tribes settled the area in the 12th century after being attacked by the Cumans. In 1206, Transylvanian Saxons settled the area and called the region Nösnerland. Tatars destroyed the Markt Nosa (Nösen market) when heading towards central Europe in 1241. Bistrița was situated on several important trade routes and flourished as a trading post in the Middle Ages. The town was named after the Bistrița River flowing through the centre. The name comes from the Slavic word *bystrica* meaning 'limpid water'. By 1349, the town had become a city with its name changed to 'civitas Bysterce'. Saxon colonists brought to the region by Hungarian king Geza II contributed to the development of the city as a prosperous craft and trade centre. Called Bistritz by the Saxons, it was one of Transylvania's (Siebenburgen) most important and influential Saxon citadels. In 1353, Bistrița was granted the right to organise an annual fair and have its own seal. Its coat of arms showed an ostrich with a horseshoe in its beak, which according to medieval heraldry, symbolised that trade was one of the inhabitants'

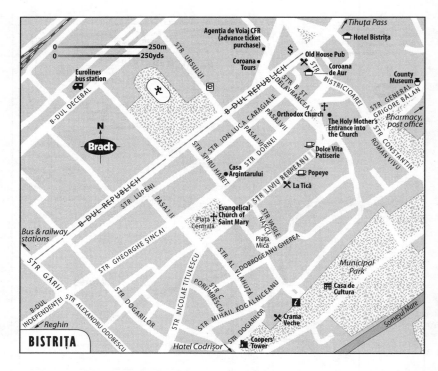

main occupations. In 1453, Ioan de Hunedoara took control of the city and built a citadel in the northeastern part. The city's defensive fortifications were completed by the beginning of the 16th century. Between the 15th and 18th centuries, Bistriţa established close economic links with the Rodna valley area and Moldavia to the east. During the 16th century, Bistriţa was an important cultural centre. In 1602, the troops of Austrian general Giorgio Basta damaged the city's defence system followed by a plague that only made matters worse. The city was devastated during the 1848–49 revolution, when it was seized in succession by the revolutionary and the Habsburg armies. In 1862–63, the Imperial Court of Vienna ordered that the medieval city gates be destroyed. In 1876, Bistriţa became the county town of Bistriţa-Năsăud County.

The first modernisation project took place in the late 19th century and electric current was provided at the beginning of the 20th century. Bistriţa became part of Romania in 1918, apart from a period of Hungarian occupation between 1940 and 1944.

GETTING THERE AND AWAY The railway and bus stations are situated next to each other to the northwest of the centre at the northern end of Strada Gării. Eight buses leave daily for Braşov (*8hrs*) from the **bus station** (✆ *0263 233 655*), four buses leave daily for Cluj-Napoca (*3hrs*), seven to Târgu Mureş (*2½hrs*) and three to Sibiu (*6hrs*). From the **railway station** (✆ *0263 223 572*) travellers can take a night train to Bucharest (*10hrs*), or one of four daily trains to Cluj-Napoca (*4hrs*).

For rail information, contact **Agenţia de Voiaj CFR** (*Piaţa Petru Rareş 7A;* ✆ *0263 213 938;* ⊕ *09.00–14.00 Mon–Fri*) or the **Bistriţa Eurolines bus station** at B-dul Decebal 15 (✆ *0263 235 502;* e *biSt.ita@eurolines.ro; www.eurolines.ro*).

TOURIST INFORMATION

ℹ Tourist Information Centre Casa de Cultura, Str Albert Berger 10; ☏0263 219 919; ⏱ 09.00–17.00 Mon–Fri. Situated in a large building in the Municipal Park to the southeast of the Piața Centrală.

ℹ Coroana Tours Piața Petru Rareş 7A; ☏0263 231 803 or 0263 212 056; ⏱ 08.00–17.00 Mon–Fri. If the tourist information centre in the park is not open – it shuts suddenly for no reason – this tourist office has maps, accommodation advice & a lot of information.

WHERE TO STAY

⌂ Coroana de Aur (6 sgl, 104 dbl, 4 apts) Piața Petru Rareş 4; ☏0263 232 470 or 0263 232 471; www.hotel-coroana-de-aur.ro. A 3-star hotel in a large tower block. Stoker's Jonathan Harker stayed at the Golden Krone Hotel & this modern block attempts to link itself to the novel with Harker & Dracula mentioned at every opportunity, as the hotel was built in the 1970s on the site of the inn where Harker stayed. The restaurant ($$) serves traditional favourites & there's a Dracula țuică, a blood-red elixir! Visits to

the Castel Dracula hotel at Piatra Fântânele can also be arranged. **$$$**

⌂ Hotel Bistrița (49 dbl) Piața Petru Rareş 2; ☏0263 231 154; e hotel@hotel-bistrita.ro; www.hotel-bistrita.ro. A pink, 3-star hotel behind a bank across from the Coroana de Aur. The restaurant ($) is not bad. **$$**

⌂ Hotel Codrişor (29 dbl) Str Codrişor 28; ☏0263 233 814; e hotel@hotel-bistrita.ro; www.hotel-bistrita.ro. The terrace restaurant ($) by a large pool is popular in summer. **$$**

WHERE TO EAT AND DRINK

✗ Crama Veche Albert Berger 10; m 0730 011 812; www.crama-veche.ro; ⏱ 10.00–midnight daily. A great restaurant in the Municipal Park behind the Casa de Cultura. Shares a huge terrace with the Corrida en Sol café-bar. **$$**

✗ Old House Pub Str Petru Rareş 7; m 0771 763 073; ⏱ 10.00–23.00 daily. A plaque by the front door reads 'Jonathan Harker stayed here 31 May 1893.' Formerly the Coronița. **$$**

🍺 Dolce Vita Patiserie Str Liviu Rebreanu 33; ⏱ 09.00–18.00 Mon–Fri, 09.00–22.00 Sat. A very popular hole in the wall dispensing pizza slices &

foietaj – little pastries stuffed with vanilla crème, nuts, poppy seeds, apples & cherries. **$**

✗ La Tică Str Rebreanu 10; ⏱ 09.00–22.00 Mon–Fri, 10.00–23.00 Sat, 12.00–23.00 Sun. A good, cheap local bistro with mămăligă served with sheep's cheese, balmoş (deep-fried mămăligă balls rolled around cheese) & ciorbă (sour soup). **$**

✗ Popeye Str Liviu Rebreanu 36; ⏱ 09.00–22.00 Mon–Fri, 10.00–22.00 Sat, 12.00–22.00 Sun. A fun fast-food-type joint with seating outside on the pedestrian street. Kebabs, sandwiches, chips & coffee. **$**

SILVER-ROOFED ROMA PALACES

If driving to Bistrița from the south on route 15A from Târgu Mureş via Reghin, you will come across some unusual and striking structures in the village of Sărățel. These huge mansions have many silver spires but they are not churches; they are homes for wealthy Roma families. The exterior walls are often brightly coloured – orange and pink being favourite hues – and richly decorated.

The style is thought to have come from western India, the homeland of the Roma's ancestors. These constructions first started appearing in the 1990s after many Roma left for western Europe to find better-paid work and returned home with their euros to build these lavish structures with shining tin roofs. Quite often the buildings appear to be unfinished and still uninhabited, as the funds ran out before completion. Other places to see the palaces are around Sibiu, Huedin and Cluj.

OTHER PRACTICALITIES

Bank

$ Banca Transilvania B-dul Republicii 3;
⊕ 09.00–18.00 Mon–Fri, 09.30–12.30 Sat. With
24hr ATM accepting Visa & MasterCard.

Internet

e Str Ursului 14; ⊕ 10.00–midnight Sun–Thu,
10.00–06.00 Fri/Sat; 1.5RON/hr

Pharmacy

✚ Farmacie Str Ştefan cel Mare 1; ⊕ 08.00–
20.00 Mon–Fri, 08.00–14.00 Sat. On the same
street as the post office; look for the green cross.

Post office

✉ Poşta Romană Str Ştefan cel Mare 9;
⊕ 07.00–20.00 Mon–Fri, 08.00–13.00 Sat.
Situated quite a long way out of the centre, to the
northeast of town.

WHAT TO SEE AND DO

'It was on the dark side of twilight when we got to Bistritz, which is a very interesting old
place. Being practically on the frontier – for the Borgo Pass leads from it into Bukovina
– it has had a very stormy existence, and it certainly shows marks of it. Fifty years ago a
series of great fires took place, which made terrible havoc on five separate occasions. At
the very beginning of the seventeenth century it underwent a siege of three weeks and
lost 13,000 people, the casualties of war proper being assisted by famine and disease.

Count Dracula had directed me to go to the Golden Krone Hotel, which I found,
to my great delight, to be thoroughly old-fashioned, for of course I wanted to see all I
could of the ways of the country.'

From Jonathan Harker's journal, Chapter 1, Dracula, *by Bram Stoker*

The older part of Bistriţa is dominated by the imposing, Saxon **Evangelical
Church of Saint Mary** (⊕ *10.00–12.00 & 14.00–17.00 Tue–Sat, 15.00–17.00 Sun*),
dating from the 14th–15th centuries, situated in the middle of the Piaţa Centrală,
flanked by lovely 15th-century arched arcades of the Şugălete **merchants'
houses**. The church was constructed originally in the Gothic style on the site of
a Roman church. Petrus Italus da Lugano converted it into the Renaissance style
in 1559–63. The nave holds a collection of 23 flags belonging to the guilds of
the town and a 500-year-old organ. In 1516, Johannes Begler made the valuable
Renaissance pews. The Saxons' Tower (76.5m) is the tallest church tower in all
Romania. The church was restored several times in 1897, 1901, 1927 and also
2007. Just northeast of the square, the **Casa Argintarului** (Silversmith's House),
built in the 15th century and restored twice in the 16th century and also after
the great fire of 1758, is the former lodging of a renowned jeweller. Its façades
are adorned with fine stone carvings in the Renaissance style made by Petrus
Italus da Lugano. Nowadays, the house holds the **Fine Arts, Music and Folk
Dance School** (Şcoala de Arte; ⊕ *08.00–20.00 Mon–Fri*). Head southeast towards
the Bistriţa River to find the lovely, shaded **Municipal Park**, with the **Casa de
Cultura** and several restaurants. Southwest of the park is the **Turnul Dogarilor**
(Coopers' Tower), the remains of the 13th-century city walls and fortifications.
The tower has a gallery with a collection of folklore masks and puppets. After a
stroll along the café-lined pedestrian street **Strada Liviu Rebreanu**, you come to
one of two Orthodox churches, the **Holy Mother's Entrance into the Church**,
a 13th-century Cistercian structure, with neo-Byzantine murals and colourful
icons. It's a bit of a hike northeast to find the excellent **County Museum** (*Muzeul
Judeţean; Str G-ral Grigore Balan 19;* ☏ *0263 211 063; http://complexulmuzealbn.
ro;* ⊕ *Oct–Mar 09.00–17.00 Tue–Sun, Apr–Sep 10.00–18.00 Tue–Sun; admission
adult/child 5/2RON*) with an overgrown garden, ponds and a small wooden

church in the back courtyard and collections of artefacts by Dacian, Celtic and Saxon craftsmen.

AROUND BISTRIȚA

LACUL COLIBIȚA Setting off for the Pasul Tihuța (Borgó Pass in *Dracula*) on Transylvania's northeast border, journey along the E576/route 17, an important highway in the direction of Bucovina and Moldova, heading northeast out of Bistrița. After 23km, at Prundu Bârgăului, turn right and drive for 5km to the lake. By **bus**, two buses leave Bistrița's bus station at 08.30 and 15.00, journey time 46 minutes. From there, it's 18km to the lake; **hitching** is an option. At the railway level crossing at **Livezile**, opportunistic mushroom sellers thrust huge buckets of fungi at their captive audience. At **Prundu Bârgăului**, a busy, industrial village of 1960s concrete buildings, it is possible to fork off to the right for a refreshing break at the gorgeous Lacul Colibița. The lake, created by a manmade dam, has been documented since 1760 and sits at an altitude of 830m and is a wonderful summer destination. Its 'beaches' are filled with campers and people enjoying watersports. Caliman Club Holidays has its own outdoor centre (*Caliman Club Colibița Center; 229A, Lacul Colibița, Bistrița-Năsăud County; contact Doru Munteanu m 0744 600 148; see also page 54 for contact details*) by the lake and offers a vast range of holidays, trips, treks and sports. Visitors can try mountain biking, hiking, rafting, kayaking, windsurfing, snowboarding and skiing. The outdoor centre comprises a **mini-hotel** of 44 beds in 23 rooms (*3 sgl, 19 dbl, 1 trpl*) all with their own bathrooms, a **youth hostel** (*20 beds*) with kitchen, toilets, showers and laundry facilities, a restaurant, bar, equipment for all the outdoor activities and a staff of specialised guides and instructors. Lacul Colibița is also the location of an all-Romanian construction project, the **Hotel Dracula Secret Castel**, a €1.5 million holiday complex in a 'macabre' style befitting the prince of darkness.

THROUGH THE MOUNTAINS TO THE PASUL TIHUȚA From Prundu Bârgăului, back on the main E576 highway, it's a wonderful drive (30km) to the Pasul Tihuța (1,200m), known in *Dracula* as the Borgó Pass, in the Bârgău Mountains. The road is dotted with haystacks shaped like ripe pears, dotting the grassy slopes between the pine forests. In the autumn, the fog can descend quite suddenly, obscuring the view, so check the weather forecast before setting out. Long logging lorries hurtle past at full tilt and the view at the Tihuța Pass is breathtaking. Between October and April, the road across the pass may be blocked by snowdrifts, but you can always stop off at the small village of **Piatra Fântânele**, at the Hotel Castel Dracula (see below) to warm up with some hot soup before heading off on a mountain hike. The surrounding region has more brown bears than any other part of Europe, and also boars, red deer and wolves. A magical light hangs over the fir- and haystack-dotted meadows and fields far below so that the scene resembles a pastoral painting. The Hotel Castel Dracula is a hulking great concrete block construction, built in 1983, during the Ceaușescu era in an attempt to lure hard-currency-laden Dracula fans from the West. In the car park at the front is a bust of Bram Stoker (1847–1912) holding a copy of the novel, acknowledging the Romanian tourist industry's debt to the Irish author. The décor is all faux-medieval banqueting hall-style with wrought-iron chandeliers, wooden beams and huge dining chairs. There's a humorous 'Dracula's Grave' room (*admission 1RON*), although we all remember the Count is supposed to be buried at Lacul

Snagov near Bucharest. Be prepared: the coffin reveals a live 'surprise' so don't be too nervous. I hope I haven't spoiled the effect!

One daily **microbus** leaves Bistriţa bus station at 12.45 (*1¼hrs*). By **car**, the hotel is easy to find on the straight road E576 all the way for 52km.

Where to stay and eat

🏠 **Hotel Castel Dracula** (124 dbl, 3 apts) 427363 Piatra Fântânele; ☎ 0263 264 010; e contact@hotelcasteldracula.ro; www. hotelcasteldracula.ro. A 3-star hotel with a great restaurant ($), featuring a heavy tome as a menu & good *mămăligă, ciorbă,* rice & meat dishes, & *clătite cu ciocolată* (chocolate pancakes). Rooms are simple & clean but the bathrooms have attracted some criticism. **$$$**

LUNCA ILVEI Lunca Ilvei is a village in northeast Transylvania in the Ilva River valley. British mechanical engineer Julian Ross relocated to Lunca Ilvei where he established an equestrian centre. In early 2008, Ross had to return to the UK for health reasons and together with Count Tibor Kálnoky (see page 155), it was decided to transfer seven of Ross's horses as well as his know-how to the 'Woodlands' region of Covasna County, near the Kálnoky Estates at Micloşoara/Miklósvár and Valea Crişului/Sepsikőröspatak. Horses are vitally important to the Romanian rural economy. Not only are they used widely in peasant agriculture, they are also more cost effective than tractors. However, there are problems: horse-drawn farm implements are outdated and limited in scope. Horse-drawn logging implements are also ineffective. Second, farriery as practised in Romania is poor, which reduces the working lives of horses and, on occasions, causes equine suffering. Horses have suffered greatly and have been abandoned in large numbers since a law came into effect (see also box, page 83) banning horses and carts from Romania's main roads.

Getting there and away It is not possible to cut across country from the Tihuţa Pass and the Hotel Castel Dracula to visit the equestrian centre at Lunca Ilvei. Although still indicated on many maps and auto atlases, the road from Poiana Stampei on the E576 just beyond the Tihuţa Pass to Lunca Ilvei via the Grădiniţa Pass was blown up in 1944 and has not been reinstated. Rumours circulate that the road will be rebuilt as a gravel track for forestry activities, but at the moment the best way of reaching Lunca Ilvei from Bistriţa is to head for Sângeorz-Băi and fork right after the village of Ilva Mică. Lunca Ilvei is about 30km further east. If approaching from the east on the main E576 highway it is possible to make a short cut to Ilva Mică at Josenii Bârgăului. The road is partly gravel track but it is passable except after snowfall. There is only one direct **bus** between Bistriţa and Năsăud (*2¾hrs*). However, there are regular buses between Bistriţa and Năsăud (*1hr*), and from Năsăud there are three daily **trains** to Lunca Ilvei (*1hr*).

Where to stay

🏠 **Casa Alexandra** (7 dbl) Str Principală 42, Lunca Ilvei; ☎ 0264 525 513; m 0722 218 295; e uionel@email.ro, ecolunca@go.ro or cornelia_ ureche@yahoo.com; www.ecolunca.go.ro or www. ruraltourism.ro/alexandra. Casa Alexandra is a wooden holiday home, built in a rustic style. Run by Cornelia Ureche, the guesthouse is a member of the Association of Ecotourism in Romania & welcomes guests who value & appreciate the natural environment. The house can accommodate 22 people & it is possible to rent the entire house for a group at a cost of 600RON per night, or 999RON for the weekend (2 nights, 3 days). Ureche offers theme-based hiking, cross-country skiing, snowshoe tours, forest-fruit collecting, farm activities such as milking & hay collecting, &

guided walks in the forest. Self-catering is possible in a large, fully equipped kitchen, & there is a large dining area & living room with a huge ceramic stove. Meals can be provided for groups of 4 or more (dinner 30RON pp). The outdoor wooden pavilion has a traditional bread oven & barbeque & is great for summer parties. To get there by car, arriving from Năsăud (a small town & railway connecting station 20km north of Bistriţa on route 17C/D) from the village sign of Lunca Ilvei, continue for about 1.7km. The house is located on the right side of the road & has a green sign 'Retea Turistica'. If coming by train, several trains leave Năsăud daily for Lunca Ilvei; get off & go down the main street, turn right & continue for 1km. The guesthouse is on the left. *B/fast not inc.* **$**

SÂNGEORZ-BĂI Sângeorz-Băi (Oláhszentgyörgy/Rumänisch-Sankt-Gören) is a well-known **spa resort** set in the heart of the mountains. The town lies on the Someşul Mare River and the spa became popular at the beginning of the 20th century attracting countless visitors to the unspoiled Transylvanian countryside around the Cormaia Valley. Members of the Aurora Bank Society named the mineral water springs Hebe after Zeus's daughter, the goddess of eternal youth and the Olympian gods' cup-bearer. Another story says that the name comes from when the hospitable locals urged travellers to *Hai bei!* ('Come on, drink!') and the two words shortened to *hebe*. The mineral-rich waters are particularly good for treating digestive problems.

By **car** from Bistriţa, head east out of town on the E576 and outside town turn left onto route 17C for Năsăud. At Năsăud, turn right onto route 17D and drive for 20km to reach Sângeorz-Băi. There are regular **buses** between Bistriţa and Năsăud (*1hr*), and from there, one daily bus (*10.00; 1hr*) to Sângeorz-Băi.

 Where to stay and eat

🏠 **Hebe Hotel** (285 dbl, 5 apts) Str Trandafirilor 10; ☎ 0263 370 521; e receptie@hotel-hebe. com; www.hotel-hebe.com. The hotel is perfect for those taking the water cures as the restaurant (**$$**) provides special diets for patients. **$**

POIANA ZÂNELOR Situated in the foothills of the Rodna Mountains, the resort's name translates as 'Fairies' Meadow, the location of many local fairy tales. The resort is a collection of wooden chalets and is ideal for anyone who wants to explore the Rodna Mountains. Many trails lead off into the hills, heading for the Ineu Peak (2,279m) where Lacul Lala Mare (2,000m) is a fantastic, deserted mountain lake, reachable only on foot. Less taxing is the hike to the Fântânele Peak (1,201m).

By **car** from Bistriţa, head east out of town on the E576 and outside town turn left onto route 17C for Năsăud. At Năsăud, turn right onto route 17D and drive for 48km to reach the village of Şanţ. The drive is very pleasant with the soaring Rodna mountain peaks to the left and the Bârgău range to the right. Two **buses** leave Bistriţa daily for Şanţ (*weekdays only; 2hrs 50mins*).

 Where to stay

🏠 **Poiana Zânelor** (36 dbl, 19 trpl, 13 quad, 5 apts) Şanţ village, Valea Mare; m 0724 028 224; e rezervari@poianazanelor.ro; www. poianazanelor.ro. Separate chalets dotted over a scenic meadow with a restaurant (**$**) & pizzeria (**$**). **$**

RODNA MOUNTAINS The Rodna Mountains (Munţii Rodnei) are a subdivision of the Eastern Carpathians in northern Romania. The name comes from the nearby Rodna Veche village.

Part of the Rodna range is in Bistriţa-Năsăud County, but the Rodna National Park is over the Transylvanian border in Maramureş County.

The Rodna Mountains have one of the longest continuous ridges in the country, stretching for more than 50km from west to east. The two highest points are the peaks of Pietrosul Rodnei (2,303m) and Ineu (2,279m). The massif has some caves, notably **Izvorul Tăuşoarelor**, the deepest cave in the country, sinking 479m beneath the surface.

The main ridge of the Rodna Mountains provides a natural border for Transylvania, between the counties of Bistriţa-Năsăud and Maramureş in the north. Route 18 travels through the famous **Prislop Pass** on a lovely journey filled with breathtaking scenery. Further west, the **Şetref Pass** can be crossed by car or train from Beclean railway station via Dealu Ştefăniţei station near the border.

For information on mountain and other emergency services, see box, page 112.

12

Sălaj County

Sălaj County (3,864km²) lies in the region between the Apuseni Mountains and the Eastern Carpathians in an area known as the Someş River plateau, from the Someş (HU Szamos) River. Other smaller rivers are the Crasna, Barcău, Almaş, Agrij and Sălaj. This region, known as the Szilágyság in Hungarian, is very beautiful with rolling hills, vast cornfields, oak forests and shadoof-style wells dotted around. These wells are also found just over the Hungarian border in the Hortóbágy National Park.

Only the southeastern chunk of Sălaj County is officially in Transylvania. The northeastern Transylvanian border leads from around Ileanda in the northeast near the meeting of three counties (Sălaj, Cluj and Maramureş), in a slight loop diagonally in a southwesterly direction, taking in the county town Zalău, before leaving Sălaj County just south of Sâg where three counties (Sălaj, Cluj and Bihor) meet. The main industries of the county are food, textiles, wood, furniture, paper, machine and car parts.

ZALĂU *Telephone code 0260, sometimes 0360*

Zalău (Zilah/Zilenmarkt) is little more than a small country town with a large industrial suburb grafted on after World War II. There's not a great deal to see in the modern industrial town and it feels a little forgotten, 517km from Bucharest and 430km from Budapest, neither here nor there. The main reason to visit would be to see the fine archaeological exhibition in the County Museum which has items found in digs at Moigrad Porolissum.

HISTORY Situated 9km to the east of Zalău is the Roman camp of **Porolissum**, a well-preserved city with an imposing fortress, an amphitheatre, temples, houses and a customs house in the ancient Roman province of Dacia. In medieval times, Zalău was the crossing point between central Europe and Transylvania, along the Salt Route. The first mention of the settlement now known as Zalău comes from 1241 when the Mongols destroyed the town. Control of the city changed hands many times over the centuries. Zalău/Zilah was part of the Central-Szolnok County of the Kingdom of Hungary until 1538. During 1538–52, Zalău was part of the semi-independent Principality of Transylvania ruled by King János I. Then between 1552 and 1570, the county was in Hungary and ruled by the Habsburgs. In 1570, the Treaty of Speyer allocated Zalău to the Principality of Transylvania. The Ottomans ruled between 1660 and 1692 and for 70 years following 1806 it was a Free Royal City. In 1862, Zalău was given back to Hungary. Before the Treaty of Trianon, Zalău was one of the most important urban centres in the region. It had some excellent schools including the Wesselényi College, the biggest hospital in the region and a tax revenue office.

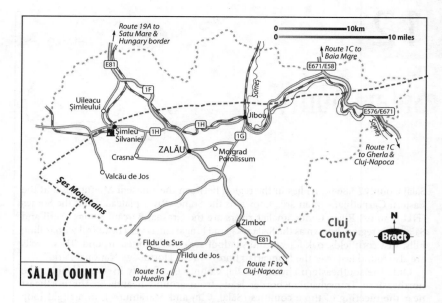

At first glance, the city appears as a collection of busy, exhaust-filled main streets lined with modern tower blocks, but there are several attractive buildings hidden away in the side streets. Zalău hosts lively pageants each year, including a 'Zalău Days' summer festival.

GETTING THERE, AWAY AND AROUND The **bus station** (☎ 0260 611 056) is about 20 minutes' walk north of the centre at Strada Mihai Viteazul 54. The **railway station**, **Gară CFR** (☎ 0260 662 131) is a further 30 minutes' walk north at Mihai Viteazul 100, almost in the village-suburb of Crişeni. Buses 1 and 2 and many maxi-taxis link (*15mins*) both stations to the centre but it is hardly convenient.

For Zalău, visitors usually have to change trains at Jibou, 76km northwest of Dej. The city is connected by bus to Cluj-Napoca (*1¾hrs*), Huedin (*2hrs*) and Târgu Mureş (*5hrs*).

By taxi
🚕 **Pro Taxi** Piaţa Iuliu Maniu 3–5; ☎ 0260 611 111

 WHERE TO STAY
🏠 **Hotel Brilliant Plaza** (17 dbl, 1 sgl) Str Maxim D Constantin 8; ☎/f 0260 615 066; e office@hotelbrilliantplaza.ro; www. hotelbrilliantplaza.ro. Smart rooms & central location, near the County Museum. **$$$**
🏠 **Hotel Porolissum** (72 dbl, 4 suites) Str Unirii 1; ☎/f 0260 613 301; e hotelporolissum@vidalis. ro; www.hotelporolissum.ro. In the centre of town, along from the County Museum, the Porolissum is modern, clean & friendly with a large restaurant ($) & a massage salon with many treatments. **$$**

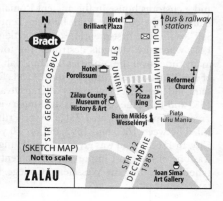

✕ WHERE TO EAT AND DRINK

✕ **Pizza King** B-dul Mihai Viteazul 1/B (in passage); ☎0360 106 080; ⊕ 09.00–midnight Mon–Fri, 10.00–02.00 Sat, 12.00–midnight Sun. Excellent pizzeria in a pub-like setting with movie memorabilia, flock wallpaper & wooden booths. Good pizza selection, salads, stews, grilled meats, tiramisu. Take-away & pizza delivery service. **$**

OTHER PRACTICALITIES

Bank

$ Banca Transilvania Str Unirii 1; ☎0260 661 205; ⊕ 09.00–18.00 Mon–Fri, 09.30–12.30 Sat. With an ATM outside.

Pharmacy

✚ **Prima Farm** Str Unirii 13; ⊕ 08.00–20.00 Mon–Sat, 08.00–16.00 Sun

Post office

✉ Piața 1 Decembrie; ⊕ 08.00–20.00 Mon–Fri, 08.00–13.00 Sat

Information

www.zalausj.ro For further information on the town of Zalău.

WHAT TO SEE AND DO At Piața Iuliu Maniu, in front of the elegant, custard-coloured town hall is a statue featuring **Baron Miklós Wesselényi**, born nearby in Jibou, gazing benevolently and putting his arm on the shoulder of a local gentleman. The statue was created by Bratislava-born Hungarian sculptor János Fadrusz in 1902. Nearby is a **modern fountain** with orange and black tiles. Here, the locals fill up plastic bottles with mineral water. The historical branch of the **Zalău County Museum of History and Art** (*Str Unirii 15;* ☎ *0260 612 223;* ⊕ *09.00–17.00 Tue–Sun; admission adult/child 2/1RON*) displays artefacts ranging from Neolithic through to modern times with a focus on the Roman period, including items from Moigrad Porolissum (see below). The history department consists of 20,000 items, mainly archaeological collections, showing almost all the stages of human existence in the area such as 100,000-year-old cave paintings, and items from the Bronze Age, Dacian and Roman times. The lapidary contains the statue of the Roman emperor Caracalla and many other sculptures. The ethnographic department displays wooden, textile, glass and pottery items as well as folk costumes from the Sălaj area. The museum's collection of works by Romanian painter Ioan Sima are housed in the '**Ioan Sima' Art Gallery** (*Str Gheorghe Doja 6;* ☎ *0260 611 065;* ⊕ *08.00–16.00 Tue–Sun*) along with work by other modern Romanian artists, such as the painter Aurel Ciupe (1900–85), sculptor Romulus Ladea (1901–70), painter Petre Abrudan (1907–79) and Imre Nagy (1893–1976) who studied in Miercurea-Ciuc and whose work was inspired by the Csík and Székely regions. Just north of here, the **Reformed Church** dates from 1907.

AROUND ZALĂU

A hire car would be really useful for those wishing to see the sights around Zalău. Public transport in this part of Sălaj is fairly limited.

JIBOU (25km northeast of Zalău) The town of Jibou (Zsibó/Siben) has a **castle** built in 1810 by Baron Wesselény's father. The building with its blend of Classicist and Baroque features, an arcaded loggia and four corner bastions, might have been influenced by the Bánffy Castle at Bonțida. The castle is used as a college and is not open to the public, but the grounds are home to one of Transylvania's most famous botanical gardens, **Grădina Botanică** (*www.gradina-botanica-jibou.ro;* ⊕ *Apr–Oct 08.00–19.00 daily, Nov–Mar 08.00–17.00 daily; admission adult/child 5/2RON*).

Several **buses** and **trains** leave Zalău daily for Jibou. By **car**, head north towards Bocşa on the E81, turn right after 5km onto the 1H road, signposted for Jibou.

MOIGRAD POROLISSUM (*www.porolissum.org*) Some 10km east of Zalău on a scenic road (note the road is in a poor state) in the direction of Creaca (Karika), you will find an **archaeological site**, which is one of the largest and best-preserved sites in Romania and can be visited. The territory covers almost 61ha, making it about the same size as ancient Pompeii and Ostia, but archaeologists have only determined key moments in the historical development of the city and less than 5% of the site has so far been excavated.

CRASNA The 14th-century **church** has a soaring spire, four turrets and beautiful painted ceiling panels dating from the 17th century. The priest's house is nearby and he has the key.

To reach Crasna from Zalău, take a minor road heading west, signed for Meseşenii de Jos; Crasna is 6km further west. Regular **buses** from Zalău (*30mins*).

ŞIMLEU SILVANIEI This is a small town with a 16th-century **ruined castle** perched on a little hill above the centre. In the town there is a mostly Baroque **Roman Catholic church** which dates from 1535 and has a bust to a prince of Transylvania, István Báthory, who was born here. Situated 10km north of Şimleu Silvaniei, **Uileacu Şimleului** has a Calvinist church, built in the 13th century. This church has a unique feature for Transylvania: a little passageway built right into the church wall.

From Zalău, **drive** north along the E81 and turn left after about 10km onto the 1H road signposted for Vârşolţ and Şimleu Silvaniei.

FILDU DE SUS On the southern county border with Cluj, Fildu de Sus (Felsüföld) has a very beautiful Romanian **wooden church** with spectacular frescoes dating from 1856 depicting biblical scenes.

Travellng by **car**, drive south from Zalău on route 1F for 30km to Zimbor, then fork right onto route 1G to Fildu de Jos (Alsófüld). Turn off the main road onto a minor road and drive for 8km to Fildu de Sus (Upper Fildu). One **bus** a day from Zalău (*1¾hrs*).

Appendix 1

LANGUAGE

Romanian originated from the Vulgar Latin spoken by Dacia's Roman conquerors in AD105, but has since acquired about a fifth of its vocabulary from German, Turkish, Greek and Hungarian influences. It is the Romance language closest to the original Latin tongue and a knowledge of French, Italian, Spanish or Latin will aid in understanding Romanian. The Romanian language is generally seen as a language with difficult grammar but easy to pronounce, being very phonetic.

The Romanian alphabet is nearly exactly the same as the English alphabet.

The letters K, Q, W and Y are not part of the native alphabet but were officially introduced in 1982 to write borrowed words such as kilogram, quasar, watt and yoga.

The Romanian alphabet is based on the Latin alphabet, and has five additional letters. These are not diacritics, but letters in their own right. These letters are ă, â, î, ş and ţ.

THE ROMANIAN ALPHABET IS AS FOLLOWS:

A, a	like the 'a' in 'father'
Ă, ă	like the 'a' in 'musical', a bit like 'er'
Â, â	no equivalent in English, like 'uh'
B, b	like the 'b' in 'bed'
C, c	before 'i' or 'e' pronounced 'ch', before other letters pronounced 'k'. As in Italian, the letter 'c' can be hardened by adding 'h' as in 'cheile' (gorge), pronounced 'key-el-eh'.
D, d	like the 'd' in 'dog'
E, e	at the beginning of the word pronounced 'ye', otherwise like the 'e' in 'ten'
F, f	like the 'f' in 'fat'
G, g	before 'i' or 'e' pronounced like the 'g' in 'gym', before other letters, or followed by 'h' pronounced 'g' as in 'garden', such as the name Gheorghe (pronounced 'gay-OR-gay')
H, h	like 'h' in 'help', never silent in Romanian
I, i	usually like the 'ee' in 'week', but at the end of a word, 'i' is almost silent, see Bucureşti (pronounced 'Boo-KOO-resht', with a soft 't' at the end)
Î, î	pronounced like â, but more slack-jawed 'uh'
J, j	like the 'j' in 'bonjour' or the 's' in 'pleasure'
K, k	like the 'k' in 'kilo
L, l	like the 'l' in 'love'
M, m	like the 'm' in 'mother'
N, n	like the 'n' in 'normal'
O, o	like the 'o' in 'chlorine'
P, p	like the 'p' in 'pig'

Q, q	like the 'k' in 'king'
R, r	like a Scottish rolled 'r' in 'rough'
S, s	like the 's' in 'sad'
Ş, ş	like the 'sh' in 'shop'
T, t	like the 't' in 'cat'
Ţ, ţ	like the 'ts' in 'cats'
U, u	like the 'oo' in 'room', but much shorter
V, v	like the 'v' in 'very'
W, w	like the 'v' in 'very'
X, x	like the 'cks' in 'licks', sometimes a bit like the 'gs' in 'pigs'
Y, y	like the 'i' in 'ship'
Z, z	like the 'z' in 'fizz'

ROMANIAN VOCABULARY
Essentials

Good morning	*Bună dimineaţa*
Good day	*Bună ziua*
Good evening	*Bună seara* (often reversed)
Good night	*Noapte bună*
Goodbye	*La revedere*
Bon voyage!	*Drum bun!* (literally 'good road')
My name is …	*Mă numesc …*
What is your name?	*Cum vă numiţi?*
How are you?	*Ce mai faceti?*
Pleased to meet you	*Încântat de cunoştinţă* (pronounced 'uhn-kun-tat de koo-nosh-tint-ser')
I/we thank you	*Mulţumesc/Mulţumim*
You're welcome (after thanks)	*Cu plăcere*
Cheers!	*Noroc!*
Yes	*Da*
No	*Nu*
Please	*Vă rog* (*ver rog*)
Do you speak English?	*Vorbiţi englezeşte?* ('Vor-beetsi ing-lez-esh-teh')
I don't understand	*Nu înţeleg* ('Noo uhnts-ell-egg')
I don't speak Romanian	*Nu vorbesc româneşte*
Excuse me	*Scuzaţi-mă*
I beg your pardon?	*Poftim/Poftiţi?*
Please, would you speak more slowly?	*Puteţi să vorbiţi mai rar, vă rog?*
Do you understand?	*Înţelegeţi?* ('unts-ele-jhets')

Questions

How?	*Cum?*	When?	*Când?*
What?	*Ce?* ('cheh')	Why?	*De ce?* ('deh cheh')
Where?	*Unde?*	Who?	*Cine?* ('chinay'
Which?	*Care?*		

How much/many?   *Câţi/câte?* ('kuhts'/'kuhteh')
How much does this cost?   *Cât costă?* ('kuht koster')
When does … open/close?   *Când se deschide/închide … ?* ('kuhnd seh des-key-deh/uhn-key-deh … ?')

Numbers

1	*unu*	6	*şase* ('shaseh')
2	*doi*	7	*şapte* ('shapteh')
3	*trei*	8	*opt*
4	*patru*	9	*nouă* ('no-wer')
5	*cinci* ('cheench')	10	*zece* ('zecheh')

11	*unsprezece* ('OON-spreh-zeh-cheh')
12	*doisprezece* ('DOY-spreh-zeh-cheh')
13	*treisprezece* ('TRAY-spreh-zeh-cheh')
14	*paisprezece* ('PIE-spreh-zeh-cheh')
15	*cincisprezece* ('CHEEN-chi-spreh-zeh-cheh')
16	*şaisprezece* ('SHY-spreh-zeh-cheh')
17	*şaptesprezece* ('SHAPte-spreh-zeh-cheh')
18	*optsprezece* ('OPT-spreh-zeh-cheh')
19	*nouăsprezece* ('NO-wer-spreh-zeh-cheh')
20	*douăzeci* ('do-wer-ZECH')
21	*douăzeci şi unu* ('do-wer-ZECH shee oonoo')
30	*treizeci* ('tray-ZECH')
40	*patruzeci* ('patroo-ZECH')
50	*cincizeci* ('cheench-ZECH')
60	*şaizeci* ('shy-ZECH')
70	*şaptezeci* ('shap-te-ZECH')
80	*optzeci* ('opt-ZECH')
90	*nouăzeci* ('no-wer-ZECH')
100	*o sută* ('o SOO-ter')
1,000	*o mie* ('o MEE-eh')

Time

What time is it?	*Cât este ceasul?* ('kuht yesht-eh chas-ool')
It is ...	*Este ...*
Today	*azi*
Tomorrow	*mâine* ('MUY-neh')
Yesterday	*ieri* ('yehr')
In the morning	*dimineaţa*
In the afternoon	*după amiaza* ('doo-per am-yazer')
In the evening	*seara* ('sara')
This week	*săptămâna asta* ('suhp-tuh-MOOHN-ah-stah')
Daily	*zilnic*

Days of the week

Monday	*luni* ('loon')
Tuesday	*marţi* ('marts')
Wednesday	*miercuri* ('mee-HER-coor')
Thursday	*joi* ('zhoy')
Friday	*vineri* ('vee-NEHR')
Saturday	*sâmbătă* ('some butter')
Sunday	*duminica* ('doo-me-neeker')

Months

January	*ianuarie* ('yan-WAH-ree-eh')
February	*februarie* ('feb-RWAH-ree-eh')
March	*martie* ('MAR-tee-eh')
April	*aprilie* ('ah-PREEL-ee-eh')
May	*mai* ('my')
June	*iunie* ('YOO-nee-eh')
July	*iulie* ('YOO-lee-eh')
August	*august* ('ow-GOOST')
September	*septembrie* ('sep-TEHM-bree-eh')
October	*octombrie* ('ok-TOHM-bree-eh')
November	*noiembrie* ('noy-EHM-bree-eh')
December	*decembrie* ('deh-CHEHM-bree-eh')

Getting around and public transport

I'd like ...	*Aş dori ...*
... a one-way ticket to Braşov	*... un bilet dus pentru Braşov*
... a return ticket	*... un bilet dus-întors*
How much is the fare to ... ?	*Cât costa pâna la ... ?*
	('Kuht koster puh-ner la')
What time does the train for Mediaş leave?	*La ce oră pleacă trenul de Mediaş?*
	('La cheh orer plak-er')
First class	*clasa întâi* ('klass-er uhn-tuy')
Second class	*clasa a doua* ('klass-er a dower')
Berth in the sleeping car	*cuşeta la vagonul de dormit*
Platform	*peron*
Ticket office	*casa de bilete*
Timetable	*orar*
Bus station	*autogară*
Railway station	*gară*
Airport	*aeroport*
Bus	*autobuz*
Tram	*tramvai*
Train	*tren*
Plane	*avion*
Car	*maşină* ('mash-een-er')
Taxi	*taxi*
Minibus	*microbus/maxi-taxi*
Motorbike/moped	*motocicletă/motoreta*
Bicycle	*bicicletă*
Arrival/departure	*sosiri/plecări*
Here	*aici*
There	*acolo*
Bon voyage!	*drum bun!*

Private transport

Is this the road to ... ?	*Care este drumul spre ... ?*
Where is the nearest service station?	*Unde este cea mai apropiată staţie de benzină?*
Please fill it up	*Faceţi plinul, vă rog*
I'd like ... litres of...	*Puneţi ... litri de...*

Diesel		*motorină*
Unleaded petrol		*benzină fără plumb*
My car has broken down		*Maşina mea are o pană de motor*

Road signs

Danger	*pericol*	Keep right	*ţineti dreapta*
Detour	*deviere*	Caution	*atenţie*
One-way	*sens unic*	Slow down	*reduceţi viteza*
No entry	*trafic interzis*	Icy road	*polei*

Directions

Where is …?	*Unde este …?*	north/south	*nord/sud*
Go straight ahead	*Mergeţi drept înainte*	east/west	*est/vest*
To the left/right	*la stânga/la dreapte*	near	*aproape*
… at the traffic lights	*… la semafor*	opposite	*vis-a-vis*
toward	*spre*		

Street signs

Entrance/exit	*intrare/iesire*	Toilets –	*Toaleta –*
Open/closed	*Deschis/închis*	men/women	*bărbaţi/femei*
Push/pull (on doors)	*Impingeti/trageti*	Information	*Informaţie*

Accommodation

Where is a cheap/good hotel?	*Puteţi să-mi recomandaţi un hotel?*
Do you have any rooms available?	*Aveţi camere libere?*
I'd like …	*Aş vrea …*
… a single room	*… o cameră cu un pat*
… a double room	*… o cameră cu pat dublu*
… a room with two beds	*… o cameră cu două paturi*
… a room with a bathroom	*… o cameră cu baie*
How much is it per day/week?	*Cât costă pe zi/pe săptămână?*
Is there hot water?	*Există apă caldă?*
Is electricity included?	*Electricitatea este inclusă în chirie?*
Is breakfast included?	*Aceasta include şi micul dejun?*
I am leaving early in the morning	*Plec mâine dimineaţă*

Food

Could we have a table for … people?	*Putem avea o masă pentru … personae?*
Waiter! (getting attention)	*Ospătar!* ('os-puh-TAHR')
I am a vegetarian	*Sunt vegetarian*
I don't eat pork	*Nu mănânc carne de porc*
Do you have any vegetarian dishes?	*Aveţi mâcăruri pentru vegetarieni?*
Please bring me a …	*Putem avea … vă rog*
… fork/knife/spoon/glass	*… o furculiţa/un cuţit/o lingură/un pahar*
Bon appetit!	*Poftă bună!*
The bill, please	*Nota de plata, vă rog*
Bread	*pâine*	Fruit	*fructe*
Butter	*unt*	Apples	*mere*
Cheese	*brânză*	Bananas	*banane*
Jam	*gem*	Grapes	*struguri*
Oil	*ulei*	Pears	*pere*

Eggs	*ouă*	Plums	*prune*
Vinegar	*oțet*	Tomatoes	*roșii*
Pepper	*piper*	Vegetables	*legume*
Salt	*sare*	Boiled/mashed/	*cartofi natur/piure/*
Sugar	*zahăr*	fried potatoes	*prăjiti*
Rice	*aroz*	Lamb	*miel*
Beans	*fasole*	Ham	*jambon* or *șuncă*
Onion	*ceapă*	Sausage/meatball mix	*mititei* ('mici')
Garlic	*usturoi*	Soup/sour soup	*supa/ciorba*
Peppers	*ardei*	Stew	*tok*
Carrots	*morcovi*	Beer	*bere*
Aubergine/eggplant	*vinete*	Red/white wine	*vin roșu/alb* ('veen-ROH-shoo'/'ahlb')
Cucumbers	*castraveti*		
Cabbage	*varză*	Fruit brandy	*țuică, palincă*
Mushrooms	*ciuperci*	Fruit juice	*suc*
Salad	*salată* ('sa-LAH-tah')	Coffee	*o cafea*
Fish	*pește*	Tea	*un ceai*
Trout	*păstrăv*	Herbal tea	*ceai din plante*
Pike	*știucă*	With milk	*cu lapte*
River perch	*biban*	With lemon	*cu lămâie*
Meat	*carne*	Water (mineral)	*apă minerale*
Beef	*vita*	Water (still)	*apă plată* ('AH-puh PLAH-tah')
Chicken	*pui*		
Pork	*porc*	Ice cream	*înghetata*

Shopping

Have you any … ?	*Aveți … ?*
I would like …	*Aș vrea …*
I/we have …	*Am/avum …*
How much is it?	*Cât costă?*
It costs too much	*Costa prea mult*
Yes, I'd like …	*Da, aș vrea …*
Do you accept credit cards?	*Acceptați cărți de credit?*
Don't you have anything …?	*Nu aveți ceva …?*
… cheaper/better	*… mai ieftin/mai bun*
… smaller/bigger	*… mai mic/mai mare*
Bookshop	*librărie*
Stationers	*papetărie*
Souvenir shop	*artizanat*
Tobacconists	*tutungerie*

Colours

Black/white/grey	*negru/alb/gri*
Red/blue/yellow	*roșu/albastru/galben*
Green/orange	*verde/portocaliu*
Purple/brown	*mov* ('mohv')/*maro* ('mah-ROH')

Communications

Where is the … ?	*Unde se află … ?*
… nearest bank?	*… o bancă in apropiere?*
… nearest post office?	*… o poșta prin apropiere?*

… church?	… biserică?
… embassy?	… ambasadă?
… exchange office?	… un birou de schimb?
… tourist office?	… oficiul de turism?

Emergencies

Emergency!	Urgenţă!
Help!	Ajutor!
Call a doctor	Chemaţi un doctor
There's been an accident	A fost un accident
I've been injured	Sunt accidentat
I'm lost	M-am rătăcit
Go away!	Pleacă de aici!
Police	poliţia
Fire/fire brigade	foc/pompieri
Ambulance	ambulanţa
Stop, thief!	Stai! hoţi! ('sty! hohtz!')
Hospital	spital
I've got diarrhoea	Am diaree
I've been vomiting	Am vărsat
Doctor	doctor
Prescription	reţetă
Pharmacy	farmacie
Painkiller/antibiotic	anti-inflamator/antibiotice
Tampons	tampoane ('tum-POAH-neh')
Condom	preservativ
Sunblock	cremă de bronzat
Soap/shampoo	săpun ('suh-POON')/şampon ('sham-pon')
Toothbrush/toothpaste	perie/pastă de dinţi
	('per-ee-ye'/'PAH-stuh deh DEENTS')
I am …	Sunt …
… diabetic	… diabetic(ă)
I've got asthma	Am astmă
I'm allergic to…	Sunt alergic(ă) la…
penicillin/peanuts/bee stings	penicilină/arahidă/înţepături de albine

Children

Is there a…?	Aveţi … ?
… baby changing room?	… o cameră de schimbat scutecele bebeluşilor?
… a children's bed?	… un pătuţ de copii?
Do you have…?	Aveţi … ?
… infant milk formula?	… lapte pentru sugari?
… nappies/potty/high chair?	… scutece/oliţă/scaun special pentru bebeluşi?
… children's menu?	… meniu pentru copii?
… babysitter?	…babysitter/îngijitoare pentru copii?
Are children allowed?	Este permis accesul copiilor?

Other

My/our	*meu/nostru*
He/his/she/her	*el/lui/ea/ei*
And/some/but	*şi/nişte/dar* (or *însă*)
This/that	*asta, acesta/acela*
Expensive/cheap	*scump/ieftin*
Good/bad	*bun/rău*
Beautiful/ugly	*frumos/urât*
Old/new (things)	*vechi/nou*
Old/young (people)	*bătrân/tânar*
Early/late	*devreme/târziu*
Hot/cold	*fierbinte/rece*
Easy/difficult	*uşor/greu*
Light/heavy	*uşor/greu* (same as above)
Fast/slow	*repede/încet* ('rep-ed-eh'/'oon-chet')
A little/a lot	*Putin/mult*
Good/very good	*Bun/foarte bună*
OK/fine	*Bine*
OK	*In regula*
Perhaps	*Poate*

Some basic Hungarian phrases

English	Hungarian
Good day	*Jó napot* ('YAW NOP-ot')
Hello/bye (informal)	*szia* ('SEE-ya')
Good evening	*Jó estét* ('YAW ESH-tate')
Goodbye	*Viszontlátásra* ('VEE-sont-lah-tah-shro')
Bon voyage!	*Jó utat!* ('YAW OOT-ot')
My name is	*A nevem* ('ah NEV-em')
What is your name?	*Hogy hivják?* ('hodge HEAVE-yak?')
I am English/American/Australian	*angol/amerikai/austrál vagyok* ('ONG-ol'/'OM-eri-koi'/'OW-stral VODGE-ok')
How are you?	*Hogy van?* ('HODGE von?')
Thank you	*Köszönöm* ('CUR-sir-nuhm')
You're welcome (after thanks)	*Kérem* ('KIR-em')
Cheers!	*Egészségére!* ('EGG-ace-sheg-ir-reh')
Yes/no	*Igen/nem* ('IG-en'/'nem')
Please	*Kérem* ('KIR-em')
Do you speak English?	*Beszél angolul?* ('BEH-sail ONG-ol-ool?')
I don't understand	*Nem értem* ('nem IR-tem')
I don't speak Hungarian	*Nem beszélek magyarul* ('nem BEH-sail-eck modge-ah-rool')
Excuse me	*Elnézest* ('EL-nay-zesht')
Sorry	*Bocsánat* ('BOTCH-ah-not')
A beer please	*Egy sört kérek* ('Edge shirt KIR-eck')
Where is the …?	*Hol van a …?* ('HOL von a ….?')
… bus station/railway station?	… *busz állomás/pályaudvar?* ('boose AH-lo-mash/PIE-ya-ood-vah')
… post office/bank/pharmacy?	… *posta/bank/gyógyszertár?* ('POSH-tah/bonk/GEORGE-sair-tah')

… tourist information centre?	… *turisztikai információs központ?* ('TUR-ist-ik-oi IN-for-mats-iosh KUZ-pont')
Two tickets, please…	*Kettő jegyet, kérek…* ('KET-tuh YEDGE-et KIR-ek')
Do you have a room available?	*Van kiadö szobája?* ('VON KEE-ah-doh SOB-ai-yah?')
WC (gents'/ladies')	*WC férfi/nöi* ('vay-tsay FER-fee'/'NUH-ee')
One/two/three/ten	*Egy/kettő/három/tíz* ('Edge'/'KET-tuh'/'HAH-rom'/'teaze')

Appendix 2

FURTHER INFORMATION
BOOKS
Literature

Bánffy, Miklós *They Were Counted* Arcadia Books, 1999; Bánffy, Miklós *They Were Divided* Arcadia Books, 2000; Bánffy, Miklós *They Were Found Wanting* Arcadia Books, 2000. The Transylvanian Trilogy is a fascinating insight into the social and political history of Hungary in the early years of the 20th century. It ranges from the intricacies of political life in Budapest to the challenging task of running an estate in Transylvania. The translation is a little clunky.

Bánffy, Miklós *The Phoenix Land* Arcadia Books, 2002. Following the success of the Transylvanian Trilogy, Bánffy's memoirs of life in the region following World War I. With a foreword by Patrick Leigh Fermor.

Cioabă, Luminiţa Mihai *Negustorul de Ploaie* (*The Rain Merchant*). A book of poetry by the daughter of the Roma emperor Florin Cioabă.

Crane, Nicholas *Clear Waters Rising* Penguin, 1997. Account of a 10,000km journey across Europe by car, bicycle, even armoured truck. The author takes in the Carpathians and the Transylvanian Alps. Good observations on geography, flora and fauna.

Dragoman, György *The White King* Doubleday, 2008. A story of life in Transylvania under Ceauşescu, narrated by an 11-year-old boy, Djata. Translated by Paul Olchváry.

Eminescu, Mihai *Poems and Prose* Center for Romanian Studies, 2000. Published to mark 150 years since the birth of Romania's greatest poet, this selection contains the best English-language renderings of Eminescu's poetry and prose.

Fermor, Patrick Leigh *Between The Woods and the Water* John Murray, 2004. In his sequel to *A Time of Gifts*, the late travel writer Fermor combines youthful enthusiasm and fire with an older man's knowledge of history. More of a Hungarian view as Fermor mostly stayed with Hungarian families.

Gerard, Emily *The Land Beyond the Forest* 1888, reprinted Cambridge University Press 2010. Victorian account of two years living in Transylvania.

Goodwin, Jason *On Foot to the Golden Horn* Vintage, 1994. On a journey on foot, mostly through eastern Europe, Goodwin meets a host of colourful characters.

Harding, Georgina *In Another Europe: Journey across Hungary and Romania* Stoughton, 1991. One woman's solo cycle ride across the region. She visited some unattractive parts of Romania at the nadir of conditions in the country under Ceauşescu.

Hoffman, Eva *Exit into History: Journey through the new Eastern Europe* Minerva, 1994. Not long after 1989, Hoffman travelled through five countries noting the changes. The passages on Romania are enlightening.

Manning, Olivia *The Balkan Trilogy* Arrow Books, 1992. The author lived in Bucharest during the early part of World War II and her experiences provide the background for her work. The trilogy was filmed by the BBC.

Marie, Queen of Romania *The Lost Princess* S W Partridge, 1924. The lovely Princess Dorinda enlists the help of the witch Carabaracola and two little imps, Jenky and Jonky, to help her find her lost sister. Six charming tipped-in colour plates plus numerous black-and-white text drawings by Mabel Lucie Attwell.

Marie, Queen of Romania *Peeping Pansy* Hodder & Stoughton, 1919. Another delightful children's story with illustrations by Mabel Lucie Attwell.

Marie, Queen of Romania *Story of my Life* Ayer Co Publishing, 1970. A fascinating inside account.

Murphy, Dervla *Transylvania and Beyond* John Murray, 1992. Murphy's excellent travelogue combines vivid descriptions of the countryside and people with serious discussions on society immediately after the fall of Ceauşescu.

Ross, Julian *Travels in an Unknown Country: A Mounted View of Transylvania* Long Riders' Guild Press, 2004. Ross lived in Transylvania for many years and this summer-long horse ride across the countryside will inspire a visit.

Simon, Ted *The Gypsy in Me: From Germany to Romania in Search of Youth, Truth, and Dad* Random House, 1997. Simon embarked on a 2,400km journey (mostly by foot), covering the lands between his mother's Germany and his father's Romania, discovering the cultures and realities of eastern Europe.

Sitwell, Edith and Sacheverall *Roumanian Journey* Oxford University Press, 1938. Account by two aristocratic food lovers of travels in the country in 1938.

Sorkin, Adam J and Bleoca, Liviu *Transylvanian Voices: An Anthology of Contemporary Poets of Cluj-Napoca* Center for Romanian Studies, 1998. Edited and translated by Sorkin and Bleoca, this is a strong selection of works from the end of the 20th century.

Starkie, Walter *Raggle-Taggle Adventures with a Fiddle in Hungary and Roumania* John Murray, 1933. Colourful details on the people, the music and the inspiring countryside.

Verne, Jules *The Castle of the Carpathians* Fredonia Books, 2001. A description of the villagers of Werst, their costumes, way of life and belief in the supernatural world. Set in and around Haţeg.

Society and history

Akeroyd, John *The Historic Countryside of the Saxon Villages of Southern Transylvania* ADEPT Foundation, 2007. Fascinating details about the Saxon villages.

Bailey, Chris *The Railways of Romania* Locomotives International, 2002. A description of the locomotives and tracks in Romania.

Blacker, William *Along the Enchanted Way. A Story of Love and Life in Romania*, John Murray, 2010. Charming account of the author's life in Romania from 1996 to 2004.

Blacker, William *The Plight of the Saxons of Transylvania and their Fortified Churches*, Mihai Eminescu Trust, 1997. Available from the MET.

Boia, Lucian *History and Myth in Romanian Consciousness* Central European University Press, 2001. Separates fact and fiction in history.

Douglas-Home, Jessica *Once Upon Another Time* Michael Russell Publishing, 2000. The director of the Mihai Eminescu Trust chronicles the difficulties of supporting dissidents in the 1980s.

Fonseca, Isabel *Bury Me Standing* Vintage, 1996. Fonseca travelled through central Europe and lived in Roma communities researching this in-depth study.

Fox, Edward *The Hungarian Who Walked to Heaven (Alexander Csoma de Kőrös 1784–1842)* Short Lives Series, Faber and Faber, 2001. The strange life of the Transylvanian who wrote the first Tibetan–English dictionary.

Hall, Donald *Romanian Furrow: Colourful Experiences of Village Life* Bene Factum Publishing Ltd, 2007. A young Englishman set out in 1933 to discover rural life.

Kurti, László *The Remote Borderland: Transylvania in the Hungarian Imagination* State University of New York Press, 2001. The Hungarian view on Transylvania.

Ogden, Alan *Fortresses of Faith: A Pictorial History of the Fortified Saxon Churches of Romania* Center for Romanian Studies, 2000. With beautiful black-and-white photographs by Ogden.

Ogden, Alan *Moons & Aurochs: A Romanian Journey* Orchid Press, 2007. Ogden takes the reader on an eccentric tour of Romania. He wanders through the mountains of Transylvania meeting Lipovans, Székelys, Saxons and Houtsouls.

Ogden, Alan *Romania Revisited: On the Trail of English Travellers, 1602–1941* Center for Romanian Studies, 1999. The story of the journeys made by English travellers to Romania between 1602 and 1941. The author interweaves the impressions of previous generations into an account of his own journeys made in 1998.

Ogden, Alan *Winds of Sorrow: Travels in and Around Transylvania* Orchid Press, 2004. An eclectic collection of essays compiled by the author during his travels to Transylvania in northern Romania between 1998 and 2004.

Pakula, Hannah *The Last Romantic: A Biography of Queen Marie of Roumania* Simon & Schuster, 1986. The fascinating life of a remarkable woman.

Pintea, Alex I *Buying Property in Romania: An Insider's Guide* Lean Marketing Press, 2006. Helpful tips on property buying.

Nature

Gorman, Gerard *Birding in Eastern Europe* Wildsounds, 2006. With illustrations by Szabolcs Kokay. Information for twitchers.

Gorman, Gerard *Central and Eastern European Wildlife* Bradt Travel Guides, 2008. A guide to the wildlife of the entire region.

Gorman, Gerard *Where to Watch Birds in Eastern Europe* Hamlyn Birdwatching Guides, 1994. With illustrations by Clive Byers and Mark Andrews, this is a useful tool.

Gorman, Gerard *Woodpeckers of Europe: A Study of the European Picidae* Bruce Coleman Books, 2004. With illustrations by Szabolcs Kokay.

Roberts, James *Romania: A Birdwatching and Wildlife Guide* Burton Expeditions, 2000. Detailed information on the wildlife and ecology of the mountain areas.

Roberts, James *The Mountains of Romania* Cicerone Mountain Walking Guide, 2005. Romania's Carpathians offer some of the finest walking in Europe.

Travel and language

Alexandrescu, Yvonne and Deletant, Dennis *Teach Yourself Romanian* McGraw-Hill, 2003. Has an accompanying cassette.

Deletant, Dennis *Colloquial Romanian: A Complete Language Course* Routledge, 1995

Evans, Andrew *Ukraine: the Bradt Travel Guide* (second edition) Bradt Travel Guides, 2006

Gall, Dana *Beginner's Romanian* Hippocrene Books Inc, 1994. Getting started with the language.

Hoffman, Christina *Roumanian Grammar* Hippocrene Language Studies, 1991

Miroiv, Mihai *Romanian–English/English–Romanian Dictionary and Phrasebook* Hippocrene Dictionary and Phrasebooks, 1996

Mitchell, Laurence *Serbia: the Bradt Travel Guide* (second edition) Bradt Travel Guides, 2007

Palin, Michael *New Europe* Weidenfeld & Nicolson, 2007. Intrepid traveller Michael Palin's *New Europe* book and BBC1 series is based on the simple idea that 'only a couple of hours from home is half of Europe that is – for him – unknown and unexplored'.

Phillips, Adrian and Scotchmer, Jo *Hungary: the Bradt Travel Guide* (second edition) Bradt Travel Guides, 2009.

Riley, Bronwen *Transylvania* Frances Lincoln, 2008. Elegant coffee-table book captures Transylvania's vanishing landscape. Beautiful photographs by Dan Dinescu.

Spinder, Stephen *Ten Years in Transylvania/Tíz esztendő Erdélyben* Spinder Fine Art Photography, February 2001. Bilingual (English and Hungarian) photo album documenting a personal journey through a 'fabled landscape'. Available through the website www.spinderartphoto.com.

Various authors *Siebenbürgen. Gästehäuser und Wanderwege in der Kirchenburgenlandschaft (Transylvania. Guest Houses and Hiking Trails in the Fortress Landscape)* Shaker Media 2008. A very useful guide (in German only) to the fortified churches of Transylvania, with walks and accommodation. Available from www.shaker-media.de.

History

Bodea, Cornelia *Transylvania in the History of the Romanians* East European Monographs, 1982. History from the Romanian viewpoint.

Boia, Lucian *Romania: Borderland of Europe (Topographics)* Reaktion Books, 2001. The author introduces the reader to the heroes and myths of Romanian history, such as the celebrated fictional Count Dracula, and provides an enlightening account of the history of Romanian communism.

Gallagher, Tom *Theft of a Nation: Romania Since Communism* C Hurst & Co Publishing, 2005. A study of the country in the 1990s.

Kinross, Patrick Balfour *The Ottoman Centuries: The Rise and Fall of the Turkish Empire* William Morrow, 1979. The Turkish influence on Transylvania is also included.

Klepper, Nicolae *Romania: An Illustrated History*, Hippocrene Books Inc, 2002. A useful study taking in all angles.

Lázár, István *Transylvania: A Short History* Simon Publications, 2001. A controversial Hungarian version of Transylvanian history.

Lehrer, Milton G *Transylvania: History and Reality* Bartleby Press, 1986. A very dry historical study.

Mackenzie, Andrew *The History of Transylvania* Unified Publishers Ltd, 1983

Makkai, László *History of Transylvania V1 From the Beginnings to 1660 (East European Monographs)* Columbia University Press, 2002

Makkai, László, *History of Transylvania V2 From 1660 to 1830 (East European Monographs)* Columbia University Press, 2002

Pascu, Stefan *A History of Transylvania* Wayne State University Press, USA, 1983

Péter, László *Historians and the History of Transylvania (East European Monographs)* Columbia University Press, 1992

Szász, Zoltán *History of Transylvania V3 From 1830 to 1919 (East European Monographs)* Columbia University Press, 2002

Tökes, László *The Fall of the Tyrants: The Incredible Story of One Pastor's Witness, the People of Romania and the Overthrow of Ceaușescu* Good News Publishing, 1991. Recollections by the Timișoara pastor who helped spark the events of 1989.

Cuisine

Klepper, Nicolae *Taste of Romania: Its Cookery and Glimpses of Its History, Folklore, Art, Literature and Poetry* Hippocrene Books Inc, 1999. Combining more than 140 tasty traditional recipes with examples of Romania's folklore, humour, art, poetry and proverbs.

Dracula, vampires and supersititions

Augustyn, Michael *Vlad Dracula: The Dragon Prince* iuniverse.com, 2004. A biography that goes beyond the vampire myth.

Belford, Barbara *Bram Stoker and the Man Who Was Dracula* Da Capo Press, 2002. A biography of the man who created the Hollywood legend.

Bibeau, Paul *Sundays with Vlad: From Pennsylvania to Transylvania, One Man's Quest to live in the World of the Undead* Three Rivers Press, 2007. A humorous examination of the vampire myth.

Bunson, Matthew *The Vampire Encyclopaedia* Gramercy Books, 2001. Information on the vampire in cinema and literature as well as in folklore.

Florescu, Radu and McNally, Raymond T *Dracula: His Life and Times* Little, Brown, 2005. A biography of the 15th-century Prince of Romania, Vlad III Drăculea, covering his career as ruler of Wallachia, terror of Transylvania and crusader against the Turks, and examining how he compares with his fictional namesake.

Florescu, Radu R and McNally, Raymond T *In Search of Dracula* Robson Books, 1998. A new edition of the study of Prince Vlad III, the inspiration behind the Dracula myth.

Kligman, Gail *The Wedding of the Dead: Ritual, Poetics and Popular Culture in Transylvania* University of California Press, 1992. Interesting study on rituals.

Knight, Amarantha *The Darker Passions: Dracula* Circlet Press, 2002. The infamous erotic re-telling of Bram Stoker's *Dracula*.

Kostova, Elizabeth *The Historian* Time Warner Paperbacks, 2006. The novel combines a search for the historical Dracula that spans countries and decades in an exciting *Da Vinci Code*-style romp with a lot of interesting historical detail.

Miller, Elizabeth *A Dracula Handbook* Xlibris Corporation, 2005. Well-researched factbook with everything you need to know about the Count.

Murray, Paul *From the Shadow of 'Dracula': A Life of Bram Stoker* Pimlico, 2005. A biography of the man who created the myth.

Newman, Kim *Anno-Dracula* Avon Books, 1994. The first part of a Gothic horror trilogy.

Stoker, Bram *Dracula* Wordsworth Editions Ltd, 1993. The classic that created the legend. First published in 1897.

Summers, Montague *The Vampire in Lore and Legend* HarperCollins, 2001. Divided into countries and their vampire myths.

Treptow, Kurt W *Vlad III Dracula: The Life and Times of the Historical Dracula* Center for Romanian Studies, 2000. A study of the man behind the legend.

Wright, Dudley *Vampires and Vampirism: Legends from Around the World* Lethe Press, 2001. A large collection of vampire stories.

CDS OF TRANSYLVANIAN MUSIC

Romania: Wild Sounds from Transylvania, Wallachia & Moldavia (World Network, Germany). Great ensembles from Transylvania and Wallachia including Taraf de Haidouks and the Moldavian Fanfare Ciocărlia.

Village Music from Romania (AIMP/VDE-Gallo, Switzerland). A three-CD box from the Geneva Ethnographic Museum. Archive recordings made by the musicologist Constantin Brailoiu in 1933–43 on his travels around Moldavia, Oltenia and Transylvania.

The Blues at Dawn (Fonó/ABT, Hungary). A sensitively produced CD of the slow, melancholy *hajnali* (morning songs) from Kalotaszeg. Sung by two native Kalotaszegi singers with guests Márta Sebestyén and András Berecz from Budapest.

The Edge of the Forest: Romanian Music from Transylvania (Music of the World, US). Included here are dances from southern districts of Maramures (Codru and Chioar) where the style belongs to the central Transylvanian tradition.

Musiques de Transylvanie (Fonti Musicali, Belgium). A superb introduction to Transylvanian music featuring a mostly Hungarian repertoire played by musicians on Budapest's dance house scene. Includes great music from Kalotaszeg, Mezőség, Gyimes plus Romanian dances from Bihor and Moldavia.

La Vraie Tradition de Transylvanie (Ocora, France). Highlighting real peasant music from Maramures and Transylvania. Featuring a track from Gheorghe Covaci, the son of a fiddler whom Bartók recorded in 1913.

Budatelke – Szászszantgyörgy (Fonó, Budapest). The second of the New Patria series archiving Transylvania's village bands. The band play a mainly Romanian repertoire plus Hungarian, Gypsy and Saxon tracks.

Hungarian Music from Transylvania: Sándor 'Neti' Fodor (Hungaroton, Hungary). On this exciting recording of both Hungarian and Romanian music from Kalotaszeg, Neti plays with some of the best dance house musicians from Budapest.

Báré – Magyarpalatka (Fono, Hungary). The band comprises two fiddles, two contras and bass and offers up Hungarian, Romanian and Gypsy dances.

Transylvanian Portraits (Koch, US). A good selection of Transylvanian music from one of Budapest's best groups, the Ökrös Ensemble, with vocals by Márta Sebestyén. Mainly Hungarian repertoire with Gyimes and Csángó songs.

Magyarpalatka – Hungarian Folk Music from the Transylvanian Heath (Hungaroton, Hungary). Traditional dance sets recorded over the years by the seminal band Palatka. Their typical lineup comprises two fiddles, two contra and bass.

Folk Music from Transylvania: Szászcsávás Band (Quintana/Harmonia Mundi, France). A marvellous recording of a real village band with a wide dance repertoire, including Hungarian, Romanian, Saxon and Gypsy tunes.

WEBSITES

www.aboutromania.com Information on all aspects of life in Romania, including long lists of facts on many themes

www.accept-romania.ro Romania's only gay and lesbian organisation

www.alpinet.org Mountain guide with trails and accommodation

www.antrec.ro Rural tourism network

www.autogari.ro Bus timetables and routes

www.beyondtheforest.com Transylvania Uncovered

www.blueair-web.com Low-cost Romanian airline

www.carpatair.ro Low-cost Romanian airline based in Timişoara

www.carpathianparks.org Carpathian network of protected areas

www.castelintransilvania.ro Castel in Transilvania (in Romanian & Hungarian)

www.cfr.ro Romanian Railways

www.cluj4all.com All about Cluj-Napoca

www.clujguide.com A good guide to Cluj-Napoca

www.dimap.hu Budapest-based map company with many mountain ranges

www.echange-roumanie.com Tourist information in French

www.eco-romania.ro Association of Ecotourism

www.fortified-churches.com An excellent online guide to the fortified churches of Transylvania

www.fundatia-adept.org Agricultural development and environmental protection

www.infofer.ro Information on Romanian railways

www.infomontan.ro *Cabanas*, accommodation, etc in the mountains

www.jiwire.com/browse-hotspot-romania-ro.htm Find Wi-Fi hotspots in Romania

www.kalnoky.org/KCT-Introduction.html Kálnoky Conservation Trust

www.meniulzilei.info Meniul Zilei, useful site with details of restaurants in Târgu Mureş and Cluj-Napoca

www.micromapper.ro Interactive web maps

www.mihaieminescutrust.org Village conservation

www.milvus.ro Birds and wildlife

A2

www.mountainguide-sibiu.ro Professional mountain guide Iulian Panescu, based in Sibiu

http://outinmures.ro Online guide to restaurants and more in Târgu Mureş

www.panparks.org The organisation behind Retezat National Park

www.psst.ro Lifestyle, subculture, mainly in Bucharest

www.ratuc.ro Public transport in Cluj-Napoca

www.riding-holidays.ro The riding centre at Ştefan cel Mare

www.romania-central.com Economy, business and other news

www.romanian-monasteries.go.ro 100 Romanian Monasteries

www.romaniatourism.com National Tourist Office

www.romaniatravel.com Useful travel information

www.rosiamontana.ro The campaign against the proposed gold mine

www.rotravel.com A web travel guide

www.roving-romania.co.uk Colin Shaw's Land Rover trips and travel advice

www.sapteseri.ro Listings magazine with some pages in English

www.sibiu.ro All about Sibiu

http://slowfoodcluj.com Slow food movement based in Cluj-Napoca

www.sor.ro Romanian Ornithological Society

www.spirit.ro Details of travel to Romania

http://szekely.blogspot.com Entertaining blog from Miercurea-Ciuc

www.tarom.ro Romania's flag-carrier airline

www.tiff.ro Transylvania International Film Festival

www.transylvaniancastle.com The estate of Count Kálnoky at Micloşoara

www.transylvanianwildlifeproject.com Transylvanian Wildlife Project

www.turism.ro Tourism in Romania

www.ursita.ro/english.htm Ursita Inn information

www.visitclujnapoca.ro Useful information for Cluj-Napoca

www.wildtransylvania.com Website of Paul White (an Englishman living in Transylvania, who formed the Transylvanian Wildlife Project), with lots of interesting information

www.wizzair.com The low-cost airline

www.zabola.com The estate of the Count Mikes family

Index

Page numbers in **bold** indicate major entries; those in *italics* indicate maps.

accommodation 83–6 *see also*
  individual towns and cities
  cabanas 86
  camping and campsites 86, 110
  hostels 86
  hotels 84
  motels 84
  pensions 84
  private guesthouses 84
  rural tourism 85
accommodation price codes 85
ADEPT 54, **192**
Agnita 212
agricultural reform 32
airports 61–3 *see also* getting
  there and away
  Băneasa-Aurel Vlaicu 62
  Cluj-Napoca 250
  Otopeni-Henri Coandă
    (Bucharest) 61
  Sibiu 195
  Târgu Mureş 177
Aiud 244
Alba County 232–46, *233*
Alba Iulia **232–6**, *235*
  getting there, away and around
    233–4
  history 232–3
  other practicalities 234
  tourist information 234
  what to see and do 235–6
  where to eat and drink 234
  where to stay 234
alcohol *see* eating and drinking
ANTREC 15
Apold 191
Apuseni Mountains and Nature
  Park 241–3, 242
architecture 45–7 *see also* castles
  and churches
Arieş River 245
Armenians 35–6, 258
arts and entertainment 105–6
Avram Iancu
  festival in 97
  town 241

Avrig 213–14
Azuga 139

Băile Bálványos 156
Băile Tuşnad 166
Băniţa 223
banks 74 *see* money
basketball 110
bears *see* brown bear
Bear Lake *see* Lacul Ursu
Bechtel motorway 32
beer 165 *see also* eating and
  drinking
Bicaz Gorges-Hăşmaş Mountain
  National Park 9, 11, **172**
Biertan 207–8
  Biertan church 208
birdwatching 110
Bistriţa **262–7**, *264*
  getting there and away 264
  history 263–4
  other practicalities 266
  tourist information 265
  what to see and do 266–7
  where to eat and drink 265
  where to stay 265
Bistriţa-Năsăud County 262–70,
  263
Blaj 243–4
Bod 149
books 284–8
bookshops 104, 117, 153, 252
Borgó Pass *see* Pasul Tihuţa
Borsec 174
Bran 140–2
Bran Castle 140
Brâncoveanu Monastery 145
Braşov **129–36**, *132–3*
  getting there, away and around
    130–1
  history 130
  other practicalities 134
  tourist information 131
  what to see and do 134–6
  where to eat and drink 134
  where to stay 131

Braşov County 128–50, *129*
brown bear 11, **13**
Bucegi
  Natural Park 9, **139**
  range *141*
Bucharest 2
  airports 61–3 *see also* airports
  Dracula destinations 50
  Gară de Nord 63
  places to visit *en route* from
    137–9
  routes to and from *138*
Bucium 238
budgeting 74–6 *see* money
business 117–18
  contacts 117
Buşteni 139
buying property 118–21

cabanas 86
Călimani National Park 9, 12,
  183–4
Câlnic 237–8
Calvinist *see* Reformed Church
Câmpia Transilvaniei 257
camping 86, 110 *see also*
  accommodation
Căpâlna 238
Căpuşa Mare 254
car hire 61–2, 65, 79
Caraiman Massif 139
Carpathian Mountains 3–5, 172
Cârţa 213
castles 107–8, 182–3
  Aiud 107, **244**
  Alba Iulia 107, **236**
  Bánffy 107, **257**
  Bornemisza 182
  Bran 107, 118–19, **140**
  Câlnic 107, **237**
  Corvin 107, **225**
  Deva 107, **221**
  Dumbrăvioara 182
  Făgăraş 107, **145**
  Kemény 183
  Lăpuşna 183

castles *continued*
  Lăzarea 107, **174**
  Mikó 165
  Orăştie 108, **222**
  Peleş 108, **138**
  Pelişor 108, **138**
  Poienari 108, **216**
  Râşnov 108, **140**
  Reghin 183
  Rupea 108, **149**
  Sighişoara 107, **187**
  Slimnic 108, **206**
  Teleki 182
castle ruins 107
caving 110
CDs (music) 288–9
Ceauşescu, Nicolae 26–7, 124, 239
cellphones *see* mobile phones
ceramics 170
charities 124–6 *see also* travelling
  positively
Cheile Bicazului-Hăşmaş 9, 11,
  172 *see also* Bicaz Gorges-
  Hăşmaş National Park
children 70
Chiurus 160
Christmas 102
churches 38–9, 105–6, *see also*
  individual village and town
  names
  opening hours 105–6
  phrases 106
  Saxon *see* Saxon fortified
    churches
  with elaborate painted ceilings
    and frescoes 38–9
cinema 42, 102, 105 *see also*
  culture
Cisnădie 202
Cisnădioara 202–3
city codes, Transylvania 115
Ciuc *see* Csík towns and villages
climate 5–6
climbing 111
Cloaşterf 191
Cluj County 247–61, *247*
Cluj-Napoca **249–54**, *248–9*
  getting there and away 250–1
  history 249–50
  other practicalities 252
  tourist information 251
  what to see and do 252–4
  where to eat and drink 251–2
  where to stay 251
Codlea 146
Comandău 160
conservation 6–16
Copşa Mare 208
Copşa Mică 14, 206
Corund 170

Corvin, Matei 20, 225, 252
Costeşti-Bildaru 223
Costeşti-Cetăţuia 223
Count Tibor Kálnoky 15, 55,
  154–5
counties, Transylvanian 3, *5*
Covasna 159–60
Covasna County 151–61, *152*
Crasna church 38, **274**
Criş 189
Cristian (Braşov) 145–6
Cristian (Sibiu) 204
Criţ 150
Csíkszereda *see* Miercurea-Ciuc
Csík towns and villages 167
cuisine, Transylvanian 87–91,
  260, 287 *see* eating and
  drinking
cultural etiquette 121–4
culture 42–7
currency 2, 72–3 *see also* money
customs regulations 57
cycling and mountain biking 111

Dacian fortresses **222–3**, 238
  see also
  Băniţa 223
  Căpâlna 238
  Costeşti-Bildaru 223
  Costeşti-Cetăţuia 223
  Luncani Piatra Roşie 223
  Sarmizegetusa Regia 17–18,
    222
Daco-Roman Continuity Theory
  17
Daneş 189
Dârjiu 38, **170**
Dealu Frumos 213
Dej 259
Densuş church 226
Deva **218–222**, *220*
  getting there and away 220
  history 218–20
  other practicalities 221
  tourist information 221
  what to see and do 221–2
  where to eat and drink 221
  where to stay 221
disabled travellers 70
Dracula 50–1, 188–9, **190–1**,
  262, 266, 287–8 *see also* Vlad
  III Ţepeş
drinking water 66
drinks 91–4, 122, 165 *see also*
  eating and drinking
driving 78–81 *see also* car hire
  best drives 82
  parking 80
  petrol and stations 79–80
  regulations 80

drugs 122

Easter 102
eating and drinking 87–94, 260
  beer 165
  breakfast 87
  cheese 260
  dinner 91
  drinks 91–4
  lunch 88
  palincă 93
  restaurant opening hours 91
  restaurant price codes 90
  Transylvanian cuisine 87–91,
    260, 287
  Transylvanian recipes 88–9
  ţuică 93
  wine 92
economy 30–2
education 41
electricity 2, 72
embassies and consulates 58
emergency telephone numbers
  69, 112
English-language press 114
entertainment *see* arts and
  entertainment
entry requirements 57
environment 14–16
  contacts 15–16
  issues 14, *see also* conservation
etiquette *see* cultural etiquette
European health insurance
  card 67
European Union 29, 30–1

Făgăraş 144
Făgăraş Mountains 12, *214–15*,
  216
Fântânele peak 269
festivals 94–103 *see* public
  holidays and festivals
Fildu de Sus 274
fishing 111
flag 2
flora 6–11
folk art 106
folk music 44–5, 105
  CDs 288–9
food 87–91*see* eating and drinking
football 111
Fundata 142

galleries 106
gay travellers 70
genealogy 36
geography 3–5
getting around 76–83
  by air 76
  by bus/coach 77

getting around *continued*
  by bicycle 84
  by car 78–81, *80*
  by horse and cart 83
  by minibus 81
  by taxi 81
  by train 76–7, *77*
  hitchhiking 82
  on foot 82
getting there and away 58–65
  by air 59–63
  by car 65
  by coach/bus 64–5
  by train 63–4
getting to Transylvania from
  Bucharest 137, *138*
Ghelinţa 157–8
Gherla 258
Ghimbav 146
gold mining 240 *see also* Roşia
  Montana
golf 112
government 29–32
Grădiştea de Munte-Cioclovina
  Natural Park 9, 223
greetings 121 *see* language
guidebooks 286–7

Hălmeag 145
Harghita County 162–74, *163*
Hărman 148
Háromszék 151, 155
  region 151 *see also* Sfântu
    Gheorghe 151–2, 155
  Hungarian-language daily
    newspaper 113–14
Hăşmaş Mountains 172 *see*
  also Bicaz Gorges-Hăşmaş
  Mountain National Park
Haţeg 225
Hayakaghak *see* Gherla
haystacks 6
health 65–8
health insurance 67 *see* European
  health insurance card
highlights 48–9
hiking 112 *see also* national and
  natural parks
  vocabulary 230
history 16–30
  ancient 18
  Ceauşescu, Nicolae 26–7
  Habsburg 22
  Magyar 19
  Ottoman 19
  Peasant revolts 20
  revolutions 24 (1848), 27
    (1989)
  religious movements 20
  Roman 18

history *continued*
  Saxon 19, 36
  Transitional period 27–30
  World War I and II 25
holidays 94–103 *see* public
  holidays and festivals
Homorod 149
Horea, Cloşca and Crişan 23, 221
horseriding 112
Hosman 215
hospitality 122
hotels 84 *see* accommodation
Huedin 254
Hunedoara 223–5
Hunedoara County 218–31, *219*
Hungarians 19, 33
hunting 112
Hunyadi, János *see* Ioan de
  Hunedoara

internet 116
Ioan de Hunedoara 19, **224**
Izvorul Tăuşoarelor cave 270

Jews 25, 36
Jibou 273–4

Kalotaszeg region 255
King's Pass *see* Piatra Cramlui

Lacu Roşu 173
Lacul Bâlea 216
Lacul Beliş 256
Lacul Colibiţa 267
Lacul Făntănele 256
Lacul Lala Mare 269
Lacul Sfânta Ana 166
Lacul Snagov 137
Lacul Ursu 181
Lacul Vidraru 216
language VII, 12, 36–7, 121, **275–83**
  greetings 121
  hiking vocabulary 230
  Hungarian phrases 282–3
  note on the use of VII
  Romanian vocabulary 276–82
Lăzarea 173
lei 72–3 *see* RON (currency)
literature 43, 284–5
local travel agents and tour guides
  53–6 *see* tour operators
Lunca Ilvei 268
Luncani Piatra Roşie 223
Lupşa 243
Lutheran Church 40

Magyars *see* Hungarians
Mălâncrav 209
Mănăstireni 256
maps 116–17

Mărginimea Sibiului region 204–5
Marie of Romania, Queen 25, 69,
  142, 285
Marin, Dan 12, 143
markets 91
Marosvásáhely *see* Târgu Mureş
media and communications 113–
  16 *see also* internet, mobile
  phones, radio *and* television
Mediaş 211–12
  church 212
Meşendorf 150
Michael the Brave *see* Viteazul,
  Mihai
Micloşoara, 154
Miercurea-Ciuc 162–6, *164*
  getting there and away 163–4
  history 162–3
  other practicalities 165
  tourist information 164
  what to see and do 165–6
  where to eat and drink 164
  where to stay 164
Miercurea Sibiului 205
Mihai Eminescu Trust 15, **52**,
  150, 192, 209
Miklósvár *see* Micloşoara
mineral water 66
mobile phones and phonecards
  115
mofettes 161
Moigrad Porolissum 274
Moldo 172
money 2, 72–6
  banks 74
  budgeting 74–6
  credit cards 74
  currency 72–3
  exchanging currency 73–4
  sample prices 75
  tipping 75–6
  travellers cheques 73–4
Moşna 209
motels 84 *see* accommodation
Moţi 34, **245**
Moţii 34
Ţara Moţilor 245
motorway 32 *see* Bechtel
  motorway
mountain biking 111 *see* cycling
mountain refuges 86 *see*
  accommodation
Mugeni 170
Murderer's Lake *see* Lacu Roşu
Mureş County 175–92, *176*
Mureş River valley 182–3
museums 106
music 105 *see also* culture
  folk 44–5, 105
  jazz 96, 101, 199
  Roma 34, 44, 105

Nagy Imre Gallery 166
narrow-gauge railways 160, 212
national and natural parks 9,
    11–12 *see also* individual
    chapters
    Apuseni Natural Park 9, 12,
        241–3, *242*
    Bicaz Gorges-Hăşmaş
        Mountain National Park 9,
        11, **172**
    Bucegi Natural Park 9, **139**,
        141
    Călimani National Park 9,
        12, **183**
    Grădiştea Muncelului
        Cioclovina Natural Park
        9, 223
    Piatra Craiului National Park
        9, 11, 12, **144**
    Retezat National Park 9, 11,
        227–31, *228–9*
natural history 6–16, 286
Negreni 254
newspapers 113–14
    English-language press 114
Nicula Monastery 258

Ocna Sibiului 205
Odorheiu Secuiesc 167–9
Orăştie 222
Orăştie Mountains 222
Our Lady's bedstraw 8

Padiş Plateau 243
palaces 108
    Avrig Palace 108, **213**
    Bánffy Palace (Cluj-Napoca)
        108, **253**
    Brukenthal Palace (Sibiu) 108,
        199–200
Păltinis 203
PAN Parks 231
paragliding 112
parking 80
Pasul Tihuţa 267
pensions 84 *see* accommodation
people 32–6
petrol and stations 79–80 *see also*
    driving
pharmacies 68
photographing people 122
Piatra Craiului National Park 9,
    11, 12, **144**
Piatra Cramlui 255
Pied Piper 157
Poiana Braşov 146–8, *147 see also*
    skiing
Poiana Zânelor 269
police 69
population 2

population migration 32
pottery 170
Prahova Valley 137–9
Praid 171
    salt mine 171
Predeal Ski Resort 139
Prejmer 148–9
prices 75 *see* money
Prislop 225–6
    monastery 225
    pass 270
private guesthouses 84 *see*
    accommodation
property, buying 118–21
public holidays and festivals
    94–103

rabies 66
radio 115
rafting 113
railway network *77 see also*
    getting around
Râmeţ Monastery 244–5
Raşinari 203
Râşnov fortress 140
recipes, Transylvanian 88–9 *see*
    also eating and drinking
Reformed Church (Calvinist) 40
religion 2, 20–1, **38–41**
restaurants *see also* eating and
    drinking
    opening hours 91
    price codes 90
Retezat National Park 9, 11,
    227–31, *228–9*
Richiş 209
Rimetea 245–6
road network *80 see also* getting
    around
Rodna Mountains 269–70
Roma 34, 37, 45, 265
    people 34
    language 37
    music traditions 45 *see also*
        music
    palaces 265
Roman Catholic Church 40
Romanian Orthodox Church 38
RON (currency) 72–3
Roşia Montana 14, 31, **239–40**
Rupea 149
rural tourism 85 *see* ANTREC
    and accommodation

Săcele 148
safety 68–9
    in the mountains 112
saints and beliefs 123–4
Sălaj County 271–4, *272*
Sâncraiu 255

Sándor Kőrösi Csoma 160
Sângeorz-Băi 269
Sânpetru 149
Sântămăria Orlea Church 226
Sarmizegetusa Regia 17–18, **222**
Saschiz 190
Saxon fortified churches 19, 46–7,
    145–6, 148–50, 190–2, 206–16,
    210–11
    see also individual town and
        village names
Saxons 19, 35, 43, 46, 189
Scărişoara Ice Cave 243
Sebeş 236
Sfântu Gheorghe **151–4**, *154*
    getting there and away 153
    history 152–3
    other practicalities 153
    tourist information 153
    what to see and do 153–4
    where to eat and drink 153
    where to stay 153
shopping 103–4
Sibiu **193–202**, *196–7*
    entertainment and nightlife
        199
    getting there, away and around
        195, 198
    history 195
    other practicalities 199
    shopping 199
    tourist information 198
    what to see and do 199–202
    where to eat and drink 198
    where to stay 198
Sibiu County 193–217, *194*
Sibiel 204–5
Sic 257
Sighişoara 184–9, *186*
    clock tower 188
    getting there, away and around
        185
    history 185
    other practicalities 187
    tourist information 185
    what to see and do 187–9
    where to eat and drink 187
    where to stay 185–7
Şimleu Silvaniei 274
Sinaia 137–8
Şinca Noua 144
skiing 113
    Bucegi 139
    Păltiniş 203
    Poiana Braşov 146–8, *147*
    Predeal 139
    Sinaia 137
    ski tour operators 53 *see also*
        tour operators
Slimnic 206

snowboarding 113
Sovata Băi 181
spas 68, **108–9**, *see also* individual
 spa resorts
sports and activities 109–13
Starkie, Walter 254, 285
Stuff your Rucksack campaign
 126
Subcetate 169
superstitions 123
Suseni church 227
Székely 33, 43, 159, 167, **168–9**
Székely gates 159

Târgu Mureş **175–80**, *178*
 getting there, away and around
  177, 179
 history 176–7
 other practicalities 179
 tourist information 179
 what to see and do 180
 where to eat and drink 179
 where to stay 179
Târgu Secuiesc 157
tax refunds 58 *see* VAT/tax
 refunds
telephone and fax 115
 city codes 115
television 114
Three Seats (Háromszék)155
ticks 67
time 2, 117
 business 117
Tinovul Mohoş peat bog 166
tipping 75–6 *see* money
toilets 121
tour operators 52–6
 local travel agents/tour guides
  53–6
 ski and wildlife tours 53

tour operators *continued*
 UK tour operators 52–3
 US and Canada tour operators
  53
tourist offices 56–7
traditions 94–103 *see* public
 holidays and feast days
Transfăgărașan Highway 4, 82,
 216–17
 Lacul Bâlea 216
 Lacul Vidraru 216
 Poienari Citadel 216
 where to stay 216–17
Transylvania, origins of the
 name 16
travel clinics 67
travellers' cheques 73–4 *see*
 money
travelling positively 124–6
ţuică 93 *see* eating and
 drinking
Turda 259–61
 fest 259
 gorge 260–1
 salt mine 259
 tourist information 260
 where to stay and eat 260

Ulpia Traiana Sarmizegetusa
 226–7
UNESCO sites **47** *see also*
 individual locations and site
 names
Unirea 245
Unitarian Church 40

Valea Viilor 206–7
vampires 287–8 *see also* Dracula
VAT/tax refunds 58
visas 57

Viscri 149–50
 church 149
 where to stay 150
visual arts 43–5 *see also* culture
Viteazul, Mihai 21, 236
Vlad III Țepeș 20, 188, **190–1**, *see*
 also Dracula
vocabulary *see* language
 hiking 260
Von Brukenthal, Samuel **22**,
 199–10, 214
Vulcan 146

websites 289–90
what to take 71–2
when to visit 48
Whitsun Pilgrimage 166
wildlife 11–14 *see also* brown
 bear, natural history *and*
 wolves
wine 92–3 *see* eating and
 drinking
wolves 123
women travellers 69–70
World War I and II 25

Zăbala 158–9
Zalău **271–3**, *272*
 getting there, away and around
  272
 history 271–2
 other practicalities 273
 what to see and do 273
 where to eat and drink 273
 where to stay 272
Zărneşti 143–4
 where to stay, eat and drink
  143–4
Zetea 169–70
 where to stay 169–70

ADVERTISERS

Apuseni Experience 246
Roving Romania 47, 150